Valuation

science &
technology books

ELSEVIER

Companion Web Site:

Companion site: http://booksite.elsevier.com/9780128023037

Valuation:Theories and Concepts
Rajesh Kumar

TOOLS FOR ALL YOUR TEACHING NEEDS
textbooks.elsevier.com

ELSEVIER

ACADEMIC
PRESS

Valuation

Theories and Concepts

Rajesh Kumar

**Professor of Finance,
Institute of Management Technology,
Dubai, UAE**

AMSTERDAM • BOSTON • CAMBRIDGE • HEIDELBERG
LONDON • NEW YORK • OXFORD • PARIS • SAN DIEGO
SAN FRANCISCO • SINGAPORE • SYDNEY • TOKYO
Academic Press is an imprint of Elsevier

Academic Press is an imprint of Elsevier
125 London Wall, EC2Y 5AS.
525 B Street, Suite 1800, San Diego, CA 92101-4495, USA
225 Wyman Street, Waltham, MA 02451, USA
The Boulevard, Langford Lane, Kidlington, Oxford OX5 1GB, UK

Notices
Knowledge and best practice in this field are constantly changing. As new research and experience broaden our
understanding, changes in research methods, professional practices, or medical treatment may become
necessary.

Practitioners and researchers must always rely on their own experience and knowledge in evaluating and using
any information, methods, compounds, or experiments described herein. In using such information or methods
they should be mindful of their own safety and the safety of others, including parties for whom they have a professional responsibility.

To the fullest extent of the law, neither the Publisher nor the authors, contributors, or editors, assume any liability for any injury and/or damage to persons or property as a matter of products liability, negligence or other-
wise, or from any use or operation of any methods, products, instructions, or ideas contained in the material
herein.

ISBN: 978-0-12-802303-7

British Library Cataloguing-in-Publication Data
A catalogue record for this book is available from the British Library.

Library of Congress Cataloging-in-Publication Data
A catalog record for this book is available from the Library of Congress.

For Information on all Academic Press publications
visit our website at http://store.elsevier.com/

Typeset by MPS Limited, Chennai, India
www.adi-mps.com

Printed and bound in the United States

Publisher: Nikki Levy
Acquisition Editor: Scott Bentley
Editorial Project Manager: Susan Ikeda
Production Project Manager: Jason Mitchell
Designer: Matthew Limbert

Working together
to grow libraries in
developing countries

www.elsevier.com • www.bookaid.org

Dedication

To
Sreelatha, Rohit, Gopika, and Gowri

Contents

Preface

Value maximization is the primary objective of the existence of any firm. Value creation is fundamental for the existence of a firm from the perspective of all its stakeholder, which includes shareholders, employees, customers, suppliers, creditors, local community, state, and others. Value has different meanings in functional areas of management. Strategic management considers value chain as steps that a firm performs to provide value for customers. In finance, value is the firm value that consists of fundamental value and shareholder value. Fundamental value is based on the present value of expected free cash flows. Companies create value by means of investing capital at a higher rate of return when compared to its cost of capital. Companies with higher returns and higher growth are valued more highly in the stock market. Valuation is an integral part of the field of finance. Valuation plays a vital role in corporate finance.

Valuation has significance in different areas of finance. It has relevance in portfolio management, mergers and acquisitions, corporate finance, legal and tax purposes. The wealth maximization principle of corporate finance is embedded in the objective of maximization of firm value. The value of a firm is directly related to the firm's financing, investment, and dividend decisions.

There are basically three approaches to valuation. Discounted cash flow valuation is based on the fundamental idea that the value of any asset is the present value of expected future cash flows on that asset. Relative valuation estimates the value of any asset by analyzing the pricing of comparable assets relative to a common variable such as earnings, cash flows, sales, etc. The contingent claim valuation employs option pricing models to measure the value of assets that have option characteristics. Discounted cash flow valuation consists of equity valuation and firm valuation. Stock price maximization is one of the significant factors for valuing maximization objectives. Stock prices are the most observable of all measures, which can be used to judge the performance of a listed company. The concept of measuring and managing shareholder value is of paramount importance on account of the increasing relevance of capital markets and corporate governance.

This book *Valuation Theories and Concepts* aims to provide a broader and more holistic perspective on valuation. This book focuses on how valuation theories are applied in the world of business and commerce. Part I focuses on concepts and theories of valuation. Part II focuses on cases on valuation. Special emphasis is given for valuation of firms from the emerging markets. Part III discusses Mergers and Acquisition valuation. Chapter 1 focuses on different approaches to valuation. This chapter also focuses on the major value drivers for shareholder wealth creation and measures of shareholder value creation. Chapter 2 discusses the theoretical perspectives on risk and return. Chapter 3 discusses the implications of capital market efficiency and its significance for wealth creation. A major thrust of this chapter is on event studies and its importance for firms in the context of wealth creation. The focus of Chapter 4 is on estimation of the cost of equity and the weighted average cost of capital. Cash flow estimation is an integral part of the valuation and capital budgeting process. Chapter 5 discusses the principles of cash flow estimation. This chapter highlights the adjustments that need to be made for cash flow estimation. This chapter also discusses reinvestment needs and estimation of growth rates, which are critical aspects of the valuation process. Chapter 6 analyzes the three basic discounted cash flow valuation models—dividend discount models, free cash flow to equity, and free cash flow to firm models. Chapter 7 focuses on relative valuation. Chapter 8 discusses mergers and acquisition valuation. Chapter 9 focuses on real option valuation. Chapter 10 outlines valuation of different industry sectors. Chapter 11 explains valuation issues in startup firms, cyclical firms, high growth, and emerging market firms.

The book focuses on case studies from both developed and emerging market firms. The case studies analyze the financial performance based on trend analyses and ratio analysis. The major emphasis of these cases are on valuation in which the value of firm is estimated using various models of discounted cash flow valuation and relative valuation. This section discusses valuation cases on firms from developed markets like Walmart, Wells Fargo, Franklin Resources, Singapore Airlines, and Pfizer. Valuation cases from emerging markets include cases of ICBC, Samsung, Tata Motors, Gazprom, and China Life Insurance. The three cases on mergers and acquisition valuation discussed are Google's Acquisition of Motorola, HP Compaq Merger, and Tata's acquisition of Corus.

Acknowledgments

I would like to thank the production and editorial staff at Elsevier who guided this book through the publishing process. I wish to acknowledge the valuable guidance and support of Scott Bentley, Senior Acquisition Editor at Elsevier. My special thanks to Susan Ikeda, Editorial Project Manager, and her team for all the cooperation and support in the publication of this book. I thank Jason Mitchell, Publishing Services Manager, and his team for all the support. I also acknowledge the content of the various Web sites and sources of information to which I referred. I thank my family for all their support. Special gratitude to my wife, Sreelatha, for her understanding and support.

Part I

Theories and Concepts

Perspectives on value and valuation

1

1.1 Introduction

Value has different meanings in functional areas of management. In marketing, value is often perceived as customer value. Strategic management considers value chain as steps a firm performs to provide value for customers. In finance, value is the firm value which consists of fundamental value and shareholder value. Fundamental value is based on the present value of expected free cash flows. Shareholder value is firm value minus the value of outstanding debt. Firm value can be based on book value or market value. Market value is based on the stock market performance of a company. The most widely used practical measure of shareholder value is Total Shareholder Return which is based on stock price appreciation plus dividends. Companies create value by means of investing capital at a higher rate of return when compared to its cost of capital. Companies with higher returns and higher growth are valued more highly in the stock market.

Knowledge assets are organizational resources which are integral for company's value creation. The strategic relevance of knowledge assets has led to the generation of new concepts and models for managing a company's knowledge assets. Intellectual Capital has emerged as a key concept to evaluate the intangible dimension of an organization. The modern economic world is based on the foundation of new technologies, globalization, and increased relevance of intangible assets. Alan Greenspan, the former Federal Reserve chief, once remarked that virtually unimaginable a half century was the idea that concepts and ideas would substitute for physical resources and human brawn in the production of goods and services. Modern era is the world of knowledge economy. Organizations create value in totally new ways. In early 2000, Microsoft achieved market value exceeding the combined value of eight US giants—Boeing, Caterpillar, Ford, General Motors, Kellogg, Eastman Kodak Company, JP Morgan & Company, and Sears Roebuck which were built mostly on intangibles (Boulton et al., 2000). Value creation is often perceived as the future value captured in the form of increased market capitalization. The new global economy has led to the emergence of new business models where companies are combining both old and new economy assets. New processes and tools are required to manage the risks on account of new business models. The greatest challenge a company faces today is identification of the combination of tangible and intangible assets which creates the greatest amount of economic value. The complex interaction of a company's mix of assets termed economic DNA creates or destroys value. In 2000, American Online's book value was a miniscule 3.3% of its market capitalization.

1.2   Application of valuation

Valuation has significance in different areas of finance. It has relevance in portfolio management, mergers and acquisitions, corporate finance, legal and tax purposes. Valuation plays a vital role in corporate finance. The wealth maximization principle of corporate finance is embedded in the objective of maximization of firm value. The value of a firm is directly related to the firm's financing, investment, and dividend decisions. Valuation also plays a critical role in corporate finance for financing decisions to raise funds for investment purposes. The pricing of IPOs are basically determined by the valuation process. Valuations of private companies are basically done for tax or legal reasons.

In portfolio management, the role of valuation is integral in fundamental analysis in which the true value of any firm can be related to the financial characteristics of its cash flows in terms of growth, riskiness, and timings. The fundamental value of a firm can be derived to understand whether it is under- or overvalued in order to facilitate long-term investment strategy. Valuation is also useful for technical analysis.

Valuation plays a pivotal role in merger and acquisition (M&A) analysis. Determining the value of target firm for acquisition is an important step in the due diligence process of M&A. The bidding firm has to decide on a fair value for the target firm before making the bid, and the target firm has to decide a reasonable value for the offer. The value of target from the bidder's point of view is the sum of the pre bid standalone value of the target and the incremental value that the bidder expects to add to the target's assets. The incremental value may arise from improved operations of the target or the synergy between the two companies. Valuation of the target requires valuation of the totality of the incremental cash flows and earnings.

1.3   Approaches to valuation

There are basically three approaches to valuation. Discounted cash flow valuation is based on the fundamental idea that the value of any asset is the present value of expected future cash flows on that asset. Relative valuation estimates the value of any asset by analyzing the pricing of comparable assets relative to a common variable such as earnings, cash flows, sales, etc. The contingent claim valuation employs option pricing models to measure the value of assets which have option characteristics. Discounted cash flow valuation consists of equity valuation and firm valuation.

In another perspective valuation can be broadly classified into earnings-based valuation, market-based valuation, and asset-based valuation. The earnings-based valuation (also known as discounted cash flow valuation) takes into account the future earnings of the business. The value of business depends on projected revenues and costs in future, expected cash outflows, number of years of projection, discount rate, and terminal value of business. Market-based valuation for listed companies and comparable listed companies are based on market multiples such as market capitalization to sales or market price to earnings. The asset-based value is based on the book value of assets net liabilities. The value of intangible assets like brands and copyrights are valued independently and added to the net asset value to get the business value.

In other words, valuation methods can be categorized as direct valuation method and indirect (relative) valuation methods. The direct valuation methods provide an estimation of a company's fundamental value. The analyst, through direct valuation method, can compare the fundamental value of the company with the market value of a company. The direct valuation method consists of discounted cash flow valuation method and nondiscounted cash flow models like real option analysis. The company can be said to be fairly valued if the market value of the firm is equal to its fundamental value. If the market value of firm is lower than the fundamental value then it is said to be undervalued. If the market value is higher than the fundamental value then the firm is said to be overvalued. Relative valuation basically identifies whether a company is fairly valued relative to some benchmark group of companies in the same sector. In other words relative valuation method doesn't give a direct estimate of a company's fundamental value. Relative valuation is also known as comparable approach as the process involves identifying a group of comparable companies in the same sector.

The basic factor that determines a company's fundamental value is its expected future cash flows. Relative valuation methods give a quick and simple way for analysts to understand the valuation of a company. Relative valuation methods are based on multiples which is a ratio between two financial variables. The numerator of the multiple is primarily the firm's market price or enterprise value. The enterprise value is equal to market value of equity and debt net of cash.

Economic income or residual income method is an alternate model of valuation. Economic income models rely on earnings to estimate a firm's fundamental value. This model is based on the premise that positive economic income leads to shareholder value creation.

1.4 Steps in value creation

Arzac (1986) suggests four steps for valuation of business units within a strategic framework:

1. Estimate the basic data for each unit—cost of equity and debt, debt capacity and tax rate, and the turnover, sales margin, ROI, and asset growth expected.
2. Set performance standards (required sales margin and ROI) and compare them against projected performance.
3. Estimate the value creation implications of the current strategy. Use return on investment (ROI) and financial leverage data to express the unit's performance in terms of return on equity (ROE) and cost of equity and to estimate the unit's contribution to the value of stockholder equity.
4. Evaluate strategic decisions having to do with the units, such as changes in production and marketing, alternative investment and growth rates, and harvest and liquidation options.

1.5 Value drivers

Every asset, financial as well as real, has value. The key to fundamental aspect of investing and managing assets lies in understanding of not only what value is, but also the sources of value. A value driver is a performance variable which impacts the results of a business such as production effectiveness or customer satisfaction. The metrics associated with value drivers are called key performance indicators (KPIs). Value drivers should be directly linked to shareholder value creation and measured by both financial and operational KPIs which must cover long-term growth and operating performance.

The three commonly cited financial drivers of value creation are sales, costs, and investments. Earnings growth, cash flow growth, and return on invested capital are specific financial drivers. Profitability, growth, and capital intensity are considered as important drivers of free cash flow and value of a firm (Miller et al., 2004). The key performance indicators also include financial measures such as sales growth and earnings per share as well as nonfinancial measures. The nonfinancial performance measures include product quality, workplace safety, customer loyalty, employee satisfaction, and customer's willingness to promote products.

The determination of value drivers is a critical step in business process valuation since these drivers can either increase or reduce the value. Many researchers consider value driver as any variable influencing enterprise's value. Value drivers include both external and internal value drivers (Jennergren, 2013). Value drivers are crucial for value maximization. The classification of value drivers are most frequently related to the analysis method of shareholder value and the concept of value-based management (Kazlauskiene and Christauskas, 2008). The major value drivers included by researchers consist of sales increase, margin of activity profit, tax rate, working capital, expenses of capital, costs of capital, period of competitive advantage, and return on capital. Relative indicators like turnover of capital, margin of gross profit are also called drivers.

The value drivers for a fast food chain consider customer satisfaction as key to profitability. The acquisition of new customers is an important performance metric for new subscription businesses like wireless telephone provider. As the company matures, the focus of these companies would be on managing the existing customers by providing them additional services. Increasing shareholder value is the primary goal of business. Corporations seek to maximize the value of shares over the long term. It is often observed that the market value (in terms of share prices) of many firms exceed the book value of firms. There are also firms in the market which trade below book value both in bull and bear markets.

Companies which cannot create fundamental value through operational efficiency and increase of cash flow cannot be successful in the market in the long run. Stock markets recognize those strategies of firms which are directed toward value creation. Shareholder value enhancement is possible through acquiring knowledge about sources of value creation and destruction in an organization. Basically value is created or destroyed at business unit level for a company. For instance, in the eighties, the tobacco business of Philip Morris consistently created value for the company while the beverages unit performed below the expectations. Companies often consider divestment of loss-making units in order to recover loss of shareholder value. SCM had to halve its investment in typewriter business due to years of value destruction on account of persistent losses and shrinking of market share.

Any value creation model must synthesize the link between strategy and shareholder value. The key determinants of value creation are present values of free cash flows, expected return on equity, cost of equity capital, expected growth rate and period in which company creates positive spread between return on equity and cost of equity. Companies create value when positive spread is generated between its return on equity and cost of equity. Growth opportunities through investments in assets at positive spread are also sources of value creation. On the other hand companies destroy value when the spread between return on equity and cost of equity is negative. It is often observed that many companies evaluate business units in terms of return on investment and pretax margin on sales rather than ROE Arzac (1986).

1.6 Empirical evidence on value drivers

The term value has attracted the interest of many researchers and economists. In scientific literature, value is referred as the best indicator of a firm's performance results which integrates the drivers reflecting enterprise's internal as well as external environment.

Executives often believe that EPS is the most important part of value creation. A survey of executive compensation by Frederic W Cook and Company found that EPS is the most popular measure of corporate performance used by companies. Another study by researchers at Stanford Graduate school of Business based on survey of 400 financial executives found that nearly two-thirds of companies placed EPS first in a ranking of most important performance measures reported to outsiders. Sales revenue and sales growth were also highly rated for measurement of performance. EPS growth is good for company which earns high returns on invested capital. At the same time EPS growth is not good for companies which have returns below the cost of capital. Mauboussin (2012) finds that the two popular measures of performance—sales growth and EPS have limited value in predicting shareholder returns since neither is both persistent and predictive.

The CEOs of companies must focus on objectives and rules to promote long-term value creation for shareholders. A US study (Carrott and Jackson, 2009) based on companies managed by CEOs with 4−8 years of service and having returns greater than 20% during the period 2003−2008 suggest that these CEOs focused on actions for value creation. Nordstrom focused on improvement of gross margin return on inventory investment as a driver for value creation. The company spends approximately $200 million on an improved inventory system. During the period 2000−2004, the inventory per square feet dropped from $63 to $52 while the sales rose from $5.5 billion to $7.1 billion. Adobe holds managers responsible for long-term performance by linking compensation to long-term stock performance of the company. During the period 2005—2009, the company achieved an average annual compound return of 28% to shareholders. But the top executives' salaries were only 10—25% of the total compensation. The rest in terms of stock option and bonuses were linked to long-term value creation. John Deer improved the operating return on operating assets to a range of 22—26% by reducing working capital investments in receivables and inventory from 58% to 35% of sales. As a result the share price of Deere quadrupled. McDonald was able to improve performance by improved service and menu items.

Rappaport (1986, 1998) presented the model of relationship between value drivers and common goals of an enterprise within the framework of general enterprise management system. This study divided drivers into three groups: operational, investment, and financial. Scarlet (1997) classified value drivers into four categories of intangible, operational, investment, and financial. Research studies by Kaplan and Norton (1996) classify value drivers into financial, purchasers, employees, operational, quality, alliances, supply, environment, innovations, and society. Damodaran (1994, 2002) introduced the value creation model which highlights cash flow, capital cost, and expected growth period as the main value drivers. Value drivers can be divided into internal and external; financial and nonfinancial.

Pratt (1989) suggests that the analysis of qualitative drivers as well as the determination of their impact on value requires highest skills of a valuer which form up during many years of practical and research work. McKinsey value driver formula (Copeland et al., 2000; Koller et al., 2000) can be split into two parts, one for existing operations and one for growth projects. The return on new invested capital (RONIC) which refers to the rate of return on growth projects can be lower than the return on invested capital (ROIC) which is the rate of return on the existing operations.

1.7 Strategic models of valuation

Value-based management focuses on the application of valuation principles. In value-based management system, the components of the employees' work should be identified and linked to profitability, growth, and capital intensity. The actual performance should be measured, evaluated, and rewarded in terms of targets for profitability, growth, and capital intensity.

Value creation is traditionally considered as a chain of activities. The field of corporate finance was revolutionized by introduction of mathematical models of capital asset pricing model and the Black Scholes Merton option pricing model. Value-based business strategy adapted by A. Brandenburger and Harborne Stuart applied mathematics to the evaluation of strategic decisions through mathematical linkages. Value capture model (VCM) defines competition in an industry as a tension between the value generated from transactions that a firm undertakes with a given set of agents and the forgone value it could have generated from transactions with other agents. Cooperative game theory could be applied effectively in studying competitive dynamics. VCM model of competition allows a firm to identify potential payoffs to investments in resources and capabilities supported by big data. The resources and capabilities which influence value are deployed with competitive intent (Ryall, 2013).

1.8 Stock price maximization

Stock price maximization is one of the significant factors for value maximization objectives. Stock prices are the most observable of all measures which can be used to judge the performance of a listed company. Stock prices are constantly updated to reflect new information about a firm. Thus managers are constantly judged about their actions with the benchmark being the stock price performance. Book value measures like sales and earnings are obtained only at the end of year or in each quarter. Stock prices reflect the long-term effects of a firm's business decisions. When firms maximize their stock prices, investors can realize capital gains immediately by selling their shares in the firm. An increase in stock price is often automatically attributed to management's value creation performance. At the same time, the stock price might have increased due to macro-economic factors.

1.8.1 Shareholder value and wealth creation

The concept of measuring and managing shareholder value is of paramount importance on account of the increasing relevance of capital markets and corporate governance. In the era of globalization of markets, investors have easy accessibility to raise funds. The shareholders of the company desire transparency in the operations of the company and place much significance to the corporate governance practices. Today no underperforming company is safe as always there is the threat of hostile takeovers. Hence the managers of firms have to perform to improve the value of the company. The criticism with accounting measures such as earnings per share (EPS) and profit or growth in earnings is that they do not consider the cost of investment made for running the businesses.

Shareholder is the main pivotal stakeholder or fulcrum of the business activity. Firms which don't create value for shareholders faces challenges like risk of capital flight, higher interest rates, lower efficiency and productivity and threat of hostile takeovers. Maximization of shareholder wealth is the main objective of any value creating organization. The value perspective is based on measurement of value from accounting-based information while wealth perspective is based on stock market information.

Economist's viewpoint suggests the firms create value when management generates revenues over and above the economic costs to generate these revenues (Armitrage and Jog, 1996). The economic costs are attributed to sources like employee wages and benefits, materials, economic depreciation of physical assets, taxes and opportunity cost of capital. Value creation occurs when management generates value over and above the costs of resources consumed, including the cost of using capital. A company which loses its value faces the daunting task of attracting further capital for financing expansion as the declining share price becomes a detrimental factor for value creation. In such a scenario, the company is compelled to pay higher interest rates on debt or bank loans.

Wealth creation refers to changes in the wealth of shareholders on a periodic (annual) basis. In the case of stock exchange listed firms, changes in shareholder wealth occurs from changes in stock prices, dividends, equity issues during the period. Stock prices reflect the investors' expectation about future cash flows of the firm. Shareholder wealth is created when firms take investment decisions with positive NPV values.

The real or true value of a stock or intrinsic value includes all aspects of company in terms of both tangible and intangible factors which affect the value of a company and subsequently the perceived value of a share of stock.

1.8.2 Value drivers for shareholder wealth creation

Value drivers are variables which affect the value of the organization. The main value drivers for shareholder wealth creation are intangibles, operating, investment, and financial. Increase in shareholder value results from improvement in cash flow from operations. Value enhancement can also result from minimizing the cost of capital by focusing on optimal capital structure decisions. The value drivers for increase in cash flow from operations are higher revenues, lower costs and income taxes and reduction in capital expenditure. No company can maintain their operation and produce great wealth for its shareholders without stable and rising revenue which comes from customer.

The strategic requirements for higher revenues consist of patent barriers to entry, niche markets, and innovative products. The strategic requirements for lower costs and income taxes are scale economies, captive access to raw materials, efficiencies in processes of production, distribution and services. The strategic requirements for reduction in capital expenditure are efficient asset acquisition and maintenance, spin offs, higher utilization of fixed assets, efficiency of working capital, and divestiture of nonperforming assets.

The value drivers for reduction in capital charge are reduced business risk, optimization of capital structure, reduction of cost of debt, and cost of equity. The strategic requirements for reduced business risks are superior operating performance and long-term contracts. The strategic requirement for optimal capital structure involves maintaining a capital structure that minimizes the overall costs which optimizes tax benefits. Companies often adopt different strategies for value creation. Companies like Sony, Apple, and Microsoft often introduce new products for enhancing shareholder value creation.

1.8.3 Measures of shareholder value creation

1.8.3.1 Economic value

Economic Value (EV) as a performance measure has been popularized by multinational companies like Coca Cola, AT&T and Kellog. EV is calculated as net operating income after taxes (NOPAT) minus the capital charge. The sequential steps for EV calculation are as follows:

- Calculation of NOPAT
- Estimation of Capital Employed
- Estimation of Weighted Average Cost of Capital (WACC)
- Calculation of capital charge and EV.

Format for calculation of EV

Revenues − cost of sales = Gross Profit − Other Operation (income/loss) −
Depreciation = Profit Before Interest and Tax − Income Tax = NOPAT
Capital Employed = Net Working Capital + Net Fixed Assets
Capital Employed * WACC = Capital Charge
NOPAT − Capital Charge = EV

1.8.3.2 Equity spread

Equity Spread is a variation of the EV measures. Equity spread is the difference between the ROE and the required return on equity (cost of equity) as the source of value creation. Mathematically, the equity spread is expressed as:

Equity value creation = (Return on equity in percent − Cost of equity in percent) * Equity Capital

1.8.3.3 Implied value

The implied value measure is similar to discounted future market value. This method is closely related to the DCF (discounted cash flow) framework. If the difference between implied value at the beginning of the year and end of the year is positive, then the management would have created value. Value would be created if the management's decisions generate cash flows over and above the cost of capital and is able to sustain this performance over a long period of time. The implied value measure is based on forecasts of future by making proforma income and balance sheet statements over a period of time.

1.8.3.4 Cash flow return on investment (CFROI)

CFROI represents the sustainable cash flow a business generates as a percentage of the cash invested in the business. This measure can be interpreted as the internal rate of return (IRR) over the economic life of the assets. The difference between this IRR and cost of capital represents the value creation potential of the firm. The calculation of CFROI involves conversion of income and balance sheet items into cash and calculating cash flows after adjusting for inflations and adjustments for monetary or near monetary assets such as inventories. The estimation of the normal life of assets is made. The value of the nondepreciating assets at the end of the horizon is also calculated.

NOPAT + Depreciation = Real Gross Cash Flow.

The capital employed is considered as the initial investment. Then IRR is calculated.

1.8.4 Measures of shareholder wealth creation

Wealth creation measures are based on stock market and don't require analysis of the financial statements of the firm. Hence these measures are applicable only to exchange listed firms and cannot be used for privately held firms. The price of a share of any company is basically considered to be the market's expectation about the firm's value creation potential. The higher the potential, higher will be the share price relative to the capital invested. Companies which create fundamental value in the operating performance are expected to create value in the market through rise in the stock prices.

The two major wealth creation measures are

a. Total Shareholder Return (TSR)

TSR is the rate of return earned by shareholder based on capital appreciation through price changes and dividends received. TSR enables measurement of a firm's contribution to the overall capital gain and dividend yield to investors. Return on Investment (ROI), free cash flow, and growth in invested capital are the key value drivers of capital gains. Companies with higher returns on the invested capital are able to achieve stock price increases as these companies are able to invest more capital at high ROIs.

The annual TSR is calculated as the change in price plus any dividends divided by the initial price.

Mathematically, TSR can be expressed as:

$$TSR = (Price_{t+1} + dividends_{t+1} - Price_t)/Price_t$$

b. Annual Economic Return

Annual Economic Return (AER) is based on a firm's annual wealth creation performance. AER calculation is based on dividends and its timings and externally raised capital. The AER method involves estimation of the cost of equity based on the riskiness of the firm.

AER is calculated as a return by the firm after adjusting for dividends paid and external dividends paid and external capital.

1.8.5 Hybrid wealth creation measure

This measure involves measuring both the book value of equity and market value of equity. The difference between the market value of equity and book value of equity is called the net wealth created.

1.8.5.1 Market value added (MVA)

The most commonly used hybrid value or wealth creation measure is market value added. MVA involves adjusting all debt and equity to reflect capital market expectations about the firm's future value creation performance.

Market value added represents the wealth generated by a company for its shareholders. It equals the amount by which the market value of the company's stock exceeds the total capital invested in a company (including capital retained in the form of undistributed earnings).

Adjustments are required for negative changes to equity. The market value of a firm's equity is obtained by multiplying the number of shares outstanding times the price per share. The market value of firm is calculated as the sum of the market value of all outstanding securities which consists of common shares, preferred shares, and debt. This measure is calculated by comparing the market value of capital (equity) with the adjusted value of capital (equity).

Market Value Added (MVA) = Market Capitalization−Total Common Shareholders' Equity = Total Shares Outstanding*Current Market Price−Total Common Equity
Market Value Added for Investors = Market Value of the company−(Book value of equity + book value of debt)

1.9   Linkage between strategic management and shareholder value

The study by Bigler and Hsieh (2013) posits that the five elements of competitive strategy, innovation, profitable growth, strategy execution, enterprise wide risk management are necessary and sufficient strategy and management factors affect shareholder value.

The ultimate test of corporate strategy is to analyze whether strategic decisions creates economic value for shareholders. Value-based management (VBM) is used to assess firm value and shareholder value. According to the basic VBM model, the present financial value must be equal to the discounted future free cash flows from operations using the firm's weighted average cost of capital as discount rate.

1.9.1   Value-based management

VBM is an approach to management whereby the company's overall aspirations, analytical techniques, and management processes are aligned to help the company maximize its value by focusing management decision making on the key drivers of shareholder value (Ittner, 2001). Coca Cola is one of the pioneering companies with VBM principles.

1.9.2   Significance of shared value

Shared values are policies and operating practices which enhance the competitiveness of a company. In this concept, businesses have to focus on value with a societal perspective. Value is defined as benefits relative to costs. The approach to value creation has undergone transformational changes. Value creation is not just optimizing short-term financial performance. Companies like GE, Google, IBM, Intel, Johnson & Johnson, Nestle, Unilever, and Walmart aim to create shared values by focusing on the interaction between societal needs and corporate performance. The next wave of innovation and productivity growth in the global economy will be based on shared value creation. Porter (2011) suggests three key ways that companies can create shared value opportunities: (i) By reconceiving products and markets, (ii) By redefining productivity in value chain, and (iii) By enabling local cluster development. The concept of shared values focuses on societal needs instead of economic needs. Societal harms or weaknesses create internal costs for firms such as wasted energy or raw materials.

Societal needs in terms of basic needs like housing, nutrition, help for aging, financial security are the greatest unmet needs in the global economy. Innovative new companies like Water Health International use innovative water purification techniques to distribute clean water at minimal cost to more than one million people in rural India, Ghana, and Philippines. Excessive packaging and greenhouse gases are costly to environment and businesses. By means of reducing its packaging and cutting 100 million from the delivery routes of its trucks, Walmart lowered carbon emissions and saved $200 million in costs. British retailer Mark and Spencer's overhaul of its supply chain with steps like stoppage of purchase of supplies from one hemisphere to ship to another is expected to provide cost savings of £175 million by year 2016 thereby contributing immensely to reduce carbon emissions (Porter and Kramer, 2011). Coca Cola had a goal of reducing its water consumption by 20% in the year 2012. Dow Chemicals reduced consumption of water by one billion gallons and had a cost savings of $4 million. This amount of water was enough to supply water to 40,000 households in US. Nespresso emerged as one of the fastest growing division of Nestle (over 30% since 2000) by redesigning procurement. The company redesigned procurement by working with growers, providing advises on farming practices, guaranteeing bank loans and securing fertilizers and pesticides for farmers. Johnson and Johnson through its employee wellness programs saved $250 million in healthcare costs. Hindustan Unilever through its Project Shakti Program is empowering underprivileged female entrepreneurs with microcredit and training.

1.9.3 Intangibles

In R&D organizations, intangible assets are a key driver of innovation and organizational value. The allocation and deployment of intangible resources is an important strategic decision for organizations (Pike et al., 2005). Intangible assets are identified as key resource and driver of organization performance and value creation. Researchers like Itami (1987) articulated the idea that intangible assets such as technology, accumulated consumer information, brand name, reputation and corporate culture are critical resources of firms and sources of competitive advantage. Hall (1992) divides intangible assets into intangible properties and intangible resources. Intangible property consists of knowledge related to legal ownership like patents, trademarks, copyrights, trade secrets, registered designs, brands, computer software, contracts, and databases. Intangible resources are formed by an individual's experience, organizational processes, relational resources such as reputation, client loyalty as well as firm's relationship. Intangible assets can be classified into human capital, process capital, and innovation capital. Intangibles are important value drivers in the R&D process.

The intangible assets consist of patents, skilled workforce, software, know-hows, strong customer relationships, brands, unique organizational skills. These intangible assets generate shareholder value and corporate growth. These soft assets provide competitive advantage for modern companies. Intangibles account for over half the market capitalization of public companies. Intangible assets absorb trillion dollars of corporate investments every year. Markets sometimes overvalue or undervalue the intangibles of a company. In case of undervaluation of intangibles, firms have to deal with high cost of capital which could lead to underinvestment in intangibles in future. The research by Federal Reserve economist Leonard Makamura finds that US Companies expenditure annually on intangibles is equal to the total corporate investments in physical assets. Financial service firms often invest substantial resources in product and service innovation.

The intangible assets can be categorized as follows:

Marketing-related intangible assets: Trademarks (Brands), trade names, service marks, internet domain names, noncompetition agreements.
Contract-based intangible assets: Licensing and royalty agreements, advertising, construction, service or supply agreements, lease agreements, employment contracts.
Technology-based intangible assets: Patented technology, computer software, unpatented technology (know-how), databases, trade secrets.
Customer-related intangible assets: Customer lists, order or production backlogs, customer contracts and customer relationships including noncontractual relationships.
Artistic-related intangible assets: Plays, books, magazines, newspapers, pictures and photographs.

Brooking (1996) identified market assets, intellectual property assets, human-centered assets and infrastructure assets as constituents of intangible assets. Sveiby (1997) suggested that the core components of intangible assets are internal organization structures, external organization structures and the competence of its personnel.

In the modern era of knowledge economy, the value of companies have shifted from the tangible assets of bricks and mortar to intangible assets such as patents, customer clients and brands. During the last few years, the brand value of Apple equaled a huge 80% of its market capitalization.

Pharmaceutical companies have spent huge amounts to create new brands. Regulatory changes have speeded up the process of branding in financial service sectors. Branding had played a key role in the reinvention and growth of IBM computers. During the dotcom crash period, IBM was well positioned as a "voice of reason." A strong brand helps customers understand an organization and imparts a sense of mission inside the company. Free cash flows are the very blood of a corporation but intangible assets are its nervous system. The four core intangible assets are firm's brands, relationships, productivity, and innovation capacity of its people.

1.9.4 Valuation of intangibles

The general techniques used for valuation consists of brand valuation, human resource valuation, valuation of research and development costs and valuation of patents and copyrights. The general methods used for brand valuation include market value of company's shares, the difference between market value and book value, brand replacement value, difference between values of branded company and value of company selling generic products and present value cash flow method.

The methods frequently used for valuing human resources mainly include balanced scorecard, competency models, benchmarking, business worth, and calculated intangible value. According to International Financial Reporting Standards, the cost involved in R&D has to be expensed in the same year in which it has been incurred. In the case of valuation of patents and copyrights, the full acquisition costs consisting of purchase consideration and related expenses are required to be capitalized. International guidelines direct companies to go through a more rigorous process of identifying and valuing acquired intangible assets. The International financial reporting standards (IFRS-3) advocates identification of more intangible assets, rigorous and detailed annual impairment test and requirement of purchase price allocation. The financial role of intangibles has become relevant as reflected in the valuation of brand and valuation of intellectual property rights.

A McKinsey Co. study in the year 1999 suggested that in a firm's market value, an average of 55% represented the market's evaluation of the firm's core intangible assets and the remainder being the evaluation of the firm's physical assets and financial performance, profits and cash flows (Bruckner et al., 2000). The study by Ocean Tomo (2010) suggests that in the context of service-based economy, the average value of the nonphysical assets have risen from 17% of a firm's value in 1975 to 68% in 1995 and further to 81% in 2009.

The report of Brand Finance "Global Intangible Tracker TM 2009" analyzes the enterprise value of 37,000 companies, on 56 stock markets in 32 countries, over a 7-year period up to December 31, 2008. At the close of 2008, tangible net assets recorded on balance sheets amounted to US$23.2 trillion, up by US$1.0 trillion on last year. Disclosed intangible assets (e.g., brands and patents) amounted to US$3.3 trillion, up by US$0.54 trillion.

Hares and Royle (1994) converted intangible benefit into cash flow for cost–benefit analysis. They advocated following steps for valuation: identification and measurement of benefits, prediction of the results in physical terms and evaluation.

Reilly (1998) presented three methods to value proprietary technology—the market approach, the cost approach and the income approach.

1.9.4.1   Market approach

The market approach involves investigating the valuation of intangible assets on the basis of benefits and costs of comparable projects in other organizations in similar markets, or benchmarks of comparable assets.

1.9.4.2   Cost approach

The cost method attempts to estimate the benefits and costs of achieving the same functionality using distinct technologies, processes or human resources through the assessment of replacement cost of the asset or benchmarking.

1.9.4.3   Income method

The income approach method values intangible assets on the basis of the future economic benefits derived from the ownership of the asset. This approach is basically used for valuation of brands, customer relationships, patented and unpatented (know-how) technology. This method is heavily reliant on prospective financial information like turnover and profits. The main methods under this approach are Relief from Royalty and Excess Earnings.

1.9.4.4 Calculated intangible value (CIV)

In this method, the valuation of intangible assets is based on residual operating income model as a variant fundamental value of equity model. The method consists of following steps:

- Determination of book value of the company's assets and discounted flow of residual operating income to ascertain company's value
- Determination of book value of tangible assets and discounted flow of residual earnings using the average industrial rate of return
- Calculation of difference between total book value of company and value of tangible assets of company to determine the value of intangible assets.

1.9.5 Brand value

Value in industry is often associated with the quality of the product. Industries characterized by highly disruptive technologies, competition, and innovation are found to be dominated by traditional players. Companies like Microsoft and Intel with their brand strength were able to convince consumers as the driving force for the entire computing experience. Firms are often faced with the strategic choice of growth or control. Firms which emphasize a high rate of return may in the process be undervaluing growth potential by means of strategic control through underinvestment (Jacobides and MacDuffie, 2013).

1.9.6 Brand valuation

Brands are defined as trademarks plus associated goodwill. Brands are a combination of physical, functional and emotional attributes. Brand valuation is the process to calculate the value of the brands. Earlier most of the company's value was in tangible assets such as property, stock, equipment, land, and building. Now the majority of most company's value is in intangible assets like brand names. Brand value is the most valuable of the identifiable intangible asset. The development of computerized software like excel in the eighties facilitated the process of brand valuation. Brands are valued for strategic management purposes, legal disputes, brand securitization and mergers and acquisitions. For multinational companies, brand valuation is central to the strategy that determines the marketing spend for each brand. The difference between book value and actual acquisition price paid for an acquisition is due to the intangible assets of which brands are an important part.

Brand valuation has become an integral part of internal accounting and budgetary control system in firms. Brand valuation can give critical insights that influence brand strategy. The brand valuation process analyzes the strength of the brand using different brand performance parameters. The process of valuation analyzes what drives brand value, revenue and profitability and what particular components could be leveraged to increase the brand value. IFRS stipulate companies to report intangible assets in their balance sheet.

Brand valuation for compliance with accounting standards such as IFRS requires knowledge of the industry in which the brand operates. Brand valuation is a useful tool to calculate the damages or lost profits related to a brand led business. Disputes which require brand valuation consist of partnership disputes, contract disputes, trademark infringement, and failure to fulfil licensing obligations.

Brand valuation provides critical insights that influence brand strategy. Brand valuation is a useful tool for maximizing the Return on Investment (ROI). Brand value can be used for securitization purpose as they can be used as collateral for loan.

Different approaches for brand valuation are explained below:
Income-based brand valuation methods

- Relief from royalty method
  This method is based on how much the brand owner would have to pay to use its brand if it licensed from a third party. The method uses discounted cash flow analysis (DCF) to capitalize future branded cash flows.
- Excess earnings method
  This method calculates the earnings above the profits required to attract the investor. This method estimates the rate of return based on the current value of assets employed. The excess earnings are attributable to the intellectual property or brand.
- Price premium method
  This method is based on a capitalization of future profit stream premiums which are attributable to the business brand above the revenues of a generic business without a brand.
- Capitalization of historic profits methods
  This method is based on the capitalization of profits earned by the brand.

Market-based brand valuation methods

- P/E ratios methods
  The brand's profits are multiplied by a multiple derived from similar transactions of profits to price paid based on the value of reported brand values.
- Turnover multiple methods
  In this method, the turnover of the brand is multiplied by a multiple derived from similar transactions.

Cost-based brand valuation methods

- Creation costs method
  This method estimates the amount that has been invested for the creation of brand.
- Replacement value method
  This method estimates the investment required to build a brand with a similar market position and share.

1.10   Challenges in valuing intangibles

A study by Lev (2004) suggests that R&D-intensive companies were systematically underpriced by the market and investors are slow to recognize the full value of investments in R&D. It has to be noted that R&D investments are reported in the corporate financial statements. Most other types of investments in intangibles like employee training, brand development are not tracked within the company.

Researchers have documented that returns from basic research have on average substantially higher than those from product line extensions. Companies have long been underinvesting in R&D. It is difficult to make generalizations about intangible intensive companies. Intangibles have to be productive and unique. A successful clinic trial in one Pharma Company will lead to value creation in form of stock price increase only for that company. Moreover intangible assets are not traded in active and transparent markets. There are no markets which generate visible prices for intellectual capital, brands or human capital to assist investors in correctly valuing intangibles intensive companies (Gross, 2001).

Many studies report positive market value effects of advertising and R&D expenditures. The study by Chauvin and Hirschey (1993) provides evidence that advertising and research and development (R&D) expenditures have large positive and consistent influences on the market value of the firm. Graham et al. (2005) reported that changes in advertising expenditures are significantly associated with the earnings up to 5 years and market values of firms. The study by Szewczyk et al. (1996) finds that firms with greater investment opportunities have significantly positive stock price reaction to announcements of R&D expenditures. In contrast firms with relatively lesser investment opportunities have negative effects to announcements of R&D expenditure opportunities.

The estimation of aggregate value of the company's intangible capital helps in determining whether it is overvalued or undervalued from intangible perspective. The value of intangible capital is obtained by subtracting from earnings the average contribution of physical and financial assets in the company's industry. The residual figure indicates the contribution of intangible assets to the company's performance and thus provides the basis for the valuation of intangible capital (Lev, 2004). According to Lev (2004), the primary benefit of having asset mentality is that it drives management to structure the intangible related investments for maximum productivity and longevity. Corporations and accounting bodies must focus on developing models on valuations which reflect the unique characteristics of intangible assets.

Dowse (2013) suggests the approach Sustainability and Intangibles Valuation Analysis (SIVA) as a comprehensive value driver model for intangibles based on revenues and costs. The approach identifies and quantifies sustainability related actions and metrics which influence intangibles. This model also uses sensitivity analysis to correlate NPV changes with the strength of factors.

1.11 Innovation and value creation

Innovation is the successful conversion of new concepts and knowledge into new products and processes that deliver new customer value in the market place. The fundamental purpose of innovation is to create value which leads to value creation for different stakeholders of a company. Innovation is profitable, radical and needs speed. According to BCG survey 2013, technology and telecommunications top the list of most innovative companies. Apple, Google, Samsung, Microsoft, IBM, GE have been consistently ranked as top innovative companies. A study by Booze & Company lists Apple, Google, 3M, GE, Toyota, Microsoft, P&G, IBM, Samsung and Intel as the most valuable companies in terms of innovation.

According to Forbes 2013 study, Apple with brand value of $104.3 billion was the most valuable brand. Six of the top ten most valuable brands came from the technology sector. The top ten most valuable brands had brand value of $476 billion and $revenues of 870 billion in the year 2013.

1.12 Review of research studies on usage of valuation methods

Academic research and teaching emphasize fundamental valuation models, although in practice they are much less common than price multiple valuations. Empirical research has analyzed the relative usefulness of company valuation models to investors. The field of financial theory has advocated discounted cash flow methods like dividend discount method and free cash flow to equity as primary valuation methods.

A study by Imam et al. (2008) used semi structured interviews along with content analysis of analysts equity reports to study the analysts valuation model preferences over a large number of industries in UK. The study finds that most analysts prefer sophisticated valuation models such as DCF. The study finds that cash flow−based valuation models play a significantly greater role than accrual models as the primary model of analysis. This study also provides strong evidence that the analysts use cash flow− and earnings-based models like Price Earning (PE) to value shares. The study finds perceived limitations in the technical applicability of the discounted cash flow method which in fact makes the analyst to rely on relative valuation methods.

Research by Liu et al. (2002), Feltham and Ohlson (1995), Ohlson (1995), and Penman (1997, 2001) have compared residual income−based accounting valuation models with DCF models for the purpose of equity valuation. Studies by Penman and Sougiannis (1998), Francis et al. (2000), Courteau et al. (2001) suggest that accrual-based income valuation models are superior to DCF models based on sample of US firms. Olhson (1995) proposes residual income valuation model. The study by Penman (1997) contrasts dividend discounting models, discounted cash flow models and residual income models on the basis of accrual accounting. The study also showed that some models which are apparently different yielded the same valuation. Penman and Sougiannis (1998) examine models that forecast dividends, cash flow, earnings or book value and also compare models that capitalize forecasted earnings rather than discount residual earnings. The findings by Penman and Sougiannis (using ex post average attributes of models) and Francis et al. (2000) using ex ante analysts' forecasts suggest that valuations using different models give the same results when forecasts are made for infinite periods. The study by Lundholm and O'Keefe (2001) dismisses the claim that accrual residual income models and earnings capitalization models are better than cash flow or dividend discount models.

The survey study by Arnold and Moizer (1984) points out that the primary analysis technique used by analysts is fundamental analysis. The study suggests PE ratio as an important valuation model. The study by Pike et al. (1993) examines the changes in the ordinary share appraisal approaches adopted by UK analysts and investigates the differences between British and German analysts in share appraisal. The findings suggest that deregulation and introduction of new technology had little impact on the equity appraisal approach employed by analysts. The study further states that British analyst regard the price to earnings and price to cash flow ratios as the most useful tools in evaluating a company's share price. Technical analysis and beta analysis were found not useful by majority of sample analysts. Barker (1999a) points out that the actual determination of share price is rarely based on direct estimation of future dividends. On the basis of ranking of valuation models used by analysts and fund managers, the study finds preferences for unsophisticated valuation models like dividend yield than dividend discount models. The study by Barker (1999b) suggests that analyst's preference between valuation models varies systematically according to the stock market sector. Analysts basically use valuation models for the determination and evaluation of share prices. This survey-based study suggests that the most dominant valuation model is the price earnings (PE) ratio. Analysts derive incremental information from earnings rather than dividends. The study by Block (1999) points that present value techniques are not widely used in practice as they are in theory. The dividend paying policy of companies is not relevant in the analytical process. Studies like Stern et al. (1995), Stewart (1991) suggest that EVA approach is a better valuation model than dividend valuation model. Myers (1984) who advocated the EVA approach suggest that discounted cash flow valuation models are useful in valuing regular dividend paying companies, but not those with much growth opportunities.

Survey-based research studies (Basu, 1977; Basu, 1983; Arnold and Moizer, 1984; Pike et al., 1993; Barker, 1999ab; Block 1999) suggest that analysts and fund managers prefer using unsophisticated valuation models like Price Earnings ratio (PE) and dividend yield methods in preference to sophisticated valuation models like DCF and residual income methods. Content analysis studies of Demirakos et al. (2004) and Bradshaw (2002) also suggest that analysts are skewed toward usage of unsophisticated models based on PE and Price/Earnings to growth (PEG) ratios. The study of Bradshaw (2002) examine through a sample of 103 sell-side analysts' reports to document the frequency with which the analysts disclose target prices as justifications for their stock recommendations. The most favorable recommendations are likely to be justified by price earnings ratio and expected growth. Further evidence by the study suggests that analyst compute target prices using price multiple heuristics such as PEG. The study by Demirakos et al. (2004) analyzes the valuation practices of financial analysts based on 104 analysts' reports for 26 large UK listed companies representing sectors like beverages, electronics and pharmaceuticals. This study finds that the use of valuation by comparatives is higher in the beverages sector than in electronics models. The study suggests that analysts typically choose either a Price Earning (PE) model or an explicit multi period DCF valuation model as their dominant valuation model.

Asquith et al. (2005) analyze a sample of 1126 analyst reports written during the years 1997–1999 (56 sell-side analysts, 11 investment banks, 46 industries). Their study finds that in 99.1% of the reports the analysts mention that they use some sort of earnings multiple (for example, a price-to-earnings ratio, EBITDA multiple, relative price-to-earnings ratio). In contrast, only in 12.8% of the reports the analysts cite using any variation of discounted cash flow valuation (asset multiple).

Lie and Lie (2002) evaluated various analysts who use multiples to estimate company value. The study finds that asset multiple (market value to book value of assets) generate more precise and less biased estimates than do the sales and the earnings multiples.

1.13   Challenges for valuation

Business Valuation requires the application of finance theory using professional judgment. One of the major challenges facing business valuation professionals is the development of reasonable assumptions for projections based on historical trends and the reasoning for assumption choices. Another challenge involved is the calculation of appropriate discount rate based on the risk of the project.

Security Analysts must initially evaluate information that is reflected in the market in the form of market price of the stock and focus on valuing private information. Generally in merger analysis, the acquirer company makes a forecast of the target firm's future cash flows. The revenue increases or cost reductions accountable to merger are included in the forecasts which are then discounted back to the present value for comparison with the purchase gain. The estimated net gain from the merger will be equal to discounted valuation of target including merger synergy benefits minus the cash paid for acquisition. Valuation can go wrong due to the tendency to make large errors. The analyst often fails to recognize the target's potential as a standalone business. The focus ought to be on valuing the target's standalone value and concentrate on changes on cash flow that accrue as a result of the merger. Managers often adjust their firms' operations and investments to manage earnings. These accounting earnings were the single most figures reported to investors. A study by Graham et al. (2005) finds that about 80% of managers were willing to decrease discretionary expenditures like R&D and advertising to meet earning targets. Many managers were also prepared to defer or reject investment projects with positive NPV to meet earnings target. This pattern indicates that firms do indeed manage their earnings.

The Dividend discount model calculates the value of equity investment in the company as the present value of expected future dividends discounted at the cost of equity capital. But the trend shows that an increasing number of companies choose to hold additional cash to buy back shares of stock than pay dividends. Thus the dividends do not represent the actual cash flows available to equity shareholders. Dividend paying companies cannot use the dividend growth model to value divisions and projects. Moreover it is observed that dividend growth models are of little use for valuing start up, expansion and growth companies. In the discounted cash flow (corporate valuation model) the value of company is the present value of the expected future free cash flows which are discounted at the weighted average cost of capital. This model is based on various assumptions for projections and calculation of appropriate discount rates.

Overreaction by stock markets is often debated (De Bondt, 1985). Studies find that stock prices have been based too much on current earning power and too little on long-term dividend paying power. The price earnings ratio (P/E) anomaly refers to the observation that stocks with extremely low P/E ratios earn large risk adjusted returns than high P/E stocks. Companies with very low P/Es are thought to be temporarily undervalued since investors become excessively pessimistic after a series of bad earnings reports or other bad news.

1.14 Review on theories of valuation

Modigliani and Miller (1958) studied the effect of leverage on the firm's value. In a no tax case scenario, the value of the firm levered is equal to the value of firm unlevered. In the presence of taxes, the value of the firm is equal to the value of the unlevered firm plus the present value of the interest tax shield. Arditti and Levy (1977), Ruback (1995, 2002) suggested that the firm's value could be calculated by discounting the capital cash flows instead of free cash flows. Myers (1974) introduced the APV (adjusted present value). According to Myers, the value of the levered firm is equal to the value of the firm with no debt (Vu) plus the present value of the tax saving due to the payment of interest (VTS). Myers proposes calculating the VTS by discounting the tax savings at the cost of debt. The argument is that the risk of the tax saving arising from the use of debt is the same as the risk of the debt. Luehrman (1997) recommends valuing companies using the Adjusted Present Value and calculates the VTS in the same way as Myers. This theory yields inconsistent results for growing companies, as shown in Fernandez (2002, 2004). Fernandez (2006) shows that this theory yields consistent results only if the expected debt levels are fixed. According to Miles and Ezzell (1980), a firm that wishes to keep a constant debt equity ratio must be valued in a different manner from a firm that has a preset level of debt. Lewellen and Emery (1986) also support the method adopted by Miles and Ezzell.

Harris and Pringle (1985) suggest that the present value of the tax saving due to the payment of interests (interest tax shields) have the same systematic risk as the firm's underlying cash flows and should be discounted at the required return to assets.

Summary—Methods of Discounted Cash Flow Valuation

Basically there are four methods to value companies by discounted cash flows.

- Using the free cash flow and the WACC (weighted average cost of capital)
- Using the expected equity cash flow (ECF) and the required return to equity
- Using the capital cash flow (CCF) and the WACC
- Using the adjusted present value method (APV)

The other methods consists of using the business's risk adjusted free cash flows discounted at the required return to assets; the business's risk adjusted equity cash flows discounted at the required return to assets; using economic profit and required return on equity; EVA discounted at WACC and the risk free rate adjusted free cash flows discounted at the risk free rate.

When Valuation Goes Wrong

An old adage states "When traveling, you should 'know before you go'". Knowing about the company's financial position is essential before buying, selling or merging a business. It is necessary to analyze the full facts for valuation. The financial models used by investment banking firms are basically discounted cash flow and relative valuation models. Forecasting future cash flows for several years is one of the most difficult parts of valuation. Often mergers and acquisitions fail due to the reason that investment bankers and management teams are simply overly optimistic about the synergies which can be achieved through the deal. Roll (1986) put forward the hubris hypothesis that managers commit errors because of over optimism in evaluating merger opportunities. In a takeover, the bidding firm identifies a potential target firm and values its stocks. When the valuation is below the market price of the stock, no offer is made. Only when the valuation exceeds the current market price, a bid is made. If there is no synergy or other takeover gains, the mean of valuations would be the current market price. Offers are made only when the valuation is too high. The takeover premium is a random error which is the mistake made by the bidder.

Initially the price set limits by the acquiring firm makes good sense for the shareholders. But when the deal gets into the bidding war, it's more about winning the bid than acquiring the firm for a price that makes economic sense. Economists often use the phrase "the winner's curse" to explain the phenomena in which the winning bidder in an auction overestimates the value of the asset being sold. Academic studies have shown that M&A transaction delivers a premium return to target firm shareholders.

The lessons of the 1999–2000 tech bubble suggest that the businesses that failed were valued on metrics which were poor indicators of business health. The dot-com bubble or dot com boom was a speculative bubble covering during the period 1997–2000. During this period, stock markets in industrialized world saw their equity value rise rapidly in the internet sector and other related fields. One interesting point observed was that companies could cause their stock price to increase by adding "e" prefix to their name or a ".com" to the end. The internet boom was referred to the steady commercial growth of internet with the advent of the World Wide Web. A combination of factors like sudden rise in stock prices, market confidence about future profits, individual speculation in stocks resulted in unrealistic valuations relative to fundamentals. Many companies were grossly overvalued. The collapse of the bubble took place during the period 2000–2001. Many companies like pet. com collapsed. During the period Cisco's stock price declined by approximately 86%. Amazon's stock price went down from $107 to $7 per share. A number of communication companies like WorldCom, NorthPoint Communications, Global Crossing had to file for bankruptcy. WorldCom was involved in illegal accounting practices to exaggerate its profits. Many dotcoms ran out of capital and were acquired or liquidated.

References
Lowenstein, R., 2004. Origins of the Crash The Great Bubble and Its Undoing. (pp. 114–115). Penguin Books, New York, NY.

Galbraith, J.K., Hale, T., 2004. Income Distribution and the Information Technology Bubble. University of Texas Inequality Project Working Paper.

Failure of AOL Time Warner Merger—A Case of Market Overvaluation

Information technologies strategically impact a business in different ways. The story of AOL illustrates how innovation creates rapid market growth that is highly valued by the stock market. In 1990s, the new electronic commerce or e-commerce had created a whole new set of companies and media industry. The booming US stock market had priced most of these companies exceedingly high. America Online was such company providing service access through internet to its subscribers. AOL was an upstart Internet company in 1993 with just 124 employees. By 2000, AOL had grown into world's premier online server with market value of $ 169.6 billion. AOL used its very high

(Continued)

Failure of AOL Time Warner Merger—A Case of Market Overvaluation (cont'd)

market value to merger with Time Warner. On January 10, 2000 Time Warner announced that it had agreed to be taken over by American Online (AOL) at a 71% premium to its share price on the announcement date. AOL has proposed the acquisition in October 1999. The deal valued at $164 billion became the largest merger on record up to that date.

The merger was structured as a stock swap deal. In December 1999, the market capitalization of American Online was $250 billion dollars whereas the market capitalization of Time Warner was $85 billion. The difference was in the stock markets' multiplication of their relative price to earnings ratio. AOL stock was 3.8 times more valuable than Time Warner's stock based on earnings. But AOL had just one fifth of Time Warner's revenue and only 15% its employees. Time Warner shareholders received 1.5 shares of the new company for every share of Time Warner stock they owned. AOL shareholders received one share of the new company for every AOL share they held. AOL owned 55% of the new company and Time Warner 45%. The merger created one of the world's largest vertically integrated media and entertainment company. The combined entity had a market capitalization of $350 billion. By 2004, the combined market value of the firm had fallen to about $78 billion. The downfall of this merger is symbolic for the burst of the internet bubble. AOL Time Warner proved to be mostly a disaster, partly because AOL's rapid growth had evaporated and huge clash of corporate cultures. In 2003, Time Warner decided to drop AOL from its name. The Time Warner President declared "the death of synergy." Ted Turner, the largest individual shareholder, lost 80% of the worth of the company.

In 2009, Time Warner completed the separation of AOL from Time Warner through a spin off involving a pro rata dividend distribution of all the AOL common stock held by Time Warner to Time Warner stockholders. Time Warner Inc. thus spun off the entire AOL Internet unit reversing a failed mega merger that triggered record losses.

The study by Andrei Shleifer and Robert Vishny argues that the high AOL valuations were based on unrealistic growth expectations (Shleifer and Vishny, 2003). The study further put forward the viewpoint that the company knew that its share price would fall when the market realized its error. Therefore, AOL had a short-run opportunity to cash in by using its stock as currency to buy another company's hard assets that were more rationally valued. In other words, the acquisition was an attempt by the management of overvalued AOL to buy hard assets in Time Warner in order to avoid even worse long-run returns. The merged company had a $100 billion loss in the year 2002 as a result of writing down of overvalued assets. After the announcement of the deal, the stock prices of the company declined rapidly. AOL contributed only 18% of the merged company's pre deal revenues and 30% of the operating cash flow. But AOL shareholders owned (55%) of the new merged company due to its high market valuation. It has been observed that even 2 years after the deal was closed in January 2001, the shares of the then combined firms traded at 90% less than their pre-merger peak value. The very high valuations for the new economy internet stocks made this deal possible. During the 1990s, many upcoming internet startups called dotcoms were tremendously overvalued.

References

The Washington Times. 2000. The AOL Time Warner debacle, January 10 (Editorials page A18).

Cha, A.E. and Dugan I.J. 2000. AOL to acquire Time Warner in record $183 billion merger: Few obstacles foreseen for all-stock deal, *The Washington Post*, January 11 (page A01).

AOL. Time Warner merger adds up to less than the sum of its parts, *The Washington Post*, April 1 (Financial Section, page E01).

1.15 Most valuable companies

According to Forbes Global 2000 list in 2014, the top global 2000 companies had revenues of $38 trillion and profits of $3 trillion, assets worth $161 trillion and market value of $44 trillion. These firms employ 90 million people worldwide.

According to Fortune study Walmart, Exxon Mobil and Chevron were the top three revenue based companies of the year 2014. In terms of market capitalization Apple and Exxon were the largest companies in the world. Apple and Exxon Mobil were the top profit maximizers. General Electric and Berkshire Hathaway were the top asset maximizers among the fortune 500 companies in 2014. In 2014, the book value of equity of Apple was approximately 26% of its market value. The book value of Walmart, Exxon and Ford were approximately 31%, 41%, and 42% of the market value of equity respectively in the year 2014. The book value of equity of General Electric was approximately 50% of its market value. The top ten companies had positive value gap as excess market value compared to the book value of equity. In terms of MVA Apple, Exxon Mobil and Walmart were the toppers. Apple created MVA of $355.52 billion dollars, while Exxon Mobil and Walmart had excess market value of $248 and $170 billion respectively.

According to Fortune Study 2014, Apple had the highest 10-year annualized returns of 49%. The highest 5-year annualized total returns were accounted by Ford Motors and Apple. In 2013, the highest total returns were provided by Valero Energy.

Appendix: Financial statement analysis

Financial Statements are the major source of information which are considered by lenders in providing funds to the firm. Financial Statement Analysis aims to evaluate management performance in terms of profitability, efficiency and risk. A firm's performance can be compared relative to the aggregate economy, its industries, major competitors within the industry and its past performance. Financial statements are evaluated to understand the performance of a company. Often in many companies managers are provided hike in compensation based on accounting measures of performance such as profit margin and return on equity. Short-term and long-term creditors and, potential investors also use the financial statements of firms for appraisal purposes.

Annual and quarterly reports provide three financial statements: the balance sheet, income statement and the statement of cash flows. The annual income statement is a summary of the profitability of the firm over 1 year. Income statement shows the revenues generated over the operating period, the expenses incurred during the year and the firm's net profits which represent the difference between revenues and expenses. Balance sheet is the summary of the firm's assets and liabilities for the specified period of 1 year. The balance sheet is the summary of the financial position of the firm during the 1-year period. The balance sheet highlights what resources or assets the firm possesses and how it has been financed.

A company's financial statement which summarizes its sources and uses of cash over a specific time period is called statement of cash flows. The statement of cash flow combines the information on balance sheet and income statement to show the effects on the firm's cash flow of income flows and changes on the balance sheet on account of cash flows. The statement of cash flows consists of cash flows from operating activities, investing activities and financing activities. The statement of cash flows monitors the implications of transactions. The statement of cash flow recognizes the cash implications of a transaction only when it is completed.

Cash Flow from operating activities = Net Income + Noncash revenues and expenses + changes in net working capital

Cash Flow from investing activities = Investments in fixed assets/noncurrent assets + equity investments in subsidiaries or joint ventures

Cash Flow from financing activities = Investments in notes payable + Long term liability and equity accounts

The total cash flows from operating, investing and financing activities represent the net increase or decrease in the firm's cash. Analyst use cash flow values to estimate the value of a firm.

Sources and uses of cash

Operations or activities which generate cash are sources of cash and which involve spending are uses or application of cash. Basically firms generate cash and use it. Firms generate cash by selling products, real assets or financial assets like securities. The sale of securities consisting of equities and bonds are sources of cash. Cash is required for the purchase of raw materials, assets, payment of salaries and wages and production process.

Table A.1 **Cash flow highlights**

A. Cash Flow Identity Statement
  Cash flow from assets = Cash flow to Bondholders + Stockholders
B. Cash flow from assets
  Cash flow from assets = Operating cash flow − Net capital spending − Change in Net
    Working capital (NWC)
  Operating cash flow = Earnings before interest and taxes (EBIT)
    + Depreciation − Taxes
  Net Capital Spending = Ending net fixed assets − Beginning net fixed
    assets + Depreciation
  Change in NWC = Ending NWC − Beginning NWC
C. Cash flow to creditors (bond holders)
  Cash flow to creditors = Interest Paid − Net new borrowing
D. Cash flow to stockholders (owners)
  Cash flow to stockholders = Dividends paid − Net new equity raised

Cash flow identity

The cash flow identity statement reflects the point that the cash flow from the firm's assets would be equal to the cash flow paid to the contributors of capital to the firm.

Cash Flow from assets = Cash flow to Creditors + Cash flow to stockholders

The three components of cash flow from assets are operating cash flow, capital spending and changes in net working capital (Table A.1).

Measures of cash flow

The traditional cash flow measure is found out by adding depreciation and deferred taxes to net income. The EBITDA (earnings before interest, taxes, depreciation, and amortization) is also viewed as a measure of cash flow.

Free Cash Flow is the amount of cash flow available for a firm after it makes the asset investments to support its operations. The major determinant of a value of a company is its ability to generate free cash flow. The free cash flow is available for distribution to investors consisting of shareholders and debt holders.

Common size statements

Common size statements are standardized financial statements which present all items in percentage terms.

The role of common size statement is to normalize balance sheet and income statement items to allow easier comparison of different sized firms. A common size balance sheet expresses all balance sheet accounts as a percentage of total assets. A common size income statement expresses all income statement items as a percentage of sales.

Common base year statements

Common base year statements are also standardized financial statements which present all items relative to a certain base year amount. This type of statements is useful for trend analysis.

Ratio analysis

The major financial ratios are ratios of short-term solvency or liquidity measures, long-term solvency measures, asset management or turnover measures, profitability and market valuation measures.

Short-term solvency or liquidity measures

Liquidity ratios focus on current assets and current liabilities. Short-term creditors of the firm would be particularly interested in liquidity ratios.

Current ratio

Current ratio examines the relationship between current assets and current liabilities. Current assets include cash, marketable securities, accounts receivables and inventories. Current liabilities consist of accounts payable, short-term notes payable, accrued taxes, and other accrued expenses. High current ratio reflects high liquidity for a firm which is seen as a good sign from the perspective of creditors. Current ratio indicates the extent to which the claims of short-term creditors are covered by current assets. Sometimes high ratios also indicate inefficient use of cash and other short-term assets. A high current ratio may also be due to large inventory holdings.

Current ratio = Current assets/Current liabilities

Quick or acid test ratio

Quick or Acid test ratio measures the ability of firm to payoff short-term obligations without depending on sale of inventories. It considers only those current assets that can be converted into cash quickly. It is a better measure of liquidity for those firms whose inventory cannot be readily converted into cash.

Quick Ratio = Current Assets − Inventory/Current Liabilities

Absolute liquid or cash ratio

It relates the firms' cash and short-term marketable securities to its current liabilities.

Absolute Liquid ratio or cash ratio = Cash/Current liabilities

Profitability measures

Net profit margin

This margin explains the relationship between net income and sales.

Net Profit Margin = Net Income/sales

Return on assets (ROA)

ROA measures the income earned per amount invested in the firm

ROA = Earnings before Interest and Taxes (EBIT)/Total Assets

Return on capital employed (ROCE)

ROCE highlights the income earned per amount of long term capital invested (debt and equity).

ROCE = EBIT/Long Term capital

Return on equity (ROE)

ROE explains the profitability of only equity investments in a firm.

ROE = Net Income/Shareholders' Equity

Long-term solvency measures

These are also called financial leverage ratios or leverage ratios. Long-term solvency ratios aim to examine a firm's capacity to meet interest and principal payments in the long term.

Debt Equity ratio = Total Long term debt/Total equity

The debt figure includes all long-term fixed obligations including capital lease obligations and subordinated convertible bonds. The equity typically is the book value of equity and includes preferred stock, common stock and retained earnings. Some analysts prefer to exclude preferred stock and consider only common stock.

Long Term Debt to Total Capital Ratio = Total Long Term Debt/Total Long Term Capital
(The long term capital include all long term debt, any preferred stock, and total equity)
Total debt to Total capital ratio = (Total Interest bearing debt/Total Invested Capital) = (Capitalized Leases + Noncurrent liabilities)/(Total Interest bearing debt + Shareholders' Equity)

Debt to equity ratio and debt to total capital ratio can also be based on market value weights.

Earnings and cash flow coverage ratios

Interest coverage ratio

This ratio is also known as times earned (TIE) ratio. This ratio measures the firm's capacity to meet interest payments from its predebt and pretax earnings. Higher the interest coverage ratio, higher would be the firm's capacity to make interest payments from the earnings.

Interest Coverage ratio = EBIT/Interest Expenses

Cash coverage ratio

It also measures the firm's ability to generate cash from operations.

Cash Coverage ratio = EBIT + Depreciation/Interest
Fixed Financial Cost Coverage = EBIT + Implied Lease Interest/Gross Interest Expense + Implied Lease Interest
Cash Flow to Long Term Debt Ratio = (Cash flow from Operating Activities)/(Book Value of Long Term debt + PV of Lease Obligations)

Operational efficiency or asset utilization ratios

These ratios measure how efficiently a firm is managing its assets. These turnover ratios measure the efficiency of the working capital management.

Total Assets turnover indicates how effectively it is using its total asset base. This ratio needs to be compared within firms in a particular sector. It is observed that capital intensive industries have low asset turnover ratios while retail firms have high ratio values.

Total Assets turnover = Sales/Average Total Assets
Fixed Assets turnover = Sales/Average Fixed Assets
Equity Turnover = Net Sales/Average Equity

Equity includes preferred and common stock, paid in capital and total retained earnings.

Inventory turnover ratio

Inventory turnover ratio can be calculated relative to sales or cost of goods sold. This ratio has to be examined relative to an industry norm and/or the firm's competitors. Certain industry sectors don't hold high inventory

Inventory turnover = Sales/Average Inventory
Days' sales in inventory = 365 days/Inventory turnover

Receivables turnover ratio

Receivable Turnover = Net Annual Sales/Average Receivables

The average collection period is useful to analyze the quality of accounts receivable. The sooner the firm is able to collect its accounts receivable, the firm would be able to pay off its own current liabilities.

Average Receivable Collection Period = 365/Annual Receivables turnover

Market value measures

EPS = Net Income/Shares Outstanding
Price Earnings ratio = Price per share/Earning per share
Price Sales ratio = Price per share/Sales per share
Market to Book ratio = Market value per share/Book Value per share
Tobin' Q = Market Value of firm's assets/Replacement cost of firm's assets
Market value of firms' assets = Market Value of firm's debt and equity

Du Pont system

Analysts often "decompose" ROE to understand the factors which affect a firm's ROE. This type of analysis is called Du Pont System.

ROE = Profit Margin * Total asset turnover * Equity Multiplier

Business risk

It is the uncertainty of operating income caused by the firm's industry. This uncertainty is due to the firm's variability of sales caused by its products, customers and the way it produces its products.

Business Risk = Coefficient of Variation of Operating Earnings = Standard deviation of Operating Earnings/Mean operating earnings
Sales Volatility = Coefficient of Variation of sales

Analysis of growth potential

The analysis of sustainable growth potential examines the ratios that indicate how fast a firm should grow. Analysis of sustainable growth potential is important for both lenders and owners.

Growth rate (g) = Percentage of Earnings Retained (RR) * Return on Equity
RR = 1−Dividend Payout ratio (DPO)
DPO = Dividends Paid/Net Income

Additional Financial Ratios for Banking/Financial Institutions

Analysis of bank performance

Profitability measures

Return on Assets = Net Income/Total Assets
Profit Margin = Net Income/Total operating Income
Asset Utilization = Total operating income/Total Assets
Net Interest Margin = Net Interest income/Earning Assets
Net Interest Income = Interest Income − Interest Expense

Efficiency measures

Efficiency Ratio = Noninterest expense/Net operating income
Overhead Efficiency = Noninterest income/Noninterest expense
Risk adjusted return on capital (RAROC) = Risk adjusted income/Capital

Expense measures

Interest expense ratio = Interest expense/Total operating income
Provision for loan loss ratio = Provision for loan losses/Total operating income
Noninterest expense ratio = Noninterest expense/Total operating income

Leverage ratios

The most widely used indicator of capital adequacy is the capital to risk weighted assets ratio (CWRA) commonly known as CAR.

Capital to Assets ratio = Core capital/Assets
Total risk based capital ratio = Total capital (Tier I plus Tier II)/Risk adjusted assets

Tier 1 (core capital) is shareholder equity capital. Tier 2 capital (supplementary capital) is the bank's loan loss reserves plus subordinated debt, which consists of bonds sold to raise funds.

Asset quality

Gross NPL (Nonperforming loans) ratio = Gross NPL/Total loan
Net NPL ratio = Net NPL/Total loan

Management quality

Total Advance to Total Deposit Ratio

Limitations of ratio analysis

Ratio analysis provides useful information about a company's operations and financial condition. But for diversified firms involved in different industries, it would be difficult to develop a meaningful set of industry averages. Inflation and seasonal factors also distort the results of a ratio analysis. Firms can also use "window dressing" techniques to showcase stronger financial statements. Companies using different accounting practices for inventory valuations and depreciation methods can distort comparisons.

Links for websites for financial analysis

1. Thomson Financials
2. http://financeyahoo.com
3. http://www.sec.gov
4. http://money.cnn.com
5. http://www.zacks.com
6. http://www.bloomberg.com
7. http://www.marketwatch.com
8. http://www.smartmoney.com
9. http://www.investor.reuters.com
10. http://www.hoovers.com
11. http://www.fool.com
12. http://www.thestreet.com
13. http://www.dnb.com

Fundamentals of valuation

Time value of money

The basic concept behind time value of money is that an amount of money earned earlier is better than that earned tomorrow. Time value of money has immense application in today's life. Its application spans in a variety of personal decisions like saving and retirement planning. Corporates investment decisions are based on time value of money. A dollar earned today is worth more than a dollar earned tomorrow since the dollar can be invested to earn a return. For example if the bank offers an annual interest rate of 10% in a saving account, then one dollar deposited will become $1.10 in a year's time. Time value of money exists due to inflation and preference of people for present consumption. On account of inflation, you might not be able to buy the same amount of goods in future compared to today as the purchasing power of money decreases due to inflation. People basically prefer present consumption compared to future. Borrowers must offer compensation for the postponement of the present consumption in the form of interest rate on savings. This interest rate is called real rate of interest. Nominal interest rate includes real rate of interest and expected inflation. In time value of money, money can be invested to earn a return which is termed discount rate.

Future value and compounding

Future value of an investment is the amount of money the investment would be worth after some period of time. The process of accumulating interest on an investment over time to earn more interest is called compounding. Earning interest on interest is called compound interest. In simple interest, interest is earned each period only on the original principal.

The future value of $1 invested for t periods at a rate of r per period is given by

Future Value $= \$1*(1 + r)^t$
Future Value $=$ Present Value$*(1 + r)^t$

Present value and discounting

Present Value is the current value of future cash flows discounted at the appropriate discount rate. The process of finding the present value is just the reverse of future value. In present value calculation, the amount of money is discounted back to the present instead of compounding the money forward as in the case of future value of money.

Present Value $=$ Future Value$/(1 + r)^t$ where r is the discount rate and t is the time period.

Discounted cash flow valuation

The process of calculating the present value of a future cash flow to determine its value today is known as discounted cash flow valuation. The rate which is used to calculate the present value of a future cash flow is called discount rate (Table A.2).

Annuities

A series of identical or level stream of cash flows for a fixed period of time is called annuity. A series of constant cash flows that occur at the end of each period for some fixed number of periods is called ordinary annuity. An annuity for which the cash flows occur at the beginning of the period is called annuity due.

Perpetuities

An annuity in which the cash flows continue forever is called perpetuity (Table A.3).

Table A.2 Time value of money calculations using spreadsheets

Factor	Formula
Future Value	= FV (rate, nper, pmt, pv)
Present Value	= PV (rate, nper, pmt, fv)
Discount rate	= RATE (nper, pmt, pv, fv)
Number of periods	= NPER (rate, pmt, pv, fv)

Table A.3 **Formulas for annuity and perpetuity calculations**

Future Value of an Annuity
A cash amount C per period for t periods at r percent per period:
$FVt = C^*\{[(1 + r)^{t-1}]/r\}$. The term $[(1 + r)^{t-1}]/r$ is called the annuity future value factor.
Present Value of an Annuity
$PV = C^*\{1-[1/(1 + r)^t]\}/r$. The term $\{1-[1/(1 + r)^t]\}/r$ is called the annuity present value factor.
Present Value of a Perpetuity
A cash amount C per period:
$$PV = C/r$$

Growing annuity

An annuity is a series of constant payments which are to be received over a specified period of time. Growing annuity represent a series of payment that grow at a constant rate.

Continuous compounding

In continuous compounding, money is continuously or instantaneously compounded and the interest is credited at the time it is earned.

Different types of interest rates

Nominal or stated interest rate

The interest rate expressed in terms of the interest payment made each period. It is also known as the quoted interest rate. This is the form of rate which is quoted by brokers, banks and other financial institutions. The quoted nominal rate must also include the number of compounding periods per year.

Annual percentage rate

Annual Percentage rate is defined as the interest rate charged per period multiplied by the number of periods per year. The Truth lending laws in the United States stipulates that lenders have to disclose the annual percentage rate on all consumer loans.

Periodic rate

Periodic rate is the rate charged by a lender each period. It can be quoted as a rate per period, say semiannually, per quarter or per month. For example, a bank could charge 1% per month for a credit card loan.

Effective annual rate

The interest rate expressed as if it were compounded once per year.

$$EAR = [1 + (\text{Quoted rate}/m)]^m - 1$$

Effective Annual Rate is used to compare the effective costs of different loans or rates of return on different investments when the period of payments differ.

Different types of loans

Pure discount loans

It is the most basic type of loan. In such type of loan, the borrower receives money today and repays a single lump sum amount in a specified period in future. Treasury bills are examples for pure discount loans.

Interest only loans

In interest only loan, the borrower pay interest each period and repay the entire original loan amount in the final period.

Amortized loans

In amortized loans, the loan is paid off by making regular principal reductions. The borrower pays the interest each period plus some fixed amount as principal reduction.

Bond valuation and interest rates

Basics of bonds

A Bond can be termed as a long-term contract in which a borrower commits to make payments of interest (known as coupon) and principal on specified time period to the holders (buyers) of the bond. There are various types of bonds like government (treasury) bonds, municipal bonds, agency bonds, corporate bonds, Eurobonds and foreign bonds. Government bonds are issued by national governments like US. Agency bonds are issued by government sponsored entities like Fannie Mae, Freddie Mac and Federal Home Loan Bank System. Corporate bonds are issued by corporations. Municipal bonds are issued by state and local governments. Eurobond is a bond issued in a currency other than the currency of the country or market in which it is issued. A foreign bond is a debt instrument issued by a borrower from outside the country in whose currency the bond is denominated and sold.

Convertible bonds have the option to convert the bonds into a fixed number of shares of common stock. Income bonds are required to pay interest under the condition that earnings are high enough to cover the interest expense.

Bonds are also classified as zero coupon bonds, floating rate and fixed rate bonds. Zero coupon bonds is a bond that makes no coupon payment which is initially priced at a deep discount. Floating rate bonds have adjustable or variable coupon payments. The value of a floating rate bond depends on the adjustments of the coupon payments. An example of floating rate bond is an inflation linked bond. Fixed rate bonds have fixed coupon payments.

Features of bond

Indenture

Indenture or deed of trust is a written agreement between the corporation (the borrower) and the lender which highlights the terms of the debt issue. This legal document includes provisions like the basic terms of bond, the total amount of bonds issued, details of collateral, repayment provisions and protective covenants.

Bonds can be issued in registered or bearer form. In registered bond, the ownership of each bond is recorded and payments are directly made to the owner of record. In bearer form, the interest payments are made to whomever who holds the bond. Collaterals are any asset pledged as security for the payment of debt. Collaterals can be in form of bonds and stocks. Mortgage securities are secured by a mortgage on the real property of the borrower.

A sinking fund is an account managed by the bond trustee for early bond redemption. A call provision is an agreement which confers the option to a corporation to buy back a bond at a specific price prior to maturity. Protective covenants which limit certain acts that might be taken during the term of the loan are basically meant to protect the lender's interests. For example the firm must limit the amount of dividends.

Bond terminology

Par value

The par value is the stated face value of bond. A bond generally has a face value of $1000.

Coupon and coupon rate

The stated interest payment made on the bond is called coupon. The annual coupon divided by the face value of the bond is called coupon rate.

Maturity date

Bonds have a specified maturity date on which the par value must be repaid.

Yield to maturity (YTM)

The market rate of interest required for a bond is called yield to maturity.

Current yield

The annual interest payment divided by the price of the bond gives the current yield.

Current yield + Capital gains yield = Yield to Maturity

Yield to call

The expected rate of return that is calculated instead of yield to maturity when a bond is likely to be called as the current interest rates are below the bond's coupon rate.

Premium and discount bond

When a bond is issued, the selling price of the bond is equal to its par value since the coupon rate will be equal to market rate of interest. In other words whenever the going market rate of interest is equal to the coupon rate, the fixed bond will sell at its par value. An increase in the market rate of interest will cause the price of the bond to fall whereas a decrease in the market rate of interest will cause the bond's price to rise. When a bond sells for more than its face value due to decrease in market interest rate, it is called a premium bond. When a bond sells for less than its face value due to increase in market interest rate, it is called a discount bond.

Value of bond

Bond Value $= C^*[1 - 1/(1 + r)^t]/r + F/(1 + r)^t$
Bond Value = Present Value of Coupons + Present Value of the Face Amount.

With Excel spreadsheet, use PV function = PV (I, N, PMT, FV, 0)
Specialized function = PRICE (settlement date, maturity date, coupon, yield to maturity, redemption, frequency)

Interest rates

The rate that is often quoted by banks and financial press is known as nominal interest rates. *Nominal interest rates* are not adjusted for inflation. Real rates are those interest rates which have been adjusted for inflation. The real risk free rate of interest is the interest rate on a riskless security in an environment of no inflation. *Real interest rate* can be the rate of interest on Treasury bill in an inflation free scenario. From the year 1997 onward, US Treasury issued TIPS (Treasury Inflation Protected Securities).

Fisher effect states the relationship between nominal interest, real interest and inflation.

$$1 + N = (1 + r)(1 + h)$$

where N is the nominal interest rate, r is the real rate and h the inflation rate

By approximation

$$N = r + h$$

Term structure of interest rates

A yield curve is a curve which plots several yields or interest rates across different maturity period. The yield curve shows the relation between the level of interest (cost of borrowing) and the time to maturity (term of debt) for a borrower in a given currency. The Wall Street Journal provides a plot of Treasury yields relative to maturity. The most frequently reported yield curve compares the 3-month, 2-year, 5-year, and 30-year US Treasury bond rates. The yield curve is used as a benchmark for determining mortgage or bank lending rates.

The term structure of interest rates describes the relationship between the long-term and short-term interest rates. The interest rates for bonds can be obtained from different sources like The Wall Street Journal, Federal Reserve Bulletin, websites of CNN Financial, Federal Reserve Board, Bloomberg, Yahoo!. The term structure of interest rates indicates what the nominal interest rates are on default free pure discount bonds of all maturities. In short, the term structure highlights the time value of money for different lengths of time.

The term structure of interest rates is upward sloping when long-term rates are higher than short-term rates. An upward sloping yield curve is called a normal yield. When short-term rates are higher than the long-term rates, then term structure is downward sloping. The term structure can also be humped when medium term rates were higher than either short- or long-term rates. The Expectation theory states that shape of yield curve is determined only by market expectations about future interest rates.

The three fundamental components which determine the shape of term structure are real rate of interest, inflation premium, interest rate risk premium. The real rate of interest depends on pure time value of money. The inflation premium arises by the need for compensation for expected future inflation. Interest rate risk premium arises due to the compensation required by investors for bearing interest rate risk. The other premiums include default risk premium, taxability premium and liquidity premium. The default risk premium arises as a result of credit risk which is the possibility of default. Investors demand extra yield on a taxable bond as compensation for unfavorable tax treatment. The liquidity premium arises when bonds have varying degrees of liquidity.

Bond ratings

Bonds are assigned quality ratings by major rating agencies like Moody's Investors Service (Moody's), Standard and Poor's (S&P), and Fitch Ratings. Triple A and double rated A bonds are considered to be the safest investments. Single A and triple B bonds are considered strong and termed investment grade bonds. Double B and lower bonds are of low grades.

Bond ratings are based on quantitative factors like financial ratios, bond contract terms and qualitative factors. The major ratios used to evaluate the ratings are the coverage ratios, leverage ratios, liquidity ratios, profitability ratios and cash flow to debt ratio.

Bond pricing theorems

- Bond prices and yields move inversely. Prices and interest rates are inversely related.
- As maturity approaches, bond prices converge toward their face value at an increasing rate, other things held constant.
- Dollar changes in bond prices are not symmetrical for a given basis point increase/ decrease in YTM, other things constant. A decrease in interest rate raises bond prices by more than a corresponding increase in rates lower the prices.
- Price volatility is inversely related to coupon. Lower coupon bonds are more sensitive to yield changes than higher coupon bonds, other things held constant.
- Price volatility is directly related to maturity. Longer maturity bonds are more sensitive to yield changes than shorter maturity bonds. Price volatility increases at a diminishing rate as maturity increases.

Duration theorems

A measure of the average maturity of the stream of payments generated by a financial asset is duration. The mathematical relationship between bond yields and prices is termed bond convexity.

The main highlights of the duration theorems are:

- The duration of a zero coupon bond is always equal to its time to maturity.
- The lower the coupon rate the longer the duration, other things held constant.
- The longer the maturity, the longer the duration, other things held constant.
- The lower the yield to maturity, the longer the duration, other things held constant.

Basics of stock valuation

The common stock holders are the owners of a corporation. Managers seek to maximize the value of firm's stocks. The stock price is the market price of a publicly listed company. The intrinsic value is considered the correct value of a stock and can be estimated. The goal of investment strategy is to purchase stocks which are undervalued (price is below the stock's intrinsic value). One of the basic models to estimate the intrinsic value is the dividend discount model. In this model, the value of stock is equal to the present value of expected future dividends.

If P_0 is the current price of stock and let P_1 be the price of the stock in one period. r is the required return in the market. If D_1 is the dividend paid at the end of the period.

$$P_0 = (D_1 + P_1)/(1 + r).$$

If the future dividends in two periods is D_2, the stock price in one period

$$P_1 = (D_2 + P_2)/(1 + r).$$

In generalization,

$$P_0 = D_1/(1+r)^1 + D_2/(1+r)^2 + D_3/(1+r)^3 + D_4/(1+r)^4 + D_5/(1+r)^5$$

The dividend growth model states that value of a stock is determined as the dividend next period divided by the discount rate less the dividend growth rate.

The components of the required return are sum of dividend yield and capital gain yield. Dividend yield is the expected cash dividend divided by its current price. The capital gains yield is the rate at which the stock price grows.

Summary highlights of stock valuation

General method

The price today of a stock P_0 is the present value of all its future dividends D_1, D_2, $D_3 \ldots$

$$P_0 = D_1/(1+r)^1 + D_2/(1+r)^2 + D_3/(1+r)^3$$

Constant growth method

Suppose if the dividend grows to D_1 at a steady rate g, then the price is

$$P_0 = D_1/r - g$$

This model is the dividend growth model.

Nonconstant growth

Suppose if the dividends grow steadily after a period of time say t, the value of the stock can be written as

$$P_0 = D_1/(1+r)^1 + D_2/(1+r)^2 + \cdots + D_t/(1+r)^t + P_t/(1+r)^t$$

Where $P_t = D_t(1 + g)/(r - g)$

Two stage growth

If the dividend grows at rate g_1 for period of time t and then grows g_2 thereafter the price is written as

$$P_0 = D_1/(r - g_1) * [1 - (1 + g_1/(1+R)^t] + P_t/(1+R)^t$$

Where $P_t = D_{t+1}/R - g_2 = D_0 * (1 + g_1) * (1 + g_2)/R - g_2$

References

Arditti, F.D., Levy, H., 1977. The weighted average cost of capital as a cutoff rate: a critical examination of the classical textbook weighted average. Financ. Manage. 24−34.

Armitrage, H., Jog V. 1996. Economic value creation: what every management accountant should know. CMA magazine 9 October, 21−24.

Arnold, J.A., Moizer, P., 1984. A survey of the methods used by UK investment analysts to appraise investments in ordinary shares. Account. Bus. Res. 14, 195−207.

Asquith, P., Mikhail, M., Au, A., 2005. Information content of equity analyst reports. J. Financ. Econ. 75, 245−282.

Arzac, E.R., 1986. Do your business units create shareholder value? Harv. Bus. Rev. 121−128.

Barker, R.G., 1999a. The role of dividends in valuation models used by analysts and fund managers. Eur. Account. Rev. 8 (2), 195−218.

Barker, R.G., 1999b. Survey and market based evidence of industry dependence in analysts preferences between dividend yield and price earnings ratio valuation models. J. Bus. Finance Account. 26 (3/4), 393−418.

Basu, S., 1977. Investment performance of common stocks in relation to their price-earnings ratios: a test of the efficient market hypothesis. J. Finance. 3, 663−682.

Basu, S., 1983. The relationship between earnings' yield. Market value and return for NYSE common stocks: further evidence. J. Financ. Econ. 12, 129−156.

Bigler, W.R., Hsieh, C.H., 2013. Linking strategic management and shareholder value. Bus. Stud. J. 5 (2), 27−48.

Block, S.B., 1999. A study of financial analysts: practice and theory. Financ. Analyst J. 86−95.

Boulton, R.E.S., Libert, B.D., Samek, S.M., 2000. Cracking the value code, Harper Business, New York, NY, 26.

Bradshaw, M.T., 2002. The use of target prices to justify sell-side analysts' stock recommendations. Account. Horiz. 16 (1), 27−41.

Brooking, A., 1996. Intellectual Capital: Core Asset for the Third Millennium Enterprise. International Thomson Business Press, New York.

Bruckner K., Leithner S., McLean R., Taylor C., Welsh J.F., 2000. What is the market telling you about your strategy. *McKinsey Quarterly*, June.

Carrott G.T., Jackson, S.E., 2009. Shareholder Value must top CEO's Agenda, Harvard Business Review, hbr.org.

Chauvin, K., Hirschey, M., 1993. Advertising, R&D expenditures and the market value of the firm. Financ. Manage. 22, 128−140.

Copeland, T.E., Koller, T., Murrin, J., 2000. Valuation: Measuring and Managing the Value of Companies. Third ed. John Wiley & Sons, New York.

Courteau, L., Kao, J.L., Richardson, G.D., 2001. Equity valuation employing the ideal versus ad hoc terminal value expressions. Contemp. Account. Res. 18, 625−661.

Damodaran, A., 1994. Damodaran on Valuation. John Wiley & Sons, New York.

Damodaran, A., 2002. Investment Valuation: Tools and Techniques for Determining the value of any Asset. Second ed. John Wiley & Sons, New York.

De Bondt, W.F.M., 1985. Does the stock market overreact? J. Finance, 40, 3, 793−805.

Demirakos, E.G., Strong, N., Walker, M., 2004. What valuation models do analysts use? Account. Horiz. 18, 221−240.

Dowse, J., 2013. Valuing intangibles and ESG performance, Keeping Good Companies, Applied Corporate Governance, 334−339.

Feltham, G., Ohlson, J., 1995. Valuation and clean surplus accounting for operating and financial activities. Contemp. Account. Res. 11 (2), 689−731.

Fernandez, P., 2002. Valuation Methods and Shareholder Value Creation. Academic Press.

Fernandez, P., 2004. The value of tax shields is NOT equal to the present value of tax shields. J. Financ. Econ. 73 (1), 145−165.

Fernandez, P., 2006. University of Navarra, Madrid, Spain, valuing companies by cash flow discounting: ten methods and nine theories. J. Manag. Sci. 1 (1), 80−102.

Francis, J., Olsson, P., Oswald, D., 2000. Comparing the accuracy and explainability of dividend, free cash flow and abnormal earnings equity value estimates. J. Account. Res. 38 (1), 45−70.

Graham, J.R., Harvey, C.R., Rajagopal, S., 2005. The economic implications of corporate financial reporting. J. Account. Econ. 40, 3−73.

Graham Jr., R.C., Frankenberger, K.D., 2000. The contribution of changes in advertising expenditures to earnings and market values. J. Bus. Res. 50, 149−155.

Gross, 2001. Valuing intangibles is a tough job, Business Week 54−55.

Hall, R., 1992. The strategic analysis of intangible resources. Strateg. Manage. J. 13 (2), 135−144.

Hares, J., Royle, D., 1994. Measuring the Value of IT. John Wiley & Sons, New York.

Harris, R.S., Pringle, J.J., 1985. Risk-adjusted discount rates extensions form the average-risk case. J. Financ. Res. 237−244.

Imam, S., Barker, R., Clubb, C., 2008. The use of valuation models by UK Investment Analysts. Eur. Account. Rev. 17 (3), 503−535.

Itami, H., 1987. Mobilizing Invisible Assets. Harvard University Press, Cambridge.

Ittner, C., 2001. Assessing empirical research in managerial accounting a value based management perspective. J. Account. Econ. 32.

Jacobides, M.G., MacDuffie, J.P., 2013. How to drive value. Harv. Bus. Rev. 92−100.

Jennergren, L.P., 2013. Technical note: value driver formulas for continuing value in firm valuation by discounted cash flow model. Eng. Econ. 58, 59−70.

Kaplan, R.S., Norton, D.P., 1996. Using the balanced scorecard as a strategic management system, Harvard Business Review, Jan−Feb.

Kazlauskiene, V., Christauskas, C., 2008. Business valuation model based on the analysis of business value drivers. Econ. Eng. Decis. 57 (2), 23−31.

Koller, T., Goedhart, M., Wessels, D., 2000. Valuation: Measuring and managing the Value of Companies. Fifth ed. Wiley, Hoboken NJ.

Lev, B., 2004. Sharpening the intangibles edge. Harv. Bus. Rev. 109−116.

Lewellen, W.G., Emery, D.R., 1986. Corporate debt management and value of firm. J. Financ. Quant. Anal. 21 (4), 415−426.

Lie, E., Lie, H.J., 2002. Multiples used to estimate corporate value. Financ. Analyst J. 58 (2), 44−56.

Liu, J., Nissim, D., Thomas, J., 2002. Equity valuation using multiples. J. Account. Res. 40 (1), 135−172.

Luehrman, T.A., 1997. What's it worth: a general manager's guide to valuation, and using APV: a better tool for valuing operations. Harv. Bus. Rev. 132−154.

Lundholm, R.J., O'Keefe, T., 2001. Reconciling value estimates from discounted cash flow model and the residual income model. Contemp. Account. Res. 18 (2), 311−335.

Mauboussin, M.J., 2012. The true measure of success. Harv. Bus. Rev. 46–56.

Miles, J.A., Ezzell, J.R., 1980. The weighted average cost of capital, perfect capital markets and project life: a clarification. J. Financ. Quant. Anal. 719–730.

Miller, T.W., Mathisen, R.E., McAllister, J.P., 2004. Estimates of the sensitivities of the value of the firm to profitability, growth and capital intensity. J. Account. Finance Res.-Winter II. 20–33.

Modigliani, F., Miller, M., 1958. The cost of capital, corporation finance and the theory of investment. Am. Econ. Rev. 48, 261–297.

Myers, S.C., 1974. Interactions of corporate financing and investment decisions – implications for capital budgeting. J. Finance. 1–25.

Myers, S.C., 1984. Financial theory and strategy. Interfaces. 14 (1), 126–137.

Ocean Tomo, 2010. Intangible asset market value study.

Ohlson, J.A., 1995. Earnings, book values and dividends in security valuation. Contemp. Account. Res. 11, 661–687.

Penman, S.H., 1997. A synthesis of equity valuation techniques and the terminal value calculation for the dividend discount model. Rev. Account. Stud. 2 (4), 303–323.

Penman, S.H., 2001. On comparing cash flow and accrual models for use in equity valuation. Contemp. Account. Res. 18 (4), 681–692.

Penman, S.H., Sougiannis, T., 1998. A comparison of dividend, cash flow and earnings approach to equity valuation. Contemp. Account. Res. 15 (3), 343–383.

Pike, R., Meerjanssen, J., Chadwick, L., 1993. The appraisal of ordinary shares by investment analysts in United Kingdom and Germany. Account. Bus. Res. 23, 489–499.

Pike, S., Roos, G., Marr, B., 2005. Strategic management of intangible assets and value drivers in R&D organizations. R&D Management. 35 (2), 111–124.

Porter, M.E., Kramer, M.R., 2011. Big idea creating shared value. Harv. Bus. Rev.63–77.

Pratt, S.P., 1989. Valuing a Business. Richard D Irwin Inc, Chicago, IL.

Rappaport, A., 1986. Creating Shareholder Value: The New Standard for Business Performance. The Free Press, New York, NY.

Rappaport, A., 1998. Creating Shareholder Value. The Free Press, New York.

Reilly, R.F., 1998. The valuation of proprietary technology. Manage. Account. 79, 45–49.

Roll, R., 1986. The hubris hypothesis of corporate takeovers. J. Bus. 59, 197–216.

Ruback, R., 2002. Capital cash flows: a simple approach to valuing risky cash flows. Financ. Manage. 31, 85–103.

Ruback, R.S. 1995. A note on capital cash flow valuation. Harvard Business School Background Note 295-069.

Ryall, M.D., 2013. The new dynamics of competition. Harv. Bus. Rev. 80–87.

Scarlett, R.C., 1997. Value based Management. CIMA Publishing, London.

Shleifer, A., Vishny, R.W., 2003. Stock market driven acquisitions. J. Financ. Econ. 70, 295–311.

Stern, J.M., Stewart III, G.B., Chew Jr., D.H., 1995. The EVA financial system. J. Appl. Corp. Finance, Finance. 8 (2), 32–16.

Stewart III, G.B., 1991. The Quest for Value. Harper Collins, New York, NY.

Sveiby, K., 1997. The new organizational wealth: managing and measuring knowledge based assets. Barrett-Kohler, Publishers, San Francisco, CA.

Szewczyk, S., Tsetsekos, G., Zantout, Z., 1996. The valuation of corporate R&D expenditures: evidence from investment opportunities and free cash flow. Financ. Manage. 25 (1), 105–110.

Risk and return

2.1 Introduction

Risk can be termed as the mixture of danger and opportunity. Risk refers to the chance that some unfavorable outcome will occur contrary to our expectations. Determination of an appropriate discount rate is one of the most important steps in the process of valuation. The discount rate must reflect the riskiness of cash flows. The discount rate is a combination of cost of equity and cost of debt. The cost of debt incorporates a default risk and the cost of equity includes risk premium for equity risk.

Capital market history provides us a perspective on the relationship between risk and return. There is a reward for bearing risk. Higher the potential reward or return greater is the risk. The study by Ibbotson and Sinquefiled (1982) has analyzed the rates of returns in US financial markets for large and small company stocks, long-term corporate, and US government bonds along with US treasury bills for the past one century. The analysis for large company stock portfolio was based on the Standard & Poor's (S&P) 500 index. The small company stock analysis was based on a portfolio comprising smallest 20% of the companies listed on the New York Stock Exchange (NYSE). The returns for corporate bonds and government bonds were based on bonds with a 20-year maturity period. The returns on treasury bills were based on 1-month maturity. The average annual returns for small company stocks and large company stocks were found to be 17.1% and 12.3% during the period 1926−2007, respectively. At the same time, the annual returns for long-term corporate bonds, long-term government bonds, and US treasury bills were found to be 6.2%, 5.8%, and 3.8%, respectively. US treasury bills are the safest risk-free assets. An asset's risks can be analyzed on a standalone basis or portfolio basis. Investments are to be undertaken when the expected rate of return is good enough to compensate for the risks undertaken.

2.2 Accounting and risk measures

Accounting statements and financial ratios measure risk in the context of risk of default and the capacity of the firm to meet its obligations at a certain period of time. The financial statements measure risks by means of disclosures like contingent liabilities. Contingent liabilities refer to potential liabilities which firm might incur under certain contingencies. The short-term liquidity risk of a firm can be analyzed through current ratio and quick ratio. The current ratio is the ratio of current assets to its current liabilities. A current ratio of less than 1 indicates the potential liquidity risks faced by the firm.

The quick or acid test ratio (cash plus marketable securities divided by current liabilities) measures how current assets can be converted quickly into cash. The turnover ratios measure the efficiency or speed with which firms turns accounts receivables into cash or inventory to sales. The calculation of accounts receivable period, accounts payable period, and inventory turnover period helps in the estimation of the amount of financing required to fund the working capital needs of the firm.

The long-term solvency or default ratios examine a firm's capacity to meet the interest and principal payments in the long run. The interest coverage ratio measures the firm's capacity to meet interest payments from earnings before interest and taxes. Higher the interest coverage ratio, higher would be the capacity of the firm to cover the interest payments from earnings. Debt ratios like debt to capital ratio and debt to equity relate debt to total capital or equity of the firm.

2.3   Measures of returns

2.3.1   Total return

With respect to stock market investments, the total return on any investment is the sum of the dividend and the capital gain. In percentage terms, the total return is equal to the dividend yield plus the capital gain yield.

Total return = Dividend income + Capital gain (loss)
Returns in percentage = Dividend yield + Capital gain yield.

Suppose P_t be the price of a stock at the beginning of a year and D_t be the dividend paid during the year. The stock price at the end of the year is P_{t+1}.

Dividend Yield = D_t/P_t
Capital gains yield = $(P_{t+1} - P_t)/P_t$

2.3.2   Historical rates of return

Historical rates of returns help investors to choose among alternative investment assets. Historical rates of returns and risk are often used by investors to estimate the expected rates of return and risk for an asset class. Suppose an investment is made at the beginning of the year and receive an amount at the end of the year. The change in wealth of investment may be due to cash inflows like interest or dividends or due to change in the price of assets. The period for which the investment is made is called holding period and the return for the holding period is called the holding period return (HPR).

HPR = Ending value of investment ÷ Begining value of investment

A HPR value of greater than 1 indicates an increase in wealth and a value of less than 1 indicates decline in wealth. Holding period yield (HPY) is the percentage return obtained by converting HPR into an annual percentage rate.

HPY = HPR − 1

Annual HPR = $(HPR)^{1/n}$

where n is the years for which investment is made.

2.3.3 Average returns

The average compound return earned per year over different years is called geometric average return. The return earned in an average year over different years is called arithmetic average return.

Geometric average return = $[(1 + R_1)^*(1 + R_2)^* \ldots \ldots(1 + R_T)]^T − 1$

where $R_1, R_2, \ldots R_T$ are rates of returns during time period ranging from 1 to T.

$$\text{Arithmetic average return} = \sum_{i=1}^{i=n} R_{i/n}$$

where ΣR_i is the sum of returns for n period.

The geometric average gives the returns earned per year on average, compounded annually, whereas the arithmetic average gives the returns earned in a particular year. The arithmetic average return is too high for longer periods of time while geometric average is too low for shorter periods of time.

2.3.4 Expected return

Expected return is the return on a risky asset expected in the future. The expected return on an asset is equal to the sum of the possible returns multiplied by their probability. Each possible outcome is multiplied by its probability of outcome and summed up. This weighted average is called expected return.

$$\text{Expected rate of return} = r = \sum_{i=1}^{n} P_i \, r_i$$

2.3.5 Portfolio returns

The expected return on a portfolio is calculated as the weighted average of the expected returns on the stocks which comprise the portfolio. The weights reflect the proportion of the portfolio invested in the stocks. This can be expressed as follows:

$$E[R_p] = \sum_{i=1}^{N} w_i E[R_i]$$

where

- $E[R_p]$ is the expected return on the portfolio,
- N is the number of stocks in the portfolio,
- w_i is the proportion of the portfolio invested in stock i, and
- $E[R_i]$ is the expected return on stock i.

For a portfolio consisting of two assets, the above equation can be expressed as follows:

$$E[R_p] = w_1 E[R_1] + (1 - w_1) E[R_2]$$

2.3.6 Determinants of rate of return

The major determinants of the expected rate of return on an investment are the real risk-free rate of return, expected inflation during the holding period, and the risk premium which is determined by the uncertainty of returns. In other words, the required return is the sum of real risk-free rate plus expected inflation and risk premium. The real risk-free rate is the fundamental interest rate which reflects the pure time value of money under the assumptions of zero inflation and no uncertainty regarding future cash flows from the investment. The real interest rate is determined by the time preference of individuals for consumption of income and the set of investment opportunities in the economy. The investment opportunities in turn are determined by the real growth rate of economy. The nominal risk rates of interest are determined by real risk-free rates of interest, expected rate of inflation, monetary environment, and capital market conditions. Treasury bills are considered as default free investment which provides real risk-free rate of interest. According to sources,[1] the annualized average rates of returns for the treasury bills for all months during the period 1926–2012 was 3.55% while the real treasury bill rate was 0.52% during the same period. The annualized average inflation during the above period was 3.04%.

Required rate of return = Real risk-free rate + Expected inflation + Risk premium
Nominal risk-free rate = [(1 + Real risk-free rate)*(1 + Expected inflation)] − 1

The above relationship is known as Fisher Effect.

For investment of assets, an investor must estimate the intrinsic value of the investment at the required rate of return and compare it with the prevailing market price of the asset. If the estimated intrinsic value is greater than the market price, then the investor should buy the asset.

---

[1] Annual rates of return from rolling over 1 month treasury bills: Kenneth French and Morningstar, annual inflation rates: Bureau of Labor Statistics.

2.4 Risk premium

The returns on government debt instruments like treasury bills can be considered as risk-free return as the probability of default is negligible. The investor would be certain of the amount and timing of the expected return. Investors require higher rates of returns on investments if they expect uncertainty about the expected rate of return. The excess return required from an investment in a risky asset over that required from a risk-free investment is called risk premium. Risk premium is equal to expected return minus risk-free rate. The risk measured by the uncertainty of returns is attributed to various risks like business risk, financial risk, liquidity risk, exchange rate risk, and country risks. In other words, the major sources of uncertainty are attributed to the above stated risks.

Business risk is due to uncertainty of cash flows due to the nature of a firm's business. Firms in the consumer goods or retail sector face less business risk compared to auto or steel sector firms whose revenues and earnings fluctuate to greater extent due to the business cycle. Investors demand risk premium which depends on the uncertainty of cash flows caused by the basic nature of business. Financial risk arises due to the uncertainty on account of fixed cost financing or financial leverage. In the case of increased financial leverage, the equity shareholders demand an increased premium as uncertainty of returns increases due to fixed financing cost of interest payments on debt issued by the firm. Liquidity risk arises when investors realize that assets cannot be quickly converted into cash. Exchange rate risk arises due to uncertainty of returns on account of exchange rate fluctuations. Country risk refers to the uncertainty of returns due to changes in the political or economic environment of a country.

Investors basically increase their required rates of return as uncertainty or risk increases.

2.4.1 Classification of risks

Risk basically means uncertainty of future outcomes. It is the probability of an adverse outcome.

The variability of returns is known as risk. The actual returns can be quite different from the expected returns. Risk can be classified into systematic and unsystematic risks. Systematic risks have market-wide effects and affect a large number of assets. Systematic risks are also known as market risks. Changes in GDP, inflation, and general interest rates contribute toward systematic risks. When recession sets in all firms are affected though cyclical firms such as automobiles, steel, and housing are affected to greater extent. Unsystematic risks are those that affect a small number of assets. They are also known as unique or firm-specific risks. Project risk, competitive and sector risk, affects few firms. Demand for products and changes in regulation for a particular sector lead to only unsystematic risks. Product defects and management turnover are specific risks which affect individual securities.

2.4.2   Diversification

When an investor puts all his/her investments in one single asset, then his/her investments are exposed to both systematic and firm-specific risks. The process of spreading an investment across assets whereby the unsystematic or firm-specific risk is diversified is called diversification. A portfolio is a group of assets formed as a result of diversification. Diversification limits or eliminates firm-specific risks. Each investment in a diversified portfolio accounts for a smaller percentage of that portfolio compared to the case in which there was only single asset. Undiversified investors are much more exposed to changes in investment values compared to diversified investors. Since the number of assets is more in a diversified portfolio, the positive performances of certain stocks in terms of prices in the portfolio are balanced out by the negative performances of certain other stocks. As a result, the risk is averaged out to zero and the overall value of portfolio remains unaffected.

There is a minimum level of risk that cannot be eliminated by diversification. Investors expect compensation for taking this nondiversifiable or systematic risk. The systematic risk principle suggests that the reward for bearing risk depends only on the systematic risk of an investment. In other words, the expected return on an asset depends only on that asset's systematic risk.

Total risk = Systematic risk + Unsystematic risk

2.4.3   Risk measures

2.4.3.1   Variance and standard deviation

The variance or standard deviation of expected returns is one of the best-known measures of risk. In finance, the variability or volatility of returns is known as risk. Volatility measures how much the actual returns deviate from the average returns in a certain period of time. The two most commonly used measures of volatility are variance and its square root standard deviation. Variance is the average squared difference between the actual and average return. The distribution of returns is often described by normal distribution. A normal distribution is a symmetric bell-shaped distribution which is defined by mean and standard deviation.

$$\text{Variance} = \sigma^2 = \sum_{i=1}^{n} (r_i - r')^2 P$$

Standard deviation is the square root of the variance. Standard deviation is a weighted average of the deviations from the expected value.

2.4.3.2   Coefficient of variation

If two investments have different expected returns and standard deviations, coefficient of variation (CV) is used as a measure of risk. CV is a measure of relative variability to indicate the risk per unit of return.

CV = Standard deviation/Expected return

2.4.4 Portfolio risk

Portfolio risk refers to the chances that an investment portfolio does not earn the expected or desired rate of return. Portfolio risk includes both systematic and unsystematic risks. Investors can reduce portfolio risk through diversification. The risk of a portfolio of assets, σ_p, is generally not the weighted average of the standard deviations of the individual assets in the portfolio.

Portfolio risk can be measured through portfolio variance and standard deviations. Portfolio standard deviation is the standard deviation of a portfolio of investments. It is a measure of the variability of the expected returns from a portfolio. Diversification leads to a reduction in risk unless the returns on the portfolio investments are perfectly correlated. On account of diversification benefits, the standard deviation of a portfolio of investments should be lower than the weighted average of the standard deviations of individual investments. The variance/standard deviation of a portfolio highlights not only the variance/standard deviation of the stocks which constitute the portfolio but also how the returns on the stocks which comprise the portfolio vary together. Covariance and correlation coefficient are two measures which analyze how the returns on a pair of stocks vary together.

Consider the case of two assets. The covariance between the returns on two stocks can be calculated using the following equation:

$$\mathrm{Cov}(R_1, R_2) = \sigma_{12} = \sum_{i=1}^{N} p_i(R_{1i} - E[R_1])(R_{2i} - E[R_2])$$

where

- σ_{12} is the covariance between the returns on stocks 1 and 2,
- N is the number of states,
- p_i is the probability of state i,
- R_{1i} is the return on stock 1 in state i,
- $E[R_1]$ is the expected return on stock 1,
- R_{2i} is the return on stock 2 in state i, and
- $E[R_2]$ is the expected return on stock 2.

The correlation coefficient between the returns on two stocks can be calculated using the following equation:

$$\mathrm{Corr}(R_1, R_2) = \rho_{12} = \frac{\sigma_{12}}{\sigma_1 \sigma_2} = \frac{\mathrm{Cov}(R_1, R_2)}{\mathrm{SD}(R_1)\mathrm{SD}(R_2)}$$

where

- ρ_{12} is the correlation coefficient between the returns on stocks 1 and 2,
- σ_{12} is the covariance between the returns on stocks 1 and 2,
- σ_1 is the standard deviation on stock 1, and
- σ_2 is the standard deviation on stock 2.

Using either the correlation coefficient or the covariance, the variance on a two-asset portfolio can be calculated as follows:

$$\sigma_p^2 = (w_1)^2\sigma_1^2 + (1-w_1)^2\sigma_2^2 + 2w_1(1-w_1)\rho_{12}\sigma_1\sigma_2$$
$$= (w_1)^2\sigma_1^2 + (1-w_1)^2\sigma_2^2 + 2w_1(1-w_1)\sigma_{12}$$

The standard deviation on the portfolio equals the positive square root of the variance.

$$\sigma_{portfolio} = \sqrt{w_1^2\sigma_1^2 + w_2^2\sigma_2^2 + 2w_1 w_2 Cov_{1,2}}$$

2.4.5 Sharpe ratio

Sharpe ratio reflects the trade-off between reward (the risk premium) and the risk (as measured by standard deviation or SD)

Sharpe ratio = Risk premium/Standard deviation of excess return

2.4.5.1 Beta as a measure of systematic risk

The level of systematic risk for different investment levels is measured by the beta coefficient. Beta is the amount of systematic risk present in a particular risky asset in relation to that in an average risky asset. Portfolio beta can be calculated like portfolio's expected return. Beta coefficient is the measure of sensitivity of a share price to movement in the market price. Beta reflects the systematic risk which is the risk inherent in the whole financial system. According to CAPM, beta coefficient is an important factor used to calculate the required rate of return on a stock. It is the slope of the security market line.

Beta coefficient is given by the following formulas:

$$\beta = \frac{\text{Covariance of market return with stock return}}{\text{Variance of market return}}$$

$$\beta = \frac{\text{Correlation coefficient}}{\text{Between market and stock}} \times \frac{\text{Standard deviation of stock returns}}{\text{Standard deviation of market returns}}$$

A stock with a beta coefficient of 1 suggests that the stock carries the same risk as the overall market and earns market return only. A coefficient of less than 1 suggests risk and return lower than overall market. A beta coefficient of greater than 1 indicates greater sensitivity compared to market returns. In other words, beta reflects the tendency of a security's returns to respond to swings in the market. A beta of 1 indicates the security price will move with the market. For example, if the market index (say NYSE Dow Jones) moves by 1% and the stock (say FORD) also moves up by 1%, then the beta for the stock will be 1. A beta of less than 1 means that the security will be less volatile than the market. A beta of greater than 1 indicates that the security's price will be more volatile than the market.

2.4.5.2 Beta estimation

Beta can be estimated by regressing stock returns on market returns (returns on a market index like S&P 500). The steps are as follows:

- Obtain the historical share price data for the company's share price for a certain period of time.
- Obtain historical values of an appropriate capital market index (say S&P 500) for the same period of time.
- Convert the share price values into daily return values by using the following formula: Return = (Closing share price − Opening share price)/Opening share price.
- Convert historical stock market index values in similar way.
- Match the share return data with index return such that there is one-on-one correspondence between them.
- Regress stock returns on market returns. The slope of regression gives the beta value of the stock.

Table 2.1 gives the average weekly returns and standard deviation values of 2014 top five of Fortune 500 companies. The weekly return data used for analysis is for the period January 2009−September 2013. The data was collected from Yahoo! Finance. The average returns were geometric mean returns. The 5-year period of analysis reveals that Apple had the highest average weekly returns of 0.7% followed by Berkshire Hathaway with average weekly returns of 0.22%. In other words, Apple and Berkshire Hathaway had an average yearly return of 36.4% and 11.4%, respectively. Standard deviation measures the total risk. Apple had the highest risk with a standard deviation of 4.30%. It can be observed from Table 2.1 that higher the

Table 2.1 Risk and return for top five 2014 Fortune 500 companies

Company	Average weekly returns (%)	Average yearly returns (%)	Standard deviation (%)
Walmart	0.12	6.24	2.31
Exxon Mobil	0.082	4.26	2.68
Chevron	0.19	9.88	3.05
Berkshire Hathaway	0.22	11.4	3.19
Apple	0.70	36.4	4.30

Table 2.2 **Beta values for top companies in different sectors**

Company	Sector	Beta
Walmart	Retail	0.49
Dow Chemical	Chemical	1.23
United Continental Holding Inc	Airlines	1.48
J P Morgan Chase	Commercial Banks	1.16
Microsoft	Computer Software	0.78
Coca Cola	Beverages	0.69
Honeywell International	Electronics, Electrical	1.12
Johnson & Johnson	Pharmaceuticals	0.77
Exxon Mobil	Petroleum Refining	0.86
General Motors	Automobiles	1.31
Intel	Semiconductors	0.71

risk, higher the return is. Walmart had the least risk and return among the top five 2014 Fortune 500 companies. *The spreadsheet risk and return.xlsx in resources website provides the calculation for risk and return.*

Table 2.2 gives the beta values for the top companies in different sectors based on Fortune 500 list. Beta values were obtained by regressing daily stock returns on market index returns. The estimation period was from January 1, 2013 to September 30, 2014. The data was collected from Yahoo! Finance. The selected market indexes were NYSE Composite index (DJ) and NASDAQ Composite based on the list of stocks. For example, Microsoft, Intel, and Apple stock returns were regressed upon NASDAQ index while the rest of stock returns were regressed on NYSE Dow Jones index. *The spreadsheet Beta.xlsx in resources website shows the workings for beta calculations.*

United Continental Holding Inc and General Motors had the highest beta values of 1.48 and 1.31, respectively. Walmart had the least beta value during the estimation period. Beta measures systematic risk. Beta is the tendency of a security's returns to respond to swings in markets. In other words, beta measures a stock's volatility which is the degree to which its price fluctuates in relation to the market index. Analysts use the Greek letter "ß" to represent beta. A beta of 1 means that the stock's price tends to move with the broader market.

A beta greater than 1 indicates that price of the stock will be more volatile than market. A beta value of 0.8 indicates that the returns tends to go up only by 0.8% when the market rises by 1% and vice versa. In that sense, United Holdings stock with a beta of 1.48 is theoretically 48% more volatile than the market. Similarly, General Motors stock with a beta of 1.31 is theoretically 31% more volatile than the market. High beta asset classes have high expected return and vice versa.

Utility stocks usually have beta less than 1 and aggressive stocks have beta greater than 1. Technology stocks also have beta greater than 1. Healthcare sector stocks have betas lesser than 1.

The Relation Between Risk and Return

In financial perspective, risk is the possibility of losing hard earned money. The relationship between risk and return is often represented by a trade-off. Risk and return are directly related. The greater the risk of the investment, the greater the potential return from that investment. This trade-off that an investor faces between risk and return while taking investment decisions is called risk return trade-off. The risk-free rate of return refers to return on investments that hold little or no risk such as US government bonds or certificate of deposit (CD) which are federally insured. The risk premium is the additional return an investor may get over the risk-free rate of return. US government securities can be considered to be default or risk-free. A 30-day treasury-bill is most commonly used to represent the risk-free asset.

Investments in government bonds and savings accounts offer lower rate of return as the risks involved in such investments are relatively low. The yield for average money market account has been 0.5% and 2-year CD rate hovered around 1.2%. Investments in stocks are considered riskier and hence the expected returns is higher. Optimally, the risky portion of the portfolio includes all risky assets; for example, stocks, bonds, real estate, etc. Stocks have a potentially higher return than bonds over the long term but are also riskier.

Recent research in empirical finance has documented that expected excess returns on bonds and stocks, real interest rates, and risk shift over time in predictable way. An important implication of time variation in expected returns is that investors, particularly aggressive investors, may engage in market timing or tactical asset allocation strategies that are aimed at maximizing short-term return based on predictions of their return forecasting model Campbell and Viceira. Crashes usually occur under the conditions of a prolonged period of rising stock prices, excessive economic optimism, overvaluation (e.g., P/E ratios exceed long-term averages), extensive use of margin debt, and leverage by market participant.

The Wall Street Crash of 1929 was the most devastating stock market crash in the history of United States. The crash heralded the beginning of the 10-year Great Depression which affected the industrialized world. The stock market had been on a 9-year boom run before the crash which saw Dow Jones Industrial Average increase in value almost tenfold peaking at 381.17 one month before the crash. Stock prices had reached the peak of the tableau before the crash. The market lost over $30 billion in a span of 2 days on October 28 and 29, 1929. The speculative bubble in shares led to the Great Depression. During the 4-year period of 1929–1932, Dow Jones Industrial Average lost 89% of its value. The global financial crisis of 2008 had affected stock market volatility. The Dow Jones Industrial Average fell over 1874 points, or 18%, in its worst weekly decline ever on both a point and percentage bases. The S&P

(Continued)

The Relation Between Risk and Return   (cont'd)

500 fell more than 20% during the 2008 Crisis. The fall in the value of world stock markets was estimated to be 10−12 trillion dollars.

According to Merton (1973)'s intertemporal capital asset pricing model (ICAPM), the conditional expected excess return in a stock market is linearly and positively related to its variance. Positive risk return relationship in a stock market emerges as essential criteria for risk-taking for investors.

The relationship between return on an asset and its variance (volatility) as a proxy for risk has been an important topic in financial research. The theoretical asset pricing models typically link the return or price changes of an asset to its own return variance or to the covariance between its return and the return on the market portfolio. Most asset pricing models postulate a positive relationship between a stock's portfolio's expected returns and volatility.

2.5   Models of risk and return

All risk and return models suggest that risk is basically the deviations of actual returns around the expected return. Risks are measured from the perspective of marginal investors who is well diversified. Models differ in their perspective on measuring market risks. Capital Asset Pricing Model (CAPM) is the most important risk return model widely used in the industry.

2.5.1   Mean−variance optimization and modern portfolio theory

The Markowitz mean−variance optimization model is a widely used tool for portfolio selection. The fundamental goal of portfolio theory is to optimally allocate the investments between different assets. Portfolio theory assumes that investors are basically risk-averse. Mean−variance optimization is a quantitative tool for allocation of assets based on the trade-off between risk and return. Harry Markowitz in the year 1952 introduced a formal model of portfolio selection signifying diversification principles. This portfolio variance model suggested not only the importance of diversifying the investments to reduce the total risk of a portfolio, but also how to effectively diversify the investments. The concept led to the identification of the efficient set of portfolios known as the efficient frontier of risky assets. Efficient frontier represents the set of portfolios which has the maximum return for any given level of risk or minimum risk for every level of return. The underlying principle behind the frontier set of risky portfolios is that in a universe of risky assets, investors can optimize their returns by combining risky assets that maximize the expected return for any given level of risk (Merton 1972). The portfolio with the highest expected return level for any risk level will be chosen by the investors. In another perspective, the frontier is the set of portfolios that minimizes the variance for any targeted expected return. It can be stated that modern portfolio theory represents a theory of finance which attempts to maximize portfolio's expected return for a given portfolio risk or equivalently minimize the risk for a given level of expected return. The Markowitz model suggests that a single asset or portfolio of assets is considered to be efficient if no other asset or portfolio of assets have higher expected return with the same or (lower risk) or vice versa. The basic assumptions of Markowitz model are as follows:

- Each investment alternative is defined by investors as a probability distribution of expected returns over a holding period.
- The utility curves of investors demonstrate diminishing marginal utility of wealth. Investors maximize one-period utility.
- Investors estimate the risk measure on a portfolio on the basis of the variability of expected returns.
- The decisions by investors are based solely on expected return and risk. The utility curve is a function of expected return and expected variance (or standard deviation) of return only.
- For a given level of risk, investors prefer higher returns.
- For a given level of expected return, investors prefer less risk.

The optimal portfolio refers to that portfolio which has the highest utility for a given investor.

2.5.2   Capital market theory

Capital market theory is based on the modern portfolio theory. The additional assumptions for capital market theory are as follows:

- All investors are Markowitz efficient in which investor's aims to invest in tangent points in efficient frontier. The selection of portfolio by investors depends on the individual investors' risk return utility function.
- Investors can borrow or lend any amount of money at the risk-free rate of return. Government treasury bills offer risk-free rate of return.
- All investors have homogenous expectations.
- All investors have the same one-period time horizon.
- All investors are infinitely divisible such that fractional shares of any asset can be bought or sold.
- There are no taxes or transaction costs involved in buying and selling assets.
- Capital markets are in equilibrium.
- The risk-free asset have zero variance.

The major factor that led to the development of capital market theory from Markowitz model was the concept of risk-free asset with zero variance. Capital market theory suggests that investors diversify their cash flows between a riskless security and the risky portfolio M. Portfolio M requires a return equal to the risk-free rate plus compensation for the number of risk units. Portfolio M is the market portfolio which contains all risky assets in the market place and have the highest level of expected return per unit of risk for any available portfolio of risky assets. It can be mathematically shows that the standard deviation of a portfolio which combines risk-free asset with risky assets is the linear proportion of the standard

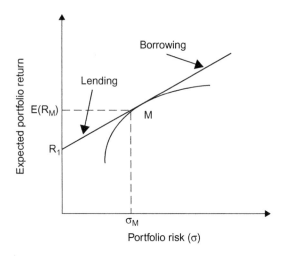

Figure 2.1 Capital market line.

deviation of the risky asset portfolio. The capital market line (CML) is given by the equation given below:

$$E(R_P) = R_F + \sigma_P[E(R_M) - R_F/\sigma_M]$$

where R_F is the risk-free rate, R_M is the return on the market index, σ_P and σ_M are the standard deviations of the specific portfolio and market portfolio, respectively. Portfolio M is the single collection of the risky assets which maximizes the risky premium. The term $E(R_M) - R_F/\sigma_M$ is the expected return per unit of risk undertaken or commonly referred to as investor's expected risk premium per unit of risk. CML represents a new efficient frontier which combines the Markowitz efficient frontier of risky assets with additional investments in risk-free assets. The implications of the CML are that investors must invest funds in two types of assets—risk-free asset and risky asset denoted by market portfolio M with the weights in these investment based on the investor's tolerance for risk. The market portfolio is a completely diversified portfolio which has only systematic risks. In real sense, market portfolio includes all assets in the economy. The proportion of each stock in the market portfolio equals the market value of the stock (price per share times number of shares outstanding) divided by the sum of the market value of all stocks.

The major limitation of CML is that it cannot explains the risk return trade-off for individual assets.

2.5.3   Capital asset pricing model

CAPM is the extension of the capital market theory which provides the scope for investors to evaluate the risk return trade-off for diversified portfolios and individual assets. CAPM considers risk in terms of a security's beta which measures the systematic risk of a stock. CAPM expresses the expected return for an investment as the sum of the risk-free rate and expected risk premium. The underlying message of CAPM is that the only significant factor that matters is the overall market risk premium $E(R_M) - R_F$ which can be related to any risky asset by adjusting it according to the asset's riskiness relative to the market denoted by beta. CAPM is a normative model for asset pricing.

The key assumptions of CAPM are:

- Investors are rational, mean−variance optimizers.
- Investors have homogenous expectations.
- All assets are publicly traded.
- Investors can borrow or lend at a common risk-free rate.

The CAPM can be graphically expressed in the form of security market line (SML). The SML shows the trade-off between risk and expected return as a straight line which intersects the vertical axis at risk-free rate. CAPM is the equation of the SML which shows the relationship between expected return and beta.

$$E(R_i) = R_F + \beta_i * E(R_M) - R_F$$

The CAPM shows that the expected return on a particular asset depends on three factors—the pure time value of money as measured by risk-free rate (R_F), the reward for bearing risk measured by market risk premium $E(R_M) - R_F$, and the amount of systematic risk measured by β_i. CAPM can be used to estimate the discount rate for future cash flows. The cost of equity can be determined by the SML approach. The key implications of the CAPM are:

- The market portfolio is efficient.
- The risk premium on a risky asset is proportional to its beta.

The SML approach can be used to identify undervalued and overvalued assets. The required or expected rate of return on a stock is compared with the estimated rate of return. If the required rate of return is greater than the estimated return, then the stock is overvalued or vice versa. Underpriced stocks plot above the SML; overpriced stocks plot below the SML. The difference between estimated return and expected return is referred to as stock's expected alpha or excess return. When alpha is positive, the stock is undervalued and when alpha is negative, the stock is overvalued. If the alpha is zero, the stock is on the SML, see Figure 2.2.

CAPM is the cornerstone of modern financial economics. This model gives the prediction of the relationship between the risk of an asset and its expected return. Hence, CAPM provides a benchmark rate of return for evaluating possible investments, and is very useful in capital budgeting decisions. The model also facilitates in estimating the expected return on assets which had not been traded in the market. CAPM is the most popular risk return model used by practitioners.

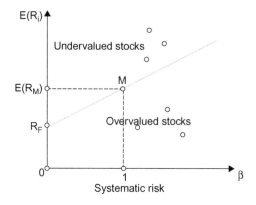

Figure 2.2 Security market line.

2.5.3.1 Arbitrage

An arbitrage opportunity arises when an investor earn riskless profits without making a net investment. The law of one price states that, if two assets are equivalent in all economic aspects, then they should have the same market price. Arbitrageurs engage in arbitrage activity when there is a violation of the law. Arbitrage involves the simultaneous purchase and sale of equivalent securities in order to profit from the discrepancies in their prices.

2.5.4 Arbitrage pricing theory

The arbitrage pricing theory (APT) was developed by Stephen Ross. The basic difference between APT and CAPM is in the way systematic investment risk is defined. CAPM advocates a single, market-wide risk factor for CAPM while APT considers several factors which capture market-wide risks. In an environment of single factor market, the APT leads to CAPM. The major assumptions of APT were as follows:

- Capital markets are perfectly competitive.
- Investors always prefer more wealth to less wealth with certainty.

The stochastic processes generating asset returns are expressed as a linear function of a set of K risk factors. APT like CAPM assumes that the unique or specific effects ($\mathcal{E}_i$) are independent and could be diversified away in a large portfolio. According to APT, the expected return on any asset can be given as:

$$E(R_i) = \lambda_0 + \lambda_1 b_{i1} + \lambda_2 b_{i2} + \cdots\cdots\cdots\cdots\cdots + \lambda_k b_{ik}$$

where

    $E(R_i)$ is the expected return on any asset,
    λ_0 is the expected return on asset with zero systematic risk,

λ_k is the risk premium related to the kth common risk factor, and
b_{ik} is the pricing relationship between the risk premium and the asset which are known as factor betas or factor loadings.

The limitation of APT is that the theory does not suggest factors for a particular stock or asset (Bodie and Kane). The investors have to perceive the risk sources or estimate factor sensitivities. In practice, one stock would be more sensitive to one factor than another. The price of an oil company stock, like Royal Dutch Shell, will be more sensitive to factor like oil price changes compared to that of a pharma company stock. Hence in APM, the real challenge for investor would be to identify each of the factors which affect a particular stock; the expected returns for each of these factors and the sensitivity of stock to each of these factors.

2.5.5 Multifactor models

In multifactor model investors identify the risk factors and choose the exact number of factors (Reilly and Brown). A two factor model can be expressed as:

$$R_i = E(R_i) + \beta_{i1}F_1 + \beta_{i2}F_2 + e_i$$

where F_1 is the deviation of GDP growth rate from expectations and F_2 is the unexpected change in interest rates.

Generally, multifactor model can be expressed by the following relationship

$$R_{it} = a_{it} + [\beta_{i1}F_{1t} + \beta_{i2}F_{2t} + \cdots\cdots\cdots\cdots + \beta_{ik}F_{kt}] + e_{it}$$

where F_{kt} is the period t return to the kth risk factor.

On the basis of nature, the risk factors can be classified as macroeconomic and microeconomic factors. At macroeconomic level, changes in asset's cash flows and returns can be related to macroeconomic variables like changes in GDP, interest rates, and inflation rates. At microeconomic level, firm variables like financial ratios are related to expected returns.

Chen et al. (1986) hypothesized that security returns are related to a set of broad economic factors given by:

$$R_{it} = a_i + [b_{i1}R_{Mt} + b_{i2}MP_t + b_{i3}DEIt + b_{i4}UI_t + b_{i5}UPR_t + b_{i5}UTS_t] + e_{it}$$

where

- R_M is the return on a value weighted index of NYSE listed stocks during time t,
- MP is the monthly growth rate in US Industrial production in time t,
- DEI is change in inflation measured by the US consumer price index,
- UI is the difference between actual and expected levels of inflation,
- UPR is the unanticipated change in the bond credit spread, and
- UTS is the unanticipated term structure shift.

Burmeister et al. (1994) developed a multifactor model based on five risk exposures consisting of confidence risk (unanticipated changes in the willingness of investors to take on investment risk), time horizon risk(unanticipated changes in investor's desired time to receive payouts), inflation risk(unexpected components of short-term and long-term inflation rates), business cycle risk (unanticipated changes in the level of overall business activity), and market timing risk (market index's total return not explained by the other four risk exposures).

2.5.6 Fama French three factor model

The Fama French (FF) three factor model is given by the equation given below:

$$R_{it} = \alpha_i + \beta_{iM}R_{Mt} + \beta_{i\,SMB}SMB_t + \beta_{i\,HML}HML_t + e_{it}$$

where

> SMB, Small minus Big, which means the return of a portfolio of small stocks in excess of the returns on a portfolio of large stocks,
> HML, High Minus Low, which means the return of a portfolio of stocks with a high book to market ratio in excess of the return on a portfolio of stocks with a low book to market ratio.

In their study, Fama and French (1996a,b) finds that firms with high ratios of book to market value are more likely to be in financial distress and small stocks are more sensitive to changes in business conditions. Fama and French (1993) analyzed the behavior of broad sample of stocks grouped into quintile portfolios by their price earnings (P/E) ratios on a yearly basis over the period July 1963–December 1991.The study identified five common risk factors to explain the average returns on stocks and bonds. The stock related factors are an overall market factor and factors related to firm size and book to market equity. The bond market factors were related to maturity and default risk. Low P/E stocks tend to have high book to market ratios, while high P/E stocks tend to have low book to market ratios.

2.5.7 Review of empirical research on models of risk and return

Hary Markowitz laid the foundation of modern portfolio management in the year 1952. The theory of CAPM was developed through the works of Sharpe (1964), Lintner (1965a,b), and Mossin (1966). Many studies like Basu (1977) provide empirical evidence that size, P/E ratio, financial leverage, and book to market ratio have explanatory powers for returns of assets. The FF study highlighted that the variables with significant explanatory powers were size and book value to market value ratio. Kothari et al. (1995) finds that β_s from annual returns produce a stronger positive relation between β and average return than β_s from monthly returns. Fama and French (1996a,b) argue that survivor bias does not explain the relation between Book Value of Equity/Market Value of Equity (BE/ME) and average return. Their study shows that annual and monthly β_s produce the same results about the β premium. Basu (1983) examines the empirical relationship between earnings yield, firm size, and returns on the common stock of NYSE listed firms. The study suggests that common stock of high P/E firms earn on average higher risk adjusted returns than the common stock of low P/E firms. The study by Basu also points out that common stock of small NYSE firms earned substantially higher returns than common stock of large NYSE firms. The paper by Fama and MacBeth (1973), tests the relationship between average returns and risk for NYSE listed based on two parameter portfolio model and models of market equilibrium.

Penttengill et al. (1995) finds significant relationship between beta and cross-sectional portfolio returns. Bali et al. (2009) examines the cross-sectional relation between conditional betas and expected stock returns for the sample period between July 1963 and December 2004. The study based on portfolio level and cross-sectional regression analysis indicates a positive relation between conditional betas and cross section of expected returns. Jagannathan and Wang (1996) employs conditional CAPM that allows for changes in betas and market risk premium in explaining the cross section of returns. Grundy and Malkiel (1996) through empirical study suggests that beta is a useful tool in forecasting short-term risk in declining markets. Reilly and David (2004) suggests that the return risk analysis using a measure of systematic risk (beta) provides results with significantly more explanatory power.

Many studies have focused on use of market index as a representative of the market portfolio. Richard Roll through a series of articles in the late 1970s and early 1980s raised concerns with testing of CAPM and use of the model to evaluate investment performance. Roll (1977) basically referred to this problem as benchmark error since the practice had been to compare the performance of a portfolio manager to the performance of an unmanaged portfolio of same risk. The benchmark has been a security market index adjusted for risk while the risk measure is one implied by CAPM. Roll (1980, 1981) demonstrated that if the benchmark employed in this evaluation process is mistakenly specified then the performance of portfolio managers cannot be measured properly Reilly and Akhtar (1995). Early tests of CAPM were done by Lintner (1965a,b) and later by Miller and Scholes (1972).

Merton and Roll showed that any portfolio that is a combination of two frontier portfolios is itself on the efficient portfolio. They suggested that every portfolio on the efficient frontier has a "companion" portfolio on the bottom half of the frontier referred to as zero beta portfolio. Black (1972) showed that some investors will choose portfolios on the high risk premium portion of the efficient frontier. Merton (1973) deduced an intertemporal model for capital market known as ICAPM from the portfolio selection behavior by an arbitrary number of investors who act so as to maximize the expected utility of lifetime consumption and who can trade continuously in time. The paper by Amihud and Mendelson (1986) studies the effect of the bid ask spread on asset pricing and suggest that liquidity is increasingly viewed as an important determinant of prices and expected returns.

APT and multifactor models have also been empirically tested (Sharpe, 1984). Basu (1983) pointed out that small stock portfolios (with low market capitalizations) outperformed large stock portfolios (with large market capitalizations) on a risk adjusted basis. Fama and French (1992) showed that firms with high book value to market price ratios (value stocks) tend to have higher risk adjusted returns than for firms with low book value to market price ratios (growth stocks). Ross (1976, 1977) through seminal work developed the theory of APT. Roll and Ross (1980) carried out large-scale empirical tests of APT using data for individual equities during the 1962–1972 period and concluded that four factors aid in the generating process of returns. Cho et al. (1984) suggested that two or three factors can explain the returns. Dhrymes et al. (1984) founds no relationship between the factor loadings for groups of 30 stocks and for a group of 240 stocks. Ross and Roll (1984) suggests that number of factors is a secondary issue compared to how well the APT model explains expected security returns. The research by Reinganum (1981) investigates empirically whether a parsimonious arbitrage pricing model can account for differences in average returns between small firms and large firms. The results were inconsistent with the APT. The small firms systematically experienced average rates of return nearly 20% greater than those of large firms even after accounting for differences in the estimated values of beta. Macroeconomic-based risk factor models were developed by researchers like Chen et al. Studies of Harvey (1989) and Ferson and Korajczyk (1995) examine how business cycles affect asset beta and led to the concept of conditional beta.

Chen (1983) compares APT model to the CAPM and suggests that APT model is superior to CAPM. Gultekin and Gultekin (1987) shows that the empirical tests of the APT model can explain the risk return relation for anomalies like January effect. The study observed that once the January returns were excluded from data, there was no significant relation between stock returns and risk factors. The main focus of the paper by Burmeister and McElroy (1988) was on the interrelationships of three nested tests: APT versus the linear factor model; CAPM versus the APT; and the existence versus nonexistence of anomalies like January effect. The study found that January effect is an important determinant of expected returns. A number of papers like Onatski (2009) and Zhang (2009) have proposed new methodologies for testing APT.

Carhart (1997) extended the FF three factor model by an additional price momentum factor. Price momentum factor indicates the tendency for firms with positive (negative) past returns to produce positive (negative) future returns.

2.5.8 Bond ratings

Credit ratings are basically opinion about the credit quality of an issue—like a bond or other debt obligation—which reflects the relative likelihood that it may default.

Credit ratings enable corporations and governments to raise money in the capital market. Investors use credit ratings to assess credit risk and compare different issuers and debt issues. Institutional investors like mutual funds, pension funds, and banks use credit ratings to supplement their own credit analysis of specific debt issues. Investment bankers utilize credit rating to benchmark the relative credit risk of different debt issues and also for the purpose of setting initial price for individual debt issues. The bond ratings are also used to determine the cost of debt for a company when valuing companies.

Credit rating agencies like Moody's, S&P, and Fitch Ratings assign credit ratings to debt securities like bonds. This credit rating is a financial indication to potential investors of the debt instruments. These rating agencies assign letter grades such as AAA, BB, CC based on the quality of the bond. AAA ratings indicate bonds of highest quality. Bond ratings below BBB−/Baa are considered to be of non-investment grade and called high yield or junk bonds. Bonds in default category for nonpayment of principal and/or interest are rated the grade D.

Investment quality ratings of bonds

Moody's	Standard & Poor's	Fitch	Remarks on credit worthiness
Aaa	AAA	AAA	Highest ratings. Capacity to pay principal and interest is extremely strong
Aa1	AA+	AA+	
Aa2	AA	AA	Capacity to pay is very strong. Along with the highest rating, this group constitute high grade bond class
A1	A+	A+	
A2	A	A	
A3	A−	A−	A ratings indicate capacity to pay interest and repay principal as strong but susceptible to adverse economic conditions
Baa1	BBB+	BBB+	
Baa2	BBB	BBB	
Baa3	BBB−	BBB−	Debt rated Baa and BBB have adequate capacity to repay principal and interest but susceptible to changes in economic environment
Ba1	BB+	BB+	
Ba2	BB	BB	
Ba3	BB−	BB−	These ratings are less speculative or vulnerable than other lower ratings
B1	B+	B+	
B2	B	B	
B3	B−	B−	They are predominantly speculative

Ratings in the category C have the highest degree of speculation. Debt rated D is in default category.

Sovereign credit rating is the credit ratings of a national government by the credit rating agency. The rating indicates the risk level of the investing environment of a country. In 2011, four nonfinancial US companies had a better rating than sovereign rating for US based on S&P. Automatic Data Processing, Exxon Mobil, Johnson & Johnson, and Microsoft had AAA rating when US had AA rating. In 1983, there were 32 nonfinancial companies which were rated AAA.[2] Berkshire Hathaway, General Electric, and Pfizer lost their AAA ratings during the financial crisis in 2008.

2.5.9 Determinants of bond ratings

Quantification is integral to rating analysis. The ratings for a bond issue is based on the synthetic ratings for a firm based on one of the financial ratios or a score based on multiple ratios such as EBIT Interest coverage ratio, EBITDA interest coverage ratio, funds flow/total debt ratio, free operating cash flow to total debt ratio, return on capital, operating income to sales, long-term debt to capital ratios. For example, say if the interest coverage ratio is above 8.5, the firm's bond issue may rated AAA. Different measures are used for different industries and different external influences play ranging roles in the credit rating processes. Ratings are not only based on a defined set of financial ratios. Comprehensive qualitative elements are also an integral part of credit rating processes. Specific risk factors weighted in a given rating will vary considerably by sector. The Bond rating agencies base ratings based on the following financial ratios for issuer firms.

The major coverage ratios analyzed are times interest earned ratio and fixed charge coverage ratio. The times interest earned ratio is the ratio of earnings before interest payments and taxes to interest obligations. The fixed charge coverage ratio measures a firm's ability to pay all of its fixed charges or expenses with its income before interest and taxes. The main leverage ratio used is the debt equity ratio. The current ratio and quick ratio are the major liquidity ratios utilized for quality ratings of bonds. The main profitability ratios considered are return on assets and return on equity. Return on assets is the ratio of earnings before interest and taxes divided by total assets. Return on equity is the ratio of net income divided by equity capital.

In 2011, 53 global corporate issuers defaulted compared to 81 defaults in the year 2010. The default rate in 2009, 2010, and 2011 were 4.06%, 1.15%, and 0.75%, respectively. The investment grade default in 2009, 2010, and 2011 were 0.32%, 0.00%, and 0.03%, respectively. The speculative grade default rate was 9.52%, 2.82%, and 1.71%, respectively.[3]

---

[2] http://money.cnn.com/2011/08/08/news/companies/aaa_companies/index.htm
[3] http://www.standardandpoors.com/ratings/articles/en/us/?articleType=HTML&assetID=1245330814766, Standard & Poor's Global Fixed Income Research and Standard & Poor's CreditPro®.

Table 2.3 Moody's financial metrics for global nonfinancial corporations 2009

	EBITA/Avg assets (%)	Operating margin (%)	EBITA margin (%)	EBITA/Interest expense	FFOplusIntexp/Intexp[a]	Debt/EBITDA	Debt/Bookcap (%)	FFO/Debt (%)	RCF/Net Debt[b] (%)	CAPEX/DepExp	Rev Vol[c]
Aaa	22	18.6	21.9	18.6	17.8	0.9	30.2	87.5	164	1.3	13
Aa	7.4	9.7	11.2	5.5	10.1	2.1	43.4	35.5	23.1	1.1	11.5
A	11.3	13.4	14	6.6	8.9	2	44.7	37.6	26.7	1.3	15
Baa	9.5	11	12.2	4.4	5.8	2.8	50.6	25.4	22.9	1.3	16
Ba	9.6	11.3	12.9	3.2	4.6	3.2	54.3	22.3	21.1	1.2	22
B	6.9	7.8	9.1	1.4	2.4	5.3	74.9	10.9	10.5	1.0	17
C	2.3	1.7	2.5	0.3	1.2	7.7	103.9	2.3	2.3	0.8	15

[a](Funds from operations + Interest expense)/Interest expense.
[b]RCF/debt = (FFO-preferred dividends − Common dividends-Minority dividends)/(Short-term debt + Long-term debt).
[c]Revenue volatility is the standard deviation of trailing 5 years of net revenue growth.
Source: Moody's Corporate Finance—Key ratios by rating and industry for global nonfinancial corporations.

Table 2.4 S&P yearly total returns by category

Returns %	2008	2009	2010
AAA	2.75	7.96	6.63
AA	2.29	9.72	7.14
A	0.57	13.55	8.80
BBB	−5.95	22.21	10.28
BB	−13.98	35.38	12.77
B	−26.50	48.99	13.76
CCC and lower	−43.18	100.79	21.01
B− and lower	−36.63	84.74	17.87
Nonfinancial by rating category			
AA	6.89	7.87	7.23
A	2.89	12.61	8.68
BBB	−5.02	21.93	10.04
BB	−13.53	35.35	12.10
B	−24.75	49.40	13.06
CCC and lower	−45.17	101.36	19.07
B− and lower	−37.24	87.30	16.80
Financial by rating category			
AA	2.43	10.25	7.30
A	−5.13	15.69	9.03
BBB	−15.65	24.58	12.73
BB	−22.91	43.56	23.19

Source: Diane Vazza, Cameron Miller, *S&P's New bond spread and total return series*, Table 3, Yearly returns by category, June 2 2011, Standard& Poor's Financial Services LLC. This material is reproduced with permission of Standard & Poor's Financial Services LLC. http://www.standardandpoors.com/ratings/articles/en/us/?assetID = 1245305949879.

Table **2.5** **Reuters corporate bond spread tables**[a]

Reuters corporate spreads for industrials 03/28/2014							
Rating	**1 year**	**2 year**	**3 year**	**5 year**	**7 year**	**10 year**	**30 year**
Aaa/AAA	5	8	12	18	28	42	65
Aa1/AA+	10	18	25	34	42	54	77
Aa2/AA	14	29	38	50	57	65	89
Aa3/AA−	19	34	43	54	61	69	92
A1/A+	23	39	47	58	65	72	95
A2/A	24	39	49	61	69	77	103
A3/A−	32	49	59	72	80	89	117
Baa1/BBB+	38	61	75	92	103	115	151
Baa2/BBB	47	75	89	107	119	132	170
Baa3/BBB−	83	108	122	140	152	165	204
Ba1/BB+	157	182	198	217	232	248	286
Ba2/BB	231	256	274	295	312	330	367
Ba3/BB−	305	330	350	372	392	413	449
B1/B+	378	404	426	450	472	495	530
B2/B	452	478	502	527	552	578	612
B3/B−	526	552	578	604	632	660	693
Caa/CCC+	600	626	653	682	712	743	775
US treasury yield	0.13	0.45	0.93	1.74	2.31	2.73	3.55

Spread values represent basis points (bps) over a US Treasury security of the same maturity, or the closest matching maturity.
[a]http://www.bondsonline.com/Todays_Market/Corporate_Bond_Spreads.php
Source: Bonds Online Group, Thomson Reuter.

Table **2.6** **Default spreads and interest rates—January 2011**

Bond rating	**Default spread (%)**	**Interest rate on debt (%)**
AAA	0.50	4.00
AA	0.65	4.15
A+	0.85	4.35
A	1.00	4.50
A−	1.10	4.60
BBB	1.60	5.10
BB+	3.00	6.50
BB	3.35	6.85
B+	3.75	7.25
B	5.00	8.50
B−	5.25	8.75
CCC	8	11.50
CC	10	13.50
C	12	15.50
D	15	18.50

Source: Bonds Online Group, Thomson Reuter.

References

Amihud, Y., Mendelson, H., 1986. Asset pricing and the bid ask spread. J. Financ. Econ. 17 (2), 223–249.

Bali, T.G., Cakici, N., Tang, Y., 2009. The conditional beta and the cross section of expected returns. Financ. Manage. 38 (1), 103–137.

Basu, S., 1977. Investment performance of common stocks in relation to their price earnings ratio: a test of the efficient market hypothesis. J. Finance. 32 (3), 663–682.

Basu, S., 1983. The relationship between earnings yield, market value, and return for NYSE common stocks: further evidence. J. Financ. Econ. 12, 129–156.

Black, F., 1972. Capital market equilibrium with restricted borrowing. J. Bus. 45 (3), 444–455.

Bodie Z., Kane A. Alan marcus, investments, McGraw Hill Education 10th Edition, Chapter 9-The capital asset pricing model, pp. 291–315, Chapter 10-Arbitrage pricing theory and multifactor models of risk and return, 325–340.

Burmeister, E., McElroy, M.B., 1988. Joint estimation of factor sensitivities and risk premia for the arbitrage pricing theory. J. Finance. 43 (3), 721–733.

Burmeister, E., Roll, R., Ross, S.A., 1994. A practitioner's guide to arbitrage pricing theory. In: Peavy, J. (Ed.), A Practitioner's Guide to Factor Models. Research Foundation of the Institute of Chartered Financial Analysts, Charlottesville, VA, pp. 312–331.

Campbell J.Y. and Viceira L.M. The term structure of the risk-return tradeoff, <http://scholar.harvard.edu/files/campbell/files/cv_termstructure_riskreturn.pdf> 29/08/2014.

Carhart, M.M., 1997. On persistence in mutual fund performance. J. Finance. 52 (1), 57–82.

Chen, N.F., 1983. Some empirical tests of the theory of arbitrage pricing. J. Finance. 38 (5), 1393–1414.

Chen, N.-F., Roll, R., Ross, S., 1986. Economic forces and the stock market. J. Bus. 59 (3), 383–403.

Cho, D.C., Elton, E.J., Gruber, M.J., 1984. On the robustness of the roll and ross arbitrage pricing theory. J. Financ. Quant. Anal. 19 (1), 1–10.

Dhrymes, P.J., Friend, I., Gultekin, N.B., 1984. A critical examination re-examination of the empirical evidence on arbitrage pricing theory. J. Finance. 39 (2), 323–346.

Fama, E.F., French, K.R., 1992. The cross-section of expected stock returns. J. Finance. 47, 427–465.

Fama, E.F., French, K.R., 1993. Common risk factors in the return on stocks and bonds. J. Financ. Econ. 33 (1), 3–54.

Fama, E.F., French, K.R., 1996a. Multifactor explanations of asset pricing anomalies. J. Finance. 51, 55–84.

Fama, E.F., French, K.R., 1996b. The CAPM is wanted dead or alive. J. Finance. 51 (5), 47–58.

Fama, E.F., Macbeth, J.D., 1973. Risk, return and equilibrium: empirical tests. J. Polit. Econ. 81 (3), 607–637.

Ferson, W.E., Korajczyk, R.A., 1995. Do arbitrage pricing models explain the predictability of stock returns. J. Bus. 68, 309–349.

Grundy, K., Malkiel, B.G., 1996. Reports of beta's death have been greatly exaggerated. J. Portf. Manage. 22 (3), 36–44.

Gultekin, M.N., Gultekin, N.B., 1987. Stock returns anomalies and the tests of APT. J. Finance. 42 (5), 1213–1224.

Harvey, C.R., 1989. Time varying conditional covariance in tests of asset pricing models. J. Financ. Econ. 24, 289–317.

Ibbotson, R.G., Sinquefiled, R.A., 1982. Stocks, Bonds, Bills and Inflation, [SBBI]. Financial Analysis Research Foundation, Charlottesville, VA.

Jagannathan, R., Wang, Z., 1996. The conditional CAPM and the cross-section of expected returns. J. Finance. 51, 3−53.

Ross, S.A., 1977. Return, risk and arbitrage. In: Friend, I., Bicksler, J. (Eds.), Risk and Return in Finance. Ballinger, Cambridge, MA, pp. 189−218.

Kothari, S.P., Shanken, J., Sloan, R.G., 1995. Another look at the cross-section of expected stock returns. J. Finance. 50, 185−224.

Lintner, J., 1965a. Security prices, risk and maximal gains from diversification. J. Finance. 20.

Lintner, J., 1965b. The valuation of risk assets and the selection of risky investments in stock portfolios and capital budgets. Rev. Econ. Stat. 47, 13−37.

Merton, R., 1972. An analytical derivation of the efficient portfolio frontier. J. Financ. Quant. Anal. 7 (4), 1851−1872.

Merton, R., 1973. An intertemporal capital asset pricing model. Econometrica. 41 (5), 867−887.

Miller, M.H., Scholes, M., 1972. Rate of return in relation to risk: an reexamination of some recent findings. In: Jensen, M.C. (Ed.), Studies in the Theory of Capital Markets. Prager, New York, 1972.

Mossin, J., 1966. Equilibrium in a capital asset market. Econometricia. 34 (4), 768−783.

Onatski, A., 2009. Testing hypotheses about the number of factors in large factor models. Econometrica. 77 (5), 1447−1479.

Penttengill, G., Dundaram, S., Mathur, I., 1995. The conditional relation between beta and returns. J. Financ. Quant. Anal. 30 (1), 101−116.

Reilly, F., David, W., 2004. Analysis of risk adjusted performance of global market assets. J. Portf. Manage. 30 (3), 63−77.

Reilly, F.K., Akhtar, R.A., 1995. The Benchmark error problem with global capital markets. J. Portf. Manage. 22 (1), 33−52.

Reilly F.K., Brown K. Analysis of investments & management of portfolios, South Western Cengage Learning 10th Edition, Chapter 7-An introduction to portfolio management, pp. 171−193, Chapter 9-Multifactor models of risk and return, pp. 229−249.

Reinganum, M.R., 1981. The arbitrage pricing theory: some empirical results. J. Finance. 36 (2), 313−321.

Roll, R., 1977. A critique of the asset pricing theory's tests Part I: on past and potential testability of the theory. J. Financ. Econ. 4 (2), 129−176.

Roll, R., 1980. Performance evaluation and benchmark error. J. Portf. Manage. 6 (4), 5−12.

Roll, R., 1981. Performance evaluation and benchmark error ii. J. Portf. Manage. 7 (2), 17−22.

Roll, R., Ross, S.A., 1980. An empirical investigation of the arbitrage pricing theory. J. Finance. 35 (5), 1073−1103.

Roll, R., Ross, S.A., 1984. A critical reexamination re-examination of the empirical evidence on arbitrage pricing theory. J. Finance. 39 (2), 347−350.

Ross, S.A., 1976. The arbitrage theory of capital asset pricing. J. Econ. Theory. 13 (2), 341−360.

Sharpe, W., 1984. Factor models, CAPMs and the APT. J. Portf. Manage. 11 (1), 21−25.

Sharpe, W.F., 1964. Capital asset prices: a theory of market equilibrium. J. Finance. 19, 425−442.

Zhang, C., 2009. Testing the APT with the maximum sharpe ratio of extracted factors. Manage. Sci. 55 (7), 1255−1266.

Efficient capital markets and its implications

3

3.1 Introduction

In efficient capital markets, the share prices reflect all new information accurately and in a timely manner. In other words, an efficient capital market incorporates all information quickly and accurately into the stock prices. The current stock prices reflect all information about the stock. The basic fundamental value of a stock is based on the expected future cash flows of the firm. Thus, the efficient market theory (EMT) states that the price of an asset reflects all relevant information, which is available about the intrinsic value of the asset. A market in which prices always fully reflect available information is called "efficient."

The theory of informationally efficient capital market is based on three fundamental assumptions. The first assumption is that the capital market consists of a number of participants who analyze and value securities in an independent manner with the objective of profit maximization. The second assumption states that new information about securities reach the market in a random manner and timings of this announcement is independent of each other. The characteristics of new information is such that it is unpredictable and not known earlier. The stock prices should follow a random walk. The third and critical assumption is that the buy and sell decisions of all profit maximizing investor's causes the security prices to adjust rapidly to reflect the effect of new information. The price changes are independent and random. According to the EMT, the stock price at any time should be an unbiased reflection of all currently available information. The expected returns should reflect the risk of its share in an efficient market. In a theoretical sense, the presence of undervalued and overvalued stocks provides the motivation for investors to trade for profit opportunities and their actions moves the prices of stock toward the present value of future expected cash flows. The investment analysts search for mispriced stocks and their subsequent trading causes prices to reflect their intrinsic values. Thus, this trading pattern makes the market efficient. Investors in an efficient market cannot earn abnormally high risk-adjusted returns.

3.2 Forms of efficient market hypothesis

The origins of the efficient market hypothesis (EMH) can be traced back to the work of two individuals in the 1960s: Eugene F. Fama and Paul A. Samuelson.

3.2.1   Weak form of efficient market

In weak form of efficiency, the future returns cannot be predicted from past returns or any other market-based indicator. In other words, past rates of return have no relation with future rates of returns. The current stock prices fully reflect all stock market information that can be obtained by examining history of past prices, trading volume, and transaction by market makers. The weak form hypothesis suggests that if past data convey information about future performance, all investors will already be in possession of such information.

3.2.2   Semi-strong form of efficient market

In a semi-strong efficient market, stock prices reflect all publicly available information about economic fundamentals of the firm. The publicly available information include contents from financial reports, economic forecasts, data on the company's product lines, patents, earning forecasts, dividend forecasts, company announcements, stock splits, political news, etc. These information would be immediately reflected in the stock prices. As a result, investors would not be able to earn excess returns from their transactions.

3.2.3   Strong form of efficient market

In strong form, the highest level of market efficiency, prices reflect all public and private information. The strong form of efficiency implies that even with privileged information, an investor cannot expect to earn excess returns. Regulatory bodies like SEC act as a monitoring agency to prevent insider trading involving profiting from privileged situation.

All forms of EMH asserts that prices should reflect available information.

3.3   Tests of EMH

Weak form tests are tests in which the information set is only the historical prices. In semi-strong form tests, the concern is whether prices efficiently adjust to other information that is publicly available like announcement of earnings, dividends, stock splits or any other announcement involving corporate restructuring. The strong form tests are concerned with whether given investors have monopolistic access to any information. The empirical work on the theory of efficient markets are concerned with whether prices fully reflect particular subset of available information. The initial studies were based on weak form tests in which the information subset of interest was just past prices. This area of study was known as random walk literature (Jones and Netter, 2008).

3.3.1 Tests for weak form of EMH

The weak form of EMH involves two types of tests. The statistical tests involve tests of independence between rates of return. The second tests involve trading rules to make investment decisions based on the comparison of risk return analysis. The statistical results are autocorrelation tests of independence and run tests. Autocorrelation tests of independence measure the significance of positive and negative correlation in returns over time. EMH suggests insignificant correlation in returns over time. The runs test also known as Wald Wolfowitz test is a nonparametric statistical test, which checks the randomness hypothesis for a two-valued data sequence. Run test enable to test the hypothesis whether the elements of the sequence are mutually independent. In the event of a series of price changes, each price is either designated a plus (+) if there is an increase in price or a minus (−) if there is a decrease in price. The result is a set of pluses and minuses. Two or more consecutive positive or negative price changes constitute one run. Many studies have observed the independence of stock price changes over time. According to EMH, investors cannot make excess returns above a buy-and-hold policy using trading rules, which depend only on past market information. Studies based on trading rules compare the risk return results from trading rule simulation that include transaction costs to the results from simple buy-and-hold policy. A popular trading technique is the filter rule wherein an investor trades a stock when the price change exceeds a filter value set for it. Studies have indicated that most trading rules tested have not been able to beat a buy-and-hold policy.

3.3.2 Tests for semi-strong form of EMH

Studies of semi-strong EMH are based on two methods. The first method consists of time series analysis of returns or the cross-section distribution of returns for individual stocks. The second method known as event studies examine how fast stock prices adjust to specific events like earnings announcement, stock splits, IPO announcement, and dividend announcement.

3.3.2.1 Event study

Research has extensively chronicled the impact of market reaction to announcement of earnings, dividends, projects, acquisitions, joint ventures, etc. The results of these studies have supported the semi-strong EMH. The efficient capital market hypothesizes that share prices fully and instantaneously reflect all information.

3.3.2.1.1 Announcement effects on stock splits

Studies on stock splits like that of Fama et al. (1969) support the strong form of EMH, suggesting that investors cannot gain from the information on a stock split after the public announcement. The study by Masse et al. (1997) examines the market reaction to Canadian stock splits, reverse splits and stock dividends, and their impact on business enterprise valuation in Canada. The study finds positive effect of stock splits on stock prices. Asquith et al. (1989) suggest that market's reaction to split announcement cannot be attributed to expectations of either future earnings increases or near term dividend cash increases.

3.3.2.1.2 Announcement effects on mergers and acquisitions

For a firm characterized by an objective of stockholder wealth maximization, the appropriate test of a merger's success is the merger's effect on stock prices. In an efficient capital market, investor's expectations of the merger's future benefit should be fully reflected in stock prices by the merger date. Formally, if the capital markets are semi-strong efficient, then the value of future benefits should be fully reflected by the first public announcement of the merger and should certainly be fully reflected by somewhat later merger date. The increase in the equity value of the acquiring firm in the wake of a successful merger is a compelling evidence for the synergy theory of mergers.

In a review of scientific literature on the market for corporate control, Jensen and Ruback (1983) indicate that corporate takeovers generate positive gains, that target firm shareholders benefit, and that bidding firm shareholders do not lose. Mandelker (1974) examined the market for acquisitions and the impact of mergers on the return to the stockholders of the constituent firms. The results were consistent with the hypothesis that the market for acquisitions is perfectly competitive. The study by Asquith et al. (1983) examines the effect of mergers on the wealth of bidding firms shareholders. Bidding firms gain significantly during the 21 days leading to the announcement of each of their first four merger bids. Bruner (2004) suggests that most of the acquisitions end up costing shareholders. Moeller et al. (2004) examined the announcement returns using a sample of 12,023 acquisitions by public firms during the period 1980–2001. The results of this study showed that the equally weighted abnormal announcement returns is 1.1% but acquiring firm shareholders lose $25.2 million on average upon announcement.

Table 3.1 gives the excess returns surrounding the announcement period for mergers and acquisitions documented by various studies during different time windows.

3.3.2.1.3 Announcement effect on initial public offerings

In a study of all initial public offerings (IPOs) made between 1960 and 1987, Ibbotson et al. (1994) an average initial return of 16.37% in the month following the initial offerings. The above study and Miller and Reilly (1987) indicate that the price adjustment to the underpricing takes place within one day after the offering. The rapid adjustment to the initial underpricing indicates support for semi-strong EMH. Studies by Ritter (1991), Loughran and Ritter (1995) observe that after IPO listing, stocks do not have positive long-run abnormal returns.

3.3.2.1.4 Announcement effects on economic events

Studies have documented proof for semi-strong EMH with respect to announcement of unexpected events, especially surprise announcements. The stock markets throughout the world witnessed huge downward swings during the time of economic recession and crisis that have affected the global community. The study by Jain (1988) observes that surprise announcements about money supply impacted stock prices within 1 hour.

Table 3.1 **Abnormal returns associated with mergers and acquisitions**

Study	Sample period	Event period	Bidding firm (%)	Target firm (%)
Period: 1970−1980				
Mandelker (1974)	1941−1962	Month after through 12 months after the effective date* 7 months preceding merger**	+0.60*	14%**
Franks et al. (1977)	1955−1972	40 months before through 40 months after announcement (for acquirer), (−40 to +2 months for acquired firms)	−0.004	0.179
Langetieg (1978)	1929−1969	Month after through 12 months after effective date	−6.59	12.9%
Dodd (1980)	1970−1977	The day before and the day of offer announcements	−1.09	+13.41
Dodd (1980)	1970−1977	20 days before through the first public announcement	+0.80	+21.78
Dodd (1980)	1970−1977	10 days before offer announcement through ten days after outcome date	−7.22	+33.96
Elgers and Clark (1980)	1957−1975	24 months before through 24 months after announcement	0.097	0.426
Period: 1982−1983				
Asquith and Kim (1982)	1960−1978	10 days before through 10 days after the public announcement	1.8	14.9
Schipper and Thompson (1983)	1960−1967	12 years before to 6 years after announcement of acquisition programs	15.1	
Asquith et al. (1983)	1962−1976	The day before and day of offer announcement	+0.20	+6.20
Eckbo (1983)	1963−1978	The day before through the day after the offer announcement	+0.07	+6.24

(*Continued*)

Table 3.1 (Continued)

Study	Sample period	Event period	Bidding firm (%)	Target firm (%)
Asquith et al. (1983)	1962–1976	19 days before through the first public announcement	+0.20	+13.30
		480 days before a merger bid until 240 days after a merger bid.	+7.0	+8.5*
		480 days before a merger bid until outcome day*(The day in which the outcome of merger reported in Press)		
Eckbo (1983)	1963–1978	20 days before through ten days after public announcement	+1.58	+14.08
Asquith et al. (1983)	1963–1979	20 days before the announcement day through the announcement day	+3.48	+20.5
Malatesta (1983)	1969–1974	Public announcement month	+0.90	+16.8
Asquith et al. (1983)	1962–1976	The day before announcement through outcome date	−0.10	+15.50
Asquith et al. (1983)	1962–1976	Day after through 240 days after outcome announcement	−7.20	−9.60
Malatesta (1983)	1969–1974	Month after through 12 months after approval for entire sample	−2.90	
James et al. (1983)	1973–1977	Seven month prior to merger		29.1
Period: 1986–1987				
Dennis and McConnell (1986)	1962–1980	19 days before through 20 days after merger announcement	3.40	18.63
Asquith et al. (1987)	1977–1983	40 days before through 40 days after announcement	8.71	

(Continued)

Table 3.1 (Continued)

Study	Sample period	Event period	Bidding firm (%)	Target firm (%)
Singh and Montgomery (1987)	1975—1980	5 days before through 25 days after announcement (Related)	−0.006	0.359
Singh and Montgomery (1987)	1975—1980	5 days before through 25 days after announcement (unrelated)	−0.019	0.219
Allen and Sirmans (1987)	1977—1983	40 days before through thc day of announcement	8	
Period: 1990—2005				
Franks et al. (1991)	1975—1984	5 days before the first announcement of a bid and ending five days after the last bid	−1.02	28.04
Cornett and Tehranian (1992)	1982—1987	From 1 day before through the day of announcement	−0.8	8
Agrawal et al. (1992)	1955—1987	1 month to 60 months after merger completion	−10.26	
Singal (1996)	1985—1988	From 1 day before through the day of announcement	1.843	18.42
Houston et al. (2001)	1985—1991	4 days before through 1 day after announcement	−3.47	20.80
Amihud et al. (2002)	1985—1998	From 10 days before through 1 day after merger announcement	−1.0	
Fueller et al. (2004)	1990—2000	2 days before through 2 days after the announcement date	1.77	
Moeller et al. (2004)	1998—2001	Acquisitions in 2 year windows immediately before and immediately after the first large loss deal a firm made	−0.65	

*denote statistical significance at 10%.
**denote statistical significance at 5%.

3.3.2.1.5   Dividend announcements

Dennis et al. (1994) find that announcement period excess returns are significantly related to yield and dividend change standardized by share prices. The evidence from the study by Impson (1997) documents significantly stronger negative market responses to dividend decrease announcements by public utilities compared with unregulated firms even when yield, price standardized dividend change, firm size, and Tobin q differences are considered. Aharony et al. (1988) analyze market reaction to dividend increase announcements by public utilities. They conclude that market response to dividend increase announcements by public utilities is significantly stronger than the response to dividend increase announcement by unregulated firms.

3.3.2.2   Event study methodology

Choosing the appropriate event date is important in event studies and is generally based on the motivation of the research. For example, to test the efficiency of stock market reaction to the announcement of the merger, the event should be centered on the date of the merger announcement (Halpern, 1973; Dodd, 1980; Asquith et al., 1983; Malatesta, 1983). The benefits of the merger to acquiring firms are likely to be reflected in stock values around the time when an acquisition programme is initiated (Schipper and Thompson, 1983).

Over time, postmerger performance should be zero in an efficient market, and the entire valuation effect associated with the combination should occur on average at the time of the announcement. A stronger test of market efficiency would use the first public announcement date.

The market's reaction to a merger bid is measured using daily stock return data to compute excess stockholder returns. These excess returns are a measure of the stockholder's return from the new information, which becomes available to market. The daily excess return for the security is estimated by

$$XR_t = R_t - E(R_t)$$

Where t = day relative to an event.

XR_t = Excess return on the security for day t over a benchmark index
R_t = Actual return on the security for day t.
$E(R_t)$ = Expected rate of return on the security for day t.

The choice of the benchmark is probably the most important factor in making accurate measurement of a merger's impact.

The methodology used for event study are based on Market Model Method and Market-Adjusted Method. The expected rate of return on the security is found out using the Market Model and Market Return-Adjusted Method.

3.3.2.2.1   Market model method

The econometric method used in market model is basically residual method. Residual analysis essentially tests whether the return to the common stock of individual firms or groups of firms is greater or less than that predicted by general market relationships between return and risk. One problem involved is the choice of reference period for obtaining the parameters to be used in calculating excess returns caused by events. If the reference period chosen is too long or far removed from the event, then the risk characteristics of the sample firm may have changed in the interval. If the reference period is too short, it may not represent a valid benchmark.

The choice of the benchmark is probably the most important factor in making an accurate measurement of a merger's impact. The expected rate of return on the security can be calculated using the market model. The model parameters can be estimated by regressing daily stock return on the market index over the estimation period.

To use the market model a clean period has to be chosen for example say -50 to -200 days (0 day being the event announcement day) to estimate the model parameters. The model parameters has to be estimated by regressing daily stock return on the market index (e.g., NYSE index) over the estimation period. The market model is given by

$$R_t = \alpha + \beta R_{mt} + \epsilon t.$$

Where R_{mt} is the return on market index for day t, β measures the sensitivity of the firm to market—this is a measure of risk and ϵt is a statistical error term where $\Sigma \epsilon t = 0$.

Thus, the predicted return for the firm in the event period is the return given by the market model on that day using these estimates.

3.3.2.2.2 The market-adjusted return method
This model assume that predicted return for a firm for a day in the event period is just the return on the market index.

$$E(R_t) = R_{mt}.$$

Where $E(R_t)$ is the expected return, R_{mt} is the market index return.

3.3.3 Tests of strong form EMH

The strong form EMH suggests that stock prices fully reflect all information which are public and private. The strong form of EMH can be tested by analyzing the actions of corporate insiders, stock exchange specialists, security analysts, and professional money managers. According to SEC regulations, corporate insiders are required to furnish monthly reports to SEC about their transactions in firms in which they are insiders. The class of insiders include corporate officers, members of the board of directors, and owners who own more than 10% of the equity class. Research studies by Chowdhury et al. (1993), Pettit and Venkatesh (1995) have documented above average profits for insiders. It can be logically concluded that insiders had private information that would have been used for strong returns. Some studies have shown that stock exchange specialists have monopolistic access to certain important information about unfilled limit orders. There has been evidence to suggest that superior analysts might possess private information. Womack (1996) suggests that analysts seem to have both market timing and stock picking ability to facilitate rare sell recommendations. Many studies have analyzed the performance of money managers through mutual funds data. The tests of strong form EMH have generally given mixed results.

3.4   Review of research studies on market efficiency

Williams (1938) suggests that stock prices are based on economic fundamentals. Keynes (1936) suggested that stock prices are more based more on speculation than on economic fundamentals and in long-run the prices driven by speculation may converge to economic fundamentals. The studies by Kendall (1953), Roberts (1959), Fama (1965) documented statistical independence in stock returns. Fama (1965) also suggested the lack of predictive power of various techniques of technical analysts. These studies advocated the random walk model of stock returns. Samuelson (1965) and Benoit (1966) suggested that randomness in stock returns is a characteristic of the well-functioning stock market. These studies points that competition implies that investing in stocks is a "fair game" in which traders cannot expect to beat the market without some additional information. The implication of fair game is that today's stock price reflects the expectation of investors. Tomorrow's price will change only if investors' expectations of future events change which are random in nature. This viewpoint led to the development of rational expectation theory of macroeconomics. Rational expectation theory is referred to as EMT.

Samuelson (1965) and Mandelbrot (1966) explained the role of "fair game" expected returns models in the theory of efficient markets. The study by Kendall et al. suggests that series of speculative prices may be well described by random walks. The study by Osborne (1962) finds deviation from the random walk model. The study observes that large daily price changes tend to be followed by large daily changes.

In an informationally efficient market, price changes must be forecastable if they are properly anticipated, that is, if they fully incorporate the information and expectations of all market participants. Having developed a series of linear-programming solutions to spatial pricing models with no uncertainty, Samuelson came upon the idea of efficient markets through his interest in temporal pricing models of storable commodities that are harvested.

Fama (1970) proposed the three forms of market efficiency. Grossman and Stiglitz (1980) suggest that market frictions like costs of security analysis and trading limit market efficiency. It means that the level of market efficiency differ across markets depending on the costs of analysis and trading.

Fama (1991) observes that lower the transaction costs in terms of costs of obtaining information and trading, the higher would be the efficiency of the market. In advanced markets, the cost of obtaining information and trading securities is comparatively less due to mandated disclosure and information provisions for technology.

3.5 Anomalies of EMH

Most of the empirical research studies of 1970s supported the semi-strong form of market efficiency. In the 1980s, anomalies in market efficiency were discussed. Anomalies were pointed out like "small firm effect" and the January effect in which it was observed that small capitalization stocks tend to earn excess returns in the month of January. Financial economists often attribute most of these anomalies to misspecifications of the asset pricing model or market frictions. Fama (1998) observes that anomalies related to under and overreaction are random occurrences due to different time periods and methods.

In the eighties many researchers challenged the logic of EMT based on long-term returns. Shiller (1981) points that stock prices are driven by speculation rather than fundamentals. De Bondt and Thaler (1985) document that prices of stocks which had performed well over 3- to 5-year horizons tend to revert to their means during the subsequent 3−5 years, resulting in negative abnormal returns. Similarly, the prices of stocks that had performed relatively poor tend to revert to their means, which results in positive excess returns. This phenomena is known as mean reversion or reversion to mean. Summers (1986) predicted that stock prices take long swings in long run, which are undetectable in short period. Jegadeesh and Sheridan Titman (1993) supported the concept of technical analysis by observing that stocks that earn relatively high or low returns over 3- to 12-month intervals tend to continue the trend over the subsequent 3−12 months. The inefficiencies led to the emergence of behavioral finance.

Fama and French (1988) suggested that stocks earn larger returns when capital are scarce and default risk premiums in interest rates are high. The higher interest rates initially drive prices down but eventually prices recover with improved business conditions. As a result of this, the mean reverting pattern in aggregate returns is observed. Advocates of EMH argue that mispriced stocks generally attract rational investors who buy underpriced and sell over priced stocks.

Lo and MacKinlay (1990) find that the variance of 2-week return is twice the variance of 1-week return. French and Roll (1986) suggest that act of trading creates volatility as they found that finds that stock return variances over weekends and exchange holidays are considerably lower than return variances over the same number of days when markets are open. Fama and French (1988) and Poterba and Summers (1988) find negative serial correlation in US stock returns indexes based on data from 1926 to 1986.

Shleifer and Vishny (1997) suggest that mispricing offers few opportunities for low-risk arbitrage trading. A classic example for inconsistency with EMT is the

1987 stock market crash and the movement of internet stock prices during the late 1990s, which led to the dotcom crash.

Niederhoffer and Osborne (1966) suggest departures from complete randomness in common stock price changes from transaction to transaction. Their study indicate that reversals (pairs of consecutive price changes of opposite sign) are from two to three times as likely as continuations (pairs of consecutive price changes of the same sign). A continuation is slightly more frequent than after a preceding continuation than after a reversal. The Niederhoffer Osborne analysis suggest the existence of market efficiency with respect to strong form tests of efficient markets model.

Deviations from EMH is observed when investors do not always react in fair proportion to new information (Agrawal et al., 1992). Overreaction tends to push prices beyond their fair or rational market values. Rational investors take the opposite side of the trade and brings prices back into equilibrium. An important implication of this phenomenon is that what goes up must come down and vice versa.

De Bondt and Thaler (1985) document that the winners and losers in one 36-month period tend to reverse their performance over the next 36-month period. Chopra et al. (1992) reconfirm the findings regarding mean reversal after correcting for market risk and the size effect. Bernard and Thomas (1990) argue that investors sometimes underreact to information about future earnings contained in current earnings.

Studies by Banz (1981), Keim (1983) have analyzed the anomaly of size effect which documents the excess returns to small market capitalization stocks. Rozeff and Kinney (1976) observe that small capitalization stocks tend to outperform large capitalization stocks by a wide margin over the turn of the calendar year which was termed "January effect." Studies suggest that the January effect is largely due to "bid ask bounce" in which the closing prices for the last trading day of December tend to be at the bid price and closing prices for the first day of January tend to be at the ask price. The effects of bid ask bounce in percentage terms are more for small market capitalization stocks on account of lowprice.

The other anomalies are the profitability of short term return reversal strategies, the profitability of medium term momentum strategies in US equities, the relation between price/earnings ratios and expected returns, calendar effects such as holiday, weekend, and turn of the month of seasonalities.

Rosenberg et al. (1985a,b) evaluate the performance of the book to price and specific return reversal strategies in detecting stock market inefficiency. The contrarian investment strategy is based on the method of buying stock which has been losers and selling stocks, which have been winners. This strategy is based on the premise that the stock market overreacts to news, which results in overvaluation of winner stocks and undervaluation of loser stocks. Investment strategies based on price earnings (PE) ratio or book to market ratio are variants of this strategy. A study by Kahneman and Tversky (1982) observes that people tend to overreact to unexpected and dramatic events. De Bondt and Thaler (1990) on the basis of half century of data find that large abnormal returns can be earned by this strategy. This study suggests the reversal effect in which losers rebound and winners fade back since market overreact to relevant news. Chan (1988) offers alternate interpretation of the evidence on the performance of contrarian strategy. The study suggests that the risk of winners and losers are not constant over time. The risk of strategy appears to correlate with the level of expected market risk premium. The study therefore suggests that the measurement of abnormal returns are sensitive to how risk are estimated. In this context it is noteworthy to point out the errors in beta estimation. Lehmann (1990) examines market inefficiency and stock price overreaction by examining returns over short time intervals on the basis of assumption that systematic changes in fundamental valuation over intervals like a week should not occur in efficient market. The study finds that the winners and losers in 1-week experience sizeable return reversals the next week. Lehmann suggests that this phenomenon reflects inefficiency in the market for liquidity around large price changes. Lo and Mackinlay (1990) suggest that the contrarian profits from contrarian investment strategy can be attributed to overreaction.

Jegadeesh (1990) rejects the hypothesis that the stock prices follow random walks. This study suggest that the predictability of stock returns can be attributed either to market inefficiency or to systematic changes in expected stock returns. Chan et al. (1996) evaluate the profitability of price momentum strategies based on past return and earnings momentum strategies based on standardized unexpected earnings and revisions of consensus forecasts. This study document violation of the concept of market efficiency and suggests that market is slow to incorporate the full impact of information in its valuation.

Jegadeesh and Titman (1993) find striking seasonality in momentum profits. They document that the winners outperform the losers in all months except January, but the losers significantly outperform the winners in January. Jegadeesh and Titman described it as a momentum effect in which good or bad recent performance of individual stocks continues over time. Jegadeesh and Titman (2001) find that positive momentum returns are sometimes associated with postholding period reversals, suggesting that behavioral models provide a partial explanation for momentum anomaly.

Lakonishok and Smidt (1988) use 90 years of daily data on the Dow Jones Industrial average to test for the existence of persistent seasonal patterns in the rates of return. The study finds evidence of persistently anomalous returns around the turn of the week, month, year, and holidays.

The critiques of EMH are based around the preferences and behavior of market participants (Malkiel, 2003). Grossman and Stiglitz (1980) observe that perfectly informationally efficient markets are impossible as in such markets, there is no reason to trade as the scope for profit making is nil and such markets would eventually collapse.

The need for more realistic assumptions has led to new strands of literature, which includes psychological approaches to risk taking behavior, evolutionary game theory, agent-based modeling of financial markets, and direct applications of principles of evolutionary psychology to the field of economics and finance.

A study by Cooper (1974) finds support for the contention that the stock market returns in January are a predictor to the return over the next 11 months of the year.

Cross-sectional return have examined the relationship between historical PE ratio and returns on the stocks. Studies like that of Basu (1977) have pointed out that low PE ratio stocks will outperform high PE stocks. This happens due to the fact that market tends to overestimate the growth potential of companies with high PE ratios while undervaluing low growth firms with low PE ratios. The existence of relationship between the historical PE and subsequent risk-adjusted market performance suggest evidence against semi-strong EMH. Peavey and Goodman (1983) by examining PE ratios with adjustments for firm size, industry effects, and infrequent trading observe that the risk-adjusted returns for stocks in the lowest PE ratio quintile were superior to those in the highest PE ratio quintile. Peters (1991) finds that stocks with low PEG (Price Earning Growth) ratio have above average rates of return while stocks with high PEG ratio have below average rates of return. Banz (1981) studied the impact of size on the risk-adjusted rates of return and finds that small firms had significantly larger risk-adjusted returns than the larger firms. James and Edmister (1983) examined the impact of trading volume by observing the relationship among returns, market value, and trading activity. The study established the relationship between size and rates of return.

Anomalies of EMH with respect to ratio of book value to market value was also documented by researchers. Rosenberg et al. (1985a,b) found a significant positive relationship between current book to market value ratio and future stock returns. Fama and French (1992) find a significant positive relationship between the book value to market value ratio and average returns. In summary, many research studies have documented evidence against semi-strong form of EMH.

3.6   Implications of EMH

EMH advocates that security prices adjusts to new information very rapidly. The technical analysis is based on the assumption that new information to the stock market is disseminated to the bulk of investors in stages. The new information passes onto the informed professionals, then to the aggressive investors and finally to the general investors. Thus, technical analyst hold the view that investors take time to analyze information. Technical analysts believe that stock prices move to a new equilibrium after the release of new information in a slow manner, which results in trends in stock price movements which persist over a period of time. Thus, the view of EMH directly contradicts the technical analysis assumptions. If the capital markets are weak form efficient, the prices fully reflect all historical information about the stock. In that case by the time the information is public, the price adjustment would have already take place and technical trading systems based on past trading data would have no value at all. In short, EMH implies that technical analysis is not valid. The information available from analyzing past prices has already been incorporated in the stock prices. The investor will not be able to earn excess returns.

Fundamental analysis aims to understand the intrinsic value of the firm is essential to get superior risk-adjusted returns. Hence, it is pertinent for a superior analyst to understand the major variables which are relevant for the valuation process. The EMH contends that fundamental analysis is also bound to be a failure. The analysts recommendation based on publicly available earnings and other company information is not likely to be more accurate than those of competitor analysts. In other words, it is difficult for analysts to get unique insights, which help them to predict evaluation of the firm's prospects with a competitive edge. Thus, EMH advocates passive investment strategy instead of active portfolio management. Passive investment strategy is based on a buy and hold strategy. An example for passive investment strategy is to create an index fund which replicates the performance of a broad-based index of stocks. Tax considerations are also an important determinant of the investment policy. Professional money managers are experts in the field of investments and are considered better and more skilled than ordinary small investors.

3.7 Behavioral finance

Behavioral finance deals with the study of influence of psychology on the behavior of financial practitioners and its subsequent effects on markets. Behavioral finance offers explanation for why and how markets are inefficient. Through a series of experiments, Kahneman and Tversky (1979) developed the prospect theory. Their research indicate that people give too much weight to recent experience when making forecasts. This is termed as memory bias. People tend to underweight outcome, which are merely probable compared to outcomes which are obtained with certainty. People also tend to overestimate the precision of their beliefs often termed overconfidence. The prospect theory predicts fourfold pattern of risk attitudes—risk aversion for gains of moderate to high probability and losses of low probability, and risk seeking for gains of low probability and losses of moderate to high probability. The conservatism bias is based on the fact that when things change, people tend to be slow to pick up on the changes. In other words, they anchor on the ways things have normally been. Decisions seem to be affected by how choices are framed. Thaler (1980) introduced mental accounting which is a specific form of framing in which people segregate certain decisions. Psychologists often describe regret avoidance as situation in which individuals who make decisions that turn out badly have more regret when such decisions are unconventional. De Bondt and Thaler (1987) suggest that regret avoidance is consistent with both the size and book to market effect.

Technical analysis can be described as a search for trends or patterns in market prices. Technical analyst often consider these trends as momentum or gradual adjustments to correct prices or reverse trends.

Behavioral biases are often considered as factors which contribute towards such trends and patterns. Technical analysts use charts and other tools to identify patterns.

References

Agrawal, A., Jaffe, J.F., Mandelker, G.N., 1992. The post merger performance of acquiring firms: a reexamination of an anomaly. J. Finance. 47 (4), 1605–1622.

Aharony, J., Falk, H., Swary, I., 1988. Information content of dividend increases. The case of regulated utilities. J. Bus. Financ. Account. 15, 401–414.

Allen, P.R., Sirmans, C.F., 1987. An analysis of gains to acquiring firm's shareholders: the special case of REITS. J. Financ. Econ. 18 (1), 175–184.

Amihud, Y., Delong, G.L., Saunders, A., 2002. The effect of cross border bank mergers on bank risk and value. J. Int. Money Financ. 21 (6), 857–877.

Asquith, P., Kim, E.H., 1982. The impact of merger bids on the participating firm's security holders. J. Finance. 37 (5), 1209–1227.

Asquith, P., Bruner, R.F., Mullins Jr, D.W., 1983. The gains to bidding firms from merger. J. Financ. Econ. 11, 121–139.

Asquith, P., Bruner, R.F., Mullins Jr., D.W., 1987. Merger returns and the form of financing, Unpublished paper. Harvard University, Cambridge, MA.

Asquith, P., Healy, P., Palepu, K., 1989. Earnings and stock splits. Account. Rev. 64, 387–403.

Banz, R.W., 1981. The relationship between return and market values of common stocks. J. Financ. Econ. 9 (1), 3–18.

Basu, S., 1977. Investment performance of common stocks in relation to their price earnings ratio: a test of the efficient market hypothesis. J. Finance. 32 (3), 663–682.

Bernard, V., Thomas, J., 1990. Evidence that stock prices do not fully reflect the implications of current earnings for future earnings. J. Account. Econ. 13, 305–340.

Benoit, M., 1966. Forecasts of future prices, unbiased markets and 'Martingale Models'. J. Bus. Spec. (Suppl., January 1966), 242–255.

Bruner, R., 2004. Where M&A pays and where it strays: a survey of the research. J. Appl. Corp. Financ. 16 (4), 63–76.

Chan, K., 1988. On the contrarian investment strategy. J. Bus. 61, 147–164.

Chan, L., Jegadeesh, N., Lakonishok, J., 1996. Momentum strategies. J. Finance. 51, 1681–1713.

Chopra, N., Lakonishok, J., Ritter, J., 1992. Measuring abnormal performance: do stocks overreact? J. Financ. Econ. 31, 235–286.

Chowdhury, M.J., Howe, S., Lin, J.C., 1993. The relation between aggregate insider transactions and stock market returns. J. Financ. Quant. Anal. 28 (3), 431–437.

Cooper, R.V.L., 1974. Efficient capital markets and the quantity theory of money. J. Finance. 29 (3), 887–908.

Cornett, M.M., Tehranian, H., 1992. Changes in corporate performance associated with bank acquisitions. J. Financ. Econ. 31 (2), 211–234.

De Bondt, W.F.M., Thaler, R., 1985. Does the stock market overreact? J. Finance. 40, 793–807.

De Bondt, W.F.M., Thaler, R.H., 1987. Further evidence on investor overreaction and stock market seasonality. J. Finance. 42, 557–581.

De Bondt, W.F.M., Thaler, R.H., 1990. Do security analysts overreact? Am. Econ. Rev. 80, 52–57.

Dennis, D.K., McConnell, J.J., 1986. Corporate mergers and security returns. J. Financ. Econ. 16 (2), 143–187.

Dennis, D.J., Denis, D.K., Sarin, A., 1994. The information content of dividend changes. cash flow signaling, over investment and dividend clienteles. J. Financ. Quant. Anal. 29, 567–587.

Dodd, P., 1980. Merger proposals, management discretion and stockholder wealth. J. Financ. Econ. 8 (2), 105–137.

Eckbo, E., 1983. Horizontal mergers, collusion and stockholder wealth. J. Financ. Econ. 11 (1–4), 241–273.

Elgers, P.T., Clark, J.J., 1980. Merger types and shareholder returns: additional evidence. Financ. Manage. 9 (2), 66–72.

Fama, E.F., 1965. The behavior of stock market prices. J. Bus. 38, 34–105.

Fama, E.F., 1970. Efficient capital markets: a review of empirical work. J. Finance. 25 (2), 383–417.

Fama, E.F., 1991. Efficient capital markets II. J. Finance. 46 (5), 1575–1617.

Fama, E.F., 1998. Market efficiency, long term returns and behavioral finance. J. Financ. Econ. 49 (3), 283–306.

Fama, E.F., French, K.R., 1988. Dividend yields and expected stock returns. J. Financ. Econ. 22, 3–25.

Fama, E.F., French, K.R., 1992. The cross section of expected stock returns. J. Finance. 47 (2), 427–465.

Fama, E.F., Fisher, L., Jensen, M., Roll, R., 1969. The adjustment of stock prices to new information. Int. Econ. Rev. 10 (1), 1–21.

Franks, J.R., Broyles, J.E., Hecht, M.J., 1977. An industry study of the profitability of mergers in the United Kingdom. J. Finance. 32 (5), 1513–1525.

Franks, J., Robert, H., Titman, S., 1991. The post merger share price performance of acquiring firms. J. Financ. Econ. 29 (1), 81–96.

French, K., Roll, R., 1986. Stock return variances: the arrival of information and the reaction of traders. J. Financ. Econ. 17, 5–26.

Fuller, K., Netter, J., Stegemoller, M., 2004. What do returns to acquiring firms tell us? Evidence from firms that make many acquisitions. J. Finance. 57 (4), 1763–1794.

Grossman, S.J., Stiglitz, J.E., 1980. On the impossibility of informationally efficient markets. Am. Econ. Rev. 70, 393–408.

Halpern, P.J., 1973. Empirical estimates of the amount and distribution of gains to companies in mergers. J. Bus. 46 (4), 554–575.

Houston, J.F., James, C.M., Ryngaert, M.D., 2001. Where do merger gains come from? bank mergers from the perspective of insiders and outsiders. J. Financ. Econ. 60 (2–3), 285–331, <http://web.mit.edu/alo/www/Papers/EMH_Final.pdf>.

Ibbotoson, R.G., Sindelar, J.L., Ritter, J.R., 1994. The market problems with the pricing of initial public offerings. J. Appl. Corp. Financ. 7 (1), 66–74.

Impson, M., 1997. Market reaction to dividend decrease announcement: public utilities versus unregulated industrial firms. J. Financ. Res. 20 (3), 407–422.

Jain, P.C., 1988. Response of hourly stock prices and trading volume to economic news. J. Bus. 61 (2), 219–231.

James, C., Edmister, R., 1983. The relation between common stock returns, trading activity and market value. J. Finance. 38 (4), 1075–1086.

James, W., Rodney, L., Philip, L.C., 1983. The abnormal returns from merger profiles. J. Financ. Quant. Anal. 18 (2), 149–163.

Jegadeesh, N., 1990. Evidence of predictable behavior of security returns. J. Finance. 45, 881–898.

Jegadeesh, N., Titman, S., 1993. Returns to buying winners and selling losers: implications for stock market efficiency. J. Finance. 48, 65−91.

Jegadeesh, N., Titman, S., 2001. Profitability of momentum strategies: an evaluation of alternative explanations. J. Finance. 56, 699−720.

Jensen, M.C., Ruback, R.S., 1983. The market for corporate control. J. Financ. Econ. 11, 5−50.

Jones S.L., Netter, J.M., 2008. The Concise Encyclopedia of Economics, Efficient Capital Markets E <http://www.econlib.org/library/Enc/EfficientCapitalMarkets.html>.

Kahneman, D., Tversky, A., 1979. On the psychology of prediction. Psychol. Rev. 80, 237−251.

Kahneman, D., Tversky, A., 1982. Intuitive prediction: biases and corrective prediction. In: Kahneman, D., Solvic, P., Tversky, A. (Eds.), Judgment Under Uncertainty: Heuristics and Biases. Cambridge University Press, New York, NY.

Keim, D., 1983. Size-related anomalies and stock return seasonality: further empirical evidence. J. Financ. Econ. 12, 13−32.

Kendall, M.G., 1953. The analysis of economic time series, part I: prices. J. R. Stat. Soc. 96, 11−25.

Keynes, J.M., 1936. The General Theory of Employment, Interest and Money. Harcourt, New York, NY.

Lakonishok, J., Smidt, S., 1988. Are seasonal anomalies real? A ninety-year perspective. Rev. Financ. Stud. 1, 403−425.

Langetieg, T.C., 1978. An application of a three-factor performance index to measure stockholder gains from merger. J. Financ. Econ. 6 (4), 365−383.

Lehmann, B., 1990. Fads, martingales, and market efficiency. Q. J. Econ. 105, 1−28.

Lo, A., MacKinlay, C., 1990. When are contrarian profits due to stock market overreaction? Rev Financ. Stud. 3, 175−206.

Loughran, T., Ritter, J.R., 1995. The new issues puzzle. J. Finance. 50 (1), 23−51.

Malatesta, P.H., 1983. The wealth effect of merger activity and the objective functions of merging firms. J. Financ. Econ. 11 (1−4), 155−181.

Malkiel, B.G., 2003. The efficient market hypothesis and its critics. J. Econ. Perspect. 17 (1), 59−82.

Mandelbrot, B., 1966. Forecasts of future prices, unbiased market and martingale models. J. Bus. 39, 242−255.

Mandelker, G., 1974. Risk and return: the case of merging firms. J. Financ. Econ. 1, 303−335.

Masse, I., Hanrahan, J.R., Kushner, J., 1997. The effect of Canadian stock splits, stock dividends and reverse splits on the value of the firm. Q. J. Bus. Econ. 36, 51−62.

Miller, R.E., Reilly, F.K., 1987. Examination of mispricing, returns and uncertainty for initial public offerings. Financ. Manage. 16 (2), 33−38.

Moeller, S.B., Schlingemann, F.P., Stulz, R.M., 2004. Firm Size and the gains from acquisitions. J. Financ. Econ. 73, 201−228.

Niederhoffer, V., Osborne, M.F.M., 1966. Market making an reversal on the stock exchange. J. Am. Stat. Assoc.897−916.

Osborne, M.F.M., 1962. Periodic structure in the brownian motion of stock prices. Oper. Res. 10, 345−379.

Peavey III, J.W., Goodman, D.A., 1983. The significance of P/Es for portfolio returns. J. Portf. Manage. 9 (2).

Peters, D.J., 1991. Valuing a growth stock. J. Portf. Manage. 17 (3), 49−51.

Pettit, R.R., Venkatesh, P.C., 1995. Insider trading and long run return performance. Financ. Manage. 24 (2), 88–103.

Poterba, J.M., Summers, L., 1988. Mean reversion in stock market prices: evidence and implications. J. Financ. Econ. 22, 27–59.

Ritter, J.R., 1991. The long run performance of initial public offerings. J. Finance. 46 (1), 3–27.

Roberts, H.V., 1959. Stock market patterns and financial analysis: methodological suggestions. J. Finance. 14, 11–25.

Rosenberg, B., Reid, K., Lanstein, R., 1985a. Persuasive evidence of market efficiency. J. Portf. Manage. 11 (3), 9–17.

Rosenberg, B., Reid, K., Lanstein, R., 1985b. Persuasive evidence of market inefficiency. J. Portf. Manage. 11, 9–17.

Rozeff, M., Kinney Jr., W., 1976. Capital market seasonality: the case of stock returns. J. Financ. Econ. 3, 379–402.

Samuelson, P.A., 1965. Proof that properly anticipated prices fluctuate randomly. Ind. Manage. Rev. 6, 41–49.

Schipper, K., Thompson, R., 1983. Evidence on the capitalized value of merger activity for acquiring firms. J. Financ. Econ. 11 (1–4), 85–119.

Shiller, R.J., 1981. Do stock prices move too much to be justified by subsequent changes in dividends. Am. Econ. Rev. 71, 421–435.

Shleifer, A., Vishny, R.W., 1997. The limits of arbitrage. J. Finance. 52, 35–55.

Singal, V., 1996. Airline mergers and competition: an integration of stock and product price effects. J. Bus. 69 (2), 233–268.

Singh, H., Montgomery, C.A., 1987. Corporate acquisition strategies and economic performance. Strateg. Manage. J. 8 (4), 377–386.

Summers, L.H., 1986. Does the stock market rationally reflect fundamental values? J. Finance. 41, 591–601.

Thaler, R.H., 1980. Toward a positive theory of consumer choice. J. Econ. Behav. Organ. 1, 39–60.

Williams, J.B., 1938. The Theory of Investment Value. Harvard University Press, Cambridge, MA.

Womack, K.L., 1996. Do brokerage analysts recommendation have investment value. J. Finance. 51 (1), 137–167.

Estimation of cost of capital

4

4.1 Introduction

The cost of capital is generally the weighted average cost of capital. The weighted average cost of capital is the weighted averages of cost of equity and cost of debt. The cost of equity is basically determined by the capital asset pricing model (CAPM). The determinants of cost of equity are the risk-free rate, beta, and risk premium. The cost of debt can be found out using different methods.

4.1.1 Risk-free rate

Risk-free rate and risk premium are two major building blocks for the calculation of cost of equity. The risk-free rate has been dismally low during the economic recession period 2008–2009. For the calculation of cost of equity, different models like CAPM and Fama French Three factor model can be utilized. The yield-to-maturity (YTM) can be considered as risk-free rate for the application of these models. The risk-free rate consists of three components—the real return, inflation, and investment rate risk. The real rate of return is required for an investor for postponing the present consumption. Real rates of return are those rates that have been adjusted for inflation. The nominal interest rates have not been adjusted for inflation. The risk-free rate also includes the expected inflation. The expected rate of inflation is based on the period of the risk-free investment. The YTM incorporates the basic components of the risk-free rate.

The long-term US treasury bonds are considered to be default risk free, but face reinvestment risk. Bonds are sensitive to interest rate fluctuations. There is an element of uncertainty regarding reinvestment of the cash flows obtained from coupon payments and the maturity period. This can be termed as the reinvestment rate risk. The horizon premium is basically the long-term premium of government bond returns in excess of the average expected interest rates on the treasury bills. The horizon premium is expected to compensate the investor for the maturity risk of the bond.

Financial analysts use YTM of different bonds based on the period of valuation. For example, if the valuation period is 20 years, then the YTM for government bond with maturity of 20 years is used. During the 2007–2009 economic crisis period, it is found that the risk-free rates were abnormally low, which results in lower discount rate for valuation.

Academic studies have suggested that the long-term real risk-free rate of interest is estimated in the range of 1.3% to 2% based on the study of inflation swap rates and yields on long-term US treasury Inflation Protected Securities (TIPS). The average yield on long-term TIPS can be used as a proxy for long-term real rate. The average monthly 20-year TIPS yield from 2004 to 2013 period was 1.7%.

Table 4.1 Yield on US treasury bonds (in %) with different maturity periods

Year	10-year bond	20-year bond	30-year bond
2000	6.03	6.23	5.94
2001	5.02	5.63	5.49
2002	4.61	5.43	5.43
2003	4.01	4.96	NA
2004	4.27	5.04	NA
2005	4.29	4.64	NA
2006	4.8	5	4.91
2007	4.63	4.91	4.84
2008	3.66	4.36	4.28
2009	3.26	4.11	4.08
2010	3.22	4.03	4.25
2011	2.78	3.62	3.91
2012	1.8	2.54	2.92
2013	2.35	3.12	3.45

NA, not applicable.
Source: http://www.federalreserve.gov/releases/h15/data.htm.

Established surveys like that of Livingston survey and survey of professional forecasters conducted by Federal Reserve Bank of Philadelphia, Blue chip Financial Forecasts, University of Michigan survey have forecasted annual inflation in the range of 2.3–3%. The Congressional Budget Office in the United States have forecasted inflation of approximately 2% per annum through 2023.[1] Based on these estimates, the nominal risk-free rate can be estimated to be in the range of 3.6–5%.

Based on the historical data from Fed Reserve, it can be observed that the average YTM for 10-year US treasury bonds was *6.56%* during the period 1962–2013. The average YTM for 20-year US treasury bonds during the period 1993–2013 was *5.28%*. The average YTM for 30-year US treasury bond was *7.37%* during the period 1977–2013.[2] *The yield on long-term treasury bond can be used as risk-free rate* (Table 4.1).

4.1.2 Risk premium

The market or equity risk premium (ERP) is an important metric in finance, which is implicit in the evaluation of financing and investment opportunities. The market risk premium is the incremental premium required by investors relative to a

[1] http://appraisal.wichita.edu/2014%20Presentations/Monday/10.30%20-%20Grabowski-%20Cost%20of% 20Capital.pdf.

[2] The returns calculated were arithmetic returns. The annual data for the yield to maturity for 20-year bonds were available from 1993 onward. For 30 yield-to-maturity calculation, the data were not available for period 2003–2005.The source of database was Historical statistics, http://www.federalreserve. gov/releases/h15/data.html.

risk-free asset like US government bond for the purpose of investing in a globally diversified market portfolio. The quantification of risk premium is an important step for the valuation process. The cost of equity has to be adjusted to new market realities in order to check under valuation and over valuation. In theory, stocks should provide a greater return than safe investments like treasury bonds. The difference between return on stock and risk-free rate is called the ERP. ERP is the compensation that investors require to make them indifferent between holding the risky market portfolio and risk-free bond.

Expected return on the market portfolio = Risk-free rate of return + market risk premium

Expected return on an asset = Risk-free rate of return + beta * market risk premium. In a macroeconomic perspective, the market risk premium represents the broader picture of the economy. The major factors that influence investor's perception about market risk include growth forecasts for economic growth, consumer demand, inflation, interest rates, and geopolitical risks.

The determination of risk premium is an important step in the calculation of the cost of equity. The estimation of risk premium is a function of the holding period of the investment. For the estimation of the equity return for a highly liquid investment of short-term period, the US treasury bill may be the appropriate rate to benchmark the ERP. The ERP is also known as market risk premium. ERP is the extra return over the expected yield on the risk-free securities that an investor is expected to receive from an investment in a diversified portfolio of common stocks.

Market or ERP = $R_m - R_f$

Where R_m is the expected return on a fully diversified market portfolio of equity securities. R_f is the risk-free rate. The returns on a market index like S&P 500 or NYSE Composite index is taken as a proxy for the market portfolio.

If the period stock returns are not correlated and the stock returns are quite stable, then arithmetic average of historical stock returns provides an unbiased estimate of expected future stock returns. The arithmetic average of realized risk premiums provides an unbiased estimate of expected future risk premiums. If the stock price exhibits volatility, then geometric mean of historical stock returns is a better estimate of expected future stock returns Cooper (1996). With respect to the period of estimation of risk premium, a shorter period will be susceptible to large errors in estimating its true value on account of high volatility of annual stock returns. JP Morgan estimates the risk premium within the range of 5−7% during the year 2008 (Table 4.2).

US-based market risk premium is a reasonable estimate for developed countries as unconstrained investors can freely invest in any developed economy market. But in emerging markets, US-based risk premium may not be the right choice due to nonmarket risks like political risk.

4.1.2.1 Estimation of ERP

Basically, there is no universally accepted methodology for estimating the ERP. A number of methods are used in practice and recommended by academicians and

Table 4.2 **Risk premium estimates**

Source	Risk premium estimate (%)
Historical US 1926–2007 geometric mean based on historical average realized returns	5.1
Dividend discount model	5.6
Constant sharpe ratio	6.0
Dividend yield methodology	6.6
Geometric academic survey	5
Arithmetic academic survey	5.8
Historical US 1926–2007, arithmetic mean	6.9
Implied from AA bonds	8.6

Source: JP Morgan, Corporate Finance Advisory.

financial advisors. The approaches for estimation of ERP can be classified as *ex post* approach and *ex ante* approach (Grabowski 2011). In *ex post* approaches, expected returns on common stocks are estimated in terms of averages of realized historical single period returns or multiyear compound returns. The *ex ante* approach consists of estimating the ERP using the returns on the diversified portfolio implied by the expected future stock prices or expected dividends.

Methods to estimate the market or ERP

1. Historical average-realized returns

    ERP = Average annual equity index returns−average return on treasury bonds.

    The choice of arithmetic or geometric method can lead to significant differences in ERP estimates. Over a long-term horizon, geometric mean is the better measure, while arithmetic average is the better estimate of annual expected return. The method can produce counterproductive results if changing risk premium environment results. In cases of increase of risk premium and constant cash flows, the equity price returns will fall. This will lead to lower realized returns which in turn would lower the average historical returns.

2. Dividend discount model

    Dividend discount model (DDM) can be used to calculate the current market cost of equity. The model uses an internal rate of return (cost of equity) based on a price level and expected dividend of an index like S&P 500 as a proxy for the broad market. Dividends are projected by applying an expected payout ratio to forecasted earnings. Earnings are forecasted by combining near term of 5 years market estimates with a perpetuity growth rate equivalent to long-term nominal GDP growth. The dividend payout is initially assumed to be the average of recent historical payout ratios, but tends to increase over the long-term period toward 80% in the terminal period as reinvestment opportunities declines (Goyal and Welch 2001). It has to be noted that the market cost of equity varies primarily with movements in the level of index and changes in expectations for future dividends. DDM are forward looking and consistent with no arbitrage.

    MRP = Cost of equity implied by DDM − 10-year government bond yield

3. Constant sharpe ratio method

    The Sharpe ratio measures a portfolio's excess return per unit of risk.

    MRP = Market (S&P 500) Sharpe ratio * Market (S&P 500) implied volatility

4. Bond market implied risk premium

The bond market implied risk premium is based on the expected return on the bond and its beta. For high-yield bonds, the expected return is likely to be significantly lower than the promised yield. For AA rated corporate bond, the default probabilities are low and the yield can be used as a proxy for expected returns.

5. Dividend yield method

The dividend yield method is related to the dividend discount method. The price of the dividend paying stock can be estimated using the constant growth valuation model. The model assumes that dividend will grow at a constant rate forever. Cost of equity is the sum of dividend yield and long-term growth rates.

MRP = (Cost of equity implied by dividend yield method − 10-year government bond yield)/Beta

6. Survey evidence

Survey method is one of the basic methods used for determining the MRP. The survey results are based on the opinion of academics, investors, and CFOs.

4.1.2.2 Other perspectives on estimation of market risk premium

4.1.2.2.1 Unconditional MRP

The unconditional ERP is the long-term average ERP, which is based on realized historical risk premium data. Practitioners, tax, and regulatory authorities use historical data to estimate the conditional ERP under the assumption that historical data are a valid proxy for current investor expectations. A widely used practice is to add the same long-term average realized risk premium, which is an *ex post* estimate of the ERP to the market interest rate of the risk-free security throughout the following year, regardless of the level of the rate on that security as of the valuation date. The first assumption made in this practice is that in future period, the difference between the expected return on common stocks and US government bond is constant. The second assumption is that the increase or decrease in ERP during the valuation period is short term in nature and the ERP is mean reverting to the long-term average of the realized risk premiums within a short span of time.

Practitioners often estimate cost of capital by adding the yield on a long-term US treasury government bond to the arithmetic average of the realized risk premium each year as reported by the Morningstar SBBI Yearbook.

4.1.2.2.2 Conditional MRP

Conditional ERP is cyclical in nature and based on current market conditions. During the times of recession or near recession, returns on stock would be low and the conditional ERP would be higher. During the boom period, stock returns will be higher and the conditional ERP will be lower.

Four *ex ante* (forward looking) approaches can be used to estimate the conditional ERP. They are bottom-up implied ERP estimates, top-down ERP estimates, top-down risk premium estimates, and survey approaches. In bottom-up implied approach, the expected growth in earnings or dividends forms the basis for estimating a "bottom-up" company by company rate of return for the companies. The top-down implied ERP estimate uses expected growth in earnings or dividends for the aggregate of the companies comprising a stock index. The top-down risk premium estimates uses the ERP or changes in ERP using the observed relationship between interest rates and other factors, which impact the ERP. Survey method relies on the opinions of investors and financial professionals about the risk premiums. Professor Damodaran (2006) calculates the implied ERP estimates for the S&P 500 data using a multistage model. Duff and Phelps recommends ERP of 5% and an expected (normalized) risk-free rate of 4% as of December 31, 2013.[3]

4.1.2.3 Research discussions on ERP

The existing empirical research that investigates the size of equity premium is generally based on the mean difference between an estimate of the return to holding equity and the risk-free rate. Goyal and Welch (2008) suggest that historical mean is a good tool for forecasting the equity premium. Siegel (1999) predicted that the ERP will decrease on account of low current dividend yields and high equity valuations.

Campbell and Shilier (2001) forecasted low returns due to the perception that the market was overvalued. Amott and Ryan (2001) suggested that the forward-looking ERP is actually negative. Arnott and Bernstein (2002) argued that the forward-looking ERP is near zero or negative.

Many studies suggest that long-term predictability is much better than short-term predictability. The implied forward looking estimates of ERP can be estimated on the basis of underlying expectations of growth in corporate earnings and dividends using the *ex ante* approach. Fama and French (2002) estimate the equity premium using dividend and earnings growth rates to measure the expected rate of capital gain. The study based on a very long period of 1872−1999 estimated a historical expected geometric equity premium of 2.55 percentage points when they used dividend growth rates and a premium of 4.32 percentage points on the basis of earnings growth. The study observed that the increase in the price earnings ratio would have resulted in a realized ERP, which was higher than the *ex ante* (expected) premium. Robert (2001) suggests that the expected ERP can be estimated on the basis of a normal or unconditional ERP (the long-term average) and a conditional ERP based on the current level of the stock market and economy relative to the long-term average. Kozhan et al. (2013) find that the skew premium accounts for over 40% of the slope in the implied volatility curve in the S&P 500 market. Skew risk is tightly related to variance risk. Elroy et al. (2003) examined the realized equity returns and equity premiums for 17 countries during the period 1900−2009. The study observes that larger equity returns were obtained in the second half of the twentieth century compared to the earlier period. This pattern was basically due to growth of corporate cash flows, lower transaction and monitoring costs, lower inflation rates and lower required rates of returns as expected by investors on account of decreased investment risks. The study also observes that increases in overall price to dividend ratio are on account of the long-term decrease in the required risk premium. Ibbotson and Chen (2003) find that the expected long-term ERP relative to the

---

[3] Valuation Handbook-Guide to Cost of Capital. Duff & Phelps.

long-term government bond yield is 6 percentage points in terms of arithmetic mean and 4 percentage points in geometric mean terms.

Survey-based studies generally support higher ERPs. Welch (2000) conducted a survey of 226 academic financial economists to elicit their view on ERP and forecasted a geometric long horizon ERP of approximately 4 percentage points. Graham and Harvey (2001) based on multiyear survey of chief financial officers of US companies suggest expected 10-year geometric average ERP in the range of 3.9 to 4.7 percentage points.

Studies have also documented long-term average or unconditional estimate of ERP. Shannon et al. (2010) observes the long range of conditional ERP estimates over the entire business cycle is in the range of 3.5−6.0% during the period 1926−2010. This study documents realized risk premiums of 6.72% during the period 1926−2010.

Academic studies indicate that ERP are lowest in periods of business expansion and highest in periods of recession. Fabio (2002) finds that ERP is positively correlated with long-term bond yields and with default premium measured as the differential rates between Aaa- and Baa-rated bonds. Mayfield (2004) suggest that the required market risk premium for the period after 1940 is 5.9% over the yield on treasury bills. Harris and Marston (1999) find an average market risk premium of 7.14% above yields on long-term US government bonds over the period 1982−1998. Fernando and Carlos (2013) estimate the ERP by combining information from 20 models and point that equity premium reached historical heights in July 2013 at 14.5%, the highest level in 50 years. The study also states that the ERP during the financial crisis in 2009 was 10.5%.

4.1.2.4   Variations in risk premium estimations

The variations in historical risk estimates by different estimators are due to differences in time period used, the choice of bonds or bills of different maturity as the risk-free rate, and the usage of arithmetic averages compared to geometric averages. There are estimates for historical risk premium, which are based on long time period from 1926 onward. At the same time, risk estimates are also based on shorter time period of 10, 20, or 50 years. Hence, the risk estimates are of different values. The disadvantage of using longer period is that the risk perception of the investor changes over the period of time. If shorter periods are used, greater standard errors in the estimation is found. For example, the annual standard deviation in stock prices between 1926 and 2010 was found to be 20%. The calculation of standard error of the estimate for 5 and 50 years comes to 8.94% $(20\%/\sqrt{5})$ and 2.83% $(20\%/\sqrt{50})$, respectively. The choice of treasury bill or treasury bond as the risk-free asset is also a factor for variation in the estimated values for risk premium. If the risk-free asset is taken as treasury bills, then the difference between the average return on stocks minus the yield on treasury bill is calculated for the risk premium. If the treasury bond rate is considered as the risk-free rate, then the difference between average return on stocks minus the yield on treasury bond rate is used as the risk premium. The two standard statistics used for estimating historical average return on the stocks are the arithmetic and geometric mean. The results vary based on these two estimates. For example, Professor Damodaran (2012) estimates the arithmetic mean of stock returns (based on S&P 500 returns) and 10-year treasury bond returns as 11.5% and 5.21%, respectively, during the period 1928−2013. This results in a risk premium of 6.29% from arithmetic mean calculations. During the same period, the geometric mean-based returns on stock and bond were 9.55% and 4.93% resulting in a risk premium of 4.62%. During the period 2004−2013, the arithmetic mean-based risk premium was 4.41%, while the geometric mean-based risk premium was 3.07%.[4] The arithmetic mean or the simple average is the unbiased measure of the expected value of repeated observations of a random variable. Hence, arithmetic return is the rate of return that investors expect over the next year for the random annual rate of return on the market. Geometric average is the compounded annual growth rate or time weighted rate of return. The use of the arithmetic mean ignores the estimation error and serial correlation in returns.

There is a paradox in the fact that if we consider a long-term period for historical risk premium estimation, then the risk assumptions would have undergone changes during the long period. At the same time, if we use a short period, the challenge would be to deal with large standard error associated with the risk premium estimates on account of stock volatility.

4.1.2.5   Risk premiums in other markets

The study by Elroy et al. (2011) provide global evidence on the long-term realized equity premium relative to both bills and bonds in 19 different countries. The study suggests considerable variation in risk premiums across countries. The study finds that the mean real returns were an annualized 5.5%, and the equity premium relative to the long-term government bonds was an annualized 3.8%. The dataset was based on two North American markets, eight euro currency markets, five other European markets, three Asia pacific market, and one African market region (Table 4.3).

The risk premium in other markets like emerging countries can be calculated by adding a country premium to the base premium of the developed market.

ERP = Base premium for matured developed equity market + country risk premium.

4.1.2.5.1   Estimation of country risk premium from default spread

The country risk premium can be estimated based on the default spread on country bonds issued by the emerging country and equity market volatility. Credit rating agencies like S&P, Moody's Investors Services, and Fitch provide sovereign ratings for all countries. These ratings that measure the default risk of a country is based on a number of factors like political stability, trade balances, and stability of national currency. These sovereign ratings can be used to estimate the default spreads over the riskless rate. The S&P gave a rating of BBB − to Brazil's long-term foreign currency sovereign credit rating in November 2014. This rating suggested a stable outlook, which reflected

---

[4] Annual Returns on Stocks, T. Bonds and T.Bills :1928-Current, http://pages.stern.nyu.edu/ ∼ adamodar/ New_Home_Page/datafile/histretSP.html.

Table 4.3 **Risk premium relative to bonds (1900–2010)**

Country	Geometric mean (%)	Arithmetic mean (%)
Australia	5.9	7.8
Belgium	2.6	4.9
Canada	3.7	5.3
Denmark	2.0	3.4
Finland	5.6	9.2
France	3.2	5.6
Germany	5.4	8.8
Ireland	2.9	4.9
Italy	3.7	7.2
Japan	5.0	9.1
The Netherlands	3.5	5.8
New Zealand	3.8	5.4
Norway	2.5	5.5
South Africa	5.5	7.2
Spain	2.3	4.3
Sweden	3.8	6.1
Switzerland	2.1	3.6
United Kingdom	3.9	5.2
United States	4.4	6.4
Europe	3.9	5.2
World ex USA	3.8	5.0
World	3.8	5.0

Source: Elroy, Dimson, Paul Marsh, Mike Staunton, Triumph of the Optimists, Princeton University Press 2002; Credit Suisse Global Investment Returns Year book 2011.

the Brazil's institutional and balance sheet strength. Moody services gave a bond implied rating of Baa3 in October 2014. The yield on Brazilian government bond with 10-year maturity was 12.29% in November 2014. The average yield on US government bond with 10-year maturity was 6.37%.[5] The average yield on Brazil government bond with 10-year maturity was 12.27%. Brazil's dollar bonds yield an average 2.05 percentage points more than US Treasuries, compared with 2.30 percentage points at the end of 2013, according to index data from JP Morgan Chase & Co.[6] The default spread is found out as the difference between the yield on dollar denominated Brazil government bond and US government bond with same maturity period. In this case, it is found to be $8.42 - 6.37 = 2.05\%$. The standard default spread with BBB − /Baa3 rating for 30-year maturity bond is 2.04 as of November 2014 (Table 4.4). The cost of equity estimated in dollars for a Brazilian company in dollar terms can be calculated as follows :

Cost of equity (in US dollars) = (US risk-free rate + beta * US risk premium) + default spread

[5] http://www.tradingeconomics.com/united-states/indicators.
[6] http://www.bloomberg.com/news/2014-07-23/brazil-planning-to-sell-benchmark-dollar-bonds-maturing-in-2045.html.

Table 4.4 **Reuters corporate spread table for industrials in percent (as of November 7, 2014)**

Rating	5 Year	10 Year	30 Year
Aaa/AAA	0.18	0.42	0.65
Aa1/AA+	0.34	0.54	0.77
Aa2/AA	0.50	0.65	0.89
Aa3/AA−	0.54	0.69	0.92
A1/A+	0.58	0.72	0.95
A2/A	0.61	0.77	1.03
A3/A−	0.72	0.89	1.17
Baa1/BBB+	0.92	1.15	1.51
Baa2/BBB	1.07	1.32	1.70
Baa3/BBB−	1.40	1.65	2.04
Ba1/BB+	2.17	2.48	2.86
Ba2/BB	2.95	3.30	3.67
Ba3/BB−	3.72	4.13	4.49
B1/B+	4.50	4.95	5.30
B2/B	5.27	5.78	6.12
B3/B−	6.04	6.60	6.93
Caa/CCC+	6.82	7.43	7.7.5
US treasury yield	1.74	2.73	3.35

Source: http://www.bondsonline.com/Todays_Market/Corporate_Bond_Spreads.php. Bonds Online Group, Thomson Reuter.

Consider the following inputs. Beta for the company = 1.5, US treasury bond rate (risk-free rate) = 6.37%, US risk premium = 4.4 %, Default spread for Brazil = 2.05%.

Cost of equity for Brazil company in US dollars = [6.37 + 1.5 * 4.4] + 2.05 = 15.02%

The cost of equity for the company in Brazilian currency can be estimated by relative inflation. The inflation rate in Brazil in September 2014 was 6.75%, and the inflation in the United States was 1.7% in September 2014.

$(1 + \text{Expected cost of equity}_{\text{Home country}}) = (1 + \text{Expected cost of equity US}) *$
$[1 + \text{inflation rate in home country}/1 + \text{inflation rate in US}]$
Expected cost of equity$_{\text{Home country}}$ = 1.1502 * [1.0675/1.017] − 1 = 0.2073 or 20.73%.

The spread values represent basis points (bps) over a US treasury security of the same maturity, or the closest matching maturity. Suppose a corporate bond has obtained a credit rating from Moody/S&P of value Ba3/BB−. Then the interest rate on the bond is calculated as the US treasury yield for the 10-year bond plus the default spread. In this case, it equals 2.73 + 4.13 = 6.86%. The default spread can vary for bonds with same rating but different maturity periods. The default spread is found to increase during periods of low economic growth.

4.1.2.5.2 Country risk premium from volatility of stock prices
Country risk premium can also be estimated from volatility of stock prices. The equity risk is measured by the standard deviation in stock prices. Relative standard

deviation of stock prices in emerging country is found out in relation to standard deviation of stock prices in the US market. Then the ERP in the emerging market is obtained as the product of risk premium in the United States and the relative standard deviation of stock prices in the United States. Another alternate approach is based on the implied equity premiums.

4.1.2.5.3 Estimation of default spread from bonds

The default spread for each ratings can be based on the sample bonds within that ratings class and obtain the current market interest rate on these bonds. The sample of bonds are required as single bonds may be mispriced or misrated. The two measures to estimate the interest rate on bond are the current yield on the bond and YTM. The current yield on the bond is the bond's annual coupon divided by its market price. The YTM is the rate required in the market on the bond. YTM is the interest rate that makes the present value of the coupons and the face value of the bond equal to the market price. YTM is considered to be a superior measure of market rate of interest.

4.1.3 Estimation of cost of equity

The cost of equity is estimated by means of standard risk return model of CAPM. The risk and return models are discussed in detail in Chapter 2. All models have two important components—the risk-free rate and risk premium.

Expected return = Riskless rate + beta * (risk premium)

4.1.4 Beta estimation

The beta can be estimated through historical market beta, fundamental beta, and accounting betas.

4.1.4.1 Historical beta estimation

Historical beta is estimated by regressing the stock returns on the market returns during the estimation period. Estimation of historical returns are based on a period of daily, weekly, or monthly returns. The market index returns are obtained from stock index like S&P 500, DJIA, or NYSE Composite Index.

Stock return$_t$ = Price$_t$ − Price$_{t-1}$ + Dividends$_t$/Price$_{t-1}$

Where Stock return$_t$ is the return to the stockholder in time period t

- Price$_t$ is the price of the stock in time period t
- Price$_{t-1}$ is the price of the stock in time period t − 1
- Dividends$_t$ is the dividend per share given in time period t

The returns on the market index like DJIA are estimated as given below:

Market return$_t$ = Index$_t$ − Index$_{t-1}$ + Dividends$_t$/Index$_{t-1}$

where Market return$_t$ is the return on the market index at time period t

- Index$_t$ is the value of index during the time period t
- Index$_{t-1}$ is the value of index during the time period t − 1

The expected return R$_i$ on a stock according to CAPM is given by

$$R_i = R_f + \beta(R_m - R_f)$$
$$R_i = R_f + \beta R_m - \beta R_f \text{ Rearranging we get}$$
$$R_i = R_f(1 - \beta) + \beta R_m$$

This expected return can be compared to the returns from the regression obtained. That is

$$R_i = a + bR_m$$

The slope of regression b corresponds to the beta of the stock, which measures the systematic risk of the stock. The comparison of the regression intercept a to R$_f$ $(1 - \beta)$ provides the measure of stock performance in relation to the CAPM. The difference between *a* and the measure R$_f$ $(1 - \beta)$ is called Jensen's alpha. Jensen's alpha, or *ex post* alpha, is determined by taking the current portfolio return and subtracting the expected return according to the CAPM. The difference between a and R$_f$ $(1 - \beta)$ provides a measure of whether the investment earned a return greater than or less than its required (expected return) as estimated from the CAPM model.

If a $>$ R$_f$ $(1 - \beta)$, then the stock has greater return than expected during the regression period

If a $=$ R$_f$ $(1 - \beta)$, then the stock has return equal to the expected return during the regression period

If a $<$ R$_f$ $(1 - \beta)$, then the stock has return less than the expected return during the regression period

R-squared (R^2) provides the measure of goodness of fit for the regression, which is an estimate of the proportion of risk of a firm which can be attributed to market risk and then balance $(1 - R^2)$ can be attributed to firm-specific risk. The standard error indicates the amount of error in the estimate.

Beta estimation services are provided by Merrill Lynch, Barra, Value Line, Standard & Poor, Morning Star, and Bloomberg. Bloomberg provides an adjusted beta which is obtained by the raw beta $* 0.67 + 1.00 * 0.33$. The values obtained for beta estimation varies based on the length of the estimation period, return interval, and choice of market index to be used for the regression analysis. Service firms usually uses 5- or 2-year data. Longer the estimation period the more data would be available for analysis, but the risk characteristics of the firm would have undergone changes during the long estimation period. The stock and market index returns can have intervals like annual, monthly, weekly, and daily returns. The usage of daily returns increases the number of observations in the regression, but at the same time exposes the estimation process to significant bias in beta estimates due to nontrading. The choice of market index must be related to the stock market in which the stock is listed. The market index for US stocks could be NYSE composite index, Dow Jones Industrial Average, and S&P 500 index. The beta of Japanese stocks can be estimated relative to Nikkei and British stocks relative to FTSE index.

4.1.4.1.1   Regression beta calculation

This section describes the beta calculation for three automobile companies one from the mature market and two from the emerging market. The stocks selected were General Motors from US, Tata Motors from India, and SAIC Motor Corporation from China. The S&P 500 index was chosen as the market index for General Motors. The BSE SENSEX and SSE Composite (also known as Shanghai Composite) was the market index chosen for estimation of beta for Tata Motors and SAIC Motor Corporation Group, respectively. The beta estimation was based on a 5-year period (October 2009−2014) with monthly returns interval.

Beta estimate for General Motors with market index S&P 500.

The slope of the regression is 1.71 which is the beta for the stock. The adjusted R^2 value of 0.4046 indicates that 40.46% of the variation comes from market sources and the rest from firm specific source. The standard error of the estimate is 0.068, which gives the beta range of 1.64 to 1.78 at 95% level of confidence.

Regression statistics

Multiple R	0.65
R^2	0.42
Adjusted R^2	0.40
Standard error	0.068
Observations	47

Similarly, the beta for Tata Motors was estimated as 1.58. The beta for SAIC Motors was 0.41 during the estimation period. The data and procedure for beta calculation are illustrated in the resources excel worksheet *beta calculation for GM TATA SAIC.xlsx*. Beta estimated from regression may have high standard errors.

4.1.4.2   Fundamental beta estimation

The historical method of beta estimation is possible only for firms which are traded and have market prices. Fundamental beta estimation method is utilized for estimating betas for private firms.

4.1.4.2.1   Fundamental beta

Fundamental beta is basically used to calculate the beta of the unlisted firms. Fundamental beta is the product of a statistical model, which can be used to predict the fundamental risk of a security using market related and financial data. Fundamental beta is an alternative to statistical beta. Fundamental beta is based on fundamental factors, which drives risks to cash flow. The major determinants of fundamental betas are company size, the degree of operating leverage, and the firm's financial leverage.

4.1.4.2.2 Determinants of beta

Nature and size of businesses

Smaller firms are assumed to have more uncertain future cash flows and hence higher betas than larger firms. The beta for a firm would be higher if it is more sensitive to market conditions. Cyclical firms are considered to have more beta than uncyclical firms. Real estate and automobile firms have higher betas, whereas food and tobacco firms have lower betas. Firms with discretionary products are found to have higher beta than firms, which sell essential consumer products. Tiffany will have a higher beta than Procter and Gamble. The elasticity of demand is also a determinant of fundamental beta. The more elastic the demand for a product of a firm, the higher would be the beta of the firm. Inelastic demand for a firm's products leads into lower beta. More competition leads to higher uncertainties for future cash flows and results in higher betas.

Degree of operating leverage

Fixed costs acts as a fulcrum in the case of operating leverage. Higher the fixed costs in relation to total costs, higher would be the operating leverage. The variability of operating income would be high for firms with high operating leverage. Firms with high operating leverage tend to have higher beta values.

The degree of operating leverage is given by

Degree of operating leverage = Percent change in operating profit/percent change in sales

Financial leverage

Another major determinant of fundamental beta is financial leverage. Higher the financial leverage, riskier the firm will be and greater would be the beta of the firm. A firm with higher leverage faces uncertainty in periods of greater variability in cash flows. A firm with higher financial leverage have greater outflows in the form of fixed interest payments. Hence, the equity risk of the investment rises and beta would be higher. An all equity firm have only unlevered beta, which is also known as asset beta. Asset beta is determined by the assets owned by the firm. The unlevered beta is determined by the size and type of businesses and degree of operating leverage. The levered beta signifying equity investment in a firm is determined by all the factors like type of businesses, operating leverage, and financial leverage of the firm.

The relationship between levered and unlevered beta is given by the following equation

$$\beta_L = \beta_u(1 + (1 - t)D/E)$$

where β_L is the levered beta for equity in the firm.

β_u is the unlevered beta of the firm (beta of firm with no debt in capital structure), t is the corporate tax rate, and D/E is the debt equity ratio.

4.1.4.2.3 Bottom-up approach for beta estimation

Bottom-up approach method is used to calculate beta values for startup firms and private companies that do not trade in the stock market. The bottom-up beta method depends on the major determinants like the nature of business the firms are in; the operating leverage of the firm; and the financial leverage of the firm. The bottom-up beta is estimated by the weighted average of the unlevered betas of the different businesses that the firm operates in.

Regression betas estimated from historical stock have high standard errors. The historical beta obtained from regression does not reflect the current mix of the business mix and represent the firm's average financial leverage over the period rather than current leverage.

A bottom-up beta is estimated from the betas of firms which are in a specified business. The procedure eliminates the need for historical stock prices to estimate the firm's beta. Hence, the standard error due to regression betas is reduced to a great extent. The problem of changing product mix is eliminated as the business finds a cost of capital for each product line. The leveraged beta is computed from the company's current financial leverage than the average leverage over the period of the regression. Bottom-up beta is considered to be a better measure of the market risk associated with the industry or sector of the business. Bottom-up betas capture both the operating and financial risk of a company.

4.1.4.2.4 Steps in bottom-up beta estimation

- Identify the business or businesses in which the firm operates
- Find sample of publicly traded firms for each of these businesses and find their regression betas. Then an average beta for these publicly traded firms is found out. This average beta is unlevered using the average debt equity ratio of the publicly listed firms in the sample.

$$\beta_u = \text{Average } \beta_L / (1 + (1 - t)\text{Average D/E})$$

- Estimate the unlevered beta for the target firm selected for analysis by the simple average of the unlevered betas for the comparable firms if the firm is in a single business. If the target firm is in multiple businesses, then the weighted average of the unlevered betas of the businesses in which the firm operates is found out. The weights can be based on value, operating income, or revenues. The weighted average is the bottom-up unlevered beta.
- The levered beta for the firm is obtained by using the current debt equity ratio of the firm based on market values.

The cash adjusted beta can be obtained from the following equation

Cash-adjusted beta = Unlevered beta/(1 − cash/firm value)

The standard error of the bottom-up beta is given by the following equation (Table 4.5)

Standard error = Average standard error of comparable firms/square root of number of comparable firms.

Table 4.5 **Estimation of bottom-up beta for Walmart in 2013**

Companies	Beta	D/E (%)	Tax rate
Big lots	1.31	6.87	0.33
Home depot	1.02	146.08	0.36
Target	0.94	86.34	0.36
Safeway	1.07	68.41	0.27
The Kroger	0.97	223.02	0.33
Costco	0.57	41.47	0.32
Family dollar	0.41	46.87	0.36
Dollar General	0.93	58.58	0.37
Dollar Tree	0.65	52.28	0.37
Amazon	1.19	29.42	0.32
Average	0.906	75.934	0.34

The average beta for the comparable firms is 0.906. The average debt equity ratio was 0.759. The average tax rate was 34%.

The unlevered beta is obtained from the following equation.

$$\beta_L = \beta_u(1 + (1 - t)D/E))$$

Using average tax rate of 34% and average debt equity ratio of 0.759, the value of unlevered beta is obtained.

$$\beta_u = \beta_L/(1 + (1 - t)D/E)$$
$$= 0.906/(1 + (1 - 0.34) * 0.759 = 0.6036$$

The levered beta for Walmart is obtained by using the Walmart's marginal tax rate of 0.31 and debt equity ratio of 0.66 in 2013.

$$\beta_L = \beta_u(1 + (1 - t)D/E))$$
$$= 0.6036(1 + (1 - 0.31) * 66) = 0.87.$$

4.1.4.3 Accounting betas

Accounting betas are estimated by regression of the company's return on assets against the average return on assets for large sample of firms as included in a market index. Betas determined by using accounting data instead of stock market data is known as accounting data. Accounting betas can also be found out by regressing changes in earnings for a firm with respect to changes in earnings of market over a period of time. Estimation of accounting betas using regression involves only few observations which would result in more standard errors. Moreover, accounting earnings are affected by other factors like changes in depreciation or inventory methods.

4.1.5 Cost of equity

The cost of equity or expected rate of return can be estimated using risk and return models like CAPM, Arbitrage Pricing, and Multifactor Model. CAPM is the most popular method adopted by practitioners.

Expected return = Riskless rate + beta * expected risk premium

The rate on the long-term government bond is the riskless rate and the beta can be estimated using historical beta method or fundamental bottom-up method. The risk premium could be either historical risk premium or an implied risk premium.

4.1.6 Cost of capital

The cost of capital basically refers to the weighted average cost of capital.

The first step involved in the calculation of cost of capital is the cost of equity calculation. The next step involved is the cost of debt calculation. The cost of debt refers to the cost of borrowing funds. The cost of debt indicates the default risk of the debt. The cost of debt is determined by the riskless rate, the default risk, and the tax advantage on account of using the debt. The after tax cost of debt is given by Pretax cost of debt $(1 - t)$.

4.1.6.1 Cost of debt calculation

Cost of debt can be estimated using one of the following methods:

If the firm has outstanding bonds that are traded, then the YTM on a long term bond can be used as the cost of debt.

If the firm's bonds are not actively traded, then the cost of debt for the firm can be estimated using the ratings of the firm and the default spread. Suppose a firm obtained a Baa3/BBB− rating by the Moody's/S&P. The default corporate spread is given as 204 basis point(bps) for a 30-year bond. 1% is equal to 100 bps. The US treasury yield for 30-year treasury bond is given as 3.55%. We need to add 204 basis spread to the US treasury yield of 3.55% to get the cost of debt for the firm. In this case, the cost of debt comes to $(3.55 + 2.04) = 5.54\%$. Suppose the tax rate for the firm is 30%, then the after tax cost of debt = $5.54(1 - 0.30) = 3.878$. Refer Table 4.6 for default spreads.

If the firms are not rated, then synthetic ratings can be used to estimate the cost of debt. The firm is assigned a rating based on its financial ratios. For example, a low market cap firm with interest coverage ratio of >12.5 gets a ratings of AAA while <0.5 gets a rating of D based on S&P ratings. Interest coverage ratios tend to be lower for large market capitalization stock. A large market cap stock firm with ICR of >8.5 gets a AAA rating while <0.2 gets a D rating. Based on the synthetic rating, the default spread can be added to the risk-free rate to get the pretax cost of debt for the firm.

Another method is to identify the current cost of the company's debt which is the interest rate the company would pay on the new debt. The interest expense obtained from the income statement divided by the total long-term debt gives the cost of debt.

Table 4.6 **Reuters corporate spreads for industrials March 2014**

Rating	1 Years	2 Years	3 Years	5 Years	7 Years	10 Years	30 Years
Aaa/AAA	5	8	12	18	28	42	65
Aa1/AA+	10	18	25	34	42	54	77
Aa2/AA	14	29	38	50	57	65	89
Aa3/AA−	19	34	43	54	61	69	92
A1/A+	23	39	47	58	65	72	95
A2/A	24	39	49	61	69	77	103
A3/A−	32	49	59	72	80	89	117
Baa1/BBB+	38	61	75	92	103	115	151
Baa2/BBB	47	75	89	107	119	132	170
Baa3/BBB−	83	108	122	140	152	165	204
Ba1/BB+	157	182	198	217	232	248	286
Ba2/BB	231	256	274	295	312	330	367
Ba3/BB−	305	330	350	372	392	413	449
B1/B+	378	404	426	450	472	495	530
B2/B	452	478	502	527	552	578	612
B3/B−	526	552	578	604	632	660	693
Caa/CCC+	600	626	653	682	712	743	775
US treasury yield	0.13	0.45	0.93	1.74	2.31	2.73	3.55

Spread values represent basis points (bps) over a US treasury security of the same maturity, or the closest matching maturity.
Source: Bonds Online Group, Thomson Reuter.

After-tax cost of debt = Pretax cost of debt $(1 - T)$ where T is the tax rate.

The cost of debt in an emerging market company can be estimated by adding the country default spread based on sovereign rating for the country in which the firm is domiciled to the company default spread based on synthetic rating and the risk-free rate.

Cost of debt for emerging market company = Riskless rate + country default spread + firm default spread.

The firm default spread can be based on the ratings obtained by the firm on its long-term bond issue given by S&P or Moody's or synthetic rating (Tables 4.7−4.10).

4.1.6.2   Cost of preferred stocks

The cost of preferred stock is given by
Preferred dividend per share/Market price per preferred share.
The cost of other hybrid securities like convertible bonds can be estimated. The hybrid components can be broken down into debt and equity components and cost can be found out separately.

Table 4.7 Business and financial risk profile matrix

Business risk profile	Financial risk profile					
	Minimal	**Modest**	**Intermediate**	**Significant**	**Aggressive**	**Highly leveraged**
Excellent	AAA/AA+	AA	A	A−	BBB	−
Strong	AA	A	A−	BBB	BB	BB−
Satisfactory	A−	BBB+	BBB	BB+	BB−	B+
Fair	−	BBB−	BB+	BB	BB−	B
Weak	−	−	BB	BB−	B+	B−
Vulnerable				B+	B	B− or below

Source: Mark Puccia, Methodology: Business Risk/Financial Risk Matrix Expanded, 18 -September , 2012, Standard & Poor's Financial Services LLC. This material is reproduced with permission of Standard & Poor's Financial Services LLC.

Table 4.8 Financial risk indicative ratios for corporates

Ratings	FFO/debt in %	Debt/EBITDA (x)	Debt/Capital%
Minimal	Greater than 60	Less than 1.5	Less than 25
Modest	45−60	1.5−2.0	25−35
Intermediate	30−45	2−3	35−45
Significant	20−30	3−4	45−50
Aggressive	12−20	4−5	50−60
Highly leveraged	Less than 12	Greater than 5	Greater than 60

Source: Mark Puccia, Methodology: Business Risk/Financial Risk Matrix Expanded, 18 -September, 2012, Standard & Poor's Financial Services LLC. This material is reproduced with permission of Standard & Poor's Financial Services LLC.

4.1.6.2.1 Estimation of Weighted Average Cost of Capital (WACC)

In weighted average cost of capital (WACC), the cost of debt, equity, and hybrid securities are estimated on the basis of weights. Ideally, the weights should be based on the market value of these securities. The market value of equity capital is based on the price at which the share is traded. The WACC that represents the overall cost of capital is obtained by multiplying the capital structure weights by the associated costs and adding them up.

Suppose the firm's capital structure consists of equity capital, debt, and preference share capital.

$$WACC = E/V * K_e + P/V * K_p + D/V * K_d(1 − T)$$

where V is the total value of the firm, E is the value of equity capital, P is the value of preference share capital, D is the value of the debt, T is the tax rate.

Table 4.9 Global Corporate Default Rates by Rating Modifier (%)

	AAA	AA+	AA	AA−	A+	A	A−	BBB+	BBB	BBB−	BB+	BB	BB−	B+	B	B−	CCC to C
1981	0.00	0.00	0.00	0.00	0.00	0.00	0.00	0.00	0.00	0.00	0.00	0.00	0.00	0.00	0.00	0.00	0.00
1982	0.00	0.00	0.00	0.00	0.00	0.33	0.00	0.00	0.68	0.00	0.00	2.86	7.04	2.22	2.33	7.41	21.43
1983	0.00	0.00	0.00	0.00	0.00	0.00	0.00	0.00	0.00	0.00	2.17	0.00	1.59	1.23	9.80	4.76	6.67
1984	0.00	0.00	0.00	0.00	0.00	0.00	0.00	0.00	1.40	0.00	0.00	1.64	1.49	2.15	3.51	7.69	25
1985	0.00	0.00	0.00	0.00	0.00	0.00	0.00	0.00	0.00	0.00	1.64	1.49	1.33	2.61	13.11	8.00	15.38
1986	0.00	0.00	0.00	0.00	0.00	0.00	0.76	0.00	0.78	0.00	1.82	1.18	1.12	4.68	12.16	16.67	23.08
1987	0.00	0.00	0.00	0.00	0.00	0.00	0.00	0.00	0.00	0.00	0.00	0.00	0.83	1.31	5.95	6.82	12.28
1988	0.00	0.00	0.00	0.00	0.00	0.00	0.00	0.00	0.00	0.00	0.00	0.00	2.34	1.99	4.50	9.80	20.37
1989	0.00	0.00	0.00	0.00	0.00	0.00	0.58	0.90	0.78	0.00	0.00	0.00	2.00	0.43	7.80	4.88	33.33
1990	0.00	0.00	0.00	0.00	0.00	0.00	0.00	0.76	0.00	1.10	2.78	3.09	4.50	4.89	12.26	22.58	31.25
1991	0.00	0.00	0.00	0.00	0.00	0.00	0.00	0.83	0.74	0.00	3.70	1.14	1.05	8.72	16.25	32.43	30.19
1992	0.00	0.00	0.00	0.00	0.00	0.00	0.00	0.00	0.00	0.00	0.00	0.00	0.00	0.72	14.93	20.83	13.33
1993	0.00	0.00	0.00	0.00	0.00	0.00	0.00	0.00	0.00	0.00	0.00	1.94	0.00	1.30	5.88	4.17	16.67
1994	0.00	0.00	0.00	0.00	0.46	0.00	0.00	0.00	0.00	0.64	0.00	0.86	0.00	1.84	6.58	3.13	28.00
1995	0.00	0.00	0.00	0.00	0.00	0.00	0.00	0.00	0.00	0.64	0.00	1.56	1.12	2.77	8	7.50	8.00
1996	0.00	0.00	0.00	0.00	0.00	0.00	0.00	0.00	0.00	0.00	0.00	0.65	0.56	2.37	3.74	3.85	12.00
1997	0.00	0.00	0.00	0.00	0.00	0.00	0.00	0.37	0.35	0.00	0.67	0.00	0.41	0.72	5.30	14.58	42.86
1998	0.00	0.00	0.00	0.00	0.00	0.00	0.27	0.00	0.27	1.06	0.55	1.06	0.72	2.60	7.56	9.46	33.33
1999	0.00	0.00	0.00	0.36	0.00	0.24	0.57	0.00	0.28	0.31	0.00	1.34	0.91	4.22	10.45	15.60	35.96
2000	0.00	0.00	0.00	0.00	0.00	0.24	0.00	0.00	0.26	0.89	0.00	0.82	2.05	5.81	10.00	11.61	45.45
2001	0.00	0.00	0.00	0.00	0.58	0.25	0.00	0.24	0.49	0.28	0.52	1.22	5.54	5.84	17.17	22.46	44.44
2002	0.00	0.00	0.00	0.00	0.00	0.00	0.00	1.10	0.88	1.07	1.58	1.77	4.78	3.27	10.23	19.85	32.73
2003	0.00	0.00	0.00	0.00	0.00	0.00	0.00	0.00	0.20	0.54	0.50	0.97	0.28	1.72	5.34	9.52	16.18
2004	0.00	0.00	0.00	0.00	0.00	0.24	0.00	0.00	0.00	0.00	0.00	0.67	0.52	0.47	2.35	2.84	9.09
2005	0.00	0.00	0.00	0.00	0.00	0.00	0.00	0.00	0.17	0.00	0.37	0.00	0.51	0.79	2.64	2.96	13.33
2006	0.00	0.00	0.00	0.00	0.00	0.00	0.00	0.00	0.00	0.00	0.39	0.32	0.50	0.55	0.82	1.57	15.24
2007	0.00	0.00	0.00	0.00	0.32	0.21	0.60	0.19	0.61	0.73	1.22	0.66	0.24	0.19	0.00	0.90	27.00
2008	0.00	0.00	0.44	0.41	0.05	0.05	0.10	0.16	0.28	0.24	0.64	0.90	0.68	3.14	3.45	7.63	23.09
Avg	0.00	0.00	0.02	0.03	0.05	0.00	0.00	0.00	0.09	0.00	0.00	0.84	0.87	2.07	7.22	9.98	22.76
Median	0.00	0.00	0.08	0.10	0.14	0.10	0.22	0.32	0.37	0.38	0.97	0.85	1.77	2.02	6.27	7.06	11.90
Stdev	0.00	0.00	0.00	0.00	0.00	0.00	0.00	0.00	0.00	0.00	0.00	0.00	0.00	0.00	4.75	7.78	0.00
Min	0.00	0.00	0.44	0.41	0.58	0.33	0.76	1.1	1.4	1.1	3.7	3.09	7.04	8.72	17.17	32.43	45.45
Max																	

Table 4.10 Interest coverage ratios and ratings high market cap firms

Interest coverage ratio	Rating	Spread (%)
More than 8.5	AAA	0.50
6.5–8.5	AA	0.65
5.5–6.5	A+	0.85
4.25–5.5	A	1.00
3–4.25	A–	1.10
2.5–3	BBB	1.60
2–2.5	BB	3.35
1.75–2	B+	3.75
1.5–1.75	B	5.00
1.25–1.5	B–	5.25
0.8–1.25	CCC	8.00
0.65–0.8	CC	10
0.2–0.65	C	12
Less than 0.2	D	14

Source: Capital IQ, Bondsonline.com.

4.1.6.2.2 Estimation of values of capital components

The market value of equity and preference share capital is based on the market price of the shares listed in the stock market and the number of outstanding shares. In other words, the market value of equity is the number of shares outstanding times the current stock price. Some analysts also use book value of equity as it is not subject to volatility and conservative in approach. Some firms issue multiple class of shares. The market values of all these shares has to be summed up and considered as equity. Other equity claims such as warrants and conversion options are also to be added to the equity value. The market value of debt is more difficult to obtain directly since firms have different types of debt. Debt in the forms of bonds outstanding are traded while nontraded debt like bank debts are stated in book value terms. Market value of traded debt are found in various sources including online.

The market value of debt that is not traded in the bond market can be estimated by converting debt into a hypothetical coupon bond similar to bonds which are traded in the bond market. In this method, the nontraded debt on the books is considered as one coupon bond with a coupon set equal to the interest expenses on the entire debt and the maturity set equal to the face value-weighted average maturity of the debt. This hypothetical coupon bond is valued at the current cost of debt. The market value of total debt is arrived at by adding the market value of traded debt and the value of nontraded debt calculated as explained above to get the total market value of debt. The debt's weighted average maturity is obtained by multiplying each component of its debt by its maturity, adding them together, and dividing by the total face value of debt.

In an alternative way, the entire book value of debt in the books is considered as one coupon bond with a coupon set equal to the interest expense on all the debt and the maturity set equal to the face value of weighted average maturity of the debt and the bond is valued at the current cost of debt for the firm.

For example, consider the current interest expense of the firm as $15,000 and a 8% current cost of debt. Suppose the total debt have two components with book value of $100,000 and $250,000.The total book value of the debt is $350,000. Suppose the maturity of first component of debt is 10 years and the maturity of second component of debt is 15 years, then the weighted average maturity period is obtained as follows

$$(100,000 * 10 + 250,000 * 15)/(350,000) = 13.57 \text{ years}.$$

Substitute the values in the bond pricing formula: $C[(1 - (1/((1 + R)^T)))/R] + [F/((1 + R)^T)]$. In the formula, C represents the annual interest expense, R represents the current cost of debt, T represents the weighted average maturity, and F represents the total face value of debt. Substituting the values, $15,000[(1 - (1/((1 + 0.08)^{13.5}))/0.08] + [$250,000/((1 + 0.08)^{13.5})]$, we get the market value of the debt as $209,609.4

Alternatively, we can use the spreadsheet to find the market value of the debt. The current cost of debt of 8% is considered as the YTM, the interest rate on the debt (15,000/250,000) is assumed as the coupon rate on the bond. Using the formulae, = price(settlement date, maturity date, coupon rate, yield, redemption, frequency), the price is obtained as 84% of the par value of 250,000 which is approximately 210,000.

4.1.6.2.3   Estimations of components of debt capital

Only interest bearing liabilities are included in the debt capital. Liabilities like accounts payable and supplier credit are not interest charged liabilities. Applying after tax cost of debt to noninterest bearing liabilities will lead to misleading results regarding the true cost of debt. Hence in the estimation of cost of debt, it would be ideal to consider only interest bearing short term and long-term liabilities. Operating leases which appears as off balance sheet items in the annual report is also considered as the part of debt. The present value of the operating leases is obtained by discounting the operating lease commitments of the firm at the firm's current pretax cost of debt.

The operating income of the firm can be adjusted after considering the operating leases as a part of debt.

Adjusted operating income = Operating income + operating lease expense for the current year − depreciation on leased asset.

4.1.7   Estimation of cost of capital–industry practices

The study by Brotherson et al. (2013) provides survey results on the practices adopted by firms with respect to cost of capital estimation. The study finds that discounted cash flow is the major investment valuation technique used by firms. WACC is the dominant discount estimation method used in discounted cash flow analysis. Majority of firms calculate WACC based on market value weights. Majority of firms use marginal tax rate for the calculation of after tax cost of debt. The CAPM model is the most widely used model for estimating cost of equity. The choice of risk-free rate has a material effect on the cost of equity and cost of capital. The long-term bond yields more closely reflect the default free holding period returns available on long-term investments. The study suggests that practitioners prefer long-term treasury bond yields of 10 years or more as the popular choice of risk-free rate. Service firms like Bloomberg estimate historical beta on the basis of time interval of weekly returns over a 2-year period. The market proxy used by Bloomberg is S&P 500. Value line estimate beta based on the time interval of weekly returns over a period of 5 years. The market index proxy used by value line is NYSE Composite index.

Survey study by Fernandez et al. (2011) suggest that US market risk premium is the most widely used premium measure. One of the most widely mentioned source was Ibbotson/Morning Star. Bloomberg uses a version of DDM for the estimation of risk premium. *The annual average risk premium (difference between stock returns and long-term government bond returns) during the period 1926–2011 based on Ibbotson study (2012) was 5.7% based on arithmetic means and 3.9% based on geometric means.*

4.1.8   Estimation of WACC—Johnson & Johnson

In this section, the WACC of Johnson & Johnson is estimated. The 30-year treasury bond rate of 3.02%[7] as of November 18, 2014 is assumed to be the risk-free rate. *The average treasury bond rate during the period 2005–2013 can also be considered as the risk-free rate.* The risk premium is assumed to be 5% approximately based on various academic studies. The historical beta estimation was based on the regression of weekly returns of the stock over the market index NYSE composite during the 2-year period November 2012 to November 2014. The beta value was 0.9034. The cost of equity is estimated using CAPM.

K_e = R_f + Beta * Risk Premium where K_e is the cost of equity, R_f is the risk-free rate.
The cost of equity for Johnson & Johnson in 2014 = 3.02% + 0.9034 * 5 = 7.5%

The equity component consists of only equity shares. The book value of equity was $74,053 million in 2013. The book value of debt was $52,364 million, respectively. The present value of the operating lease commitments were added to arrive at the total book value of debt. The total operating lease commitments amounted to $992 million. The present value of these commitments for the period 2014–2018 and beyond were estimated using the current cost of debt (Yield on long term bond) as the discount rate of 4%. The present value of future lease commitments is arrived at 927.769 million dollars.

Total book value of debt = 52,364 + 927.769 = $53,291.769.

---

[7] http://www.bondsonline.com/Todays_Market/Composite_Bond_Yields_table.php.

The book value weights of equity and debt in the capital structure are 58% and 42%, respectively.

The market price per share at year end 2013 was 92.35 and number of shares 2877 million. Hence, the market capitalization was $265,690.95 million.

The yield on the long-term bond issued by Johnson and Johnson is estimated as the cost of debt. The yield on the long term bond maturing in 2043 was found to be 3.846%.[8] The coupon rate on the bond was 4.5%.[9] The price of the bond is 111% of the par value. Hence the market value of debt = 53,291.769 * 1.115 = $59,420.32 million. The market value weights for equity is 82% and 18% for debt.

$$\text{WACC} = K_e\,(E/V) + K_d\,(D/V)(1 - T)$$

The cost of capital using market value weights is calculated as follows:

$$7.35\% * 0.82 + 3.8\% * 0.18(1 - 0.35) = 6.63\%.$$

The cost of capital based on book value weights is 5.42%.

The detailed calculation of the cost of capital of Johnson and Johnson is given in the resources website for Chapter 4 *Cost of Capital.xlsx.*

4.1.8.1   Estimation of cost of capital of Chevron corporation

The risk-free rate is taken as 3.45%, which was the yield on 30-year US treasury bond in 2013 as given by Federal Reserve historical database. The risk premium was taken 5.28% based on the average YTM on a 20-year US treasury bond during the time period 1993–2013. The yield on 2043 maturity bond issued by Chevron is 6.32%.[10] The cost of debt is assumed to be 6.32%.

$$\text{Cost of equity} = R_f + \text{beta} * \text{Risk Premium}$$
$$3.45\% + 0.98 * 5.28 = 8.62\%$$

The WACC based on book value weights is 7.42%, whereas based on market value weights is 8.04%. The detailed calculation is given in resources Web site *Cost of Capital.xlsx.*

---

[8] www.finra.org.

[9] Alternatively, the interest paid divided by the debt gives us the interest rate which can be considered as the coupon on the bond amount.

[10] http://quotes.morningstar.com/stock/cvx/s?rbtnTicker = Ticker&t = CVX&x = 11&y = 10&SC = Q& pageno = 0&TLC =

References

Amott, R.D., Ryan, R., 2001. The death of the risk premium: consequences of the 1990s. J. Portf. Manag. 27 (3), 61−74.

Arnott, R.D., Bernstein, P.L., 2002. What risk premium TB 'Normal'? Financ. Anal. J. 58 (2), 64−84.

Brotherson, W.T., Eades, K.M., Harris, R.S., Higgins, R.C., 2013. Best practices in estimating the cost of capital: an update. J. Appl. Finance. (1), 15−33.

Campbell, J.Y., Shilier, R.J., 2001. Valuation Ratios and the Long-Run Stock Market Outlook: An Update. National Bureau of European Research, Cambridge, MA, NBER Working Paper No. 8221.

Cooper, I., 1996. Arithmetic versus geometric mean estimators: setting discount rates for capital budgeting. Eur. Financ. Manage. 2 (2), 157−167.

Damodaran, A., 2006. Estimating discount rates. Discounted Cash Flow Valuation, Damodaran on Valuation, second ed. Wiley Finance, 72 (Chapter 2).

Damodaran, A., 2012. Investment valuation. Riskless Rates and Risk Premium, third ed. Wiley Finance, 162.

Damodaran, A., 2012. Investment Valuation, Tools and Techniques for Determining the Value of Any Asset. third ed. John Wiley and Sons, Inc, Chapter 4, 47−65.

Elroy, D., Marsh, P., Staunton, M., 2002. Triumph of the Optimists 101 Years of Global Investment Returns. Princeton University Press, pp. 176−196.

Elroy, D., Marsh, P., Staunton, M., 2003. Global evidence on the equity premium. J. Appl. Corp. Financ. 27−38.

Elroy, D., Marsh, P., Staunton, M., 2011. Equity Premia Around the World. London Business School, <https://www.fairr.de/docs/dimson-marsh-staunton-2011.pdf>, 1−19.

Fama, E.F., French, K.R., 2002. The equity premium. J. Finance. LVII (2), 637−659.

Fernandez, P., Aguirreamalloa, J., Corres, L., 2011. US Market Risk Premium Used in 2011 by Professors, Analysts and Companies: A Survey with 5,731 Answers,. IESE Business School Working Paper, 1−17.

Fernando, D., Carlo, R., 2013. The Equity Risk Premium: A Consensus of Models, <http://ftp.ny.frb.org/research/economists/duarte/Duarte_Rosa_EquityRiskPremium.pdf>, 1−22.

Fabio Fornari, 2002. "The Size of the Equity Premium," Economic Working paper 447, Bank of Italy, Economic Research and International Relations Area.

Fornari, F., 2002 The Size of the Equity Premium. Economic Working paper 447, Bank of Italy, Economic Research and International Relations Area.

Goyal, A., Welch, I., 2001. Predicting the Equity Premium with Dividend Ratios. Yale School of Management and UCLA, Working Paper.

Goyal, A., Welch, I., 2008. A comprehensive look at the empirical performance of equity premium prediction. Rev. Financ. Stud. 21 (4), 1455−1508.

Grabowski, R.J., 2011. Developing the cost of equity capital: risk free rate and ERP during periods of "Flight to quality", <www.duffandphelps.com/sitecollectiondocuments/articles/Article_Grabowski_Risk_Free_Rate_and_ERP_During_Flight_to_Quality_01_29_11.pdf>, 1−27.

Graham, J.R., Harvey, C.R., 2001. Expectations of Equity Risk Premia, Volatility and Asymmetry from a Corporate Finance Perspective.. Fuqua School of Business, Duke University, Working Paper.

Harris, R., Marston, F.C., 1999. The Market Risk Premium: Exceptional Estimates Using Analysts Forecast. Darden Business School, Working Paper N0-99-08.

Ibbotson, R.G., Chen, P., 2003. Long run stock returns : participating in the real economy. Financ. Anal. J. 59 (1), 88–98.

Kozhan, R., Anthony, N., Schneider, P., 2013. The skew risk premium in the equity index market. Rev. Financ. Stud. 26 (9), 2174–2203.

Mayfield, S., 2004. Estimating the market risk premium. J. Financ. Econ. 73, 465–496.

Shannon, P., Graboswski Roger, J., 2010. Chapter 7, 9, Cost of Capital: Applications and Examples. fourth ed. John Wiley & Sons.

Robert, A., 2001. Historical Results, Equity Risk Premium Forum. CFA Institute (AIMR), Nov 08, 27.

Siegel, J.J., 1999. The shrinking equity risk premium. J. Portf. Manage. 26 (1), 10–17.

Welch, I., 2000. Views of financial economists on the equity premium and other issues. J. Bus. 73 (4), 501–537.

Zenner, M., Hill, S., Clark, J., Mago, N., 2008. The Most Important Number in Finance, The Quest for the Market Risk Premium. Capital Structure Advisory & Solutions JP Morgan, pp. 1–11.

Principles of cash flow estimation

5.1 Introduction

Cash flow estimation is an integral part of the valuation and capital budgeting process. Cash flow estimation is a necessary step for assessing investment decisions of any kind. Project cash flows consider all kinds of inflows of cash. The estimation of cash flows is done through the coordination of wide range of professionals involved in the project. The engineering department is responsible for forecasting of capital outlays. The production team is responsible for forecasting operational costs. The marketing team is basically involved in forecasting revenues. The finance manager has the responsibility to collect data and set norms for better estimation. Forecasting cash flows is one of the major challenges faced by valuation professionals. Cash flow estimation is based on a number of principles. The consistency principle states that consistency has to be maintained between the flow of cash in a project and the rates of discount that are applicable on the cash flows. The separation principle suggests that project cash flows can be segregated into investment and financing flows. The posttax principle suggests that the forecast of cash flows should be based on after-tax method. The incremental cash flow principle suggests that only cash flows relevant to the valuation of a project are the incremental cash flows resulting from it.

The discounted cash flow (DCF) model is based on the assumption that a stock's value is basically equal to the present value of its estimated future cash flows. In this DCF model, the major step of valuation is the estimation of future cash flows. The most important variable in estimating cash flows are the firm's future sales growth and profit margins. Hence, estimation of growth rates is an important determinant of cash flow estimation. A firm's revenue growth rate is based on a number of factors like industry trends, economic environment, and company's competitive advantage. The costs incurred by firms are a major factor for determining the company's future operating profits. Companies that are heavily dependent on oil and natural gas face wide swings in profit margin if the price of the raw materials increases. Operating leverage is a factor that determines the profitability position of a firm. As a company grows, it must be able to spread its fixed costs across a broader base of production.

DCF model focusses on free cash flow, which is defined as operating cash flow minus capital expenditures and non cash working capital. Free cash flow represents the residual cash flow after all expenses necessary to keep the firm growing at its current rate. It is vital to estimate how much the company reinvests in itself every year with respect to capital expenditures and working capital. DCF consists of two models: the free cash flow to equity and the free cash flow to firm model.

5.2   Adjustments to financial statements

5.2.1   Invested capital

The fundamental rule of accounting is given by

Assets = Liabilities + equity
Operating assets = Operating liabilities + debt + equity
Operating assets − Operating liabilities = invested capital
Invested Capital = Debt + equity.

In terms of operating method, invested capital can be defined as operating assets minus operating liabilities. In terms of financing method, invested capital equals debt plus equity component. From the investment perspective, total funds invested would be equal to invested capital plus nonoperating assets. In financial perspective, total funds invested would be equal to debt and equity and its equivalents. Only interest-paying liabilities are considered as debt.

Nonoperating items, like deferred tax assets, prepaid pension assets, intangible assets related to pensions, and nonconsolidated subsidiaries, must not be included in invested capital. Invested capital is the capital necessary to operate a firm's core business. Pension assets are considered as nonoperating assets and hence are not a part of invested capital. Nonoperating assets like excess real estate and discontinued operations are not included in invested capital.

Total funds invested = Invested capital + nonoperating assets = net debt + equity + equity equivalents.

5.2.2   Debt

Debt consists of only short-term or long-term interest-bearing liability. The short-term debt includes commercial paper, notes payable, and current portion of the long-term debt. The long-term debt includes fixed debt like straight bonds, floating debt and convertible debt with maturities greater than 1 year. *Unfunded pension expenses and unfunded medical expenses are considered as debt equivalent.* The net interest expenses associated with these liabilities are treated as nonoperating expenses.

5.2.3   Equity

The original investor fund of common stock, additional paid up capital, and retained earnings constitute the equity capital. Stocks repurchased and held in treasury should be deducted from total equity. *Deferred taxes and reserves are considered as equity equivalents.* Deferred taxes arises from tax incentives are provided by governments. It also arises from nonoperating items like pensions.

5.2.4   Return on Invested Capital

The ratio return on invested capital (ROIC) is the measure of net profit to the invested capital.

ROIC = Net operating profit after taxes/invested capital.

5.2.5 Free cash flow

Free cash flow is the after-tax cash flow available for all shareholders. Free cash flow is independent of financing and nonoperating items. Net investments in nonoperating assets and the gains, losses, and income-associated with nonoperating assets are not included in free cash flow.

5.2.6 Operating working capital

Operating working capital equals operating current assets minus current liabilities. The operating working capital is often referred to noncash operating working capital as excess cash and marketable securities are not included in working capital calculation. Operating current assets include trade accounts receivables, inventory, and prepaid expenses. The noninterest-bearing operating liabilities are liabilities required for the ongoing operations of the firm. The operating liabilities include accounts payable, accrued salaries, deferred revenues, and taxes.

5.2.7 Net capital expenditure

The net capital expenditure is the investments in net property, plant, and equipment. The production equipment and other facilities form part of operating assets.

5.2.8 Provisions and reserves

Provisions are noncash expenses that reflect future costs or expected losses. Firms make provisions by reducing current income and setting up a corresponding reserve as a liability. Provisions are categorized into four categories: current operating provisions, long-term operating provisions, nonoperating restructuring provisions, and provisions for smoothing income.

Companies need to create a provision or liability when products or services are sold as some of its products will be returned or due to applications of warranties. Provisions must be deducted from revenues to determine operating income and the reserves must be netted against operating assets. As provisions and reserves are treated as operating items, they form a part of free cash flow. Provisions for plant closure reserve like decommissioning expenses are treated as debt equivalent. One-time restructuring provisions are considered as nonoperating and considered as debt equivalents.

5.2.9 Earnings adjustments

The earnings reported in the financial statements have to be adjusted in order to get a measure of earnings, which is suited for proper valuations. The income statement provides the measure of operating income (EBIT) and net income (income after tax). Updated earnings is vital for proper valuation. On account of regulatory stipulations like that of SEC's 10 −Qs, firms have to file quarterly reports with SEC.

The recent estimate of revenues and earnings can be obtained by adding the values of the most recent four quarter to obtain more recent values for valuation. The revenues and earnings obtained by this process is called trailing 12-month revenues and earnings.

5.3   Adjustments of expensed investments

The expenses incurred by a company can be classified into operating expenses, capital expenses, and financial expenses. Operating expenses are accountable only in the current year of operations. Capital expenditures are basically expenditures in which the benefits are obtained over multiple periods. Financial expenses are expenses incurred for raising funds primarily through debt instruments. The operating income is equal to revenues less operating expenses. The net income is obtained as revenues less operating and financial expenses.

When a firm builds a factory or purchases equipment, the asset is capitalized on the balance sheet and depreciated over time. For intangible assets, such as brand name or patent, the entire amount have to be expensed. On the basis of FASB, stipulation development costs can be capitalized and straight line amortized over the economic life of the product.

Adjustments have to be made for certain misclassification in the form of capital expenses and adjustments to finance expenses. Research and Development (R&D) expenses are often treated as operating expenses instead of capital expenses. For adjustment, first the amortizable life of the research asset has to be estimated. In other words, the first step involved in capitalizing expenses like R&D is to choose an amortization period. The amortizable life of assets vary across firms and is a function of the time involved in converting research initiatives into products. Studies have shown that new drugs development time for pharma companies is approximately 15 years. At the same time, software research products development takes a much shorter duration. For example, suppose the amortizable period for R&D expenses for a pharma company is 10 years. On the basis of financial statements for the prior 10 years from the year of analysis, treat the R&D expenses as capital expenses. This involves the removal of R&D expenditure from income statement and placing the amount on balance sheet. The process is repeated in which R&D amortization is eliminated from the income statement as an expense and from the balance sheet as a deduction to the accumulated R&D.

The adjusted operating income (EBITA) = Operating income (EBITA) + annual R&D expenditure − annual amortization of research asset.

Adjusted net income = Net income + annual R&D expenses − annual amortization of research asset.

Adjusted book value of equity = Book value of equity + value of research asset

Adjusted book value of capital = Book value of capital + value of research asset

Table 5.1 shows the capitalization of R&D expenses of IBM.

Table 5.1 **Capitalization of R&D expenses: IBM**

Value in million dollars	2009	2010	2011	2012	2013
Operating income (EBITA)	18,138	20,091	21,414	22,361	19,926
Annual R&D expenses	5820	6026	6258	6302	6226
Annual amortization	5815	5891	6088.6	6119	6149
Adjusted EBITA	18,143	20,226	21,583	22,544	20,003

Table 5.2 **Adjusted invested capital invested**

Value in million dollars	2009	2010	2011	2012	2013
Invested capital	73,020	72,890	74,310	75,588	86,069
Accumulated R&D	11,228	11,363	11,532	11,715	11,792
Adjusted invested capital	84,248	84,253	85,842	87,303	97,861

IBM's R&D operations differentiate the company from its competitors. IBM annually spends approximately $6 billion for R&D, focusing its investments on high-growth, high-value opportunities. The amortization period for capitalizing the R&D expenses is estimated to be 5 years. R&D expenses are amortized linearly over time with a 5-year life. Each year annual R&D expenditure is added to the operating income (EBITA) and the current amortization of the accumulated R&D asset is subtracted to get adjusted operating income.

For example, the operating income of $19,926 million in year 2013 is adjusted by adding the annual R&D expenses of $6226 million and subtracting the annual current amortization of the accumulated R&D asset of amount $6149 million to get adjusted operating income of $20,003 million (Table 5.1).

The adjusted invested capital is obtained by adding the accumulated R&D expenses to the invested capital.

The detailed calculation of adjusted operating income and adjusted invested capital is given in resources Web site *Capitalization of R&D IBM.xlsx*.

A portion of operating expenses such as advertising expenses can also be treated as capital expenses and adjusted.

5.3.1 Adjustment for financing expenses: case of operating leases

In financial statements, operating leases are considered as operating expenses instead of capital expenses. The future operating lease commitments are discounted at the firm's pretax cost of debt. The present value of the operating lease commitments is added to the debt of the firm to get the total debt outstanding.

Adjusted debt = Debt + present value of lease commitments.

The operating income can be adjusted in two ways. In the first method, the operating lease expense is added to the operating income. The depreciation on the leased asset is subtracted to arrive at the adjusted operating income.

Adjusted operating income = Operating income + operating lease expenses − depreciation on the leased asset.

On the basis of the assumption that the depreciation on the leased asset approximates the principal portion of the debt which is being repaid, the adjusted operating income is found out by adding back the imputed interest expense on the debt value of the operating lease expense.

Adjusted operating income = Operating income + debt value of operating lease expense ∗ interest rate on debt.

5.3.2   Adjustment for operating lease: case of IBM in 2013

Lease commitments in the year 2013 = $832 million.

Year	Lease commitments in millions dollars
2014	1492
2015−2016	2302
2017−2018	1419
After 2018	778

The present value of the future lease commitments is $7879.95 million dollars.

The adjusted debt = Interest-bearing debt + present value of lease commitments
Interest-bearing debt in 2013 = $39,718 million
Adjusted debt = $39,718 million + $7879.95 million = $47,597.95 million
Adjusted operating income = Operating income + operating lease expense in current year—depreciation on leased assets
19,926 + 832 − 1313.3255 = $19,444.675 million.

The detailed calculation of adjustment of operating leases is given in the instructor resources Web site *Adjustment for Operating lease IBM.xlsx*.

5.3.3   Summary of adjustments for operating income

Adjustments have to be made with respect to financing expenses that are treated as operating expenses by accountants. The most significant example is the case of operating leases. The second adjustment is for treatment of capital expenditure as operating expenses. For example, the treatment of R&D expenses. The third adjustment is made to correct for the incidence of one-time or irregular income and expenses. One-time expenses has to be removed from the operating income and not to be used in forecasting future operating income.

5.4 Reflections on managed earnings

Corporate earnings are often manipulated by firms by practicing managed earnings by means of falsely inflating stock prices due to improperly reporting income, failure of capitalizing expenses, hiding losses in subsidiaries, or prematurely recognizing revenues. Firms might time gains and losses from asset sales in order to show inflated earnings. Managed earnings are the results of misapplications of accounting principles like premature recognition of revenues. A survey of 169 public company chief financial officers conducted in year 2012 suggest that 20% of firms manage earnings to misrepresent their economic performance and 10% of firms manage the EPS number.[1] Managed earnings are the culmination of series of aggressive interpretations of accounting rules and aggressive operating activities. Firms resort to managed earnings when it becomes more difficult for the company to maintain the sales and earnings growth, which analysts expected. Earnings management can be defined as the acceleration or deferral of expenses or revenues through operating or accounting practices with the aim to produce consistent growth in earnings. Accounting literature defines earnings management as distortion of the application of generally accepted accounting principles.

There are different techniques to manage and manipulate earnings like "cookie-jar," reserves, capitalization practices, "big bath losses," change of time of operating activities, merger and acquisition practices, and revenue recognition practices.

The accounting principles state that the accrual of expenses has to be reflected in the period in which the expense was incurred. In many industry sectors like insurance and banking, the accrual of expenses or reserves are based on estimates. During periods of strong earnings, firms often establish additional expense accruals and subsequently reduce the liability to generate earnings when required in future. Under the cookie-jar technique, the firm would overestimate expenses during the current year to manage earnings (McGregor, 2014). When the actual expenses turn out lower than estimates, the difference is placed into the "cookie jar" to be utilized when the firm requires a boost in earnings to meet the analyst's prediction in future. Techniques to manage earnings under this category include estimation of sales returns and allowances, estimates of bad debt and write-downs, estimation of pension expense, warranty costs, inventory write-downs, estimation of completion for long-term contracts, and termination of pension plans.

Capitalization practices involving intangible assets, software capitalization, and R&D investments are used to manage earnings (Musfiqur et al., 2013). Firms may allocate more expenses to a project, which can be capitalized to reduce current operating expenses.

"Big bath loses" is an earnings management technique in which a one-time charge is taken against income in order to reduce assets, which results in lower expenses in future. The asset reduces or removes the asset from the financial books and results in lower net income for that particular year. The purpose of one-time "big bath" is to take one-time charge in a single year so that future years will show

---

[1] Herb Greenberg, CFOs concede earnings are managed: Study, http://www.cnbc.com/id/48243380#.

increased net income. Analysts usually do not consider nonrecurring charges as a part of the firm's ongoing operations or operating income. Generally, nonrecurring charges include writing down assets, discontinuance of operating division, or product line and establishing reserves. Firms may take other write-offs or create other accruals not directly tied to the event and attribute those expenses to the one-time event. Corporations employ this big bath technique to clean up balance sheet during bad years. General Motors had huge write-downs on balance sheet assets, which resulted in massive losses. Big bath technique is called one-time event in which that an out of the ordinary or nonrecurring event occurs in the firm and the expenses associated with that particular event are actually inflated. The firm would report all of its expenses to the one-time event instead of placing in the current account. For example, consider the case of a retail chain dealer who is facing tough situation and needs to wind up one of his stores. This would be a one-time event and nonrecurring in nature. The losses incurred led to decrease in the reported net earnings. The retail dealer would charge a major part of the business expenses to this business unit which is to be closed.

Earnings management techniques can also be based on operating activities. Executives can plan for certain events to occur in certain periods. For example, in periods of high income, managers would decide to purchase new equipment to level off the income. In other words, managers modify the timing of events in such a way that accounting systems record these activities in the period, which is most advantageous to management. A firm could accelerate its sales and delivery process to report higher fourth quarter revenues and profits than in the future period. In this process, a firm could inflate its growth in the near term and reduce profits in future period.

Corporate restructuring activities undertaken by firms can also be used to manage earnings. Restructuring activities like M&A create one-time charge along with other merger-related expenses. Firms establish accruals for restructuring the transaction that results in allocation of more expenses than required for the transactions.

In merger and acquisition accounting, the pooling method consolidates the balance sheet by adding the balance sheet of the two individual companies. The purchase method of accounting in mergers and accounting considers the transaction as a purchase. The fair value of the purchased company is assessed and compared to the purchase price. Any excess or premium paid above the fair value of assets is recognized as goodwill. The goodwill is amortized over a period of time. Firms can identify certain expenses, which can be revalued on the seller's balance sheet to increase goodwill. If the valuations prove to be excessive, then the company is able to reduce its operating expenses in the near term by reducing its estimate for the liability. The additional goodwill created would be amortized over long period of time and would not have significant impact on near-term results.

The timings of revenue recognition is also an area of earnings management. Earnings can be managed through techniques like timings sales of securities that have gained value. The company can sell portfolio securities that has unrealized gain and report the gain as operating earnings to manipulate earnings. Timing of sales of securities can also be done which has lost value. In case the manager wants to show lower earnings, then securities can be sold, which has unrealized loss and report the loss in operating earnings. Managers can also manage earnings by means of change of its holding from available to sale securities to trading securities and vice versa.

The studies by Badertscher et al. (2006a) and Phillips et al. (2003) find that firms manage earnings in ways that minimize their current income tax costs, regardless of whether the earning management aims to increase or decrease reported earning. Phillips et al. (2003) suggest that deferred tax expense, which proxies for the temporary differences between book and taxable income, is incrementally useful beyond accrual based measures in finding out income enhancement earnings management to avoid reporting a loss or an earnings decline. In other words, firms manage earnings upward in a book tax nonconforming manner to minimize current tax costs (Badertscher et al., 2006b). These studies suggest that financial analysts can use deferred tax expenses to improve their ability to detect upward earnings management and evaluate earnings quality.

5.4.1 Tax effect on valuation

There are basically two methods of measurement of tax rates. Effective tax rate is the actual taxes due on the basis of tax statements divided by the company's pretax reported income

Effective tax rate = Taxes due/taxable income

Marginal tax is the amount of tax paid on the additional dollar of income. The marginal tax rate increases as the income level increases. In the United States, the federal corporate tax rate on marginal income is 35%. When firms have global operations, the marginal tax rate of the country in which the company is incorporated can be used for tax purpose based on the assumption that income generated in other countries will eventually be repatriated to the country of origin. In case of net operating losses, the tax rate used for the computation of after-tax operating income and cost of capital has to be zero in the years of reported losses. In the case of firms with current positive earnings but having a large net operating losses carried forward, the firm will be valued ignoring the tax savings on account of net operating losses and then add the tax savings from the net operating losses to the estimated value of firm. The expected tax savings are estimated by multiplying the tax rate by the net operating loss.

When R&D expenses are capitalized, the tax saving benefit is added to the after-tax operating income of the firm. Firms are allowed to deduct their entire R&D expense for tax purposes. The tax benefit is estimated as the difference between the entire R&D expense and the amortized amount of research asset.

5.5 Estimating reinvestment needs for valuation

The reinvestment needs of a firm are its investments in capital expenditure and working capital. Reinvestment needs consists of net capital expenditure calculated as the difference between capital expenditure and depreciation. The second type of reinvestment need is investments in noncash working capital.

Recall that cash flow from assets consists of three components: operating cash flow, capital spending, and change in working capital. Operating cash flow is the cash flow that results from the firm's daily operational activities. Capital spending refers to the net spending on fixed assets, which is the purchases of fixed assets less sales of fixed assets. Change in net working capital is the net change in current assets relative to current liabilities for the period.

5.5.1 Net capital expenditures

Net capital expenditure refers to capital expenditure less depreciation. The data on capital expenditure and depreciation are obtained from financial statements. Firms usually incur large capital expenditures in 1 year and smaller expenditures in the following years. In accounting statements, R&D expenses are treated as operating expenses. These expenses have to be capitalized as explained in the Section 5.3. Acquisitions are not considered as capital expenditures in accounting statements. Serial acquirers involved in a large number of acquisitions have to consider the investments made in acquisition as capital expenditures.

Capital expenditures would be very high in certain years when new product is introduced or new plant or machinery is purchased. In other period, small investment in capital expenditure may be observed. Hence, it is necessary to normalize capital expenditures to estimate future cash flows for valuation. The normalization technique involves averaging the capital expenditure for a certain period, say 5 years.

The amortization of R&D asset is added to the depreciation for the current period.

Adjusted net capital expenditure = Net capital expenditure + R&D expenses in the current period − amortization of the research asset.

This adjustment nullifies the impact in cash flows of capitalizing R&D.

Acquisition of firms is also considered as part of capital expenditures.

Adjusted net capital expenditure = Net capital expenditures + acquisition of other firms − amortization of the acquisitions.

Details of acquisition can be found in the statement of cash flows in annual report under the category other investment activities. As firms do not undertake acquisitions every year, the normalized measure of acquisition can be used to estimate the cost of acquisition.

5.5.2 Working capital investments

Generally, working capital refers to the difference between current assets and current liabilities. Increase in working capital indicates outflow of cash and decrease in working capital indicates inflow of cash. In valuation, the focus is on noncash working capital. Cash and other market securities (investments in treasury bills and other short-term government securities) are excluded from the current assets. The cash and marketable securities are added to the value of the firm obtained through different valuation model at the end of analysis to get the total value. All interest-bearing debt, which includes short-term debt and portion of long-term debt, is excluded from the current liabilities. For forecasting purposes, noncash working capital as percentage of revenues can be estimated. There can be variations in working capital on a yearly basis. Hence, the changes in the noncash working capital has to be estimated in relation to expected revenue changes. Noncash working capital changes can also be negative. When noncash working capital decreases, cash flow to the firm increases as current assets like inventory are better managed. Working capital changes from year to year can be estimated using working capital as a percentage of revenues. Working capital becomes negative when the nondebt current liabilities exceed noncash current assets. Negative noncash working capital is considered as a source of default risk for a firm. In long run, change in cash flow has to be assumed to be zero or positive in the long run.

Working capital = Current assets − current liabilities
Noncash working capital = Noncash current assets − noninterest current liabilities
Noncash current assets = Current assets − cash and marketable securities
Noninterest-bearingcurrent liabilities = Current liabilities − interest-bearing current liabilities.

5.5.3   Estimation of net capital expenditure for China National Petroleum Corporation

The Company and its subsidiaries (the "Group") is one of the largest oil companies in the world. The Group is involved in a broad range of petroleum- and gas-related activities including: the exploration, development, production and sales of crude oil and natural gas; the refining, transportation, storage and marketing of crude oil and petroleum products; the production and sales of basic petrochemical products, derivative chemical products, and other chemical products; and the transmission of natural gas, crude oil and refined products, and the sales of natural gas (Tables 5.3−5.7).

The working capital at China Petroleum was negative during the past years except in 2007. The noncash working capital was also negative in period 2007−2013 except in period 2008.

Working capital becomes negative when company's current liabilities exceed its current assets. In other words, the liabilities that need to be paid within 1 year exceed the current asset which can be monetized over the same period. For some businesses, negative working capital is considered a positive sign. Dell Computers for years had a negative working capital on account of its business models, which allowed the firm to collect cash up front but pay suppliers later. Top companies like Walmart are found to have negative working capital as they sell goods on the shelf faster than they pay the vendor for the merchandise. Companies like McDonald and

Table 5.3 **Details of capital expenditure for the period 2012–2014[2] in RMB millions**

Activity	2012	%	2013	%	2014	%
Exploration & production	227,211	64.45	226,376	71.03	225,700	76.12
Refining & chemicals	36,009	10.21	26,671	8.37	25,300	8.53
Marketing	14,928	4.23	7101	2.23	6400	2.16
Natural gas & pipeline	72,939	20.69	57,439	18.02	37,200	12.5
Others	1429	0.42	1109	0.35	1900	0.69
Total	352,516	100	318,696	100	296,500	100

Others include Research and Development expenses.

Table 5.4 **Calculation of adjusted capital expenditure in RMB millions**

Year	CAPEX	DDA	NET CAPEX	Acquisitions	Adjusted CAPEX
2007	182,387	66,625	115,762	1652	117,414
2008	232,214	75,285	156,929	13,003	169,932
2009	266,836	86,112	180,724	25,864	206,588
2010	276,212	113,209	163,003	21,120	184,123
2011	284,391	138,073	146,318	6569	152,887
2012	352,516	151,975	200,541	22,127	222,668
2013	318,696	163,365	155,331	32,676	188,007
Average	*273,321.714*	*113,520.6*	*159,801.14*	*17,573*	*177,374.14*

CAPEX is the capital expenditure. DDA refers to Depreciation, Depletion and Amortization. Net CAPEX is CAPEX minus DDA.
NET CAPEX + acquisitions = Adjusted CAPEX.
The normalized 7-year Capex is Rmb 159,801.14 million and the adjusted capex is Rmb 177,374.14 million.

Amazon.com are found to have negative working capital. The products for these companies are delivered and sold to customers before the company pays for the creditors. Firms like Amazon, Walmart, and McDonald's often have negative working capital as customers usually pay up front. They can use the cash generated to pay off their accounts payable than keeping a large cash balance on hand. Negative working capital indicates managerial efficiency for businesses with low inventory and receivables. In other scenarios, it is the sign of trouble for the company. Companies will not be able to operate with negative working capital for long period of time as the firms will not be able to meet payments requirements on certain liabilities if the additional funds are not acquired. Wireless and broadcasting firms are found to have negative working capital. Companies with subscriptions or longer-term contracts often have negative working capital due to high deferred revenue balances. Changes in working capital can also be negative. When noncash working capital decreases, the tied-up cash is released and the cash flow of the firm is increased.

[2] The capital expenditure values for the year 2014 are estimated values.

Table 5.5 Estimation of working capital and noncash working capital at China National Petroleum Corporation

Current assets	2007	2008	2009	2010	2011	2012	2013
Cash at hand and bank	92,590	45,879	88,284	52,210	64,299	49,953	57,250
Notes receivable	4735	4314	4268	5955	12,688	9981	14,360
Accounts receivable	18,565	16,756	28,785	45,005	53,822	64,450	64,027
Advances to suppliers	20,441	37,394	36,402	37,935	39,296	32,813	11,445
Other receivables	15,714	6157	4815	5837	8576	14,165	17,802
Inventories	88,496	90,670	114,781	134,888	182,253	214,117	227,017
Other current assets	61	25,813	18,378	8050	24,486	32,561	39,052
Total current assets	240,602	226,983	295,713	289,880	385,420	418,040	430,953
Noncash current assets	148,012	181,104	207,429	237,670	321,121	368,087	373,703

Current liabilities	2007	2008	2009	2010	2011	2012	2013
Short-term borrowings	18,734	87,217	74,622	97,175	99,827	143,409	110,894
Other interest bearing liabilities	11,652	5544	14,229	5093	37,871	7838	81,873
Notes payable	1143	433	2002	3039	2458	2265	832
Accounts payable	104,468	118,197	156,760	209,015	232,618	278,427	298,075
Advances from customers	12,433	12,968	21,193	29,099	34,130	38,131	46,804
Employee compensation payable	11,585	6363	5105	5696	5991	4161	4836
Taxes payable	22,895	15,186	34,963	57,277	119,740	72,045	69,718
Other payables	16,299	18,426	17,125	19,845	21,995	23,642	27,025
Other current liabilities	13	3	62,554	3497	5408	4830	5432
Total current liabilities	199,222	264,337	388,553	429,736	560,038	574,748	645,489
Nondebt current liabilities	168,836	171,576	299,702	327,468	422,340	423,501	452,722
Working capital	41,380	−37,354	−92,840	−139,856	−174,618	−156,708	−214,536
Noncash working capital	−20,824	9528	−92,273	−89,798	−101,219	−55,414	−79,019

Table 5.6 **Estimation of noncash working capital needs for Caterpillar (values in million dollars)**

Current assets	2007	2008	2009	2010	2011	2012	2013
Cash and short-term investments	1122	2736	4867	3592	3057	5490	6081
Receivables	15,752	18,128	13,912	16,792	17,953	18,566	17,176
Inventories	7204	8781	6360	9587	14,544	15,547	12,625
Other current assets	1399	1988	1650	1839	2574	2535	2453
Total current assets	25,477	31,633	26,789	31,810	38,128	42,138	38,335
Noncash current assets	24,355	28,897	21,922	28,218	35,071	36,648	32,254
Current liabilities							
Short-term debt	5468	7209	4083	4056	3988	5287	3679
Short-term portion of long-term debt	5132	5492	5701	3925	5660	7104	7352
Accounts payable	4723	4827	2993	5856	8161	6753	6560
Other payables	5971	7514	5627	6662	8785	8216	7857
Other current liabilities	951	1027	888	1521	1967	2055	1849
Total current liabilities	22,245	26,069	19,292	22,020	28,561	29,415	27,297
Noninterest-bearing current liabilities	11,645	11,651	9508	14,039	18,913	17,024	16,266
Working capital	3232	5564	7497	9790	9567	12,723	11,038
Noncash working capital	12,710	17,246	12,414	14,179	16,158	19,624	15,988

Table 5.7 **Net working capital as percentage of revenues**

	2007	2008	2009	2010	2011	2012	2013
Revenues	44,958	51,324	32,396	42,588	60,138	63,068	52,694
Noncash working capital	12,710	17,246	12,414	14,179	16,158	19,624	15,988
Change in noncash working capital		4536.00	−4832.00	1765.00	1979.00	3466.00	−3636.00
Working capital as % of revenues	28.27	33.60	38.32	33.29	26.87	31.12	30.34

The average working capital as percentage of revenue was 31.69% during the 7-year period 2007–2013. This average value can be used to estimate the changes in working capital for the future estimated period. The noncash working capital estimation of caterpillar is given in *Noncash working capital caterpillar.xlsx.*

5.6   Forecasting growth

Estimation of growth is one of the most critical aspects of the valuation process. Basically, growth is estimated through three methods of historical growth rates, analyst's estimates, and fundamental estimates. The value of the firm is the present value of the expected future cash flows generated by the firm. A firm's fundamental growth rate can be estimated by determining how much the firm is reinvesting back into the firm in the form of capital expenditures and working capital. No firm can grow without reinvesting some of its profits in the long run.

5.6.1   Revenue forecast models

In top-down forecast, revenues are estimated by analyzing the size of the market, determining the market share of the company, and forecasting prices. In bottom-up approach, the forecast of revenues is made based on forecasts of demand from existing and potential customers and customer turnover. Many industry sector reports provide forecasts of future revenues.

5.6.2   Forecast of income statement items

The forecast of most line items in the income statement is directly related to revenues. The forecast ratios based on the income statements can be estimated from historical values. The forecast of operating expenses such as cost of goods sold, selling, general and administrative expenses can be related to revenues. Depreciation can be forecasted as a percentage of revenue or as a percentage of property, plant, and equipment. When assets are fully depreciated, they must be removed from gross property, plant and equipment, else overestimation of depreciation and its tax shield take place in later years. Future nonoperating income from nonconsolidated subsidiaries can be estimated by forecasting nonoperating income growth rate or by forecasting return on equity (ROE) on the basis of the competitive position of the subsidiary. Interest expense must be related to debt. Future interest expense can be estimated based on the past ratio of interest expense to debt. Taxes can be estimated as a percentage of earnings before taxes. To find average tax rate, taxes are divided by earnings before taxes. The marginal tax rate is equal to the tax rate on the next dollar of income.

5.6.3   Forecast of balance sheet items

Operating working capital are estimated as percentage of revenues. Inventories and accounts payable can be estimated as a percentage of cost of goods sold. Property, plant, and equipment reflecting capital expenditure can be forecasted as a percentage of revenues. The average of capital expenditure as a percentage of revenue for the past years can also be used to forecast capital expenditures. Depreciation is forecasted as a percentage of capital expenditure.

5.6.3.1 Estimation of historical growth rates to forecast future growth

Historical growth rates are determined on the basis of assumption that future growth rate is a good indicator of past growth rates. Historical data can be collected from the firm's financial statement, foot notes, and external reports. Historical ratios and forecasted ratios can also be determined from historical and forecasted financial statements. The forecasting process involves forecasting of revenues, income statement items which includes forecast of operating expenses, depreciation, interest income, interest expense, and taxes. The revenue forecasts are based on economic growth and other trends facing the industry sector. The average historical growth rate of revenues for a period of time can be used to estimate future growth of revenues. The average growth rates can be based on arithmetic or geometric average. Geometric average is a more accurate measure of growth if the past earnings are volatile in nature. The method of estimating future growth rate in earnings using historical growth rates is not a useful method when the earnings are negative.

Table 5.8 gives the arithmetic and geometric mean growth rates of net sales, operating income, net income, and net EPS of Procter and Gamble during the period 2005–2014. The arithmetic and geometric mean values differ much in the case of changes in operating income and net income compared to net sales. This can be attributed to the greater volatility in operating income and net income compared to other variables. In case of increased volatility, geometric average is a better measure for estimation of growth rates. The standard deviation values for

Table 5.8 **Estimating growth—Procter and Gamble (value in million dollars except per share)**

Year	Net sales	% Change	Op. income	% Change	Net income	% Change	Net EPS	% Change
2005	55,292		10,026		6923		2.53	
2006	66,724	20.68	12,916	28.83	8684	25.44	2.64	4.35
2007	74,832	12.15	15,003	16.16	10,340	19.07	3.04	15.15
2008	81,748	9.24	16,637	10.89	12,075	16.78	3.64	19.74
2009	79,029	−3.33	16,123	−3.09	13,436	11.27	4.26	17.03
2010	75,785	−4.10	15,306	−5.07	12,736	−5.21	4.11	−3.52
2011	79,385	4.75	15,233	−0.48	11,797	−7.37	3.93	−4.38
2012	82,006	3.30	13,035	−14.43	10,756	−8.82	3.66	−6.87
2013	82,581	0.70	14,330	9.93	11,312	5.17	3.86	5.46
2014	83,062	0.58	15,288	6.69	11,643	2.93	4.01	3.89
Arithmetic average		4.89		5.49		6.58		5.65
Geometric average		4.63		4.80		5.95		5.25
Standard deviation		7.97		12.88		12.37		9.78

changes in operating income and net income are higher compared to the variables of net sales and EPS. The standard deviation of year-to-year changes in operating income and net income was 12.88% and 12.37%. Geometric mean of 4.80% was the realistic average for change in operating income compared to the arithmetic average of 5.49%.

Linear and log linear models of growth can be estimated through regression. The estimation of linear and log linear models of growth for EPS of Procter and Gamble are estimated as given in Table 5.9. In linear model, EPS is regressed against time variable in which years are denoted as 1, 2, ..., n. In log linear regression ln(EPS) is regressed against the time variables.

The t statistic for intercept and slope is 9.4 and 3.358, respectively. The R^2 for the regression is 0.585. The regression suggests that earnings per share increases by 15.5 cents a year from 2005 to 2014. The growth rate in earnings per share is found out in the following manner.

Growth rate in earnings per share = Slope on linear regression/average EPS
That is 0.155/3.568 = 0.0434 = 4.34%

Hence, through the linear regression methodology, the growth rate of earnings is arrived at 4.34%.

Log linear regression: ln(EPS) = 0.9928 + 0.048t. The R^2 value is 0.606. The t statistics for intercept is 11.69 and for the slope it is 3.51. The growth rate of earnings per share is estimated as 4.8% through the log linear regression.

The detailed calculation of growth rate of net sales, operating income, net income, and EPS including the regression results are provided in the excel sheet *Estimation of growth rate Procter and Gamble.xlsx*.

Time series models are considered to be better models in forecasting earnings per share compared to other models like averages of past growth.

Historical growth rates often have disturbances associated with them. In such cases of higher volatility, historical growth rates are not ideal measures of

Table 5.9 Estimation of linear and log linear regression

SL	Year	EPS	ln(EPS)
1	2005	2.53	0.93
2	2006	2.64	0.97
3	2007	3.04	1.11
4	2008	3.64	1.29
5	2009	4.26	1.45
6	2010	4.11	1.41
7	2011	3.93	1.37
8	2012	3.66	1.30
9	2013	3.86	1.35
10	2014	4.01	1.39

Linear regression: EPS = 2.712 + 0.155t

estimation of growth rate of earnings (Knill et al., 2012). Revenue growth are found to be less volatile than earnings growth. Growth rates are also a function of the firm sizes. It would be difficult for large firms to sustain higher growth rate in the long run.

5.6.3.2 Analysts estimation of growth rates

Basically analysts follow companies with very high market capitalization, trading volume, and institutional holdings. Analyst's predictions on growth rate are based on macroeconomic information, firm specific, and competitor's information. The Institutional Brokers Estimate System is a central location in which investors would be able to research different analysts estimates for any given stock.

Analysts are assumed to be better informed than the rest of market. Larger the number of analysts following a stock, more informative would be their consensus forecast. Research shows that there is an intimate link between an analyst's experience and the forecasting experience. Studies of Clement and Tse (2005) and Bernhardt et al. (2006) suggest that analysts who are experienced and highly specialized often provide superior forecasts. Superior forecasters produce better estimates either by resolving information asymmetry or by offering better assessment. Analysts often incorporate information from other forecasts and improve the accuracy of their own forecasts. Buyside analysts work for mutual funds, pension funds, trusts, and hedge funds. Sell side analysts work for brokerage firms.

5.6.3.3 Estimation of growth rate through fundamentals

The growth rates in earnings per share, net income, and operating income can be estimated using the fundamental relationship between fundamentals and growth in equity income.

The growth is based on the retention ratio (RR) and the ROE of its projects. RR is the percentage of earnings retained in the firm. Firms with high RR and high returns on equity are expected to have higher growth rates in earnings.

Growth rate in EPS = Retained Earnings t − 1/Net Income t − 1 * ROE, where ROE is Return on Equity
*Growth rate in EPS = Retention Ratio * ROE*

The growth rate in net income is found out by estimating how much equity the firm reinvests back into its businesses in the form of net capital expenditures and investments in working capital.

Equity reinvested in business = Capital expenditure − depreciation + change in working capital − (new debt issued − debt repaid)
Equity reinvestment rate = Equity reinvested/net income
*Expected growth rate in net income = Equity reinvestment rate * ROE*

The growth rate in operating income is estimated from the reinvestment rate and the return on capital employed.

*Expected growth operating income = Reinvestment rate * return on capital.*
Reinvestment rate = (Capital expenditure − depreciation + change in noncash working capital)/EBIT(1 − T)

where EBIT is the earnings before interest and tax. T is the tax rate.

Return on Capital = EBIT(1 − T)t/Capital Employed t − 1

where EBIT(1 − T)t is the earnings before interest and tax in the year t and capital employed t − 1 is the sum of the book value of equity and debt minus cash in the year t − 1.

Capital employed = Book value of equity + book value of debt − cash at the end of year t − 1.

The reinvestment rate measures how the firm plow back to generate the future growth. The reinvestment rate can be negative if the depreciation exceeds its capital expenditures or if the working capital declines take place. The negative reinvestment could be considered as a temporary phenomenon.

5.6.3.3.1 Estimation of growth rate of EPS: Apple Inc
Apple Inc had an EPS of $6.38, $5.72, and $6.49, respectively, during the period 2012−2014. The average growth rate in EPS during the 5-year period was 43%. At the same time, the 3-year average growth rate in EPS during the period 2012−2014 was 21% (Tables 5.10 and 5.11).

5.6.3.3.2 The growth rate in EPS can also be estimated through fundamentals
The average expected growth rate is the product of the ROE and RR. Note that Apple started paying dividends only in the year 2012. Hence, it can be assumed that in prior years 2009−2011, the RR was 100%. The average expected growth rate during the 3-year period 2012−2014 was 29%. This rate is comparable to the actual growth rate of EPS for Apple during the period 2012−2014. RR is the

Table 5.10 Growth rate of EPS: Apple Inc

Year	EPS	Change
2009	1.3	
2010	2.2	0.69
2011	4.01	0.82
2012	6.38	0.59
2013	5.72	−0.10
2014	6.49	0.13
	Average	0.43 (5 years)
	Average	0.21 (3 years)

retained earnings in t − 1 period divided by net income in period t − 1. ROE is for the period t.

5.6.3.3.3 Estimation of growth rate of net Income: Apple Inc

Apple Inc had net income of \$41,733 million, \$37,037 million, and \$39,510 million in the years 2012, 2013, and 2014, respectively. The average 5-year (2010–2014) growth rate of net income was 42%. The average growth rate of net income was 19% during the 3-year period (2009–2013) (Table 5.12).

5.6.3.3.4 Estimation of expected growth rate of net income: Apple Inc

The expected growth rate of net income is obtained from fundamentals. The relationship between growth rate and fundamental variables is determined as follows.

*Expected growth in net income = Equity reinvestment rate * return on equity.*

The capital expenditure is adjusted to account for R&D expenses. Similarly, the net income is also adjusted.

Adjusted capital expenditure in a year = Capital expenditure in the year + current R&D expenses + current acquisitions expenses.
Adjusted net income in a year = Net income + current year R&D expenses − amortization of research asset.
Adjusted book value of equity = Book value of equity + value of research asset.

Table 5.11 **Estimation of growth rate from fundamentals**

Year	Return on equity	Retention ratio	Expected growth rate ($ROE_t * RR_{t-1}$)
2011		1	
2012	0.43	0.94	0.40
2013	0.31	0.71	0.22
2014	0.34	0.72	0.24
Average			0.29

Table 5.12 **Growth rate of net income**

Year	Net income (in million dollars)	Change
2009	8235	
2010	14,013	0.70
2011	25,922	0.85
2012	41,733	0.61
2013	37,037	− 0.11
2014	39,510	0.07
Average		0.42 (5 years)
		0.19 (3 years)

The capitalized costs related to internal use of software in Apple are amortized using straight line method over the estimated useful lives of the assets which range from 3 to 5 years. For calculation of value of research asset, the amortizable life of the asset is assumed to be 5 years. Based on the methodology[3], the value of research asset is arrived at by cumulating one fifth of the R&D expenses from 4 years, two-fifths of R&D expenses from 3 years, three-fifths of R&D expenses from 2 years, four-fifths of R&D expenses from previous year, and current year's entire R&D expenses. The details of calculation of value of R&D assets are given in the excel sheet 1 *Expected growth rate from fundamentals.xlsx* (Tables 5.13–5.18).

The return on the capital employed was 31% and 28% in the year 2013 and 2014, respectively. The return on capital employed in 2013 is found out by dividing the EBIT(1 − T) in the year 2013 by adjusted book value of capital in the year 2012. The average return on capital employed during the 2-year period was

Table 5.13 Estimation of equity reinvestment rate (values in US$ millions except rate)

	2012	2013	2014
Capital expenditure	9402	9076	9813
R&D expenses	3381	4475	6041
Acquisition expenses	350	496	3765
Adjusted capital expenditure	*13,133*	*14,047*	*19,619*
Depreciation and amortization	3277	6757	7946
Change in working capital	2093	10,517	−24,545
New debt issued	0	16,960	12,027
Equity reinvested	11,949	847	−24,899
Net income	41,733	37,037	39,510
Amortization of research asset	677	957	1046
Adjusted net income	*44,437*	*40,555*	*44,505*
Equity reinvestment rate	0.2689	0.0209	−0.5595
Equity reinvestment rate (%)	26.89	2.09	−55.95

Table 5.14 Adjusted ROE

	2012	2013	2014
Adjusted net income	41,733	37,037	39,510
Book value of equity	118,210	123,549	111,547
Value of R&D asset	7148.4	9616.6	12,977.6
Adjusted book value of equity	125,358.4	133,165.6	124,524.6
ROE	0.33	0.28	0.32

[3] Damodaran, A. Measuring earnings. Investment Valuation, third ed. Wiley Finance, 233 (Chapter 9).

Table **5.15** **Calculation of expected growth rate in net income**

	2012	2013	2014
Equity reinvestment rate	0.27	0.02	−0.56
ROE	0.33	0.28	0.32
Growth rate in net income (%)	8.95	0.58	17.75

The two average growth rate for the period 2012−2013 was 4.77%.

Table **5.16** **Calculation of growth rate in operating income (values in million US dollars)**

Year	Operating income before tax	Tax	Operating income after tax	Growth rate
2010	18,385	4527	13,858	
2011	33,790	8283	25,507	0.84
2012	55,241	14,030	41,211	0.616
2013	48,999	13,118	35,881	−0.129
2014	52,503	13,973	38,530	0.074
Average				0.350

The average growth rate in operating income during the 5-year period 2011−2014 was 35%.

Table **5.17** **Calculation of reinvestment rate**

Year	EBIT(1 − T)	Equity reinvested	Reinvestment rate
2012	41,211	11,949	0.2899
2013	35,881	847	0.02361
2014	38,530	−24,899	−0.646

Table **5.18** **Calculation of adjusted book value of capital (values in million dollars)**

Year	Adjusted book value of equity	Book value of debt	Cash and cash equivalents	Adjusted book value of capital
2012	125,358.4	0	10,746	114,612.4
2013	133,165.6	16,960	14,259	135,866.6
2014	124,524.6	28,987	13,844	139,667.6

29.83%. The growth rate in operating income is obtained by multiplying reinvestment rate by ROCE. In 2013, the growth rate in operating income was 0.74%.

The detailed calculations of the growth rate from fundamentals is given in the resources excel sheet 1 *Expected growth rate from fundamentals.xlsx.*

5.6.3.3.5 Estimation of growth rate of Indian Oil Corporation

Indian Oil Corporation (IOC) or Indian Oil is India's flagship national oil company, which has business interest spanning the entire hydrocarbon value chain consisting of refining, pipeline transportation, and marketing of petroleum products, exploration and production of crude oil and gas, marketing of natural gas and petrochemicals. IOC is the leading Indian corporate in the Fortune 500 listing ranked at 96th position in the year 2014. The company has established subsidiaries in Sri Lanka, Mauritius, and United Arab Emirates. IOC with 34,000 strong workforce has been involved in meeting India's energy needs for the past 55 years.

Table 5.19 analyses the growth rate of revenues, operating income (EBITDA), net income, and earnings per share of IOC during the 5-year period 2009−2013.

Very high volatility is observed in the operating income and net income during the 5-year period of analysis. The operating income increased by 69% in the year 2009 compared to the previous year 2008. Similarly, there was exponential growth rate of 246% in net income during the year 2009. For the next 2 years (2010−2011), the growth rate was negative, followed by positive growth rates of 27% and 40% in the next two consecutive years. Geometric mean is a better measure of estimates of growth rates when the earnings exhibit high volatility. The growth rate in operating income and net income are same because no new equity is issued by the firm during the 5-year period. The workings for estimation of growth rates are given in sheet 2 *Expected growth rate from fundamentals.xlsx.*

5.6.3.3.6 Estimation of growth rate from fundamentals

The growth rate in EPS can be determined from the fundamental variables of RR and ROE. The average RR during the 6-year period 2008−2013 was 64%. Table 5.20 gives the average growth rate of EPS determined as the product of RR in year $t - 1$ and ROE in year t.

Table 5.19 Actual growth rates at IOC

Year	Change in revenues (%)	Change in operating income (%)	Change in net income (%)	Change in EPS (%)
2009	−5	69	246	247
2010	21	−13	−27	−27
2011	23	34	−47	−47
2012	11	−21	27	27
2013	10	10	40	40
Arithmetic mean	12	16	48	48
Geometric mean	12	11	19	19

Table 5.20 **Estimation of expected growth rate in EPS**

Year	ROE (%)	RR (%)	Growth rate(%) $(RR_{t-1} * ROE_t)$
2008	6.93	64	
2009	21.62	64	14
2010	14.06	64	9
2011	6.99	64	4
2012	8.41	65	5
2013	11.04	65	7
Arithmetic mean			8

Table 5.21 **Growth rate in net income**

Year	ROE (%)	Reinvestment rate (%)	Growth rate in net income (%)
2011	6.99	81.79	5.72
2012	8.41	76.36	6.42
2013	11.04	−8.72	−0.96
Average			3.73

The 5-year average expected growth rate of EPS is 8% during the period 2009–2013 based on fundamentals. The actual growth rate in terms of geometric mean was estimated as 19% during the above period.

5.6.3.3.7 Estimation of growth rate in net income

The reinvestment rate was negative in the year 2013 as the change in working capital was negative. Hence, the growth rate in net income was −0.9% in the year 2013. IOC had an equity reinvested rate of 81.79% in the year 2011 and 76.36% in the year 2012 (Table 5.21).

The average expected growth rate in net income is 3.73% during the period 2011–2013. The actual growth rate during the same period based on arithmetic mean was 7% and −2% during the 3-year period 2011–2013.

5.6.3.3.8 Estimation of growth rate in operating income

The average reinvestment rate was approximately 16% of operating income during the period 2011–2013. The average expected growth rate in operating income from fundamental variable calculation was 2.08% during the 3-year period of 2011–2013. At the same time, the average actual growth rate was 8% in terms of arithmetic mean and 5% in terms of geometric mean values (Table 5.22).

Forecasting of growth rates is one of the most important step in the process of valuation. Forecasting of growth rate for earnings is essential for DCF valuation.

Table 5.22 **Expected growth rate in operating income**

Year	Reinvestment rate (%)	ROCE (%)	Expected growth rate (%)
2011	20	16.48	3.34
2012	33	10.69	3.57
2013	−6	11.45	−0.68

The growth rate of earnings can be estimated using historical growth rates based on past years. The average historical growth rate can be used to estimate the future expected growth rate. The growth rates can also be estimated from analyst's estimates. The future growth rate can also be estimated from the fundamentals of the firm. In this method, reinvestment rate is a determinant of future growth rate. The future expected growth rate in EPS is determined as a function of RR and ROE. The expected growth rate in net income is determined as a function of reinvestment rate (expressed as reinvested equity divided by net income) and ROE. The expected growth rate in operating income is determined as a function of reinvestment rate expressed as ratio of reinvestment of equity to earnings before interest and after tax and return on capital employed. In case of volatility of earnings, determination of growth rates from fundamental variables is a better method for forecasting growth rates.

References

Badertscher, B., Collins, D., Lys, T., 2006a. Earnings Management and the Predictive Ability of Accruals with Respect to Future Cash Flows.. University of Iowa and Northwestern University, Working Paper.

Badertscher, B., Philips, J., Pincus, M., Rego, S.O., 2006b. Do Firms Manage Earnings in a Book Tax Conforming Manner? <https://tippie.uiowa.edu/accounting/mcgladrey/winter-papers/badertscher.pdf>.

Bernhardt, D., Campello, M., Kutsoati, E., 2006. Who herds? J. Financ. Econ. 80, 657−675.

Clement, M., Tse, S., 2005. Financial analyst characteristics and herding behavior in forecasting. J. Financ. Econ. 60, 307−341.

Knill, A., Minnick, K., Nejadmalayeri, A., 2012. Experience, information asymmetry, and rational forecast bias. Rev. Quant. Financ. Account. 39, 241−272.

McGregor, S., Earnings Management and Manipulation <http://webpage.pace.edu/pviswanath/notes/corpfin/earningsmanip.html#types>, 2014.

Musfiqur, M.D., Mohammad, M., Sharif, M.J., 2013. Techniques, motives and controls of earnings management. Int. J. Inf. Technol. Bus. Manage. 11 (1), 22−33.

Phillips, J., Pincus, M., Rego, S., 2003. Earnings management: new evidence based on deferred tax expense. Account. Rev. 78 (2), 491−521.

Discounted cash flow valuation models

6

6.1 Introduction

Discounted cash flow (DCF) analysis uses future free cash flow (FCF) projections and discounts the cash flow to get the present value that can be used to estimate the potential for investment. The DCF valuation models are based on the assumption that the value of any firm is the present value of the expected cash flows. The three basic DCF valuation models are the dividend discount models (DDMs), the free cash flow to equity (FCFE), and the free cash flow to firm (FCFF) models. DCF analysis signifies the net present value of projected cash flows that are available to capital providers net of the cash needed to be invested for future growth prospects. The major principle underlying DCF is that the value of a business or an asset is based on its ability to generate cash flows. DCF is based on the fundamental expectations of the business. DCF analysis must yield the overall enterprise value of the business. In theoretical sense, the DCF is the most appropriate method of valuation. The DCF method basically depends on future expectations and hence is forward looking. DCF analysis focuses on the fundamental expectations of the business and assets. DCF analysis focuses on cash flow generation and factors in synergies of businesses. All valuation approaches are based on the estimated growth rate of the variables. The DDM provides a means for developing explicit returns estimates for both individuals and the aggregate market value.

The basic valuation model is given by

$$\text{Value} = \sum_{t=1}^{t=n} \frac{CF_t}{(1+r)^t}$$

Where value refers to the value of asset; t is the time period ranges from 1 to n, CF_t is the cash flow in period t, r represents the discount rate that reflects the riskiness of the cash flows. According to the model, the value of any asset is the present value of the expected cash flows on the asset.

Valuation models can be classified into equity valuation and firm valuation models. In equity valuation models, the future cash flows to the equity shareholders are discounted by the cost of equity to arrive at a value. In firm valuation models, the future cash flows to the main stakeholders (equity shareholders and debt holders) are discounted by the cost of capital (weighted average cost of capital (WACC)) to arrive at the value of the firm.

6.2   Dividend discount model

DDM is the simplest and most direct version of the equity valuation model. This model of valuation assumes that the value of a firm's equity is the present value of the forecasted future dividends. In financial theory, the value of any financial claim is basically the present value of expected cash flows that the claim holders receive from the firm. In this scenario, it can be stated that as shareholders receive cash payoffs from the company in the form of dividends, the value of the equity is the present value of future dividends. Dividends is the most straightforward measure of cash flow as it goes directly to the equity investor. The cost of equity is used as the discount rate for discounting estimated future dividends. DDM prices a stock by the sum of its future cash flows discounted by the required rate of return which is the cost of equity. The value obtained by the DDM model is the intrinsic value of the stock. One of the biggest disadvantages of this method is that the model cannot be used to value stocks which do not pay any dividends. Firms in their high growth stage usually do not pay dividends. For example, Apple started paying dividends only in the year 2012. Growth companies like Intel, Google, and Apple retain a very high percentage of their earnings for reinvestment purposes rather than paying out large dividends to shareholders. The DDM is a specialized case of equity valuation wherein the value of a stock is the present value of expected future dividends. In the narrowest sense, the only cash flow stockholders in a publicly listed company receive from investments is dividends.

The DDM is a heuristic model that relates the present stock price to the present value of its future cash flows. Bonds are also priced in terms of its future cash flow. But in bond pricing, the cash flows and interest rates on those cash flows are known with certainty if the bonds are held to maturity unless the bond issuer defaults. The DDM depends on the projections about the growth rate and capitalization rates of the expected cash flows. The capitalization rates (cost of equity) in a bear market will be higher than that in a bull market. The investors in such a market will demand a higher required rate of return to compensate for the greater risk. The dividend models will give wrong intrinsic values for a stock if either the capitalization rates or growth rates are miscalculated.

The basic premise behind the dividend valuation model is that the value of a stock today is the present value of all future dividends. The dividend valuation model can be modified for patterns including a constant dividend, a constantly growing dividend, and a dividend that grows at different rate depending on the period in the future. The dividend valuation model can be related to fundamental factors that drive the value of a company's equity, including the return on equity and the dividend payout.

DDM provides an estimation of the price per share of a company based on the present value of future dividends. On the basis of this estimated value, investors would be able to determine whether the stock is undervalued or overvalued.

DDM assumes that the value of a share of common stock is the present value of all future dividends.

$$V = \frac{D_1}{1+k} + \frac{D_2}{(1+k)_2} + \cdots + \frac{D_n}{(1+k)_n}$$

$$= \sum_{t=1}^{t=n} \frac{D_t}{(1+k)^t}$$

Where V is the value of the common stock, D_t is the dividend received during the period t, and K is the required rate of return on the stock. The above version of the model assumes that the stock is never sold and held for perpetuity. In this case, the value is equal to the sum of the present value of expected future dividends. The future dividends are based on estimated growth rates. The growth rates can be estimated on the basis of historical growth rates or fundamentals.

In the next scenario, it is assumed that the stock is not held for an infinite period and the stock could be sold at the end of a time period. The future cash flows include the dividends and the sale price of the stock when it is sold. If the stock pays no dividends, then the expected future cash flow is the sales price of the stock.

The assumption of sale of stock imply the following formulae

$$V = \frac{D_1}{1+k} + \frac{D_2}{(1+k)_2} + \cdots + \frac{D_n}{(1+k)_n} + \frac{P_n}{(1+k)_n}$$

6.2.1 Special cases of DDM

There are three basic versions of DDM.

The zero growth DDM model assumes that dividends has a zero growth rate. In other words, all dividends paid by a stock remain the same. The formula used for estimating value of such stocks is essentially the formula for valuing the perpetuity.

$$V = \frac{D}{K}$$

where V is the intrinsic value of the stock, D is the annual dividends, and K is the required rate of return which is the cost of equity.

6.2.1.1 The constant growth DDM (Gordon growth model)

This model assumes that dividends for some firms grow at a steady rate. It can be assumed that dividends grow by a specific percentage each year. The constant growth DDM is given by the formula:

$$V_0 = \frac{D_0(1+g)}{r-g} = \frac{D_1}{r-g}$$

V is the intrinsic value of the stock, D_0 is the current dividend, D_1 is the next year forecasted dividend, k is the required return on the stock (cost of equity), and g is the dividend growth rate in perpetuity. The constant growth model is often used to value stocks of mature companies that have consistently increased the dividend over a period of years. If k and g remains the same in future, then the value of the stock increases annually by the percentage of dividend increases. It has to be noted that the zero growth rate and constant growth rate DDMs value stocks in terms of only dividends paid not the capital gains in the stock price.

The Gordon growth model suggests that the value of the stock is related to its expected dividends in the next time period, the cost of equity, and the expected growth rate in dividends. The model is useful for valuing companies with stable growth rate. The major disadvantage of the model is that it is not practical for valuing dividend paying stocks with unstable growth characteristics. The model results are highly sensitive to assumptions for the growth rate and required return. When the earnings are volatile, it is difficult for firms to maintain a constant dividend growth rate. In reality, dividend growth rates are rarely constant. In Gordon model, the required return must be higher than the growth rate in dividends. If the growth rate exceeds the required rate of return (cost of equity), then value becomes negative. Gordon model is suited for firms that grows at a rate similar to the nominal growth rate of economy with established dividend policies. The Gordon model is not suitable for firms that have multistage growth rates. Gordon model is simple to understand and applicable to stable, mature firms that have constant growth in dividends. This model can be used to value an entire stock market using the data for the entire stock market.

The appropriate application of the constant dividend growth model requires an understanding of the fundamental nature of the model and parameters. The simplicity of constant growth dividend model have led to its extensive application for common stock valuation. The sensitivity of DDM to error increases geometrically when the estimates of required rate of return (cost of equity) and growth rates converge.

The simple DDM $P = D_0(1 + g)/(k - g)$ cannot be used for high-growth companies when the growth rate g exceeds the discount rate k.

Expected return is given by the following relation

Expected return = Dividend yield + capital gains yield.

The implied growth rate can be estimated by setting the intrinsic value equal to the current stock price by means of algebraically transforming the constant growth rate DDM formula.

Implied growth rate (g) is given by

$$g = k - \frac{D_1}{P}$$

Where D_1 is the dividend next year, k is the expected rate of return or cost of equity, and P is the stock price.

The implied return on equity is given by

Return on equity = Implied growth rate/earnings retention rate.

Nonconstant growth DDM considers abnormal growth rates over some finite length of time. This model allows for supernormal or abnormal growth rates over some period of time. The nonconstant growth model primarily consists of two- and three-stage growth model. In the two-stage growth model, the assumption made is that there would be an initial high rate of growth for some time period followed by sustainable steady rate of growth in perpetuity. In the two-stage model, the dividend is assumed to grow at a rate of g_1 for t years and then grow at a rate g_2 in perpetuity (forever). In the three-stage growth model, three different stages in terms of rates of growth are assumed: an initial high rate of growth, a transition to slower growth, and a sustainable steady rate of growth. The present value of each stage is added to obtain the intrinsic value of the stock.

6.2.1.2 Two-stage DDM model

In the two-stage DDM model, the first stage of rapid growth suddenly transits to a second stage of constant growth. This model would be suitable to value stocks that have first mover advantage. For example, pharma firms with patents can be considered to have a high growth rate before the patent expires and then the growth rate falls to a steady state. The model assumes that earnings eventually will decline to the long-term stable growth rate of economy.

Value of the Stock = PV of dividends during abnormal growth phase + PV of terminal price.

The model assumes that dividends grow at rate g_S for n years and rate g_L thereafter:

$$V_0 = \sum_{t=1}^{n} \frac{D_0(1+g_S)^t}{(1+r)^t} + \frac{V_n}{(1+r)^n}$$

$$V_n = \frac{D_{n+1}}{r - g_L}$$

$$D_{n+1} = D_0(1+g_S)^n(1 + g_L)$$

The basic assumption of two-stage valuation model is that the dividends will exhibit a high rate of growth during the initial period. The model values the dividends over the short-term period of high growth and the terminal value at the end of the period of high growth. The short-term growth rate, g_S, lasts for n years. The intrinsic value per share in year n, V_n, represents the year n value of the dividends received during the sustainable growth period or the terminal value at time n. V_n can be estimated by using the Gordon growth model, where g_L is the long-term or sustainable growth rate. The dividend in year n + 1, D_{n+1}, is determined by assuming n years of growth at rate g_S followed by 1 year of growth at g_L.

The terminal value V_n is estimated by multiplying the dividend in the nth year by the growth rate in the stable state, which is considered equal to the nominal growth rate of economy. In stable phase of the growth cycle of a firm, the firms have higher payout ratios compared to their high-growth phase state when the payout ratios are smaller as the retention ratio (RR) for reinvestment purposes would be higher. The relationship between growth rate and RR is given by

Expected growth rate = Retention ratio * return on equity.

In the stable phase growth stage, the RR (1 − Dividend payout ratio) will be lower and the return on equity would be lower as cash flows generated would be lesser. A stable firm will pay more of its earnings as dividends than high-growth firms. The return on equity will also be lower for firms in the stable phase growth period than in the high growth period. The average return on equity of the industry can be considered as the return on equity for the firm in the stable phase growth period. The cost of equity for the firm in the stable growth period can be estimated by means of adjustment for betas. Firms can be considered to have a beta value of approximately 1 close to the market beta value. Firms with stock buyback schemes should include buybacks along with dividends to find out the payout ratios.

6.2.1.3 Financial characteristics of high growth and stable growth firms

Stable growth firms are expected to have lower risk, more leveraged, lower excess returns, and higher dividend payout ratios. A high-growth firm is expected to have higher betas, higher returns on capital, and lower debt ratios. High-growth firms tend to reinvest more than stable growth firms. Hence, the dividend payout ratios of high-growth firms will be lower than that of low-growth firms.

6.2.1.4 Two-stage H-model

Another version of the two-stage DDM model is known as the H-model. H-model assumes an initially high growth rate which declines linearly over a specified period till it reaches a steady state of rate of growth in perpetuity. The steady state is reached when competition leads to decline in growth rates and the industry matures.

$$V_0 = \frac{[D_0 \times (1 + g_L)] + [D_0 \times H(g_S - g_L)]}{r - g_L}$$

H is the half-life in years of high growth period; g_S and g_L are the short-term and long-term growth rates, and r is the required rate of return.

The model assumes that the high growth period lasts $2 \times H$ years. H-model suggests that stocks with longer high growth periods and higher growth rates will have higher values.

One of the major limitations of the two-stage dividend model is the exact determination of the length of the high growth period which is based on subjective factors. The assumption of transition of high growth into stable growth phase is not based on realistic factors.

6.2.1.5   Three-stage dividend growth model

This model is designed to value the stock in a firm with three stages of growth—an initial period of high growth, transition period of declining growth, and a final period of stable growth. The value of the stock is estimated as the present value of expected dividends during the high growth and transitional period and the terminal value at the beginning of the final stable growth phase.

6.2.2   Reflections on terminal value

Terminal value is the value of the firm's expected cash flow beyond the explicit forecast horizon. In practice, forecasts of dividends are made for a finite number of years and the truncation of the forecast horizon usually requires a terminal value or continuing value calculation at the horizon. Terminal values often have a significant effect on the valuation. A high-quality estimate of terminal value is critical as it accounts for a large portion of the value of firm in DCF valuation. Firms that reinvest their earnings are expected to earn higher rates of returns. As the firm becomes bigger in size, it would be difficult for the firm to maintain the high growth rate. The theory of life cycle of a firm suggests that in the long run, the high-growth firm matures and will grow at a rate, which would be approximately equal to the growth rate of the economy in which it operates. Based on the stable phase growth rate, the value of all cash flows beyond the high growth period can be estimated as the terminal value of the firm. The terminal value of cash flows of a firm can be estimated in three different ways. The terminal value can be estimated either on the basis of liquidated value of the firm or the value of the firm on the basis of the assumption of ongoing concern. If the firm is liquidated, then the liquidation value is based on the book value, salvage value, or breakup value of the firm. The firm must make assumptions for the salvage value of capital assets and recovery of net working capital.

On the basis of ongoing concern, the terminal value of the firm can be estimated using DCF valuation or by using multiples from comparable firms. In DCF valuation, the terminal value is determined using the Gordon growth model.

$$V_n = \frac{D_{n+1}}{r - g_L}$$

The terminal value of cash flows can also be determined using a multiplier of income or cash flow measure like net income, EBITDA. The multiple is determined by analyzing how comparable companies are valued by market. The commonly used multiples are price earnings ratio, market/book values, or cash flow multiples.

6.2.3   Practical difficulties in estimation of parameters in the DCF models

Valuation using DCF models involves formulation of critical assumption regarding the high growth rate, the length of high growth period, stable growth rate and period, return on equity, cost of capital, etc. The estimation of high growth period for a firm is a challenging task for analysts. In the long run, all firms will be become stable growth firms as postulated by the life cycle of a firm. It is also assumed that during the high-growth phase firms earn return on equity higher than the cost of equity. In practical terms, it would be difficult to assume that excess returns are possible particularly in the context of competitive market. The high growth rate period of a firm is the function of size of the firm, the current growth rate, abnormal returns along with the magnitude, and sustainability of competitive advantage. Practical difficulties may arise from three types of structural assumptions in the model—the rate of return, time horizon assumption, and risk adjustment procedures. Standard DDMs cannot handle dynamic betas, risk premiums, or risk-free rates as the future expected cash flows are valued at constant discount rates.

6.2.4   Research studies related to DDM

Accrual accounting classify standard equity valuation into DDM, the residual income model and the DCF model. Gordon and Shapiro (1956) and Gordon (1962) presented the special case of the general model for dividends referred to as the Gordon growth or constant growth model.

Financial economists suggest that DDM provides good approximate description of stock price determination for the aggregate market. Research based on volatility tests of LeRoy and Porter (1981) and Shiller (1981) suggest that stock price fluctuations are explained by changes in the expected present value of future dividends. Their studies based on the simple DDM model suggest that stock market volatility was far greater than could be justified by subsequent changes in dividends. Their studies suggest that aggregate stock prices are too volatile to be measured by dividends in the DDM. The studies by Flavin (1983) and Marsh and Merton (1986) challenged the statistical validity of the volatility tests.

West (1988) devised a variance bounds test that is free from small sample bias and valid even when dividends are nonstationary. This inequality test suggest that if discount rates are constant, the variance of the innovation in the expected that presents discounted value of future dividends is larger when less information is used. Campbell and Shiller (1987) derived testable implications of the present value model taking into account the nonstationarity and cointegration of prices and dividends. These research studies suggest strong evidence against simple present value model. Time varying discount rate might explain the failure of simple DDMs. Cochrane (2010) suggests that dividend growth is unpredictable and all movement in the dividend payout ratio is driven by news about future discount rates.

Researchers have explored the basis for valuation errors resulting from the implementation of various forms of DDM. Jacobs and Levy (1988) finds that DDM-expected returns are not generally predictive and sometimes negatively correlated with actual returns. Hickman and Petry (1990) suggests that dividend discount approaches produce errors averaging 88% of the actual price and 4.21 times those of price earnings methods. In addition, high degree of error in growth and required return estimates are found irrespective of specific modeling assumptions. Gehr

(1992) suggests that price estimation bias in DDM is the result of required return and growth prediction error. In this context, this study suggests a probability weighted range of parameter estimates. Good (1989) suggests that the reliability of DDM is primarily dependent on the estimation of required return and growth rates.

Foerster et al. (2005) on the basis of share price, dividend payments, and earnings for Bank of Montreal over a period of more than 120 years compare the actual share price to the expected price using commonly used fundamental valuation methods and suggest that dividend-based models perform well at explaining actual prices than earnings-based models. This study provides evidence on the ability of DCF-based techniques to explain the value of equity for a large mature dividend paying company. The study by Einhorn and Shangquan (1984) uses DDM for asset allocation and for calculating the Standard & Poor's 500 monthly excess returns for the 1968−1982 period.

Nasseh and Strauss (2004) examine whether there has been a stable relation between prices and dividends over the 20-year period for firms in the S&P 100. The study suggest a close link between stock prices and dividends based on DDMs. During the period mid-1990s, the present value model parameters indicate a 43% overvaluation of stock prices. The reason attributed for the overvaluation had been a short-run decline in long-term interest rates.

6.2.5   Estimation of value of ICBC through dividend models

Industrial and Commercial Bank of China (ICBC) Ltd is one of the largest bank in the world by total assets and market capitalization. It is one of China's "Big Four" state-owned commercial banks. The bank provides various financial products and services worldwide. ICBC Ltd was established in 1984. The bank with presence in 39 countries spanning six continents provides wide range of products and services to over 4.38 million corporate customers and 393 million personal customers. The bank has a wide distribution network consisting of 17,125 domestic institutions, 383 overseas institutions, and 1771 correspondent banks worldwide. In 2012, ICBC topped the Fortune Global 2000 list, which was the first by a Chinese company. ICBC is ranked among the top four card issuing banks in the world. ICBC is one of the leading international settlement banks of the world. ICBC Ltd provides various financial products and services worldwide. It operates through Corporate Banking, Personal Banking, Treasury Operations, and Others segments.

The Bank paid amount of 101,764 million CNY[1] as dividends in the year 2014. During the period 2009−2014, the bank paid a cumulative dividend of CNY 465,132 million. The payout ratio was 30.2% in the year 2014. The dividend payout was 6.6% of earnings in the year 2007, which peaked at 41.6% in 2009. The average growth rate of net income for ICBC during the 5-year period 2010−2014 was 17%. The average increase in the dividends during the 5-year period of 2010−2014 was 13%. The average increase in dividends per share and dividend payout was 8% and 31.90% during the period 2010−2014 (calculations based on Table 6.1).

[1] Chinese Yuan.

Table 6.1 Financial highlights of ICBC during the period 2009–2014

Year	Net income (million CNY)	Dividends (million CNY)	EPS	DPS	Dividend payout (%)
2009	129,350	56,367	0.39	0.16	41.6
2010	166,025	66,364	0.48	0.15	31.3
2011	208,445	67,432	0.59		
2012	238,691	79,519	0.67	0.18	27.3
2013	262,965	93,686	0.74	0.22	29.1
2014	278,049	101,764	0.78	0.24	30.2
Average	213,920	77,522	0.61	0.19	31.90

6.2.5.1 Valuation of ICBC using the stable DDM model

The China government 10-year bond had an average yield of 3.73% during the period 2005–2014.[2] This rate is considered as the risk-free rate for the cost of equity calculation. The risk premium is obtained as difference between the returns on market index and risk-free rate. The average returns on the SSE composite index during the period 2005–2014 is considered as the returns on the market index. SSE composite index takes December 19, 1990 as the base day and the total market capitalization of all the listed stocks on the same day as the base period with a base of 100 points. It was published from July 15, 1999 and is the most widely used index in China's securities market.

Risk-free rate = 3.73%
Return on market index = 11.98%
Risk premium = 11.98 − 3.73 = 8.25%
Beta = 1.19. Estimation of beta given in spreadsheet *DDM ICBC.xlsx*.
Cost of equity = 3.73 + 1.19 ∗ 8.25 = 13.55%

ICBC paid a dividend per share (DPS) of 0.24 CNY in the year 2014. The growth rate for the model is assumed to be the average 5-year GDP growth rate of China during the period 2009–2013.[3] The average annual growth rate of GDP of China was 8.86% during the 5-year period 2009–2013.

Value per share = Dividends in year 2014(1 + growth rate)/(cost of equity − growth rate)
Value per share = 0.24(1.0886)/(0.1355 − 0.0886) = 5.57 CNY.

ICBC was trading at 5.460 in Hong Kong Stock exchange on December 23, 2014. The 52-week range of ICBC stock in the year 2014 was 4.330–5.690.[4] ICBC was undervalued by approximately 2% based on the valuation done as above.

---

[2] http://www.tradingeconomics.com/china/government-bond-yield.

[3] http://data.worldbank.org/indicator/NY.GDP.MKTP.KD.ZG.

[4] In terms of Hong Kong dollars, ICBC paid dividend of 0.30 in the year 2014. Value of ICBC per share is equal to 0.30 ∗ (1.0886)/(0.1355 − 0.0886) = 6.96 HKD. The exchange rate of 1 Chinese Yuan (CNY) = 1.25 HKD (Hong Kong Dollar).

The average dividend paid by ICBC during the 5-year period 2010−2014 was 81,753 million CNY.

The value of equity is determined as follows

Value = 81,753(1.0886)/(0.1355 − 0.0886) = 1897.576 billion. The market capitalization of ICBC on 26/12/2014 was 1624 billion CNY.[5]

6.2.5.2 Estimation of growth rate from fundamentals

The growth rate of ICBC can be estimated from the fundamentals.

The dividend payout ratio in 2014 was 30.2%. The return on equity was 20.88%.[6]

Retention ratio in 2014 = 1 − 0.302 = 0.698
Return on equity = 0.2088.

Growth rate = Retention ratio ∗ return on equity = 0.698 ∗ 0.2088 = 14.57%. The implied growth rate (g) can be estimated from the market price and DPS in the year 2014.

$$5.460 = 0.24(1 + g)$$

Solving the implied growth rate is 21.75%.

6.2.5.3 Valuation of ICBC using the two-stage DDM model

The actual average growth rate in EPS during the period 2010−2014 was 15%. The average ROE during the period 2010−2014 was 22%. The average dividend payout during 2010−2014 was 31.90%. Hence, the RR during the above period is 68.1%.

The estimated growth rate from fundamentals = Average ROE ∗ average retention ratio = 0.22 ∗ 0.681 = 15%.

The high growth rate period is considered to be 5 years, wherein EPS will grow by 15%. The dividend payout during this period is estimated to be the average payout during the period 2010−2014 (31.90%).

Current year EPS (2014) = 0.78

The cost of equity is estimated in the previous section as 13.55%. This estimate is considered as the cost of equity during the high-growth phase period.

The high growth period is the period 2015−2019. Table 6.2 shows the present value calculation of ICBC using DPS during the high growth period.

Estimation of present value of ICBC during the stable phase growth period.

The inputs for the stable phase period are given below:

[5] http://quotes.morningstar.com/stock/s?t = 601398&region = chn&culture = en-US.
[6] http://financials.morningstar.com/ratios/r.html?t = 601398&region = chn&culture = en-US.

Table 6.2 **Calculation of present value of ICBC during the high growth period**

	1	2	3	4	5
EPS	0.90	1.03	1.19	1.36	1.57
Payout ratio	0.319	0.319	0.319	0.319	0.319
DPS	0.29	0.33	0.38	0.44	0.50
Cost of equity	0.1355	0.1355	0.1355	0.1355	0.1355
PV	$0.25	$0.26	$0.26	$0.26	$0.27
Sum					$1.29

Value of the share of ICBC in high growth period = 1.29 CNY.

Table 6.3 **Estimation of average ROE of Chinese banking sector[a]**

Year	Average ROE of all China banks (%)
2007	16.7
2008	17.1
2009	16.2
2010	17.5
2011	19.2
2012	19
2013	18.5
Average	17.74

[a]Data collected from http://www.statista.com/statistics/278023/return-on-equity-of-banks-in-china-since-2007/.

The Chinese government 10-year bond yield averaged 3.73% from 2005 until 2014. The risk-free rate is assumed to be 3.73% (Table 6.3).

Stable phase growth rate = Retention ratio * return on equity
RR = Stable phase growth rate/stable phase growth rate

The average ROE for Chinese banks for the period 2007−2013 was 17.74%. This is the average ROE of all banks in China during the period 2007−2013. It is assumed that in the long run, the average ROE of all Chinese banks would be 15%. The growth rate is assumed to be 3% in the stable phase period which is set below the risk-free rate of 3.73%.

RR = Growth rate/return on equity
RR = g/ROE = 3%/0.15% = 20%.
Dividend payout ratio = 1 − RR = 1 − 0.20 = 0.80.

The RR is assumed to be 20%. The bank in the long run will retain 20% of earnings and payout 80% of earnings as dividends.

The stable phase is assumed to begin in the year 2020 after 5 years of high-growth period.

EPS in 2020 = EPS in 2019 $(1 + g)$ where g is the growth rate.
= $1.57(1 + g) = 1.57 * 1.03 = 1.6171$
DPS = EPS $*$ DPO = $1.6171 * 0.80 = 1.29$

Cost of equity calculation in stable phase.
The cost of equity in the stable phase growth period is assumed to be the same as the high-growth period cost of equity that 13.55%.

The terminal or continuing value = DPS in year 2020/(cost of equity − growth rate)
= $1.29/(0.1355 − 0.03) = 12.23$
The present value of the terminal price = $12.23/(1.1355)^5 = 6.48$.
The value of ICBC today = $1.29 + 6.48 = 7.77$ CNY

The detailed calculations for the estimation of value of ICBC through DDM models is provided in the spreadsheet DDM ICBC.xlsx.

6.2.6 Valuation of Reliance Industries Ltd using DDM

Reliance Group founded by Dhirubhai Ambani is India's largest private sector enterprise with businesses in the energy and materials value chain. Reliance Industries Ltd (RIL) is a Fortune Global 500 company and is the largest private sector company in the world. Reliance had adopted backward vertical integration as its strategy for growth. Starting with textiles businesses in late 1970s, the company expanded into petrochemicals, petroleum refining and marketing, oil and gas exploration and production, thereby fully integrated along the materials and energy value chain. Reliance is the world's largest polyester yam and fiber producer in the world. It is also among the top 10 petrochemical producers in the world.

RIL had an average net income of 170,355.3 million INR during the last 10-year period 2005−2014. During the same period, the company had an EPS of INR 58.425. The company paid total dividend of 15,837 million INR during this 10-year period. The 5-year (2010−2014) average net income was INR 213,568.2 million. The average EPS during the 5-year period was INR 72.08. The average dividend paid during the 5-year period was INR 2105.6 million. The average dividend payout in percent during the 5-year period was 10.92%. The geometric mean-based growth rate of net income was 8.5% during the period 2010−2014. The average growth rate of EPS during the 5-year period was 7.2%. The average growth rate of DPS was 6.8% and 6.7% based on arithmetic and geometric mean values.

In section 6.2.6.1 and 6.2.6.2, RIL is valued using both the constant growth DDM and two-stage DDM.

The cost of equity for the Gordon model is estimated as given below.

The India government 10-year bond yield of 7.98% is assumed as the risk-free rate. The average yield on 10-year government of India bond during the period 1994−2014 were 9.21%.[7] The risk premium is estimated as the difference between the average returns on market index BSE SENSEX and the risk-free rate. The average returns on BSE SENSEX during the period 2005−2014 was 17.01%.

---

[7] http://www.tradingeconomics.com/india/government-bond-yield.

Risk premium = 17.01% − 7.98% = 9.03%

Beta value is estimating by regressing the stock returns on the market index returns based on 3 years of weekly data.[8] The estimated beta value was 1.14.

Cost of equity = Risk-free rate + beta * risk premium
= 7.98 + 1.14 * 9.03 = 18.27%

Estimation of value per share of RIL through constant growth DDM

Dividend per share paid in year 2014 = INR 9.5.

The growth rate for the constant growth DDM is based on the average growth rate of GDP of India during the past 10 years. The 10-year average growth rate is calculated as 7.53%.[9]

Value = Current DPS (1 + growth rate)/(cost of equity − growth rate) = Current DPS (1 + g)/(r − g) = 9.5(1.0753)/(0.1827 − 0.0753) = INR 95.11

Reliance paid DPS of INR 9.5 during the year 2014 which was 95% of the par value of the share. Reliance Industries was trading at INR 894.75 on December 29, 2014.

6.2.6.1   Estimation of value of equity

The amount of dividend paid in the year 2014 was INR 2531 million. Applying the Gordon model to value the equity in stable growth phase.

Value = Dividend 2014(1 + g)/(r − g) = 2531(1.0753)/(0.1827 − 0.0753) = INR 25,340.64 million.

The market value of Reliance was INR 2892.5 billion in December 2014. The dividend yield was 1.07%. Hence in terms of market value of RIL, the dividend paid was very less.

6.2.6.2   Valuation of RIL using the two-stage DDM

The average growth rate of DPS was 8% during the period 2010−2014. The average growth rate of earnings per share was 10% during the period 2010−2014. The average dividend payout was 10.92% during the above 5-year period. In the two-stage DDM, value is estimated as the combination of value in high and stable growth period. The high growth period is assumed to be 10 years followed by stable phase growth period. The value of RIL share in the stable period is determined by the Gordon model.

[8] The index chosen was NSE index.
[9] Data collected from http://data.worldbank.org/indicator/NY.GDP.MKTP.KD.ZG.

6.2.6.3   Estimation of growth rate from fundamentals

The growth rate of the company can be estimated from its fundamental variables of ROE and RR (Table 6.4).

g = ROE * RR

Expected ROE for the next 10 years is assumed to be 13%.

Expected retention ratio = (1 − payout ratio).

The average payout ratio during the 5-year period 2010−2014 was 10.92%.

Expected retention ratio = 1 − 0.1092 = 0.8908.

RIL is expected to reinvest 89% of its earnings back to the firm.

Expected growth rate = ROE * retention ratio
= 0.13 * 0.8908 = 12%

The expected growth rate in EPS for the high growth period is estimated to be 12% from the fundamentals of the firm.
The EPS in the current year (2014) was INR 76.55[10]

EPS next year = EPS 2014(1 + g) where g = 12%

The high growth period is 2015−2024 (10-year period) (Table 6.5).

Table 6.4 Average ROE RIL

Year	ROE (%)
2010	18.64
2011	13.02
2012	12.13
2013	11.82
2014	11.76
Average	13

Table 6.5 Present value of RIL share in high growth period

	1	2	3	4	5	6	7	8	9	10
EPS	85.74	96.02	107.55	120.45	134.91	151.10	169.23	189.53	212.28	237.75
Payout	0.1092	0.1092	0.1092	0.1092	0.1092	0.1092	0.1092	0.1092	0.1092	0.1092
DPS	9.36	10.49	11.74	13.15	14.73	16.50	18.48	20.70	23.18	25.96
COE	0.1827	0.1827	0.1827	0.1827	0.1827	0.1827	0.1827	0.1827	0.1827	0.1827
PV	7.92	7.50	7.10	6.72	6.37	6.03	5.71	5.41	5.12	4.85
Sum										62.71

[10] 1US$ = 63.67 Indian Rupees (INR) as of December 29, 2014.

6.2.6.4 Inputs for stable growth estimates

The risk-free rate is assumed to be 7% which is approximately equal to the 10-year yield on India government bond with rate of 7.98% in 2014.

> Growth rate in stable period = Retention ratio $*$ ROE. The growth rate in stable period is assumed to be the risk-free rate of 7%.
> Retention ratio = Growth rate/ROE

The average ROE of the oil and gas refining and marketing sector in India in the year 2014 was 17.3%.[11] Hence, the average ROE in the stable phase is proxied as taken as 17.3%.

> Retention ratio in stable phase period = Growth rate in stable growth phase/return on equity
> = 7%/17.3% = 0.40
> Dividend payout ratio = 1 − Retention ratio = 1 − 0.40 = 0.60

RIL is expected to retain 40% of its earnings and payout 60% of its earnings as dividends during the stable period on the basis of fundamental assumptions on growth rate and return on equity.

The stable phase starts from 2025 onward. EPS in 2024 = 237.75

> EPS in 2025 = 237.75(1 + 7%) = INR 254.39
> DPS in 2025 = 254.39 $*$ 0.60 = INR 152.64

Assume that in the stable period, the beta will drop to1, the value of market beta. Hence, the cost of equity in the stable period is estimated as follows:

> Cost of equity = 7% + 1 $*$ 9.03% = 16.03%
> Terminal or continuing value = DPS in 2025 (1 + g)/(r − g)
> = 152.64(1.07)/(0.1603 − 0.07) = INR 1808.69
> Present value of terminal value of RIL share = 1808.69/$(1.1827)^{10}$ = INR 337.77
> Value of RIL stock = PV of RIL during high growth period + PV of RIL during stable phase period.
> Value = 337 + 62.71 = INR 400.48.

RIL was trading at INR 894.75 on December 29, 2014.

The comparison of estimated value from DDM with the market value of RIL suggests that DDM is not suited to analyze the value of RIL.

The spreadsheet *DDM RELIANCE INDUSTRIES.xlsx* provides the estimation of value of RIL through dividend models in detail.

6.3 FCF valuation models

Dividends are the cash flow that is actually paid to the shareholders while FCF is the cash flow available to the shareholders. Many analysts suggest that FCF models are more significant and relevant than DDMs.

---

[11] *Source*: Industry Center Yahoo Finance : https://biz.yahoo.com/ic/122.html.

FCF can be categorized as FCFE and FCFF. FCF to equity is the cash flow available to common stockholders. FCF to firm is the cash flow available to common stockholders, debt holders, and preferred stockholders.

FCFF is the cash flow available to all the suppliers of capital for the firm after the firm pays for all operating expenses and expenditures incurred for investment purposes. The investment expenditures include capital expenditures and working capital investments. The main suppliers of capital for the firm are common stockholders, bondholders, and preferred stockholders.

6.3.1 FCFE

FCFE is the residual cash flow available to shareholders. It is a measure of potential dividends which a firm can pay to its shareholders. It is the residual cash flow after taxes, interest expenses, and reinvestment needs. The reinvestment needs for a firm consists of capital expenditures and working capital.

FCFE = net income − capital expenditure + depreciation & amortization − change in noncash working capital + new debt issued − debt repayment.

Thus the basic formula for calculation of FCF to equity is net income minus net capital expenditure (Capital expenditure − depreciation and amortization) minus change in noncash working capital plus net borrowing.

The cash flow from operations stated in the firm's financial statements is not the same as FCF. The unadjusted financial earnings measure like EBITDA does not give an exact description of the FCF available to the firm's providers of capital.

Net income often known as bottom line is the firm's earnings after expenses which include interest expenses and taxes. The capital expenditure which is the capital used for long-term or fixed assets can be found in the firm's cash flow statement. Depreciation is normally the largest noncash adjustment and is added back to net income to get FCFE.

The difference between capital expenditures and depreciation is known as net capital expenditure. High-growth firms tend to have high net capital expenditures in relation to income, whereas low-growth firms have lesser net capital expenditures or even negative net capital expenditures. Increases in working capital is a cash outflow while decreases in cash outflow is a cash inflow. High-growth firms require high working capital requirements. In FCFE estimation, only changes in noncash working capital is considered to measure cash flow effects. Noncash working capital is obtained as the difference between noncash current assets and current liabilities (excluding short-term debt). In other words, for the estimation of working capital, we need to deduct cash and cash equivalents from current assets and interest bearing short-term debt from current liabilities. In FCFE valuation, the effects of changes in the levels of debts on cash flows are also considered. Repayment of debt which is a cash outflow may be partially or fully financed by the issue of new debt which is a cash inflow. Hence, the net effect of the cash flow effects need to be estimated in FCFE valuation. Net borrowing is the difference between the amount a company borrows and the amount which it repays. Interest is excluded in net borrowing as it is accounted in the calculation of net income. Net borrowing is obtained by comparing changes of long-term debt on a company's balance sheet.

The equity reinvestment rate in the firm can be obtained as the ratio of equity reinvestment to the net income. The equity reinvestment is obtained as capital expenditure minus depreciation plus changes in noncash working capital plus net borrowing.

FCFF is considered to a more preferable method of equity valuation when FCFE is negative or when capital structure is unstable.

As mentioned earlier, FCF to equity is the amount available to the shareholders, but it is not the amount that is paid out to shareholders. Ideally, if a company don't have enough investment opportunities, it should pay its FCFE as dividends to shareholders. Positive FCFE signals the ability of the firm to payout dividends or buyback of stocks without comprising on firm's operations or growth opportunities. Negative FCFE often implies that firm must issue new equity to raise funds. FCFE valuation method is more popular that DDMs among analysts. The ratio of cash flow returned to shareholders (dividends plus stock buybacks) to FCFE measures how much of the cash available have been actually paid out to the shareholders through dividends and stock buyback schemes. If the ratio is less than 1, the firm pays out cash less than it can afford. In this case, the firm uses the excess cash to increase cash balance or make investments in marketable securities. A ratio greater than 1 indicates that the firm is paying beyond its capacity and is using the cash reserves or issue of new securities to fund the payout schemes.

Firms may pay less cash than its FCFE in order to build up cash reserves for future unexpected capital expansion plans. Volatility of earnings may also force firms to adopt conservative approach with respect to dividend payout policy. Restrictions placed by bondholders may also become detrimental factor for payment of dividends. A firm may also payout much less in dividends if dividends are taxed at a higher rate than capital gains. Dividend policy is often sticky and managers are reluctant to change the level of dividends.

6.3.1.1   FCFE valuation models

Basically, there are two ways of estimating equity value through FCFs. In the first method, the FCFF estimated is discounted by the WACC to get the firm value. The value of the firm's debt is then subtracted to calculate the equity value. In the second method, the value of equity is obtained by discounting the FCFE cash flows by the required return on equity (cost of equity).

6.3.1.2   The constant growth or single-stage FCFE model

The constant growth FCFE model values organizations which are in steady state. The equity value is given by:

$$\text{Firm value} = \frac{\text{FCFF}_1}{\text{WACC} - \text{g}}$$

Equity value = Firm value − debt value

$$\text{Equity value} = \frac{FCFE_1}{r - g}$$

Where $FCFF_1$ is the expected FCFF next year, WACC is the weighted average cost of capital, g is the growth rate of FCFF/FCFE in the stable period for ever, $FCFE_1$ is the expected FCFE next year, and r is the cost of equity of the firm.

The expected growth rate in FCFE = Equity reinvestment rate ∗ noncash ROE
Equity reinvestment rate = Capital expenditures − depreciation + changes in noncash working capital − net debt issues/net income.
Noncash ROE = Net income − after-tax income from cash and marketable securities/ book value of equity − cash and marketable securities.

The constant growth model can be used to value firms which are growing at a comparable rate to that of the growth rate of the economy.

6.3.1.3 Two-stage FCFE model

This model assumes that the FCFE will have an initial high growth phase followed by stable growth phase. The model makes the assumption that there would be initially high growth earnings and large capital expenditures. The FCFE might be low or negative in the initial phase. In the stable phase on account of increased competition, earnings growth slows down and stabilizes. During this period, capital expenditure declines and increases in FCFE may be observed. The growth rates are determined using the growth rate in sales or net income or FCF. Expected growth rate in FCFE in high growth period can also be determined from fundamentals.

The growth rate of FCFE in the stable period can be assumed to be that of the economic growth rate. The reinvestment rate is obtained as follows:

Reinvestment rate = Growth rate of economy/average ROE of the industry sector of the firm.

$$\text{Equity value} = \sum_{t=1}^{n} \frac{FCFE_t}{(1+r)^t} + \frac{FCFE_{n+1}}{(r-g)} + \frac{1}{(1+r)^n}$$

$FCFE_t$ is the FCF to equity in initial high growth period; $FCFE_{n+1}$ is the FCFE at the beginning of the stable growth period; r is the cost of equity, g is the stable growth rate.

FCFE models can be applied to companies which do not pay dividends or pay unsustainable dividends. FCFE model can be more useful when valuing a company on the basis of control perspective for majority shareholder on how to use the equity cash flows. The models of DDM reflects the viewpoint of small shareholders who does not have control over the firm in real sense.

6.3.1.4 Three-stage FCFE model

This model can be applied to cover three stages of the growth life cycle of a company—an initial high phase of growth rate followed by slower growth period and finally the matured period. The model estimates the present value of expected FCF to equity over all the three stages of growth.

Estimation of FCFE from cash flow from operations (CFO)

FCFE = CFO − fixed capital investment + net borrowing

Estimation of FCFE from FCFF

FCFE = FCFF − (interest expense ∗ (1 − tax rate) + net borrowing.

Estimation of FCFE on FCF basis

FCFE = Change in cash balance + net payments to stockholders.

Where net payments to stockholders = cash dividends + share repurchases − stock issuances

6.3.2 FCFF

FCFF is the sum of the cash flows to all the suppliers of capital to the firm which includes stockholders, bondholders, and preference shareholders. The FCFF approach of valuation is more appropriate when the firm's FCFE is negative and when the capital structure is unstable. When the financial leverage is unstable, the ROE used for estimation of growth rate will be more volatile. FCFF growth rate estimated from historical data can be a better estimate of the fundamentals than the FCFE growth rate.

FCFF = FCFE + interest expense (1 − T) + principal repayments − new debt issues + preferred dividends.
FCFF = EBIT (1 − T) + Depreciation − capital expenditure − change in working capital.

FCFF is the cash flow prior to debt payments and is often termed as unlevered cash flow. The after-tax cost of debt is considered in the cost of capital estimation.

6.3.2.1 FCFF models

6.3.2.1.1 Single-stage FCFF model
The FCFF approach says that the value of the firm is equal to next period's FCFF discounted by the WACC minus the stable growth rate (g) in FCFF.

Firm value = $FCFF_1$/WACC − g

where $FCFF_1$ is the FCFF next period, WACC is the weighted average cost of capital, and g is the growth rate in the stable growth period. The assumption made is that growth rate used in the model is less than the growth rate of the economy.

Expected growth rate in operating income = Reinvestment rate ∗ return on capital.

Growth in operating income can be expected to be lower than growth in net income as return on capital employed will be lower than return on equity. Note that capital employed consists of both equity and debt. Finance theory suggests that in a scenario whereby firms borrows funds and invests in projects to give returns higher than the after-tax cost of debt, then return on equity will be higher than return on capital. Hence during the high growth stage, the growth rate in equity income would be more than the growth rate in operating income. In stable phase, the growth rates in equity income and operating income are expected to converge (Damodaran, 2012).

6.3.2.1.2 Two-stage FCFF model
This model is used when a firm's growth rate is expected to decelerate in the future and stabilize at a rate g. Analysts often use growth rates of sales, earnings, or some measures of fundamentals to forecast growth rates of FCFs. The terminal value is estimated using the one-stage growth model. Then the present value of terminal price is estimated using the discount rate (WACC) of the initial high growth period. The present value of terminal price is added to the present value of cash flows in the high growth period to get the value of the firm.

$$\text{Firm value} = \sum_{t=1}^{n} \frac{\text{FCFF}_t}{(1+\text{WACC})^t} + \frac{\text{FCFF}_{n+1}}{(\text{WACC} - g)} \frac{1}{(1+\text{WACC})^n}$$

Reinvestment rate in stable growth period = Growth rate/return on capital

6.3.2.1.3 Three-stage FCFF model
The three-stage model of FCFF is based on an initial high growth phase, a transition phase, and a stable phase period.

6.3.2.1.4 Adjustments for estimation of FCFF
The adjustments for capital expenditures like R&D expenses and operating leases have been discussed in detail in Chapter 5. Depreciation is added back to $\text{EBIT}(1 - T)$ to determine FCFF. The amortized expenses of intangibles and restructuring expenses in the form of noncash event must be added back to net income to determine FCFF. Restructuring income which is noncash in nature (e.g., capital gain) must be subtracted to find out FCFF. Similarly, capital loss would be added back. Adjustments must reflect the additional shares which will result on the exercise of ESOPs for the determination of forecasted FCFF per share. Changes in deferred tax liabilities needs to be added back to the net income if the firm tends to consistently defer taxes in future.

6.3.2.1.5 Determination of FCFF from EBITDA
FCFF = EBITDA(1 − tax rate) + depreciation (tax rate) − capital expenditure − change in working capital.

In estimation of FCFF with EBITDA, the depreciation tax shield is added back since the depreciation tax shield saves the firms on taxes. EBITDA refers to earnings before interest, taxes, depreciation, and amortization.

6.3.2.1.6   Determination of FCFF from cash flow from operations

FCFF = CFO + interest (1 − tax rate) − fixed capital investment.

6.3.2.1.7   Determination of FCFF on uses of FCF Basis

FCFF = Change in cash balance + net payments to debt holders + net payments to stockholders.

6.3.2.1.8   Forecasting FCFE and FCFF

The growth rate for forecasting FCFE and FCFF can be based on historical FCF under the assumption that firm fundamentals are unchanged. Alternately, forecasting of growth rates can be based on each component of FCF. Capital expenditure can be related to sales. A firm is assumed to maintain a constant target debt financing ratio for net new investment in fixed capital and working capital while forecasting FCFE. FCFF can be forecasted as the after-tax EBIT minus the change in capital expenditures and working capital investments.

6.3.2.1.9   Advantages and disadvantages of DCF method

DCF is the most sound method of valuation. DCF is forward looking as the model depends on future expectations than historical results. DCF analysis is focused on cash flow generation and is less affected by accounting practices and assumptions. DCF method allows different operating strategies to be incorporated into the valuation. Different components of business or synergies can be valued separately in the DCF analysis.

The correctness of DCF depends on the assumptions made with respect to FCF, growth rate, discount rate, and terminal value. It is difficult to make exact realistic assumptions. Hence, analysts analyze difference scenarios for estimation of various parameters or inputs for DCFs. The terminal value represents a large percentage of total DCF valuation. Hence, valuation predominantly depends on the terminal assumptions rather than operating assumptions for the DCF.

6.3.2.1.10   Zero growth valuation model

This model assumes that FCF is constant in perpetuity. The value of the firm at time zero is the discounted or capitalized or discounted value of its annual cash flows.

Value of firm = $FCFF_0/WACC$
Value of equity = $FCFE_0/Ke$

Where $FCFF_0$ and $FCFE_0$ are the FCFF and FCFE at time period 0. WACC and Ke are the weighted average cost of capital and cost of equity.

6.4   Adjusted present value method

Adjusted present value (APV) method is used to value companies as well as projects. In the APV method, the value of the firm is obtained as its value as an all equity firm plus the discounted value of the interest tax shield from the debt funds. The APV is basically an investment appraisal technique in which instead of using weighted average cost of capital as the discount rate, the unlevered (ungeared) cost of equity is used to discount the cash flows from the project along with an adjustment for tax shield of debt capital raised. In a theoretical sense, the APV method converges the impact of growth as well as the tax shield of debt on the cost of equity, systematic risk, and cost of capital. The difference between APV and NPV is that in APV the discount rate used is cost of equity rather than WACC in NPV. APV calculation includes tax shields. APV analysis is suited for highly leveraged transactions.

6.4.1   Steps in APV estimation

In the APV approach, the value of the firm is estimated as follows:

1. Estimation of value of unlevered firm

   The first step involves the estimation of the value of the company with no leverage by calculating the NPV with cost of equity as the discount rate. The expected FCFF is discounted by the unlevered (ungeared) cost of equity. If the firm is in stable growth phase, then the value of the firm is obtained as follows:

   Value of unlevered firm = $FCFF_1/Re - g$, where Re is the unlevered cost of equity, g is the expected growth rate.

   The cost of equity is obtained through the CAPM model.

   $R_e = R_f + \beta_u (R_m - R_f)$ where β_u is the unlevered beta, cost of equity, R_f is the risk-free rate, $R_m - R_f$ is the risk premium.

   $\beta_u = \beta_L/[1 + (1 - T)D/E$

   where β_u is the unlevered beta of the firm, β_L is the current beta or levered beta which can be estimated from regression estimation. T is the tax rate and D/E is the debt equity ratio.

2. Expected tax benefits from borrowed funds

   The next step is to calculate the expected tax benefit from a given level of debt financing. The estimated tax benefit is discounted at the cost of debt. The NPV of the tax effects is then added to the base NPV.

   Value of tax benefits = Tax rate * cost of debt * debt/cost of debt.

   = Tax rate * Debt

3. Estimation of expected bankruptcy costs.

   The third step involves the evaluation of the effect of borrowing the amount on the probability that the firm will go bankrupt and the expected cost of bankruptcy. In the APV method, the primary benefit of borrowing is the tax benefit and the most significant cost of borrowing is the increased risk due to bankruptcy.

   Present Value of expected bankruptcy cost = Probability of bankruptcy * Bankruptcy costs.

   The probability of bankruptcy can be based on empirical estimates of default probabilities (for example Altman study) for the ratings of bonds (Altman and Kishore, 2000).

Another method used is a statistical approach like probit to estimate the probability of default based on firm characteristics. The bankruptcy costs are estimated to be 25–30% of the firm value (Shapiro, 1989; Titman, 1984).

Theoretically, the APV method brings together the impact of growth as well as the tax shield of debt on the cost of equity, systematic risk, and cost of capital. Therefore, it comes up to be a more flexible technique to approach valuation as compared to other methods. The APV method takes care of financing side effects such as subsidies on loans.

Current firm value = Value of unlevered firm + present value of tax benefits − expected bankruptcy costs.

6.5 Value of nonoperating assets

Cash and near-cash investments that exceed the operating cash requirements are considered as nonoperating assets and added to the value of the estimated operating assets. The current market value of the marketable securities are estimated and added to the value of operating assets. With respect to crossholdings, firms have minority passive (<20% of overall ownership of the firm) minority active (between 20% and 50% of overall ownership) and majority activity investments (> 50% of overall ownership). The value of the equity in each holding is found out, and the value of the proportional holdings is estimated and added to the value of equity of parent company.

With respect to overfunded pension plans (pension assets greater than liabilities), the after-tax portion of the excess funds is added to the estimated value of the firm.

6.6 Estimation of total value of firm

The sum of the value of the operating assets, cash and marketable securities, and other nonoperating assets owned by the firm are added to get the firm value.

6.6.1 Estimation of equity value of firm

The value of debt is subtracted from the total value to get the equity value. A number of adjustments with respect to nonequity claims are required to be made. If the operating leases are capitalized as debt, then the debt value of operating leases must be subtracted from the value of operating assets to estimate the value of equity. Other nonequity claims like expected liabilities on lawsuits, unfunded pension and health care obligations, and present value of deferred tax liabilities are deducted from the value of operating assets to arrive at equity value.

Value of equity = Value of operating assets + cash and marketable securities + value of minority holdings in other companies − value of interest bearing debt − present value of operating lease commitments − unfunded healthcare or pension obligations − expected litigation payouts.

The effects of options outstanding must be incorporated into the value per share. The value of equity estimated is divided by the fully diluted number of shares based on the assumption that all options outstanding will be exercised. A more effective method is to estimate the value of the option using option pricing model.

Value of equity per share = Value of equity − value of options outstanding/number of shares outstanding.

6.7 Theoretical perspectives on free cash flow valuation

Cash flow is the basis for the DCF valuation. There are several popular cash flow metrics like EBITDA and cash earnings. EBITDA refers to earnings before interest, taxes, depreciation, and amortization. The discounted FCF methodology has become the primary valuation model for professional analysts with the development of CAPM. Cash earnings refer to net income plus depreciation and amortization. In their classical paper titled "Dividend Policy, Growth and the Valuation of Shares," Miller and Modigliani (1961) suggest that the DCF was the most reliable method to estimate the value of a cash generating assets. M&M state that the value of the company is the present value of its future expected stream of operating profits net of the new capital investment required to sustain the business. They suggest the usage of 5- or 10-year forecasting period. M&M provide two basic analytical approaches to valuation. In the DCF approach, the operating profits net of new investments is termed as cash receipts. The valuation measure is arrived as cash receipts minus cash outlays which include capital additions. The cash flows are estimated for a number of years and then a terminal value is added. The second method known as investment opportunities approach expresses a company's value as the sum of two components: the capitalized present value of the firm's current operating profit (assumed to continue forever at the present level) plus a "growth" term, which reflects the firm's expected ability to earn returns in excess of its cost of capital on its new investments above and beyond those currently held by the firm. Stern (1974) defined FCF as net operating profit after taxes minus the amount of new capital invested. Some companies consider FCF as CFO minus capital expenditures. Amount spend on M&A and other strategic investments, financing payments like preferred and common dividends are also included in expenditures. FCF includes interest, taxes, capital expenditures and excludes issuance or repurchase of debt. The reported cash flows are defined differently in different sets of accounting standards such as GAAP. Under IFRS, companies when reporting cash from operations can choose to include or exclude both interest paid and interest received. The appropriate measure for valuing the firm's enterprise value is FCFF and that for valuing equity is FCFE. Price to FCF multiple and its reciprocal known as the "cash flow yield" is an emergent popular valuation tool.

6.8 Research studies on FCF models

The study by Deloof et al. (2009) suggests that discounted FCF model is the most popular method adopted by investment banks to determine the offer price for an initial public offering (IPO), which tends to produce the least biased estimates. O'Brien (2003) developed a variant of the FCF methodology to value firms with expected declining growth or negative earnings or even negative FCF. Jensen (1986) suggests the existence of agency conflict between shareholders and managers when firms generate substantial FCF. Estridge and Lougee (2007) and Lauricella (2008) suggest that the increased popularity of the FCF-based valuation method is due to the perception that cash is less vulnerable to manipulation than earnings. Hackel et al. (2000) suggest that FCF captures information about permanent earnings which GAAP earnings fail to capture. Studies by Damodaran (1994) and Koller et al. (2010) suggest that the after-tax cash flow generated by a firm, which is available for distribution to all claimholders is the correct metric to value an enterprise. The paper by Chen et al. (2011) examine the effect of shareholder rights on reducing the cost of equity and the impact of agency problems from FCF on this effect. The study finds that firms with strong shareholder rights have a significantly lower implied cost of equity after controlling for risk factors, price momentum, analysts' forecast biases, and industry and year effects than do firms with weak shareholder rights. Habib (2011) based on accounting-based valuation framework regresses stock returns on FCF variable interacted with growth and earnings quality proxies and finds that firms with positive FCF and attractive growth opportunities command a valuation premium. The study by Tole et al. (1992) points that FCF is a better measure of performance in capital intensive companies. Accounting standards like US GAAP does not require firms to disclose FCFs. Many cash flow studies like Dechow (1994), Bowen et al. (1986), Livnat and Zarowin (1990) focused on operating cash flows to explain performance as measured by abnormal stock returns.

Burgstahler et al. (1998) find that cash flow have more predictive ability than earnings. Nunez (2013) points that significant difference exists between operating cash flow and net income. Nunez (2014) suggests that FCF have better explanatory power for firm performance in terms of stock returns. Awasthi et al. (2013) finds that FCF measured as cash distributed to claimholders, adjusted for accounting distortions and omissions plus net change in surplus cash produces more accurate valuation.

6.9 Estimation of value of Hyundai Motors through FCFE and FCFF valuation models

Hyundai Motor Company is a major South Korean multinational automotive manufacturer, which is headquartered in Seoul, South Korea. The company was established in 1967. Along with its 32.8% stake in subsidiary Kia Motors, Hyundai Motor Company forms the Hyundai Motor Group. In 2013, Hyundai Motors ranked among the top 50 global brands and sold 4.62 million vehicles worldwide. Hyundai vehicles are sold in 193 countries through 6000 dealerships and show rooms. The company paid an average dividend of €0.83 per share during the period 2010—2014. The average dividend yield was 2.5% during the period 2010—2014.

6.9.1 Valuation of Hyundai Motors through FCFE model

(Tables 6.6–6.10).

Table 6.6 Estimation of adjusted capital expenditure in millions of Korean won

Year	R&D expenses	Amortization	Adjusted R&D expenses	CAPEX	Adjusted CAPEX = CAPEX + adjusted R&D expenses
2009	663,384	110,703	552,681	7,646,317	8,198,998
2010	952,324	88,488	863,836	2,875,945	3,739,781
2011	632,003	124,192	507,811	3,662,411	4,170,222
2012	686,606	84,468	602,138	3,798,645	4,400,783
2013	722,732	40,791	681,941	4,162,157	4,844,098

Table 6.7 Estimation of change in working capital (CWC) in million Korean won

	2008	2009	2010	2011	2012	2013
Noncash current assets	28,121,670	22,818,876	29,760,280	33,178,346	35,528,675	36,600,566
Noncash current liabilities	26,470,280	21,086,254	15,586,313	16,963,300	18,141,609	17,941,630
Working capital	1,651,390	1,732,622	14,173,967	16,215,046	17,387,066	18,658,936
Change in working capital		81,232	12,441,345	2,041,079	1,172,020	1,271,870

Noncash current assets = Total current assets − total cash.
Noncurrent liabilities = Total liabilities − short-term debt.

Table 6.8 Estimation of FCFE

Year	Net income	Depreciation & amortization	Adjusted CAPEX	Change in working capital	Debt issued	Debt repaid	FCFE
2009	3,056,017	3,682,010	8,198,998	81,232	23,364,329	27,563,022	−5,740,896
2010	5,567,132	2,154,780	3,739,781	12,441,345	32,888,633	27,043,429	−2,614,010
2011	7,655,871	2,334,757	4,170,222	2,041,079	43,978,974	39,998,261	7,760,040
2012	8,561,825	2,523,919	4,400,783	1,172,020	23,448,538	20,595,164	8,366,315
2013	8,541,834	2,551,338	4,844,098	1,271,870	23,632,277	17,533,905	11,075,576
Total	33,382,679	13,246,804	25,353,882	17,007,546	147,312,751	132,733,781	18,847,025

Table **6.9** **Calculation of year end accumulated R&D in million Korean won**

	2009	2010	2011	2012	2013
Beginning balance[a]	696,355	1,249,036	2,112,872	2,620,683	3,222,821
Annual R&D expense	663,384	952,324	632,003	686,606	722,732
Annual amortization	110,703	88,488	124,192	84,468	40,791
Ending balance (accumulated R&D)	1,249,036	2,112,872	2,620,683	3,222,821	3,904,762

[a]The R&D expenses in 2008 is the beginning balance of R&D in the year 2009. The R&D expenses in 2008 was 696,355 in the year 2009.

Table **6.10** **Adjusted book value of equity in million Korean won**

Value in million dollars	2009	2010	2011	2012	2013
Book value of equity	29,765,639	32,887,973	40,327,702	47,917,575	56,582,789
Accumulated R&D	1,249,036	2,112,872	2,620,683	3,222,821	3,904,762
Adjusted book value of equity	31,014,675	35,000,845	42,948,385	51,140,396	60,487,551

6.9.2 Inputs for valuation models

The average ROE of the auto industry is 10.7%.[12] The growth rate of South Korean economy is taken as a proxy for estimation of growth rate in the long run or stable growth period.[13]

Year	GDP growth rate (%)
2005	3.9
2006	5.2
2007	5.5
2008	2.8
2009	0.9
2010	6.5
2011	3.7
2012	2.3
2013	3
Average	3.8

[12] The data of ROE of firms collected from http://biz.yahoo.com/p/330qpmd.html.
[13] http://data.worldbank.org/indicator/NY.GDP.PCAP.CD.

The average growth rate of South Korean economy was estimated to be 3.8%. The relationship between reinvestment rate and return is given by the following equation:

The growth rate g = ROE * Reinvestment rate
Reinvestment rate = g/ROE = 3.8%/10.7% = 35.51%.

Hence, it is assumed that the reinvestment rate in the stable growth period is equal to 35.51%.

6.9.3 Estimation of FCFE in the stable phase period

The interest income from cash and cash equivalents is deducted from net income to get the adjusted net income. The expected net income in the next period is estimated by multiplying by 1 + g. The FCFE in the stable phase is obtained by deducting the reinvestment from the expected net income in the stable period.

Net income in year 2013	8,541,834
Interest income from cash and equivalents	3,722,401
Adjusted net income in 2013	4,819,433
Expected net income next period	5,002,571.4
Equity reinvestment	1,775,912.86
FCFE in stable phase period	3,226,658.58

6.9.4 Cost of equity calculation

The South Korea government 10-year bond averaged 4.86% from 2000 until 2015.[14] The risk-free rate is assumed to be 4.86%. The beta value is estimated by regressing the Hyundai weekly returns on the KOSPI Composite market index for the 5-year period (2010–2014). The beta value is 1.229.

The South Korean risk premium = US Market risk premium + default spread for Korea

The US risk premium is assumed to be 5%. The default spread is based on sovereign rating for South Korea. S&P had given sovereign rating of A + for South Korea. The default spread for a S&P rating of A + is 0.72%. The default spread is obtained from bondsonline.com.

South Korean risk premium = 5 + 0.72 = 5.72%
Cost of equity = Risk-free rate + beta * risk premium
= 4.86 + 1.229 * 5.72 = 11.89%

The cost of equity for Hyundai is estimated to be 11.89%.

---

[14] www.tradingeconomics.com.

6.9.5   Zero growth valuation model

In this model, no growth is assumed. The value of operating assets is obtained by discounting the current period FCFE by the cost of equity.

Net income in 2013	8,541,834
Interest income from cash and cash equivalent	3,722,401
Adjusted net income in 2013	4,819,433
Depreciation & amortization	2,551,338
Adjusted CAPEX	4,844,098
Change in noncash working capital	1,271,870
Debt issued	23,632,277
Debt repaid	17,533,905
FCFE in 2013	7,353,175

The value of the operating assets = FCFE in 2013/cost of equity = FCFE/Ke
= 61,843,355.76 million Korean Won.

Adding the value of cash and cash equivalents in 2013, the value of firm = 61,843,355.76 + 22,255,539 = 84,098,894.76 million KRW.

6.9.6   Constant growth rate model (stable growth model)

Value of operating assets = Stable phase FCFE/(cost of equity − growth rate)
= 3,226,658.58/(0.1189 − 0.038) = 39,884,531.37.

The value of operating assets of Hyundai Motors is estimated to be 39,884.531 billion KRW. The market capitalization of Hyundai Motors on Korea Stock Exchange was 37,226.7 billion KRW on January 4, 2015.

The adjusted value of Hyundai Motors = Value of operating assets + value of cash and cash equivalents in 2013.
The adjusted value of firm = 62,140.07 billion KRW.

6.9.7   Two-stage FCFE model

In the two-stage FCFE model, the present value of the FCFE in the high growth period and the present value of the terminal price of FCFE is estimated.
Estimation of growth rate of net income

Year	Net income in million KRW
2009	3,056,017
2010	5,567,132
2011	7,655,871
2012	8,561,825
2013	8,541,834

The geometric mean-based growth rate of net income during the period 2010−2013 was 29%.

6.9.8 Valuation inputs from fundamentals

The growth rate in net income can also be estimated from fundamentals based on ROE and reinvestment rate.

g = Reinvestment rate * noncash ROE
Noncash-adjusted ROE in 2013 = Net income − interest income from cash/(book value of equity − cash and cash equivalents)
8,541,834 − 3,722,401/(60,487,551 − 22,255,539) = 0.126

The noncash ROE is estimated as 12.6%.

Actual reinvestment rate in 2013 = CAPEX − depreciation + Change in working capital/net income.

The actual reinvestment rate in the year 2013 was 73.96%.
The expected growth rate in high growth period is given by

g = Reinvestment rate * noncash ROE
g = 0.1261 * 0.7396 = 9.32%

The growth rate estimated from fundamentals is assumed as the growth rate of net income in the high growth period. The length of high growth period is assumed to be 5 years. The reinvestment rate is assumed to be 73.96% in the high growth period (Tables 6.11 and 6.12).

Adjusted net income in 2013 = 4,819,433 million KRW.
Growth rate = 9.3 %
PV of FCFE during the high growth phase = 5,852,369.97 million KRW.

Table 6.11 Estimation of present value of FCFE in high growth period

	High growth period				
	1	**2**	**3**	**4**	**5**
Net income	5,267,640.269	5,757,530.814	6,292,981.18	6,878,228.429	7,517,903.673
Reinvestment	3,895,946.743	4,258,269.79	4,654,288.881	5,087,137.746	5,560,241.557
FCFE	1,371,693.526	1,499,261.024	1,638,692.299	1,791,090.683	1,957,662.117
PV of FCFE	$12,25,930.40	1,197,552.89	1,169,832.254	1,142,753.288	$11,16,301.14
Sum					*5,852,369.971*

Table 6.12 Estimation of FCFF in millions of KRW

Year	EBIT	1 − Tax rate	EBIT (1 − t)	DEP&AMORT	Adjusted CAPEX	CWC	FCFF
2009	5,001,367	0.758	3,791,036	3,682,010	8,198,998	81,232	−807,184
2010	5,751,607	0.78	4,486,253	2,154,780	3,739,781	12,441,345	−9,540,093
2011	8,101,600	0.758	6,141,013	2,334,757	4,170,222	2,041,079	2,264,469
2012	8,436,947	0.758	6,395,206	2,523,919	4,400,783	1,172,020	3,346,322
2013	8,315,497	0.758	6,303,147	2,551,338	4,844,098	1,271,870	2,738,517

The cost of equity is assumed to be the same in the high growth and stable phase period. The cost of equity is 11.89%.

Stable phase growth period inputs	
Net income at the end of high growth period	7,517,903.673
Net income in the stable period	7,803,584.013
Reinvestment	2,770,272.325
FCFE in the stable phase period	5,033,311.688
Terminal value	62,216,460.92
Present value of terminal price	35,477,167.15

Growth rate of net income = 3.8% (average growth rate of Korean economy).
Reinvestment rate = 35.5% (estimated in the constant stable growth model as discussed in the section 6.9.2).

The value of the operating assets is obtained by adding the sum of the present value of FCFE in the high growth period to the present value of the terminal price.

Present value of operating assets	41,329,537.12
Value of cash and cash equivalents	22,255,539
Value of Hyundai Motors	*63,585,076.12*

Based on the two-stage FCFE model, the value of Hyundai Motors is estimated as 63,585.076 billion KRW.

6.9.9   FCFF valuation of Hyundai

FCFF = EBIT $(1 - T^{15})$ + depreciation − capital expenditure − change in working capital

The actual reinvestment rate was 63.12% in the year 2011, 47.67% in the year 2012, and 56.55% in the year 2013. Workings for adjusted CAPEX is given in the FCFF calculation.

6.9.10   One-stage or constant growth FCFF model

The inputs for the stable phase growth can be determined through fundamentals

Reinvestment rate = CAPEX − Depreciation + Change in noncash working capital/EBIT(1 − T)

The average reinvestment rate during the period 2012−2013 was 52%.

Return on Capital Employed = EBIT(1 − T) in year 2013/Book Value of Equity in 2012 + Book Value of debt in 2012 − Cash and Cash Equivalents in 2012.
Adjusted book value of equity in 2012 = 51,140,396 million Won.
Book value of debt in 2012 = 45,207,252 million Won.

---

[15] http://www.kpmg.com/global/en/services/tax/tax-tools-and-resources/pages/corporate-tax-rates-table.aspx.

6.9.11 Cost of debt calculation

The cost of debt for emerging market company can be calculated as follows.

Cost of debt = Risk-free rate + country default spread + company default spread.

The risk-free rate is 4.86% based on the 10-year bond yield of South Korea. The default spread for South Korea based on S&P rating of A + is 0.72% (country default spread).[16] The company default spread for Hyundai Motors based on S&P rating of BBB + is 1.15% (company default spread)[17]

Cost of debt for Hyundai Motors = 4.86% + 0.72% + 1.15% = 6.73%
Tax rate = 24.2%
After-tax cost of debt (K_d) = 6.73 * (1 − 0.242) = 5.10%
Cost of equity calculated K_e = 11.89% (calculation given in Section 6.3.1)
Weight of debt in Hyundai Motors (W_e) = 45.9%
Weight of equity in Hyundai Motors (W_d) = 54.1%
WACC = $W_e * K_e + W_d * K_d$ = 0.54 * 0.1189 + 0.46 * 0.510 = 0.0877
Thus the weighted average cost of capital is estimated to be 8.77%.
Book value of debt in 2012 = 88,702,115 million KRW
EBIT(1 − T) in 2013 = 6,303,147 million KRW.
Book value of debt in 2012 = 33,988,810 million KRW
Adjusted book value of equity in 2012 = 51,140,396 million KRW
Return on capital = EBIT(1 − T) in 2013/book value of debt in 2012 + adjusted book value of equity in 2012 − cash and marketable securities.
Cash and cash equivalents in 2012 = 3,594,881
Return on capital = 7.73%
Reinvestment rate in 2013 = Adjusted CAPEX − Depreciation + change in noncash working capital/adjusted EBIT(1 − T)

Adjusted CAPEX in 2013	4,844,098
Depreciation in 2013	2,551,338
Change in Noncash working capital in 2013	1,271,870
Adjusted EBIT(1 − T) in 2013	6,303,146.726
Reinvestment rate	0.56
Expected growth rate = Return on capital * reinvestment rate	
6.79% * 56.55%	0.0437

The stable rate growth rate is estimated to be 4.37%.

FCFF in the year 2013 = 2,738,517 million KRW
Value of operating assets = Expected FCFF next period/cost of capital − expected growth rate.
Expected FCFF next period = FCFF in year 2013 * (1 + g) = 2,738,517 * 1.0437 = 2,858,190
WACC = 0.087
Growth rate = 4.37%

---

[16] http://www.standardandpoors.com/en_US/web/guest/ratings/entity/-/org-details/sectorCode/CORP/entityId/310520.
[17] http://www.bondsonline.com/Todays_Market/Corporate_Bond_Spreads.php.

Value of operating assets = 64,921,473 million KRW

Value of Operating assets of Hyundai Motors using constant growth model is estimated as 64,921,473 million KRW.

Cash and cash equivalents in year 2013	3,722,401
Value of the firm	68,643,873.65
Book value of debt	33,988,810
Minority interests	4,651,704
Value of equity	39,306,767.65

Adding Cash and Cash Equivalents to the Value of operating Assets, subtracting the value of debt and adding minority interests.

The value of firm is arrived at 68,643.87 billion KRW. Deducting the book value of debt and adding the value of minority interests, the value of equity is estimated as 39,306.767 billion.

The market price of Hyundai Motors 4.5% coupon bond is 101.2. Based on the ratio of market price of bond to the face value of bond, the book value of debt is multiplied by the ratio to get the market value of debt as 34,396,676 million KRW. Adjusting the market value of debt, the value of equity is estimated as 38,898,902 million KRW.

Value of equity = 38,898.902 billion KRW.

The market capitalization of Hyundai Motors on Korea Stock Exchange was 37,226.7 billion KRW on January 4, 2015. Based on the calculations, it can be stated that Hyundai Motors is undervalued in the market.

Zero growth valuation model	
FCFF IN 2013	2,738,517
WACC	0.087738
Value of the firm	31,212,262

According to zero growth model, the value of Hyundai Motors is estimated to be 31,212.262 billion KRW
The market capitalization of Hyundai Motors as on January 11, 2015 on Korea Stock Market Exchange was 37,670 billion KRW.

Detailed Calculation for Hyundai Valuation given in the resources spreadsheet HYUNDAI FCFE AND FCFF.xlsx.

Table 6.13 **Estimation of FCFF value in millions of rand**

	2010	2011	2012	2013	2014
EBIT(1 − T)	18,501	22,037	26,287	29,184	32,342
Adjusted CAPEX	16,108	24,466	29,849	32,367	40,124
Depreciation & amortization	6712	7400	9651	12,030	13,516
Change in noncash working capital		1958	5178	4424	−5310
FCFF		3013	911	4423	11,044

Table 6.14 **Operating income, capital expenditures, and working capital as percent of revenues**

	2010	2011	2012	2013	2014	Average
Revenues in millions of ZAR	122,256	142,436	169,446	181,269	202,683	
EBIT(1 − T) as % of revenues	15.1361	15.471	15.513	16.099	15.956	15.63
CAPEX as % of revenues	13.1756	17.1768	17.6156	17.855	19.796	17.12
Noncash working capital as % of revenues	14.3698	13.7086	14.5792	16.068	11.751	14.09

6.10 Estimation of value of Sasol through the two-stage FCFF model

Sasol is a South African headquartered international integrated energy and chemicals company, which develops and commercialize technologies and produces a range of product streams which includes liquid fuels, high-value chemicals, and low-carbon electricity. Sasol was established in the year 1950 and is one of the largest investor in the capital projects in South Africa. The company is listed on the JSE in South Africa and on the New York Stock Exchange in the United States (Table 6.13).

The method employed is two-stage FCFF model in which the value of Sasol Ltd in high growth and stable phase is estimated. The growth rate is estimated using historical parameters. The average reinvestment rate in 2014 was 72.90%.

The average growth rate in depreciation during the 5-year period 2010−2014 was 19.42% (Tables 6.14 and 6.15).

The average growth rate in revenues on basis on geometric mean is estimated as 13.5%.

Table 6.15 **Estimation of FCFF**

Year	1	2	3	4	5	6	7	8	9	10
REVENUES	230,045.2	261,101.3	296,350.0	336,357.2	381,765.5	433,303.8	491,799.8	558,192.8	633,548.8	719,077.9
EBIT(1 − T)	35,887.1	40,731.8	46,230.6	52,471.7	59,555.4	67,595.4	76,720.8	87,078.1	98,833.6	112,176.2
CAPEX	39,107.7	44,387.2	50,379.5	57,180.7	64,900.1	73,661.6	83,606.0	94,892.8	10,7703.3	12,2243.2
Depreciation and amortization	161,38.1	192,68.9	230,07.1	274,70.4	32,799.7	39,162.8	46,760.4	55,832.0	66,663.3	79,596.0
Noncash working capital	32,206.3	36,554.2	41,489.0	47,090.0	53,447.2	60,662.5	68,852.0	78,147.0	88,696.8	100,670.9
Change in working capital	8388.3	4347.9	4934.8	5601.0	6357.2	7215.4	8189.4	9295.0	10,549.8	11,974.1
FCFF	4529.1	11,265.6	13,923.3	17,160.4	21,097.8	25,881.2	31,685.8	38,722.2	47,243.8	57,554.9

6.10.1 Inputs for estimation of FCFF in the high growth period

The high growth period is assumed to be 10 years. The high growth period is estimated from 2015 to 2024.

Revenues in year 2014 = 202,683 million rand
1 + growth rate = 1.135
EBIT as percent of revenues = 15.6%
CAPEX as percent of revenues = 17%
Noncash working capital as percent of revenues = 14%
Growth rate in depreciation (based on average 4-year period) = 19.40%
Noncash working capital in 2014 = 23,818 million rand
Depreciation and amortization in 2014 = 13,516 million rand

6.10.2 Estimation of cost of capital

The South African 10-year government bond rate of 7.19% in 2014 is considered as risk-free rate (http://www.tradingeconomics.com/south-africa/government-bond-yield).

Beta of Sasol is estimated by regressing 3 years of weekly stock returns (SSL ADR listed on NYSE) on market index returns NYSE Composite Index. The beta for Sasol is 1.33.

Emerging market risk premium = US risk premium + default spread for South Africa.

US risk premium is assumed to be 5%. The default spread is based on sovereign rating for South Africa. The default spread is obtained from bondsonline.com and rating from S&P. S&P have given a rating of BBB − for South Korea for foreign currency rating. The default spread for a S&P rating of BBB − is 1.65%.

Risk premium = 5 + 1.65 = 6.65%.
Cost of equity = Risk-free rate + beta ∗ Risk premium
= 7.19 + 1.33 ∗ 6.65 = 16.03%

6.10.3 Cost of debt calculation

Cost of debt = Risk-free rate + country default spread + company default spread.

The risk-free rate is 7.19% based on the 10-year government bond rate of South Africa. The default spread for South Africa based on S&P rating of A + is 1.65% (country default spread). The company default spread for Sasol based on S&P rating of BBB + is 1.32% (company default spread). Sasol's foreign currency credit rating by S&P was BBB + /Stable/A-2.

Cost of debt = 7.19 + 1.65 + 1.32 = 10.16%.

The cost of debt is estimated to be 10.16%. The corporate tax rate is 28% (http://www.kpmg.com/global/en/services/tax/tax-tools-and-resources/pages/corporate-tax-rates-table.aspx).

After-tax cost of debt = 10.16 * (1 − 0.28) = 7.315%

The weight of debt in capital structure was 13% and that of equity in capital structure was 87% in the year 2014.

Weighted average cost of capital (WACC) = Weight of equity * cost of equity + weight of debt * after cost of debt
WACC = 0.87 * 10.16% + 0.13 * 7.315% = 14.9%.

The WACC is 14.9% during the high growth period (Table 6.16).

The sum of the present value of FCF to firm in the high growth period = 105,899.9306 million rand.

6.10.4   Stable growth rate inputs

The value of Sasol in the stable phase growth period is estimated by the constant growth model.

Value of Sasol = Expected FCFF in the next period/(WACC − growth rate in the stable phase period)

The stable phase growth rate is estimated based on the annual GDP growth rate of South African economy.

Year	GDP growth rate (%)
2005	5.3
2006	5.6
2007	5.5
2008	3.6
2009	−1.5
2010	3.1
2011	3.6
2012	2.5
2013	1.9
Average	3.29

Source: http://data.worldbank.org/indicator/
NY.GDP.MKTP.KD.ZG.

The average growth rate of FCFF in the stable growth period is assumed to be 3.29%.

FCFF in year 2014 = 57,554.88 million rand
FCFF in stable phase period = FCFF in 2024 (1 + stable growth rate) = 59,448.43 million rand.

Estimation of WACC in stable period
Assume that beta falls to 1 in the stable phase period.

Cost of equity = Risk-free rate + beta * risk premium = 7.19 + 1 * 6.65 = 13.84%
After-tax cost of debt = 7.13%

Table 6.16 Estimation of present value of FCFF in high growth period

Year	1	2	3	4	5	6	7	8	9	10
FCFF	4529.1	11,265.6	13,923.3	17,160.4	21,097.8	25,881.2	31,685.8	38,722.2	47,243.8	57,554.9
PV	3941.8	8533.3	9178.8	9845.7	10,535.1	11,247.7	11,984.6	12,746.8	13,535.2	14,351.0

WACC = 0.87 * 13.84% + 0.13 * 7.13% = 12.96%
Terminal value of Sasol Ltd in the stable phase period = 614,771.77 million rand.
Present value of the terminal price = 153,289.93 million rand
Value of operating assets = 259,189.863 million rand
Value of debt = 2484.8 million rand
Value of equity = 256,705.063 million rand.

The value of Sasol's equity is arrived at 256.705 billion rand.

The market capitalization of Sasol was 247.83 billion rand on January 15, 2015 as quoted by quotes.wsj.com.

Two-stage FCFF MODEL is an appropriate model for valuation of Sasol.

The detailed calculation for FCFF model of Sasol is given in the spread sheet Sasol.xlsx.

References

Altman, E.I., Kishore, V., 2000. The Default Experience of US Bonds. Salmon Center, New York University, Working Paper.

Awasthi, V., Chipalkatti, N., De Mello e Souza, C., 2013. Connecting free cash flow metrics to what matters for investors: accuracy, bias, and ability to predict value. J. Appl. Financ.104–116.

Bowen, R., Burgstahler, D., Daley, L., 1986. Evidence on the relationships between earnings and various measures of cash flow. Account. Rev. 61, 713–725.

Burgstahler, D., Jiambalvo, J., Pyo, Y., 1998. The Informativeness of Cash Flows for Future Cash Flows. University of Washington, Working Paper.

Campbell, Y.J., Shiller, R.J., 1987. Cointegration and tests of present value model. J. Polit. Econ. 95, 1062–1088.

Chen, K.C.W., Chen, Z., Wei, K.C.J., 2011. Agency costs of free cash flow and the effect of shareholder rights on the implied cost of equity capital. J. Financ. Quant. Anal. 46 (1), 171–207.

Cochrane, J.H., 2010. Discount rates, Working Paper. University of Chicago

Damodaran, A., 1994. Damodaran on Valuation: Security Analysis for Investment and Corporate Finance. John Wiley & Sons, New York, NY.

Damodaran, A., 2012. Firm valuation: cost of capital and adjusted present value approaches. In: Investment Valuation, third ed. Wiley Finance, pp. 380–422 (Chapter 15).

Dechow, P., 1994. Accounting earnings and cash flows as measures of firm performance: the role of accounting accruals. J. Account. Econ. 18, 3–43.

Deloof, M., De Maeseneire, W., Inghelbrecht, K., 2009. How do investment banks value initial public offerings (IPOs)? J. Bus. Financ. Account. 26 (1–2), 130–160.

Einhorn, S.G., Shangquan, P., 1984. Using the dividend discount model for asset allocation. Financ. Analyst J. 40 (3), 30–32.

Estridge, J., Lougee, B., 2007. Measuring free cash flows for equity valuation: pitfalls and possible solutions. J. Appl. Corp. Financ. 19 (2), 60–71.

Hickman, K., Petry, G.H., 1990. A comparison of stock price predictions using court accepted formulas, dividend discount, and P/E models. Financ. Manage. 76–87.

Jacobs, B.I., Levy, K.N., 1988. On the value of 'value'. Financ. Analyst J. 47–6.

Flavin, M.A., 1983. Excess volatility in the financial markets: a reassessment of the empirical evidence. J. Polit. Econ. 96, 929−956.

Foerster, S.R., Sapp, S.G., 2005. The dividend discount model in the long run: a clinical study. J. Appl. Financ. 15 (2), Fall/Winter, 1−21.

Gehr, A.K., 1992. A bias in dividend discount models. Financ. Analyst J. 75−80.

Good, W.R., 1989. Bias in stock market valuation. Financ. Analyst J. 6−7.

Gordon, M.J., 1962. The investment. In: Irwin, R. (Ed.), Financing and Valuation of the Corporation. Homewood, III, pp. 1−256.

Gordon, M.J., Shapiro, E., 1956. Capital equipment analysis: the required rate of profit. Manag. Sci. 3 (1), 102−110.

Habib, A., 2011. Growth opportunities, earnings permanence, and valuation of free cash flow. Australas. Account. Bus. Financ. J. 5 (4), p101−p122.

Hackel, K.S., Livnat, J., Rai, A., 2000. A free cash flow investment anomaly. J. Account. Auditing' Financ. 15 (1), 1−24.

Jensen, M.C., 1986. Agency costs of free cash flow, corporate finance and takeovers. Am. Econ. Rev. 76 (2), 323−329.

Koller, T., Goedhart, M., Wessels, D., 2010. Valuation: Measuring and Managing the Value of Companies, fifth ed. John Wiley & Sons, Hoboken, NJ.

Lauricella, T., 2008. Cash flows reign once again. Wall St. J. 1−3, Online (May 12).

LeRoy, S., Porter, R., 1981. The present value relation: tests based on implied variance bounds. Econometrica. 64, 555−574.

Livnat, J., Zarowin, P., 1990. The incremental information content of cash-flow components. J. Account. Econ. 13, 25−46.

Marsh, T.A., Merton, R.C., 1986. Dividend variability and variance bounds tests for the rationality of stock market prices. Am. Econ. Rev. 76, 483−498.

Miller, M., Modigliani, F., 1961. Dividend policy, growth, and the valuation of shares. J. Bus. 34 (4), 411−433.

Nasseh, A., Strauss, J., 2004. Stock prices and the dividend discount model: did their relation break down in the 1990s. Q. Rev. Econ. Finance. 44 (2), 191−208.

Nunez, K., 2013. Free cash flow and performance predictability in electric utilities. J. Bus. Policy Res.19−38.

Nunez, K., 2014. Free cash flow and performance predictability: an industry analysis. Int. J. Bus., Account. Financ. 8 (2), 120−135.

O'Brien, T.J., 2003. A simple and flexible DCF valuation formula. J. Appl. Financ. 13 (2), 54−62.

Shapiro, A., 1989. Modern Corporate Finance. Macmillan, New York, NY.

Shiller, R.J., 1981. Do stock price move too much to be justified by subsequent changes in dividends? Am. Econ. Rev. 71, 421−436.

Stern, J., 1974. Earnings per share don't count. Financ. Analyst J. 30 (4), 39−43.

Titman, S., 1984. The effect of capital structure on a firm's liquidation decision. J. Financ. Econ. 13, 137−151.

Tole, T., McCord, S., Pugh, W. 1992. How cash flow pays dividends. Public Utilities Fortnightly; 130−138.

<www.morningstar.com>.

West, K. 1988. Bubbles, fads and stock price volatility tests: a partial evaluation. J. Financ. 43, 639−656.

Relative valuation

7.1 Introduction

Valuation multiple is an expression of market value of an asset relative to a key statistic that is assumed to relate to that value. The basic objective of relative valuation is to value assets based on how similar assets are currently priced in the market. In other words, relative valuation involves the use of similar comparable assets in valuing another asset. In relative valuation, a firm's value is compared to that of its competitors to determine its financial worth. Relative valuation is a very useful tool in valuing an asset. Relative valuation models are alternate models to absolute value models like discounted cash flow valuation models. In discounted cash flow models, a company's intrinsic worth is based on its estimated future free cash flows discounted to their present value. Relative valuation is also known as comparable valuation. Price earnings (P/E) ratio is the most commonly used relative valuation measure in industry.

Relative valuation is a major component of many equity research reports and acquisition valuations. Most of the sell-side analysts determine the target price-based on multiples like price-to-earnings or price-to-sales (P/S). Damodaran (2012) based on sample of 550 sell-side reports find that 67% of price targets were derived using multiples. Damodaran suggests that approximately 85% of equity research reports are based on multiples and comparables while 50% of all acquisition valuation are based on multiples. In relative valuation, the benchmark might be the multiple of a similar company or the median average value of the multiple for a peer group companies, an economic sector, an equity index, or a median or an average own past value of the multiple. The benchmark can be based on the stock's historical price ratios, the company's industry sector or subsector, and the market. Companies with low stock price ratios signify buy targets for value managers. Some companies may be undervalued compared to its competitors. For example, Goldman Sachs Large Cap Value selects stocks on an industry-by-industry basis on the criteria of low-value stocks compared to their industry peers. In some cases, managers select companies that are attractively valued compared to the relative broader equity market. Some of the common metrics used in relative valuation include P/E ratio, return on equity, operating margin, enterprise value (EV) and price-to-free cash flows. Empirical research advocates the use of forward-looking multiples as they are considered to be more accurate predictors of value. DCF approach is used for pure intrinsic valuation. The terminal value can be calculated using the earnings before interest, tax, depreciation, and amortization (EBITDA) multiple assumption.

The major choices for value drivers include measures of cash flow, book value, earnings, and revenues. The most widely used measures are based on earnings and cash flows. One of the most widely used multiple is the price earnings ratio commonly known as P/E or PER. Other commonly used multiples are based on the EV of companies such as EV/EBITDA, EV/EBIT, and EV/OPAT. P/B ratio is a commonly used benchmark multiple, which compare market value to the accounting book value of the firm's assets. The P/S ratio and EV/Sales ratio measure value relative to sales.

There also exists other industry-specific value drivers like EV/Number of subscribers for telecom businesses, EV/Number of audiences for broadcasting companies. In real-estate sector, the sales comparison approach involves valuation multiples based on the surface areas of the properties being valued. Equity price-based multiples are more significant when investors acquire minority positions in companies.

7.2   Advantages and disadvantages of relative valuation

Relative valuation requires far fewer assumptions than discounted cash flow valuation. Relative valuation is simple and easy to understand. Relative valuation is more likely to reflect market perceptions than discounted cash flow valuation. Mutual fund managers basically focus on relative value strategies to compare a stock's price ratios like P/E, price/book (P/B), P/S with a benchmark and make a decision about the firm's prospects. Thus, the value obtained is relative in nature. Portfolio managers are often judged for performance based on how they perform on a relative basis. Hence, relative valuation is more significant in mutual fund industry. Another advantage of relative valuation is that the technique provide information on how the market is currently valuing the stock at different levels—aggregate market, alternate industries, and individual stocks within industries. The relative valuation approach provides information on how the market is currently valuing the securities. At the same time, relative valuation does not provide guidance on whether current valuations are appropriate. Valuation could be too high or low. Suppose assume that market has been significantly overvalued. In that context, it would not be proper to compare the value of an industry to the overvalued market. In this scenario, the point that an industry is undervalued relative to market is not correct as markets are overvalued. Relative valuation techniques are appropriate when there are a good set of comparable companies and the aggregate market is fairly valued.

A portfolio of stocks which are undervalued on a relative basis may still be overvalued in other estimation methods. Relative valuation is built on the assumption that markets are correct in the aggregate even if there are errors in individual securities valuation. Relative valuations are not suited when the market is over- or undervalued. Relative valuation ignores important variables of growth, risk, and cash flow measures. Relative valuation depends on market sentiments. The biggest limitation of relative valuation is the assumption that the market has valued the business correctly. Relative valuation does not account for growth. The major challenge involved in a market multiple valuation is identifying appropriate comparable companies, which are priced similar to the companies being valued. It is also necessary to make adjustments to the financial numbers, which are used to measure the market multiples of comparable companies as well as those used to value the company. In the process, the characteristics of the comparable companies must be aligned with those of the company being valued. Controlling for the differences in value drivers across companies is necessary when trying to ensure the comparability of the comparable companies and the company being valued.[1]

The usage of industry averages has its own limitations as companies even in the same industry may have different growth rates and rates of returns.

7.3 Drivers of relative valuation

Relative valuation measure like P/E ratio reflects the market potential of a firm in terms of earnings. P/E ratio is a technically simple model with company earnings as the value driver. The three important drivers for PE valuation are investment risk, earnings growth, and accounting measurement principles. The EV/EBITA is determined by factors like the growth rate of company, return on capital, and cost of capital. The EV/EBITA multiple increases with growth when the firm's return on invested capital is greater than the cost of capital.

Multiples reflect the market's perception of a company's growth prospects as two firms with similar prospects and operating characteristics must trade at similar multiples. If a firm is trading at a lower multiple than its peer companies, then it can be termed as "undervalued in the market." If all the value drivers like discount rate, growth rate, and return on invested capital are equivalent, then the multiples for the firms must be equal. If drivers like growth are higher for a firm, then its multiple should be higher than the comparative peer firm. Hence, it can be stated that the firm trades at a premium in comparison with its peer group, which is accounted by its higher growth rate.

7.4 Steps in relative valuation

The first step of an effective valuation process involves selection of businesses, which are as similar as possible. The process of relative valuation starts with the selection of a peer group. The peer group selection is on the basis of examination of the industry of the firm. The product profile, revenues, and profits of the firm is compared with the peer group firms. Peer group valuation may not be appropriate if the firms gave negative earnings. Peer group selection is based on defining industry attributes, matching companies on size, growth, margins, asset intensity, and risk.

---

[1] Holthausen, R.W., Zmijewski, M.E. Valuation with market multiples: how to avoid pitfalls when identifying and using comparable companies, J. Appl. Corp. Financ. 24 (3), 26–35.

Then the equity value is estimated by means of incorporating the effect of dilutive securities such as options, restricted stocks, convertible debt, warrants, etc. The equity value is unlevered to arrive at EV. The next stage involves identifying and measuring value drivers such as earnings and computing multiples for peer companies. The focus is on appropriate value drivers in terms of revenues, EBITDA, EBIT, and net income. The value drivers have to be adjusted to remove nonrecurring items. The next step involves identification and adjustment for differences between the selected company and its peers. The adjustments in differences between peer company and selected firm must be in terms of business strategy, size, growth, margins, asset intensity, and risk factors. Finally, the range of values for the firm is selected based on the company's value drivers and the adjusted multiples of the peer firms.

In summary, for relative valuation, a list of comparable peer companies is selected, and their market values are obtained. These market values are converted into comparable trading multiples like P/E, P/B, EV/Sales, and EV/EBITDA multiples. Then the company's multiples are compared with the peers to assess if the firm is over- or undervalued.

7.5 Relative valuation techniques

In relative valuation, the value of any firm can be standardized with respect to earnings, book value of assets, revenues, or firm-specific measures. Multiples are classified as earnings multiples, book value multiples, revenue multiples, and sector-specific multiples. In earnings multiple, the value of any asset is a multiple of the earnings that asset generates. The value of the operating assets can be expressed as a multiple of EBITDA or operating income. Book value multiples like P/B ratio indicates whether a firm is under- or overvalued. Tobin Q is a measure of replacement value multiple. Ratios like P/S and values to sales are examples for revenue multiples. Industry-specific multiples are also used for relative valuation of firms in specific sectors.

The numerator of the multiple can be either equity value or firm value. The equity value is based on either book value or market value. The firm value can be based on the EV, which is the sum of the value of debt and equity net of cash. The denominator of the multiple is an equity measure or a firm measure. The equity measure is based on earnings per share, net income, or book value of equity. The analyst's choice for the comparison stocks and benchmark value of the multiple must be based on either one of the following: (i) the firm's peers within its industry, (ii) the firm's industry or sector, (iii) the representative broad market equity index, and (iv) the average historical price multiple for the firm.

The selection of company's peer within it industry for the method of comparables is based on the law of one price, which states identical assets should sell for the same price.

7.5.1 Forward multiples

Forward multiples are basically applied to a firm's next 12 months EBITDA or EBIT. This measure basically focus on a firm's predicted earnings for the next year. Forward multiples are used to value high-growth companies that expect better future earnings in the future period. Forward multiple is basically useful for companies that have recently engaged in a major restructuring activity like M&A or introduced a new product. A firm recovering from a downturn may focus on forward multiple if the future business in next 12 months is expected to recover. Firms with project backlog in future use forward multiples for valuation purposes. Many publicly traded firms are valued based on projected rather than historical earnings and cash flows. Projections or forward estimates are made by equity analysts for estimation of valuation multiples. Forward estimates are obtained from sources like Bloomberg, First Call, and IBES. The projections are provided on a calendar year basis for consistency.

7.5.1.1 Equity price-based multiples

Equity value multiples are calculated using denominators relevant to equity holders.

7.5.1.1.1 Earnings multiplier—P/E ratio

The earnings multiple technique consists of a detailed assumption of future earnings per share and an estimate of earnings multiplier (P/E) ratio.

P/E = Share price/Earnings per share

Investment analysts and advisors highlight the significance of P/E ratio. The P/E ratio valuation plays an important role among investment analysts and advisors. In earning-based valuation model, the value of equity of firm is estimated as a function of the observed P/E ratio for some peer company or the mean/median P/E ratio for peer companies. The drawback for PE-based valuation is that earnings per share can be subjected to distortions due to differences in accounting rules and capital structure between firms.

P/E ratio is the most commonly used equity multiple. Stock market valuation basically focusses on price earning multiple commonly called P/E ratio (Kenth and Stina, 2008). P/E ratio is a useful indicator of expectations of growth opportunities. P/E multiples do vary with growth prospects. In other words, P/E ratio reflects the market optimism regarding the firm's growth prospects. Analysts must decide if they are more or less optimistic than the perception conveyed by the market multiple. Mathematically, it can be proved that P/E ratio increases with ROE. High ROE projects give the firm good opportunities for growth. Higher reinvestment rate increases P/E ratio only if the investments undertaken by the firm offer an expected rate of return greater than the market capitalization rate. A common thumb rule in Wall Street is that the growth rate ought to be roughly equal to the P/E ratio. Riskier firms will have higher required rates of return. The P/E ratio for such firms will be lower. P/E ratio is based on earnings growth and risk. Forward P/E also known as estimated P/E ratio is a forward-looking indicator, which can be used to compare current earnings to future earnings. Forward P/E ratio uses the current share price and divides by the total EPS earnings over the estimated future 12 months. Trailing P/E is found out by dividing the current share price by the total EPS earnings over the past 12 months. In other words, the trailing P/E (also referred to as the current P/E) uses the past four quarters of earnings, referred to as the trailing 12-month (TTM) EPS. The forward P/E (also referred to as the leading or prospective P/E), which uses next year's expected earnings (based on the analyst or database estimates).

The P/E ratio of a high-growth firm is a function of the expected growth rate in abnormal growth rate. Firms with higher cost of equity will often have lower P/E ratio compared to a firm with lower cost of equity. The rise of market interest rates will lead to higher cost of equity and lower PE ratio. If the P/E ratio of a company's stock is greater than that of market index like DJIA or S&P 500, then the firm would be overvalued and vice versa.

The forward P/E is preferred over the trailing P/E when trailing earnings are not representative of the firm's future. The trailing P/E is preferred when forecasted earnings are not available, which is often the case for small firms that are not widely followed.

If earnings are zero or negative, the analyst may use a longer-term or future (positive) earnings figure. Regardless, the analyst should use the same definition of earnings when making comparisons across firms.

When analyst use trailing P/E, adjustments have to be made with respect to potential dilution of EPS, transitory nonrecurring earnings, transitory earning components, which are attributable to business cycles and differences in accounting methods. Basic EPS utilizes the actual number of shares outstanding during the period. Diluted EPS utilizes the number of shares that would be outstanding and the accompanying earnings if all executive stock options, equity warrants, and convertible bonds were exercised.

Disadvantages of P/E ratio

The earnings which forms the denominator of the P/E ratio is an accounting measure, which is influenced by accounting rules, use of historical cost in depreciation, and inventory valuation. In times of inflation, historic cost depreciation and inventory costs tend to underrepresent the true economic values. P/E ratios are generally inversely related to inflation rate. P/E measure might be distorted if the firms use earnings management to improve the apparent profitability of the firm. P/E ratios can also be affected by business cycles as reported earnings can fluctuate substantially over a business cycle. P/E ratio cannot be used if earnings are negative. One of the major flaws of P/E multiples is that they are affected by capital structure. Unlevered companies (all equity firms) with high P/E ratio can increase its P/E ratio artificially by swapping debt for equity. Earnings include many nonoperating items like restructuring charges and write-offs, which are one-time events that often make P/E ratios misleading. In 2002, AOL Time Warner wrote-off nearly $100 billion in goodwill and other intangibles. The company had an EBITDA of $6.4 billion but recorded a loss of $98 billion due to the write-off. P/E ratio in this case was misleading as earnings were negative.[2]

---

[2] Goedhart, M., Koller, T., Wessels, D. The right role for multiples in valuation, Mckinsey Finance, 7–11.

7.5.1.1.2   Price earning growth ratio

Price earning growth (PEG) is calculated by dividing the P/E by the projected earnings growth rate of the firm. Suppose a company has a P/E ratio of 25 and analysts expect its earnings to grow by 15%, then its PEG would be 1.66. The firm is trading at a premium compared to its growth rate. PEG ratio is obtained by dividing the P/E ratio by the growth rate in earnings per share. It is most suited for valuing high-growth companies like technology firms. PEG ratios can be used to compare valuation of firms that are in the same businesses. If the expected growth rate in earnings per share is based on earnings in the most recent period, then the current PE ratio should be used to compute the PEG. Basically, a forward P/E is used in the PEG ratio, but trailing P/E is more effective in calculating PEG.

PEG ratio = PE ratio/Expected growth rate in EPS

PEG relies heavily on earnings estimates by analysts, which may go wrong. Hence for calculation of PEG, good margin of errors have to be provided in earnings estimate. Firms with PEG ratio of 1 is considered to be fairly valued, while those higher than one is considered to be overvalued. PEG ratio of <1 indicates undervaluation. The P/E ratio of any firm that is fairly priced will be equal to its growth rate. In theory, the lower the PEG ratio the better—implying that we are paying less for future earnings growth. PEG ratio combines prices and forecasts of earnings and earnings growth into a ratio, which can be used as a basis for stock recommendations.

PEG ratios allow expected level of growth to vary across companies. The drawback of PEG ratio is that there is no standard yardstick to measure the duration of the expected growth rate.

7.5.1.1.3   P/B ratio

P/B = Share price/Book value per share

The P/B ratio is also known as the market-to-book ratio. It links the market price of a stock with the book value of shareholder's equity. It measures how many times book value investors are ready to pay for a share. It is the ratio of price per share divided by the book value per share. Academic research by Fama and French (1992), Rosenberg et al. (1985), and Fairfield (1994) have advocated the importance of P/B ratio. Fama and French (1992) suggest a significant inverse relationship between P/B value ratios and excess rates of return for a cross-section of stocks. Book value is a reasonable measure for value of firms that have consistent accounting practice. P/B ratio is a relevant measure when firms have negative earnings or cash flows. This ratio is not appropriate for comparison of firms with different levels of assets, for example, heavy manufacturing firms and service firms. It is most useful when assets are core driver of earnings like capital intensive industries. P/B ratio is considered to be an important relative measure for valuation in the banking industry as banks rely on large asset base to generate profits. Ideally, the current price has to be matched with the future book value of the firm, which is an expected value at the end of the year. P/B ratio is a function of the firm's return on equity relative to its cost of equity. The share price must reflect the future value creation potential while the accounting or book value of equity reflects the accumulation of past share issues and past retained profits or earnings. A higher P/B ratio reflects expected future prospects on account of perceived growth opportunities or competitive advantages. During the period of boom, high P/B ratio reflect overoptimism and overpricing. The difference between the market value and the book value of a company is often known as market value added or market goodwill. Companies having more intangible assets are set to have higher market value. The lowest P/B ratio are found to be in capital intensive industries like utilities and retail, whereas the highest P/B are found in sectors like pharmaceuticals and consumer products that have more intangibles. Hence, it is observed that new economy firms have higher P/B ratios than traditional brick and mortar type firms that have more tangible assets in their balance sheet. The book value for tangible assets can be significantly impacted by the differences in accounting policies.

7.5.1.1.4   Price-to-cash flow (P/CF) ratio
P/CF = Share price/Cash flow per share

This metric compares the stock market's price to the amount of cash flow that the company generates on a per share basis. Many analysts prefer P/CF instead of P/E ratio. Cash flow used are either operating cash flow or free cash flow. The major variables that affect P/CF ratios are the expected growth rate of cash flow variable used and the risk of the stock as indicated by the variability of the cash flow. Cash flows are less prone to manipulation in comparison with earnings per share. P/CF is driven by the growth rate and volatility of cash flows. P/CF ratio provides a reliable indication of long-term returns. A high P/CF ratio indicates that specific firm is trading at a high price but would not generate enough cash flows to support the multiple. It is unaffected by differences in accounting for depreciation. P/CF ratios are more stable than P/E ratios because cash flow is more stable than earnings.

7.5.1.1.5   P/S ratio
P/S = Share price/Sales per share

The P/S ratio is a major valuation benchmark. Strong and consistent sales growth is an important requirement for a growth company. Sales growth basically drives the growth of all subsequent earnings and cash flows. P/S ratio is mathematically equal to P/E ratio times the net profit margin. Thus, P/S ratio is impacted significantly to a great extent by the profit margin of the firm. The three major variables that affect P/S ratio are sales growth rate, volatility of sales growth, and profit margin. Sales are always positive. Hence, P/S can be used even if EPS is negative. P/S are of limited use for comparing valuations of different firms. P/S multiple assumes that comparable firms have similar growth rates and returns on incremental investments. P/S is obtained in the same way as P/E ratio is obtained except that a company's annual sales is used as denominator instead of its earnings. The advantage for P/S ratio is that sales is much harder to manipulate and is subject to fewer accounting estimates than earnings. As sales is more stable than earnings, P/S can be used for screening cyclical firms and firms with fluctuating earnings patterns. P/S ratio is useful to compare companies in similar industries. P/S is useful for valuing the stocks of mature and cyclical firms. The differences in the P/S ratio are significantly related to differences in long-term stock returns.

7.5.1.1.6 Dividend yield

Dividend yield is an important measure of valuation. Dividend yield is equal to a company's annual dividend per share divided by its stock price per share. Mature companies with few growth opportunities usually have high dividend yields. Utility companies are considered as dividend paying companies.

Dividend yield = Annual dividends per share/Stock price

Best yielding stocks have strong cash flows, health balance sheets, and relatively stable businesses.

7.5.1.2 EV-based multiples

EV multiples are expressed as a ratio of capital investment to a financial metric, which is attributable to the providers of capital. EV equals market value of equity plus debt minus cash. Cash and short-term investments known as nonoperating assets are subtracted from the value of the firm to get the EV. EV multiples are better than equity value multiples as EV multiples allow for direct comparison of different firms regardless of capital structure. EV multiples are less affected by accounting differences. It is not an appropriate measure for comparison of firms in different industries.

7.5.1.2.1 EV/EBITDA

This ratio is also known as the "enterprise multiple" and the "EBITDA multiple." It is one of the most commonly used firm value metric. EBITDA refers to Earnings before Interest, Taxes, Depreciation and Amortization. EBITDA is a proxy for cash flow. Basically, there will be very few firms with negative EBITDA though earnings may be negative. This multiple is not affected by methods of depreciation. It ignores variations in capital expenditure and depreciation. EV/EBITDA is often in the range of 6.0× to 18.0×. This ratio compares the value of the firm inclusive of debt and other liabilities to the actual cash earnings exclusive of the noncash expenses. This multiple can be used to compare the value of two different companies within the same industry. A low EV indicate undervaluation. The EV/EBITDA multiple is a better measure as it is not affected by changes in capital structure. It can also be used to make comparison of companies with different capital structures. This ratio also removes the effect of noncash expenses like depreciation and amortization. This multiple is difficult to be used for firms with crossholdings. EV/EBITDA ratio is not usually appropriate for comparison of firms in different industries. EV/EBITDA is more relevant than P/E in determining the relative value when firms have different degrees of financial leverage as the financial variable EBITDA is pre interest while EPS is postinterest. EBITDA is calculated before depreciation and amortization. Hence, the multiple EV/EBITDA is particularly useful in for comparison of capital intensive companies.

7.5.1.2.2 EV/EBIT

EBIT refers to Earnings before Interest and Taxes. As in the case of consulting firms, when depreciation and amortization are small, EBIT and EBITDA will be similar. EBIT takes into account depreciation and amortization charges. EV/EBIT is often in the range of $10.0\times$ to $25.0\times$. The EV/EBIT is a modified multiplier of the P/E ratio. It is also known as EBIT multiple. EBIT is the profits of the firm before the impact of interest income, interest expense, and tax expense. The major difference between EBIT Multiple and PE ratio is that EBIT multiple takes into account distortions in earnings due to cash holdings and borrowings.

7.5.1.2.3 EV/Sales

EV/Sales would be the most appropriate multiple to use when a firm's EBITDA is negative. EV/Sales is a commonly used valuation metric when operating costs exceed revenues as would be the case of new internet firms. EV/Sales multiples are often in the range of $1.00\times$ to $3.00\times$. This multiple is applicable even when earnings are negative or highly cyclical. This measure basically compares the EV of a company to the company's sales. The ratio suggests how much it costs to buy the company's sales. EV/Sales is considered to be a better valuation method than P/S as the former also considers the amount of debt along with the market value of equity while the latter considers only the market value of equity. Generally, the lower the EV/Sales, the firm is considered to be undervalued and attractive for buy. A high EV/Sales is not always a bad sign as it can be an indicator that investors believe that the sales turnover would witness huge growth in future. A lower EV/Sales multiple might signal that future sales would be low.

7.5.1.2.4 EV/EBITDAR

EV refers to enterprise value and EBITDAR is earnings before interest, tax, depreciation and amortization and rental costs. This measure is a proxy for operating free cash flows. It is used in the transport, hotel, and retail industries.

7.5.1.2.5 EV/Invested capital

This measure is the ratio of EV to the invested capital.

7.5.1.2.6 EV/capacity measure

The capacity measure could be subscribers, production capacity, and audience.

7.5.1.2.7 Value-to-book ratio

Value-to-book ratio is obtained by dividing the market value of both debt and equity by the book value of equity and debt.

Value-to-book ratio = Market value of equity + Market value of debt/Book value of equity + Book value of debt

7.5.1.2.8 Tobin q ratio

Tobin's q or the q ratio is the ratio of the market value of a company's assets (market value of outstanding stock plus debt) divided by the replacement cost of the company's assets or book value. It was developed by Nobel Laureate James Tobin. A fairly priced company ought to have a tobin q value of 1 as for such a company the market value must be equal to its total asset value. If the tobin q value is less than 1, it suggests that the market value of the company is less than the total asset value and is thus undervalued. If the tobin q is more than 1, it indicates that the market value is higher than the total asset value and the company would be overvalued. The tobin q is also called simply a q ratio. q is one of the methods for measuring the value of the stock market. The data from which q is calculated are published in the "Flow of Funds Accounts of the United States Z1," which is published quarterly by the Federal Reserve.

7.6 Industry-specific multiples

EV/Revenues is used by different industry sectors to value new companies. EV/Number of subscriber is an important multiple for subscriber-based businesses like cable and direct to home businesses. Consumer and industrial companies focus on relative valuation measure of EV/EBITDA. Media industry subsectors like gaming, chemicals and bus, and rail industries use EV/EBITA. EV/Reserves is used in oil and gas industry with upstream operations. EV/Reserves indicates how much the oil field is worth on a per barrel basis. EV/EBITDAX is a relevant valuation measure in the Oil and Exploration industry. EBITDAX refers to earnings before interest, taxes, depreciation, depletion, amortization and exploration expenses.

EV/Production ratio in oil and gas sector gives value on a barrel per day production basis. This ratio gives the value per ton of cargo handled for container ports. EV/Capacity is a commonly used relative valuation ratio in the oil and gas sector, which gives value in terms of barrel per day of refining capacity. P/B book value is a very important value measure for technology, banks, and insurance sectors. EV/FFO is a value measure relevant for real-estate businesses. PEG ratio is used as a value measure in high-growth technology firms to account for differences in growth across companies. EV/EBITDA is used in specialty retail industry.

7.7 Research studies on relative valuation

In a study by Goldman Sachs (1999), the P/E ratio was found to be the primary valuation metric for approximately 50% of US investment analysts. Researchers have basically focused on earnings and cash flow-based value drivers. Boatsman and Baskin (1981) compare the valuation accuracy of P/E multiples based on two sets of comparable firms in the same industry. Their results suggest that valuation errors are smaller when comparable firms are chosen based on similar historical growth earnings. Beatty et al. (1999) examine the different linear combinations of value drivers, which are derived from earnings, book value of assets, and dividends. The results of this study suggest that the best performance is achieved by using weights derived from harmonic mean book and earnings multiples and coefficients from price-scaled regressions on earnings and book value. Baker and Ruback (1999) examine the econometric problems with different ways of computing industry multiples and comparing the relative performance of multiples based on EBITDA, EBIT, and sales. The study suggests that absolute variation errors are proportional to value and also demonstrates that industry multiples that are estimated using harmonic mean are close to minimum variance estimates based on Monte Carlo simulations. The study also suggests that industry-adjusted EBITDA performs better than EBIT and sales. Kim and Ritter (1999) investigate how IPO pricing are determined using multiples, which include value drivers of book value, cash flows, sales, past earnings, and forecasted earnings. The study suggest that forward P/E multiples based on forecasted earnings is the most dominating multiple with respect to valuation accuracy. Tasker (1998) examines the industry patterns in the selection of comparable firms by investment bankers and analysts in acquisition transactions and suggests systematic selection of industry-specific multiples in different industries. Liu et al. (2002) examine the valuation properties of a comprehensive list of value drivers. The study suggest that multiples based on forward earnings are the major determinant of performance of stock prices. In terms of ranking of relative performance, forward earning measures were followed by historical earning measures, cash flow measures, book value measures, and the lowest ranking attributed by sales-based measures. Alford (1992) examine the effect of choosing comparables based on industry, size, risk, and earnings growth on the appropriateness of valuation using P/E multiples. Alford suggests that pricing errors decline when the industry definition used to select comparable firms is narrowed from a broad single digit SIC code to classifications based on two and three digits. The study also points out that controlling for size and earnings growth over and above industrial controls does not reduce valuation errors. Kaplan and Ruback (1995) analyze the valuation properties of the DCF approach for highly leveraged transactions. They find that though DCF valuations approximate transacted values reasonably well but simple EBITDA multiples also result in similar valuation accuracy. Liu et al. (2007) point out that valuations based on cash flow multiples are better than earnings multiple. Their study suggest that stock prices are better explained by reported earnings than reported operating cash flows. Penman (1996) explains the relationship between PE ratio and market-to-book ratio. Penman (1997) investigate approximate benchmark valuations that combine earnings and book value together. Huang et al. (2007) reexamine the P/E anomaly by decomposing P/E ratios into a fundamental component and a residual component, which enables them to capture factors that potentially provide better measures of investor overreaction. Their study suggest that firm specific and macroeconomic factors determine P/E multiples. Da and Schaumburg (2011) document that within-industry relative valuations implicit in analyst target prices do provide investors with valuable information although the implied absolute valuations themselves are much less informative.

Many studies have explored the linkage between P/B value ratios and excess return. Fama and French (1992) find positive relationship between book-to-price ratios and average returns. Rosenberg et al. (1985) find that average returns on US stocks are positively related to the ratio of a firm's book value to market value. Chan et al. (1991) finds that market-to-book ratio has a direct impact on the cross-section of average returns on Japanese stocks. Capaul et al. (1993) suggest that value stocks characterized by low P/B value ratios earned excess return in all markets.

7.8 Principles of relative valuation

Discounted cash flow valuation might give erroneous results when estimates like return on invested capital, growth rate, and weighted average cost of capital are not estimated correctly. Many analysts often base valuation for a firm by means of multiplying a company's earnings by an industry average P/E ratio. The industry average yardstick may not be an appropriate method as firms in the same industry can have different expected growth rates, return on invested capital, and capital structure.[2] In relative valuation, it is very important to use peer companies for comparison with similar prospects for ROIC and growth. The use of Standardized Industrial Classification code published by US government and Global Industry Classification Standard developed by Morgan Stanley Capital International and Standard & Poor's are suited for selection purposes. Forward-looking multiples are better predictors of value than historical multiples. The study by Liu et al. compared the historical and forward industry multiples for companies listed on major stock exchanges of NYSE, NASDAQ, and American Stock Exchange. The comparison of individual companies against industry mean suggest that the dispersion of historical earnings-to-price (E/P) ratios was nearly twice that of 1-year forward E/P ratios. The median pricing error was 23% for historical multiples and 18% for 1-year forecasted earnings. Kim and Ritter based on the study of IPO pricing find that the average prediction error was 55% for historical earnings multiples, 43.7% for 1-year forecasts, and 28.5% for 2-year forecasts. EV multiples are less affected by changes in capital structure as EV includes both debt and equity in the capital structure. The EV/EBITA multiple has to be adjusted to account for nonoperating items like excess cash, operating leases, employee stock options, and pensions. Basically, EBITA excludes interest income from excess cash. Hence, for calculation of EV, excess cash must not be included in EV calculation. In EV calculation, the value of the leased asset is added to the market value of debt and equity. The implied interest expense is added to EBITA. The present value of all employee grants options that are currently outstanding are added to determine the EV. The present value of pension liabilities is added to the EV. The nonoperating gains and losses related to pension plan assets are adjusted with EBITA. In this process, pension interest expense is added to EBITA and returns on plan assets are deducted from EBITA.

7.9   Cases of relative valuation

7.9.1   Relative valuation of America Movil

America Movil is the leading wireless services provider in Latin America. The company has third largest equity subscribers in the world. The company has operations in 18 countries in the Americas. The company has more than 265 million mobile customers and more than 31 million fixed lines. The company has more than 19 million television subscribers. The company had an ROE of 28.55% in the year 2010, 29.81% in 2011, and 30.95% in 2012. The America Movil was trading at 15.30 Mexican peso on January 20, 2015 on Mexican stock exchange BMV MEX. Its telecommunications services include mobile and fixed voice services, mobile and fixed data services, Internet access, paid TV, and other related services (Tables 7.1 and 7.2).

Comparatively, P/B ratio is higher for America Movil than for the market index S&P 500. The higher value reflects future potential for America Movil envisaged by market on account of growth opportunities or competitive advantages. P/CF is also higher for America Movil compared to the market index. The dividend yield is much lesser for America Movil compared to the market index. The dividend yield is only 1.4% (Table 7.3).

In terms of forward valuation, Morning star assigns a P/E ratio of 12.4 and PEG ratio of 2.4.

Table 7.1 **Past financial highlights during 2010−2012**

Year	2010	2011	2012
P/E	13.30	14.22	13.63
P/B	1.70	2.41	1.70
Marcap (in million peso)	0.26	0.36	0.28

Source: Data from Annual Reports.

Table 7.2 **Current valuation of America Movil**

	America Movil	S&P 500
P/E	17.6	18.6
P/B	5.7	2.7
P/S	1.5	1.8
P/CF	5.6	1.5
DIV YIELD %	1.4	2.1

Source: Data from Morningstar.com.

Table 7.3 Equity price-based relative valuation—historical values of America Movil

	2012		2013		2014	
	American Movil	S&P 500	American Movil	S&P 500	American Movil	S&P 500
P/E	12.1	15	14.9	18.6	17.1	18.6
P/B	4.5	2.1	5.3	2.6	5.5	2.7
P/S	1.4	1.3	1.4	1.7	1.4	1.8
P/CF	5.3	9.2	5.9	11.2	5.3	11.5

The P/E ratio for the company has shown growing trend during the period 2012–2014. The P/B ratio for America Movil have been higher than that of market index during the period of analysis. The P/CF ratio for America Movil had been lower than that of S&P 500 during the period of analysis.
Source: Data from Morningstar.com.

7.9.1.1 EVs for America Movil

Market price of America Movil as on January 20, 2015 = 15.30 Mexican pesos
Market value of equity = Share price*Number of shares = 15.30*3643 million = 55,737.9 million
Book value of debt = 490,319 million
Total cash and cash equivalents = 48,164 million
Enterprise value = Market value of equity + Book value of debt − Total cash and cash equivalents = 55,737.9 + 490,319 − 48,164 = 497,892.9 million
EBITDA in the year 2014 = 241,557 million
EV/EBITDA = 497,892.9/241,557 = 2.06
EBIT in 2014 = 152,975 million
EV/EBIT = 497,892.9/152,975 = 3.25
EV/Sales = 497,892.9/796,415 = 0.625

America Movil had a wireless subscriber base of 269.883 million. Hence, the EV/Number of subscriber ratio was 497,892.9/269.883 = 1844.8

Lower the enterprise multiple, more attractive the stock would be. These enterprise multiples suggest how much sources of finances are required to generate one unit of sales and operating earnings.

7.9.2 Relative valuation of TSMC

Taiwan Semiconductor Manufacturing Co. Ltd is the world's first dedicated semiconductor foundry established in the year 1987. It is listed on both the Taiwan Stock Exchange and New York Stock Exchange. TSMC manufacturers more than 8600 products for various applications in market segments of computer, communications, and consumer market segments. TSMC has the broadest range of technologies in the dedicated IC foundry segment and delivers the largest portfolio of process-proven IPs and libraries, and the IC industry's most comprehensive design ecosystem. TSMC commanded a 49% share of the global foundry market in 2013.

The total capacity of the manufacturing facilities owned by TSMC exceeded 16.4 million eight inch equivalent wafers in 2013. The market capitalization of TSMC as of December 31, 2014 was NT $3.66 trillion or US$ 115.4 billion. In May 2009, TSMC established the New Businesses organization to explore nonfoundry-related business opportunities. In August 2011, the New Businesses organization was formally separated from the main TSMC organization as two subsidiaries, TSMC Solid State Lighting Ltd and TSMC Solar Ltd. These subsidiaries are engaged in developing, designing, manufacturing, and selling solid-state lighting devices, related products and systems, and solar-related technologies and products (Table 7.4).

7.9.2.1 Enterprise valuation

In enterprise valuation, the numerator of the multiple is EV, which is calculated as the sum of market value of equity + book of debt − cash and cash equivalents. Table 7.5 compares the EV multiples of Taiwan Semiconductors with its peer companies. The data and detailed calculation for the various EV-based multiples are given in the spreadsheet *EV Multiples TAIWAN.xlsx*.

It is often stated that lower the EV multiple, more attractive would be the firm. Lower the EV multiple, more undervalued would be the firm. A low ratio might indicate that the firm would be undervalued. EV-based multiples are ideal for comparison of transnational companies since the multiples do not consider tax effects of different countries. A firm with lower enterprise multiple is a good takeover target. Taiwan Semiconductors is the most undervalued firm when compared to its peer group. The EV/EBITDA multiple for Taiwan Semiconductor is the lowest compared to other peer companies. Similarly, with respect to other enterprise multiples, of EV/EBIT and EV/Sales, Taiwan Semiconductors had the least multiple values.

Table 7.4 Current relative valuation on basis of equity multiples: TSMC versus industry peers

Company	Market cap ($ million)	Net income ($ million)	P/S	P/B	P/E	P/CF	Div yield %
TSMC	122,957	224,549	5.7	4.1	17.3	10.5	1.7
Intel Corp	178,459	10,668	3.4	3.2	17.6	8.0	2.4
Texas Instrument	58,064	2507	4.7	5.6	23.9	15.7	2.3
Avago Technologies	26,860	263	6.6	8.3	90.9	24.3	1.2
Broadcom	25,059	430	3.0	2.9	58.5	15.2	1.1

Among the three major selected companies in terms of market capitalization, TSMC is the largest semiconductor company. In terms of P/S, TSMC is the most valuable company. It occupies second position in terms of P/B ratio. The P/CF for TSMC is 10.5.
Source: Data from Morningstar.com.

7.9.3 Relative valuation of Sberbank

Sberbank is the largest bank in Russia and the third largest bank in Europe. The bank offers corporate and retail banking services, export and import transaction, foreign exchange, securities, and derivative financial instruments trading services. In 2011, Sberbank acquired Volksbank International AG, and in 2012, Turkish DenizBank was acquired. By 2013, Sberbank had about 19,000 branches and 250,000 employees.

The peer banks selected for comparison of Sberbank for relative valuation are from other emerging markets. The peer banks are State Bank of India, Bank of China, and Siam Commercial bank.

The forward P/E ratio for Sberbank given by morningstar.com is 16.5 (Tables 7.6 and 7.7).

Table 7.5 EV multiples: Taiwan Semiconductors versus peer comparison

Company	EV/EBITDA	EV/EBIT	EV/Sales
Taiwan Semiconductors	1.3	2.4	0.9
Intel	7.7	12.3	3.2
Texas Instruments	12.4	16.8	4.6
Avago Technologies	29.0	71.3	7.3
Broadcom	26.5	49.5	2.9

Table 7.6 Current relative valuation on basis of equity multiples: Sberbank versus industry peers

Company	P/S	P/B	P/E	P/CF	Div yield %
Sberbank	1.3	0.8	4.5	4.4	5.35
State Bank of India	1.9	0.1	14.9	9.4	0.5
Bank of China	3.1	1.4	8.3	2.7	3.6
Siam Commercial Bank	3.5	2.1	11	106.3	3.0
S&P 500	1.8	2.7	18.6	11.5	2.1

Sberbank have the least equity multiples among the three peer banks and the S&P 500 except for P/CF and dividend yield. Sberbank has the highest dividend yield among the peer group and market index.
Source: Data from Morningstar.com.

Table 7.7 EV multiples: Taiwan Semiconductors versus peer comparison

Company	EV/EBITDA	EV/Revenues
Sberbank	3.2	1.0
State Bank of India	28	3.3
Bank of China	45.1	18.8
Siam Commercial Bank	6.6	3.7

7.9.3.1   EV multiples for Sberbank

In terms of EV multiples, Sberbank is the most undervalued bank among the selected peer banks as its EV multiples like EV/EBITA and EV/Revenues are the least. The data and calculations for EV multiples are given in the spreadsheet *EV Multiples Sberbank.xlsx*.

References

Alford, A., 1992. The effect of the set of comparable firms on the accuracy of the price earnings valuation method. J. Account. Res. 30, 94−108.

Da, Z., Schaumburg, E., 2011. Relative valuation and analyst target price forecasts. J. Financ. Mark. 14, 161−192.

Damodaran, A., 2012. Investment Valuation, third ed. Wiley Finance.

Baker, M., Ruback, R., 1999. Estimating Industry Multiples, Working Paper. Harvard University.

Beatty, R.P., Riffe, S.M., Thomson, R., 1999. The method of comparables and tax court valuation of private firms: an empirical investigation. Account. Horiz. 13, 177−199.

Boatsman, J., Baskin, E., 1981. Asset valuation with incomplete markets. Account. Rev. 56, 38−53.

Capaul, C., Rowley, I., Sharpe, W.F., 1993. International value and growth stock returns. Financ. Anal. J. 49, 27−36.

Chan, L.K., Hamrao, Y., Lakonishok, J., 1991. Fundamentals and stock returns in Japan. J. Finance. 46, 1739−1789.

Fairfield, P., 1994. P/E, P/B and the present value of future dividends. Financ. Anal. J. 50 (4), 23−31.

Fama, E.F., French, K., 1992. The cross section of expected stock returns. J. Finance. 47 (2), 427−465.

Goldman Sachs, 1999. Accounting/Portfolio Strategy, Goldman Sachs Investment Research, pp. 1−40.

Huang, Y., Tsai, C.H., Chen, C.R., 2007. Expected P/E, residual P/E, and stock return reversal: Time — Varying fundamentals or investor overreaction? Int. J. Bus. Econ. 6 (1), 11−28.

Kaplan, S.N., Ruback, R.S., 1995. The valuation of cash flow forecasts: an empirical analysis. J. Finance. 50 (4), p1059−p1093.

Kenth, S., Stina, S., 2008. P/E ratios in relative valuation—a mission impossible. Invest. Manage. Financ. Innov. 5 (4), 237−248.

Kim, M., Ritter, J.R., 1999. Valuing IPOs. J. Financ. Econ. 53 (3), 409−437.

Liu, J., Nissim, D., Thomas, J., 2002. Equity valuation using multiples. J. Account. Res. 40 (1), 135−172.

Liu, J., Nissim, D., Thomas, J., 2007. Is cash king in valuations? Financ. Anal. J. 63 (2), 56−68.

Penman, S.H., 1996. The articulation of price-earnings ratios and market-to book ratios and the evolution of growth. J. Account. Res. 34, 253−259.

Penman, S.H., 1997. Combining Earnings and Book Value in Equity Valuation, Working Paper. Columbia University, Department of Accounting.

Rosenberg, B., Reid, K., Lanstein, R., 1985. Persuasive evidence of market inefficiency. J. Portf. Manage. 11 (3), 9−17.

Tasker, S.C., 1998. Industry Preferred Multiples in Acquisition Valuation, Working Paper. Cornell University, Ithaca, NY.

Mergers and acquisition valuation $\boxed{8}$

8.1 Introduction

Corporate restructuring activities like Mergers and acquisitions (M&A) have great relevance in the global corporate arena. M&A signify a major force in the modern financial and economic environment. Acquisitions remain the quickest route companies take to operate in new markets and to add new capabilities and resources. In times of boom or bust, M&A have emerged as a compelling strategy for growth. M&A are transactions of great significance not only for companies but for other stakeholders like competitors, employees, communities, and the economy as a whole. Events like M&A are of great significance in the modern political environment. The historic corporate battle between Mittal Steel and its unsolicited hostile bid on Arcelor stirred up passions in Europe with politicians, ministers, and even ordinary citizens joining in the discussions.

The economic perspective on M&A suggests that competitive advantage over competitors can be obtained through cost reduction or increased market power. Economies of scale are cost savings that result from large-sized operations. Economies of scope stem directly from cost savings due to consolidation of value chain activities.

8.2 Types of mergers and acquisitions

A merger is a combination of two companies into one larger company. The method of exchange involve either cash or stock or hybrid. In a merger, the acquiring company takes over the assets and liabilities of the target or merged company. All the combining companies are dissolved and only the new entity exist to operate. In general, when the combination involve firms of similar size, it is termed consolidation. When two firms differ significantly by size, the term merger is used. Merger commonly takes two forms. In the first form, amalgamation two entities combine together and form a new entity, thus removing both existing entities. In the second form, absorption, one entity gets absorbed into another. The latter does not lose its identity. Thus, in any type of merger, at least one entity loses its entity.

Thus A + B = A, where Company B is merged into Company A (Absorption)

A + B = C, where C is an entirely new company (Amalgamation or Consolidation)

Acquisition is a more general term which envelops in itself a range of acquisition transactions. It could be acquisition of control leading to takeover of a company. It could be acquisition of tangible assets, intangible assets, rights, and other kinds of obligations. An acquisition also known as a takeover is the buying of one company (the target) by the acquirer. An acquisition can be friendly or hostile. In a friendly takeover, the companies proceed through negotiations. In a hostile acquisition, the target firm's management does not want to be acquired. In a hostile takeover, an outside group launches a hostile attack to takeover the control of the target company without the concurrence of the existing controlling group. The buyer buys the shares and the control of the target company. The ownership control of the company results in effective control of its assets. Asset acquisition involves buying assets of another company. The assets may be tangible assets like a manufacturing unit or intangible assets like brands. A firm can also be acquired by its own management or by a group of investors usually by a tender offer. After this transaction, the acquired firm ceases to exist as a publicly traded firm and becomes a private business. These acquisitions are called management buyouts, if managers are involved, and leveraged buyouts, if funds are predominantly raised from debt.

Horizontal mergers take place when two merging companies produce similar products in the same industry. Horizontal mergers are meant to attain market power. Vertical mergers refer to a firm acquiring a supplier or distributor of one or more of its goods or services. Vertical mergers involve combinations of companies that have a buyer–seller relationship. Vertical mergers occur when two firms each working at different stages in the production of the same product combine. Conglomerate mergers occur when companies in the different industry sectors. A pure conglomerate merger occurs when a firm in an industry with low demand growth relative to the economy acquires a firm operating in an industry with high expected demand growth. The motive of conglomerate merger is the realization of financial synergy, which involves capturing the investment opportunities available in the acquired firm's industry by lowering the cost of capital of the combined firm and also by utilizing the acquiring firm's internal funds available at a lower cost. The opportunity for utilizing the cash flows of the acquiring firm would be enhanced if the cash flows of the acquired firm are low. The industry of the acquirer firm may be growing at a lower rate than the average industry growth rate in the economy. The acquirer firm may have internal cash flows in excess of current investment opportunities in its own industry. The acquiring firm may supply lower cost internal funds to the combined firm. Thus in a nutshell, a pure conglomerate merger occurs to internalize the investment opportunities in the acquired firm's industry by initially lowering the cost of capital of the combined firm.

8.3   Synergies in mergers

Synergic effect occurs when two factors combine to produce a greater effect, more than the sum of those together operating independently. The principle of synergy aims to maximize the shareholder value of the merged entity. Synergy is the ability of a merged company to create more shareholder value than the standalone entity. If synergy exists in a takeover, the value of the combined firm must be greater than the sum of the values of the bidding and target firms operating independently.

$$V(AB) > V(A) + V(B)$$

Where V(AB) = Value of a firm created by combining A and B (Synergy)
V(A) = Value of firm A operating independently
V(B) = Value of firm B operating independently

The value created by the combination of firms may result from more efficient management, economies of scale, improved production techniques, combination of complementary resources, redeployment of assets to more profitable uses, exploitation of market power, or any number of value creating mechanism, which falls under the general rubric of corporate synergy (Weston et al., 2006).

Basically, operating synergies can be classified into cost-based and revenue-based synergy. Cost-based synergy aims for reducing incurred costs by combining similar assets in the merged businesses. Cost synergy can typically achieve economies of scale particularly for sales and marketing, administrative, operating, and/or research and development (R&D) costs. Revenue-based synergy focuses on enhancing capabilities and revenues and combining complementary competencies. Revenue-based synergy can be exploited if merging business develops new competencies that allow them to command a price premium through higher innovation capabilities (product innovation, time to market, etc.) or boost sales volume through increased market coverage (geographic and product line extension). Revenue synergy is achieved through product cross-selling, higher prices due to less competition, or increasing market share.

M&A create three types of synergies by customizing resources differently. Companies created modular synergies when they manage operations independently and pool-only the results for greater profits. In a collaboration between an airline and a hotel chain, where the hotel's guests earn frequent flyer miles, clubbing of consumer's choice of hotel and airline benefits both the organizations. Firms can also create sequential synergies when one company completes its task and passes on the results to a partner to do its part. When a biotech firm partner with a pharmaceutical firm that is familiar with FDA approval process, then both firms can create sequential synergies. Companies create reciprocal synergies by working closely together and executing tasks through an iterative knowledge sharing process (Dyer et al., 2004).

Operating synergy facilitate firms to increase their operating income or growth or both (Kumar, 2010). Operating synergy may result from economies of scale, which may arise from merger, allowing the combined firm to become more cost efficient and profitable. The source of operating synergy may be attributed to greater pricing power, reduced competition, and higher market share, which may result in higher margins and operating income. For example, firm with good product line when acquired by a firm with strong marketing skills may be result in operating synergy. Higher growth in new or existing markets, arising from the combination of two firms, may also become a source of operating synergy.

The resultant feature of corporate merger or acquisition on the cost of capital of the combined or acquiring firm is called financial synergy. It is the result of the lower cost of internal financing as compared to external financing. Debt capacity may increase because when two firms combine their earnings and cash flows may become more stable and predictable. This would allow the firms to borrow more than they could as individual entities, which creates a tax benefit for the combined firm. A combination of a firm with excess cash or cash slack (and limited project opportunities), and a firm with high return projects (and limited cash) can yield a payoff in terms of higher value for the combined firm.

8.4   Drivers of value creation in different types of M&A

The basic drivers of value creation in a horizontal merger would be increased market power and revenue growth. Value creation in a horizontal merger can be achieved through revenue enhancement, cost savings, and new growth. Revenue growth can be achieved through lowering prices for products that are highly price sensitive. As a result of horizontal merger, market share may increase and contribute to revenue enhancement, if the price elasticity of products are unchanged. Acquired firms involved in horizontal mergers with target firms in terms of network externality can realize revenue enhancement. Acquisition can also facilitate revenue growth by acquiring firms whose products are complementary in nature. Value creation in horizontal mergers through revenue growth can be achieved through leveraging marketing resources and capabilities of the merging firms (Sudarsanam, 2003). Cost savings in horizontal mergers results due to combination of functional areas like production, marketing, sales and distribution, R&D of the acquirer and target firms. The same activities can be carried out at a lower cost than either firm's individual costs. This would lead to reduction in production and fixed costs. The profit margin may be improved and pricing pressure be eased by reducing supply to match the demand. M&A in steel industry were basically motivated to reduce excess capacity and enhance cost savings. In horizontal mergers, cost savings may also result from economies of scale in production, marketing, sales and distribution, logistics, branding, and R&D. Economies of scope exist when the cost of production of two or more goods by a multiproduct firm is less than the combined costs of separate production of those goods by firms specializing in the production. Scope economies are realized when costs are spread over an increased range of output of different products. R&D activity often generate spillovers when ideas developed in one research project provide stimulus for other projects. Learning economies arise when managers and workers over time become experienced and effective in using the available resources of the firm and facilitate lowering the cost of production. New growth opportunities arise due to horizontal mergers due to creation of new technologies and products.

Vertical integration refers to the degree to which a firm owns its upstream suppliers and downstream buyers. Vertical integration is the process in which several steps in the production and/or distribution of a product or service are controlled by a single company or entity in order to increase its power in the market.

Vertical integration refers to the degree of integration between the firm's value chain and the value chain of its suppliers and distributors. Expansion of activities downstream is referred to as forward integration, whereas expansion upstream is referred to as backward integration. A merger or an acquisition can be termed vertical if there is a kind of buyer—seller relationship between the partnering firms. Vertical mergers can create value if they improve economic efficiency by cutting out intermediaries and reducing overhead expenses and redundant assets. Vertical mergers may increase the ability of firms to provide a package of services and products, which could lead to revenue enhancement. Vertical mergers have blurred the boundaries segregating banking, insurance, and asset management industries. The modern concept of bancassurance is based on the backward integration of banks to source insurance industry products and forward integration of insurance companies to acquire distribution channels. The financial supermarket giant, Citigroup has been built on the basis of this model. In the 1990s, Travelers Group diversified its business, from insurance into securities by buying Smith Barney (brokerage firm), Salomon Brothers (investment bank and securities trading firm), and Citibank (commercial bank) to form a full-fledged financial institution called Citigroup (Gart, 1998).

In conglomerate mergers, the merging firms do not have any relation between their products and markets. Conglomerate merger may result in transfer of scarce resources like management capabilities, from one firm to another. The main synergy effect in conglomerate mergers is based on specific risk reduction, which lowers the cost of capital. In unrelated acquisitions, value creation is also associated with coinsurance effect. If the merger reduces the probability that one of the firms would default on its debt, then the value of the debt would increase and the merger would be beneficial. Conglomerate diversification might promote knowledge transfer across divisions. General Electric practices total quality management and extends its productivity enhancing techniques to new businesses that it acquires. When diversification takes place in a related field, it may be possible for the diversified firm to reduce costs through improved bargaining power with its suppliers. The cost of financing may be lowered due to the portfolio diversification effect. Lewellen (1971) suggested that combining two unrelated businesses whose cash flows are imperfectly correlated can reduce the risk of default of the entire enterprise. Diversification can bring aggregation of resources that can be shaped into core competencies to facilitate competitive advantage (Prahalad and Hamel, 1990). The diversified firm internalizes the capital market by acting as an allocator of resources among the businesses in its portfolio. This close proximity to the companies and access to better information about them permit internal capital market to operate more efficiently than the external markets (Bruner, 2004).

8.5   Empirical evidence on value creation in M&A

The study by Eckbo (1983) found little evidence indicating that horizontal mergers would have collusive anticompetitive effects. The study by Edward Fee and Thomas

(2004) investigates the upstream and downstream product market effects of a large sample of horizontal M&A from 1980 to 1997. The study finds evidence consistent with improved productive efficiency and buying power as sources of gains to horizontal mergers. Haugen and Udell (1972) finds that there is some indication that horizontal acquisitions were associated with increased rates of returns during the decade 1962—1971. A study by Joseph and Goyal (2006) based on vertical mergers between 1962 and 1996 found that vertical mergers generate positive wealth effects that are significantly larger than those for diversifying mergers. Vertical mergers can enhance change the pricing incentive of an upstream producer. In his study, Chen (2001) found that vertical integration can also change the pricing incentive of a downstream producer and the incentive of a competitor in choosing input suppliers. The study also finds that competitive effects of a vertical merger depends on the cost of switching suppliers and the degree of downstream product differentiation. Haugen and Udell (1972) found that vertical mergers in the 1970s were associated with increased rates of returns during the decade 1962—1971. Lubatkin (1987) found no significant differences in returns to bidding firm shareholders for strategically related and unrelated acquisitions. Singh and Montgomery (1987) despite controlling for the type and degree of strategic relatedness between bidding and target firms found that these acquisitions did not generate abnormal returns for shareholders of bidding firms. The study also states that shareholders of related target firms obtain higher abnormal profits than shareholders of unrelated firms. The study further concludes that strategically related acquisitions create more economic value than unrelated acquisitions. Rumelt (1974) in his study of diversification strategies showed that related diversification strategies outperformed unrelated diversification strategies.

Arnould (1969) and Markham (1973) find no significant relationship between diversification and firm performance. In contrast, studies by Rumelt (1974,1982), Montgomery (1982), and Christensen and Montgomery (1981) report a systematic relationship between a firm's diversification strategy and its economic performance. Teece (1980) suggests that diversification leads to economies of scope. Elgers and Clark (1980) examined the risk-adjusted common stock returns associated with 377 mergers during the period 1957—1975. They found that both the buyer and seller stockholders appear to benefit more from conglomerate mergers than from nonconglomerate mergers though these differences are not statistically significant. Amihud and Lev (1981) argues that managers diversify to protect the value of their human capital. Jensen (1986) suggests that companies diversify to increase the private benefits of managers. Morck et al. (1989) suggests that managers diversify as they are better at managing assets in other industries.

8.6 M&A valuation

Valuation is an integral part of M&A process. In valuation, investors make decisions based on expectations of future performance. Analysts have to base estimates on forecasts of the future rather than on past results. The economic reality is that the real value is based on cash flows rather than accounting profits. Warren Buffet had once said that accounting consequences do not influence the operating and capital allocation process. In generic form, free cash flow equals earnings plus noncash charges minus investments. Intrinsic value is the present value of future expected performance.

The two major methods of valuation as discussed by in Chapter 6 & 7 are discounted cash flow valuation and relative valuation. In an M&A Scenario, the concept of opportunity cost must take into account different alternative strategies for the acquirer and target firms. This include decisions of make or buy for the buyer as well as the scope for different kinds of deals like joint venture and strategic alliances. The value of target to the seller ought to be the target's value in its highest alternative deployment. The aim of all valuation analysis is to assess the true or intrinsic value of an asset. General M&A valuation involves many estimates and estimators.

From a buyer's perspective, it is worthwhile for an acquirer to accept the deal if the intrinsic value of the target is greater than the amount paid to the target as a part of deal. From the seller's perspective, the proposed deal must be accepted if the payment to the target is greater than the intrinsic value of target to the seller.

8.6.1   Enterprise value

Enterprise value (EV) is the intrinsic value of the firm. It is the net asset value that is equal to the total assets less current liabilities. EV of a firm is an economic measure, which reflects the market value of the business. It is a fundamental metric in business valuation. It is the sum of the claims of both creditors and equity holders.

In general form, Enterprise value = Market value of equity + Value of debt.

The EV measures the value of the ongoing operations of a firm. EV can be considered as the theoretical takeover price of the firm. EV is an alternate to market capitalization.

Enterprise value = Market capitalization + Debt + Preferred share capital + Minority interest − Cash and cash equivalents.

8.6.2   Book value of assets

Book value is obtained from the audited financial statements. This method is basically backward looking and ignores the operating aspects of the firm. The book value ignores intangible assets like brand names and patents. In tangible book value, the intangible or soft assets are deducted from the total assets.

8.6.3   Liquidation value

Liquidation value is the most conservative valuation approach. Liquidation value refers to the worth of a firm when the assets of the firm are sold. In other words, liquidation value refers to the estimated amounted of money received when its assets are sold and its debts paid. This value is often stated on a per share basis. Liquidation value above the stock's market price indicates that it is better to liquidate the firm. The calculation of liquidation value is often related to bankruptcy procedures. Intangible assets, like goodwill, intellectual property, and brands, are not considered as part of estimation of liquidation value. The liquidation value is estimated for plant and machinery, fixtures, real estate, and inventory owned by the firm. The liquidation value is obtained by subtracting company's liabilities from its assets. Receivables are often sold for 80–90% of book value. Inventories liquidation value is often based on 80–90% of the book value, depending on the degree of obsolescence and condition. The equipment value depend on its age, condition, and purpose. The book value will always understate the market value. Prepaid assets like insurance can be liquidated with a portion of the premium recovered. The liquidation value of a project also refers to abandonment value, which would be the cash value generated from liquidating a project or selling an investment. The overall value of a business would be lower when standard book method is used. Liquidation value is smaller than the book value of the firm. The liquidation values are basically appraiser specific and based on subjective estimates. The physical conditions of the assets will affect values.

A variation of liquidation value is bust-up value, which is estimated in M&A by investors in valuing acquisition targets or taking companies private. Breakup value estimation is often used in private equity/hedge or LBO deals. Target firms are viewed as a number of independent operating units whereby income, cash flow, and balance sheet items reflect intracompany sales, fully allocated costs, and operating liabilities specific to each unit. The after-tax cash flows are valued using market-based multiples or discounted cash flow methods in order to determine the operating unit's current market value. Each unit's equity value is determined by deducting the operating liabilities from the current market value. The aggregate value of equity in the business is determined by adding up the equity value of each operating unit less the unallocated liabilities and breakup costs.

8.6.4 Replacement cost valuation

Replacement cost valuation is generally used for valuing firms in inflationary environment setting. Under inflationary conditions, historical cost is not ideal for valuation of firms. In this method, liabilities are deducted from the replacement cost to arrive at the value of the business. Replacement cost is the actual cost incurred to replace an existing asset. This method is used in insurance industry to determine the value of an insured item. Usually for property insurance, a contractual stipulation is made that the lost asset must be actually repaired or replaced before the replacement cost is paid. Replacement cost valuation is highly subjective in nature. Replacement cost valuation is often used to value existing utility generation assets.

8.6.5 Discounted cash flow valuation

The discounted cash flow valuation is based on the assumption that the value of any firm is the present value expected future cash flows from the assets of the firm. The basic models of discounted cash flow valuation are the free cash flow to the firm (FCFF) and free cash flow to the equity (FCFE). In the FCFE model, the future cash flows to the equity shareholders are discounted by the cost of equity. In the FCFF model, the future cash flows to the equity shareholders and debtors are discounted by the WACC. The discounted cash flow valuation involves one-, two-, and three-stage models of valuation.

8.6.6 Adjusted present value method

In adjusted present value (APV) method, the present value of cash flows from the assets and the side effects associated with financing like interest tax shields are estimated. The APV measures the profitability of a project or investment in which tax deductions are applied on the basis of debt financing through an unlevered equity cash flow. APV is the net present value of a project which is the combination of the present value of unlevered cash flows plus the present value of all benefits of financing. The first step involves the estimation of the value of unlevered firm by discounting the expected FCFF at the unleveraged cost of equity. The second step involves the calculation of the expected tax savings from the given level of debt by discounting the expected tax saving at the cost of debt to reflect the riskness of the cash flow. The third step involves evaluation of the effect of a given level of debt on the default risk of a firm and the expected bankruptcy costs.

> Value of operating assets = Unlevered firm value + PV of tax benefits − Expected bankruptcy costs.
> Adjusted present value = Value of the operating assets + Value of cash and marketable securities.

In a technical sense, the APV valuation model combines the impact of both growth and tax shield of debt on the cost of capital, the cost of equity, and the systematic risk. The disadvantage of this method is that in the case of firms with high-debt ratios,[1] the firm value estimated may be more as the tax benefits are more due to usage of high leverage.

8.6.7 Relative valuation

In relative valuation, the value of target firm is estimated by applying the valuation multiples of peer firms to the target firm. Multiples can be classified into equity price-based multiples, earnings-based multiples, and EV multiples. Multiples are also classified into forward and lagged multiples. A multiple is a ratio between two financial variables. The numerator of the multiple is either the company's market price in case of price multiples or its EV in case of EV multiples. The important

---

[1] http://strategiccfo.com/wikicfo/adjusted-present-value-apv-method-of-valuation/

equity price-based multiples are P/E, PEG, P/S, and P/B ratios. The major enterprise-based multiples are EV/EBITDA, EV/EBIT, and EV/Revenues. Relative valuation do not provide a direct estimate of a firm's fundamental value. Relative valuation method indicate whether a firm is fairly priced relative to some benchmark. Relative valuation is also known as comparable valuation approach as this indirect valuation process involves identification of a group of comparable companies. It is interesting to point out that most valuations on Wall Street are based on relative valuations. Approximately 85% of equity research reports are based on multiples and comparable. Almost 50% of all acquisition valuations are based on multiples. In same or comparable industry method, the target firm's earnings or revenues are multiplied by the market value to earnings or revenue ratios for the average firm in target's industry or a comparable industry. Relative valuation provides reasonable estimate of the target company's value. The method is sensitive to market mispricing and estimates of takeover premium.

8.6.8 Venture capital valuation approach

In this valuation approach, valuation is based on risk assessment of factors, which include market, technology trends, financials, funding phase, etc. A mix of different assessment methods is used to value startup companies and high-growth potential technology companies. The analysts project the performance of the firm into future and assume that the private equity investor will exit typically in a 5-year time period. The exit value at that horizon is estimated using an exit multiple.

8.6.9 Real options valuation approach

The option valuation approach suggests that the equity in a levered firm is equivalent to a call option on the asset value of the firm. The total M&A value consists of a standalone of a target value plus synergistic real options value. The value of a call option requires the estimation of parameters. The first parameter is the value of underlying assets, which could be the EV. The exercise price of the call option is the par value of the debt outstanding. The term of the option is the duration of the debt outstanding. The risk free rate is another parameter for estimation. The risk-free rate is the yield to maturity on government securities with a life equal to the duration of the firm's outstanding debt. Volatility of returns is another parameter for estimation on the underlying assets. Volatility is measured as the standard deviation of the price changes on the underlying asset. Real options are strategic management options in terms of the choice to adopt corporate investment decisions (Titman and Martin, 2014). M&A often contain embedded options like the option to accelerate growth by increasing initial investment known as option to expand; delay the timings of the initial investment or abandon the project. The existence of the real option will increase the value of the expected NPV. Expand, delay, and abandon options for a firm exist prior and after the deal is closed. The acquirer have the opportunity to expand, delay, and abandon new investments in the target firm. Real options can be valued using decision tree framework and the Black Scholes model.

8.6.10   Firm valuation using weighted average method

In weighted average method, the analyst assigns weights to different methodologies to arrive at the weighted firm value. The weights are assigned for different valuation techniques like relative valuation, discounted cash flow valuation, and liquidation value to arrive at the weighted value.

8.7   Valuation of M&A synergies

In synergy, the whole would be greater than sum of the parts. Mathematically, we can state $2 + 2 = 5$. Ideally, M&A activities must lead to value creation through the realization of synergies. Synergy must result in real measurable improvements in competitive advantage. Synergies must lead to increased shareholder wealth creation for firms. Estimation of synergy must be the central focus of the analysis of M&A. In the absence of synergy, if the buyer is perceived to have overpaid the target firm, then the buyer's share price is expected to fall following the announcement of the deal. In traditional merger valuation, the focus is on cost and revenue synergies as a primary source of value creation. Financial synergies have become relatively more important as the source of value creation particularly in the context of recent credit crisis. Financial synergies can be derived from increased size, scale, diversity, improved credit profile, and market access. The cost for debt can be lowered with a better credit profile and rating. The factors that slow down M&A activity include credit market challenges, valuation differences, concerns about the economy, friction costs, and execution risk. Horizontal mergers will provide the opportunity to increase profitability through cost synergies. The increased scale contributes to revenue synergies and leads companies to greater pricing and buying power. Friction costs trigger change in control clauses whereby firms renegotiate bank deals or acquirer purchase target firm bondholders at par. The uncertainty and risk around an M&A transaction in an uncertain capital market environment may prevent firms from accessing capital markets when the deal gets closed. When two firms merger and are able to achieve a better credit quality, then financial synergy results as the cost of capital is reduced. This happens since the higher the ratings, lower coupon needs to be given on a bond issue. Corporations also receive a tax deduction for payments to debt holders thereby creating a tax shield on debt for corporations. This tax benefit is incorporated for the weighted average cost of capital calculation. When two firms merge, the cash flows may become less volatile. In such a scenario, the merger may improve the credit profile and reduce the likelihood of default. Mergers which enhance the scale and size, reduce the business risk can lead to increase in the debt capacity due to improvement in ratings as they could access more stable debt markets, thereby creating financial flexibility synergies. Financial synergies also signify improved bank market access for large firms and access of less expensive commercial papers. Large firms in a given industry have a cost of capital and capital access advantage. There can also be sizable valuation differences. Large firms often use this valuation advantage to absorb and integrate smaller firms with less dilution via stock acquisitions.[2]

The quantification of synergies is situation specific and basically focus on what the merging firms brings to the mix and on the degree of redundancy or overlap between two operations. The quantum of synergies depends on how management rationalize redundancies and manage the overall combination of two businesses as well as on postmerger business strategies and tactics.

The synergy value can be factored into the value of a business in different ways.[3] In the first method, synergies can be valued separately by performing two discounted cash flow analysis one for business on its own (intrinsic value) and for synergy value. The annual incremental cash flow from synergies are capitalized using a suitable discount rate. The resulting value of annual synergies plus one time benefits is added to the intrinsic value of the entity. A single discounted cash flow analysis can also be done by adding the synergy cash flows to the intrinsic cash flows and converting it to present value using a single discount rate.

Synergies should be measured as a bundle of value of assets in place and growth options. Revenue synergies will be achieved through combination of two firms, which results in cross-selling of products, efficient exploitation of brands, and geographic and product line extension.

The initial offer price for the target firm lies between the minimum and maximum offer prices. The minimum offer price can be stated as the target's standalone value or its current market value. The maximum price is the sum of the minimum price plus the present value of net synergy. The determination of initial offer price also requires the estimation of the anticipated synergy which the acquirer firm shares with the target firm's shareholders. The target company are often purchased at a premium to the current market value to make the offer attractive to the target shareholders. The extent of premium offered to the target firm depends on its financial performance. Target firms which are doing extremely well will command a high premium. The cost of sales for the merged firms can be reduced from factors like elimination of duplication of resources and bulk purchases of raw materials. Sales and administration expenses can be reduced by elimination of overlapping jobs.

8.7.1   Estimation of value of synergy

Value of synergy can be estimated using discounted cash flow techniques. In the first step, the value of the firms involved in the merger are estimated independently by discounting expected cash flows to each firm at the weighted average cost of capital. Then the value of the combined firm with no synergy is estimated by adding the values obtained from each firm. The third step involves building in the effects of synergy into

---

[2] A shifting landscape for synergies, How financial considerations are affecting value creation in mergers and acquisition, https://www.jpmorgan.com/cm/BlobServer/cfa_jun2009.pdf?blobkey=id&blobwhere=1320675767611&blobheader=application/pdf&blobheadername1=Cache-Control&blobheadervalue1=private&blobcol=urldata&blobtable=MungoBlobs.

[3] http://www.duffandphelps.com/sitecollectiondocuments/reports/DUF_sharing_synergies.pdf.

expected growth rates and cash flows and then the value of the combined firm with synergy is estimated. The synergy value is estimated as the difference between the value of the combined firm with synergy and the value of the combined firm without synergy.

Hostile takeovers basically take place for control purposes. Firms pay large premium over the market price to control the management of firms in a hostile takeover. The value of control is the difference between the value of firms managed optimally minus the value of the firm with current management.

8.8   Payment to target firms

A firm can raise funds for an acquisition from either debt or equity. The mix of debt and equity depends on the excess debt capacities of both acquiring and target firms. The chances are more that the acquirer firm will finance the acquisition of the target with more debt if the target firm is unlevered. If the acquiring firm have unused debt capacity or is underlevered, then the acquirer firm might use more debt to finance the transactions.

A firm can use cash balances to finance the acquisition. It can also issue stock to the public to raise funds to finance the acquisitions. The firm can also issue stock as payment for the target firms in which the payment is structured in terms of stock swap based on exchange ratios. In the stock swap method, the shares in the acquiring firm is exchanged for shares in the target firm. When an acquisition is a stock swap, the stockholders in the target firm would be able to defer capital gains taxes on the exchanged shares. In the stock swap, the target firm shareholders will be offered a number of shares per share of acquirer firm. The stock swap is normally based on the market price at the time of announcement of the deal.

8.8.1   Types of exchange of shares

The exchange of the acquirer's shares for the target's shares requires the determination of the appropriate exchange ratio for listed companies. There are two ways to structure an offer for exchange of shares. These approaches have a significant impact on the allocation of risk between the two sets of shareholders. Companies can either issue a fixed number of shares or they can issue a fixed value of shares.

In fixed shares offer, the number of shares to be issued is fixed, but the value of the deal may fluctuate between the announcement of the offer and the closing date, depending on the acquirer's share price. Both the acquiring and selling shareholders are affected by fluctuations. However, the fluctuations in the acquirer's share price will not affect the proportional ownership of the two sets of shareholders in the combined company. Hence, the interests of the shareholders in the deal's shareholder value added do not change, even though the actual shareholder value may vary. In fixed share deal, shareholders in the acquired company are particularly vulnerable to fall in the price of the acquiring company's stock as they bear a portion of the price risk from the deal when it is announced (Rapport and Sirower, 1999).

In fixed value offer, the acquirer issues a fixed value of shares. In this deal, the number of shares issued is not fixed until the closing date, and depends on the prevailing price.

8.9 Bootstrapping

The phenomena whereby shareholder value increases by the application of the bidder's higher bid to the target's earnings is known bootstrapping. In other words, a high PE (Price Earnings ratio) firm buys a low PE firm resulting in a higher EPS for the merged firm.

8.10 Empirical studies involving methods of payment

In studies covering more than 1200 major deals, researchers have consistently found that, at the time of announcement, shareholders of acquiring companies fare worse in stock transactions than in cash transactions. If the acquirer believes in undervaluing its shares, then it should not issue new shares to finance a transaction because that would affect the current shareholders. Research consistently shows that the market takes the issuance of stock by a company as a sign that the stock is overvalued. Myers and Majluf (1984) have found that differential stock returns of bidders in mergers and tender offers may be due to the method of acquisition financing. The Myers and Majluf model suggests that the managers will prefer cash offer if they believe that their firm is undervalued, while a common exchange offer will be preferred in the opposite case. De Angelo and Masulis (1980) suggests that the market participants interpret a cash offer as a good news and a common stock exchange offer as a bad news about the bidding firm's true value. If such information effects are important, the bidding firm's stock price change at the proposal's announcement will reflect both the gain from the takeover (weighted by the probability that the takeover bid will go through) and the information effects.

Cash offers and exchange offers have different tax implications. Cash offers and exchange offers have different tax implications. Cash offers generate tax obligations for the target firm's shareholders but allow the acquiring firm to raise the depreciation basis of acquired assets to their market value. Common stock exchange offers are, in general, tax-free acquisitions as any capital gains realized by the target firm's stockholders are deferred until the stock is sold, but the depreciation basis of the acquired assets remains the same (Travlos, 1987).

The study by Travlos (1987) provides direct confirmation of a differential return relationships across different methods of payment for bidding firms announcing takeover bids. The results on pure stock exchange bidding firms show that their stockholders experience significant losses at the announcement of the takeover proposal. On the other hand, the results on the cash financing bidding firms show that their stockholders earn normal rates of returns at the announcement period.

Their findings are consistent with the signaling hypothesis, which implies that financing a takeover through exchange of common stock conveys negative information that the bidding firm is overvalued. Carleton et al. (1983) argues that cash takeovers and security exchange mergers may well be motivated by different considerations. The study finds that lower dividend payout ratios and lower market-to-book ratios increase the probability of being acquired in a cash takeover relative to being acquired via an exchange of securities even though neither variable can be shown as to be an important explanatory factor for the simple categorization of firms into those that have been acquired and those that have not been acquired. Fishman (1989) argues that when the fixed costs of collecting information about the target are high, cash financing is more likely than stock financing as a means to signal high valuation in order to deter competing offers for the target firm.

8.11 Empirical studies on performance of merged companies

Two main research approaches explain M&A value creation. The event studies examine the abnormal returns to shareholders in the period surrounding the announcement of a merger or acquisition. The accounting studies examine the reported financial results of acquirers before and after the acquisitions to see how the financial performance changes. It can be stated that a given merger is successful if other things equal, it increases the total current wealth of the owners of the acquiring firm. The efficient market hypothesis assumes that investor's anticipation of future benefits will be reflected in the merging firm's stock prices at the time of acquisition announcement. The post takeover accounting performance measures represent actual economic benefits generated by takeovers, whereas the takeover announcement returns represent the investor's expectation of takeover benefits.

McKinsey and Co examined 115 mergers in the United Kingdom and United States during the 1990s and suggested that 60% of the acquisitions earned return on capital less than the cost of capital. KPMG in their 1999 study examined 700 expensive deals during the period 1996–1998 and suggested that 17% created value for the combined firm, 30% were value neutral, and 53% destroyed value.

For a firm characterized by the objective of stockholder wealth maximization, the appropriate test of the success of a merger is its effect on stock prices. In an efficient capital market, the investor's expectation of the merger's future benefit should be fully reflected in the stock prices by the date of the merger. The increase in the equity value of the acquiring firm in the wake of a successful merger is compelling evidence for the synergy theory of M&A. The questions concerning the impact of a merger on the market value of merging firms have occupied a prominent position in the literature of economics and finance for the last half-century in the western context. In response to these questions, a number of carefully conducted empirical investigations have documented the effect of a merger on the wealth of the common stockholders of merging firms. In the context of mergers as corporate investment, it follows that there is an incentive for the stockholders to acquire firms, which increases the variability of the firm's cash flow. The profitability of a merger can be enhanced by positive synergistic effects due to the effective integration of productive facilities and distribution networks. In an efficient capital market, if there is certainty about the scope, timing, and success of a firm's merger program, then the entire net present value of a merger program should be capitalized in stock prices when the program is first announced. If there is uncertainty about the program, the market reaction should be ongoing as new information is released (Asquith et al., 1983). In an efficient capital market, the investor's expectations of future benefits should be fully reflected in stock prices by the merger date. Postmerger stock prices could experience a merger-related increase (or decrease) as actual merger benefits are realized to be greater than or less than expectations. The change in the equity value for the buying firm when measured from some base date reflects the expected net present value of the merger. The change in the value of the equity for the selling company is the difference between the price actually paid for the company and the value of the equity without the merger. The sum of the increases in the values of the equities for the merger partners is the market's expectation of the expected total economic gain (or loss) from the merger (Mandelker, 1974).

Jensen and Ruback (1983) reviewed 13 studies that examine returns around takeover announcements and reported an average excess return of 30% to target stockholders in successful tender offers and 20% to target stockholders in successful mergers. Jarrell et al. (1988) reviewed the results of 663 tender offers and found that premiums averaged 19% in the 1960s, 35% in the 1970s, and 30% between 1980 and 1985.

Many of the empirical studies like Franks et al. (1977) on the profitability of the acquiring firm suggest that mergers are unsuccessful. The study by Mandelker (1974) suggests that the market for acquisitions is perfectly competitive, and suggest that there are resources which earn positive gains when combined across firms.

The study by Asquith et al. (1983) examines the effect of mergers on the wealth of bidding firms' shareholders. Bidding firms gain significantly during the 21 days leading to the announcement of each of their first four merger bids. The results fail to support the capitalization hypothesis that bidder's gains are captured at the beginning of merger programs. The study by Langetieg (1978) employs four alternative two-factor market industry models in combination with a matched nonmerging control group to measure stockholder gains from mergers. Moeller et al. (2004) examines the announcement returns using a sample of 12,023 acquisitions by public firms during the period 1980−2001. The results of this study show that the equally weighted abnormal announcement returns are 1.1% but acquiring firm shareholders lose $25.2 million on average upon announcement. Moeller et al. (2004) finds that acquisition announcements in the 1990s were profitable in the aggregate for acquiring firm shareholders until 1997, but the losses of acquiring firm shareholders from 1998 through 2001 wiped out all gains made earlier, thereby making acquisitions announcements in the later merger wave costly for acquiring firm shareholders.

Lev and Mandelker (1970) examines the profitability of mergers along such aspects as risk, growth, capital structure, income tax savings, earnings per share, etc. The conclusion drawn is that the long-run profitability of acquiring firms is probably somewhat higher than that of comparable nonmerging firms. Palepu (1985) finds that there is no significant cross-sectional difference between the (i) profitability of firms with predominantly related and unrelated diversification and (ii) profitability of firms with high and low total diversification. Moreover, the study finds that the superior profitability growth of related diversifiers is significantly greater than that of unrelated diversifiers. Herman and Louis (1988) examined the postmerger performance of a sample of hostile acquisitions between 1975 and 1983. The study by Healy et al. (1992) examines the postmerger cash flow performance of acquiring and target firms and explores the sources of merger-induced changes in cash flow performance based on 50 largest US mergers between 1979 and mid-1984. The study finds that merged firms show significant improvements in asset productivity relative to their industries, leading to higher operating cash flow returns. These improvements were particularly strong for transactions involving firms in overlapping business. The study further suggests that postmerger cash flow improvements do not come at the expense of long-term performance as ample firms maintain their capital expenditure and R&D rates relative to their industries after the merger. The study also found strong positive relation between postmerger increases in operating cash flows and abnormal stock returns at merger announcements, indicating that expectations of economic improvements explain a significant portion of the equity revaluation of the merging firms. Cornett and Tehranian (1992) examines the postacquisition performance of large bank merger between 1982 and 1987. The results of their study indicate better performance for merged banks due to the improvements in ability to attract loans and deposits, in employee productivity and in profitable asset growth. Furthermore, the study finds a significant correlation between announcements period abnormal return and the various performance measures indicating that the market participants are able to identify in advance the improved performance associated with bank acquisitions. Switzer (1996) examined the change in operating performance of merged firms using a sample of 324 combinations, which occurred between 1967 and 1987. The results are not sensitive to factors such as offer size, industry relatedness between the bidder's and target's businesses or bidder's leverage. The study also found positive association between the abnormal revaluation of the firms involved around the merger and changes in operating performance observed. The study by Healy et al. (1997) finds that strategic takeovers that are generally friendly transactions involving stock and firms in overlapping business are more profitable than financial deals that are usually hostile transactions involving cash and firms in unrelated business. Ghosh (2001) compares the post- and preacquisition performance of merging firms relative to matched firms to determine whether operating cash flow performance improves following acquisition. The result finds no evidence of improvement of operating performance following acquisitions. Moreover, the study also indicates that cash flows increases significantly following acquisitions that are made with cash, but decline for stock acquisitions.

8.12   Principles of evaluation of bids

In an M&A transaction, the acquiring firm shareholders basically aim to minimize the amount paid to the target shareholders. The upper limit perceived by the acquirer shareholders will be the premerger value of target plus the value of synergies. The target shareholders aim to maximize the gain with the minimum threshold value for acceptance being a premium above the current market value.

Target shareholder gain = Premium = Price paid for the target company − Premerger value of the target company.
Acquirer's gain = Synergies − Premium.

Synergies are created when the market value of the combined firm is more than the individual market values of the firm.

8.13   Illustration of financial variables in merger analysis

8.13.1   Case 1

Share exchange ratio (SER) is stated as the fixed number of shares of the acquirer's stockm which can be exchanged for each share of the target's stock.

SER = Target firm share price/Acquirer firm share price.

Consider a merger involving exchange of shares based on the market price of the firms. Suppose the target firm market price is $50 per share and the acquirer firm's market price is $75 per share, then

SER = $50/$75 = 0.667. The acquiring firm will give 0.667 shares of its own stock for each share of the target company.

8.13.2   Case 2

Acquirer firm X is evaluating the acquisition of the target firm Y. X was trading at $40 per share. Y was trading at $20 per share. The exchange was based on exchange of shares. Acquired offered a premium of 20% to the target firm's Y share price. The earnings of X was $200 million and that of Y was $150 million. X had 100 million shares and Y had 75 million shares. Assume the merger results in no synergy. The EPS of the combined firm can be determined as follows.

Exchange ratio is based on the share price of target X plus the premium offered to target firm.

Adding the premium of 20% to the target's share price ($20*1.20 = 24$), the SER = 24/40 = 0.60

New shares issued to target shareholders = 75 ∗ 0.60 = $45 million.
Total earnings of the merged company = 200 + 150 = $350 million
Total shares of the merged company = 100 + 45 = $145 million.
Earnings per share of the merged firm = 350/145 = $2.41 per share.

The postmerger share price of the acquired firm is calculated as given below. Assume that the acquirer company does not expect any change in its P/E multiple after the acquisition.

Premerger EPS of the acquirer company X = Earning of X/Number of shares of X = 200/100 = $2 per share.

Premerger P/E = Premerger price per share /Premerger EPS = $40/$2 = 20
Postmerger share price = Postmerger EPS*Premerger P/E = 2.41 * 20 = $48.20

The acquisition results in an increase in the share price of the acquirer from $40 to $48.20.

References

Amihud, Y., Lev, B., 1981. Risk reduction as a managerial motive for conglomerate mergers. Bell J. Econ. 12 (2), 605−617.

Arnould, R.J., 1969. Conglomerate growth and public policy inn. In: Gordon, L. (Ed.), Economics of Conglomerate growth. Oregon State University, Department of Agricultural Economics, Corvallis, OR, pp. 72−80.

Asquith, P., Bruner, R.F., Mullins Jr., D.W., 1983. The gains to bidding firms from merger. J. Financ. Econ. 11 (1−4), 121−139.

Bruner, R.F., 2004. Valuing firms. Applied Mergers and Acquisitions. John Wiley & Sons, pp. 247−295 (Chapter 9).

Carleton, W.T., Guilkey, D.K., Harris, R.S., Stewart, J.F., 1983. An empirical analysis of the role of the medium of exchange in mergers. J. Finance. 38 (3).

Chen, Y., 2001. On vertical mergers and their competitive effects. Rand J. Econ. 32 (4), 667−685.

Christensen, H.K., Montgomery, C.A., 1981. Corporate economic performance: diversification strategy versus market structure. Strateg. Manage. J. 2, 327−343.

Cornett, M.M., Tehranian, H., 1992. Changes in corporate performance associated with bank acquisitions. J. Financ. Econ. 31, 211−234.

De Angelo, H., Masulis, R., 1980. Optimal capital structure under corporate and personal taxation. J. Financ. Econ. 8, 3−30.

DePamphilis, D., 2013. Mergers, Acquisitions and Other Restructuring Activities, seventh ed, Chapter 7, M&A cash flow valuation basics. Academic Press, Elsevier, pp. 217−251.

Dyer, J.H., Kale, P., Singh, H., 2004. When to ally & when to acquire. Harv. Bus. Rev. 111−112.

Eckbo, B.E., 1983. Horizontal mergers, collusion and stock holder wealth. J. Financ. Econ. 11 (1−4), 247−271.

Edward Fee, C., Thomas, S., 2004. Sources of gains in horizontal mergers: evidence from customer, supplier, and rival firms. J. Financ. Econ. 74 (3), 423−460.

Elgers, P.T., Clark, J.J., 1980. Merger types and stock holder returns, additional evidence. Financ. Manage. 9, 66−72.

Fishman, M.J., 1989. Preemptive bidding and role of the medium of exchange in acquisitions. J. Finance. 44, 41−57.

Franks, J.R., Broyles, J.E., Hecht, M.J., 1977. An industry study of the profitability of mergers in the United Kingdom. J. Finance. 32 (5), 1513−1525.

Gart, A., 1998. The long reach of banking's acquisition wave. Mergers Acquis. 25−35.

Ghosh, A., 2001. Does operating performance really improve following corporate acquisitions. J. Corp. Finance. 7, 151−178.

Haugen, R.A., Udell, J.G., 1972. Rates of returns to stockholders of acquired companies. J. Financ. Quant. Anal. 7 (1), 1387−1398.

Healy, P.M., Palepu, K.G., Ruback, R.S., 1992. Does corporate performance improve after mergers. J. Financ. Econ. 31, 135−175.

Healy, P.M., Palepu, K.G., Ruback, R.S., 1997. Which takeovers are profitable? Strategic or financial? Sloan Manage. Rev. 38 (4), 45−57.

Herman, E., Louis, L., 1988. The efficiency effects of hostile takeovers. In: John C., Jr., Louis, L., Rose-Ackerman, S. (Eds.), Knights, Raiders and Targets. Oxford University Press, Oxford, England, pp. 211−240.

Jarrell, G.A., Brickley, J.A., Netter, J.M., 1988. The market for corporate control: the empirical evidence since 1980. J. Econ. Perspect. 2, 49−68.

Jensen, M.C., Ruback, R.S., 1983. The market for corporate control. J. Financ. Econ. 5−50.

Joseph, P.H., Goyal, V.K., 2006. On the pattern and wealth effects of vertical mergers. J. Bus. 79 (2), 877−902.

Kumar B.R., 2010. Types and Characteristics. Mergers and Acquisitions, Text and Cases, first ed. McGraw-Hill Education, pp. 64−80 (Chapter 4).

Langetieg, T.C., 1978. An application of a three-factor performance index to measure stockholder gains from merger. J. Financ. Econ. 6 (4), 365−383.

Lev, B., Mandelker, G., 1970. The microeconomic consequences of corporate mergers. J. Bus. 45 (1), 85−104.

Lewellen, J., 1971. A pure financial rationale for the conglomerate merger. J. Finance. 26, 521−537.

Lubatkin, M., 1987. Merger strategies and stock holder value. Strateg. Manage. J. 8, 39−53.

Mandelker, G., 1974. Risk and return: the case of merging firms. J. Financ. Econ. 1−4, 303−335.

Markham, J.W., 1973. Conglomerate Enterprise and Economic Performance. Harvard University Press, Cambridge, MA.

Moeller, S.B., Schlingemann, F.P., Stulz, R.M., 2004. Firm size and the gains from acquisitions. J. Financ. Econ. 73 (2), 201−228.

Montgomery, C.A., 1982. The measurement of firm diversification: some new empirical evidence. Acad. Manage. J. 25 (2), 299−307.

Myers, S.C., Majluf, N.J., 1984. Corporate financing and investment decisions :when firms have information that investors do not have. J. Financ. Econ. 187−221.

Palepu, K., 1985. Diversification strategy, profit performance and the entropy measure. Strateg. Manage. J. 6, 239−255.

Prahalad, C., Hamel, G., 1990. The core competencies of the corporation. Harvard Bus. Rev. 68 (3), 79−91.

Rapport, A., Sirower, M.L., 1999. Stock or cash? Harv. Bus. Rev. 147−158.

Rumelt, R., 1974. Strategy, Structure and Economic Performance. Harvard University Press, Cambridge, MA.

Singh, H., Montogomery, C.A., 1987. Corporate acquisition strategies and economic performance. Strateg. Manage. J. 8 (4), 377−386.

Sudarsanam, S., 2003. Creating Value from Mergers and Acquisitions—The Challenges. Pearson Education Ltd, Harlow.

Switzer, J.A., 1996. Evidence on real gains in corporate acquisitions. J. Econ. Bus. 48, 443−460.

Teece, D.J., 1980. Economies of scope and the scope of the enterprise. J. Econ. Behav. Organ. 1, 223–247.

Titman, S., Martin, J., 2014. Valuation-the Art and Science of Corporate Investment Decisions, 3rd ed. Prentice Hall, pp. 259–315 (Chapter 8 and 9).

Travlos, N.G., 1987. Corporate takeover bids, methods of payment and bidding firms stock returns. J. Finance. XLII (4), 943–963.

Weston, J.F., Chung, K.S., Hoag, S.E., 2006. Mergers Restructuring and Corporate Control. Prentice Hall, pp. 1–40 (Chapter 1).

Real options valuation

9

9.1 Introduction

The real options valuation is a dynamic approach to valuation in terms of flexibility and growth opportunities. The real options approach is an extension of financial options theory. Options are contingent decisions that provide an opportunity to make decisions after uncertainty become relevant. Uncertainty and the firm's ability to respond in terms of flexibility are the sources of value of an option. The investment opportunities can be considered as corporate real options, which are integral for corporate resource allocation and planning. The opportunity to invest can be considered as a call option, which involve the right to acquire an asset for a specified price (investment outlay) in a future period. The underlying asset can be embedded corporate real options to expand production scale, delay the production, or abandon a project. The values derived from the options pricing help the management to set the course for future plans to capitalize on favorable investment opportunities by expansion. Similarly, if the situation is undesirable, the investment can be abandonment. The option to delay flexibility for a firm is an important criteria for the evaluation of many investment opportunities under uncertainty. The decision to delay an investment project would be based on the assumption that new information would affect the desirability of the investment and the value of the project increases if the option to delay is exercised. If the market conditions turn out to be unfavorable, then management has the option to discontinue the project. The option to delay a project is valuable when the project have a premium over the zero NPV value. The ability of the option-pricing theory to quantify flexibility in strategic investment projects is advocated by practitioners. A number of strategic decisions can be considered as real options. Investments in computer business, valuation of an aircraft purchase option, development of commercial real estate are all examples for real options before firms. Mining companies might acquire rights to an ore mine, which could be turned profitable if the price of products increases. The development of a worn-out farmland would become a strategic option for a real-estate developer to build a shopping mall if a new highway becomes feasible in the region (Brealey et al., 2008). The acquisition of patent to market a new drug is a viable strategic option for a pharmaceutical company.

The value of flexibility of an investment project is basically a collection of real options, which can be valued with the techniques estimated for financial options.

Strategic investment options by pioneering firms like development of technology provide such firms with cost or timing advantage, which could lead into value creation. Valuation of a gold mine concession license to develop a mine can be considered as considered as analogous to the valuation of a simple call option. The multistage R&D Investment can be considered as a compound option.

Pioneering firms that make strategic investments on a large scale in a new geographic market have first mover advantage and competitors would have to overcome entry barriers to reach out to the market. In this context, the option before the competitor firms is to delay its entry into the market or stay out to avoid market share war. In this context, the strategic project can lead to higher term profits for the pioneer firm. In high-effort R&D projects, flexibility effect is a relevant factor in option valuation. The scenario in which management has to wait to invest in business under uncertain conditions results in flexibility effect. Flexibility is an integral component of value for many investment projects and option pricing framework is a useful tool for analyzing such flexibility.

9.2 Real options as strategic investments

Strategic investments facilitate firms to invest or divest in subsequent periods of time on the basis of new opportunities. Similar to financial options, these strategic investments provide the firms different options on the future market conditions. These strategic options which are based on value of real assets called strategic real options. Unlike financial options, real options require the purchase the sale or restructuring of the real or nonfinancial assets. These investment opportunities also involve investment in intangibles like Intellectual Property Rights and Patents. Amazon has the ability to adapt rapidly to the digital business environment. Amazon is more than an Internet book seller as it delivers a broad range of products to customers. Amazon provided a wide range of IT-based business initiatives in collaboration with other firms. Amazon developed the ability to acquire strategic digital options and nurture them by capitalizing on those likely to prove successful while exercising discipline to eliminate nonprofitable ones. Lotus's development of notes illustrates the importance of organizational architecture as a strategic initiative to capture the value of options (Kulatilaka and Venkatraman, 2001).

Future growth opportunities are considered analogous to ordinary call options on securities. Derivative options give the owner the right (no obligation) to buy a security at a fixed predetermined price (exercise price) on or before the fixed date (maturity date). By way of analogy, an opportunity to undertake capital investment in productive assets like plant, equipment, or brand names at some future point in time is termed as call option on real assets or growth option. The cost of investment is the option's exercise price. Current investment may affect future opportunities by creating growth opportunities. The value of the option is the present value of the expected cash flows plus the value of new growth opportunities. The value of growth options can be estimated as the difference between the total market capitalization of a firm and its capitalized value of its earnings, which includes estimated earnings. Growth options are more valuable for small high-growth companies that market innovative products. At the time of its Initial Public Offering (IPO), Genentech had revenues of $9 million. The IPO was priced at $35 per share. After listing, its market capitalization value was $262 million, which was basically attributed to the value of the growth option (Kester, 1984).

Myers (1987) suggests strategic investment opportunities as growth options. Dixit and Pindyck (1994) provide various expositions to the real options approach to investment.

9.3   Limitations of discounted cash flow methods

The major drawback of discounted cash flow valuation is that discounted cash flow valuation assumes that the future firm decisions are fixed at the beginning and ignores the flexibility in decision making during the course of the investment project. Moreover when there are exit options in the investment project, the choice of an appropriate discount rate for NPV calculation is a challenging task. The risk neutral valuation or certainty equivalent approach can effectively capture the flexibility embedded in real options valuation. The NPV method have major shortcomings in analyzing projects when future decisions are contingent on intermediate developments in a uncertain environment. Option theory provides a better analytical tool to evaluate such projects.

9.4   Different types of real options

Real option analysis deals with investments in real tangible assets where the sponsors have multiple options to continue or abandon the project. Basically, there are three main types of options associated with investment projects. They are the option to postpone or delay, the option to expand, and the option to abandon. Another variation of abandonment option is to temporarily suspend an investment.

9.4.1   The option to delay

The option to delay becomes valuable when an investment project that has a negative NPV presently will have a positive NPV in future as the riskiness of the project and cash flow may change due to new changes in the scenario. A project with exclusive rights that have negative NPV today might still be valuable on account of the option characteristics. The option to delay can be valued using the binomial option pricing model. Generally, the Black Scholes model is applied for valuation of options to delay. Examples include patents for pharmaceutical firms. A product patent provides a firm with exclusive right to develop and market a product and can be considered as a real option. The value of the firm can be estimated as the value of commercial products plus the value of existing patents plus the value of options to obtain new patents in future minus the cost of obtaining these patents. The strategic decision to develop the undeveloped reserves of the natural resource oil and mining companies can also be considered as options. In this case, the variables required for estimation of value of option include available reserves of the resource, estimated cost of developing the resource, time of expiration of option, variance in value of underlying asset, and the cost of delay. By using the Black Scholes model, the value of the option to delay can be estimated as a call option.

9.4.2   Option to expand

Firms can exercise options to expand for further investments or enter into a new market. Entering a large market or acquisition of a proprietary technology can be viewed as an option to expand. Options to expand are valued as call option. Consider the case of a firm with two projects—one initial project and the other the final project. The initial project may result in negative NPV, but the second project may be conditional on the initial project as it is a project for expansion. In another case, if the initial investment becomes successful, the firm can exercise the option to expand its market by entering into a new geographic market. An initial investment could serve as a platform to extend a company's scope into related market opportunities. For example, Amazon's huge investment to develop its customer base, brand name, and information infrastructure for its core book business created a portfolio of real option for expansion into a variety of businesses (Rappaport and Michael, 2001).

9.4.3   Abandonment option

The option to abandon a project is valuable in research and development as it provides the flexibility to abandon a project in the presence of negative results. An abandonment option can be applicable in the valuation of pharmaceutical firms on account of procedures used by pharmaceutical researchers and high costs involved in the development stages. In the context of dotcom bubble, many dotcom firms exercised abandoned options. In abandonment option, firms have to bail out and recover the value of the project's plant, equipment, or other assets. The option to abandon is equivalent to a put option. The abandonment option is exercised when the value recovered from the disposal of project's assets is greater than the present value of continuing the project. Abandonment options can be valued with binomial method.

9.5   Solution approach to option valuation

The three main solution methods for option valuation are the dynamic programming approach, partial differential equations, and the simulation approach. The dynamic programming techniques involve finding out possible future outcomes and the value of the optimal future strategy using the risk neutral distributions. The partial differential equations (PDE) is a flexible method in which the PDE has to be solved numerically. Simulation approach to option valuation is applicable for American option. The most important tool for valuing real options valuation problems is the simulation approach. Simulation approach can be easily applied to multifactor models and path-dependent problems. The real options approach are applicable to natural resource investments and pharmaceutical R&D investments. Option-pricing methods were first developed to value financial options. Then it was applied to value options on real assets.

Schwartz (2013) proposed a model on the Black Scholes option pricing framework which was extended by Merton (1972) and Cox and Ross (1976) to value commodity-linked bonds.

9.6 Real options in different industry sectors

Real options valuation in R&D Investment projects is mainly applicable in pharmaceutical industry. The new drug development in the pharma industry is characterized by a number of public policy issues like financing of research, cost of product development, prices charged for its products, and patent protection. There exist a trade-off between promoting innovative efforts and securing competitive market outcomes. Regulation also has important effects on the cost of innovation in the pharmaceutical industry. The average span of new drug development is between 10 and 12 years. In the United States, the average time from discovery to Food and Drug Administration approval is around 15 years. The odds of a compound making it through this process are around one in 10,000, while the cost of getting it through is around $200 million. The cost of research process is increasing significantly as many of the drugs are focusing on complex and difficult targets. There is also a high probability of failure for either technical or economic reasons. Approximately, 80% of projects that start clinical trials are later abandoned. The economic reasons comprise the high cost of production and inefficacy of the drugs. Even if the drug have been approved, there is uncertainty about the level and duration of future cash flows as the time to complete and length of the patent are also uncertain.

Real options valuation is applicable in natural resources investment projects. The valuation of mining and other natural resources project have option characteristics as traditional valuation methods are difficult on account of uncertainty of output prices. The techniques of continuous-time arbitrage and stochastic control theory may be used to value natural resources investment projects and to determine optimal policies for development, management, and abandonment of such projects. In natural resources, industries price swings in the range of 25−40% is commonly observed.

In technological innovation-based firms, investors' expectations are formed on the basis of timings and significance of future innovations. Firms in the technology market have the option to adopt the new innovation or wait to adopt new technologies that are evolved in the near future, which could be more valuable. Firms in the rapidly changing high-technology markets are faced with valuable innovations, which are undergoing volatile and unpredictable change. These types of changes are relevant in a number of sectors like computer and semiconductor industry.

A firm have the option to choose a current version of innovation or wait to respond to future technological innovations. Bypassing a current innovation to wait for future innovation can result in the firm losing important learning that results from using the technological innovations (Grenadier and Weiss, 1995).

Offshore oil and gas industry often faces decision problems with respect to timing option. Companies buy licenses from government to explore and develop oil fields. The exploration phase involves the estimation of the amount and quantity of oil and gas reserves within that sector. The license for exploration usually expires after a certain time. When the exploration time expires, the oil companies have three possible option strategies. The firm can abandon the project and return the field to the government. The next strategy of action could be to start and develop the reserve immediately. The third strategy would be to postpone development and thus extend the exploration phase. In order to extend the exploration phase, the company have to undertake further drilling at additional costs. The first two options can be analyzed on the basis of NPV analysis as it does not contain any real option. The third alternative provides an option to the management to postpone the investment and wait for the oil prices to increase. The deferment of investment could lead to higher NPV in the future due to increase in oil prices. If the NPV is negative initially, the firm could exercise the option to wait, which finally may result in positive NPV. Discounted cash flow analysis assumes that project starts immediately without considering future NPV. The risk of an option changes over time with changing prices. Decision tree analysis (DTA) can be used as a basic framework to determine the value of options embedded in the investment project (Kemna, 1993). When the oil company decides to postpone the investment, it is exercising the option to delay by incurring the costs of extra drilling. The oil firm buys the right to start development at the expiration date of the extended license. The benefit of exercising the option at the expiration date is the market value of the developed project. The cost is equal to the investment outlay. The option to wait is similar to a European call option on an installed project with maturity date.

Consider a case in which the management have decided to abandon crude distiller in a refinery as the supply of distillates from crude oil has exceeded the demand. This case can be considered as an option to abandon and valued as a put option.

9.7   Factors affecting the value of real growth options

The NPV of an investment opportunity is estimated as the present value of the project's cash inflow minus the present value of its outflow. The major factors that affect the value of the growth option are the length of time the project could be deferred; project risk, level of interest rates, and the exclusivity of owner's rights to exercise the option. The option to delay a project gives the decision maker the flexibility to examine the course of future events and avoid errors if unfavorable scenarios occur. During the deferred time interval, positive turn of events can make the investment project more profitable. In this context it can be argued that the longer a project can be deferred, the more valuable the growth option will be. Thus the firm's investment opportunity with negative NPV currently (out of money growth option) can delay the investment (option to delay) so that in future it becomes in the money growth option. Project risk is an important determinant of the value of a firm's growth option. Higher the risk or variance of a growth option, higher would be the value of the option. Higher interest lowers the value of an option. Exclusivity of owner's right to exercise the option is also an important determinant of value of a growth option. In this context, two types of growth options can be highlighted—the proprietary and the shared options. Proprietary options results from patents possessed by the firm or a firm's unique knowledge of a market or a superior technology difficult to be imitated by competitors. Shared growth options represent collective opportunities of industry sectors, which could generate cash flow opportunities. Proprietary growth options are more valuable than shared growth options since counter investments in shared options by different firms can reduce or preempt profits. Compound growth options might become more valuable than simple growth options. A simple growth option requires the evaluation of only one cash flow from one investment opportunity while compound growth option involves estimation and valuation of cash flows from different investment opportunities like R&D investments, expansion into existing and new markets.

Strategic investments, which could lead to future comparative advantage, may be investments in research to develop new technology, advertisement investments that increases brand awareness and recognition, organizational and logistic planning, which would result in lower cost in building production capacity.

9.8   Real options in mergers and acquisitions

The operating synergies acquiring from a merger can be valued as a real option (Kinnunen). The target firm's value is equal to the value of existing assets plus the value of the future growth opportunities. The value of these synergistic future growth opportunities can be valued as real options (Collan and Kinnunen). The major sources of value for the target firm are the cash flows from economic capital, strategic capital consisting of intangibles, and human capital. The strategic capital can be valued as real options (Luehrman, 1998). The synergies are dependent on management decisions on the redeployments and additional investments. Real options in mergers and acquisitions can be valued using DTA and Black Scholes model (Kulatillaka and Perotti, 1998). The options to expand, delay, and abandon exist for an acquirer firm. An acquirer can use the option to delay to purchase additional stakes in the target firm. If the bidding for a target firm turns competitive due to simultaneous bidding by number of acquirers, acquirers have the option to abandon the bid if the proposal is not attractive. Examples of option to delay or abandon include scenarios like an acquiring firm choosing to delay a merger due to outstanding litigation or delay in regulatory approval. General Electric Honeywell deal was opposed by the European Union regulatory commission. When GE found the deal unattractive, it abandoned the option to acquire Honeywell UK. The due diligence of the potential target enables acquirer firms to take optimal decision regarding the option to acquire or postpone the acquisition. The time the options are available may be limited by the existence of competing bidders.

9.9   Empirical studies on real options

Black and Scholes (1973) introduced the option pricing formulae for European financial options. Myers (1977) suggests that growth opportunities can be viewed as real options whose value depends on future investment by firms. The general theory of real options have been discussed by studies of McDonald and Siegel (1986), Majd and Pindyck (1987), and Dixit (1989). Real option valuation of interrelated projects are found in studies by Trigeorgis (1993). The study by Ekern (1985) and Paddock et al. (1988) apply real-option analysis to petroleum sector. Brennan et al. (1985) discusses real option in natural resources. Benaroch and Kauffman (1999) examines real option application in information technology. Kester (1984) suggests that the difference between the total value of a firm's equity and the capitalized value of its current earnings stream estimates the value of its growth options.

McDonald et al. (1986) suggest that the option to delay investments is significant in corporate acquisition based on a rule for timing of acquisition investment with the practical intention to minimize the lost NPV of suboptimal investment financing. Smith and Triantis (1995) suggest that the success of an acquisition program is determined by the options acquired, created, or developed and the actions taken for the optimal exercise of these options. The study suggest three classes of real options important in acquisitions: growth options, flexibility options, and divestiture options. Dapena and Fidalgo (2003) analyzes embedded options in tender offers and acquisitions. The study calculates the value of control premium and presents a model for optimal acquisition timing.

Smit et al. (2005) research the distribution of value gains in acquisitions with a real options game model that examines the bidding process, the likelihood of a bidding contest (war), and the expected value distribution for the acquirer. Alvarez and Stenbacka (2006) focus on the option to divest parts of the acquired company. The study suggest divestment option as an embedded sequential option.

9.10   Real option valuation using decision tree approach

The discrete-time approach to real option valuation has typically been implemented in the finance literature using a binomial lattice framework (Brandão et al., 2005). Real option valuation problems can be solved by using binomial decision tree to determine the cash flows and probabilities that give the correct project values when discounted to each period and to each uncertain state. Project flexibilities, or real options, can then be modeled easily as decisions that affect these cash flows. In the decision tree approach, binomial lattice is augmented with decision nodes to represent investment alternatives. A binomial lattice can be viewed as a probability tree with binary chance branches, with the feature that the outcome resulting from moving up u and then down d in value is the same as the outcome from moving down and then up. Thus, this probability tree is recombining, since there are numerous paths to the same outcomes, which significantly reduces the number of nodes in the lattice. The backward induction is used to determine optimal exercise strategy and associated option value.

The binomial lattice model can be used to accurately approximate solutions from the Black−Scholes Merton continuous-time valuation model for financial options, with the added advantage of allowing a solution for the value of early-exercise American options, whereas the Black−Scholes−Merton model can value only European options. DTA can be used to model managerial flexibility in discrete time by constructing a tree with decision nodes that represent decisions the manager can make to maximize the value of the project as uncertainties are resolved over the project's life.

9.11   Real option valuation using Black Scholes model

The basic formula for valuing a call option is given by the formula:

$$C(S,t) = N(d_1)S - N(d_2)Ke^{-r(T-t)}$$

$$d_1 = \frac{1}{\sigma\sqrt{T-t}}\left[\ln\left(\frac{S}{K}\right) + \left(r + \frac{\sigma^2}{2}\right)(T-t)\right]$$

$$d_2 = \frac{1}{\sigma\sqrt{T-t}}\left[\ln\left(\frac{S}{K}\right) + \left(r - \frac{\sigma^2}{2}\right)(T-t)\right]$$

$$= d_1 - \sigma\sqrt{T-t}$$

$N(.)$ is the cumulative distribution function of the standard normal distribution. $T-t$ is the time to maturity. S is the spot price of the underlying asset. K is the strike price. r is the risk free rate and σ is the volatility of returns of the underlying asset.

References

Alvarez, L., Stenbacka, R., 2006. Takeover timing, implementation uncertainty, and embedded divestment options. Rev. Finance. 10, 1−25.

Benaroch, M., Kauffman, R., 1999. A case for using real options pricing analysis to evaluate information technology project investments. Inf. Syst. Res. 10 (1), 70−86.

Black, F., Scholes, M., 1973. The pricing of options and corporate liabilities. J. Polit. Econ. 81, 637–659.

Brandão, L.E., Dyer, J.S., Hahn, W.J., 2005. Using binomial decision trees to solve real-option valuation problems. Decis. Anal. 2 (2), 69–88.

Brealey, R.A., Myers, S.C., Allen, F., 2008. Brealey, myers, and allen on real options. J. Appl. Corp. Finance. 20, 58–71.

Brennan, M., Rennan, M., Schwartz, E., 1985. Evaluating natural resource investments. J. Bus. 58 (2), 135–157.

Collan M., Kinnunen J. Acquisition Strategy and Real Options, <http://www.realoptions.org/papers2009/34.pdf>

Cox, J.C., Ross, S.A., 1976. The valuation of options for alternative stochastic processes. J. Financ. Econ. 3, 145–166.

Dapena, J., Fidalgo, S., 2003. A Real Options Approach to Tender Offers and Acquisitions Processes, CEMA Working Papers. Universidad del CEMA, Argentina.

Dixit, A., 1989. Entry and exit decisions under uncertainty. J. Polit. Econ. 97 (3), 620–638.

Dixit, A., Pindyck, R.S., 1994. Investment Under Uncertainty. Princeton University Press, Princeton, NJ.

Ekern, S., 1985. An option pricing approach to evaluating petroleum projects. Energy Econ. 10, 91–99.

Grenadier, S.R., Weiss, A.M., 1995. Investment in technological innovations: an options pricing approach. J. Financ. Econ. 44, 397–416.

Kemna, A., 1993. Case studies on real options. Financ. Manage. 22 (3), 259–270.

Kester, W.C., 1984. Today's options for tomorrow's growth. Harv. Bus. Rev. 62 (2), 153–160.

Kinnunen J. Valuing M&A Synergies as (Fuzzy) Real Options, <http://www.realoptions.org/papers2010/238.pdf>.

Kulatillaka, N., Perotti, E., 1998. Strategic growth options. Manag. Sci. 44 (8), 1021–1031.

Kulatilaka, N., Venkatraman, N., 2001. Strategic options in the digital era. Bus. Strategy Rev. 12 (4), 7–15.

Luehrman, T., 1998. Strategy as a portfolio of real options. Harv. Bus. Rev.89–99.

Majd, S., Pindyck, R., 1987. Time to build, option value, and investment decisions. J. Financ. Econ. 18 (1), 7–27.

McDonald, R., Siegel, D., 1986. The value of waiting to invest. Q. J. Econ. 101 (4), 707–727.

Merton, R., 1972. An analytic derivation of the efficient portfolio frontier. J. Financ. Quant. Anal. 7 (4), 1851–1872.

Myers, S., 1977. Determinants of corporate borrowing. J. Financ. Econ. 5, 146–175.

Myers, S.C., 1987. Finance theory and financial strategy. Midland Corporate Financ. J. 5, 6–13.

Paddock, J., Siegel, D., Smith, J., 1988. Option valuation of claims on real assets: the case of offshore petroleum leases. Q. J. Econ. 103 (3), 479–508.

Rappaport, A., Michael, M., 2001. Expectations Investing: Reading Stock Prices for Better Returns. HBS Press, pp. 118–134 (Chapter 8).

Schwartz, E., 2013. The real options approach to valuation: challenges and opportunities. Lat. Am. J. Econ. 50 (2), 163–177.

Smit, H., van den Berg, W., de Maeseneire, W., 2005. Acquisitions as a real options bidding game. FMA Annual Meeting. Chicago, IL.

Smith, K.W., Triantis, A., 1995. The value of options in strategic acquisitions. In: Trigeorgis, L. (Ed.), Real Options Capital Investment: Models, Strategies and Applications. Praeger Publishers, Westport, CT.

Trigeorgis, L., 1993. The nature of option interactions and the valuation of investments with multiple real options. J. Financ. Quant. Anal. 28 (1), 1–20.

Valuation of different industry sectors

10

10.1 Valuation of internet companies

Yahoo purchased Geocities using shares, which were worth more than $5 billion when Geocities had a market capitalization of $3 billion. The lifetime value (LTV) of a customer is an important yardstick for valuing internet stocks. The internet business is one of the most dynamic developing sectors of the world economy. Internet companies run businesses with the use of information technology often termed e-commerce. E-commerce businesses include internet technologies (www and e-mails), electronic data interchange, electronic money transfer, smart cards, bulletin board systems, data input technologies (consisting of bar codes, sign, and voice recognition technologies), satellite identification, etc.

Valuation of start-up internet companies is difficult due to a number of reasons. High marketing costs initially results in losses for such companies. Successful companies develop at a very fast rate often signifying increase in revenues manifold times making forecasting of revenues a difficult process in valuation. The internet business is a very risky business. The development model of internet companies have a high level of operational leverage in terms of fixed costs. Higher operational leverage makes the business riskier. Discounted cash flow valuation method and return to economic fundamentals are suitable to value internet companies. Simple relative valuation methods like price to earnings (P/E) is not suited to value internet companies (Athanassakos, 2007). Kossecki (2009) suggests that the value of an internet company is the sum of the value of one-deal customers and value of relation-oriented customers. The customer LTV provided by one-deal customer will be equal to the profit generated from the single transaction. It is important to assess the number of transactions carried out by nonregistered users or registered users who carry out only one transaction. The average revenues and costs related to the single transactions are then estimated. The forecasted profits can be estimated on the basis of historical data from past period transactions. Then the forecasting of the number of transactions with one-deal customers is made. It is difficult to forecast sales revenues for start-up companies due to lack of knowledge related to specific markets. New clients become profitable only if the future discounted cash flows are higher than the acquisition costs. To estimate the customer LTV, it is important to determine retention and churn rates. These rates basically represent the percentage of clients retained and clients lost in comparison to the previous period. Perotti and Jansen (2002) based on academic studies suggest that web traffic is not a major value driver for internet companies, and traditional accounting data remain important for valuing internet companies.

The estimation of cash flows for discounted cash flow analysis for valuation of internet companies must incorporate scenario analysis based on probabilistic assumptions of cash flow generation (Zarzecki, 2011). The value of the internet company can be estimated as the mean of values obtained in all scenarios weighted with the probability level assigned to each scenario. The profit or loss made by internet companies depend on a number of factors like average annual revenue per customer, income from advertisements and retailers, total number of customers, return on sales per customer, average cost of acquiring customers, and customer churn ratio. The churn ratio indicate the share of customers lost every year.

Internet companies with high growth prospects and high risk can be valued using the Black Scholes option valuation model. Studies of Schwartz and Moon (2000) and Perotti and Rossetto (2000) suggest that internet companies have the characteristics of call option as they have large growth potential upside and limited downside potential on account of bankruptcy.

Market capitalization was a central metric to value internet companies till the collapse of dotcoms. Then the focus shifted on to other metrics like revenues, registered users, traffic, strategic positioning, proprietary technology, and brand image. The right valuation model for internet companies must encompass discounted cash flow valuation along with other attributes like intellectual assets, business models, and company-specific risk factors.

Internet companies are often links in supply chain rather than single business sector, which makes valuation more challenging. The business plans of these companies often change frequently. An internet company's strategic position in the market place is a key determinant of value. The success of business model of an internet company depends on product/service delivery methods, marketing practices, and customer relationship capital. The main focus is on business-to-customer model. The value of the brand basically depends on the relationship capital the firm has built over a period of time.

Pioneering internet companies such as Amazon.com and eBay have gained competitive advantage by adopting sophisticated software platform for enabling rapid ordering, inventory control, customer data collection, and marketing innovations. The initial public offerings (IPOs) of LinkedIn, Facebook, Twitter, and Groupon have made the issue of valuation of internet companies more relevant in the modern period.

10.1.1 Analysis of valuation methods

Earlier Web traffic measures were considered as the standard internet company performance benchmark. But the disadvantage is that the number of people viewing a webpage may not accurately represent the customer base.

Studies of Xu and Cai (2006) and King (2000) suggest that revenues' trend is a solid measure for most businesses. The study by Xu and Cai (2006) suggests that revenues were more relevant for valuation of dotcom companies than other key performance parameters like earnings and operating cash flows.

Studies point out that traditional measures of value measured in terms of revenues, profits, and assets are not significant methods for valuation of internet companies. King (2000) suggests that relative valuation method is commonly used for valuation of e-businesses. Kettell (2002) advocates for discounted cash flow techniques for valuation of internet companies. Market capitalization-to-revenue ratio method is a primary method for valuation as most firms' earnings were initially negative. Kettell (2002) introduced a modified discounted cash flow approach to valuation by using probability-weighted scenarios to address high uncertainty and exploiting classic analytical techniques to understand the underlying economics to forecast future performance. Gollotto and Sungsoo (2004) suggest that relative valuation ratio of P/E is not relevant in valuation of internet stocks. Their study finds a positive and significant correlation between the market appreciation of the value of web company stock and their R&D expenditures. This study highlights the significance of the potential future growth of a company and returns to investors.

Revenue per share is an important valuation variable for internet companies. The growth rate of revenues and stock price is another indicator of valuation metric.

Recent IPOs and valuation of internet companies

Facebook is a leading social network company located in Palo Alto, California. Facebook held its initial public offering (IPO) on May 18, 2012. Facebook was the largest venture backed IPO on record to date. Facebook had priced its IPO at $38 per share making it the third largest IPO in US history. It was labeled as one of the biggest IPOs in the technology and internet history. The IPO valued the company at $104 billion at the time of listing. However the stock fell as soon as it opened and the share prices crashed more than 50% over the next couple of months. It took more than a year for the shares to trade above the $38 listing. The share price was originally set conservatively between $28 and $35 a share. But 3 days before the market debut, the underwriting banks Morgan Stanley, J P Morgan and Goldman Sachs increased the IPO range to between $35 and $38 citing high demand. It was said that some large investors felt that Facebook was overpriced. Prior to the offering, Facebook had also expanded its number of shares by 25% to 421.2 million. There were concerns that the company would not be able to make much from mobile advertisements revenues compared to online advertisements. Facebook faced a number of lawsuits following its IPO. There was also a lack of confidence in the stock, as 57% of the shares sold in the IPO came from Facebook insiders.

LinkedIn IPO was offered for $45 per share which amounted to a value of $4.3 billion. The shares of LinkedIn rose as much as 171% in their first day of trade on the New York Stock Exchange, which closed at $94.25, more than 109% above the $45 IPO price. LinkedIn shares were undervalued to the extent

(Continued)

Recent IPOs and valuation of internet companies   (cont'd)

that it had a 143% rise in stock price on the first day of trading reflects the true value of the firm. Ovide (2011) pointed out that at the current stock price, LinkedIn is valued at $10.5 billion, which is 43 times its 2010 revenue.

In November 2013, Twitter raised about $1.8 billion through the sale of 70 million shares through its IPO which was offered at $26 a share. The offering's underwriters also have the option to buy another 10.5 million shares from Twitter. Twitter has become one of the most valuable companies in the world at a $24.9 billion valuation.

Source: Samantha Nielson, Why Facebook is a leading social media player, http://marketrealist. com/2014/01/facebook/;   www.reuters.com/article/2011/05/19/us-linkedin-ipo-risks-idUSTRE74H 0TL20110519; http://www.wsj.com/articles/SB10001424052702303448404577409923406193162.

10.2   Valuation of financial institutions

The changing landscape of financial institutions in the context of competition, diversification, new products, and new geographic markets have dramatically changed the risk profile of these institutions. Basically, the financial institutions can be divided into depository and nondepository institutions. Deposit-taking institutions consist of commercial banks, savings institutions, and credit unions. The nondepository institutions consist of finance companies, insurance institutions, pension funds, investment banks, and investment companies. The commercial banking industry provides commercial, industrial, and consumer loans and accepts deposits from individual and institutional customers. These deposits from then used to extend credit to other customers. Banks collect interest on loans and interest payments from the debt securities they possess and pay interest on the deposits, certificates of deposits and short-term borrowing. The retail customer market is the largest segment of a commercial bank's customer base.

The value of any financial claim is the present value of expected net flows to the owners of that claim. Unlike manufacturing firms that invest in plant and machinery, financial services reinvestment basically focusses on intangible assets like brand names and human capital.

Financial services firms raises funds from equity investors and bond holders and uses these funds to make investments. Financial services firms differ from nonfinancial firms in a number of ways. Globally, financial services firms are heavily regulated. Financial services firms are heavily regulated all over the world. Banks and insurance companies are required to maintain minimum regulatory capital as reflected by capital adequacy ratios. Regulatory provisions also constrain the financial services firms in terms of the investments in certain area. Banking regulations are essential in the context of preventing systemic dangers of bank failures and maintaining stability and security of payment services.

The Glass Steagall Act was enacted to prevent a repeat of the mass bank collapses during the Great Depression. Commercial banks were barred from underwriting and distributing the securities of private companies. Commercial banks were not allowed to affiliate with brokerage businesses and underwriting insurance. Glass Steagall Act created the FDIC, providing government protection for depositors whose funds were secured from the activities of the securities businesses. Many conditions were imposed on the banks that received protection. However, gradually the restrictions were eased and finally the law was repealed by the Gramm Leach Biley Act 1999. The global crisis, which led to the collapse of the global financial system, can be attributed to the systemic failure of the financial regulation. Financial services firms invest in intangible assets. *Net capital expenditures and working capital changes are not major factors in the valuation of financial service firms. In discounted cash flow valuation, the dividend discount model can be used to value financial services firms. In free cash flow to equity model the reinvestments can be considered as training and development expenses and investments in regulatory capital. Asset-based valuation models can also be used to value financial services firms.* In relative valuation, operating earnings-based multiples are not suited for valuation of financial services firms. The most popular multiples are P/E, price-to-book, and price-to-sales ratios.

There are certain complex issues to be considered in the valuation of financial service firms. The provisions set by banks and insurance firms to meet future losses understate the net income and reduce the return on equity (ROE) and retention ratio. In discounted cash flow models, the growth rate estimation would be understated and hence the equity value will be lower. The incorporation of regulatory risk in the estimation of discount rates is another complex factor in the cost of capital estimation for financial services firms. Risk-adjusted return on capital is an important metric to evaluate the economic performance of business units within a bank or insurance company.

10.2.1 Bank's performance evaluation

The main source of income for a bank are net interest income and fee-based (noninterest) income. Net interest income is the difference between the interest income a bank earns from lending and the interest expense it pays to borrow funds. Fee income is the revenue from services provided to customers in retail banking, private banking services, mergers, and acquisitions or asset management. Banks also derive income from other financial activities like proprietary trading or capital gains on their securities portfolios. A major cost metric is the provision for loan losses. The quantum of loans repaid in a timely manner is an important value driver for banks. Another major cost metric for valuation of banks is the noninterest expenses, which include selling, general, and administrative expenses.

The framework for a bank's performance can be analyzed along the six dimensions of deposit mobilization, quality of lending, capital adequacy, liquidity analysis, earnings performance analysis, and loan growth. The major profitability measures in banking sector can be analyzed by ratios like ROE, return on assets (ROA), equity multiplier, profit margin, asset utilization, and net interest margin.

Return on equity = Net income/Total equity capital
Return on asset = Net income/Total asset
Equity multiplier = Total assets/Total equity capital
Profit margin = Net income/Total operating income

The profit margin measures the ability to pay expenses and generate net income from interest and noninterest income.

Asset utilization measures the amount of interest and noninterest income generated per dollar of total assets. Asset utilization measures the extent to which the banks generate revenue.

Net interest margin is a measure of the net return on the bank's earning assets, which include investment securities, loans, and leases. It is the ratio of interest income minus interest expense divided by earning assets

Asset utilization = Total operating income/Total assets
Net interest margin = Net interest income/Earning assets

Efficiency ratio

An efficiency ratio measures a bank's ability to control noninterest expense relative to net operating income. Net operating income is the net interest income plus noninterest income.

Efficiency ratio = Noninterest expense/Net operating income

Overhead efficiency ratio is the ratio that measures a bank's ability to generate noninterest income to cover noninterest expense. The higher the ratio, the better the efficiency position of the bank.

Expense ratio

Profit margin represent a bank's ability to control expenses.

Interest expense ratio = Interest expense/Total operating Income
Provision for loan loss ratio = Provision for loan losses/Total operating income
Noninterest expense ratio = Noninterest expense/Total operating income
Tax ratio = Income taxes/Total operating income

The lower the value of these expense ratios, the higher the bank's profitability as measured by the profit margin ratio.

Productivity ratios

The main productivity ratios used to analyze a bank's performance is asset per employee and average personnel expense.

Assets per employee = Average assets/Number of employees
Average personnel expense = Personnel expense/Number of employees
Net income per employee = Net income/Number of employees

Leverage ratios
Capital to assets ratio: This ratio measures the ratio of a bank's book value of primary or core capital to the book value of its assets. Core capital consists of a bank's equity, cumulative preferred stock, and minority interests in equity accounts of consolidated subsidiaries.

Capital asset ratio = Core capital/Assets
Total risk-based capital ratio = Total capital (Tier 1 + Tier II)/Risk-adjusted assets

10.2.1.1 CAMEL rating system

CAMEL is an internal supervisory tool for evaluating the soundness of a financial institution. The CAMEL-based rating reviews different aspects of a bank with respect to a financial statement, funding sources, macroeconomic data, and cash flow. CAMEL is an acronym for five components of bank factors:

Capital adequacy
Asset quality
Management quality
Earning ability
Liquidity

A sixth factor that measures the sensitivity to market was included later in the rating system. Each component in the CAMEL model is scored from 1 to 5. After computing the rating for each of the elements, the composite rating is the average of the sum of five elements.

Banks with ratings of 1 or 2 are considered to present few, if any supervisory concerns, while banks with ratings of 3, 4, or 5 present moderate to extreme degrees of supervisory concerns.

10.2.1.2 Capital adequacy

Maintaining an adequate level of capital is a critical element that is essential to maintaining balance along with a bank's risk exposure for the purpose of absorbing potential losses. The most widely used indicator of capital adequacy is the capital to risk weighted assets ratio known as CAR.

10.2.1.3 Asset quality

Poor asset quality is a major contributing factor for bank failures. The asset quality of banks can be analyzed by assessing the credit risk and evaluating the quality of loan portfolio. Nonperforming loans (NPLs) and provisions for loan losses are considered as important asset quality indicators. Under general classification, loans are divided into five categories: standard, special mention, substandard, doubtful, and loss. The latter three categories are classified as NPLs.

Gross NPL ratio = Gross NPL/Total loan
Net NPL ratio = Net NPL/Total loan

A high net NPL ratio is indicative of the high probability of a large number of credit defaults that affect the profitability. The higher the ratio, the higher the credit risk.

10.2.1.4 Management quality

The management quality can be assessed by the total asset growth rate, loan growth rate, and earnings growth rate and comparing it to nominal GNP growth.

The ratios that can be used to assess the management efficiency are as follows:

Total advance to total deposit ratio
This ratio measures the efficiency and ability of banks to convert the deposits available with the banks (excluding other funds such as equity) into high earning advances. Total deposits include demand deposits, savings deposits, term deposits, and deposits of other banks. Total advances include the receivables.

Business per employee ratio
Revenue per employee is a measure of how efficient is the employees of a bank. This ratio indicates the productivity potential of the human resources of the bank.
Business per employee = Total income/Number of employees

Profit per employee
This ratio indicates the surplus earned per employee. The higher value for this ratio is indicative of the efficiency of the management.
Profit per employee = Net profit/Number of employees

10.2.1.5 Earning ability

Strong earnings and profitability profile of banks reflect the ability to support the present and future operations. Consistency in profits helps banks to absorb loan losses and provide sufficient provisions. It also increases shareholder value. The profitability ratios measure the ability of banks to generate profits from revenues and assets. The single best indicator used to gauge earnings is the ROA, which is the net income after taxes to total asset ratio. ROE is another measure of earnings, which is the ratio of net income to total equity.

Net interest income margin
The net interest income margin is used to gauge the earning ability of a bank
Operating profit to average working fund

This ratio of the operating profit to average working fund indicates how much a bank can earn from its operations net of the operating expenses for every amount of money spent on working funds. Average working funds are the total resources (total assets or liabilities) employed by a bank. The higher the ratio, the better the earning potential of the bank. This ratio determines the operating profits generated out of the working funds employed.

Net profit to average asset
Net profit to average asset indicates the efficiency of banks in using their assets for generation of profits. A higher ratio indicates better income generating capacity

of assets and better efficiency of management. It is determined by dividing the net profit by average assets.

Interest income to total income
Interest income is a basic source of revenue for banks. The interest income to total income indicates the ability of the bank to generate income from its lending. In other words, this ratio measures the income from lending operations as a percentage of the total income generated by the bank in a year.

Other income to total income
Fee-based income accounts for a major portion of a bank's other income. The bank generates higher fee income through innovative products and adapting technology for sustained service levels. A higher ratio indicates an increasing proportion of fee-based income.

10.2.1.6 Liquidity

Fund management practices should ensure that an institution is able to maintain a level of liquidity sufficient to meet its financial obligations. The ratios suggested to measure liquidity are as follows:

Liquidity asset to total asset
Liquidity is essential for banks to meet their financial obligations as they come due. The proportion of liquid assets to total assets indicates the overall liquidity position of the bank. Liquid assets include cash in hand, balance with central banks, and money at call and available at short notice.

Liquidity assets to demand deposits
The liquidity asset to demand deposit ratio measures the ability of a bank to meet the demand from deposits in a particular year. Demand deposits offer high liquidity to the depositor and hence banks have to invest these assets in a highly liquid form.

Liquidity asset to total deposit
The liquidity asset to total deposit ratio measures the liquidity available to the deposits of a bank. Total deposits include demand deposits, savings deposits, term deposits, and deposits of other financial institutions.

Sensitivity to market risk
Sensitivity to market risk refers to risk factors due to changes in market conditions that would adversely impact earnings and/or capital. Market risk arises from changes in interest rates, foreign exchange rates, commodity prices, and equity prices. Sensitivity analysis is used to analyze a bank's exposure to interest rate risk, foreign exchange volatility, and equity price risks. Risk sensitivity is evaluated in terms of management's ability to monitor and control market risk.

10.2.2 Valuation of insurance companies

The major activities of insurance companies include underwriting insurance policies, collection of premiums, investigation, and settling of claims made under policies (Nissim, 2010). The major source of revenue for insurance companies are premium income that customers make for their policies. On account of time lag between when customers pay premiums and when insurers will payout any benefits and claims. During this period, insurers invest the funds received from customers and derive investment income in the form of interests or dividends. Like banking sector, insurance sector earns profits from the spread between investment returns and its sources of funding. Insurance companies also realize capital gains or losses on their investment portfolios. Insurers also derive fee-based income from their investment products.

The major costs incurred by insurance companies are reinsurance costs, benefits and claims, commissions, and other policy acquisition costs. Reinsurance cost occurs when an insurer transfers the underlying risk of a policy to a reinsurer. This cost is generally netted against premium by insurers. Commissions and other policy acquisition costs are costs incurred to sell policies to customers.

The performance of insurance companies can be measured by parameters such as growth in the number of policies, market share, and growth in the number of branches. The average number of policies per agent represents the efficiency of the insurance company. The financial indicators used to evaluate the performance of insurance companies include growth in gross and net premium, profit from underwriting, average profit per branch and employee, average annual cost per employee, and return on investment. Insurers have four primary sources of revenues: net premiums earned, net investment income, fee income, and realized gains and losses. The major relative valuation ratios are value-to-book and value-to-earnings ratio. The major value drivers for the value-to-book ratio are profitability, accounting quality, book value growth, equity risk, and long-term interest rates. The major value drivers for value-to-earnings ratio are earnings growth, accounting quality, earnings payout, equity risk, and long-term interest rates.

The major profitability ratios used to evaluate insurance companies are ROE, recurring ROE, and one-time ROE. Recurring ROE is a summary measure of recurring profitability from all business activities. Recurring income excludes "One-time items." These one-time items include other comprehensive income, extraordinary items, income from discontinued operations, impairment charges, asset write downs, restructuring charges, realized gains, and losses.

Recurring ROE = Recurring income/Beginning of period common equity
One-time ROE = One-time items/Beginning of period common equity

The combined ratio highlights the underwriting profitability of a Property and Casualty (PC) insurance company. The loss and expense ratio indicates the average cost of insurance protection per dollar of net premiums earned during the period. The losses and loss expenses reflect not just the cost of protection provided during the year but also the adjustment to the previous year balance of the loss reserve. The underwriting expense ratio indicates the operational efficiency in underwriting. Underwriting expenses include commissions to agents and brokers, taxes, salaries, employee benefits, and other operating costs. The different lines of business have intrinsically different underwriting expense ratios. For example, for boiler and machinery insurance requires a number of skilled inspectors and hence have high underwriting expense ratio. In contrast, the underwriting expense ratio for group health insurance are quite low. The underwriting expense ratio is an important determinant of overall profitability.

The combined ratio highlights the cost of protection and the cost involved in generation and maintenance of business. When the combined ratio is under 100%, underwriting results are considered profitable and if it is over 100%, the underwriting results are considered unprofitable. The disadvantage of the combined ratio is that it does not reflect the investment profits generated by insurers. The operating ratio measures the overall operational profitability from underwriting and investment activities. An operating ratio of greater than 100% suggest that the insurance company will not be able to generate profits from its underwriting and investment activities. Net investment income is earned primarily on funds obtained.

Combined ratio = Loss ratio + Loss expense ratio + Underwriting expense ratio + Policy holder dividend ratio
Loss ratio = Losses/Net premium earned
Loss expense ratio = Loss expenses/Net premium earned
Underwriting expense ratio = Underwriting expenses/Net premium earned
Policy holder dividend ratio = Policy holder dividends/Net premium earned
Operating ratio = Combined ratio − Net investment income ratio
Net investment income ratio = Net investment income/Net premium earned
Net investment income = Investment income − Investment expense

---

Underwriting leverage measures the efficiency of the use of capital resources by an insurance company to generate business. Insurers with low underwriting leverage have more potential for growth. Policy holder's surpluses measure the cushion available to absorb such losses.

Underwriting leverage = Net premiums written/Policy holder surplus

Net premiums written is equal to direct insurance and reinsurance assumed during the period, less reinsurance ceded. This ratio is an important profitability measure which indicate the efficiency with which the insurer uses its capital resources to generate business.

Investment yield measures the profitability of investments. Basically, high-risk investments generate high yields, whereas low-risk investments have low yield. PC insurers invest in short-term higher credit quality investments and hence reap lower investment yields.

Investment yield = Net investment income/Investment assets

Investment return
Investment return has two components: investment yield and net capital gains.

Investment return = Net investment income + Net gains (losses) on investment assets/Beginning period investment assets
Recurring revenue per employee = Recurring revenue/Number of employees

The major ratios to evaluate the accounting quality are the recurring revenue to equity ratio, loss development ratio meant for PC insurers, premium growth, revenue mix ratios.

Recurring revenue to equity ratio = Recurring revenue/Equity

Financial service companies require few operating assets to generate revenue. They are required to have equity capital at levels sufficient to support their operations.

Reserve development ratio = Reserve development/Beginning of period loss reserve

Revenue mix ratios

Net premiums earned ratio = Net premiums earned/Net premiums earned + Net investment income + Fee income
Net investment income ratio = Net Investment Income/Net premiums earned + Net investment income + Fee income
Fee income ratio = Fee income/Net premiums earned + Net investment income + Fee income

Insurers have basically four primary sources of revenues—net premiums earned, net investment income, fee income, and realized gains and losses.

Growth measures

In addition to earnings, dividends and assets, other growth metrics such as growth in assets under management (AUM) are important indicators of future revenues for life insurers. Premium revenue being the primary source of revenue is an important indicator of growth potential of an insurer. Asset growth is a leading indicator of revenue and earnings growth. Premium growth is driven by exposure growth in terms of increase in the number of policy holders and rate level growth in terms of an increase in the average price per exposure.

10.2.2.1 Valuation models in insurance

The valuation models in insurance focus on equity and book values rather than free cash flows. It has to be noted that life and health insurers have high leverage ratios and earn a major part of their profits from the spread between return on invested assets and cost of liabilities. The book values of major assets and liabilities of insurers are often close to fair values. Regulatory compliance creates a scenario in which the insurers' ability to write premiums is directly related to their surplus. Insurers are required by regulators to maintain minimum equity capital at levels commensurate with the scope and riskiness of their activities.

Embedded value (EV) is an important value metric for life insurance companies.
Embedded value (EV) = Adjusted net worth (ANW) + Value of in-force business (VIF).

In ANW estimation, the statutory capital and surplus are adjusted to include some assets and subtract surplus notes and debt (nonequity surplus). VIF is the discounted value of after-tax profits expected to be generated by the business in force until the material portion of in force business has run off.

The discounted cash flow valuation of insurance companies involve free cash flow valuation.

10.2.3 Investment banks

Investment banks offer services in equity capital markets, leveraged debt capital markets, commercial real estate, asset finance and leasing, and corporate lending services. Equity capital market services include IPOs and right issues. Market making and trading securities are activities carried out by the investment banks on the sell side. Underwriting and research activities are performed as an insider function. On the buy side, investment banks offer asset management services for pension funds, mutual funds, and hedge funds. Investment banks can be valued using the relative valuation methods.

10.2.4 Mutual funds

The vast majority of investment companies are mutual funds both in terms of number of funds and AUM. Mutual funds represent the second largest pool of private capital in the world after the banking industry. Mutual funds enables investors to make diversified investments across a large number of firms.

Mutual funds are basically in the business of investing in securities and the value placed on those securities has a direct impact on their shareholders. Every business day, a fund must determine the value of each portfolio security it holds to calculate its net asset value (NAV) per share. The fund's NAV then is used to process purchases, redemptions, and exchanges by shareholder.

The rate of return on an investment in a mutual fund is measured as the increase or decrease in NAV plus income distributions such as dividends or distributions of capital gains expressed as a fraction of NAV at the beginning of the investment period if the NAV at the start and end of the period as NAV0 and NAV1.

Rate of return = NAV1 − NAV0 + Income and capital gain distribution/NAV0

The risk-adjusted performance measures for mutual fund portfolio are evaluated by the following measures. The Sharpe ratio divides the average portfolio excess return over the sample period by the standard deviation of returns over that period. It measures the reward to total volatility trade-off. Treynor measure gives excess return per unit of systematic risk. Jensen's alpha is the average return on the portfolio over and above that predicted by the CAPM, given the portfolio's beta and the average market return. The information ratio divides the alpha of the portfolio by the nonsystematic risk of the portfolio termed the tracking error in the industry.

The value of the mutual fund can be considered as the current value of AUM. Real option valuation can also be applied for mutual fund industry due to the volatility of AUM. The critical parameters also include the fees, age and size of assets, and variables of flows into and out of fund.

10.2.5 Pension funds

A pension fund is established by an employer based on the contributions made by the employer and employees. Pension funds are operated by intermediary financial institutions on behalf of the company or in-house pension funds of the company. A pension fund's cash inflows consist of contribution payments by the active workforce and the employer; cash outflows include benefit payments to retirees, disabled, widows and orphans, and the fund's operating costs.

In traditional sense, most pension funds have assets valued at book value which is equal to initial cost adjusted for realized capital gains and losses. Current market value of assets has been well accepted as the correct approach to valuation of pension funds.

For valuation purposes, the use of discount rates must reflect the market yields of government bonds (Tobler Oswald). The choice of discount rate can make a large difference to the measured value of accrued liabilities. The standard approach to fair valuation of pension fund cash flows is to discount the expected cash flow at a riskless interest rate. Actuarial valuation methods consider benefit payouts only. Benefits are either attributed to specific years of service and in valuing the fund's liabilities only those benefits accumulated up to valuation date are considered.

10.3 Valuation of biotechnology companies

The valuation of biotechnology and life science companies is challenging in the context of the long lead times and uncertainty associated with product development. There is no standard methodology to define the company's worth. The market value of biotechnology firms is based on the company's intellectual property. The ability of these firms to convert these intangibles into revenue stream is hampered by factors like government regulations and lengthy approval process. The failure rate in product development is also very high. On average, the Food and Drug Administration approves only 1 out of every 5 new molecular entities.[1] Biotech projects take between 10 and 20 years to become successful and cost over $200–300 million before a product reaches the market.

The major value drivers for biotechnology companies are intellectual property rights, R&D and technology, sources of finances, market opportunity, therapeutic areas, and alliances and partnerships. The major valuation models for valuation of biotechnology firms are the discounted cash flow, the royalty or licensing model, and the relative valuation model. The sensitivity analysis is based on market, pricing, costing, R&D, and development stages. The discount rate in the traditional discounted cash flow model covers the risks of production to market. There is an additional risk factor of R&D and regulatory arrival. The risk-adjusted discounted cash flow valuation incorporates these additional risk factors. In this model, different probabilities of success at different stages of product development are incorporated in the model. The cash flows are also adjusted to incorporate the changes.

[1] Loh, J., Brooks, R., 2006. Valuing biotechnology companies using the price earnings ratio. J. Commer. Biotechnol. 12 (4), 254–260.

10.4   Valuation of real estate and construction sectors

The valuation of housing industry faces unique challenges. The roots of the global financial crisis can be found in real estate. Housing prices began to show unusual upward movements after the United States emerged from the 2001 to the 2004 economic recession. The immediate trigger was the bursting of the US housing bubble which peaked in 2005–2006. Many economists had been of the opinion that this housing bubble characterized by unexpected and temporary inflation in housing prices was doomed to contract and bust. During the 1980s, the large inflow of foreign funds and steadily decreasing interest rates made easy credit conditions for almost two decades prior to the crisis, which in turn led to a boom in the housing construction activities and debt-financed consumption. Home purchases were promoted by the government as contributors to individual wealth and retirement plans in the United States. The value of the US subprime mortgages was estimated at $41.3 trillion by March 2007. After the economic crisis of 2008, the housing industry was plagued by a large number of contract cancellations and competitions from a large inventory of homes for sale including resales of homes in developing projects.

The development of home community takes 5 years and series of communities in a master plan requires 10 years. Companies have to evaluate the possibility of impairment on their land holdings. The impairment tests often leave the potential for distortions in the valuation of these companies.[2] The earnings capitalization model and discounted cash flow valuation model can be used to value real estate businesses. The projection of future cash flows in discounted cash flow valuation must be adjusted for few factors like removal of realized holding gains or losses; recognition of deferred tax liabilities, and incorporation of potential of future price declines. The purchase of land at different times in the business cycle and the increases in land values timings create challenges for forecasting of cash flows. The realized holding gains and losses result from the sale of inventory with a replacement cost above or below its market value. The earnings capitalization model will show errors in the estimated value of a firm unless appropriate adjustments are made for unrealized holding gains in earnings. The adjustment depends on the nature of the expectations for future holding gains. If the future holding gains are expected to be different from past holding gains, then the past holding gains must be replaced by expected future holding gains.

10.4.1   Real estate valuation methods

The real estate investment valuation must consider factors like economic and social trends, government regulations. The main value drivers are demand and supply factors, utility, and the scope of transferability. Three basic approaches are used for valuing investment properties.[3] The sales comparison or market approach is used

[2] Lippitt, J.W., Mastracchio Jr., N.J., Lewis, E., 2008. Valuing companies that have experienced large holding gains. CPA J. 60–63.
[3] Jilliene   Helman,   "http://www.nuwireinvestor.com/articles/jilliene-helman-peer-to-peer-lending-and-crowdfunding-expert-60793.aspx"

for valuation of single family homes and land. This method provides an estimate of value derived by comparing property with currently sold properties with similar characteristics. The differences must be adjusted while making the comparison. The differences are based on property characteristics like location, size of the lot, square footage of the usable building space, and type and quality of construction. Other factors like age, design, land terrain, and interior layout also play a major role in comparative valuation. The cost approach provides separate estimates of value for the buildings and land. Cost analysis starts with simple estimate using current local building costs. The local builders provide a generalized per square foot cost of new construction. Construction cost indexes breakdown costs by material types and region. The building's current replacement cost has to be adjusted to reflect the actual state (and value) of the subject property. This involves reductions to reflect the property's physical deterioration, functional obsolescence, and economic depreciation.

Earnings or income capitalization approach estimates the value of income generating assets like apartment complexes, office buildings, and shopping centers. The income approach requires determining the amount, certainty, and length of time of future income from the property and applying an appropriate capitalization rate to find the present value of future cash flows. Choosing a capitalization depends on the property's type, location, age and quality of tenants. There are three ways in which the capitalization rates are estimated. In the first method, the average capitalization rate of similar properties that have sold recently is used. The second method involves the usage of survey methods to obtain an average capitalization rate used by other real estate investors. The third method involves estimation of the capitalization rate from the discounted cash flow model. The sources of cash flows from a real estate investment is rents and lease income. In the case of leased property, the terms of the lease can affect the projected lease revenues. The expenses included on real estate investments include property taxes, insurance, repairs and maintenance, and advertising. Discounted cash flow valuation is an effective valuation method in real estate business valuation.

Property value = Operating income after taxes/Capitalization rate

The value of an asset can be standardized using its income. The gross income multiplier method is used to appraise properties which are not purchased as income properties but could be rented such as one and two family homes. The gross income multiplier method relates the sales price of a property to its expected rental income.

Real estate investments can also be valued using standardized value measures and comparable assets. The major relative value ratios are P/E ratio and book value per share.

10.5   Valuation of oil companies

The economic theory states that exploration and development of new oil and gas fields is a function of increases in petroleum prices (Antill and Arnott, 2002).

Return on average capital employed is an important valuation metric in the oil and gas industry (Osmundsen et al., 2006). It is considered as the single most important performance indicator, which is a vital input for valuation analysis among stock market analysts. This measure has been widely reported by international oil and gas companies. On account of production depreciation method in oil sector, return on average capital employed will fall in the first years of project cycle. Later in the project cycle, when investment fall and capital asset depreciates, the return on capital employed will increase. In other words, return on capital employed is boosted in periods of divestment. Enterprise value to debt-adjusted cash flow is an important market-based valuation multiple used by oil and gas analysts. Enterprise value is the sum of the company's debt and equity at market values. Debt-adjusted cash flow is the cash flow from operations plus after-tax debt service payments. Total shareholder return and EVA are also important valuation indicators.

Important financial indicators in oil and gas sectors include enterprise value/EBITDA, reserve replacement efficiency, reserve replacement ratio, margin per BOE, per share growth of reserves and production, enterprise value/discretionary cash flow, and finding costs/depreciation, depletion, and amortization (Quirin et al., 2000). EBITDA represent earnings before interest, taxes and depreciation, depletion, and amortization. BOE represent barrels of oil equivalent. A margin measure is vital to exploration and production analysts. In the context of high volatility in the oil market, the oil producers requires to focus on ways to decrease costs to increase margins. Firms operating with higher gross margins typically possess the ability to earn higher future profits. Margin per BOE is a common measure of margin within the industry. Margin is obtained as total annual revenues from oil and gas operations minus total production costs. Firms that are able to process crude oil more efficiently than its competitors is considered more valuable by analysts. The two main fundamental variables to measure production efficiency are finding costs and reserve replacement efficiency. Finding costs are defined as the amount spent per BOE to acquire, explore, and develop reserves which include discoveries, acquisitions, and revisions to previous reserve estimates. Lower finding costs indicate signs of efficiency. Reserve replacement efficiency indicates an oil firm's ability to generate maximum cash flow from the newly found reserves. Firms with high levels of reserve replacement and low finding costs are considered to be more valuable. Reserve replacement efficiency indicates a firm's internal growth potential. A higher reserve replacement efficiency is considered as a positive sign by oil analysts. Reserve replacement efficiency is the discretionary cash flow per BOE divided by finding costs per BOE.

References

Antill, N., Arnott, R., 2002. Oil Company Crisis, Managing Structure, Profitability and Growth, SP 15. Oxford Institute for Energy Studies, Oxford, UK.

Athanassakos, G., 2007. Valuing internet ventures. J. Bus. Valuation Econ. Loss Anal. V2.I1, Berkeley Electronic Press.

Gollotto, J.C., Sungsoo, K., 2004. Market valuation of dot com companies; R&D versus hype. Managerial Finance. 29 (11), 61−72.

Kettell, B., 2002. Valuation of Internet and Technology Stocks: Implications for Investment Analysis, first ed. Butterworth Heinemann, pp 95−128 (Chapter 6 and 7).

King, A.M., 2000. Valuing red-hot internet stocks. Strateg. Finance. 81 (10), 28−34.

Kossecki, P., 2009. Valuation and Value Creation of Internet Companies—SSRN Electronic Journal 09/2009. Avaliable from: http://dx.doi.org/10.2139/ssrn.1478713.

Nissim D., 2010. Analysis and Valuation of Insurance Companies. Centre for Excellence in Accounting and Security Analysis, Columbia Business School. <http://www.columbia.edu/~dn75/Analysis%20and%20Valuation%20of%20Insurance%20Companies%20-%20Final.pdf>.

Osmundsen, P., Asche, F., Misund, B., Mohn, K., 2006. Valuation of international oil companies. Energy J. 27 (3), 49−64.

Ovide, S., 2011. Three reasons to fear the LinkedIn IPO. Wall Street J [Online].

Perotti, E.C., Jansen, P.D., 2002. Valuation of Internet Companies: A Survey of the Evidence. Available at SSRN: http://ssrn.com/abstract=310659 or http://dx.doi.org/10.2139/ssrn.310659, Pages 12.

Quirin, J.J., Berry, K.T., O'Bryan, D., 2000. A fundamental analysis approach to oil and gas firm valuation. J. Bus. Finance Account. 27 (7&8), 785−820.

Tobler-Oswald, J. An Investment Based Valuation Approach for Pension Fund Cash Flow, Discussion Paper PI-0619. The Pensions Institute. <http://www.pensions-institute.org/workingpapers/wp0619.pdf>.

Xu, L., Cai, F., 2006. Before and after 2000: revenue and high tech valuation. Competition Forum. 4 (2), 348−353.

Zarzecki, D., 2011. Valuing internet companies. Selected issues. Folia Oecon. Stetinensia. 9 (1), 105−120 (ISSN (Online) 1898−0198, ISSN (Print) 1730-4237, DOI: 10.2478/v10031-010-0015-5).

Valuation issues

11

11.1 Valuation of closely held or private companies

Closely held companies can be valued basically by three methods—discounted income approach, comparative analysis, and capitalized earnings (Peterson, 2013). The cash flow projections incorporate expectations of future revenue growth and operating profitability as well as capital expenditure needs, working capital requirements, taxes, and depreciation estimates. The cash flow projections also include a residual component or terminal value which reflects the expected value of business at the end of the projection period. In comparative analysis (market approach) method, a private company is compared to similar companies with quoted prices in actively traded stock markets. The market value of closely held firms is estimated by examining the market prices and valuation multiples of similar public companies. The valuation multiples in terms of financial variables like earnings, operating cash flow, assets are estimated for each of the comparable companies and compared with the private firms. Minority interest valuation is estimated by examining the relative valuation ratios like price earnings multiples, cash flow multiples, and market to book value multiples. The valuation multiples are adjusted for differences in growth and profitability and risk aspects. The fair market value of closely held companies is affected by factors like the nature of the business and history of the enterprise; general economic outlook; book value of stock; dividend paying capacity; intangibles; and market prices of stocks of comparable companies. The analyst has to assign prime importance to earnings while valuing stocks of companies. In the absence of sales of the closely held stock, the next important variable will be the selling price of comparable stock.

Profitable closely held companies are valued using the methodology of capitalized earnings. The valuation of profitable companies often involves determination of goodwill which is difficult and requires exhaustive analysis. The risk factors for small closely held companies are attributed by its small size, market share, intensity of competition, cyclicality of business, and industry overcapacity. A risky business must be assigned lower price earnings multiple than a nonrisky stable business. Determination of proper capitalization rate is one of the most difficult problems in valuation.

Cost approach can also be used as a valuation approach. The cost method involves estimation of investment required to replace or reproduce the assets of business using current prices for labor, materials, and operating facilities. This method involves estimation of value of the firm's net working capital needs, machinery and equipment, real estates, and intangible assets. This method of valuation is suited for holding companies and highly capital-intensive businesses. It is basically a valuation based on the sum of the parts of a business.

Valuation.

The ownership level is a major factor for the valuation of closely held firms. The main investor would have paid significant premiums to gain control of the company's operations and cash flows. The valuation would involve a control premium if a new investor acquires more than 50% of ownership and acquires control of the firm. To account for control disadvantage in closely held firms, a valuation discount can be applied from the perspective of minority owners since the minority owners have less control over the cash flows. The minority interest discount factor is significant for closely held companies due to limited dividends and stock sales which are not efficiently priced. Investors in privately held companies require higher return due to risk of ownership on account of changing market conditions. Lack of marketability discount arises due to the inability to sell an ownership position which leads to increased risk conditions. Private securities are considered to be non-marketable. Privately held companies' values should be reduced for the lack of marketability. Private companies tend to be smaller and exhibit higher earnings growth rates than public companies. The most sophisticated discounted cash flow (DCF) method or enterprise value/EBITDA analysis may not yield the true value of a firm when it is privately held.

The major determinants of value of closely held companies are the following factors[1] (i) The size of the markets and the growth potential of the company's products and services, (ii) the breadth of the products or services offered as well as the stability of the firm's earnings, (iii) the cost and availability of equipment and other operational factors, (iv) the quality and efficiency of operating facilities, (v) government regulatory policy and its impact on firm revenues, net income, and capital expenditures, (vi) efficiency of management, and (vii) firms' financial condition as reflected by the growth rate in revenues and cash flow margins.

11.2 Valuing firms with negative earnings

Valuation of firms with negative earnings is often considered difficult. In this case earnings growth rates cannot be estimated. The historical growth rates for earnings will be negative and the fundamentals will yield low estimates for expected growth. Negative earnings may be due to firm-specific factors or the firm may be a cyclical firm. Recessions tend to affect revenues and earnings. Negative earnings may be due to strategic choices. If negative earnings are due to specific temporary events, then the earnings prior to the event must be taken into account to estimate cash flows and fundamentals. Adjustments to earnings need to be made on account of activities like acquisitions. In the case of high probability of bankruptcy, the estimation of liquidation value is the best estimate of valuation of distressed firms. The life cycle of a firm is also a determinant of negative earnings for firms. Firms with huge investment in infrastructure require a long gestation period to generate earnings. These firms often borrow huge funds to finance these infrastructure investments. Thus in the initial period these firms are characterized by negative earnings and high leverage. Energy and telecom companies have such financial characteristics.

---

[1] http://www.bluewaterpartners.com/library/articles/valuing-closely-held-companies.

11.3 Valuing cyclical firms

Cyclical firms are subject to significant swings in profitability. Valuation of cyclical industries like automobiles, oil companies, airlines, steel, chemical, paper, and infrastructure is often a challenging task. Economic downturns affect the value of these firms immediately. The share prices of cyclical companies are less stable. Cyclical companies can be valued using modified DCF approach involving scenario analysis. Cyclical companies have historically reported lower earnings/revenues during economic downturns and higher earnings/revenues during the economic boom. The major valuation issues for cyclical firms are the volatile earnings and cash flows. The volatility in revenues will be magnified at operating income level since these companies tend to have higher operating leverage in terms of fixed costs. The earnings of the cyclical firms must be normalized for the economic cycle covering 5 or 10 years. In this way the year-to-year swings in earnings and cash flows will be smoothened out. The normalized earnings can be on the basis of absolute average of the company, relative average, or sector average. Failure to consider earnings cycles in industries can result in under- or over-valuation of business enterprises.

Ben Graham has suggested that investors must pay for a cyclical business based on the average earnings for the past 10 years. Historically this time frame would have covered an entire business cycle averaging out the highs and lows. The usage of simple earnings capitalization method for firms experiencing cyclic earnings will lead to likely errors if valuation is not adjusted for the cycle.

Copeland et al. (2005) suggest that volatility of earnings of cyclical companies introduces additional complexity in the valuation of cyclical companies. Their study suggests that big fluctuations in earnings are driven by changes in product prices of cyclical industries like primary metal, electronics, chemicals, etc. The share prices of cyclical companies are more volatile than the share prices of noncyclical firms. Copeland et al. (2005) suggest a probabilistic approach to DCF analysis of cyclical firms. Copeland et al. (2005) advocate a combination of the DCF method with a probabilistic approach, by assigning a 50% probability to a future development of expected cash flow in line with the long-term historical trend of the company by means of incorporating the—historical cyclical behavior of earnings and a 50% probability of future development of expected cash flow in line with analysts estimations.

11.4 Valuing startup firms

The value of startup firms is the present value of the expected cash flows from its operations. The startup firms have limited financial statements. Hence valuation inputs cannot be based on historical financial variables. The current financial statement is not a valuable indicator to determine the expected growth rate. In the life cycle stage of firms, startup firms highlight the initial stage of the life cycle of firms. The value of startup firm depends on its future growth potential. In the expansion phase of life cycle, the firm establishes its presence in the market and revenue increases. In high growth stage, the revenues grow rapidly. In this stage, the information of current operations and operating history of firms is vital for valuation. In mature growth stage, the revenues level off. In mature stage, the need for new projects declines. The existing assets contribute to firm valuation. Venture capital firms often provide sources of finance for startup firms.

Venture capital firms estimate the exit or terminal value of startup firms at the time of the initial public offerings. In this venture capital method, the earnings of the startup firm are forecasted for future years when the company is expected to go public. The startup firms have higher betas.

The determinants of startup firms are the market forces of the industry, the size of recent exits, and the willingness of the investor to pay a premium to get the deal. DCF valuation methods, relative valuation methods, and asset-based valuation methods like book value and liquidation value can be used for valuation of startup firms.

11.5   Valuing multibusiness firms

In multibusiness valuation, the values of individual business units are determined as stand-alone firms and added to get the consolidated business value. The important factors to be considered are the allocation of the corporate overhead costs, treatment of intercompany transactions and intercompany receivables, and valuation of financial subsidiaries. Decisions need to be taken regarding which cost to be allocated at individual levels and which to be retained at corporate levels. Many firms like General Motors have financial subsidiaries which provide financing for customers. Each business unit must be valued at its own cost of capital. The levered beta of each division is estimated to find out the cost of equity of each business unit. The firm's value is estimated by DCF valuation of each business unit and adding the business unit values. The valuation of foreign subsidiaries follows the same basic approach as the business valuation of domestic companies. The valuation of foreign subsidiaries involves dealing with issues like foreign exchange translation, understanding foreign taxes, accounting regulations, transfer pricing, etc. Other factors to be considered include political risks, effect of foreign exchange hedging on value.

If the multinational company is considered as a portfolio of companies, then the weighted average of the risk parameters of each of these companies must be estimated to derive the value of the consolidated company.

11.6   Valuation in emerging markets

During the peak of the financial turmoil in 2009, emerging markets grew at 2.5%, while developed economies contracted by 3.2%. According to the International

Monetary Fund's (IMF) April 2014 "World Economic Outlook" analysis, the emerging market's share of global GDP reached 50.4% in 2013, up from 31% in 1980. The reasons which propelled the rise of emerging markets can be attributed to lower labor costs, rising productivity, and huge improvements in communications and transport which led to connectivity to global markets, rising middle class, and boom in world trade.

The discount rate for estimation of DCF valuation for emerging market firms must factor in additional risk factors like high levels of inflation, macroeconomic volatility, ex appropriation risks, civil unrest, regulatory changes, capital controls, accounting controls, and corruption issues (James and Koller). Macroeconomic volatility is an important factor which is very relevant in the context of financial crisis. Assessment of nonperforming loans is an important element of M&A Valuation in the banking sector of Asian markets. In DCF valuation, these additional risks need to be incorporated. These risks can be included either in the assessment of the actual cash flow or as an extra risk premium added to the discount rate to calculate the present value of future cash flows. The additional risk is incorporated into a country risk premium equal to the difference between the interest rate on a local bond denominated in US dollars and a US government bond of similar maturity. In principal terms equity markets might be expected to factor in a sizable country risk measure when valuing companies in emerging markets. The major macroeconomic variables that have to be forecast are inflation rates, growth in the gross domestic product, foreign-exchange rates, and, often, interest rates.

Emerging market companies are characterized by the following features. The emerging market local currency is often volatile in nature. Some emerging market currencies have their exchange rate pegged to some strong currency like dollars. For example, countries in the Gulf region have pegged their currencies to US dollar. The effects of exchange rates, interest rates, and inflation estimates are major challenges while analyzing emerging market firms. Emerging market economies face considerable country risks. Market risk measures like beta estimated would be of not much help in estimation of cost of equity if the stocks are not liquid and actively traded. Information gaps are often encountered due to differences in accounting standards. Lack of corporate governance practices is often a valuation challenge for emerging market companies. The valuation of emerging market firms operating in a high inflationary setting is impacted by inflation. To take into account inflation impact on cash flows, the estimation of future cash flows in DCF valuation must be done in both nominal and real terms. In real cash flow estimation, the cash flows are adjusted for inflation. The real cash flows are discounted by the real discount rates while the nominal cash flows are discounted by nominal discount rates. The real problem in relative valuation of emerging firms is the lack of comparable firms. The sample of comparable firms can be widened to include similar firms from other emerging markets. In relative valuation the focus can be on revenue multiples rather than on earnings multiples.

11.7 Valuing high growth companies

Koller et al. (2005) define them as companies whose organic growth—through new products, new technologies, and a rapidly growing end-product market—exceeds 15% annually. High growth is a key driver of value.

Net asset approach can be used to value companies with strong investments in intangible assets. A company with high growth opportunities requires high reinvestments in the high growth period. For high growth firms, traditional DCF analysis fails to take into account the value of options embedded in the project. High growth firms trade at higher multiples than low growth firms. DCF valuation, relative valuation, and real option valuation methods can be used to value high growth firms. Some emerging markets trade at similar or higher multiples relative to developed market indexes like S&P 500 on account of higher growth expectations or declining perceived risk in emerging markets.

Mckinsey research on the basis of analysis of the life cycles of about 3000 software and online service companies around the globe during the period 1980–2012 suggests that growth yields greater returns. The research shows that high growth companies offer a return to shareholders which was five times greater than medium growth companies. Moreover companies whose growth was greater than 60% when they reached $100 million in revenues were eight times more likely to reach $1 billion in revenues than those growing less than 20%. The study further states that growth is more important than margin or cost structure (Kutcher et al., 2014).

11.8 Errors in valuation

If the cash flow projections are to be used in a DCF valuation, the forecasts must be equal to the expected cash flows. The challenge in practice is that the cash flow forecasts may be a biased measure of the expected cash flows (Fernandez). The determination of the risk adjusted rate of return is an important step in valuation process. The estimation of unsystematic risk premium is a highly subjective factor. Errors in valuation occur due to miscalculation of discount rates. The errors would be due to wrong calculation of cost of equity and weighted average cost of capital. The cost of equity calculation might be misleading due to selection of wrong risk-free rate or risk premium. Valuing different sectors of a diversified company using the same WACC could lead to errors in valuation. Errors would also creep in due to wrong forecast of expected cash flows. Wrong estimation in residual value may also result in valuation errors. Conceptual errors with respect to estimation of free cash flow also result in wrong estimation.

References

Copeland, T., Koller, T., Murrin, J., 2005. Valuation: Measuring and managing the value of companies, fourth ed. McKinsey & Company, Inc.

Fernandez, P., Company valuation methods. The most common errors in valuations, Working
Paper 449, University of Navarra.

James, M., Koller, T.M., Valuation in emerging markets, Corporate Finance, <http://finance.
wharton.upenn.edu/ ~ bodnarg/courses/readings/McK_valuation_in_em.pdf>, 78−85.

Kutcher, E., Manyika, J., Nottebohm, O., Sprague, K., 2014. Grow fast or die slow, How
software and online services companies become multibillion giants. McKinsey & Co.

Peterson, D., 2013. Three approaches to valuing a privately Held company, Financial
Executive, Page 64.

Part II

Case Studies on Valuation

Valuation of Walmart

12

Walmart Stores, the American multinational retail giant operates a chain of discount department stores and warehouse stores. The first Walmart store was opened in 1962 in Rogers, Arkansas. It is estimated that more than 245 million customers visit approximately 11,000 stores in 27 countries and ecommerce websites in 11 countries in a week. In the fiscal year 2015, Walmart registered a net sales of $482.2 billion. The company employs around 2.2 million associates around the world. Walmart businesses consist of Walmart US, Walmart International, Sam's Club, and Global ccommerce. Walmart's operation distribution is one of the largest in the world. Walmart logistics has a fleet of 6500 tractors, 55,000 trailers, and more than 7000 drivers in the United States. Walmart became an international company in the year 1991 with more than 6100 stores in 26 countries. There are 600 Sam's Club in the United States and 100 Clubs internationally which cater to the customers' needs of merchandise in bulk. Walmart Global ecommerce is the platform for all online and mobile innovation for Walmart (www.walmart.com).

Walmart focuses on delivering improved comparable store sales by concentrating on merchandizing efforts, price leadership through the combination of digital and physical interaction. Walmart has more than 10,900 physical points of distribution globally. In fiscal 2014, consolidated net sales increased $7.5 billion to more than $473 billion and diluted earnings per share from continuing operations were $4.85.

In terms of ownership, financial institutions, mutual funds, and promoters own 84.82%, 14.65%, and 0.53% of the corporation (Annual Reports of Walmart stores). Walmart had been an innovator of the wholesale club and hypermarket concepts. In the early 1990s many Walmart stores were redesigned as supercenters. The growth of the chain was facilitated by its effective use of computer technology. In the early 1990s, the investments in computerization and information systems enabled the company to reduce its costs to 15% of its annual revenues.

12.1 Financial highlights

The net sales growth during the period 2010–2014 was $68 billion. The earnings per share growth rate during the period 2010–2014 was 30%. The total CAGR return during the 5-year period 2010–2014 was 12%. The return on investment was 18.1% and 17% during the period 2013 and 2014, respectively. During the same period, the return on assets was 8.9% and 8.1%, respectively. The average growth rate of revenues during the 5-year period 2010–2014 was 8.2%. The average gross profit margin during the 5-year period 2010–2014 was 24.56%. The average growth rate in operating income during the 4-year period 2010–2014 was approximately 4%. In 2014, the growth rate in operating income was −3% (calculations based on data given in Table 12.1).

Valuation.

Table 12.1 Operating results 5-year summary: amounts in million dollars

	2010	2011	2012	2013	2014
Total revenues	407,697	421,395	446,509	468,651	476,294
% change from previous fiscal year	8.1%	3.4%	6%	5%	1.6%
Gross profit margin	24.9%	24.8%	24.5%	24.3%	24.3%
Operating income	23,969	25,508	26,491	27,725	26,872

Source: Annual Reports.

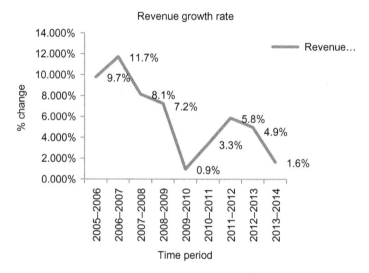

Figure 12.1 Revenue growth rate during the last decade.

The revenue growth rates have been fluctuating during the past 10 years. The growth rate ranged from 0.95% in 2009 to 11.71% in 2006. The net income growth rate has also been fluctuating to a great extent during the past 10 years (Figure 12.1 & Figure 12.2).

The average growth rate in net revenues during the period 2005−2014 was 5.9% while the average growth rate in net revenues during the 5-year period 2010−2014 was 3.3%. The average growth rate in operating income during 2005−2014 was 5% while the average growth rate for operating income during the period 2010−2014 was 3.4%.

The market capitalization of the past 10 years was based on the stock price of Walmart share price on 31 January every year during the period 2005−2014. In 2005, the market capitalization was $221.86 billion. In 2014, the market capitalization rose to $241.51 billion. On a comparative basis, the wealth created for stock holders increased by 8.85% during this period. The average growth rate of market capitalization during the 3-year period 2012−2014 was 9.9%. The market

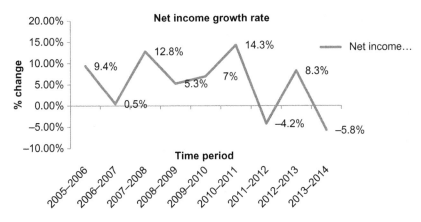

Figure 12.2 Net income growth rate during the period 2005−2014.

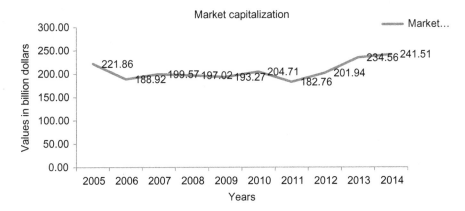

Figure 12.3 Market capitalization during the decade 2005−2014.

capitalization increased by 16% in the year 2013 compared to the previous year and by 3% in the year 2014 (Figure 12.3).

12.2 Equity value creation

Equity value creation is estimated as the product of the equity spread and equity capital. Equity spread is obtained as the difference between the return on equity and cost of equity[1] (Table 12.2).

---

[1] The beta estimated from market regression is 0.54. The risk premium is estimated as the difference between the return on market index DJIA and the risk free rate of 10-year treasury bond yield for the period of 5 years (2010−2014). Detailed calculation given in the resources excel file *Walmart.xlsx*. Applying CAPM, the cost of equity is estimated as 6.02%.

Table 12.2 **Equity value creation**

Year	2010	2011	2012	2013	2014
ROE	0.20	0.23	0.21	0.21	0.20
COE	0.06	0.06	0.06	0.06	0.06
Equity spread	0.14	0.17	0.15	0.15	0.14
Equity capital	72,929	71,247	75,761	81,738	81,339
Equity value creation in million dollars	9944.674	12,099.93	11,138.19	12,078.37	11,125.39

The equity value created has been fluctuating over the 5-year period 2010−2014. The value created increased by 21% in the year 2011 compared to the previous year. In 2012, the value decreased by approximately 8%. It was followed by a further increase of 8.4% in 2013 and then decreased by 7.8% in the year 2014.

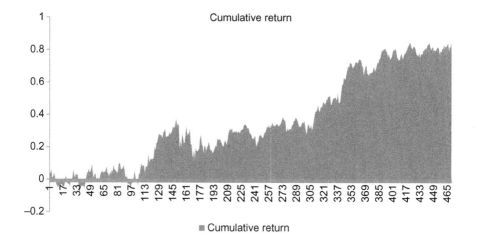

Figure 12.4 Returns of Walmart in the past decade.

12.2.1 Analysis of wealth creation

The detailed return analysis of the share price of Walmart during the 471 weeks' period (2005−2014) is given in the worksheet value and wealth of resources excel file *Walmart.xlsx*. The adjusted closing price of Walmart on 1/11/2005 was $39.32. Walmart was trading at 78.77 on 3/11/2014. The analysis reveals that the cumulative return during the 471 weeks (2005−2014) for Walmart was approximately 85%. The average weekly return was 0.18%. The average yearly return was 9.4% during the 9-year period. The cumulative weekly returns generated by Walmart stock during the period 2005−2014 is shown in Figure 12.4.

The wealth in terms of returns was showing an increasing trend at a higher rate during the post-2009 period. The cumulative return for the period 2010−2014 was approximately 56%. Table 12.3 highlights the average yearly returns generated by Walmart during the period 2010−2014. Table 12.4 illustrates the excess value created by Walmart during the period 2005−2014.

Table 12.3 Average yearly returns during the 5-year period 2010–2014

Year	Average yearly returns in percent (%)
2010	3.85
2011	14.18
2012	18.18
2013	16.19
2014	3.43

The maximum average yearly returns for the Walmart stock was during the period 2011–2013.Walmart shares gave an average yearly returns of 14.18%, 18.18%, and 16.19% in the years 2011, 2012, and 2013 respectively. The average yearly return during the 5-year period was approximately 11%.

12.3 Ratio analysis

The financial health of Walmart is analyzed through ratio analysis to understand the liquidity, efficiency, leverage, and profitability position of the firm (Tables 12.5–12.12).

12.4 Standardized income statements of Walmart

A standardized financial statement presents all items in percentage terms. Balance sheet items are shown as a percentage of assets and income statements as a percentage of sales (Tables 12.13–12.14).

12.5 Valuation of Walmart

Estimation of discount rate is an important step in the valuation process. This involves estimation of cost of equity and cost of capital. The cost of equity is estimated using the capital asset pricing model. Beta is estimated using bottom-up approach and market regression. Detailed calculation of bottom-up beta is given in the excel file *Walmart.xlsx*. The average unlevered beta from bottom-up beta estimation is 0.59. The levered beta is estimated as 0.79.

The market beta is estimated by regressing the daily stock returns of Walmart on the daily market index returns DJIA during the period 2011–2014. The beta value estimated from regression is 0.54. The regression results for beta are given in the excel file *Walmart.xlsx*. The risk free rate is taken as the average of the 10-year Treasury bond yield during the 5-year period 2010–2014. The return on market index (Rm) is the average returns on the market index DJIA during the 5-year period 2010–2014.

Table 12.4 Market value added in millions

	2005	2006	2007	2008	2009	2010	2011	2012	2013	2014
Book value of equity (BV)	49,396	53,171	61,573	64,608	67,079	72,929	71,247	75,761	81,738	81,339
Market value of equity (MV)	221,861	188,924	199,568	197,021	193,267	204,709	182,761	201,935	234,565	241,505
Excess value (MV-BV)	172,465.6	135,753	137,995	132,413	126,188	131,780	111,514	126,174	152,827	160,166
BV as percent of MV	22.26	28.14	30.85	32.79	34.71	35.62	38.98	37.52	34.85	33.68

The excess value is determined as the difference between the market value of equity and book value of equity. The excess value increased by 21% in the year 2014 compared to the previous year 2012. In 2014, the increase in excess value was 4.8%. The last row highlights book value of equity as percentage of the market value of equity. On the basis of average values for a 10-year period (2005–2014), it can be concluded that book value as percentage of market value is 33%. In 2011, book value as percent of market value was approximately 39%. In 2014, the book value was approximately 34% of the market value. In other words 66% of the value was not found in books and can be attributed to the market value of Walmart.

Table 12.5 Liquidity ratios

Year	2005	2006	2007	2008	2009	2010	2011	2012	2013	2014
Current ratio	0.90	0.90	0.90	0.81	0.88	0.87	0.89	0.88	0.83	0.88
Quick ratio	0.17	0.18	0.20	0.16	0.20	0.22	0.21	0.20	0.20	0.20
Cash ratio	0.13	0.13	0.14	0.10	0.13	0.14	0.13	0.11	0.11	0.10

The current ratio is showing a fluctuating trend during the past 10 years of analysis. The quick ratio is showing increasing trend whereas the cash ratio has been showing decreasing trend. The latest current ratio is 0.88 while the quick and cash ratio are 0.20 and 0.10, respectively. The average current, quick, and cash ratio for the 10-year period was 0.87, 0.19, and 0.12, respectively.

Table 12.6 Leverage ratios

Year	2005	2006	2007	2008	2009	2010	2011	2012	2013	2014
					Leverage ratios					
Debt equity ratio	0.57	0.68	0.61	0.63	0.61	0.58	0.71	0.73	0.61	0.66
Long-term debt to total long-term capital ratio	0.36	0.40	0.38	0.39	0.38	0.37	0.42	0.42	0.38	0.40
Total debt to total capital ratio	0.59	0.62	0.59	0.60	0.59	0.57	0.61	0.61	0.60	0.60

The different leverage ratios have been fluctuating over the 10-year period. The average debt equity ratio was 0.64 during the 10-year period. The average long-term debt to long-term capital ratio was 0.39 during the period. The total debt to total capital ratio during the 10-year period was 0.60.

Table 12.7 Profitability ratios

Year	2005	2006	2007	2008	2009	2010	2011	2012	2013	2014
					Operating profitability ratios					
Gross profit margin in percent	23.7	23.9	24.2	24.6	24.8	25.4	25.3	25	24.8	24.8
Operating profit margin in percent	6.1	6.00	5.9	5.8	5.6	5.9	6.1	5.9	5.9	5.6

The gross profit margin had been in the range of approximately 23.7 to 25.4% during the 10-year period. The operating profit margin was in the range of 5.6–6.1% during the 10-year period. Both the gross profit margin and operating profit margin were stable during the 10-year period of analysis. The 10-year average gross profit margin was 24.7% while the 10-year average operating profit margin was 5.9%.

Table 12.8 General profitability ratios

Year					General profitability ratios					
	2005	2006	2007	2008	2009	2010	2011	2012	2013	2014
ROA in percent	14.4	13.5	13.6	13.4	14	14	14.1	13.7	13.7	13.1
ROCE in percent	22.4	20.9	20.6	20.9	21.1	20.8	20.9	20.2	21.1	19.8
ROE in percent	20.8	21.1	18.3	19.7	20	19.7	23	20.7	20.8	19.7
EPS (Basic)	2.4	2.7	2.7	3.1	3.4	3.7	4.5	4.5	5.04	4.90
EPS (Diluted)	2.4	2.7	2.7	3.1	3.4	3.7	4.5	4.5	5.02	4.88

The general profitability ratios—return on assets (ROA), return on capital employed (ROCE), and return on equity (ROE) were generally stable during the last 10 years. The return on assets ranged from 13.1% to 14.4% during the period 2005–2014. The return on capital employed ranged from 19.8% to 22.4% during the 10-year period. The return on equity ranged from 18.3% to 23% during the 10-year period. The basic EPS ranged from 2.4 to 5.04 during the 10-year period. The diluted EPS ranged from 2.4 to 5.02 during the 10-year period. EPS has consistently improved over the 10-year period except in the year 2014. The average ROA, ROCE, and ROE during the 10-year period from 2005–2014 were 13.75%, 20.88%, and 20.38%, respectively. The average EPS (basic) and EPS (diluted) were 3.7 and 3.69, respectively, during the 10-year period.

Table 12.9 Decomposition of ROE using DuPont analysis

Year					DuPont ratio					
	2005	2006	2007	2008	2009	2010	2011	2012	2013	2014
Net profit margin in percent	3.6	3.6	3.2	3.4	3.3	3.5	3.9	3.5	3.6	3.4
Total asset turnover	2.36	2.26	2.31	2.31	2.47	2.39	2.33	2.31	2.31	2.33
Financial leverage	2.43	2.60	2.46	2.53	2.44	2.34	2.54	2.55	2.48	2.52

DuPont analysis explains the three factors which contribute to the return on equity. These factors are operating efficiency which is measured by profit margin, asset efficiency which is measured by total assets turnover, and financial leverage which is measured by the equity multiplier. Equity multiplier is obtained as the ratio of assets by equity. The average net profit margin was 3.50% while the average total asset turnover ratio was 2.34 while financial leverage was 2.49.

Table 12.10 Earnings and coverage ratio trend

Year	2005	2006	2007	2008	2009	2010	2011	2012	2013	2014
				Earnings and cash flow coverage ratios						
Interest coverage ratio	17.65	15.89	13.41	12.24	12.00	12.71	12.75	12.27	13.44	12.13
Cash coverage ratio	38.55	35.46	30.90	29.72	30.69	34.59	36.00	34.79	40.12	39.55
Cash flow to long-term debt ratio	0.54	0.49	0.53	0.51	0.57	0.62	0.46	0.44	0.52	0.43

The debt capacity of Walmart is analyzed through the earnings and cash flow coverage ratios. Walmart has maintained satisfactory coverage ratios during the last decade. The Interest Coverage Ratio (ICR) was highest in the year 2005 and lowest in the year 2009. The cash coverage ratio peaked in the year 2013 and the cash flow to long-term debt ratio was highest in the year 2010. The average ICR during the 5-year period 2010–2014 was 12.66 times. The average cash coverage ratio and cash flow to long-term debt ratio during the above period were 37.01 and 0.49.

Table 12.11 Asset utilization ratios

Year	2005	2006	2007	2008	2009	2010	2011	2012	2013	2014
				Operational efficiency or asset utilization ratios						
Total assets turnover	2.4	2.3	2.3	2.3	2.5	2.4	2.3	2.3	2.3	2.3
Fixed asset turnover	3.5	3.3	3.3	3.3	3.5	3.3	3.3	3.2	3.3	3.3
Equity turnover	5.8	5.9	5.7	5.8	6.0	5.6	5.9	5.9	5.7	5.9
Inventory turnover	7.4	7.4	7.8	8.1	8.8	9.2	8.7	8.2	8.0	8.0
Receivable turnover	165.8	121.2	122.8	103.2	103.6	98.5	82.9	75.2	69.2	71.3
Average receivable collection period in days	2.2	3.0	3.0	3.5	3.5	3.7	4.4	4.9	5.3	5.1

The total asset and fixed asset turnover ratios have remained almost steady over the 10-year period of analysis. The equity and inventory turnover has also been maintained in a narrow range. The receivable turnover ratio has shown a declining trend over the period 2005–2014. The average receivable collection period has increased from 2.2 days in the year 2005 to 5.1 days in the year 2014. The average total assets turnover, fixed assets turnover, and equity turnover during the 10-year period from 2005–2014 were 2.3, 3.3, and 5.8, respectively. The average receivable turnover ratio during the above period was 101.4 and average collection period was 3.9 days during the 10-year period of analysis.

Table 12.12 Market valuation ratios

						Market valuation ratios				
	2005	2006	2007	2008	2009	2010	2011	2012	2013	2014
Market to book ratio	4.52	3.57	3.27	3.12	2.89	2.87	2.67	2.70	2.92	3.00
Price earnings ratio	21.74	16.89	17.83	15.84	14.47	14.58	11.60	13.02	14.05	15.24
Earnings yield ratio	0.05	0.06	0.06	0.06	0.07	0.07	0.09	0.08	0.07	0.07
Price/Sales ratio	0.00018	0.00015	0.00014	0.00013	0.00012	0.00013	0.00012	0.00013	0.00015	0.00016

The market to book ratio moved in the range of 2.67−4.52 during the period 2005−2014. The price earnings ratio was in the range of 11.60−21.74. The earnings yield ratio was in the range of 0.05−0.09. The price to sales ratio was highest in the year 2005.

Table 12.13 Standardized income statement

Year	2005	2006	2007	2008	2009	2010	2011	2012	2013	2014
Net revenue (%)	100.0	100.0	100.0	100.0	100.0	100.0	100.0	100.0	100.0	100.0
Cost of sales (%)	76.3	76.1	75.8	75.4	75.2	74.6	74.7	75.0	75.2	75.2
Operating expense (%)	17.6	17.9	18.4	18.8	19.2	19.5	19.2	19.0	18.9	19.2
EBIT (%)	6.1	6.0	5.9	5.8	5.6	5.9	6.1	5.9	5.9	5.6
Interest expense (%)	0.3	0.4	0.4	0.5	0.5	0.5	0.5	0.5	0.4	0.5
EBT (%)	5.7	5.6	5.4	5.3	5.2	5.4	5.6	5.4	5.5	5.2
Net income (%)	3.6	3.6	3.2	3.4	3.3	3.5	3.9	3.5	3.6	3.4

Variables like cost of sales, operating expenses, earnings before interest and taxes, interest expenses, earnings before tax, and net income were almost constant as a proportion of revenues. The average cost of sales was approximately 75 of net revenues. The average operating expense as percentage of revenues was approximately 19. The average earning before interest and tax (EBIT) as percentage of revenues was approximately 6. The interest expense as percentage of revenues averaged around 5.4 during the 10-year period 2005−2014. The average of net income as percentage of revenues was 3.5 during the period 2005−2014.

Table 12.14 Components of Free Cash Flow to Firm (FCFF) as percentage of revenues

Year	2005	2006	2007	2008	2009	2010	2011	2012	2013	2014
Net revenue (%)	100	100	100	100	100	100	100	100	100	100
EBIT(1 − T) (%)	4.14	4.08	4.00	3.96	3.83	3.99	4.12	4.03	4.02	3.84
CAPEX (%)	31.32	32.34	33.04	34.05	32.44	35.16	36.62	36.04	36.64	37.51
Change in WC (%)	0.34	− 0.03	− 0.27	0.01	0.27	− 0.66	0.24	0.49	0.52	0.34
FCFF (%)	0.27	1.13	1.24	1.68	3.90	3.02	2.56	2.55	2.57	3.24

After tax earnings as percent of revenues ranged from 3.83 to 4.14. Capital expenditure as percent of revenues ranged from 31.3 to 37.51. FCFF as percent of revenues ranged from 0.27% to 3.9% during the ten year period of analysis.

Table 12.15 Economic Value Added (EVA) in millions of dollars

Year	2005	2006	2007	2008	2009	2010	2011	2012	2013	2014
Net income	10,267	11,231	11,284	12,731	13,400	14,335	16,389	15,699	16,999	16,022
Net noncash WC	9491	9384	8435	8464	9567	6853	7850	10,043	12,491	14,120
Net fixed assets	68,567	77,865	88,440	97,017	95,653	102,307	107,878	112,324	116,681	117,907
Capital employed	78,058	87,249	96,875	105,481	105,220	109,160	115,728	122,367	129,172	132,027
Capital charge	4683.48	5234.94	5812.5	6328.86	6313.2	6549.6	6943.68	7342.02	7750.32	7921.62
Economic value	5583.52	5996.06	5471.5	6402.14	7086.8	7785.4	9445.32	8356.98	9248.68	8100.38

The cost of equity is estimated as 6% for the calculation of capital charge. Total capital employed is the sum of net noncash working capital and net fixed assets. Capital charge is determined as cost of equity multiplied by capital employed. For example in the year 2005, capital charge was determined by multiplying 0.06 * 78,058 = 4683.48 million. Economic Value = Net Income − Capital Charge.
Economic Value Added has been increasing over the 10-year period of analysis. In 2014, the EVA decreased by 12% compared to the previous year. The average growth rate in EVA had been approximately 5% during the 10-year period of analysis.

Table 12.16 Walmart's dividend rate in US dollars

Year	2003	2004	2005	2006	2007	2008	2009	2010	2011	2012	2013	2014	2015
% change	0.3	0.36	0.52	0.60	0.67	0.88	0.95	1.09	1.21	1.46	1.59	1.88	1.92
		20	44	15	12	31	8	15	11	21	9	18	2

The average growth rate in dividends during the 12-year period 2003—2015 was 17%. The maximum year-on-year growth rate in dividend was in the year 2005 (44%) while the least year-on-year growth rate was in the year 2014 (2%).

Source: http://stock.walmart.com/stock-information/dividends-stock-splits/.

Risk Premium = Average return on market index − Average risk free rate = Rm − Rf = 10.9 − 2.47 = 8.43%

Cost of Equity = Rf + beta(Rm − Rf). The beta estimated from regression is taken for calculation.

Cost of Equity = 2.47 + 0.54(8.43) = 6.48%.

The yield to maturity of the fixed long-term bond of Walmart maturing in 2038 is 3.85%. This is estimated as the cost of debt. The corporate tax rate in 2014 is approximately 40%.[2]

The after tax cost of debt = 3.85 ∗ (1 − 0.40) = 2.31%.

The market value of equity is considered for the estimation of the WACC for Walmart. In early 2015, the market capitalization of Walmart was 266.2 billion and the book value of debt was 55.7 billion.

Total Value = 266.2 + 55.7 = 321.9 billion
Weight of Equity = 0.83
Weight of debt = 0.17
WACC = 0.83 ∗ 6.48 + 0.17 ∗ 2.31 = 5.76%. *The weighted average cost of capital is estimated as 5.76%.*

12.6 Discounted cash flow valuation

The three general models used in discounted cash flow valuation are the dividend discount model, free cash flow to equity, and free cash flow to firm models.

12.6.1 Dividend discount model (DDM)—stable stage growth model

The 10-year average annual growth rate of US GDP is 1.71%.[3]

The 4-year average growth rate of GDP (2.15%) is taken as the growth rate of dividends in the stable growth period.

Value = Current dividend(1 + growth rate)/(Cost of Equity-growth rate)
= 1.92(1 + .0215)/(0.0648−0.0215) = $45.30

Walmart was trading at $83.16 on 5/3/2015.

12.6.2 Two stage growth DDM model

12.6.2.1 Estimation of historical growth rate

The average EPS for Walmart during the 10-year period (2005−2014) was $3.70 while the average EPS for the 5-year period (2010−2014) was $4.53. The average

[2] http://www.kpmg.com/global/en/services/tax/tax-tools-and-resources(pages/corporate-tax-rates-table.aspx).
[3] http://data.worldbank.org/indicator/NY.GDP.MKTP.KD.ZG?page=2&order=wbapi_data_value_2005%20wbapi_data_value%20wbapi_data_value-first&sort=as.

Table 12.17 **Analysis of growth rates of EPS and DPS**

	Growth rate of EPS in percent	Growth rate of DPS in percent
10-year arithmetic mean	8	16
10- year geometric mean	8.2	15
5-year arithmetic mean	8	15
5-year geometric mean	7.6	15

The detailed calculation is given in DDM Valuation sheet in excel file *Walmart.xlsx*. On the basis of the average values for 10 years and 5 years, it can be observed that the growth rate in EPS was approximately 8% while the growth rate of DPS was 15%.

DPS for Walmart for the 10-year period (2005−2014) was $1.09 while the average DPS for Walmart for the 5-year period (2010−2014) was $1.45. The 10-year average Dividend Payout (DPO) was 30.29% while the 5-year average (2010−2014) DPO was estimated to be 34.38% (Table 12.17).

12.6.2.1.1 Estimation of growth rate from fundamentals
The expected growth rate from fundamentals is estimated as follows:

Expected growth rate = Expected Return on Equity (ROE) ∗ Retention Ratio
Retention Ratio = 1 − DPO where DPO is the dividend payout ratio.

The 5-year average (2010−2014) DPO of 34.38% is estimated as the expected DPO for the estimation of growth rates from fundamentals.

The average return on equity (ROE) during the 5-year period 2010−2014 was 0.21.

Retention Ratio = 1 − 0.3438 = 0.6562
Expected growth rate = 0.6562 ∗ 0.21 = 0.1378.

The estimated growth rate of earnings from fundamentals is estimated to be approximately 14%.

The valuation of the company using two stage DDM involves estimation of inputs for the high growth period and stable growth period.

The high growth period is estimated as 10-year period. The growth rate in EPS is assumed to be 8% based on the average growth rate estimated from historical estimation method.

Current dividend = $4.90. The average DPO for the period 2005−2014 is 30%. This value is assumed as the future DPO for the high growth period of 10 years. The present value of dividend calculation in high growth phase is given in Table 12.18.

12.6.2.2 Estimation of inputs for stable phase

The 4-year average growth rate of US GDP is estimated as 2.15%. This growth rate is assumed to be the growth rate of earnings in the stable phase. The industry sector

Table 12.18 Present value of dividends in high growth phase

	1	2	3	4	5	6	7	8	9	10
EPS	5.29	5.72	6.17	6.67	7.20	7.78	8.40	9.07	9.80	10.58
Payout ratio	0.30	0.30	0.30	0.30	0.30	0.30	0.30	0.30	0.30	0.30
DPS	1.59	1.71	1.85	2.00	2.16	2.33	2.52	2.72	2.94	3.17
Cost of equity	0.0648	0.0648	0.0648	0.0648	0.0648	0.0648	0.0648	0.0648	0.0648	0.0648
PV	1.49	1.51	1.53	1.56	1.58	1.60	1.62	1.65	1.67	1.69
Sum										15.90

PV of dividends in high growth stage = $15.90.

ROE is estimated as 19.70%.[4] The estimation of retention ratio from fundamentals in stable phase is given below.

Expected growth rate = Retention Ratio * Return on Equity
2.15% = Retention Ratio * Return on Equity

Retention Ratio = 2.15%/19.70% = 10.91%. In the stable period, the retention ratio is estimated as 10.91% from fundamentals.

The average DPO during the 5-year period 2010−2014 was 34.38% for the stable period. For estimation of DPS in stable phase period, we assume DPO as 40%.

EPS in the year 2024 = $10.58.

Year 2024 is the end of the high growth period. The Stable Phase assumed to begin in 2025.

EPS 2025 = EPS 2024 $(1 + g)$ where g is the growth rate of US economy assumed to be 2.15% in the long run.

Stable phase inputs	
Year	2025
EPS	10.80747
DPO	0.40
DPS	4.3230

The terminal or continuing value = DPS in year 2025/(Cost of Equity − Growth rate)
= 4.3230/ (0.0648 − 0.0215) = $99.83
The present value of the terminal value (discounted to ten year high growth period)
= $55.64
Value of Walmart Stock = PV of dividends in high growth stage + PV of terminal value.
= 15.90 + 55.64 = $71.94

Walmart Stock was trading at $83.57 on 6/3/2015.

12.6.3   Valuation using Free Cash Flow to Equity (FCFE) model

Three models are used for valuation of Walmart using FCFE. They are the two stage growth model, the stable phase one stage model, and the perpetuity model.

12.6.3.1   Estimation of growth rates from historical rates and fundamentals

The historical growth rates are estimated as the percentage year-to-year changes in net income and operating income for a period of 10 years (2005−2014) and then estimating the geometric mean for the 10-year period.

---

[4] https://biz.yahoo.com/p/sum_conameu.html.

Table 12.19 Ten-year growth rate in percent

	Historical	Fundamental	Average
Net income	5.9	8.93	7.42%
Operating income	5.99	3.66	4.8%

Table 12.20 Five-year growth rate in percent

	Historical	Fundamental	Average
Net income	3.6	7.7	5.65%
Operating income	3.3	3.13	3.21%

Table 12.21 Revenue growth rate

10-year growth rate	5-year growth rate
5.5%	3.5%

The growth rate from fundamentals is estimated as follows.

Growth rate in net income = Retention Ratio $*$ Return on Equity
Retention Ratio = Net Capital Expenditure + Change in noncash working capital/Net Income
Return on Equity = Net Income/Shareholder Equity
Growth rate in operating Income = Retention Ratio $*$ Return on Capital Employed (ROCE)
Retention Ratio = Net Capital Expenditure + Change in NonCash Working Capital/EBIT$(1 - T)$
ROCE = EBIT$(1 - T)$/Capital Employed

The growth rate in net income and operating income based on fundamentals is estimated for each of the 10-year period and then the geometric mean is found out. The detailed calculations are given in the worksheet Historical Growth Rate and Fundamental Growth Rate in excel file *Walmart.xlsx* Table 12.19—Table 12.20 gives the average historical and fundamental growth rate of net income and operating income during five year and 10 year period of analysis. Table 12.21 gives the average historical growth rate of revenues during the two periods of analysis.

12.7   Two stage FCFE model

Two stage FCFE model valuation assumes high growth stage for a period and then stable steady state growth phase thereafter. The high growth period is assumed to be 10 years.

Reinvestment Rate = Net Capital Expenditure + Change in Working Capital/Net Income.

The historical average reinvestment rate for the 10-year period is estimated as 47.22% while the historical average reinvestment rate for the 5-year period 2010−2014 is estimated as 32.8%.

Net Income in 2014 = 16022 million
High growth period = 10 years
Growth rate of net income in the high growth period = 7.42%

Reinvestment rate in high growth period is assumed to be the 10-year average reinvestment rate of 47.25%. Table 12.22 illustrates the present value calculation of FCFE in the high growth period.

FCFE = Net Income − Reinvestment
Value of Operating Assets in the stable growth Phase − Inputs
Net Income in 2024 (End year of high growth period) = $32,776.93 million.
Growth rate of net income in stable phase = Four-year average growth rate of US GDP that is equal to approximately 2%.
The reinvestment rate in the stable growth period can be estimated from fundamentals.
Growth rate of net income = Reinvestment rate * Return on Equity.
The industry sector ROE is estimated as 19.70%.[5]
Reinvestment rate = 2.15/19.70 = 0.1091.
Thus reinvestment rate from fundamentals is estimated as 10.91%.
The average reinvestment rate for the last five-year period is 32.79%.

For our estimation purposes, the reinvestment rate in the long run is assumed to be the average reinvestment rate obtained from the historical method that is approximately 33%.

Net Income in 2025 = $33,432.46 million
Reinvestment = $11,032.71 million
FCFE = $22,399.75 million
Terminal Value = $499,994.43 million
Present Value of terminal value = $266,860.78 million.
Value of Operating Assets = PV of operating assets in high growth phase + PV of terminal value of operating assets in stable growth phase.
 = $88,730.24 + $266,860.78 = $355,591.01 million

Value of Operating Assets = $355,591.01 million

Adding the Value of cash and equivalents in current year of estimation (2014)	7281.00
Value of Walmart Equity in 2014	362,872.01
Number of shares in millions	3283.00
Value per share	110.53

[5] https://biz.yahoo.com/p/sum_conameu.html.

Table 12.22 Present value of FCFE in high growth period

Year	1	2	3	4	5	6	7	8	9	10
Net income	17,210.83	18,487.88	19,859.68	21,333.26	22,916.19	24,616.57	26,443.12	28,405.20	30,512.87	32,776.93
Reinvestment	8132.12	8735.52	9383.70	10,079.97	10,827.90	11,631.33	12,494.38	13,421.46	14,417.33	15,487.10
FCFE	9078.71	9752.35	10,475.98	11,253.30	12,088.29	12,985.24	13,948.75	14,983.75	16,095.54	17,289.83
PV of FCFE	8526.22	8601.48	8677.42	8754.02	8831.30	8909.26	8987.91	9067.26	9147.30	9228.06
Sum										88,730.24

The present value (PV) of operating assets of Walmart in the high growth phase = $88,730.24 million.

Walmart share was trading at $82.59 on 8/3/2015 with market capitalization of $266.2 billion. The estimated value of equity from FCFE two stage model was $362.87 billion with a value of $110.53 per share. So it can be stated that the stock is undervalued in the market.

12.7.1 One stage FCFE model

Value = Current FCFE (1 + Growth rate)/(Cost of Equity − Growth Rate)

In this model the firm is assumed to have a constant growth rate equal to the growth rate of the economy. The growth rate of economy is assumed to be 2% based on 4-year average growth rate of US economy.

Current Net Income (year 2014) = $16,022 million
Reinvestment (at five year average reinvestment rate of 33 per cent) = $5287.26 million.
FCFE = $10,734.74 million
Cost of equity = 6.48%
Value = 10,734.74 * (1.02)/(0.0648 − 0.02) = $244,407.02 million.

If we assume that the operating assets of Walmart will grow at 2%, then the value of Walmart in 2014 arrived at $244.407 billion

12.7.2 Zero growth FCFE model

Under the assumption of zero growth, value of Walmart in perpetuity is estimated as given below.

Value = Current FCFE/Cost of Equity = 10,734.74/0.0648 = $165,659.57 million.

The value of operating assets of Walmart is estimated as $165.66 billion under zero growth FCFE model.

Detailed calculation of models under FCFE given in worksheet Valuation-FCFE of Walmart.xlsx.

12.7.3 Valuation using FCFF model

In this section, Valuation of Walmart is carried out using the Free Cash Flow to Firm (FCFF) model.

The 10-year average reinvestment rate is estimated to be 41.2% while 5-year average reinvestment rate is estimated as 29.6%. The 10-year average growth rate of operating income is estimated to be 5.99% from historical data while the 10-year average growth rate of operating income from fundamental is estimated as 3.66%. The average growth rate of operating income for computation purposes is the average of these two values that is 4.8%.

12.7.4 Two stage FCFF model

Current year EBIT$(1 - T)$ (Year 2014) = \$18,272.96 million.
High Growth Period = 10 years
Growth rate of operating income in the high growth period = 4.83%

Reinvestment rate in high growth period is assumed to be the 10-year average reinvestment rate of 41.22%. Table 12.23 gives the present value calculation of FCFF in the high growth phase.

WACC = 5.76% (See the computation of WACC in worksheet COE & WACC).
Value of FCFF in the stable growth Phase — Inputs
EBIT$(1 - T)$ in 2024 (End year of high growth period) = \$29,286.32million.
Growth rate of operating income in stable phase = Four year average growth rate of US GDP that is equal to approximately 2%.

The reinvestment rate in the stable growth period can be estimated from fundamentals.

Growth rate of operating income = Reinvestment rate * Return on Capital Employed
The industry sector ROCE is estimated as 8.87%.[6]
Reinvestment rate = 2/8.87 = 0.225
Thus reinvestment rate from fundamentals is estimated as 22.5 per cent.
The average reinvestment rate for the last five year period is 29.57 per cent.

For our estimation purposes, the reinvestment rate in the long run is assumed to be the average reinvestment rate obtained from the historical method and fundamental estimation method that is approximately 26%.

EBIT $(1 - T)$ in 2025 (beginning of stable growth period) = \$29,872.04 million
Reinvestment = \$7766.73 million
FCFF = \$22,105.31 million
Terminal Value = \$587,907.24 million
PV of terminal Value = \$335,810.59 million
Value of Operating Assets = Present Value of FCFF in high growth phase + PV of terminal Value in stable growth phase.
Value of Operating Assets = 102,348.39 + 335,810.59 = \$438,158.98 million

Value of operating assets of Walmart	438,158.98
Adding the Value of cash and equivalents in 2014	7281.00
Value of Walmart in 2014	445,439.38
subtracting value of interest bearing debt in 2014	53,544.00
Value of Equity	391,895.98
Number of shares in millions	3283.00
Value per share	119.37

The value of Walmart in 2014 is estimated as \$445.44 billion. The value of equity is estimated to be \$391.895 billion and the value per share is \$119.37.

---

[6] The ROCE of the industry sector discount and variety stores is estimated by finding out the current average ROCE of the 11 companies in the sector. ROCE = EBIT$(1 - T)$/Total Capital Employed. The calculations are given in the worksheet Industry-ROCE of file *Walmart.xlsx*.

Table 12.23 Present value of FCFF in high growth phase

Year	1	2	3	4	5	6	7	8	9	10
EBIT(1 − T)	19,155.54	20,080.76	21,050.66	22,067.40	23,133.26	24,250.60	25,421.90	26,649.78	27,936.96	29,286.32
Reinvestment	7895.92	8277.29	8677.08	9096.18	9535.53	9996.10	10,478.91	10,985.04	11,515.62	12,071.82
FCFF	11,259.63	11,803.47	12,373.58	12,971.22	13,597.73	14,254.50	14,942.99	15,664.74	16,421.35	17,214.50
PV of FCFF	10,646.40	10,552.78	10,459.98	10,368.00	10,276.83	10,186.46	10,096.89	10,008.10	9920.09	9832.86
Sum										102,348.39

Present value of FCFF in high growth phase = $102,348.39 million.

12.7.5   One stage FCFF model

Value = Current FCFF (1 + Growth rate)/(WACC − Growth Rate)

In this model the firm is assumed to have a constant growth rate equal to the growth rate of the economy. The growth rate of economy is assumed to be 2%.

Current EBIT(1 − T) (year 2014) = $18,272.96 million
Reinvestment (at average reinvestment rate of 26 per cent) = $4750.97 million.
FCFF = $13,521.99 million
WACC = 5.76%
Value = 13,521.99 ∗ (1.02)/(0.0576 − 0.02) = $366,819.95 million.

If we assume that the operating assets of Walmart will grow at 2%, then the value of Walmart in 2014 arrived at $366.820 billion.

12.7.6   Zero growth model

Under the assumption of zero growth, value of Walmart in perpetuity is estimated as given below.

Value = Current FCFF/WACC = 13,521.99/0.054 = $234,756.78 million.

The value of operating assets of Walmart is estimated as $234.757 billion under zero growth FCFF model.

Detailed calculation of models under FCFF given in worksheet Valuation-FCFF of *Walmart.xlsx*.

Summary: Discounted Cash Flow Valuation for Walmart

Dividend Discount Model (DDM)

- Value of Walmart stock using DDM Stable State growth model=$45.30
- Value of Walmart stock using two stage growth DDM model=$71.94

Free Cash Flow to Equity Model (FCFE)
Two Stage FCFE Model

- Value of Walmart = $362.872 billion
- Value per share = $110.53

One Stage FCFE Model

- Value of Walmart = $244.407 billion

Zero growth or perpetuity FCFE Model

- Value of Walmart = $165.66 billion

Free Cash Flow to Firm Model (FCFF)
Two Stage FCFF Model

(Continued)

Summary: Discounted Cash Flow Valuation for Walmart   (cont'd)

- Value of Walmart = $445.439 billion
- Value of Equity = $391.895 billion
- Value per share = $119.37

One Stage FCFF Model

- Value of Walmart = $366.820 billion

Zero growth or perpetuity FCFF Model

- Value of Walmart = $234.757 billion

Walmart share was trading at $82.59 on 8/3/2015 with market capitalization of $266.2 billion

---

12.8   Relative valuation

Various relative valuation ratios are examined in comparison with peer group. Walmart is the biggest discount and variety store with current market capitalization of 266 billion dollars approximately. The next largest firm (Costco Wholesale Corp)

Table 12.24 **Walmart comparison with peer group: price multiples**

Company	Market capitalization in mil	P/S	P/B	P/E	DIV yield%
Walmart Stores Inc	266,203	0.6	3.4	17.4	2.3
Costco Wholesale Corp	65,875	0.6	5.3	31.1	1
Target Corp	49,180	0.7	3	32.4	2.6
Dollar General Corp	21,640	1.2	4.1	21.4	
Dollar Tree Stores	16,372	2	10.3	27.2	
Family Dollar Stores	9018	0.9	5.3	36.4	1.2
Dollarama Inc	6593	3.8	11.8	30.7	0.6
Lawson Inc	6563	1.6	3	19.5	3.1
Don Quijote Holdings	6379	1.2	3.7	34.5	0.3
Big Lots	2593	0.5	3.6	24.9	1
Industry Average	**25,410**	**0.6**	**3.7**	**20.3**	**1.9**

The forward P/E ratio suggested by Morning star by 16.1 while that of S&P was 18.5. The PEG ratio of Walmart Stores was 3.2.
Data: Morningstar.com

Table 12.25 **Price multiples trend**

Year	2010	2011	2012	2013	2014
P/E	13.3	13.4	14	15.1	18.1
P/B	2.9	3	3.1	3.5	3.5
P/S	0.5	0.5	0.5	0.5	0.6
P/CF	7.7	8.6	8.5	11.3	11

Price multiples have been increasing over the 5-year period of analysis. The P/E ratio increased from 13.3 in year 2010 to 18.1 in the year 2014. The P/B ratio increased from 2.9 in 2010 to 3.5 in 2014. The P/S ratio improved marginally from 0.5 to 0.6 in year 2014. The Price to Cash Flow (P/CF) increased from 7.7 to 11 in 2014.

Table 12.26 **Enterprise value multiples in year 2014**

Enterprise value multiples	Walmart	Costco Wholesale	Target Corp
EV/SALES	0.66	0.58	0.86
EV/EBITDA	8.71	14.94	9.65
EV/EBIT	11.63	20.14	14.72

Enterprise value multiples are lower for Walmart compared to other peer companies. Detailed workings given in the worksheet Relative Valuation of *Walmart.xlsx*.

is approximately 25% of Walmart's size in terms of market capitalization. The third largest firm Target Corp is approximately 18% the size of Walmart in terms of market capitalization. The average market capitalization of industry sector is approximately $25 billion. The Price-to-Sales ratio of Walmart is the same as that of the industry average. Walmart's Price-to-book ratio of 3.4 is comparable to the industry average of 3.7. Walmart P/E ratio was 17.4 which is lower compared to the industry average of 20.3. Walmart's dividend yield of 2.3% was higher when compared to the dividend yield of industry sector with value 1.9% (Tables 12.24–12.26).

References

Annual Reports of Walmart Stores.
<www.walmart.com>.

Valuation of Tata Motors

13

The Tata Group founded by Jamsetji Tata is a global enterprise headquartered in India which consists of over 100 operating companies in more than 100 countries across six continents. The Group exports products and services to over 150 countries. In 2013, the Tata Group had revenues of $103.27 billion. Tata Group is known for it's strong values and business ethics. Each Tata company operates independently and has its own board of directors and shareholders. There are 32 publicly listed Tata enterprises with a combined market capitalization of approximately $137 billion as of early 2015 with a shareholder base of 3.9 million. The three major flagship companies of Tata Group are Tata Steel, Tata Motors, and Tata Consultancy Services. Tata Steel is one among the top 10 best steel makers. Tata Motors is among the top five commercial vehicle manufacturers in the world (www.tata.com). Tata Consultancy Services is among the top 10 global IT service companies in the world. Tata Group with its pioneering and entrepreneurial spirit has established industries of national importance in sectors like steel, hydropower, hospitality, and airlines in India.

Tata Motors is the largest automobile company in India. Tata Motors has operations in the United Kingdom, South Korea, Thailand, Spain, South Africa, and Indonesia. Tata Motors had acquired two iconic British brands Jaguar and Land Rover in the year 2008. In 2005, Tata Motors set up an industrial joint venture with Fiat Group Automobiles to produce Fiat and Tata cars and Fiat powertrain.

Tata Motors is the market leader in commercial vehicles and among the top three in passenger vehicles in India. Tata Motors is the world's fifth largest truck and fourth largest bus manufacturer. The commercial and passenger vehicles of Tata Motors are marketed in several countries in Europe, Africa, Middle East, South Asia, South East Asia, South America, CIS, and Russia. The company earlier known as Tata Engineering and Locomotive Company started manufacturing commercial vehicles in 1954 with a 15-year collaboration agreement with Daimler Benz of Germany. Some of the landmark achievements of Tata Motors include the development of Tata Ace, India's first indigenous light commercial vehicle; the Prima range of trucks; the Ultra range of international standard light commercial vehicles; Tata Safari, India's first sports utility vehicle; Tata Indica, India's first indigenously manufactured passenger car; and Nano, the cost-effective and affordable car. Tata Motors makes passenger cars, multiutility vehicles, and light, medium, and heavy commercial vehicles. Tata Motors automotive operations include all activities relating to development, design, manufacture, assembly and sale of vehicles, as well as sale of related parts and accessories.

Tata Motors has a joint venture with Marcopolo, the Brazil-based maker of bus and coach bodies. Tata Daewoo Commercial Vehicle Company is a 100% subsidiary of Tata Motors in the business of heavy commercial vehicles.

Table 13.1 **Production performance (2013–2014)**

Domestic & International	Units produced	Units sold
Commercial vehicles	443,202	432,600
Passenger vehicles	562,224	587,946

Source: 69th Annual Report 2013–2014.

Tata Motors has over 4500 engineers, technicians, and scientists at R&D centers in India, South Korea, Italy, Spain, and the United Kingdom. Tata Motors had a consolidated revenue of US\$38.6 billion in the years 2013–2014. Tata Motors operates in over 175 markets and has over 6600 sales and service touch points.

During the past year Tata Motors has been losing market share in domestic business in both commercial and passenger vehicles businesses. In 2013, the Indian economy was hamstrung by rising inflation and interest rates. Tata Motors focuses on keeping inventory levels low in order to reduce its burden on the channel partners. Tata Motors focuses on strong pipeline of new products and technologies to meet the changing market needs (Table 13.1).

13.1 Global industry trends

The global vehicle sale has been growing at a CAGR of 6% for the last 5 years. Asia Pacific region has been the largest contributor to the total sales in the year 2013. The contribution from Asia Pacific rose from 35% in 2008 to 48% in 2013. The highest sales came in from China (within Asia Pacific). This region accounted for 47% in the year 2008 and for 61% in the year 2013. Major demands also came in from regions of North America and Europe. The number of passenger cars and light commercial vehicles sales worldwide rose by nearly 5% to 76.28 million units in 2013, mostly on the back of increased demand in the United States and China. The strongest momentum for growth was generated in China, where the market grew by 19.30 million to 21.99 million units registering a growth of 13.94% in the year 2013.

13.2 Business overview

Jaguar Land Rover sales were growing in all markets. In the year 2013, Jaguar Land Rover sold 372,062 vehicles which represented an increase of 18.33% over the previous year 2012 (Annual Reports). Tata Motors' total Jaguar Land Rover sales in China went up by 44.7% on a year-to-year basis to 28,908 units from 19,981 units. In domestic market, the Company's Commercial Vehicle sales expanded from 529,984 to 537,143 vehicles, registering a growth of 1.35% from the previous year 2012. This represented a market leadership share of 59.5% in the domestic Commercial Vehicles market. Tata Motors' Commercial Vehicles (domestic + export) sales surged from 581,148 to 585,054. Slowdown in economic activity, sluggish infrastructure spending, and weak macro outlook coupled with higher operating costs for transport operators, adversely affected demand in the Medium and Heavy Commercial Vehicle industry. The domestic passenger car industry was affected mainly by weak sentiments, high cost of ownership, high interest rates, and fuel prices. The overall growth in domestic passenger vehicle industry grew by 3% in the year 2013. In 2013, despite difficult economic conditions and rising competition, Tata Motors retained its market leadership in commercial vehicles on the back of new offerings and introduction of innovative technologies. The company aims to integrate its products and services and deliver maximum value to its customers at the best price.

13.3   Competitor analysis

The major competitors of Tata Motors are Maruti Suzuki, Mahindra & Mahindra, Ashok Leyland, and Eicher Motors. Maruti Suzuki India Limited (MSIL) is engaged in the business of manufacture, purchase, and sale of motor vehicles, automobile components, and spare parts (automobiles). The other activities of the company consist of facilitation of pre-owned car sales, fleet management, and car financing. The Company's portfolio includes the Maruti 800, Alto 800, Alto K10, A-star, Estilo, WagonR, Ritz, Swift, Swift DZire, SX4, Omni, Eeco, Kizashi, Grand Vitara, Gypsy, Ertiga, and Stingray. Ashok Leyland, established in the year 1948 is the second largest commercial vehicle manufacturer in India, the fourth largest manufacturer of buses, and the 16th largest manufacturer of trucks globally. Ashok Leyland is the market leader in the bus segment in India. Ashok Leyland claims to carry over 60 million passengers a day which is more people than the entire Indian rail network. Ashok Leyland primarily focuses on the 16 ton to 25 ton range of trucks. Ashok Leyland has a joint venture with Nissan Motors of Japan in the Light Commercial Vehicle (LCV) segment. Eicher Group has diversified business interests in design and development, manufacturing, and local and international marketing of trucks, buses, motorcycles, automotive gears, and components. VE Commercial Vehicles (VECV) is a 50:50 joint venture between Volvo Group (Volvo) and Eicher Motors Ltd Mahindra & Mahindra Ltd operates in nine segments. These include sales of automobiles, spare parts, and related services.

Table 13.2 provides the comparative financial highlights of Tata Motors with peer companies. Tata Motors had the highest market capitalization of 1.62 trillion Indian Rupees (INR) in the year 2014. Maruti Suzuki and Mahindra and Mahindra had a market capitalization of 990.78 billion and 769.73 billion. Tata Motors has the higher EBITDA margin among the peer group. The net profit margin is also comparable with the margin of other peer group members (Figure 13.1).

13.4   Financial performance analysis

The average sales growth during the period 2006−2014 was 33% while the average sales growth during the period 2010−2014 was 27%. The average net income

Table 13.2 Comparison of financial highlights (values in Indian rupees)

Name	Market capitalization	Price per share	Revenue in million	EBITDA margin %	Net profit margin%
Tata Motors	1.62 trillion	533.75	2,328,337	14.96	6.06
Maruti Suzuki Ltd	990.78 billion	3280.25	4,44,506	12.37	6.37
Mahindra & Mahindra	769.73 billion	1240.7	669,309.7	4.35	6.46
Eicher Motor Ltd	343.09 billion	12,689	68,098	10.57	7.72
Ashok Leyland	134.89 billion	47.4	114,867.2	3.7	−2.02

Source: Google Finance.

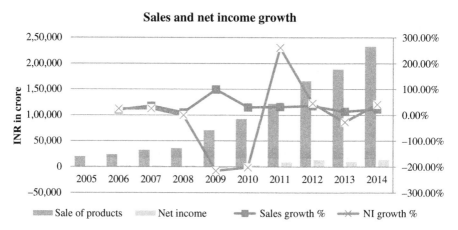

Figure 13.1 Sales and income growth analysis.

growth during the period 2006–2014 was −5.2% while the average net income growth during the 5-year period 2010–2014 was 23.7%. The maximum growth in sales was accounted in the year 2009 when the sales growth was approximately 99% compared to the previous year 2008. At the same time the expenses increased by 121% which resulted in huge negative net income growth rate. In the year 2014, sales increased by 23% while the expenses increased by 20.78% and the net income increased by approximately 41% (Figure 13.2).

Tata Motors dependence on debt for funding purposes over the past 5 years is showing fluctuating trend.

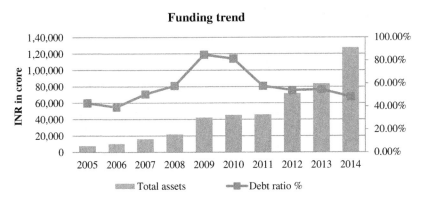

Figure 13.2 Funding trend of Tata Motors.

13.5   Wealth creation in stock market

The return analysis of the stock price of Tata Motors is examined for a period of 5 years (2010−2014). The analysis is done on the basis of weekly prices of Tata Motors. The excess returns of Tata Motors over the returns of Bombay Stock Exchange index BSE SENSEX is also examined for the period of 5 years. The 5-year cumulative weekly excess return of Tata Motors was approximately 117.14%. The 5-year average returns for Tata Motors based on arithmetic mean was 33.8% while the 5-year average return for geometric mean was 26.8%. On an average return basis, Tata Motors' stock outperformed the market index BSE SENSEX over the 5-year period of analysis. The average yearly return of Tata Motors ranged from −18.80% to 67.90%. In the year 2011, Tata Motors had an average yearly return of −18.8%. But even then its performance was better than the market index as the excess return was 0.3%. The average excess returns of Tata Motors over the market index ranged from 0.3% to 54.90%. The highest average excess returns of 54.90% was made in the year 2010. The detailed return analysis of Tata Motors is given in the worksheet wealth creation of *Tata Motors.xlsx*. The data for analysis was taken from yahoo finance. Tables 13.3 highlights the average returns of Tata Motors during the period 2010−2014. Table 13.4 highlights the excess value created by Tata Motors in stock market.

Table 13.3 Return analysis of Tata Motors

Year	Average yearly returns (%)	Average yearly excess returns (%)
2010	67.90	54.90
2011	−18.80	0.3
2012	65.10	43.20
2013	20.10	13.60
2014	34.10	4.30

Table 13.4 **Estimation of excess value in millions of INR**

Year	2010	2011	2012	2013	2014
Book value of equity	147,791.5	200,133	196,260.1	191,348.4	191,766.5
Number of shares	570.56	634.6	3173.54	3190.11	3218.68
Market price	228.83	173.39	311.83	361.15	485.05
Market capitalization (MV)	130,561.2	110,033.3	989,605	1,152,108	1,561,221
Excess value	−17,230.3	−90,099.7	793,344.9	960,759.8	1,369,454
BV as percent of MV	113.19	181.88	19.83	16.60	12.28

The market value added or excess value is estimated as the difference between the market value of equity and book value of equity. The market capitalization is based on the closing stock price of Tata Motors on the last day of trading. The average increase in the book value of equity had been 7.8% during the 4-year period from 2011−2014. During the same period, the average growth rate in market value of equity had been approximately 208% mainly due to the huge increase in market value of equity during the period 2012. The excess value had been negative in the years 2010 and 2011. In the years 2013 and 2014, the excess value increased by approximately 21% and 42.5%, respectively. In the years 2010 and 2011, the book value as percent of market value was above 100%. The book value as percentage of market value was 19.83%, 16.61%, and 12.28 % in the years 2012, 2013, and 2014, respectively, signifying the greater valuation of the stock in the market.

13.6 Ratio analysis

In this section, the liquidity, efficiency, leverage, and profitability position of the firm is examined using ratio analysis (Tables 13.5−13.12). The common size statement analysis is given in Table 13.13.

13.7 Estimation of cost of equity and WACC

The cost of equity is estimated using the CAPM model.

Cost of Equity = Risk free rate + Beta*Risk Premium

Risk free rate is assumed to be the average of 10-year government bond yield during the period 2012−2015. Risk free rate = 8.30%.[1] Beta is estimated by regressing the weekly returns of Tata Motors on the weekly returns of market Index BSE SENSEX for the period 2012−2014. The market-based beta value is estimated as 0.27.

---

[1] http://www.investing.com/rates-bonds/india-10-year-bond-yield-historical-data.

Table 13.5 Liquidity ratios

Year	2005	2006	2007	2008	2009	2010	2011	2012	2013	2014
Current ratio	1.1	1.4	1.7	1.4	1.0	1.0	0.8	0.9	0.9	1.0
Cash ratio	0.3	0.2	0.1	0.3	0.1	0.2	0.2	0.2	0.2	0.3

The average current ratio during the period 2005–2014 was 1.1 and the average cash ratio during the same period was 0.2.

Table 13.6 Operational efficiency ratios

Year	2006	2007	2008	2009	2010	2011	2012	2013	2014
Total asset turnover	2.6	2.5	1.9	2.2	2.2	2.7	2.8	2.4	2.2
Fixed asset turnover	2.8	3.0	2.6	1.3	1.7	1.8	1.8	1.9	1.7
Working capital turnover	11.2	6.4	5.7	22.9	143.4	−19.8	−15.2	−17.9	−53.0

The average total asset turnover during the period 2006–2014 was 2.4 times, while the average fixed asset turnover was 2.1. The average working capital turnover during the period 2006–2014 was 9.3.

Table 13.7 Long-term solvency ratio

Year	2005	2006	2007	2008	2009	2010	2011	2012	2013	2014
Debt to total capital	0.4	0.3	0.5	0.6	0.8	0.8	0.6	0.5	0.5	0.5
Debt to equity	0.6	0.5	0.9	1.3	5.5	4.2	1.6	1.2	1.2	0.8
Interest coverage ratio	12.1	10.6	8.5	5.1	−0.1	2.6	5.4	5.5	4.8	5.0

The average debt to total capital ratio during the 10-year period was 0.6. The average debt to equity ratio during the 10-year period was 1.8. The average interest coverage ratio during the 10-year period 2005–2014 was 5.9. The ICR was high during the 3-year period 2005–2007 and became negative in the year 2009.

Table 13.8 Profitability ratios in percent

Year	2005	2006	2007	2008	2009	2010	2011	2012	2013	2014
EBITDA margin	13.1	13.5	12.8	12.7	3.2	10.3	14.3	13.3	13.1	14.8
Operating profit/ EBIT margin	10.4	10.9	10.6	10.5	−0.3	6.2	10.5	9.9	9.1	10.1
Net profit margin	7.0	7.2	6.7	6.0	−3.5	2.7	7.6	8.1	5.2	6.0
Return on assets		19.0	16.4	11.5	−7.8	5.9	20.3	23.0	12.7	13.2
Return on equity		32.1	30.4	25.3	−32.3	34.8	66.6	51.6	27.9	26.9

Most of the profitability ratios were negative in the year 2009 reflecting the extent to which economic recession affected the firm. The EBITDA Margin was in the range of 3.2% to 14.8% during the 10-year period of analysis. The net profit margin and return on assets peaked during the period 2012. The return on equity was highest during the period 2011. The average EBITDA margin during the 10-year period from 2005–2014 was 12.1%. The average operating profit/EBIT margin during the 10-year period of analysis was 8.8%. The average net profit margin and return on assets during the 10-year period were 5.3% and 12.7%. The average return on equity during the 10-year period was 29.3%.

Table 13.9 **Dividend payout trends**

Year	2005	2006	2007	2008	2009	2010	2011	2012	2013	2014
Dividend payout in %	37.7	33.8	31.7	31.2	−14.6	39.0	16.0	11.0	7.6	5.5

DPO is dependent on the net income of the company. The DPO had been fluctuating over the period of 10 years. The maximum dividend payout had been in the year 2010. The arithmetic mean of the DPO during the period 2005−2014 was 19.9 and while the geometric mean of the DPO was 19%.

Table 13.10 **Sustainable growth rate**

Year	2006	2007	2008	2009	2010	2011	2012	2013	2014
Sustainable growth rate in %	21.2	20.8	17.4	−37.0	21.3	56.0	45.9	25.7	25.4

The sustainable growth rate is the maximum growth rate that a firm can sustain without having to increase the financial leverage. Sustainable Growth Rate = Return on Equity * (1 − Dividend Payout Ratio). The average sustainable growth rate during the period 2006−2014 as 21.9%.

Table 13.11 **Three step DuPont analysis**

Year	2006	2007	2008	2009	2010	2011	2012	2013	2014
Net profit margin	7.2%	6.7%	6.0%	−3.5%	2.7%	7.6%	8.1%	5.2%	6.0%
Asset turnover ratio	2.6	2.5	1.9	2.2	2.2	2.7	2.8	2.4	2.2
Equity multiplier ratio	1.7	1.9	2.2	4.1	5.9	3.3	2.2	2.2	2.0
Return on equity	32.1%	30.4%	25.3%	32.3%	34.8%	66.6%	51.6%	27.9%	26.9%

Table 13.12 **Five step DuPont analysis**

Year	2006	2007	2008	2009	2010	2011	2012	2013	2014
Tax burden (times)	0.7	0.7	0.7	1.2	0.7	0.9x	1.0x	0.7x	0.7x
Interest burden (times)	0.9x	0.9x	0.8x	9.1x	0.6x	0.8x	0.8x	0.8x	0.8x
Operating profit margin	10.9%	10.6%	10.5%	−0.3%	6.2%	10.5%	9.9%	9.1%	10.1%
Asset turnover (times)	2.6x	2.5x	1.9x	2.2x	2.2x	2.7x	2.8x	2.4x	2.2x
Equity multiplier (times)	1.7x	1.9x	2.2x	4.1x	5.9x	3.3x	2.2x	2.2x	2.0x
Return on equity	32.1%	30.4%	25.3%	32.3%	34.8%	66.6%	51.6%	27.9%	26.9%

The five step DuPont analysis explains the variations in the return on equity. In 2009, operating profit margin was negative and the increase in interest burden affected the return on equity.

Table 13.13 Common size statement analysis

Year	2005	2006	2007	2008	2009	2010	2011	2012	2013	2014
Net sales	100%	100%	100%	100%	100%	100%	100%	100%	100%	100%
Operating expenses	87%	87%	87%	87%	97%	90%	86%	87%	87%	85%
EBITDA	13%	13%	13%	13%	3%	10%	14%	13%	13%	15%
D&A	3%	3%	2%	2%	3%	4%	4%	3%	4%	5%
EBIT	10%	11%	11%	10%	0%	6%	11%	10%	9%	10%
Interest	1%	1%	1%	2%	3%	2%	2%	2%	2%	2%
EBT	10%	10%	9%	8%	−3%	4%	9%	8%	7%	8%
Taxes	2%	3%	3%	2%	0%	1%	1%	0%	2%	2%
Net income	7%	7%	7%	6%	−3%	3%	8%	8%	5%	6%

Net income as a percentage of sales varied from −3% to 7% during the 10-year period from 2005–2014. EBITDA as percentage of sales varied from 85 to 97% during the 10 year period of analysis.

Risk premium is estimated as the difference between the average returns on the market index BSE SENSEX and the average risk free rate assumed as the average of the 10-year government bond yield during the period 2012–2015.

Risk free rate (R_f) = 8.30%
Beta = 0.27
Average returns on market index (R_m) = 18.36%
Risk Premium = $R_m - R_f$ = 18.36 − 8.30 = 10.06%
Cost of Equity = R_f + Beta ($R_m - R_f$) = 8.30 + 0.27(10.06) = **11.016%**

The estimation of bottom up beta is given in the excel sheet Bottom-up beta of *Tata Motors.xlsx*.

WACC calculation is based on the market value weights. The weight of equity and debt in the most recent year based on market values are 0.97 and 0.03, respectively. The weight of equity and debt in capital structure based on book value weights are 0.74 and 0.26, respectively.

Cost of debt = Riskless rate in mature market like US + Country default spread + Firm Default Spread.

Tata Motors has a current rating of BB given by S&P.[2] India's sovereign rating was BBB + given by Standard & Poor.[3] The spreads were taken for 10-year bond yields. The spreads were taken from bondsonline.com. The tax rate is 30% for domestic companies in India.[4]

WACC Calculation

Risk free rate = 2.735%
Country default spread = 1.15%

---

[2] http://www.tatamotors.com/investors/credit-ratings.php.
[3] http://www.standardandpoors.com/ratings/sovereigns/ratings-list/en/us/;
   jsessionid = 0GBcVCmF2YsdWbLJ8T9KVv5G2f23PHJpfwLmDGQFWvV1Dfr2H5Ww!26805723?
   subSectorCode = &start = 50&range = 50.
[4] http://www.kpmg.com/global/en/services/tax/tax-tools-and-resources/pages/corporate-tax-rates-table.aspx.

Firm default spread = 3.30%
Cost of debt = 7.18%
After tax cost of debt = 5.026%
WACC = 0.97*11.016% + 0.03*5.026% = 10.85%.

The weighted average cost of capital is estimated as 10.85%.

13.8   Valuation of Tata Motors

In this section valuation of Tata Motors is done using the discounted cash flow valuation models like DDM, FCFE, and FCFF models.

13.9   Valuation using dividend discount models

13.9.1   Two stage DDM valuation

The average DPO during the period 2005−2014 was 20% while the average DPO during the period 2010−2014 was 16%. The average EPS during the period 2004−2014 was INR 42.19. The average growth rate of DPS during the period 2005−2014 was 1.41% and 10.67% during the period 2010−2014.

13.9.1.1   Estimation of growth rate from fundamentals

Expected growth rate = Expected return on Equity * Retention Ratio

Retention Ratio = 1 − Dividend Payout Ratio. The average DPO during the period 2005−2014 was 20%. Hence the retention ratio is 80%. The average ROE during the past 10 years is estimated as 22%.

The expected growth rate = 0.22*0.80 = 0.176

The expected growth rate in the high growth period is estimated as 17.6%.

13.9.1.2   Estimation inputs for high growth period (Table 13.14)

High growth period = 10 years
Estimated growth rate in EPS = 17.6%
Expected DPO in future = 20%. The 10 average DPO during the period 2005−2014 was 20 per cent.
EPS in year 2014 (current year) = INR 43.51
Cost of Equity = 11.02%

13.9.1.3   Inputs for stable phase growth period

The stable phase period is assumed to be the average growth rate of Indian economy during the period 2005−2013. The average growth rate of Indian economy during this period was 7.5%.

Table 13.14 **PV of dividends in high growth phase**

Year	1	2	3	4	5	6	7	8	9	10
EPS	51.17	60.17	70.76	83.22	97.86	115.09	135.34	159.17	187.18	220.12
Payout ratio	0.20	0.20	0.20	0.20	0.20	0.20	0.20	0.20	0.20	0.20
DPS	10.23	12.03	14.15	16.64	19.57	23.02	27.07	31.83	37.44	44.02
Cost of equity	0.11	0.11	0.11	0.11	0.11	0.11	0.11	0.11	0.11	0.11
PV		9.22	9.76	10.34	10.96	11.61	12.29	13.02	13.79	14.61	15.48
SUM										121.08

Present value of dividends in high growth phase = Rs 121.08.

Growth rate in stable phase = Retention Ratio $*$ Average ROE of industry sector.
7.5 % = Retention Ratio $*$ Average ROE of industry sector.

The average return on equity of the automobile sector in India is 12.70%.[5]

Retention Ratio = 59 per cent.
DPO = 1 − 0.59 = 0.41

The stable phase begins after the 10-year period.

EPS in the year 2024 = Rs 220.12
EPS in the year 2025 = 220.12 $*$ (1.075) = Rs 236.63. The growth rate is assumed to be 7.5% in the long run.

Year 2025	
EPS	236.63
DPO	0.41
DPS	97.02

Terminal or Continuing Value = DPS in year 2025/(Cost of Equity − Growth Rate)
= 97.02/(0.11 − 0.075) = Rs 2756.19
The present value of the terminal price = Rs 968.94

13.9.1.4 According to the two stage DDM model

Value of Tata Motors per share = PV of dividends during the high growth phase + PV of terminal value of dividends
= 968.94 + 121.08 = Rs 1090.02

13.9.2 One stage or constant growth DDM model

Value = Current Dividend $*$ (1 + Stable growth rate)/(Cost of equity − Stable growth rate)

The current dividend per share is very low. The average dividend per share for the past 10 years is considered for estimation.

[5] https://biz.yahoo.com/ic/330.html.

Value = 10.45(1.075)/(0.11 − 0.075) = Rs 320.96

Tata Motors was trading at Rs 498.45 in Bombay Stock Exchange on 31/12/2014.

Data and calculations given in the excel sheet DDM VALUATION of *Tata Motors.xlsx*.

13.10   FCFE valuation

The inputs for estimation of FCFE is given in the table below (Table 13.15)

Reinvestment Rate = Capex-Depreciation + Change in Noncash Working Capital/Net Income

The reinvestment rate is estimated as 34.18%.

13.10.1   General formula for FCFE calculation

FCFE = Net Income-Capex-Depreciation − Change in Working Capital + Net Debt Issued
Net Debt Issued = New Debt Issued − Debt Repaid.

Estimation of FCFE in millions Indian rupees	Year 2014
Net Income	139,910.2
Capex-Depreciation	6272.1
Change in noncash working capital	41,543
New debt issued	−23,722.9
FCFE	147,538.7

Table 13.15 **Inputs for FCFE (value in millions of Indian rupees)**

	2013	2014
Net sales		2,306,771.0
Net income		139,910.2
Capex-Depreciation		6272.1
Current assets	741,535.5	958,453.3
Cash and bank balances	211,148	297,117.9
Short-term loan and advances	126,670.5	140,552.4
Noncash current assets	403,717	520,783
Non-interest-bearing current liabilities	671,372.9	746,896
Noncash working capital	−267,656	−226,113
Change in noncash working capital		41,543
New debt issued		
Debt repaid		23,722.9
Net debt issued		−23,722.9

13.10.2   Estimation of growth rate from fundamentals

Expected growth rate in net income = Retention Ratio * Average ROE
Growth Rate = 0.3418 * 0.2223 = 7.6%

The average ROE of Tata Motors during the past 10 years was 7.6%. The average GDP growth rate of Indian Economy was 7.5%.

13.11   Stable stage or constant growth model

The stable stage growth model of FCFE is used to value Tata Motors.

Value = FCFE(1 + g)/(Cost of Equity − Growth Rate)
Cost of Equity = 11.02%
Growth rate = 7.5.%
= 68,372/(0.1102 − 0.075) = Rs 1,942,385.51 million
Value of Operating Assets of Tata Motors = Rs 1,942,385.51 million
Adding Cash and Bank Balance = 297,117.9 million
Value of Tata Motors = 2,239,503.4 million

The Value of Tata Motors is estimated as 2.2 trillion INR (Indian Rupees)
Tata Motors Stock was trading at Rs 557.05 in Bombay Stock Exchange with market capitalization of 1.71 trillion rupees on 13/3/2015.
The detailed calculation is given in the excel sheet FCFE of *Tata Motors.xlsx*.

13.12   Valuation using FCFF model

Estimation of FCFF in millions of INR	2014
EBIT(1-T)	155,801.8
Capex-Depreciation	6272.1
Change in noncash working Capital	41,543
FCFF	107,986.4

Free Cash Flow to Firm (FCFF) is estimated as INR 107986.4 million.

13.12.1   Constant growth FCFF model

Value = Current FCFF(1 + Growth Rate)/(WACC − Growth Rate)
WACC = 10.85%
Growth Rate = 7.5%
Value of Operating Assets of Tata Motors = 107,986.4 * 1.075/(0.1085 − 0.075) = Rs 3,465,236 million
Value of operating assets of Tata Motors = Rs 3,465,236 million
Adding Cash and bank balance in 2014 = Rs 297,117.9 million

Value of Tata Motors = Rs 3,762,354 million
Less book value of debt = Rs 549,544.7 million
Value of Equity = Rs 3,212,809 million
Number of Shares = 3218.68 million
Value per share = Rs 998.176

The detailed calculation is given in the excel sheet FCFF of *Tata Motors.xlsx*.

Summary Discounted Cash Flow Valuation

Valuation using Dividend Discount Models
  Two stage DDM Valuation

    Value of Tata Motors per share = Rs 1090.02

  One Stage or Constant Growth DDM Model

    Value of Tata Motors per share = Rs 320.96

  FCFE Valuation
  Stable Stage or Constant Growth Model

    Value of Tata Motors = Rs 2,239,503.4 million

  FCFF Valuation
  Stable Stage or Constant Growth Model

    Value of Tata Motors = Rs 3,762,354 million
    Value of Equity = Rs 3,212,809 million
    Value per share = Rs 998.176

Tata Motors Stock was trading at Rs 557.05 in Bombay Stock Exchange with market capitalization of 1.79 trillion rupees on 13/3/2015.
Exchange Rate 1US dollar = 62.79 Indian Rupees as on 17/03/2015.

13.13   Relative valuation (Tables 13.16–13.18)

The detailed calculation is given in the excel sheet Relative Valuation of *Tata Motors.xlsx*.

Table 13.16 **Comparison with peer group in current period**

Name	Market cap	Sales turnover	Net profit	Total assets
Tata Motors	1,792,474.7	342,881.1	3345.2	336,921.8
Eicher Motors	428,846.7	30,312.2	5589.2	12,336.6
Ashok Leyland	208,460.5	99,434.3	293.8	83,318
SMLIsuzu	17,575.8	8812.7	174	2764.1

Values in millions of INR Tata Motors had the highest market capitalization and sales turnover among the peer group.
Source: Data from MoneyControl.com.

Table 13.17 **Price multiples of Tata Motors during 2005–2014**

Ratios	2005	2006	2007	2008	2009	2010	2011	2012	2013	2014
P/E	18	21.3	20.4	13.4	–	7.2	6.3	7.9	7.2	8.5
P/B	4.4	3.8	3.4	0.8	10.1	6.7	2.1	2.8	2.2	2.0
P/CF	19.4	59.5	19	3	15.7	5.9	3.9	4.2	2.1	3.2

The Price to Earning ratio (P/E) had been drastically reduced in the period 2010–2014 compared to the period 2005–2008. The P/B ratio was highest in the year 2010 while the P/CF ratio was highest in year 2006. Morning star estimates the current P/E, P/B, P/S, P/CF values as 9.8, 2.4, 0.8, 4.8, respectively. The current dividend yield is 0.3%. Morning star has suggested forward P/E ratio of 13.1 in comparison to S&P 500 ratio of 18.5. The PEG ratio is 1.1.

Table 13.18 **Enterprise value multiples**

Year	Tata Motors	Eicher Motors	Ashok Leyland
EV/Sales	4.78	141.46	21.35
EV/EBITDA	68.87	504.56	287.42
EV/EBIT	526.28	536.21	587.02

Lower the EV/Sales ratio, the more attractive the company as it would be considered undervalued. Tata Motors is the most undervalued company among the peer firms in terms of EV/Sales. A low EV/EBITDA also indicates undervaluation of the firm. Hence it can be stated that in terms of enterprise multiples Tata Motors is the most undervalued company among the peer firms.

References

<www.tata.com>
Annual Reports. Tata Motors.

Valuation of Samsung Electronics

14

Samsung Electronics Co., Ltd is a South Korean multinational electronics company headquartered in Suwon, South Korea. The company was established in the year 1969. It is the flagship subsidiary of the Samsung Group, which contributes to approximately 70% of the group's revenue. Samsung is a global leader in technology and ranks as a top global brand. Samsung Electronics has assembly plants and sales networks in 80 countries and employs approximately 1 lakh people. Table 14.1 gives the financial highlights of Samsung during the year 2014.

Exchange Rate: Won/U.S. Dollar yearly average exchange rate: 1,126.88/1$. Won/Euro: 1,453.68/1€.

Samsung's business divisions are organized in a two-pronged business framework of set (brand products) and component businesses. The set business is comprised of CE and IM divisions, and the component business is comprised of DS division. The CE division is responsible for the production and sales of CTVs, monitors, printers, air conditioners, and refrigerators, and the IM division focuses on the production and sales of handheld phones (HHPs) (such as feature phones and smartphones), network systems, and computers. The DS division is comprised of the Semiconductor business which manufactures and sells DRAM, NAND, and Mobile AP, etc., and the Display Panel ("DP") business which manufactures and sells TFT-LCD and OLED panels for TV, Monitor, Notebook PC, and Mobile devices.

The consolidated domestic subsidiaries of Samsung include Samsung Display for display panel production, Samsung Electronics Sales for domestic retail sales, Samsung Electronics Service for after service care, and Samsung Electronics Logitech for logistics. Samsung has over 141 overseas subsidiaries for product manufacturing, sales, and R&D.

In 2013, Samsung had realized sales revenue of KRW 229 trillion, operating profit of KRW 37 trillion and net profit of KRW 30 trillion registering an increase of 14%, 27%, and 28%, respectively, over the year 2012.

14.1 Strategies for growth

The CRT TV business has become stagnant as the penetration rate in major countries is over 90%. The industries have been revived due to strong momentum owing to the launch of Flat Panel TVs (LCD, PDP). Competition between manufacturers is now focused on large size and high resolution screens. The company focuses on smart TV sales and portfolio product mix within LCD and PDP categories. Fourth-generation mobile communication technology with ultra-high speed data transmission is the common trend in the market. Currently the company focuses on consolidating its market leadership in premium smartphone and tablet categories and creating demand with new products such as Galaxy S, VR and Circle, and advanced features such as Flexible Display. The company strengthened market leadership by maintaining its wide range of product line-up from premium to mass market models and by leading new markets such as the LTE market.

Samsung Electronics had market leadership position in core businesses which include the mobile communications, TV, and memory chip businesses. Improved cost savings and advanced process technology development facilitated the consolidation of memory business. Since 1993, Samsung has had market leadership in memory business.

Samsung focuses on sustaining its market leadership by developing premium products and differentiated technologies. The company has strategic plans to broaden its product lines and lead the LTE market to maintain the leading smart phone position. The focus in TV segment is on introduction of high value added premium products. The company is moving ahead with mass production of next-generation V-NAND flash memory. Samsung Electronics has made a mark in the global printer market with a strategy that combines intuitive user convenience with

Table 14.1 **Financial highlights in 2014 (amount in billion dollars)**

Year	2014
Revenues	195.883
Total assets	218.887
Total liabilities	59.214
Total shareholder equity	159.673
Net income	22.22

Figure 14.1 Financial highlights for the period 2011–2013.

differentiated small-size products. Samsung has also launched second-generation A3 multifunction printers. In 2013, the company invested KRW 14.8 trillion and registered 7643 domestic and 11,289 overseas patents including approval for 4676 US patents in the year 2013. Samsung had a market share of 26.8% and 27.2% in the top global flat TV panel and top global mobile phone market in the year 2013. Samsung focuses on producing devices which can be integrated with most of the software and operating systems. This provides Samsung products an edge over competitors especially as Android and other OS are gaining market share while iOS and OSX are losing it.

14.2 Growth trend analysis

In this section the growth rate of major financial parameters is analyzed. Samsung Electronics had a revenue of $82,154.71 million in the year 2005. By 2014 the revenue made by Samsung Group reached $195,883 million. During the period 2006−2014, the cumulative growth rate in revenues was approximately 100%. In the same period, the cumulative growth rate in net income was 201.48%.

Table 14.2 Growth rate of financial parameters in % (year on year)

Growth rate in percent	2006	2007	2008	2009	2010	2011	2012	2013	2014
Revenues	11.53	14.12	− 14.36	33.74	15.39	4.70	30.31	15.21	− 9.83
Operating income	26.25	− 2.26	− 53.24	115.53	61.05	− 7.82	91.14	26.56	− 31.04
Net income	8.69	− 6.90	− 48.20	106.1	67.91	− 14.71	80.50	28.55	− 20.48
Total assets	14.48	14.11	− 21.56	26.77	21.78	13.71	24.40	18.16	9.11

Table 14.3 Average growth rate 2010−2014 period

Revenue	11.16%
Operating income	27.98%
Net income	28.36%
Total assets	17.43%

Samsung has grown in size to become a global Electronics behemoth with asset base of $ 200.60 billion at the end of 2013. The size of the balance sheet has grown by 2.58 times since the world financial crisis of 2008. The major sources of funds have been the reserves and the equity issues. The debt level is very low. The average debt equity ratio of the company was 0.054 during the period 2005−2014. The debt equity ratio was 0.02 in the years 2013 and 2014.

Table 14.4 Common size income statement analysis (% of sales)

Fiscal period	2005	2006	2007	2008	2009	2010	2011	2012	2013
Sales	100.00%	100.00%	100.00%	100.00%	100.00%	100.00%	100.00%	100.00%	100.00%
Cost of goods sold	68.53%	69.97%	71.95%	74.00%	69.39%	66.40%	67.97%	62.98%	60.21%
Gross profit	31.47%	30.03%	28.05%	26.00%	30.61%	33.60%	32.03%	37.02%	39.79%
EBITDA	17.81%	19.80%	19.00%	14.30%	17.51%	20.24%	19.03%	22.78%	24.11%
Operating income	9.40%	10.64%	9.11%	4.97%	8.01%	11.19%	9.85%	14.44%	16.08%
Net income	9.48%	9.23%	7.53%	4.56%	7.02%	10.22%	8.32%	11.53%	13.04%
EPS (Basic)	0.06%	0.06%	0.05%	0.03%	0.05%	0.07%	0.05%	0.08%	0.09%
EPS (Diluted)	0.06%	0.06%	0.05%	0.03%	0.05%	0.07%	0.05%	0.08%	0.09%

Samsung has been reducing its costs of goods sold over the past years. Cost of goods sold accounted for 60.21% of sales revenues. Gross profit, EBITDA, and net income have been consistently increasing over the period 2009–2013 except the fall in year 2011 compared to the previous year 2010. Net Income which was 9.48% of sales in 2005 improved to 13.04% in the year 2013. The EPS which was 0.06% of sales in 2005 improved to 0.09% of sales in the year 2013. The company has on an average spent approximately 6% of its revenues on research and development during the period 2005–2013 (see worksheet FCFE of Samsung.xlsx for details of estimation).

Table 14.5 Common size balance sheet statement analysis (% of assets)

Fiscal period	2005	2006	2007	2008	2009	2010	2011	2012	2013
Cash, cash equivalents, marketable securities	13.53%	12.03%	12.66%	12.71%	18.62%	16.74%	17.27%	19.99%	25.46%
Total inventories	7.88%	8.30%	8.53%	9.01%	8.77%	9.95%	10.10%	9.80%	8.94%
Total current assets	44.85%	43.00%	44.87%	46.50%	48.33%	45.72%	45.94%	48.20%	51.74%
Property, plant and equipment	39.32%	41.52%	40.03%	40.36%	38.83%	39.44%	39.87%	37.82%	35.27%
Total assets	100%	100%	100%	100%	100%	100%	100%	100%	100%

On an average cash and cash equivalents accounted for 16.5% of the total assets during the period of analysis. Cash and cash equivalents as a percentage of total assets have been increasing over the period of analysis. It has increased from 13.53% of total assets in 2005 to about 25.46% of total assets in the year 2013. On an average basis inventories accounted for 9% of total assets. The average of current assets as percent of total assets had been 46.57% during the period 2005–2014. Fixed assets like plant, property, and equipment accounted for 39% of the total assets on an average.

The average growth rate of revenues, operating income, and net income during the period 2006–2014 was 11.20%, 25.13%, and 22.39% respectively. The average growth rate of total assets was 13.44 % during the period 2006–2014 (Tables 14.2–14.3).

Fiscal period	2005	2006	2007	2008	2009	2010	2011	2012	2013
Total current liabilities	33.45%	31.37%	31.91%	30.59%	30.49%	29.75%	28.48%	25.92%	23.97%
Long-term debt	6.50%	5.34%	4.36%	5.85%	1.23%	0.91%	3.19%	3.01%	1.07%
Other long-term liabilities	4.17%	4.37%	3.79%	3.80%	3.16%	2.81%	2.89%	3.98%	4.88%
Total liabilities	44.12%	41.08%	40.06%	40.24%	34.89%	33.46%	34.56%	32.91%	29.92%
Total equity	55.72%	58.77%	59.82%	59.64%	65.01%	66.45%	65.36%	67.09%	70.08%
Total liabilities and stockholders' equity	100%	100%	100%	100%	100%	100%	100%	100%	100%

On an average equity has been 63% of the total liabilities and stockholders' equity. Long-term debt accounts only for 3.5% of the total liabilities and stockholder' equity on an average basis. Equity component as percentage of total liabilities has increased from 55.7% in 2005 to 70.8% in 2013.

14.3 Ratio analysis (Tables 14.6–14.12)

Table 14.6 Liquidity ratios

	2005	2006	2007	2008	2009	2010	2011	2012	2013
Current ratio	1.34	1.37	1.41	1.52	1.58	1.54	1.61	1.86	2.16
Quick ratio	0.78	0.8	0.84	0.96	0.89	0.8	0.9	0.97	0.86
Cash ratio	0.40	0.38	0.40	0.42	0.61	0.56	0.61	0.77	1.06

The liquidity position of the firm is analyzed using current ratio, quick ratio, and cash ratio. Generally current assets must be twice that of current liabilities. The current ratio has been consistently increasing year on year except in the year 2010. The average quick ratio and cash ratio during the period of analysis were 0.87 and 0.58. The cash ratio has been consistently increasing year on year except in 2010.

Table 14.7 Efficiency ratios

	2005	2006	2007	2008	2009	2010	2011	2012	2013
Receivables turnover	10.9	10.41	9.75	10.47	8.56	7.52	7.26	7.91	8.38
Inventory turnover	9.42	9.52	9.63	10.28	9.79	8.85	7.71	7.57	7.47
Fixed assets turnover	2.75	2.72	2.77	3.04	3.17	3.2	2.87	3.08	3.18
Asset turnover	1.08	1.1	1.13	1.22	1.25	1.25	1.14	1.19	1.16

The various efficiency ratios have been fluctuating over the period of analysis.

Table 14.8 Leverage ratios

Year	2005	2006	2007	2008	2009	2010	2011	2012	2013
Total equity to total asset	0.56	0.59	0.60	0.60	0.65	0.66	0.65	0.67	0.70
Long-term debt to total asset	0.07	0.05	0.04	0.06	0.01	0.01	0.03	0.03	0.01
Debt to equity	0.12	0.09	0.07	0.10	0.02	0.01	0.05	0.05	0.02
Interest coverage ratio	38.23	34.38	17.31	10.81	23.78	34.26	27.64	108.80	121.14

Samsung Electronics maintained very low debt levels in its balance sheet over the period 2005–2013. All the leverage ratios had very low values indicating that the firm faces very less financial risk. The interest coverage ratio is high on account of low interest charges as debt level is low.

Table 14.9 Profitability ratios

Year	2005	2006	2007	2008	2009	2010	2011	2012	2013
Return on equity in %	18.4	16.6	13.3	8.8	13.1	17.7	13.5	19.1	19.9
Return on assets in %	10.3	9.7	8.0	5.3	8.5	11.8	8.8	12.8	13.9
Return on capital in %		20.29	8.79	4.7	10.07	14.47	10.3	15.93	16.72
Gross margin in %	31.47	30.03	28.05	26	30.61	33.6	32.03	37.02	39.79
Operating margin in %	9.4	10.64	9.11	4.97	8.01	11.19	9.85	14.44	16.08
Net margin in %	9.48	9.23	7.53	4.56	7.02	10.22	8.32	11.53	13.04

The average ROE and ROA during the analysis period were 15.6% and 9.9% respectively. The average ROCE during the period was 11.3%. The average gross margin, operating margin, and net margin were 32%, 10.4%, and 9% respectively. On an year-to-year comparison, it is observed that the profitability ratios were the least during the year 2008.

Table 14.10 Cash flow ratios

Year	2005	2006	2007	2008	2009	2010	2011	2012	2013
Operating cash flow growth % YOY		10.61	− 2.97	− 6.81	30.42	26.16	− 1.79	65.8	23
Cap Ex as a % of sales	14.31	13.68	12.44	11.61	6.32	14.8	13.71	11.74	10.53
Free cash flow/sales %	3.26	4.59	3	0.07	7.23	0.29	0.17	7.14	9.89
Free cash flow/net income	0.34	0.5	0.4	0.02	1.03	0.03	0.02	0.62	0.76

The average capital expenditure as a percent of sales was 12% approximately during the period 2005–2013. The average free cash flow as percent of sales during the period was approximately 4%.

Table 14.11 Earnings per share ratios

Year	2005	2006	2007	2008	2009	2010	2011	2012	2013
Revenue per share ($)	611.66	697.39	816.45	699.85	933.38	1065.79	1110.56	1441.97	1637.04
EBITDA per share ($)	108.97	138.08	155.16	100.07	163.4	215.76	211.31	328.5	394.63
EBIT per share ($)	57.47	74.17	74.37	34.8	74.8	119.22	109.37	208.29	263.32
Earnings per share (diluted) ($)	50.06	55.64	51.93	27.57	56.74	94.45	78.18	144.35	185.36
Free cash flow per share ($)	19.96	31.98	24.52	0.49	67.53	3.05	1.84	102.94	161.88

The average growth rate of revenues per share was approximately 14% during the period of analysis. The average growth rate of EBITDA per share was 21.5%. The average growth rate EBIT per share was 32% during the period of analysis. The growth rate of EPS during the period of analysis was 28% during the 10-period of analysis.

Table 14.12 Dividend ratios and estimation of fundamental growth rate

Year	2005	2006	2007	2008	2009	2010	2011	2012	2013
Dividends per share	5.60	5.87	8.49	3.69	7.03	4.47	4.82	7.50	8.94
Dividend payout ratio	0.112	0.106	0.164	0.134	0.124	0.047	0.062	0.052	0.048
Dividend yield %	2.28	1.14	0.85	1.18	0.6	—	1.63	0.57	0.52
Return on equity %	18.42	16.57	13.29	8.8	13.13	17.71	13.5	19.09	19.88
Retention ratio	0.888	0.894	0.836	0.866	0.876	0.953	0.938	0.948	0.952
Growth rate	9.78%	9.03%	6.38%	4.21%	7.07%	10.82%	8.17%	12.50%	13.29%

The average dividend payout ratio during the period 2005–2013 was 9.4%. The average dividend yield during the period was 1.09%. The year-to-year growth rate was obtained by multiplying the return on equity by the retention ratio. The average fundamental growth rate during the period 2005–2013 was 9%.

14.4   Stock market wealth creation (Tables 14.13 and 14.14)

Table 14.13 **Market capitalization 2005–2015 in million dollars**

Year	Market capitalization
2005	66,400
2006	100,991
2007	86,681
2008	79,576
2009	87,900
2010	85,696
2011	108,873
2012	176,645
2013	180,008
2014	186,470
2015	189000

The average market capitalization during the period 2005–2015 was $122.57 billion. The 5-year average market capitalization. The 5-year period (2011–2015) average market capitalization was $168.199 billion. The average growth rate of market capitalization during the past 10 years was 13.38% while the average growth rate of market capitalization during the last 5 years was 19.2%.

Table 14.14 **Stock return analysis**

Year	Yearly average returns in percent	Yearly average excess returns in percent
2010	17.59	−2.96
2011	16.34	25.26
2012	40.93	30.42
2013	−12.45	−9.98
2014	6.39	7.51

The data was taken from yahoo finance. The weekly returns of Samsung Electronics were subtracted from the corresponding weekly returns of market index KOSPI Composite Index to get the excess returns. The analysis was done for a 5-year period of 2010–2014. The cumulative total return (on the basis of weekly returns) made by Samsung Electronics during the period 2010–2014 was 69%. The cumulative excess return of Samsung Electronics over that of KOPSI Composite Index returns was approximately 51%. The stock of the company outperformed the market index for 3 years on the basis of average excess returns. The average excess return was highest in the year 2012 wherein the excess return was 30.42%. In the same year Samsung made the highest average return of 40.93%. In the year 2013, both the average returns and excess returns were negative for the company. In the year 2010, though the average yearly return was 17.59%, the excess return was negative to the tune of −2.96%. The detailed calculations are given in the worksheet stock return analysis of *Samsung.xlsx*.

14.5   Discounted cash flow valuation

The models used for valuation are DDM, FCFE, and FCFF models.

14.6   Estimation of cost of equity and cost of capital

Beta is estimated by regressing the weekly returns of Samsung on the weekly returns of KOPSI Composite index during the period 2010–2014. The beta regression value is estimated as 1.21. The risk free rate is assumed as the average of the yield on the South Korean 10-year government bond for the period 2010–2014. The yield data was collected month wise. The average yield was 3.74%.[1]

Risk free rate = 3.74%.
Equity risk premium = Base premium for matured developed equity market + Country risk premium.

The country risk premium can be measured by estimating the default spread on the sovereign ratings for a country by credit rating agencies. S&P's sovereign rating for South Korea is currently A+. The default spread for rating of A+ is 0.72%. Assuming the base premium for matured markets is 5%, the equity risk premium = 5% + 0.72% = 5.72%.

Cost of Equity = Risk free rate + Beta * Risk Premium
       = 3.74% + 1.21*5.72% = 10.6%.

The yield to maturity on the long-term bond is unavailable. Hence the cost of debt for Samsung is determined in the following manner

Cost of debt = Riskless rate in mature market like US + Country default spread + Firm Default Spread.

The 10-year US Treasury bond yield of 3% is assumed as the risk free rate in mature markets.[2]

Country default spread = 0.72%
Firm default spread = 0.89%
Cost of debt = 3% + 0.72% + 0.89% = 4.61%
The corporate tax rate in South Korea is 24.2 %[3]
After tax cost of debt = 4.61(1−0.242) = 3.49%
The market value of equity in 2014 = 163.3 trillion KRW
Debt Value = 13.9 trillion KRW.
The weight of equity in the capital structure is 92 per cent while that of debt is 8%
Weighted Average Cost of Capital = (0.92*10.60) + (0.08*3.5) = 10.03%
The weighted average cost of capital is estimated as 10.03%
*The estimation of regression beta, cost of equity, and WACC is given in **Samsung.xlsx**.*

---

[1] http://www.investing.com/rates-bonds/south-korea-10-year-bond-yield-historical-data.
[2] http://www.treasury.gov/resource-center/data-chart-center/interest-rates/Pages/TextView.aspx?data=yield
Year&year=2014.
[3] http://www.kpmg.com/global/en/services/tax/tax-tools-and-resources/pages/corporate-tax-rates-table.
aspx.

14.7   Dividend discount model

In the first section, valuation is done using two stage DDM model.

Average growth rate in EPS is estimated as 16.75% on basis of fundamental estimation for a 5-year data. (Growth Rate = Retention Ratio*Return on Equity)

High growth period = 10 years
Average DPO based on five years of data = 5%
Expected DPO = 5%
Cost of Equity = 11%
EPS in the year 2014 = KRW 161058.62
EPS in year 2014 = 161058.62*(1.1675)

Table 14.15 gives the details of present value calculation of dividends in the high growth period.

14.7.1   Inputs for stable phase growth period

The stable phase period growth rate is assumed as the average growth rate of South Korean economy during the period 2005−2012.[4]

The growth rate in EPS in stable phase = 3.73%.
The average ROE of Consumer electronics sector is 15 per cent currently[5]
Growth rate in stable phase = Retention Ratio* Average ROE
3.73% = Retention Ratio * Average ROE
3.73% = Retention Ratio*15%
Retention Ratio = 3.73/15 = 0.25
DPO in stable = 0.75
EPS at the end of high growth period = Krw 757,796.97
EPS in stable phase period = 757,796.97(1.0373) = krw 786,062.8
DPO = 0.75
DPS in stable phase = 0.75*786,062.8 = 590,595.18
Terminal Value = 590,595.18/(0.11−0.0373) = 8,123,730.17
Present Value of terminal value = 2861051.7
Value of dividend per share = PV of dividend per share in high growth phase + Present Value of terminal value of dividend per share
 = 109,760.72 + 2,861,051.7 = krw 2,970,812.4

14.8   Constant growth DDM

Current EPS = 161,058.62
DPO in stable phase = 0.75
DPS = 120,793.97
Value = DPS(1 + growth   rate)/(Cost   of   equity-growth   rate) = 120,793.97(1.0373)/ (0.11−0.0373)

[4] http://data.worldbank.org/indicator/NY.GDP.MKTP.KD.ZG?page=1.
[5] https://biz.yahoo.com/p/314conameu.html.

Table 14.15 PV of dividends per share in the high growth phase

Year	1	2	3	4	5	6	7	8	9	10
EPS	188,035.9	219,532.0	256,303.6	299,234.4	349,356.2	407,873.3	476,192.1	555,954.3	649,076.6	757,797.0
Payout ratio	0.05	0.05	0.05	0.05	0.05	0.05	0.05	0.05	0.05	0.05
DPS	9401.8	10,976.6	12,815.2	14,961.7	17,467.8	20,393.7	23,809.6	27,797.7	32,453.8	37,889.8
Cost of equity	0.11	0.11	0.11	0.11	0.11	0.11	0.11	0.11	0.11	0.11
PV	8500.7	8973.4	9472.4	9999.1	10,555.1	11,142.0	11,761.6	12,415.6	13,106.0	13,834.8
Sum										109,760.72

PV of dividends per share in high growth phase = KRW 109,760.72.

= 17,223,515.54 krw
Value per stock = 17,223,515 krw

Samsung Electronics was trading at 1,345,000 in Korean Stock Market on 22/12/2014.

14.9   FCFE valuation

The models used for FCFE Valuation are the two stage FCFE model, one stage FCFE growth model and Zero growth FCFE growth model in perpetuity.

The average growth rate of revenues during the period 2005−2014 was 11.72% while the average growth rate of revenues during the 5-year period 2010−2015 was 9.75%.

In the case of Samsung, the company incurs Research and Development expenses which are treated as operating expenses. This needs to be adjusted in the capital expenditures.

Estimation of Adjusted Net Capital Expenditure = Net Capital Expenditure + R&D Expenses in current period −Amortization of Research Asset + Net Acquisitions.

Adjusted Depreciation and Amortization = Depreciation and Amortization + Amortization of Research Asset.

Adjusted Net Income = Net Income + Current Year's R&D Expense −Amortization of Research Asset

Adjusted Operating Earnings = Operating Earnings + Current Year's R&D Expense- Amortization of Research Asset.

Adjusted Book Value of Equity = Book Value of Equity + Value of Research Asset.

Table 14.16 **Estimation of amortization and value of research asset in year 2014 (millions of Korean Won)**

Year	R&D expenses	Unamortized portion %	Amount	Current amortization
Current (2014)	15,325,507	100	15,325,507	
−1	14,780,432	80	11,824,345.6	2,956,086.4
−2	11,532,795	60	6,919,677	2,306,559
−3	9,979,841	40	3,991,936.4	1,995,968.2
−4	9,099,352	20	1,819,870.4	1,819,870.4
−5	7,386,712	0	0	1,477,342.4
	Value of research asset		39,881,336.4	
	Amortization expense current year			10,555,826.4

The value of research asset is estimated by adding the amount of unamortized portion of the R&D expenses for the last 5 years to the R&D expenses in the current year.

Table 14.17 **Value of R&D assets and amortization amount in millions of krw 2008–2014**

Year	R&D expenses	Value of R&D assets	Amortization
2008	7,057,910	18,526,452.8	5,154,203.8
2009	7,386,712	20,063,309.6	5,849,855.2
2010	9,099,352	22,816,003.6	6,346,658
2011	9,979,841	25,729,305.6	7,066,539
2012	11,532,795	29,342,545.8	7,919,554.8
2013	14,780,432	35,111,655.8	9,011,322
2014	15,325,507	39,881,336.4	10,555,826.4

Table 14.18 **Adjusted -net income, book value of equity, ROE**

Year	Net income(NI)	Adjusted NI	BV of equity	Adjusted BV of equity	Adjusted ROE
2008			62,923,954	81,450,406.8	
2009	9,571,598	11,108,454.8	73,045,202	93,108,511.6	0.14
2010	15,799,035	18,551,729	89,349,091	112,165,094.6	0.20
2011	13,734,067	16,647,369	101,313,630	127,042,935.6	0.15
2012	23,185,375	26,798,615.2	121,480,206	150,822,751.8	0.21
2013	29,821,215	35,590,325	150,016,010	185,127,665.8	0.24
2014	25,016,352	29,786,032.6	168,088,188	207,969,524.4	0.16

The values are in millions of KRW.
Adjusted ROE = Adjusted Net Income in year t / Adjusted Book Value of Equity in year t − 1.

The Research assets are amortized linearly over time. The life of research asset is assumed to be 5 years. Every year 20% of the R&D expenses are amortized. The amortization value is 20%. The unamortized portion of the current R&D expenses is 100%. The value of research asset and amortization expense calculation is given in the Table 14.16. The detailed calculation for the rest of years of analysis is given in worksheet FCFE of *Samsung.xlsx* (Tables 14.16−14.18).

14.10   Estimation of adjusted net capital expenditure (Table 14.19)

Adjusted Net Capital Expenditure (CAPEX) = Net Capital Expenditures + Research & Development expenses in current period −Amortization of Research Asset + Acquisitions

Table 14.19 Adjusted net capex in millions of krw

Year	2009	2010	2011	2012	2013	2014
Capex	8,622,218	22,879,140	22,629,356	22,965,271	23,157,587	22,558,730
Dep & amortization	11,137,736	11,393,896	13,592,064	15,622,016	16,445,413	17,570,832
Net capex	−2,515,518	11,485,244	9,037,292	7,343,255	6,712,174	4,987,898
R&D expenses	7,386,712	9,099,352	9,979,841	11,532,795	14,780,432	15,325,507
Amortization of research asset	5,849,855.2	6,346,658	7,066,539	7,919,554.8	9,011,322	10,555,826
Acquisitions	136,084	−277,664	96734	702210	348,222	−1,040,465
Adjusted net capex	−842,577.2	13,960,274	12047328	11658705.2	12,829,506	8,717,114

The average of the adjusted net capex as percent of adjusted net income was 51.28% during the 5-year period 2010−2014.

14.11   Estimation of noncash working capital in millions of krw

Noncash current assets are obtained by subtracting cash and cash equivalents from total current assets. Noninterest-bearing current liabilities are obtained by deducting the short-term debt and current portion of long-term debt. Noncash working capital is obtained as the difference between the noncash current assets and noninterest-bearing current liabilities (Tables 14.20).

14.12   Estimation of two stage FCFE valuation

14.12.1   Inputs

High growth period = 10 years
Growth rate in adjusted net income = 11 per cent. (Estimated from fundamentals Table 14.21)
Average reinvestment rate = 58 per cent
Adjusted capex as per cent of adjusted net income = 51.29 per cent
Non-cash working capital as per cent of adjusted net income = 6.47 per cent.
Cost of Equity = 11 per cent.
Adjusted Net Income in 2014 = Krw 29786032.60 million. = Krw 29.79 trillion. (See the worksheet FCFE of Samsung.xlsx for details of calculation of adjusted net income.)

Table 14.23 gives the present value calculation of FCFE in high growth period.

14.12.2   Stable phase inputs

Growth rate in stable phase = Reinvestment rate*Average ROE
3.73% = Reinvestment rate * 15%
Reinvestment rate = 25%
Net income at end of high growth period = 84.58 Trillion krw
Net Income in stable period = 87.73 Trillion krw
Reinvestment rate = 0.25
Reinvestment = 21.93 Trillion krw
FCFE = 65.80 Trillion krw
Terminal Value = 905.05 Trillion krw
PV of terminal value = 318.75 Trillion krw
Value of Operating Assets = PV of FCFE in high growth phase + PV of terminal value = 126.59 + 318.75 = 445.34 Trillion krw
Value of Operating Assets = 445.34 trillion krw
Adding Cash and cash equivalents in 2014 = 58.53
Value of Samsung = 503.87 trillion krw.
Number of shares = 131 million
Value per share = 3,846,309.58 krw

Table 14.20 Estimation of changes in noncash working capital in millions of krw

Year	2009	2010	2011	2012	2013	2014
Total current assets	54,211,297	61,402,589	71,502,061	87,269,017	110,760,271	115,146,026
Cash and cash equivalents	20,883,464	22,479,963	26,877,634	36,189,397	54,496,009	58,530,542
Noncash current assets	33,327,833	38,922,626	44,624,427	51,079,620	56,264,262	56,615,484
Total current liabilities	34,204,424	39,944,721	44,319,014	46,933,052	51,315,409	52,013,913
Short-term debt	8,014,333	9,553,655	9,684,014	9,429,469	8,844,537	8,029,299
Capital leases/current portion of long-term debt				13,293	19,811	1,778,667
Noninterest-bearing current liabilities	26,190,091	30,391,066	34,635,000	37,490,290	42,451,061	42,205,947
Noncash working capital	7,137,742	8,531,560	9,989,427	13,589,330	13,813,201	14,409,537
Change in noncash working capital		1,393,818	1,457,867	3,599,903	223,871	596,336

The average change in noncash working capital as percent of adjusted net income during the period 2010—2014 was 6.47%. The average reinvestment as percent of adjusted net income during the 5-year period was estimated as 58%. The average growth rate of revenues during the 5-year period 2010—2014 was 9.3%.

Table 14.21 **Estimation of growth rate from fundamentals**

Year	2010	2011	2012	2013	2014
Adjusted ROE	0.20	0.15	0.21	0.24	0.16
Reinvestment rate	0.83	0.81	0.57	0.37	0.31
Growth rate	0.16	0.12	0.12	0.09	0.05

Growth rate = Adjusted ROE*Reinvestment Rate. The 5-year average growth rate was 11% during the period
2010–2014.

Table 14.22 **Estimation of FCFE**

Year	2010	2011	2012	2013	2014
Adjusted net income	18,551,729	16,647,369	26,798,615.2	35,590,325	29,786,032.6
Adjusted net capex	13,960,274	12,047,328	11,658,705.2	12,829,506	8,717,113.6
Change in noncash working capital	1,393,818	1,457,867	3,599,903	223,871	596,336
Net debt issued	−158,558	3,740,877	388,035	−3,136,848	−883,446
FCFE in millions of KRW	3,039,079	6,883,051	11,928,042	19,400,100	19,589,137

Free Cash Flow to Equity (FCFE) = Adjusted Net Income-Adjusted Net Capex −Change in non-cash working
capital + Net debt issued.
Net debt issued = New debt issued-Repayments.

14.13   Constant growth FCFE model

Net Income in 2014 = krw 29.79 trillion
Reinvestment rate (stable stage) = 0.25
Reinvestment = krw 7.45 trillion
FCFE in year 2014 = krw 22.34 trillion
Value = FCFE in 2014 *(1 + growth rate)/(Cost of Equity-Growth rate) where growth rate
is the stable phase growth rate.
Value = 22.34*1.0373/(0.11−0.0373) = 318.75 trillion krw.
Value per share = 2,433,170.79 krw.

Table 14.23 PV of FCFE in high growth period (values in trillion krw)

Year	1	2	3	4	5	6	7	8	9	10
Net income	33.06	36.70	40.74	45.22	50.19	55.71	61.84	68.64	76.19	84.58
Adjusted net capex	16.86	18.72	20.78	23.06	25.60	28.41	31.54	35.01	38.86	43.13
Change in noncash working capital	2.15	2.39	2.65	2.94	3.26	3.62	4.02	4.46	4.95	5.50
FCFE	14.05	15.60	17.31	19.22	21.33	23.68	26.28	29.17	32.38	35.94
NPV	126.59									

The present value of FCFE in high growth period was 126.59 trillion krw.

14.14   Zero growth FCFE model

FCFE in year 2014 = Krw 22.34 trillion
Value = 22.34/0.11 = 203.09 trillion krw.
Number of shares = 131 million
Value per share = 1,550,279.28

SAMSUNG was trading at 1,464,000 krw on 21/03/2015. The market capitalization was 246.14 trillion krw.

14.15   FCFF valuation model (Tables 14.24 and 14.25)

Adjustments to operating earnings are made to incorporate the effects of capitalizing R&D expenses.

Adjusted operating earnings = Operating earnings + Current year's R&D Expenses-Amortization of Research Asset.
Adjusted Book Value of Equity = Book Value of equity + Research Value of Asset

The 5-year average reinvestment rate as percent of EBIT (1-T) was 63.5%. The average of the adjusted net capital expenditure as percent of EBIT (1-T) was 56.5%. The average of the change in noncash working capital as percent of EBIT (1-T) was 6.99%. On the basis of past growth rate for 5 years, the average growth rate of operating income after tax was 21.8%. The details of estimation of reinvestment rate and growth rates are given in the worksheet FCFF of Samsung.xlsx.

Table 14.24 **Estimation of adjusted operating income in millions of Krw**

Year	EBIT	Taxes	EBIT (1-T)	R&D expenses	Amortization	Adjusted operating income
2009	10,309,038	2,431,046	7,877,992	7,386,712	5,849,855.2	9,414,848.8
2010	16,352,670	3,182,131	13,170,539	9,099,352	6,346,658	15,923,233
2011	15,644,291	3,432,875	12,211,416	9,979,841	7,066,539	15,124,718
2012	29,049,338	6,069,732	22,979,606	11,532,795	7,919,554.8	26,592,846.2
2013	36,785,013	7,889,515	28,895,498	14,780,432	9,011,322	34,664,608
2014	25,025,071	4,480,676	20,544,395	15,325,507	10,555,826.4	25,314,075.6

Table 14.25 **Adjusted ROCE**

Year	2009	2010	2011	2012	2013	2014
Adjusted ROCE	10.27597	16.24179	12.90945	19.38105	21.20405	12.7932
Average	15.46759					

Adjusted ROCE = Adjusted operating income in year t/ Book value of capital in year t − 1.
The average adjusted ROCE during the period 2009−2014 was 15.47%.

The growth rate of after tax operating income from fundamentals is estimated as given in Table 14.26.

14.16 Two stage FCFF valuation model

14.16.1 High growth inputs

High growth period = 10 years
Growth rate in EBIT (1-T) = 10 per cent
Capex as per cent of EBIT (1-T) = 56.5 per cent
Change in non-cash working capital as per cent of EBIT (1-T) = 6.99 per cent.
Adjusted EBIT (1-T) in the year 2014 = Krw 25,314,075.6 million

Table 14.28 gives the details of estimation of the present value of FCFF in high growth period.

14.17 Stable phase inputs

Growth rate = Reinvestment rate*Average Return on Capital Employed of industry.
3.73% = Reinvestment Rate*9.96%[6]

Table 14.26 Estimation of growth rate from fundamentals

Year		2010	2011	2012	2013	2014
Adjusted ROCE		0.1624	0.1291	0.1938	0.212	0.1279
Reinvestment rate		0.9643	0.8929	0.5738	0.3766	0.3679
Growth rate		0.16	0.12	0.11	0.08	0.05
Average	0.10					

The 5-year average growth rate of after tax operating income is estimated as 10%.

Table 14.27 Estimation of FCFF 2010–2014 in millions of Krw

Year	2010	2011	2012	2013	2014
Adjusted EBIT (1-T)	15,923,233	15,124,718	26,592,846	34,664,608	25,314,076
Adjusted net capex	13,960,274	12,047,328	11,658,705	12,829,506	8,717,113.6
Change in noncash working capital	1,393,818	1,457,867	3,599,903	223,871	596,336
FCFF	569,141	1,619,523	11,334,238	21,611,231	16,000,626

[6] http://csimarket.com/Industry/industry_ManagementEffectiveness.php?ind=1001&hist=1.

Table 14.28 Present value of FCFF in high growth period (trillions of krw)

Year	1	2	3	4	5	6	7	8	9	10
EBIT(1-T)	27.85	30.63	33.69	37.06	40.77	44.85	49.33	54.26	59.69	65.66
Net capex	15.73	17.31	19.04	20.94	23.03	25.34	27.87	30.66	33.72	37.10
Change in WC	1.95	2.14	2.36	2.59	2.85	3.14	3.45	3.80	4.18	4.60
FCFF	10.16	11.18	12.30	13.53	14.88	16.37	18.01	19.81	21.79	23.97
Sum PV	92.40									

The present value of FCFF in the high growth phase = 92.40 trillion Krw.

Reinvestment Rate $=$ 37 per cent.

Adjusted EBIT(1-T) in 2024 = 65.66 trillion krw

Adjusted EBIT(1-T) in 2025 = 68.09 trillion krw

Reinvestment = 25.19 trillion krw

FCFF = 42.90 trillion krw.

Terminal Value = FCFF $(1 + g)$/(WACC-g) $= 42.90*(1.0373)/(0.10-0.0373) =$ Krw 709.65 trillion.

PV of terminal value = krw 273.60 trillion

	Values in trillion krw
Value of operating assets	92.40 + 273.60 = 366
Add cash and cash equivalents	58.53
Value of Samsung	424.53
Subtract value of debt	10.32
Value of equity	414.21
Number of shares	131 million
Value per share	3,161,888.536 krw

14.18   FCFF one stage growth model

In this model the growth rate of operating income is assumed to be the growth rate of South Korean economy in terms of average annual GDP growth rate (3.73%).

	Value in krw trillions
EBIT(1-T) in 2014	25.31
Reinvestment rate in stable phase	0.37
Reinvestment	9.37
FCFF	15.95
Value = FCFF*(1 + g)/(WACC-g)	263.84
Value of operating assets	263.84
Add cash and cash equivalents	58.53
Value of SAMSUNG	322.37
Subtracting	10.32
Value of equity	312.05

14.19   FCFF zero growth model

FCFF IN 2014	15.95
WACC	0.1
Value = FCFF/WACC	159.5

Value = Krw 159.5 trillion.

Summary of Discounted Cash Flow Valuation

Dividend Discount Model

Two stage Model

- Value of dividend per share = krw 2970812.4
  Constant Growth DDM
- Value per share = krw 17223515.54
  FCFE Valuation
  Two stage Model
- Value of Samsung = 503.87 trillion krw.
- Value per share = 3846309.58 krw

  Constant Growth FCFE Model

- Value of Equity = 318.75 trillion krw
- Value per share = 2433170.79 krw

Zero Growth FCFE Model

- Value of Equity = 22.34/0.11 = 203.09 trillion krw.
- Value per share = 1550279.28 krw.

FCFF Valuation Model

Two Stage Model

- Value of Equity = 414.21 trillion krw.
- Value per share = 3161888.536 krw

FCFF One Stage Model

- Value of Equity = 312.05 trillion krw.
  FCFF Zero Growth Model
- Value of Equity = krw 159.5 trillion

Samsung Electronics was trading at 1345,000 in Korean Stock Market on 22/12/2014. Samsung was trading at 1464000 krw on 21/3/2015. The market capitalization was 246.14 trillion krw.

Detailed calculations for FCFE and FCFF are given in the excel worksheet FCFE and FCFF of **Samsung.xlsx.**

14.20   Relative valuation

The current Valuation of Samsung Electronics versus the S&P 500 is given below.

Valuation ratios	Samsung Electronics	S&P 500
Price/Earning	9.64	19.5
Price/Book	1.2	2.8
Price/Sales	0.9	1.8
Price/Cash flow	4.6	11.8
Dividend yield	1.4	2.2

The relative valuation ratios based on market prices were lower for Samsung Electronics compared to S&P 500. The forward price to earnings ratio as estimated by Morning star was 14.

Detailed calculations for relative valuation given in the worksheet Relative Valuation of *Samsung.xlsx.*

Table 14.29 Trend of price multiples of Samsung

	2010	2011	2012	2013	2014
Price/Earnings	9	11.9	8.6	6.9	8.2
Price /Book	1.4	1.4	1.6	1.2	1.1
Price/Sales	0.8	0.8	1.0	0.8	0.8
Price/Cash flow	5.3	6.0	5.2	3.8	4.2

Table 14.30 Current price multiple comparison of Samsung Electronics with competitors

Price multiples	Samsung	Panasonic	Sony	LG
P/E	14.1	67.3	6.8	18.29
P/B	1.2	2.2	0.5	0.8
P/S	0.9	0.4	0.1	0.2
P/CF	4.6	5.6	1.5	6.8
DIV Yield in %	1.36	1.1	0.3	0.67

Samsung Electronics has the highest dividend yield and price to sales ratio among all the competitors.

Table 14.31 Current enterprise value multiples

	Samsung	Panasonic	Sony	LG
EV/Revenues	0.7	0.9	1.8	0.5
EV/EBITDA	2.9	14.4	12	14.3
EV/EBIT	5.1	21.3	276.3	25.4

Samsung has the lowest EV/EBITDA and EV/EBIT multiples among the peer groups indicating the stock to be undervalued.

Valuation of Industrial and Commercial Bank of China (ICBC)

Industrial and Commercial Bank of China (ICBC) was established in 1984. ICBC is the largest bank in China. The bank has a presence in 39 countries spanning six continents and provides a wide range of products and services to over 4.38 million corporate customers and 393 million personal customers. The bank has a wide distribution network consisting of 17,125 domestic institutions, 383 overseas institutions, and 1771 correspondent banks worldwide. By 2012, the bank had approximately 315 million e-banking customers with annual transactions that amounted to RMB332.6 trillion. Almost 75% of the transactions were conducted through e-banking channels. In 2012, ICBC topped the Fortune Global 2000 list, which was the first by a Chinese company (www.icbc.com.cn).

The bank has issued about 470 million cards, which had an annual consumption of RMB4.13 trillion, of which 77.13 million credit cards were issued with an annual consumption of RMB1.3 trillion. ICBC is ranked among the top four card-issuing banks in the world. It is one of the leading international settlement banks of the world with a business volume of US$2 trillion in 2012. Internet banking amounted to RMB300 trillion in 2012. The bank had 4.38 million corporate customers in 2012, and domestic branches disbursed an aggregate of US$146.1 billion in international trade finance (Annual Reports of ICBC).

15.1 Business segments

15.1.1 Personal banking

ICBC provides products and services to more than 250 million personal customers through a network of more than 16,000 branches in China, 190 overseas subsidiaries, and more than 1000 correspondent banks throughout the world.

The personal banking unit provides services in a wide spectrum of activities. ICBC Happy Loan is an ICBC brand of all personal loan services, which covers 20 or more personal loan products under three major categories of personal housing loans, personal consumer loans, and personal business loans. The other types of personal/private loans in this category include new and secondhand housing loans, car loans, pledge loans, credit loans, business loans, commercial housing, and vehicle loans. The personal banking unit also provides investment and financing services such as smart money planner, "Roll Over" account services, personal insurance, and precious metal services, which include accumulation plan and metal trading. The other services provided by the personal banking division include convenient banking.

15.1.2 Corporate banking

The different types of corporate deposits offered by ICBC include current deposits, time deposits, foreign exchange deposits, corporate agreement deposits, structured deposits, and group account deposits. The loan financing consists of professional financing, working capital loans, project loans, domestic trade financing, real estate development loans, fixed assets support financing, and merging and acquiring loans. The professional financing consists of aircraft financing, commodity financing, lease financing, overseas M&A loan and global syndication, shipping finance and offshore engineering finance, export credit and overseas project finance, and natural resource-backed structured finance. ICBC plays a major role in financing aviation market sector. The lease finance division offers aircraft leasing, ship leasing, and equipment leasing. The bill services include bill discounting services such as discounting of banker's acceptances, bill rediscounting, and bill agency services. ICBC has the largest market share in RMB settlement among all banks in China. ICBC settlement is carried out through electronic exchange, Internet banking, SWIFT-PCC system, and all functional banking system (NOVA). The settlement services include corporate settlement, domestic settlement, agency services, and cash management. The corporate wealth-management segment provides loans pledged under gold. The physical gold leasing facilitates qualified clients to lease gold from ICBC and pay leasing fees in RMB as agreed in the contract. In agency gold trading business, ICBC is a key market maker in China's gold market and is among the four gold clearing banks designated by Shanghai Gold Exchange. OTC book-entry bond trading service provided by ICBC facilitates clients to trade RMB bonds.

The corporate e-banking includes Bank Enterprise Interlink, corporate Internet banking, and corporate telephone banking. The investment banking segment provides various services such as restructuring, M&A services, banking syndicate loan management, private equity, structured financing consultancy, asset securitization, credit asset transfer, corporate listing consultancy, and institution financial consultancy. In the M&A field, ICBC has completed major strategic deals such as the merger of Bao and Bayi steel, and equity transfer of Changyu Group. ICBC has organized major banking syndicate loan projects such as the syndicate loan for Hynix ST semiconductor for an amount of US$0.75 billion, CNOOC—Shell South China Petrochemical project with US$2.6 billion and the international syndicate loan for debt restructuring of Yuehai Group involving HK$14 billion.

The Asset custody services of the corporate division offer safe keeping of customers' assets under their trust, services associate portfolios, which include settlement, account checking, valuation, and related services on investment management. ICBC is the largest asset custodian in China in terms of product offerings and services. The basic asset custody services include account opening, asset custody, investment settlement, accounts checking, asset valuation, and trading supervision. The value-added services include investment appraisal, performance evaluation, and advisory services. The custody services are provided for securities investment fund, corporate annuity fund, pension insurance fund, trust funds, industry investment, and private equity funds. In institutional banking, ICBC has more than 400,000 government clients providing services covering fiscal taxation, industrial and commercial customs, court and judiciary, social security, education, and research. Institutional banking services are also offered to 7000 financial institutions which include banks, securities companies, insurance firms, trust companies, futures companies, and stock exchanges. The financial services provided to institutional clients cover more than 75 products under categories of assets, liabilities, and intermediaries. The integrated financial service solutions create a one-stop service model which is led by customer departments and supported by product and service departments. ICBC has a leading market share in key segments such as institutional deposit, third-party depository, property insurance, asset custody settlement, fiscal and Bank Futures transfer. The financial products and services to institutional customers are offered through 16,648 outlets across China, 239 overseas institutions, and a global network of 1669 correspondent banks. The corporate annuity services include trusteeship management service, account management services, and trusteeship services. The small business finance segment provides comprehensive financial services for small businesses including settlements and loans. The products include small business working capital loans, revolving loan, and online and trade finance for small businesses. ICBC is also involved in trust agency businesses of national development banks and agency trust businesses of the Chinese Export and Import bank. ICBC undertakes underwriting of super short-term commercial papers, SME collective notes, and private placement notes.

15.1.3 E-banking

The e-banking services cover both corporate and personal banking services. The Personal Banking@ Home consists of personal Internet, telephone, and mobile banking. SMS banking is provided in account management, remittance service, wealth management, payment service, credit card, and security service. Corporate Internet banking based on an Internet or private network provides services such as account inquiry, transfer and settlement, and online payment to corporate clients.

15.1.4 International banking

The international banking division ICBC Global Services provides a collection of product and services on the settlement, finance, and smart investment in RMB and foreign exchange. Global Services aims to minimize exchange risk and financial cost during international settlement and trade financing. The two main services of ICBC Global Services are categorized as Services Mart and Commercial Package. Services Mart includes products such as Invitation to Tender, Contract Negotiation, Enter Agreement, Goods Collection, Production and Sales, Payment against Import, and Export Collection to Contract Completed. Also included are international settlement, trade financing, and foreign exchange guarantee. Commercial package is a product portfolio involved in export and import services.

15.2 Strategy

The key component of ICBC's growth strategy is business transformation. The ICBC is in the process of implementing two 3-year plans. The economic boom and restructuring of China's economy provided a window of opportunity for ICBC to reorient its businesses. ICBC focuses on emerging businesses and intermediary business while limiting the scale of high capital-consuming businesses such as loans. Using diversified operations, the firm is aiming for capital savings and sustainable development. The bank is focusing on becoming the main linkage for promoting economic and trade relations between China and the rest of the world. The bank is actively involved in the promotion and development of sectors such as advanced manufacturing, service industry, cultural industries, and strategic emerging industries. The bank also focuses on financial services to small- and medium-sized enterprises. The bank facilitates corporates to have a wide range of financing tools which consist of investment banking, financial leasing, bond issuance, and syndicated loans. ICBC also has priorities in lending to local government financing vehicles and controlled loans to the real estate industry. The bank has built an integrated production line-based centralized processing system. The bank is providing controlled lending to industries with high-energy consumption, high pollution, and overcapacity. The bank also focused on improving the fund price management system to accommodate interest rate liberalization. The bank introduced more than 500 new products through independent R&D, which include multiple currency credit cards and personal account-based foreign exchange trading. The bank is leveraging its advantages in integrated financial services such as corporate wealth management, cash management, e-banking, and asset custody to improve market competitiveness. The bank puts emphasis on establishing first-class treasury trading platforms and enhancing the core competitiveness of innovative net fee and commission-based businesses. The bank focuses on establishing a global and multifunctional service chain to follow and serve multinational companies. Another priority area is focus on improving corporate governance and strengthening comprehensive risk management and internal control mechanism.

ICBC implements a comprehensive capital management that is composed of capital adequacy ratio management, economic capital management, book capital management, and aggregate capital and structure management. The economic capital management of the bank includes three major procedures of measurement, allocation, and evaluation. The economic capital indicators include Economic Capital (EC), Risk-Adjusted Return on Capital (RAROC), and Economic Value-added (EVA).

Table 15.1 **Financial highlights in millions of CNY**

Year	2008	2009	2010	2011	2012	2013	2014
Total assets	9,757,146	11,785,053	13,458,622	15,476,868	17,542,217	18,917,752	20,150,956
Total loans and advances	4,571,994	5,728,626	6,790,506	7,788,897	8,803,692	9,922,374	10,646,115
Return on average total assets (%)	1.21	1.2	1.32	1.44	1.45	1.51	1.51
Non-performing loans (%)	2.29	1.54	1.08	0.94	0.85	0.94	1.06
Core capital adequacy ratio (%)	10.75	9.9	9.97	10.07	10.62	10.57	11.79
Capital adequacy (%)	13.06	12.36	12.27	13.17	13.66	13.12	14.2

The total assets grew from 18.9 trillion in 2012 CNY to 20.15 trillion CNY in the year 2013. The total loans and advances increased from 9.9 trillion in 2012 to 10.6 trillion in the year 2014. The return on total assets has been consistently increasing over the period 2008–2014. The capital adequacy ratio improved from 13.06% in year 2008 to 14.2% in 2014. The core capital adequacy ratio improved from 10.75% in year 2008 to 11.79% in year 2014.
Source: Annual Reports.

The Table 15.1 gives the financial highlights of ICBC during the period 2008–2014.

15.3   Growth analysis (Tables 15.2–15.13)

Table 15.3 gives the year on year growth rate analysis of revenues, operating income and net income during the period 2005–2013. The bank witnessed highest growth rate of revenues in year 2007 when the revenues grew by 42% relative to the previous year. In 2009, the revenue growth rate fell by 10% in 2009. The highest growth rate of operating income of 29% approximately was registered in the year 2010. Net income registered the highest growth rate of 66.79% in the year 2007. The average growth rate of revenues during the period 2005–2013 was approximately 18%. The average growth rate of revenues during the 5-year period 2009–2013 was 14%. The average growth rate of operating income during the period 2005–2013 was approximately 27% while the average growth rate during the period 2009–2013 was 36.8%. The average growth rate of net income was 27.8% during the period 2005–2013. At the same time the average5-year growth rate of net income was 19% approximately.

CAR = Tier I capital + Tier II capital/Risk Weighted Assets. It is also known as capital to risk weighted asset ratio (CRAR). Risk weighted assets mean fund-based assets such as cash, loans, investments, and other assets. Degrees of credit risk expressed as percentage weights have been assigned by the national regulator to each such asset. Basel III rule requires banks to hold 4.5% of common equity and 6% of Tier 1 capital of risk weighted assets. The 5-year period analysis reveals that ICBC is adequately capitalized with respect to current regulatory requirements.

Table 15.2 Operating highlights for the decade 2004–2014 (values in millions of CNY)

	2004	2005	2006	2007	2008	2009	2010	2011	2012	2013
Revenues	139,342	162,378	178,889	254,157	309,758	309,454	380,821	475,214	536,945	589,637
Operating income	84,005	91,666	103,001	113,185	143,531	309,411	380,748	470,601	529,720	578,901
Net income	30,763	37,405	48,719	81,256	110,766	129,396	166,025	208,445	238,691	262,965
Operating cash flow	120,764	367,494	396,221	296,129	370,913	403,862	278,176	348,123	533,508	−1947

Financial parameters have consistently improved over this decade. The revenues improved from 139.342 billion CNY in the year 2004 to 589.637 billion CNY in the year 2014. The operating income increased by 6.89 times in year 2013 compared to the year 2004. The net income increased by approximately 8.5 times in year 2013 compared to 2004. The operating cash flow has been drastically reduced in the year 2013.

Source: Annual Reports.

Table 15.3 Year-on-year growth rate analysis

Growth rate in %	2005	2006	2007	2008	2009	2010	2011	2012	2013
Revenues	16.53	10.17	42.08	21.88	−0.10	23.06	24.79	12.99	9.81
Operating income	9.12	12.37	9.89	26.81	15.65	29.21	26.35	13.45	9.62
Net income	21.59	30.25	66.79	36.32	16.10	28.43	26.10	14.53	10.11

The table above gives the year-to-year growth rate of revenues, operating income, and net income during the 10-year period from 2005–2014.

Table 15.4 Operating margin in percent

Year	2004	2005	2006	2007	2008	2009	2010	2011	2012	2013	2014
Operating margin %	60.3	56.5	57.6	44.5	46.3	53.6	56.3	57	57.3	57.2	56.7

The 10-year average operating margin was 54% while the 5-year average operating margin was 56.9% suggesting improvement in the latter period.

Table 15.5 Growth rate analysis of assets and loans

Growth rate in percent	2009	2010	2011	2012	2013	2014
Assets	20.8	14.2	15.0	13.3	7.8	6.5
Loans and advances	25.3	18.5	14.7	13.0	12.7	7.3

The average growth rate of total assets during the period 2009–2014 was 12.9%. During the same period, the average growth rate of loans and advances was 15.3%. The highest growth rate in both assets and loans and advances was registered in the year 2009.

Table 15.6 Per share data analysis in yuan

Year	2009	2010	2011	2012	2013
Net asset value	2.02	2.35	2.74	3.22	3.63
Basic EPS	0.38	0.48	0.6	0.68	0.75
Diluted EPS	0.38	0.48	0.59	0.67	0.74

The net asset value per share improved from 2.02 yuan in 2009 to 3.63 yuan in the year 2013. The basic EPS improved from 0.38 in year 2009 to 0.74 in year 2014. The average growth rate in net asset value during the 4-year period from 2010–2013 was 15.8% while the average growth rate in basic EPS was 18.74% during the period 2010–2013.

Table 15.7 Five-year operating results analysis (values in millions of CNY)

	2009	2010	2011	2012	2013
Net interest income	245,821	303,749	362,764	417,828	443,335
Net fee and commission income	55,147	72,840	101,550	106,064	122,326
Operating expenses	120,819	139,480	169,613	189,940	204,140
Impairment losses	23,285	27,988	31,121	33,745	38,321
Operating profit	165,307	213,280	269,867	306,035	336,440

The net interest income grew from cny 245.821 billion in 2009 to cny 443.335 billion in 2013. During this period the net interest income increased 1.8 times. The net fee and commission income increased from cny 55.14 billion in 2009 to cny 122.326 billion by 2013 registering an increase of approximately 2.2 times. The operating expenses and impairment losses also grew by approximately 1.6 times. The operating profit grew from cny 165 billion in 2009 to cny 336 billion by 2013.

Table 15.8 Growth rate analysis of income and expenses

Year	2010	2011	2012	2013
Growth rate in %				
Net interest income	23.57	19.43	15.18	6.10
Net fee and commission income	32.08	39.42	4.45	15.33
Operating expenses	15.45	21.6	11.98	7.48
Impairment losses	20.20	11.19	8.43	13.56
Operating profit	29.02	26.53	13.40	9.94

The average growth rate of net interest income during the 4-year period of analysis was 16%. The average growth rate in net fee and commission income during the 4-year period from 2010−2013 was 22%. The average rate of increase of operating expenses and impairment losses during the period 2010−2013 was 14.13 % and 13.35 % respectively. The average growth rate of operating profit during the 4-year period was 19.72%. The highest growth rate of net interest income of 23.57% was registered in the year 2010. The trend shows that the growth rate of net interest income has been declining over the 4-year period. The growth rate fell from 23.57% in the year 2010 to approximately 6% in 2013. The growth rate of net fee and commission income peaked in 2011, then bottomed in year 2012, and then again rose by 15.33%. The operating expenses growth rate was the maximum in year 2011 and then registered declining rates in the following 2 years. The rate of increase of impairment losses was highest in the year 2010. The impairment losses declined by 8.43% in year 2012 and then increased by 13.56% in the year 2013. The operating profit grew by 29 % and 26.5% in the years 2010 and 2011 and then declined in the following 2 years.

Table 15.9 Deposit growth rate

Growth rate	2010	2011	2012	2013
Due to customers	14.06	10.01	11.27	7.17
Due to banks and other financial institutions	4.63	27.99	10.85	−14.63

The deposit from customers amounted to 9.7 trillion yuan in the year 2009. The deposits grew to 14.6 trillion yuan by year 2014. The deposits due to banks and other financial institutions grew from 1 trillion yuan in 2009 to 1.26 trillion yuan in 2014. The average growth rate of deposits from customers was 10.6% while the average growth rate of deposits due to banks and other financial institutions was 7%.

Table 15.10 Risk weighted assets: 2009–2013 in millions of CNY

	2009	2010	2011	2012	2013
Risk weighted assets	5,921,330	7,112,357	8,447,263	9,511,205	11,982,187

The growth of risk weighted assets averaged around 19% during the 4-year period from 2010–2013. The risk weighted assets increased by 25.9% in the year 2013.

Table 15.11 Financial indictors: profitability

Profitability in percent	2009	2010	2011	2012	2013
Return on average total assets	1.2	1.32	1.44	1.45	1.44
Return on weighted average equity	20.15	22.79	23.44	23.02	21.92
Net interest spread	2.16	2.35	2.49	2.49	2.4
Net interest margin	2.26	2.44	2.61	2.66	2.57
Return on risk weighted assets	2.43	2.55	2.68	2.66	2.45
Ratio of net fee and CI to OI	17.82	19.13	21.58	20.02	21.13
Cost to income ratio	33.18	30.99	29.91	29.24	28.8

Return on average total assets is calculated by dividing net profit by the average balance of total assets at the beginning and at the end of the reporting period. Return on average total assets was 1.2% in 2009 and improved to 1.45% in the year 2012 before falling to 1.44% in the year 2013. Returns on weighted average equity is calculated by dividing net profit attributable to equity holders of the parent company by the weighted average balance of equity attributable to equity holders of the parent company. The return on weighted average equity peaked in the year 2011 with 23.44%. The average net spread during the period 2009–2013 was 2.4%. The average net interest margin during the period 2009–2013 was 2.5%. The average return on risk weighted assets was 2.6% during the 6-year period from 2009–2013. Net interest spread is calculated by the spread between yield on average balance of interest generating assets and cost on average balance of interest bearing liabilities. The net interest margin is estimated by dividing net interest income by the average balance of interest generating assets. Return on risk weighted assets is calculated by dividing net profit by the average balance of risk weighted assets at the beginning and at the end of reporting period. The ratio of net fee and commission income to operating income was highest in year 2011. The cost to income ratio has been consistently declining over the 5-year period from 2009–2013. The cost to income ratio has declined from 33.18% in year the 2009 to 28.8% in year 2013. The cost to income ratio is calculated by dividing operating expenses less business tax and surcharges by operating income.

Table 15.12 Financial indictors: asset quality

Asset quality in percent	2009	2010	2011	2012	2013
Nonperforming loans (NPL)	1.54	1.08	0.94	0.85	0.94
Allowance to NPL	164.41	228.2	266.92	295.55	257.19
Allowance to total loans ratio	2.54	2.46	2.5	2.5	2.43

NPL ratio is estimated by dividing the balance of NPL by total balance of loans and advances to customers. Allowance to NPL ratio is obtained by dividing allowance for impairment losses on loans by total balance of NPL. Allowance to total loans ratio is calculated by dividing allowance for impairment losses on loans by total balance of loans and advances to customers. The NPL ratio has been declining over the 5-year period. The NPL ratio has been reduced from 1.54% in the year 2009 to 0.94% by year 2013.

Table 15.13 **Financial indicators: capital adequacy**

Capital adequacy in percent	2009	2010	2011	2012	2013
Capital adequacy ratio	12.36	12.27	13.17	13.66	13.12
Total equity to total assets ratio	5.76	6.11	6.19	6.43	6.76
Risk weighted assets to total assets ratio	50.24	52.85	54.58	54.22	63.34

Capital Adequacy Ratio (CAR) is a measure of a bank's capital. It is expressed as a percentage of a bank's risk weighted credit exposures. CAR has been fluctuating over the period of analysis.

15.4   Stock market wealth creation (Tables 15.14–15.16)

Table 15.14 **Market capitalization in millions of CNY**

Year	Market capitalization
2009	1,764,114.35
2010	1,458,878
2011	1,471,737.92
2012	1,455,745.3
2013	1,253,712.42
2014	1,711,244.95

The market capitalization of ICBC was cny 1764.1 billion in the year 2009. In 2014, the market capitalization fell by 2.9% compared to the year 2009. The year-on-year analysis reveals that the market capitalization decreased by 17% in year the 2010 compared to the previous year. It was followed by an increase of 0.8% in year 2011 and decrease of approximately1% consecutively in the years 2012 and 2013. In 2014, the market capitalization increased by 36% compared to the previous year 2013.

Table 15.15 **Excess value added**

Year	2010	2011	2012	2013	2014
MV	1,458,878	1,471,737.9	1,455,745.3	1,253,712.42	1,711,245
BV	820,430	956,742	1,124,997	1,274,134	1,530,859
Excess value	638,448	514,995.92	330,748.3	−20,421.58	180,385.95
BV as % of MV	56.2	65.0	77.3	101.6	89.5

The above table highlights the excess value created in terms of market value for the 5-year period 2010–2014. Excess value is obtained as the difference between the market capitalization and book value of equity. The excess value created in the year 2010 amounted to cny 638.448 billion. The excess value increased to cny 180.385 billion in 2014. In 2010, book value as percent of market value was 56.2%. By 2014, the book value was 89.5% of the market value.

Table 15.16 Yearly returns

Average yearly returns in %	2010	2011	2012	2013	2014
ICBC	−17.30	1.01	0.29	−16.29	34.43
SSE composite index	−8.1	−21.8	−2.1	−8.8	52.1
Excess returns	−9.2	22.8	2.4	−7.5	−31.4

The weekly returns were estimated and then the yearly returns are calculated. The returns of ICBC were compared with the returns of market index Shanghai Stock Exchange Composite index. In the years 2011 and 2012, ICBC outperformed the SSE Composite index. ICBC made average yearly returns of 1.01% and 0.29% in the years 2011 and 2012. SSE Composite index made negative returns during the years 2011 and 2012. The excess returns of ICBC over SSE Composite index were 22.8% and 2.4% during the 2-year period from 2011−2012. ICBC stock underperformed the market index in all other years of analysis. In 2014, ICBC registered average yearly returns of 34.4% but SSE Composite index outperformed by registering average yearly returns of 52% thereby resulting in negative excess returns of 31.4%. The 5-year average return for ICBC was 0.43% while the 5-year average return for market index was 2.2%.

15.5 Valuation of ICBC

Dividend Discount Model is used to value ICBC.

15.5.1 Estimation of cost of equity

The risk free rate is estimated as the average 10-year government bond yield during the period 2012−2015.[1]

The risk free rate is estimated as 3.8%.

Beta is estimated by regressing the weekly returns of ICBC on the weekly returns of market index Shanghai Stock Exchange (SSE) Composite index for the 3-year period from 2012−2014.

Beta = 0.24.

The average yearly return on the market index SSE Composite index for the 3-year period from 2012−2014 is estimated as 14.28%.

Risk Premium = Returns on Market Index − Risk Free Rate
14.28% − 3.8% = 10.48%
Cost of Equity = Risk free rate + Beta * Risk Premium
= 3.8% + 0.24*10.48% = 6.32%

15.5.2 Estimation of historical growth rates

	2009	2010	2011	2012	2013	2014
EPS	0.39	0.48	0.59	0.67	0.74	0.78
DPO	0.42	0.31	0.00	0.30	0.32	0.34
Retention ratio	0.58	0.69		0.70	0.68	0.66

The average growth rate of EPS during the 5-year period from 2010−2014 was 15%. The average retention ratio during the 5-year period was 66%. The average DPO during the 5-year period was 34%.

[1] http://www.investing.com/rates-bonds/china-10-year-bond-yield-historical-data

15.5.3 Estimation of growth rates from fundamentals

Year	2009	2010	2012	2013	2014
Retention Ratio	0.58	0.69	0.7	0.68	0.66
ROE	20.14	22.1	22.92	21.9	19.67
Growth Rate	11.68	15.25	16.04	14.89	12.98

The growth rate from fundamentals is estimated as the product of the return on equity and retention ratio. The growth rate for the year 2011 is excluded as the retention ratio would be 100% as dividends were not paid. The average growth rate from fundamentals for the 5-year period was estimated as 14.17%.

For estimation purposes, the growth rate from historical trend is assumed as the growth rate.

15.6 DDM

The high growth period is assumed to be 10 years. The growth rate in EPS is assumed to be 15% based on historical growth rates. The retention ratio in high growth period is assumed to be 66%.

Current EPS = 0.78 (EPS in year 2014)
EPS in the year 2015 = 0.78 * (1 + growth rate) = 0.78 * (1.15) = 0.90 CNY

The cost of equity is assumed as 6.32% (Table 15.17).
Table 15.17 highlights the present value calculation of dividends in high growth phase.

15.6.1 Stable phase inputs

The growth rate of Chinese economy is assumed to be 7.7% on the basis of the average growth rate of Chinese economy for the past 2 years.[2]
The average ROE of the Asian banking industry sector is assumed to be 19%.

Growth rate in stable period = Retention Ratio *Average ROE of industry sector.
7.7 = Retention Ratio* 19
Retention Ratio = 7.7/20 = 41%

Table 15.17 Present value of dividends in high growth phase

	1	2	3	4	5	6	7	8	9	10
EPS	0.90	1.03	1.19	1.36	1.57	1.80	2.07	2.39	2.74	3.16
Reinvestment	0.59	0.68	0.78	0.90	1.04	1.19	1.37	1.57	1.81	2.08
DPS	0.30	0.35	0.40	0.46	0.53	0.61	0.71	0.81	0.93	1.07
COE	0.063	0.063	0.063	0.063	0.063	0.063	0.063	0.063	0.063	0.063
PV of DPS	0.29	0.31	0.34	0.36	0.39	0.42	0.46	0.50	0.54	0.58
SUM										4.19

The sum of the present value of dividends in the high growth phase was estimated as CNY 4.19.

[2] http://data.worldbank.org/indicator/NY.GDP.MKTP.KD.ZG

We assume the retention ratio to be 41% in the stable phase and dividend payout to be 59%.

In this case, we cannot use the stable state growth model for valuation as the cost of equity estimated is lower than the growth rate.

Value of ICBC per share = CNY 4.19

ICBC was quoting at 4.33 CNY in Shanghai Stock Exchange on 24/12/2014.

15.7 Relative valuation (Tables 15.18–15.26)

Table 15.18 Current valuation in year 2015

Ratio	ICBC	S&P
P/E	6	19.5
P/B	1.1	2.8
P/S	2.5	1.8
P/CF	8.3	11.8
Div. yield %	5.6	2.2

The Price to Sales ratio valuation is higher for ICBC compared to the valuation for S&P. The dividend yield of 5.6% was higher for ICBC compared to the S&P dividend yield of 2.2%.

Table 15.19 Valuation trends of ICBC

Year	2010	2011	2012	2013	2014
P/E	8.8	7.2	6.2	4.8	6.2
P/B	1.8	1.5	1.3	1	1.1
P/S	3.8	3.1	2.8	2.2	2.6
P/CF	5.2	4.3	2.8		8.5

The various valuation ratios like P/E, P/B, P/S, P/CF have been fluctuating over the 5-year period. The Price to Cash Flow ratio was the maximum in the year 2014.

Table 15.20 PE ratio comparison with peer banks

Year	ICBC	ABC	CCB	BC
2010	8.8	8.1	8.2	8.3
2011	7.2	6.9	6.7	6.8
2012	6.2	6.2	6	6.1
2013	4.8	4.9	4.8	4.9
2014	6.2	6.7	7.4	7.2

The PE ratio was on the higher side for all the banks during the year 2010. The PE ratio was the lowest for all banks during the period 2013. ICBC had the highest PE ratio in the years 2010, 2011, and 2012 among all the peer banks. CCB had the highest PE ratio in the year 2014. The peer banks used for comparison are Agriculture Bank of China Ltd (ABC), China Construction Bank Corporation (CCB), and Bank of China Ltd (BC). (Annual Reports of China Construction Bank, Agricultural Bank of China, Bank of China and ICBC.)

Table 15.21 P/B ratio comparison with peer banks

Year	ICBC	ABC	CCB	BC
2010	1.8	1.6	1.6	1.4
2011	1.5	1.3	1.4	1.1
2012	1.3	1.2	1.2	1
2013	1	1	1	0.8
2014	1.1	1.2	1.4	1.1

ICBC had the highest Price to Book ratio among all the peer banks in all years except in 2013.

Table 15.22 P/S ratio comparison with peer banks

Year	ICBC	ABC	CCB	BC
2010	3.8	2.7	3.4	3.1
2011	3.1	2.2	2.8	2.6
2012	2.8	2.1	2.5	2.3
2013	2.2	1.7	2	1.9
2014	2.6	2.3	3	2.7

The above table gives the price to sales or revenue ratio for the banks during the period 2010–2014. ICBC had the highest P/S ratio in 4 out of 5 years of comparison. The P/S ratio value was highest for ICBC in the year 2010.

Table 15.23 Current market valuation

Banks	ICBC	ABC	CCB	BC
Market capitalization in billions of CNY	1678.7	1182.3	1497.6	1271.8
Dividend yield in %	5.56	4.86	5.01	4.54

ICBC has the highest market capitalization among the peer banks. ICBC has the highest dividend yield among the peer banks.

Table 15.24 Comparison of profitability measures in year 2014

Profitability measures	ICBC	ABC	CCB	BC
Net income in millions of CNY	275,811	179,461	228,473	169,595
Net margin in %	41.86	34.45	40.78	37.16
ROA in %	1.4	1.18	1.44	1.16
ROE in %	19.67	19.15	20.41	16.43

ICBC had the highest net income in comparison to the peer banks in the year 2014. ICBC had the highest net margin among all the peer banks.

Table 15.25 **Per share ratios**

Per share ratio	ICBC	ABC	CCB	BC
EPS	0.74	0.51	0.86	0.56
Net assets per share	3.63	2.6	4.3	3.31

The per share ratios discussed are for the year 2013. ICBC had an EPS of 0.74 and net assets per share of 3.63. China Construction Bank had the maximum EPS and net assets per share during the period.

Table 15.26 **Efficiency, regulatory, and risk indicators**

Banks	ICBC	ABC	CCB	BC
Cost to income %	28.08	36.3	29.65	30.61
Nonperforming loans to total loans ratio	0.94	1.22	0.99	0.96
Loan to deposit %	66.6	61.17	70.28	72.52
Tier 1 capital adequacy ratio %	11.79	9.25	10.75	9.7
Capital adequacy ratio %	14.2	11.86	13.34	12.46

The values given in the table 15.26 are for the year 2013. ICBC is the most capitalized bank in terms of regulatory requirements. ICBC has the highest Tier 1 capital adequacy ratio and capital adequacy ratio. ICBC has capital adequacy ratio of 14.2. The cost to income ratio is the most commonly used efficiency measure in the financial sector. It helps in measuring how costs are changing compared to income. Lower the ratio better the efficiency position. It can be observed that ICBC has the least cost to income ratio in comparison to different peer banks. The nonperforming loan to total loan ratio is the least for ICBC compared to other peer banks. The loan to deposit ratio of 66.6% for ICBC is less than the regulatory stipulated requirement of 75%.

References

Annual Reports of China Construction Bank. Agricultural Bank of China, Bank of China. Annual Reports of ICBC.
www.icbc.com.cn.

Valuation of Gazprom

16

Gazprom is a Russian-based global vertical integrated energy company with major businesses in geological exploration, production, transportation, storage, processing, and sales of gas. Gazprom Gas Concern was reorganized into a Russian joint stock company in the year 1993.

Gazprom has the world's largest natural gas reserves. Gazprom accounts for 18% of the global natural gas reserves and 72% of the Russian gas reserves. The company owns the world's largest gas transmission network with a total length of over 168 thousand kilometers. Gazprom sells more than half of overall produced gas to Russia and exports gas to more than 30 countries (Gazprom website). Gazprom is the only producer and exporter of liquefied natural gas in Russia. Gazprom is one of the five largest oil producers of Russia. Gazprom is the largest owner of power-generating assets in Russia. In 2013, the group's gas reserves were estimated at 35.7 trillion cubic meters while oil and condensate reserves were estimated at 3.2 billion tons. In 2013, the group produced 487.4 billion cubic meters of natural and associated gas, 14.7 million tons of condensate, and 33.8 million tons of oil. The Yamal Peninsula, Eastern Siberia, the Far East, and the Russian continental shelf are the strategic regions of gas production for Gazprom. The revenues of Gazprom are primarily derived from the sales of natural gas, crude oil, and other hydrocarbon products to Western and Central Europe, Russia, and other former Soviet Union countries. The principal businesses of Gazprom are production of gas, transportation and distribution of gas, gas storage, production, and sale of crude oil and gas condensate, refining, electric and heat generation, and sales. Gazprom is the largest gas exporter to the European market. The firm has more than 70% of the market share of the European gas market (Annual Reports of Gazprom).

Gazprom's Central Asian business strategy focuses on expanding the share of Russian gas in the traditional European market as well as diversifying Gazprom's export portfolio in different geographical areas. The natural gas from sources like Central Asia and Transcaucasia is critical for sharpening Gazprom's resource base to meet the demand in Russia, CIS, and Europe. The company also focuses on optimizing the gas flows through the Unified Gas Supply System. In collaboration with gas transmission firms and firms from Uzbekistan and Kazakhstan, Gazprom expanded the operations of the Central Asia Center Gas Transmission System. The firm focuses on new markets like LPG. In 2010, the LNG sales totaled 1.82 million tons. Gazprom has a rich resource base and branched gas transmission infrastructure. The distinct competitive advantage of

Valuation.
© 2016 Elsevier Inc. All rights reserved.

Gazprom is that it is an energy producer and supplier with a potent resource base and manifold gas transport infrastructure. On account of Russia's strategic geographical location, the firm has the potential to emerge as the energy bridge between the European and the Asian markets by supplying its own natural gas and providing gas transit services to other producers. Gazprom focuses on its reserve build-up strategy by accelerating exploration activities in Yamal, the continental shelf, Eastern Siberia, and the Far East. Gazprom's focus in gas processing and gas chemistry is to increase the recovery of valuable components from natural gas and associated petroleum gas. The focus of Gazprom in the domestic refining sector is aimed at maintaining compliance of products with technical regulations, raising of the processing efficiency to 90% as well as recovery of 77% of light petroleum products. Gazprom engages in establishing gas exchange trading in the domestic markets. Gazprom's export strategy is based on the long-term contract system under the take or pay principle with the contractual gas price pegged to the petroleum product price. In power industry, Gazprom focuses on achieving synergies by the combination of natural gas and electric power businesses. Gazprom invests heavily in the R&D sector. Gazprom initiated the Innovative Development Program in the year 2011 to develop new technologies, innovative products and services at oil and gas production, transmission and processing facilities as well as power plants. Gazprom pioneered the development of the Russian Arctic shelf by launching oil production at the Prirazlomnoye oil field in the year 2012. The oil business development strategy envisages the growth of crude oil production to 100 million tons of oil equivalent per annum by 2020. The Group's strategic focus in its Russian oil refining business is on programs to upgrade its refining capacities and increase their operational efficiency. Capacity upgrades are expected to boost domestic oil refining to 40 million tons per annum by 2025, with a 95% processing depth, and a 77% yield for light products. The Group aims to increase its total sales of motor fuels in Russia and the FSU countries to 24.7 mm tons by 2025. To this end, the retail distribution network in Russia and the FSU countries is planned to be expanded to 1880 gasoline stations by 2025. The Group also plans to develop premium distribution channels: sales of jet fuel, lubricants, bitumen products, petrochemical products, and bunker fuel. The Group is the leader in the Russian electricity market.

In the recent 9-month period, the Russian rouble significantly depreciated against major currencies. Russian rouble significantly depreciated against the US dollar by approximately 20% and by 11% against the Euro. These depreciations had a positive effect on the firm's foreign sales but had a negative effect on the foreign currency denominated debt. The world market prices for crude oil declined significantly in late 2014. As a result the export revenues linked to oil product indices may decline for Gazprom in future (Tables 16.1–16.3).

Table 16.1 **Financial highlights in millions of Russian roubles (RR)**

Year	2008	2009	2010	2011	2012	2013
Net sales	3,285,486	2,991,001	3,597,054	4,637,090	4,766,495	5,249,965
Sales profit	1,260,306	856,912	1,113,822	1,656,843	1,350,677	1,587,209
Net profit	742,928	779,585	968,557	1,307,018	1,224,474	1,139,261
Net assets	4,913,099	5,649,321	6,536,361	7,570,220	8,479,945	9,634,354
Short-term borrowings	964,845	1,047,892	1,011,261	1,311,577	1,492,066	1,391,465
Long-term borrowings	1,290,624	1,671,315	1,688,371	1,904,343	1,984,825	2,410,417
Capital expenditures	801,331	810,870	1,110,834	1,628,109	1,545,162	1,475,169

Net sales rose from 328.54 billion roubles in the year 2008 to 524.99 billion roubles in year 2013. The net profit rose from 742.928 billion roubles in the year 2008 to 1139.261 billion roubles by year 2013. The capital expenditure rose from 801.331 billion roubles in the year 2008 to 1475.169 billion roubles by year 2013.
Source: Annual Reports.

Table 16.2 **Per share ratios in RR**

Year	2008	2009	2010	2011	2012	2013
Net assets per share (RR)	207.8	246.2	284.6	329.9	369.5	419.8
Earnings per share (RR)	31.49	33.18	42.2	56.95	53.35	49.64
Dividends per share (RR)	0.36	2.39	3.85	8.97	5.99	7.2

The net asset per share rose from 207.8 RR in the year 2008 to 419.8 RR in year 2013. The earnings per share rose from 31.49 RR to 49.64 RR in year 2013. The dividends per share rose from 0.36 RR in the year 2008 to 7.2 RR in year 2013.

Table 16.3 **Average market capitalization in billions of dollars**

Year	2005	2006	2007	2008	2009	2010	2011	2012	2013
Market capitalization	160.3	272	330.9	241.1	144.5	150.9	128	112	100.4

The market capitalization fell from 241.1 billion dollars in the year 2008 to 100.4 billion dollars in the year 2013. The market capitalization peaked in the year 2007.

16.1   Growth rate analysis (Table 16.4)

Table 16.4 **Growth rate in percent**

Year	2009	2010	2011	2012	2013
Net sales	−9.0	20.3	28.9	2.8	10.1
Operating profit	−32.0	30.0	48.8	−18.5	17.5
Net profit	4.9	24.2	34.9	−6.3	−7.0
Capital expenditure	1.2	37.0	46.6	−5.1	−4.5
EPS	5.4	27.2	35.0	−6.3	−7.0

The growth rate of net sales has been fluctuating over the period of analysis. All the financial variables registered maximum growth in the year 2011. The operating profit registered growth of 48.8% in the year 2011. The average growth rate of net sales, operating profit, and net profit during the 5-year period 2009–2013 were 10%, 5%, and 8.9% respectively. The average increase in capital expenditures during the 5-year period was 13%. The average growth rate of EPS during the 5-year period from 2009–2013 was 10%.

16.2   Ratio analysis (Tables 16.5–16.9)

Table 16.5 Liquidity ratios

Year	2007	2008	2009	2010	2011	2012	2013
Current liquidity ratio	2.8	2.72	2.59	2.6	2.53	1.7	1.99
Quick liquidity ratio	2.34	2.26	2.05	2.17	2.21	1.36	1.62

The liquidity ratios have been decreasing over the period of 7 years. In 2007 the current liquidity ratio was 2.8 and decreased to 1.99 in the year 2013. The quick liquidity ratio also decreased from 2.34 in year 2007 to 1.62 in year 2013.

Table 16.6 Profitability ratios

Year	2007	2008	2009	2010	2011	2012	2013
Return on equity in %	7.73	3.62	10.62	5.89	11.7	7.06	7.51
Return on assets in %	6.08	2.8	8.4	4.66	9.26	5.54	5.79

The profitability ratios have been fluctuating over the 7-year period of analysis. The ROE and ROA peaked in the year 2011.

Table 16.7 Leverage ratios

Year	2007	2008	2009	2010	2011	2012	2013
Debt to capital ratio in %	19.84	21.54	18.41	16.04	16.57	16.51	14.09
Debt equity ratio in %	22.89	20.48	19.28	16.29	15.99	14.25	16.41

The debt to capital ratio was highest in the year 2008 and decreased during the period 2010–2013. The debt equity ratio peaked in the year 2007.

Table 16.8 Efficiency or asset utilization ratios

Year	2005	2006	2007	2008	2009	2010	2011	2012	2013
Total assets turnover	0.30	0.37	0.37	0.41	0.31	0.34	0.37	0.37	0.36
Fixed assets turnover	0.38	0.47	0.46	0.51	0.39	0.43	0.47	0.47	0.46
Equity turnover	0.40	0.48	0.51	0.54	0.42	0.45	0.49	0.49	0.48
Average collection period	109.00	95.00	103.00	94.00	112.00	99.00	89.00	89.50	90.98

The average total assets turnover ratio during the period 2005–2013 was 0.35. The average fixed assets turnover ratio was 0.45 while the equity turnover ratio was 0.47 during the same period. The average collection period during the 9-year period was 98 days.

Table 16.9 Market indicator ratio

Year	2007	2008	2009	2010	2011	2012	2013
P/E	22.51	14.86	6.95	12.57	4.6	6.12	5.23

The P/E ratio was highest in the year 2007 and lowest in year 2011.

16.3   Stock wealth creation (Tables 16.10 and 16.11)

Table 16.10 **Stock return analysis**

Year	Average yearly returns in %
2010	4.97
2011	−9.2
2012	−21
2013	−0.6
2014	−3.03

The stock price return analysis was done on the basis of daily stock price listed in the Moscow Interbank Currency Exchange or MICEX. The average daily return for each year was estimated and then the yearly average was calculated. Gazprom had an average yearly return of 4.97% in the year 2010. The average yearly return was negative in other years. The 5-year total cumulative daily return was −20.62% during the period 2010−2014. At the same time the market index MICEX index outperformed Gazprom stock. The 5-year total cumulative return for MICEX index was 7.7%. The average yearly return of market index MICEX was 3.8%. The average daily return on market index MICEX was −0.03% in the year 2014. The Moscow Exchange Indices are capitalization weighted composite indices calculated based on prices of the 50 most liquid Russian stocks of the largest and dynamically developing Russian issuers with economic activities related to the main sectors of the Russian economy presented on the Exchange. The MICEX Index was launched on September 22, 1997. The index is calculated in real time and denominated in roubles.

Table 16.11 **Excess value in billions of dollars**

Year	2008	2009	2010	2011	2012	2013
Market value of equity	86	144.5	150.9	128	112	100.4
Book value of equity	212.4	170.7	266.7	299.0	335.7	337.3
Excess value	−126.4	−26.2	−115.8	−171.0	−223.7	−236.9

The excess value obtained as the difference between the market value of equity minus book value of equity. The book value was higher than the market value in all years of analysis.

16.4   Estimation of cost of capital

The beta is estimated by regressing the Gazprom daily stock returns on the daily returns of the market index MICEX during the period 2009−2014. The beta value is obtained as 1.08. The beta value estimated by regressing the 2-year (2013−2014) stock returns on market index returns was 1.19. The value for estimation purposes is taken as 1.08.

Cost of Equity = Risk free rate + beta (Return on market index − Risk free rate)

The return on market index is calculated by finding out the average yearly returns on the market index MICEX. The average return on the market index MICEX during the period 2009−2014 was 10.7%.

Rm = 10.7%

The risk free rate is estimated as the average yield on the 10-year government bond yield during the period 2012−2014.[1]

Risk free rate = 8.23%
The risk premium Rm − Rf = 10.7 − 8.23 = 2.47 per cent.

Risk premium can also be estimated in the following manner.

Risk Premium = Mature market risk premium + Country risk premium.

The mature market risk premium is assumed to be 5%. Currently Moodys and S&P's sovereign rating for Russia is Ba1 and BB + respectively.[2]

The default spread for these ratings are 2.48%. Hence the risk premium = 5 + 2.48 = 7.48%.
Assuming the risk premium of 2.47%, the cost of equity = 8.23 + 1.08 ∗ 2.47 = 10.90%
Assuming the risk premium of 7.48, the cost of equity = 8.23 + 1.08 ∗ 7.48 = 16.31%

For our estimation purposes we assume cost of equity as 16.31%.

16.4.1 Estimation of cost of debt

The yield on any long-term traded bond of Gazprom was not obtained. The cost of debt is obtained in the following manner.

Cost of debt = Riskless rate + Country default spread + Firm default spread based on synthetic ratings.

In 2013, Gazprom had an Interest Coverage Ratio (ICR) of 5.9% According to Capital IQ, a firm with ICR of 5.9% gets a rating of A + which has a default spread of 0.85%.

Riskless rate = 8.23%
Country default spread for Russia based on sovereign S&P rating of BB + = 2.48%
Firm default spread = 0.85%
Cost of debt = 8.23 + 2.48 + 0.85 = 11.56%
Tax rate in Russia = 20%[3]
After tax cost of debt = 11.56 ∗ (1 − 0.20) = 9.248%
After tax cost of debt = 9.25%

16.5 WACC estimation

The weight used for calculation of WACC is based on book value weights.

---

[1] http://www.investing.com/rates-bonds/russia-10-year-bond-yield-historical-data
[2] http://countryeconomy.com/ratings
[3] http://www.kpmg.com/global/en/services/tax/tax-tools-and-resources/pages/corporate-tax-rates-table.aspx

WACC = Weight of Equity * Cost of Equity + Weight of debt * after tax of cost of debt

Equity in 2013 = 11039185 million roubles

Debt in 2013 = 1811382 million roubles

Total Capital = 12850567 million roubles

Weight of Equity = 86%

Weight of debt = 14%

WACC = 0.86 * 16.31% + 0.14 * 9.25% = 15.32%

The weighted average cost of capital is calculated as 15.32%.

16.6   Valuation using discounted cash flow valuation

The models used for valuation are Dividend Discount Model and FCFE.

16.6.1   DDM

16.6.1.1   Estimation of growth rates

The growth rate for EPS is estimated using both the historical growth rate and fundamental estimation methods. The 8-year (2006–2013) average growth rate of EPS was 17% while the 5-year (2009–2013) average growth rate in EPS was 10.8%. The average dividend payout in both periods was 11%. Detailed calculation of growth rates given in the worksheet DDM of Gazprom.xlsx.

16.6.1.2   Estimation of growth rates from fundamentals (Table 16.12)

Growth rate = Retention Ratio * Return on Equity

The two stage DDM assumes a high growth period and stable growth period (Table 16.13).

EPS in year 2013 = RR 49.64

Length of high growth period = 10 years

Growth rate in high growth period = 8 per cent

Cost of equity = 16.31%.

Table 16.12 Estimation of growth rate from fundamentals

Year	2005	2006	2007	2008	2009	2010	2011	2012	2013
Retention ratio	0.92	0.88	0.84	0.99	0.93	0.91	0.84	0.89	0.85
ROE	0.12	0.12	0.08	0.04	0.11	0.06	0.12	0.07	0.08
Growth rate	0.11	0.11	0.07	0.04	0.10	0.05	0.10	0.06	0.06

The average growth rate in both the 9- and 5-year period was 8%.

Table 16.13 **Present value of dividends in high growth period**

Year	1	2	3	4	5	6	7	8	9	10
EPS	53.61	57.90	62.53	67.53	72.94	78.77	85.07	91.88	99.23	107.17
DPO	0.11	0.11	0.11	0.11	0.11	0.11	0.11	0.11	0.11	0.11
DPS	5.897	6.369	6.879	7.429	8.023	8.665	9.358	10.107	10.915	11.789
PV of stock	5.070	4.708	4.372	4.059	3.769	3.500	3.250	3.018	2.802	2.602
Sum										37.150

The present value of dividends in the high growth period is estimated as 37.15 Russian rouble (RR).

16.6.1.3 Stable period inputs

The growth rate in the stable period is assumed to be the average GDP growth rate of Russian economy. The average GDP growth rate of Russian economy for the past 4 years is assumed to be 3.375%.[4]

Year	Annual GDP growth rate in %
2010	4.5
2011	4.3
2012	3.4
2013	1.3
Average	3.375

The average ROE of the oil and gas refining sector is assumed as 18.4%.[5]

Growth rate in stable period = Retention Ratio * Average ROE of Industry sector
3.375 = Retention Ratio * 18.4
Retention Ratio = 18%
EPS at end of high growth period = 107.17 RR
EPS in stable period = 107.17 * (1 + growth rate) = 107.17 * 1.03375 = 110.79 RR
Reinvestment in stable period = 110.79 * 0.18 = 20.32 RR
DPS in stable period = 110.79 − 20.32 = 90.47 RR
Terminal Value of DPS = DPS in stable period/ (Cost of Equity − Growth Rate)
= 90.79/(0.1632 − 0.03375) = 698.85 RR
Present Value of the terminal value of DPS = 154.11 RR
Value of Gazprom stock = 37.15 + 154.11 = 191.26 RR

Gazprom was trading at RR 143.94 in Moscow Exchange on 4/4/2015.

16.7 FCFE valuation

Estimation of growth rate from historical data.

[4] http://data.worldbank.org/indicator/NY.GDP.MKTP.KD.ZG
[5] http://biz.yahoo.com/ic/122.html

The average growth rate in net sales revenues was 9.8% during the 5-year period from 2009−2013. The average growth rate in net profit was 8.9% during the 5-year period from 2009−2013. The 6-year (2008−2013) average net capex as percentage of sales was 17.96%. During the same period the average net capex as percentage of net income was 70.8% Data from (Table 16.14).

Estimation of Noncash working capital in millions of roubles
The average noncash working capital as percentage of sales during the period 2008−2013 was 28.3% (Table 16.15).

Non cash current assets = Current assets-cash and non-cash equivalents
Non-interest bearing current liabilities = Current liabilities-interest bearing current liabilities.
Non-cash working capital = Non cash current assets-Non-interest bearing current liabilities.

Table 16.14 Estimation of net capex values in millions of roubles

Year	2008	2009	2010	2011	2012	2013
Capex	801331	810870	1110834	1628109	1545162	1475169
Depreciation	340444	363988	439400	472715	585734	683185
Net capex	460887	446882	671434	1155394	959428	791984
Net capex as % sales	14.03	14.94	18.67	24.92	20.13	15.09
Net capex as % of net profit	62.04	57.32	69.32	88.40	78.35	69.52

Table 16.15 Estimation of noncash working capital in millions of roubles

Year	2008	2009	2010	2011	2012	2013
Current assets	1756951	1861870	2203596	2646938	2791016	3237134
Cash and cash equivalents	252820	231688	445323	517955	438746	699612
Noncash current assets	1504131	1630182	1758273	2128983	2352270	2537522
Current liabilities	843133	951331	1013838	1301980	1495248	1417303
Interest bearing current liabilities	373451	336986	190005	366037	325447	330479
Noninterest current liabilities	469682	614345	823833	935943	1169801	1086824
Noncash working capital	1034449	1015837	934440	1193040	1182469	1450698
Change in noncash working capital		−18612	−81397	258600	−10571	268229
Noncash working capital as % of sales	31.5	34.0	26.0	25.7	24.8	27.6

Table 16.16 **Reinvestment rate calculation**

Year	2009	2010	2011	2012	2013
Net capex	446882	671434	1155394	959428	791984
Change in noncash working capital	−18612	−81397	258600	−10571	268229
Net debt issued	223261	−2230	47598	5174	302522
Reinvestment	205009	592267	1366396	943683	757691
Net income	779585	968557	1307018	1224474	1139261
Reinvestment rate in percent	26.3	61.1	104.5	77.1	66.5

Table 16.17 **Estimation of growth rate from fundamentals**

Year	2009	2010	2011	2012	2013
Reinvestment rate	0.549	0.609	1.082	0.775	0.931
ROE	0.1062	0.0589	0.1167	0.0706	0.0751
Growth rate	0.06	0.04	0.13	0.05	0.07

The average growth rate of net income based on 5 years of historical data (2009−2013) was from 8.9%. The average growth rate of net income based on fundamentals was 7%. We take the average of these two values to get the growth rate for estimation. Hence for estimation purposes the growth rate is assumed to be 7.95%.

16.7.1 Estimation of historical reinvestment rate

The average historical reinvestment rate during the 5-year period from 2009−2013 was 67.1% (Table 16.16).

Reinvestment in millions of roubles = Net Capex + Change in non-cash working capital-Net Debt Issued.
Reinvestment Rate = Reinvestment /Net Income

16.7.2 Estimation of growth rate from fundamentals

The average growth rate for the 5-year period from 2009−2013 was 7% (Table 16.17).

Growth Rate = Reinvestment Rate ∗ Return on Equity

16.7.3 Estimation of FCFE (Table 16.18)

FCFE = Net Income-Net Capex-Change in non-cash working capital + Net debt Issued
Net debt issued = New debt issued−debt repaid

Table 16.18 Estimation of FCFE in millions of RR

Year	2009	2010	2011	2012	2013
Net income	779585	968557	1307018	1224474	1139261
Net capex	446882	671434	1155394	959428	791984
Change in noncash working capital	−18612	−81397	258600	−10571	268229
Net debt issued	223261	−2230	47598	5174	302522
FCFE in millions of Russian rouble (RR)	574576	376290	−59378	280791	381570

FCFE is estimated as 574.576 billion RR in the year 2009. In 2013, the FCFE was 381.57 billion RR.

16.7.4   FCFE two stage model

16.7.4.1   High growth period inputs

High growth period = 10 years
Growth rate in high growth period = 7.95 per cent
Net Income in year 2013 = RR 1139261 million
Reinvestment Rate = 67 %
Cost of equity = 16.31%
Net income in first year of high growth period = Net Income in 2013 ∗ (1 + growth rate) = 1139261 ∗ 1.0795 = RR 1229832 million.

Table 16.9 gives the present value calculations of FCFE in the high growth phase.

16.7.4.2   Stable period inputs

Growth rate = Average GDP growth rate of Russian Economy

The average ROE of the oil and gas refining sector is assumed as 18.4%.[6]

Growth rate in stable period = Retention Ratio ∗ Average ROE of Industry sector
3.375 = Retention Ratio ∗ 18.4
Retention Ratio = 18%
Net Income at the end of high growth period = RR 2448216 Million
Net Income at the beginning of the stable period = 2448216 ∗ 1.03375 = 2530843.088 million
Reinvestment = 2530843.088 ∗ 0.18 = 455551.76
FCFE in stable period = Net Income −Reinvestment = 2075291.33
Terminal Value = FCFE in stable period /(Cost of Equity − Growth rate)
   = 2075291.33/(0.1631 − 0.03375) = 16043999.48 million RR
Present Value of terminal value = 3541131.722 million.
Value of Operating asset = PV of FCFE in high growth phase + PV of FCFE in stable phase
   = 3541131.722 + 2552049 = 6093181

[6] http://biz.yahoo.com/ic/122.html

Table 16.19 PV of FCFE in high growth period (millions of RR)

Year	1	2	3	4	5	6	7	8	9	10
Net income	1229832	1327604	1433148	1547084	1670077	1802848	1946174	2100895	2267916	2448216
Reinvestment	823988	889495	960209	1036546	1118952	1207908	1303937	1407600	1519504	1640305
FCFE	405845	438109	472939	510538	551125	594940	642238	693295	748412	807911
PV OF FCFE	348934	323853	300576	278971	258920	240309	223037	207006	192127	178317
SUM										2552049

The PV of FCFE in high growth phase is calculated as RR 2552.049 billion.

Value of Gazprom = Value of operating assets + Value of cash and cash equivalents in current year 2013 + Value of minority interests
= 6093181 + 699612 + 291268
= RR 7084061 million

The equity value of Gazprom is arrived at RR 7.08 trillion using two stage FCFE model.

16.7.4.3   One stage or stable state FCFE model

Net Income in 2013 = 1139261 million
Reinvestment = 1139261*0.18 = 205066.98
FCFE in stable stage = RR 934194.02 million
Value = FCFE $(1 + g)$/(Cost of Equity − Growth Rate) = 934194.02   (1.03375)/ (0.1631 − 0.03375) = RR 7465968.83 million

The equity value of Gazprom on the basis of stable state FCFE is calculated as RR 7.46 trillion.

The market capitalization of Gazprom in MCX was RR 3.41 trillion on 3/4/2015.

16.8   Relative valuation

The current price multiple values are given below (Tables 16.20−16.22).
(The data for relative valuation is obtained from morning star.com)

Table 16.20 Price multiples[a]

Ratio	Gazprom	Industry
P/E	3.95	10.26
P/S	0.62	0.56
P/B	0.34	0.71
P/CF	2.59	4.46
Dividend yield in %	5	3.66

[a]http://www.reuters.com/finance/stocks/financialHighlights?rpc=66&symbol=GAZP.MM

Table 16.21 Trend of price multiples

Year	2009	2010	2011	2012	2013
P/E	8.7	6.3	4.2	3.7	3.9
P/B	1.1	1.1	1.1	0.8	0.8
P/S	1.1	0.6	0.5	0.5	0.5
P/CF	7.5	3.7	3.7	2.8	2.5

The price to earning, price to book, price to sales, and price to cash flow multiples have been decreasing over the 5-year period.

Table 16.22 Comparison with peer companies

	Gazprom	Lukoy	Centrica PLC
P/E	3.95	6.6	
P/B	0.62	0.4	4.6
P/S	0.34	0.3	0.4
P/CF	2.59	2.4	10.6
Dividend yield in %	5	5.4	7.5

The above table provides the comparison of price multiples of Gazprom with the peer group. Data obtained from Morningstar.com.

The detailed calculations for all models of valuation is given in the resources file *Gazprom.xlsx.*

References

Annual Reports of Gazprom.
<Morningstar.com>.
Gazprom Website.

Valuation of Singapore airlines

17

Singapore Airlines founded in 1972 has evolved from a regional airline to one of the most famous travel brands around the world. Singapore Airlines' history can be traced back to May 1, 1947, when a Malayan Airways Limited (MAL) Airspeed Consul took off from Singapore Kallang Airport. The federation of Malaysia was established in the year 1963. The Airlines became known as Malaysian Airways Ltd. In 1966, the airlines was renamed as Malaysia Singapore Airlines (MSA). In 1968, the annual revenues of MSA reached S$100 million. In 1969, the Airline purchased five B737-100s. In 1972, MSA split to become two new entities—Singapore Airlines and Malaysian Airline System. Singapore Airlines expanded its fleets to include B747s, B727s, and DC10s. In 1989, Singapore Airlines became the first airline to operate a B747-400 on a commercial flight across the Pacific. Trade winds, a Singapore Airlines subsidiary, became Singapore's second airline in February 1989. It has since been renamed SilkAir and has an established network of more than 30 destinations in the region. Singapore Airlines has a network which spans over six continents. The Airlines was the first to offer free headsets, choice of meals, and free drinks in the Economy class starting in the 1970s.The Airline was the first to introduce satellite-based inflight telephones in the year 1991. In 1999, Singapore Airlines launched Kris Flyer, its first proprietary frequent flyer program, which allows First, Business, and Economy Class customers to earn mileage credits. In February 2004, Singapore Airlines inaugurated its first A340-500 by setting a record for the world's longest nonstop commercial flight from Singapore to Los Angeles.

The Singapore Airlines Group with its subsidiaries covers a range of airline-related services from cargo to engine overhaul. The main subsidiaries are SIA Cargo, SIA Engineering Company, SilkAir, and Trade winds Tours and Travel. The Company has organized into business units based on the nature of the services provided, and has four reportable operating segments. The airline operations segment provides passenger air transportation. The engineering services segment is in the business of providing airframe maintenance and overhaul services, line maintenance, technical ground handling services, and fleet management program. The cargo operations segment is involved in air cargo transportation and related activities and other services provided by the Group, such as training of pilots, air charters, and tour wholesaling.

Singapore Airlines maintains a modern fleet of 106 aircrafts. The average age of the fleet stands at 7 years. Singapore Airlines the flag carrier airlines of Singapore has strong presence in Southeast Asia, East Asia, South Asia, and Oceania. The subsidiaries of SIA are SilkAir, Singapore Airlines Cargo, Scoot, and Tiger Air. SilkAir manages regional flights to secondary cities with short haul aircraft. Singapore Airlines Cargo operates SIA's freighter fleet and manages the cargo hold capacity in SIA's passenger aircraft. Scoot and Tiger Air operate as low cost carriers. SIA is ranked among the top 15 carriers worldwide in terms of revenue passenger kilometers.

SIA focuses on service excellence, product leadership and network connectivity. In 2013, SIA introduced all new cabin products on new Boeing 777-300 fleets. SIA owns 40% of Tiger Airways. SIA follows the portfolio approach as its strategy for growth. SIA serves all the sectors of the market spectrum. The premium market is covered by Singapore Airlines and SilkAir whereas the low cost market is covered by Scoot and Tiger. SIA established a joint venture with Tata Sons of India. In this joint venture, 49% is owned by SIA and 51% owned by Tata Sons. Scoot has established a new base in Bangkok through a joint venture with local carrier Nok Air. Singapore has increased its equity holding in Virgin Australia to 19.9% with the purchase of 255.5 million shares for a total consideration of AUD 122.6 million.

The Singapore government investment and holding company Temasek Holdings is the major shareholder of SIA (Table 17.1). SIA is listed and traded in the Mainboard of Singapore Stock Exchange (Tables 17.2−7.7).

In 2014, SIA Group had a net profit of Singapore $359 million. This result was approximately 5% lower than the previous period due to exceptional items and losses from associated companies. The Group registered improvement in revenues on account of growth in passenger carriage. The higher nonfuel variable costs were partially mitigated by lower net fuel cost in the year 2014. The average jet fuel costs decreased 5.2% on a year-on-year basis. Hence the Group's operating profit rose 13.1% to $259 million in the year 2013/2014. In the year 2013, the parent airline company carried 18.6 million passengers which was an increase of 2.3% compared to the previous year. Passenger carriage in terms of revenue passenger kilometers rose 1.4% on account of 1.9% growth in capacity in available seat kilometers (Annual Reports of Singapore Airlines). The passenger load factor decreased by 0.4 percentage points to 78.9%. SIA Cargo's load factor of 62.5% was 0.9 percentage points lower, as a 5.1% reduction in freight carriage

Table 17.1 Major shareholdings

Name	Share in percent
Temasek Holdings (Pte) Ltd	56.26
DBS Nominees Pte Ltd	10.86
Citibank	8.43
HSBC	3.2
DBSN Service Pte Ltd	2.04

Table 17.2 Financial highlights 2009−2013

Profitability ratios in %	2009	2010	2011	2012	2013
ROE	1.6	7.9	2.5	2.9	2.7
ROA	1.2	4.9	1.7	2	1.9
ROS	2.2	7.9	2.7	2.9	2.8

Table 17.3 Per share data

Per share data	2009	2010	2011	2012	2013
EPS basic (cents)	18.2	91.4	28.3	32.2	30.6
EPS diluted (cents)	18	90.2	27.9	31.9	30.3
NAV ($)	11.3	11.89	10.96	11.14	11.26

Table 17.4 Dividend highlights

Year	2009	2010	2011	2012	2013
Gross dividends (cents per share)	12	140	20	23	46
Dividends cover (times)	1.5	0.7	1.4	1.4	0.7

The year 2010 dividend includes 25 cents per share special dividends. The year 2013 includes 80 cents per share special dividends.

Table 17.5 Market value ratios

Year	2009	2010	2011	2012	2013
P/E	83.52	14.97	38.06	33.76	34.22
P/B	1.35	1.15	0.98	0.98	0.93
P/Cash earnings	9.1	5.82	6.53	6.39	6.23

Cash earnings is defined as profit attributable to owners of the parent plus depreciation and amortization.
Source: Annual Reports.

Table 17.6 Operating characteristics

Year	2012	2013
Passengers carried (thousands)	18,210	18,628
Revenue passenger Km (million)	93,765.6	95,064.3
Available seat Km (million)	118,264.4	120,502.8
Passenger load factor (%)	79.3	78.9
Passenger yield (cents/pKm)	11.4	11.1
Passenger breakeven load factor (%)	80.7	82

Revenue passenger mile is used to measure the number of revenue passengers flown for each mile. Yield measures average earnings made by an airline by transporting revenue passengers or cargo per mile per kilometer flown. The passenger breakeven load factor is the load factor necessary for an airline to break even. It is a function of the percent of seats filled at a particular yield versus the airlines operating costs. Passenger load factor or load factor measures the capacity utilization of airline services. It is generally used to assess how efficiently the airline fills the seats and generates fare revenue. As per statistics of International Air Transport Association, the Worldwide load factor for the passenger airline industry during the year 2013 was 79.5%.

Table 17.7 SIA group financial highlights in millions of Singapore dollars

Year	2009	2010	2011	2012	2013
Total revenues	12,707.3	14,524.8	14,857.8	15,098.2	15,243.9
Operating profit	63.2	1271.3	285.9	229.2	259.3
Net profit	215.8	1092	335.9	378.9	359.5

(in load ton–kilometers) outpaced a 3.6% reduction in cargo capacity in terms of capacity ton kilometers.

SIA faces challenges due to economic uncertainty in different key markets. Air cargo industry faces challenges due to overcapacity. Yields would remain under pressure on account of promotional activities undertaken to support loads.

The total aircraft orders of SIA stood at 118 by March 2014. By March 2014, SIA's passenger aircraft fleet comprised of 103 aircrafts, with an average age of 6 years and 9 months. SIA Cargo's fleet consisted of nine Boeing 747-400 freighters with an average age of 12 years and 3 months. By 2014, Silk Air comprised of 16 Airbus A320S, 6 Airbus A319s, and 2 Boeing 737–800 NGs, with an average age of 5 years and 11 months. SIA was ranked 18th in *Fortune* magazine's annual list of the Top 50 most admired companies in the world.

The total staff strength of SIA group was 23,817 by March 2014. Of this 59.5% were employed by the parent airline. The SIA has 7733 cabin crew and 2156 pilots.

SIA Engineering Company (SIAEC) focuses on its line maintenance business. SIAEC was the first in the world to service the Airbus A380, which included the first A380 "C" check. SIAEC's line maintenance network covers 34 airports in seven countries and handles 650 flights daily round the clock for more than 80 airlines worldwide.

SIA cargo focuses on its strategy to pursue new and high growth business areas within the airfreight industry. The major thrust areas are carriage of niche and specialized types of cargo such as express traffic, time sensitive pharmaceuticals, jet engines, and charters. Charters focus on specialized needs such as the transportation of racing cars, horses, and equipment for the events management industries.

In 2013–2014, Scoot carried more than 2 million guests in its first full year of operations with an average load factor of about 80%.

Financial highlights of SIA during the past decade (Tables 17.8 and 17.9).

17.1 Growth rate analysis (Tables 17.10–17.12)

17.2 Ratio analysis (Tables 17.13–17.16)

17.3 Stock wealth creation

The weekly returns of SIA are estimated based on stock prices for the 5-year period 2010–2014. The data was collected from yahoo finance. The weekly returns of Singapore stock exchange index was also estimated for the same period. Excess returns were estimated as the difference between stock returns and index returns. The cumulative weekly return for SIA during the 5-year period 2010–2014 was −13.8%. At the same time the cumulative weekly return for the Singapore Stock Exchange index during the 5-year period 2010–2014 was 18.15%. The stock index outperformed the SIA returns during all the years of analysis except in 2014.

Table 17.8 Financial highlights in millions of Singapore dollars

Year	2004	2005	2006	2007	2008	2009	2010	2011	2012	2013
Revenues	9260.1	10,302.8	11,343.9	12,759.6	13,049.5	10,145	11,739.1	12,070.1	12,387	12,479.7
Operating profit	697.9	651	1027	1644	822.9	−38.6	851.3	180.6	187.2	255.6
PAT	1283.6	746	2213.2	758.8	1218.71	279.81	1011.2	390.2	−694.1	538.5

The revenues of SIA increased steadily till 2008, then fell in 2009, and again showed increasing trend from the year 2010 onwards. The revenues peaked in the year 2008. SIA had a net income of 1218.71 million dollars in the year 2008.

Table 17.9 **Operating characteristics**

Year	2004	2005	2006	2007	2008	2009	2010	2011	2012	2013
Passengers carried in, thousands	15,944	16,995	18,346	19,120	18,293	16,480	16,647	17,155	18,210	18,628
Revenue passenger km (million)	77,593.7	82,741.7	89,148.8	91,485.2	90,128.1	82,882.5	84,801.3	87,824	93,765.6	95,064.3
Passenger load factor %	74.1	75.6	79.2	80.3	76.5	78.4	78.5	77.4	79.3	78.9
Passenger yield (cents/pkm)	10.1	10.6	10.9	12.1	12.5	10.4	11.9	11.8	11.4	11.1
Passenger unit cost (cents/ask)	7	7.5	7.9	8.4	9.2	8.6	8.9	9.2	9.2	9.1
Passenger breakeven load factor (%)	69.3	70.8	72.5	69.4	73.6	82.7	74.8	78	80.7	82

The trend of passenger breakeven load factor has shown increasing trend over the 10-year period from 2004—2013. The passenger load factor has improved from 69.3% in the year 2004 to 82% in year 2013. The passengers carried by SIA had peaked in year 2007 when 19120 thousand passengers were carried by SIA. The revenue passenger km had been fluctuating over the period of analysis. The revenue passenger km was highest in the year 2013 with value of 95064.3 million.

Table 17.10 Growth rate analysis

Year	2006	2007	2008	2009	2010	2011	2012	2013	2014
Growth rate in revenues	0.11	0.09	0.10	0.00	−0.21	0.14	0.02	0.02	0.01
Growth rate in operating income	−0.11	0.08	0.62	−0.57	−0.93	19.17	−0.77	−0.20	0.13
Growth rate in net income	−0.06	0.68	−0.03	−0.46	−0.76	3.10	−0.65	0.11	−0.04

The average growth rate of revenues during the period 2006−2014 was 3%. The 5-year average growth rate (2010−2014) of revenues based on geometric mean was −1%. It can be observed that there have been huge fluctuations in operating income and net income during the 10-year period of analysis. The average growth rate of operating income was −17% during the period 2006−2014. The average growth rate of net income during the same period was 12%. These values were based on geometric means.

Table 17.11 EPS and operating margin

Year	2005	2006	2007	2008	2009	2010	2011	2012	2013	2014
EPS	1.14	1.02	1.71	1.66	0.89	0.18	0.9	0.28	0.32	0.3
Operating margin %	11.3	9.1	9.1	13.3	5.6	0.5	8.8	1.9	1.5	1.7

Both EPS and operating margin are showing a declining trend over the period 2005−2014. The EPS decreased from 1.14 Singapore dollar in 2005 to 0.3 Singapore dollar in the year 2014. The operating margin decreased from 11.3% in the year 2005 to 1.7% by year 2014. The average EPS during the 10-year period of analysis was $0.84. The average operating margin during the 10-year period is 6.28%.

Table 17.12 **Common size statement margin as percent of revenues**

Year	2010	2011	2012	2013	2014
Revenues	100	100	100	100	100
COGS	58.79	55.5	63.95	64.58	64.54
Gross margin	41.21	44.5	36.05	35.42	35.46
Operating margin	0.5	8.75	1.92	1.52	1.7
EBT margin	2.25	9.77	3.02	3.19	2.41

Margins as percent of revenues have been declining over the period 2010−2014. Cost of goods sold as percent of revenues is showing increasing trend. The gross margin, operating, and earning before tax margin have been fluctuating over the 5-year period from 2010−2014. The average cost of goods sold as percent of revenues during the period 2010−2014 was 61.47%. The average gross margin during the 5-year period was 38.5%. The average operating margin during the same period was 2.88%. The average earning before tax margin during the 5-year period was 4.13%.

The cumulative excess weekly return during the 5-year period of analysis was −32% approximately (Table 17.17).

17.4 Excess value added (Table 17.18)

17.5 Estimation of cost of capital

The cost of capital is estimated based on weighted average cost of capital. The cost of equity is estimated using the Capital Asset Pricing Model (CAPM).

The risk free rate is estimated as 2.33% based on the average 10-year Singapore government bond yield during the period May 2013−April 2015.[1] Risk premium is taken as the difference between the returns on the market index and the risk free rate. The return on the market index is estimated on the basis of the average weekly returns of Singapore stock exchange index during the 3-year period 2012−2014. The average yearly return on the market index is estimated as 7.5%.

Risk free rate = 2.33 %
Return on Market Index = 7.5 %
Cost of Equity = Risk free rate + beta * (Return on market index − Risk free rate)
= 2.33 + 0.70 (7.5 − 2.33) = 5.95%
The cost of equity is estimated as 5.95%.
Estimation of cost of debt
Cost of debt = Risk free rate + Country default spread + default spread for the firm based on synthetic ratings.

The latest sovereign rating given by S&P has been AAA. The default spread for 10-year AAA rating is 0.42%. Singapore Airlines had an Interest Coverage Ratio (ICR) of 12.29 in the year 2014. The synthetic rating can be arrived for Singapore

[1] http://www.investing.com/rates-bonds/singapore-10-year-bond-yield

Table 17.13 Profitability ratios

Year	2005	2006	2007	2008	2009	2010	2011	2012	2013	2014
Net margin %	11.57	9.3	14.69	12.83	6.64	1.7	7.52	2.26	2.51	2.36
Return on assets %	6.64	5.49	8.63	7.81	4.14	0.91	4.64	1.44	1.7	1.6
Return on equity %	11.63	9.58	14.9	13.56	7.17	1.53	7.73	2.43	2.85	2.66
ROCE %	11.56	9.38	14.62	12.21	6.93	1.79	7.47	2.7	2.91	2.65

The profitability position of SIA has deteriorated in the post-2010 period. The net margin has decreased from 11.57% in year the 2005 to 2.36% in the year 2014. The average net margin was 11% during the 2005−2009 period. The average net margin in the post-2009 5-year period was 3.3%. The average ROA during the 5-year period from 2005−2009 was 6.5% while the average ROA during the 5-year period from 2010−2014 was 2.1%. The return on equity also declined in the post-2009 period. The average ROE was 11.4% during the period from 2005−2009 while the average ROE during the period 2010−2014 was 3.4%. The average return on capital employed (ROCE) during the period 2005−2009 was 10.9%. In the period 2010−2014, the average ROCE declined to 3.5%.

Table 17.14 Liquidity ratios

Year	2005	2006	2007	2008	2009	2010	2011	2012	2013	2014
Current ratio	1.27	1.23	1.57	1.4	1.16	1.45	1.57	1.37	1.35	1.36
Quick ratio	1.08	0.99	1.34	1.28	1.01	1.33	1.48	1.28	1.27	1.29

The average current ratio during the first 5-year period of analysis was 1.33 which improved to 1.42 in the post-2009 period on the basis of average values. The average quick ratio during the period 2005−2009 was 1.14 while the average quick ratio value was 1.33 during the period 2010−2014.

Table 17.15 Leverage ratio

Year	2005	2006	2007	2008	2009	2010	2011	2012	2013	2014
Financial leverage	1.76	1.73	1.72	1.75	1.71	1.64	1.69	1.67	1.67	1.67

The financial leverage declined from 1.76 in the year 2005 to 1.67 in the year 2014. The average financial leverage during the 10-year period was 1.70.

Table 17.16 Efficiency ratio

Year	2010	2011	2012	2013	2014
Days inventory	22.79	18.54	13.36	10.88	9.61
Payables period	148.61	121.4	110.39	113.93	114.61
Inventory turnover	16.02	19.69	27.32	33.56	38
Fixed assets turnover	0.82	1	1.09	1.14	1.17

The 5-year average days' inventory and payable period were 15 and 121 days respectively. The inventory turnover ratio and fixed assets turnover have improved over the 5-year period.

Table 17.17 Yearly returns in percent

Year	SIA	Index returns
2010	9	10
2011	−39	−17
2012	7	18
2013	−3	1
2014	12	6

The above table analyzes the yearly returns for the stock of SIA and Singapore stock exchange index returns during the period 2010–2014. The average yearly return of the stock SIA was lower than the index returns in all years of analysis except in year 2014. The worst performance for SIA was in year 2011 when SIA registered a negative yearly returns of 39%. The average yearly index return was −17% during the same year. SIA stock returns were double that of index returns in the year 2014. The average yearly returns were negative during 2011 and 2013. SIA stock returns were highest during the year 2014. The calculation of estimation of returns is given in the work sheet stock return analysis of Singapore Airlines.xlsx.

Table 17.18 Excess value creation in millions of Singapore dollars

Year	2010	2011	2012	2013	2014
Market value of equity	18,577.44	12,261.2	12,927.6	12,294.21	13,607.02
Book value of equity	13,469	14,204	12,893	13,105	13,237
Excess value	5108.44	− 1942.8	34.6	− 810.79	370.02
BV as % of MV of equity	72.50	115.85	99.73	106.59	97.28

The market value of firm was in excess of book value of equity during the period 2010, 2012, and 2014 respectively. The excess value found as the difference between market value and book value of equity amounted to Singapore dollar 5108.44 million in the year 2010. In the same year book value of equity was 72.50% of the market value of equity. In the years 2011 and 2013, the market value of equity was lower than the book value of equity signifying lower wealth creation in the market. The market capitalization was calculated on the basis of the closing stock price on the last day of trading in the year.

Airlines on the basis of this ICR. An ICR of value more than 8.5 has a synthetic rating of AAA with default spread of 0.5%.

Pretax cost of debt = 2.33 + 0.42 + 0.5 = 3.25%.
The tax rate in Singapore is 17%.[2]

The cost of debt obtained as above is very low. Alternately the cost of debt can be based on the interest paid on the debt amount. SIL had paid interest of 43 million dollars in the year 2013. The amount of debt was 945 million dollars.

Hence the cost of debt = 43/945 = 4.5%
After tax cost of debt = 4.5 * (1 − 0.17) = 3.78%
Debt Value in year 2013 = 945 million
Market Value of equity in year 2013 = 13,607.02 million
Total Value = 945 + 13,607.02 = 14,552.02 million.
Market Value Weights
Weight of Equity = 0.94
Weight of Debt = 0.06
Cost of Equity = 5.95%
Cost of Debt = 3.78%
Weighted Average Cost of Capital (WACC) = 0.94 * 5.95 + 0.06 * 3.78 = 5.79%.

17.6   Valuation models

The valuation model used is Dividend Discount Model.

17.7   Stable stage dividend discount model

The growth rate of revenues was 3% during the 9-year period from 2006−2014. Hence it can be assumed that one stage or stable phase growth model can be assumed to value Singapore Airlines.

The average GDP growth rate of 3.06% is assumed as the growth rate of Singapore Airlines in the stable period.

Dividends in year 2014 = $0.41
Cost of Equity = 5.95%
Value of Stock = Current Dividend * (1 + growth rate)/(Cost of Equity − Growth Rate)
= 0.41 * (1.0306)/(0.0595 − 0.0306) = **$14.62**

Singapore Airlines was trading at $11.60 on Singapore Stock Exchange on 31/12/2014.

---

[2] http://www.kpmg.com/global/en/services/tax/tax-tools-and-resources/pages/corporate-tax-rates-table.aspx

17.8   Stable stage FCFE and FCFF models

The average growth rate of revenues for Singapore Airlines during the 9-year period 2006–2014 was 3%. This is equal to the average annual growth rate of Singapore GDP during the past 3 years. Hence it is assumed that Singapore Airlines is in the stable growth stage. The models examined are the stable stage FCFE and stable stage FCFF models.

Inputs

Net Income in year 2014 = $ 424.4 million
Capex in year 2014 = 2574.6 million
Depreciation in 2014 = 1601.2 million
Net Capital expenditure = 2574.6 − 1601.2 = 973.4 million.

Estimation of change in noncash working capital in million dollars

	2013	2014
Total current assets	7499.5	7310.7
Cash and bank balance	5059.6	4883.9
Noncash current assets	2439.9	2426.8
Total current liabilities	5401.6	5391.4
Interest bearing liabilities	78.9	117.5
Noninterest bearing current liabilities	5322.7	5273.9
Noncash working capital	− 2882.8	− 2847.1

Change in noncash working capital = 35.7 million.

17.9   Estimation of FCFE in year 2014

Net Income in 2014 = 424.4 million
Net Capex = 973.4
Change in Non-Cash Working Capital = 35.7
FCFE in year 2014 = Net Income in 2014 − Net Capex − Change in non-cash working capital
    = 424.4 − 973.4 − 35.7 = −584.7 million

17.10   Estimation of FCFF

EBIT $(1 − T)$ = 215.22 million
Net Capital expenditure = 973.4
Change in Non-Cash Working Capital = 35.7
FCFF = 215.22 − 973.4 − 35.7 = −793.88 million

Since both FCFE and FCFF are both negative, the models cannot be applied.

17.11   Relative valuation (Tables 17.19 and 17.20)

Table 17.19 Price multiples

Year	2010	2011	2012	2013	2014
P/E	15.4	22.4	46.5	30.8	38.3
P/B	1.3	0.9	1	0.9	1.1
P/S	1.4	1.2	1	0.9	1
P/CF	5.4	10.9	7.5	6.8	9.4

The price to earnings multiple has improved over the 5-year period. It increased from 15.4 in year 2010 to 38.3 by 2014. Other price multiple ratios were fluctuating over the period of time. The price to cash flow was 5.4 in the year 2010. By 2014, the price to cash flow ratio rose to 9.4.

Table 17.20 Comparison with peer group

Relative valuation ratios	Singapore Airlines	Japan Airlines	Cathay Pacific Airways
Dividend yield in percent	1.3	2.4	1.8
P/E	39.7	8.7	25.7
P/B	1.1	2	1.6
P/S	0.9	1.1	0.8
P/Cash flow	8.5	5.8	7.9

On the basis of current valuation, the price to earnings ratio was highest for Singapore Airlines. The price to cash flow ratio was highest for Singapore Airlines. Singapore Airlines had the lowest price to book ratio among all the competitor airlines.
Source: morningstar.com.

17.12   Enterprise value multiples

Enterprise Value = Market Value of Equity + Book Value of debt-Cash and Cash Equivalents

The enterprise value multiples of Singapore Airlines are compared with other peer airlines like Japan Airlines and Cathay Pacific Airways. The enterprise value multiples are based on the year 2014. The enterprise value multiples considered are EV/Sales, EV/EBITDA, and EV/EBIT (Tables 17.21 and 17.22).

Table 17.21 **Enterprise value and income items**

Values	Singapore Airlines	Japan Airlines	Cathay Pacific Airways
Market value of equity	13,607.02	2,610,000	66,405.92
Book value of equity	945	53,433	33,697
Cash and bank balance	5321	368,832	21,989
Enterprise value	9231.02	2,294,601	78,113.92
SALES	15,244	1,309,343	105,991
EBITDA	1861	244,843	17,732
EBIT	259	166,793	4435

The values are for the period 2014. The values given are in millions of Singapore dollars, Japanese yen, and Hong Kong dollars.

Table 17.22 **Enterprise value multiples**

EV multiples	Singapore Airlines	Japan Airlines	Cathay Pacific Airways
EV/Sales	0.61	1.75	0.74
EV/EBITDA	4.96	9.37	4.41
EV/EBIT	35.64	13.76	17.61

In terms of EV/Sales, Singapore Airlines is the most attractive among the three airlines. Singapore Airlines has the highest EV/EBIT among the three airlines.

The detailed calculations for all analysis are given in the resources file *Singapore Airlines.xlsx*.

Reference

Annual Reports of Singapore Airlines.

Wells Fargo

18

Wells Fargo & Company was established in 1852 and headquartered in San Francisco. This diversified, community-based financial services company provides banking, insurance, investments, mortgage, consumer and commercial finance through more than 8700 branches. The bank has offices in 36 countries and has more than 70 million customers. The bank possesses about 12,500 ATMS. Wells Fargo serves one in three households in the United States and was ranked Number 29 in *Fortune*'s 2014 rankings of America's largest corporations. Wells Fargo Bank is one of the "Big Four" Banks of the United States along with JPMorgan Chase, Bank of America and Citigroup. In March 2015, Wells Fargo became the world's biggest bank by market capitalization. The present-day Wells Fargo was formed as a result of a merger between San Francisco-based Wells Fargo & Company and Minneapolis-based Norwest Corporation. In the year 2008, Wells Fargo acquired Charlotte-based Wachovia for $14.8 billion in an all-stock transaction. Wells Fargo had record earnings for the sixth consecutive year in the year 2014. In 2014, Wells Fargo was the most profitable bank in the United States. Wells Fargo processes more than 20,000 customer transactions like account openings or online bill payments every minute. The cross sell strategy of the bank is to increase the number of products the customers use by offering them financial products which satisfy their needs.

Wholesale banking provides financial solutions to businesses throughout the world globally with annual sales generally in excess of $20 million. Products and business segments include Middle Market Commercial Banking, Government and Institutional Banking, Corporate Banking, Commercial Real Estate, Treasury Management, Wells Fargo Capital Finance, Insurance, Real Estate Capital Markets, Commercial Mortgage Servicing, Corporate Trust, Equipment Finance, Wells Fargo Securities, Principal Investments, Asset Backed Finance, and Asset Management (https://www.wellsfargo.com). Wealth, Brokerage, and Retirement division provides a full range of financial advisory services to clients. Wealth Management provides affluent and high net-worth clients with a complete range of wealth management solutions, including financial planning, private banking, credit, investment management, and fiduciary services.

18.1 Current financial highlights

In 2014, the net income was $23.1 billion which represented a 5% increase compared to the previous year 2013. The diluted EPS per share also rose by 5% to $4.10 in the year 2014. The revenues of the bank amounted to $84.3 billion in the year 2014. The deposits in the year 2014 amounted to $1.2 trillion which represented 8% growth rate compared to the previous year 2013. The total loans increased by 5% to $862.6 billion in the year 2014. The growth rate in loans was attributed to the growth in multiple portfolios like commercial loans, residential mortgages, credit cards, and automobile lending. The net interest income growth rate of 2% in the year 2014 was accounted by the growth in trust and investment fees, card fees, and mortgage servicing.

The capital position of the bank remained well above the minimum regulatory levels. The common equity tier 1 capital amounted to $137.1 billion with a common equity tier 1 capital ratio of 11.04% according to Basel III General Approach. Under the Basel III Advanced Approach, the common equity tier 1 capital ratio was 10.43% in the year 2014. The credit performance of the bank improved with the total net charge off ratio decreasing to 35 basis points of average loans and the total net charge offs down by $1.6 billion. In 2014, the stock price increased by approximately 21% (Annual Reports of Wells Fargo). The company paid $12.5 billion in capital to shareholders through common stock dividend and additional net share repurchases.

The nonstrategic or liquidating loan portfolio is presently 8% of the total loans. The core loan portfolios increased by $60.3 billion in the year 2014 compared to the previous year. In 2014, the federal funds sold and other short-term investments increased by $44.6 billion and the investment securities portfolio increased by $48.6 billion. In 2014, the primary consumer checking customers increased by 5.2% and the primary small business and business banking checking customers increased by 5.4% compared to the previous year. In 2014, the net charge off was of $2.9 billion which was 0.35% of average loans. The net losses in the commercial portfolio were only $44 million or one basis point of average loans. Net consumer losses declined to 65 basis points in 2014 from 98 basis points in 2013. Losses on the consumer real estate portfolios declined by $1.4 billion in the year 2014. The Community banking reported net income of $14.2 billion in 2014, up $1.4 billion, or 11%, from $12.7 billion in 2013. Wealth, Brokerage, and Retirement reported net income of $2.1 billion in 2014, up $371 million, or 22%, from 2013, which was up 29% from $1.3 billion in 2012.

In the year 2014, the return on equity was 13.41% and return on assets was 1.45%. In 2014, Wells Fargo had notable accomplishments. The bank was awarded "Most Respected Bank" by *Barron's* magazine, "Most Admired" among the world's largest banks by *Fortune* magazine, Best US Bank by *The Banker* magazine, and "Most Valuable Bank Brand" by Brand Finance.

In the year 2014, Wells Fargo made $18 billion in new loan commitments to small businesses. Wells Fargo continues to be the largest small business lender in dollars for the 12th consecutive year in the United States. Since 2012, Wells Fargo has deployed more than $37 billion to support environmental opportunities, such as clean technology, renewable energy, "greener" buildings.

In 2014, Wells Fargo introduced two credit cards Propel 365 and Propel World on American Express network. In 2014, Wells Fargo introduced innovative features on mobile services for customers which enabled the commercial card customers to easily photograph their receipts and upload them for out-of-pocket expense reimbursement. Wells Fargo was one of the first banks to offer Apple Pay™ as a convenient mobile-payment option. Wells Fargo has more than 14 million active mobile users in the digital market segment. Approximately more than 4500 bank locations of Well Fargo have fully digitized processing of deposits, withdrawals, payments, and other teller transactions.

18.2 Financial highlights

The following section discusses the financial highlights of Wells Fargo during the 6-year period from 2009 to 2014 (Tables 18.1–18.3).

Table 18.1 **Income highlights**

Year	2009	2010	2011	2012	2013	2014
Net interest income	46,324	44,757	42,763	43,230	42,800	43,527
Noninterest income	42,362	40,453	38,185	42,856	40,980	40,820
Revenues	88,686	85,210	80,948	86,086	83,780	84,347
Provision for credit losses	21,668	15,753	7899	7217	2309	1395
Noninterest expense	49,020	50,456	49,393	50,398	48,842	49,037
Net income	12,275	12,362	15,869	18,897	21,878	23,057

The values given are in millions of dollars. The net interest income rose from $46,324 million dollars in the year 2009 to $43,527 million in the year 2014. The noninterest income rose from $42,362 in the year 2009 to $40,820 in year 2014. The net income rose from $12,275 in year 2009 to $23,057 in year 2014.
Source: Annual Reports of Wells Fargo.

Table 18.2 **Per share data**

Year	2009	2010	2011	2012	2013	2014
Earnings per share	1.76	2.23	2.85	3.4	3.95	4.17
Diluted earnings per share	1.75	2.21	2.82	3.36	3.89	4.1
Dividends per share	0.49	0.2	0.48	0.88	1.15	1.35

The EPS rose from $1.76 in year 2009 to $4.17 in year 2014. The DPS rose from $0.49 in year 2009 to $1.35 in year 2014. The diluted EPS improved from $1.75 in year 2009 to $4.1 in year 2014.

Table 18.3 **Balance sheet highlights in millions of dollars**

Year	2009	2010	2011	2012	2013	2014
Investment securities	172,710	172,654	222,613	235,199	264,353	312,925
Loans	782,770	757,267	769,631	798,351	822,286	862,551
Allowance for loan losses	24,516	23,022	19,372	17,060	14,502	12,319
Assets	1,243,646	1,258,128	1,313,867	1,421,746	1,523,502	1,687,155
Core deposits	780,737	798,192	872,629	945,749	980,063	1,054,348
Long-term debt	203,861	156,983	125,354	127,379	152,998	183,943
Total equity	114,359	127,889	141,687	158,911	171,008	185,262

Core deposits are noninterest-bearing deposits, interest-bearing checking, savings certificates, certain market rate and other savings, and certain foreign deposits (Eurodollar sweep balances). The investment securities increased from $172.710 billion in year 2009 to $312.925 in year 2014. The loans increased from $782.770 billion in year 2009 to $862.551 billion in year 2014. The core deposits improved from $780.737 billion in year 2009 to $1054.348 billion in year 2014. The total equity improved from $114.359 billion in year 2009 to $185.262 billion in year 2014. The total assets improved from $1243.646 billion in year 2009 to $1687.155 billion in year 2014.
Source: Annual Reports of Wells Fargo.

18.3   Growth analysis (Tables 18.4 and 18.5)

Table 18.4 Year-on-year growth rate of income items in percent

Year	2010	2011	2012	2013	2014
Net interest income (%)	−3.4	−4.5	1.1	−1.0	1.7
Noninterest income (%)	−4.5	−5.6	12.2	−4.4	−0.4
Noninterest expense (%)	2.9	−2.1	2.0	−3.1	0.4
Revenues (%)	−3.9	−5.0	6.3	−2.7	0.7
Net income (%)	0.7	28.4	19.1	15.8	5.4

After registering negative growth in the years 2010 and 2011, the net interest income growth rate was 1.7% in the year 2014. The highest growth rate in noninterest income was in the year 2012 when the growth rate was 12.2%. The highest revenue growth rate of 6.3% was registered in year 2012. The highest net income growth rate of 28.4% was registered in year 2011. In year 2012, the net income growth rate was 19.1%. The 5-year average growth rate in net interest income was −1.2%. The average growth rate in net noninterest income during the 5-year period from 2010 to 2014 was −0.74%. The average increase in net interest expense was 0.01% during the period 2010−2014. The average growth rate in revenues and net income during the 5-year period from 2010 to 2014 was −1% and 13.4%. The average growth rate calculations were based on geometric mean values.

Table 18.5 Growth rate in per share values

Year	2010	2011	2012	2013	2014
EPS (%)	26.70	27.80	19.30	16.18	5.57
DPS (%)	−59.18	140.00	83.33	30.68	17.39

The highest growth rate in earnings per share was registered in the year 2011. In the same year, DPS increased by over 140%. The average growth rate in EPS during the period 2010−2014 was 19%. During the same period, the average growth rate in DPS was 22%. The average growth rate was based on geometric mean values.

Table 18.6 Growth rate in balance sheet items

Year	2010	2011	2012	2013	2014
Investment securities (%)	−0.03	28.94	5.65	12.40	18.37
Loans (%)	−3.26	1.63	3.73	3.00	4.90
Allowance for loan losses (%)	−6.09	−15.85	−11.93	−14.99	−15.05
Assets (%)	1.16	4.43	8.21	7.16	10.74
Core deposits (%)	2.24	9.33	8.38	3.63	7.58
Long-term debt (%)	−23.00	−20.15	1.62	20.11	20.23
Total equity (%)	11.83	10.79	12.16	7.61	8.34

The year-on-year growth rate analysis shows that the investment securities registered the highest growth rate of 28.94% in the year 2011. The allowance for loan losses has been declining over the 5-year period. The growth rate of total equity has been fluctuating over the 5-year period. The average growth rate based on geometric mean for investment securities was 13% during the period 2010−2014. The average growth rate of loans during the 5-year period was 2%. The average decrease in allowances for loans during the 5-year period was 13%. The average growth rate in assets and core assets during the 5-year period was 6%. The long-term debt declined by 2% on an average basis. On an average basis, the total equity increased by 10% during the 5-year period.

Table 18.7 Profitability, efficiency, and regulatory ratios in percent

Year	2012	2013	2014
ROA	1.41	1.51	1.45
ROE	12.95	13.87	13.41
Efficiency ratio	58.5	58.3	58.1
Tier 1 capital ratio	11.75	12.33	12.45
Total capital ratio	14.63	15.43	15.53
Tier 1 leverage	9.47	9.6	9.45
Common equity tier 1	10.12	10.82	11.04

The ROA, ROE, and Efficiency ratio were almost stable during the period 2012−2014. The tier 1 and total capital ratio has increased over a period of 3 years. The common equity tier 1 ratio has improved from 10.12% in 2012 to 11.04% in the year 2014. The efficiency ratio is noninterest expense divided by total revenue (net interest income and noninterest income).

18.4 Stock wealth creation

The stock wealth creation is examined for the 5-year period from 2010 to 2014. The return for Wells Fargo and NYSE Composite Index is examined for the period January 1, 2010 to December 31, 2014. The analysis is based on the weekly returns. The average weekly returns are then converted into yearly returns. Excess returns are obtained as the difference between the Wells Fargo weekly returns and the NYSE Composite index weekly returns. The average weekly returns are then converted into yearly returns (Tables 18.8 and 18.9).

18.4.1 Cost of equity estimation

The risk-free rate is estimated as 2.18%.[1] The risk-free rate is based on the average monthly yield on the 10-year US government bond. Beta is estimated by regressing

Table 18.8 Yearly returns and excess returns in percent

Year	Wells Fargo	NYSE composite index	Excess returns
2010	12.73	8.9	3.83
2011	−7.44	−3.66	−4.19
2012	25.38	11.45	10.003
2013	27.05	17.52	9.35
2014	19.91	5.78	14.13

Wells Fargo had the highest yearly returns of 27.05% in the year 2013. The bank registered yearly stock returns of 25.38% and 19.91% in the years 2012 and 2014, respectively. In terms of performance, Wells Fargo stock outperformed the NYSE Composite index in 4 out of 5 years of analysis. In the year 2011, the excess return was −4.19%. The highest excess return was registered in the year 2014 when Wells Fargo outperformed the market index by 14.13%. In the years 2012 and 2013, the excess returns generated amounted to 10% and 9.35% respectively. The total cumulative weekly returns for Wells Fargo during the period 2010−2014 amounted to 78%. During the same period the total cumulative weekly returns for NYSE Composite index was 44.2%. The total cumulative weekly excess return was 33.66% during the period 2010−2014.

---

[1] http://www.investing.com/rates-bonds/u.s.-10-year-bond-yield-historical-data

Table **18.9** **Excess value creation in millions of dollars**

Year	2009	2010	2011	2012	2013	2014
Total equity BV	114,359	127,889	141,687	158,911	171,008	185,262
Total equity MV	123,155.37	163,100.37	146,701.88	186,998.88	243,521.14	291,861.68
Excess value	8796.37	35,211.37	5014.88	28,087.88	72,513.14	106,599.68
BV as % of MV	92.86	78.41	96.58	84.98	70.22	63.48

Excess value is obtained as the difference between the market value of equity and book value of equity. The excess value created was highest in the year 2014 with value of 106.599 billion dollars. The book value as percentage of market value was approximately 63% in the year 2014. The excess value created was the lowest during the year 2011 when the value amounted to $5.014 billion dollars.

the weekly returns of the stock Wells Fargo on the weekly returns on the market index NYSE Composite index during the 3-year period from 2012 to 2014. The beta value estimated is 1.024.

The average yearly NYSE Composite index returns during the 2-year period from 2013 to 2014 is assumed as the returns on the market (Rm)

Returns on market index (Rm) during the period 2012−2014 = 11.74%
Risk premium = Rm − Rf = 11.74 − 2.18 = 9.56%
Cost of equity = Risk-free rate + Beta * Risk premium
= 2.18 + 1.024 * 9.56 = 11.97%.

The cost of equity is estimated as 11.97%.

18.5   Dividend discount model

The dividend discount model used is two-stage and one-stage model (Table 18.10).

Table **18.10** **EPS and DPS trends**

Year	2009	2010	2011	2012	2013	2014
Earnings per share	1.76	2.23	2.85	3.4	3.95	4.17
Dividends per share	0.49	0.2	0.48	0.88	1.15	1.35
DPO	0.28	0.09	0.17	0.26	0.29	0.32

The average dividend payout was 24% during the 6-year period from 2009 to 2014. The average growth rate in EPS during the 5-year period from 2010 to 2014 based on geometric mean was 19%. The average growth rate of DPS during the period 2010−2014 based on geometric mean was 22%.

18.6 Estimation of growth rate from fundamentals (Table 18.11)

Table 18.11 **Estimation of growth rate from fundamentals**

Year	2009	2010	2011	2012	2013	2014
DPO	0.28	0.09	0.17	0.26	0.29	0.32
Retention ratio	0.72	0.91	0.83	0.74	0.71	0.68
ROE	0.1073	0.0967	0.112	0.1295	0.1387	0.1341
Growth rate	0.077	0.088	0.093	0.096	0.098	0.091

The 6-year average growth rate is estimated as 9.1%.

18.6.1 High growth rate inputs (Table 18.12)

High growth period = 10 years

This growth rate is estimated as the average growth rate of EPS during the period 2010−2014. It is calculated as 19%.

Growth rate in high growth rate = 19%
EPS in the year 2014 = $4.17
Average DPO = 24%

18.6.2 Stable phase inputs

The average growth rate of the US economy during the past 4 years is assumed to be the growth rate of EPS during the stable growth period. The average growth rate is calculated as 2.15%. The average ROE of the banking sector is estimated as 9.65%.[2]

Growth rate = Retention ratio * Return on equity
Retention ratio = 2.15%/9.65% = 25.91%
The Dividend Payout (DPO) ratio in the stable phase = 1 − 0.2591 = 0.74
EPS at the end of high growth period = $23.75
EPS at the beginning of the stable period = 23.75 * 1.0215 = $24.26
DPO in the stable period = 0.74
DPS in the stable period = $17.95

The cost of equity in the stable period is recalculated under the assumption that beta falls to 1.

= 2.18 + 1 * 9.56 = 11.74%

The cost of equity is assumed to be 11.74% in the stable phase period.

Terminal value = DPS in stable phase/(Cost of equity − Growth rate)

[2] http://www.bankregdata.com/allIEmet.asp?met = ROE

Table 18.12 Present value of dividends in the high growth period

Year	1	2	3	4	5	6	7	8	9	10
EPS	4.96	5.91	7.03	8.36	9.95	11.84	14.09	16.77	19.96	23.75
DPO	0.24	0.24	0.24	0.24	0.24	0.24	0.24	0.24	0.24	0.24
DPS	1.191	1.417	1.687	2.007	2.388	2.842	3.382	4.025	4.789	5.699
PV	1.064	1.130	1.201	1.277	1.357	1.442	1.533	1.629	1.731	1.840
Sum										14.204

The present value of dividends in the high growth period is $14.20.

Terminal value = 17.95/(0.1174 − 0.025) = $187.17
Present value of the terminal price = $60.43
Value of stock of Wells Fargo = PV of dividends in high growth period + PV of dividends in the stable phase period = 14.20 + 60.43 = $74.63

Wells Fargo was trading at $54.35 in NYSE on April 22, 2015.

18.7 Relative valuation (Tables 18.13–18.15)

Table 18.13 Price multiples

Year	2010	2011	2012	2013	2014
P/E	14	9.8	10.2	11.7	13.4
P/B	1.4	1.1	1.2	1.6	1.7
P/Revenues	1.9	1.8	2.1	2.9	3.5
P/CF	8.7	10.7	3.1	4.2	16.5

Price/revenues have been consistently increasing over the 5-year period except in 2011.

Table 18.14 Comparison with peers

	WFC	JPM	BoA	Citi
P/E	13.3	12	23.31	21.11
P/B	1.7	1.1	0.7	0.8
P/S	3.4	2.5	2	2.1
P/CF	16.5	6.6	6.2	3.6
Div yield%	2.6	2.5	1	0.1

The competitor banks selected for the peer comparison are the three of the four big banks in the United States. Based on current calculation, Wells Fargo has the highest P/B, P/S, and P/CF ratio compared to the other peer banks. Wells Fargo had the highest dividend yield compared to the peer banks. The peer banks used for comparison are JP Morgan Chase, Bank of America, and Citigroup Data from Morningstar.

Table 18.15 Peer comparison current market capitalization in billions of dollars

Banks	WFC	JPM	BoA	Citi
Market cap	278.87	233.99	163.3	160.37

Wells Fargo had the highest market capitalization compared to the other peer banks.
Data obtained from google finance.

Details of calculation for all analysis are given in the resources file *Wells Fargo.xlsx*.

References

Annual Reports of Wells Fargo.
<https://www.wellsfargo.com/>.

Valuation of China life insurance 19

China Life Insurance Group and its subsidiaries is the largest commercial insurance group in Mainland China. It is one of the largest institutional investors in Chinese capital market with assets exceeding 1 trillion RMB yuan. The subsidiary companies are China Life Insurance Company Limited, China Life Asset Management Company Limited, China Life Property & Casualty Insurance Company Limited, China Life Pension Company Limited, China Life Insurance (Overseas) Company Limited, China Life Investment Holding Company Limited, and Insurance Professional College. Its business covers life insurance, property & casualty insurance, pension plans (corporate annuity), asset management, industrial investment, and overseas operations. Through capital operation, it has invested in several banks, security firms, and other nonfinancial institutions. China Life Group has been listed for nine consecutive years on the Fortune Global 500 list (China Life Insurance website).

China Life is the only life insurance company in China with shares listed on the Shanghai Stock Exchange, the Hong Kong Stock Exchange, and the New York Stock Exchange.

The company is the largest life insurance company in China. The company has an extensive services and distribution network in China in both urban and rural areas. The distribution network comprises exclusive agents, direct sales representatives, and other agencies. The products and services offered by China Life Insurance include individual life insurance, group life insurance, and accident and health insurance. China Life is a leading provider of individual and group life insurance, annuity products, and accident and health insurance in China. By 2014, the company had approximately 186 million long-term individual and group life insurance policies, annuity contracts, and long-term health insurance policies. The company also provided individual and group accident and short-term health insurance policies and services. In 2013, China Life has been ranked as one of the "World's 500 Most Influential Brands" published by World Brand Lab for seven consecutive years. The brand was also ranked as No. 5 on the "China's 500 Most Valuable Brands," with brand value estimated at RMB 155,876 million, ranking No. 1 among all seven insurance companies that made the list.

In 2013, the company had a total of 653,000 exclusive individual agents and 17,000 direct sales representatives in the group insurance channel. In 2013, the number of intermediary bancassurance outlets was 88,000 with a total of 54,000 sales representatives. As on December 31, 2014, the company had approximately 197 million long-term individual and group life insurance policies, annuity contracts, and long-term health insurance policies in force.

In a strategic perspective, the company is involved in diversified investment types and channels strengthening its investment capabilities and improving portfolio allocations. In the year 2013, the company implemented the "innovation driven development strategy" through the introduction of innovation product packages like Ruixin (2013), Insurance Package Plan, and Golden Account Annuity Insurance (Universal) Package Plan.

19.1 Financial highlights

The company's total revenue highlight was RMB 240,999 million which was a 2.6% decrease year on year in the first half of 2014. The net profit attributable to the company was RMB 18,407 million which was a 13.6% increase year on year. The company has a leading position in the life insurance market with market share of approximately 25.7%.

During the Reporting Period 2013, net profit attributable to equity holders of the company was RMB 24,765 million, an increase of 123.9% from 2012; and 1-year new business value was RMB 21,300 million, an increase of 2.2% from 2012. In 2013, the company's embedded value was RMB 342, 224 million, an increase of 1.4% from 2012 (Annual Reports of China Life Insurance).

In the year 2013, the number of in-force policies increased by 18.8% from the end of 2012.

The Persistency Rate for long-term individual policy is an important operating performance indicator for life insurance companies. It measures the ratio of in-force policies in a pool of policies after a certain period of time. It refers to the proportion of policies that are still effective during the designated month in the pool of policies whose issue date was 14 or 26 months ago. In 2013, the Policy Persistency Rate (14 months and 26 months) reached 89% and 88% respectively. Surrender Rate = Surrender payment/ (Liability of long-term insurance contracts at the beginning of the period + Premium of long-term insurance contracts). In the year 2013, the Surrender Rate was 3.86% which was a 1.14 percentage point increase from 2012. During the period 2013, the gross written premiums from the exclusive individual agent channel increased by 10% year on year (Tables 19.1–19.3).

Equity holders' equity refers to equity attributable to equity holders of the company.

Investment assets = Cash + Cash equivalents + Securities at fair value through profit or loss + Available for sale securities + Held to maturity securities Term deposits + Securities purchased under agreements to resell + Loans + Statutory deposits + Investment properties

Ratio of assets and liabilities = Total liabilities/Total assets

Gross investment yield = (Investment income + Net realized gains/(losses) and impairment on financial assets + Net fair value gains (losses) through profit or loss + Total income from investment properties − Business tax and extra charges for investment)/(Investment assets at the beginning of the period + Investment assets at the end of the period)/2).

Table 19.1 Financial highlights (RMB millions)

Year	2009	2010	2011	2012	2013	2014
Total revenues	339,290	385,838	370,899	371,485	417,883	440,776
Net premium earned	275,077	318,088	318,276	322,126	324,813	330,105
Benefits, claims, and expenses	298,249	346,601	352,599	363,554	391,557	404,275
Insurance benefits and claims	237,038	279,632	290,717	300,562	312,288	315,294
Net profit	32,881	33,626	18,331	11,061	24,765	32,211
Net cash flow from operating activities	149,700	178,600	133,953	132,182	68,292	78,247
Total assets	1,226,257	1,410,579	1,583,907	1,898,916	1,972,941	2,246,567
Investment assets	1,172,145	1,336,245	1,494,969	1,790,838	1,848,681	2,100,870
Total liabilities	1,013,481	1,200,104	1,390,519	1,675,815	1,750,356	1,959,236
Total equity holders equity	211,072	208,710	191,530	221,085	220,331	284,121

The total revenues increased from RMB 339.290 billion in the year 2009 to RMB 417.883 billion in the year 2013. The total revenues amounted to RMB 440.766 billion in the year 2014. The net premium earned increased from RMB 275.077 billion in year 2009 to 324.813 billion in year 2013. The benefits, claims, and expenses improved from RMB 298.249 billion in year 2009 to RMB 391.557 billion in year 2013. The benefits, claims, and expenses amounted to RMB 404.275 in year 2014. The total assets increased from RMB 1226.257 billion in year 2009 to RMB 1972.941 billion in year 2013. The average growth rate in total revenues during the period 2010−2014 was 5.4%. The net premium earned improved by 3.7% on an average basis during the same period. The average growth rate in benefits, claims, and expenses during this period was approximately 5.9%. The total assets and investment assets grew by 12.9% and 12.4% respectively on average terms during the period 2010−2014. The average growth rate of total equity during the same period was 6.1%.
Source: Annual Reports.

Table 19.2 Per share data in RMB

Year	2009	2010	2011	2012	2013	2014
Earnings per share	1.16	1.19	0.65	0.39	0.88	1.14
Equity holders equity per share	7.47	7.38	6.78	7.82	7.8	10.05
Net cash inflow from operating activities per share	5.3	6.32	4.74	4.68	2.42	2.77

The EPS has decreased from RMB 1.16 in the year 2009 to RMB 0.88 in the year 2013. The equity holders' equity per share has improved from RMB 7.47 in year 2009 to RMB 7.8 in year 2013. The equity holders' equity per share was RMB 10.05 in year 2014. The net cash inflow from operating activities per share was 2.77 in 2014.
Source: Annual Reports.

Table 19.3 Financial ratios

Year	2009	2010	2011	2012	2013	2014
Weighted average ROE %	17.13	16.02	9.16	5.38	11.22	12.83
Ratio of assets and liabilities %	82.65	85.08	87.79	88.25	88.72	87.21
Gross investment yield %	5.78	5.11	3.51	2.79	4.86	5.36

The weighted average ROE has been fluctuating over the 5-year period of analysis. The ROE had decreased from 17.13% in year 2009 to 11.22% in year 2013. In year 2014, the weighted average ROE improved to 12.83%. The ratio of assets and liabilities has improved over the 5-year period of analysis. The gross investment yield has been fluctuating over the period of analysis. The gross investment yield was 5.36% in year 2014.
Source: Annual Reports.

Table 19.4 Solvency ratio

Solvency ratio	2009	2010	2011	2012	2013	2014
Actual capital	147,119	123,769	113,685	176,024	168,501	236,151
Minimum capital	48,459	58,385	66,826	74,718	74,485	80,193
Solvency ratio (%)	303.59	211.99	170.12	235.58	226.22	294.48

The solvency ratio has decreased during the period 2009–2011. It had declined from 303.59% in year 2009 to 170.12% in year 2011. The solvency ratio improved to 235.58% in the year 2012.

In 2013, the solvency ratio decreased primarily due to the combined effect of the comprehensive income during the period 2013, dividend distribution in the previous year 2012, and business development of the company. The company's solvency ratio increased due to a significant increase in the comprehensive income during the reporting period 2014.

19.2 Solvency ratio

The solvency ratio of an insurance company is a measure of capital adequacy, which is calculated by dividing the actual capital of the company (which is its admissible liabilities determined in accordance with relevant rules) by the minimum capital it is required to meet (Table 19.4).

19.3 Gross written premium

The gross written premium can be categorized by business and channels. The different insurance businesses are individual life, group life, short term, and supplementary major medical insurance businesses.

Other channels mainly include supplementary major medical insurance business, telephone sales etc. The company's channel premium breakdown was presented based on the groups of sales personnel which include exclusive individual agent team, direct sales representatives, bank assurance sales team, and other distribution channels (Tables 19.5 and 19.6).

19.4 Analysis of cash flows

The principal cash inflows come from insurance premiums, deposits from investment contracts, proceeds from sales and maturity of financial assets, and investment income. The primary liquidity risks with respect to these cash flows are the risks of early withdrawals by contract holders and policy holders as well as the risks of default by debtors, interest rate changes and other market volatilities. The principal cash outflows primarily relate to the liabilities associated with various life insurance, annuity and accident and health insurance products, dividend and interest payment on the insurance policies and annuity contracts, operating expenses, income taxes and dividends.

Table 19.5 **Gross written premium by business—RMB in millions**

Year	2009	2010	2011	2012	2013	2014
Individual life insurance business	261,715	302,781	302,012	305,841	303,660	285,619
Group life insurance business	190	473	438	469	2060	33,192
Short-term insurance business	14,065	14,975	15,802	16,432	18,056	12,199
Supplementary major medical insurance business					2514	

Table 19.6 **Gross written premium by channels—RMB in millions**

Year	2011	2012	2013	2014
Exclusive individual agent channel	160,588	179,761	197,698	205,417
Group insurance channel	12,809	13,562	17,658	17,440
Bancassurance channel	144,363	128,863	107,658	99,825
Other channels	492	3276	556	8328

19.5 Estimation of embedded value

The embedded value of a life insurer is the sum of adjusted net worth and value in-force business which allows for the cost of capital to support a company's desired solvency margin.

Adjusted net worth is equal to the sum of the

- Net assets, defined as assets less PRC solvency policy reserves and other liabilities
- Net-of-tax adjustments for relevant differences between the market value and the book value of assets, together with relevant net-of-tax adjustments to certain liabilities.

The "value of in-force business" and the "value of half year's sales" are defined as the discounted value of the projected stream of future after-tax distributable profits for existing in-force business at the valuation date and for half year's sales in the 6 months immediately preceding the valuation date. Distributable profits arise after allowance for PRC solvency reserves and solvency margins at the required regulatory minimum level (Table 19.7).[1]

19.6 Stock return analysis

The stock return analysis is based on weekly returns during the period 2010−2014. The yearly returns were then estimated (Tables 19.8 and 19.9).

[1] Interim Report 2014, China Life Insurance.

Table 19.7 Embedded value in millions of RMB

SL	Year	2009	2010	2011	2012	2013	2014
1	Adjusted net worth	159,948	144,655	110,266	128,507	107,522	194,236
2	Value of in-force business	149,387	183,008	215,608	245,134	271,837	300,712
3	Cost of solvency margin	−24,106	−29,564	−33,020	−36,046	−37,135	−40,042
4	Value of in-force business after cost of solvency	125,282	153,444	182,588	209,088	234,702	260,670
5	Embedded value (1 + 4)	285,229	298,099	292,854	337,596	342,224	454,906

The embedded value has been consistently improving except in the year 2011. The embedded value improved from 342.22 billion RMB in the year 2009 to 454.91 billion RMB in the year 2014 registering a growth rate of approximately 33%. The second highest growth rate of 15% was registered in the year 2012 when the embedded value improved from 337.596 billion RMB to 342.22 billion in the year 2013. The embedded value decreased by 1.75% in year 2011 compared to the previous year 2010. The 5-year average growth rate of embedded value during the period 2010−2014 was 9.78%.

Table 19.8 Stock returns

Year	Average yearly returns (%)
2010	−30.17
2011	−15.98
2012	24.29
2013	−35.78
2014	95.74

The average yearly returns were negative during the years 2010, 2011, and 2013. The average yearly returns were approximately 24% in the year 2012. By the end of 2014, the stock price of China Life almost doubled compared to the start of the year. The average yearly returns were approximately 96% in the year 2014. The cumulative weekly returns during the 5-year period from 2010 to 2014 were approximately 40%.

Table 19.9 Excess value creation

Year	2010	2011	2012	2013	2014
Market value of equity	602,044.5	498,594.6	610,524	411,821.1	965,249.8
Book value of equity	208,710	191,530	221,085	220,331	284,121
Excess value	393,334.5	307,064.6	389,439	191,490.1	681,128.8
BV as % of MV	34.67	38.41	36.21	53.50	29.43

The excess value created as the difference between market value and book value of equity improved from RMB 393.33 billion to RMB 681.128 billion by the year 2014. The book value as a percent of market value which was 53.5% in the year 2013 declined to 29% by 2014 signifying increased excess value creation.

The detailed calculations are given in the worksheet stock return analysis of *China Life Insurance.xlsx*.

19.7 Estimation of cost of equity

The beta of China Life was estimated by regressing the weekly stock returns on weekly market index (SSE Composite index) returns during the 3-year period from 2012 to 2014. The beta value estimated was 0.72.

> The risk free rate = Average 10 year government bond yield during the period 2012−2015. The risk free rate = 3.8%.

The 3-year average returns on the market index (Rm) is estimated as 14.9%.

> Risk premium = Rm − Rf = 14.9 − 3.8 = 11.1%
> Cost of equity = Rf + Beta * (Rm − Rf) = 3.8 + 0.72*11.1 = 11.79%
> The cost of equity is estimated as 11.79%.

19.8 Discounted cash flow model

Dividend Discount Model (DDM) is employed to estimate the value of China Life Insurance (Table 19.10).

19.8.1 Estimation of growth rate from fundamentals

The growth rate of Chinese economy is assumed to be 7.7% based on the average growth rate for the past 2 years.[2]

Since the growth rate of the economy of China is comparable to the growth rate of earnings for China Life based on fundamental estimation, the stable stage Dividend Discount Model is used for estimation of value of China Life (Table 19.11).

Table 19.10 Dividend trends

Year	2009	2010	2011	2012	2013	2014
Earnings per share	1.16	1.19	0.65	0.39	0.88	1.14
Dividends per share	0.23	0.63	0.4	0.23	0.14	0.3
DPO	0.20	0.53	0.62	0.59	0.16	0.26

The average DPO during the 6-year period was 39%. The average growth rate in DPS during the 5-year period from 2010 to 2014 was 5.45%.

Table 19.11 Growth rate from fundamentals

Year	2009	2010	2011	2012	2013	2014
Retention ratio	0.80	0.47	0.38	0.41	0.84	0.74
ROE	16.79	16.02	9.16	5.36	11.22	11.59
Growth rate	13.46	7.54	3.52	2.20	9.44	8.54

The growth rate from fundamentals is estimated for the period 2009−2014.
Growth rate = Retention ratio*ROE.
The average growth rate during the period 2009−2014 is estimated as 7.45%.

[2] http://data.worldbank.org/indicator/NY.GDP.MKTP.KD.ZG.

19.8.2   Stable stage inputs

Growth rate in stable period = 7.5%
EPS in year 2014 = 1.14.

Average DPO during the past 6 years = 0.39. The firm's earnings growth rate is same as that of Chinese economy. We assume that the average dividend payout in the long run will be 39%.

EPS next year = 1.14*1.075 = 1.22
DPO = 0.39
DPS = 0.478
Cost of Equity = 11.79%
Value = 0.478*1.075/(0.1179 − 0.075) = 11.98
China Life was trading at 14.3 on January 6, 2014.

19.9   Relative valuation

The peer competitors for comparison are China Pacific Insurance Group, Ping An Insurance, and New China Life Insurance (Tables 19.12 and 19.13).

Table 19.12 Peer comparison

Companies	Market cap	Net profit margin (%)	ROE (%)	ROA (%)	EPS
China Life Insurance	1.01 trillion	8.09	12.77	1.41	1.14
China Pacific Insurance	311.29 billion	6.09	10.23	1.45	1.22
Ping An Insurance	787.68 billion	12.15	16.63	1.30	4.73
New China Life Insurance	188.78 billion	4.51	14.61	1.06	2.57

The peer comparison is based on the most recent data available. The market capitalization values of all insurance companies except New China Life Insurance are given in currency CNY. The market capitalization of New China Life Insurance is stated in Hong Kong dollars. China Life Insurance had the highest market capitalization among the peer competitors. Ping An Insurance had the highest net profit margin, Return on Equity, and EPS among the peer groups. China Life Insurance had the second highest return on assets after China Pacific Insurance.
Data Source: Google Finance.

Table 19.13 Price multiple comparison

Companies	P/E	P/S	P/B	Div yield in (%)
China Life Insurance	33.7	2.27	3.76	0.79
China Pacific Insurance	29.37	1.43	2.69	1.15
Ping An Insurance	18.26	1.79	2.61	0.82
New China Life Insurance	19.18	1.2	3.4	0.3

The price multiple comparison was based on the year 2014. China Life Insurance had the highest P/E, P/S, and P/B ratio among the peer competitors. China Pacific Insurance had the highest dividend yield of 1.15% among the peer competitors. China Pacific had the third highest market capitalization in the year 2014.

All detailed calculations and analysis given in the resource file *China Life Insurance.xlsx*.

References

Annual Reports of China Life Insurance.
China Life Insurance website.

Valuation of Franklin resources

20

Franklin Resources, Inc., known as Franklin Templeton Investments is a leading global investment management firm with offices in 35 countries and clients in more than 150 countries. The company was established in the year 1947 in New York. The company's first line of mutual funds, was a series of conservatively managed equity and bond funds. Franklin Templeton consists of independent multiclass investment management groups of Franklin, Templeton, and Mutual Series.

Franklin Templeton manages investments for individuals, institutions, pension plans, trusts, and partnerships. Franklin offers investment choices through Franklin Templeton, Mutual Series, Bissett, Fiduciary Trust, Darby and Balanced Equity Management brand names (Annual Reports of Franklin Resources).

Franklin Templeton provides services which consist of investment management, fund administration, sales, distribution, shareholder services, transfer agency, trustee, custodial and fiduciary services as well as private banking services. The investment solutions offered include mutual funds, retirement savings vehicles, and 529 college savings plans. The sponsored investment products (SIP) include a wide range of equity, hybrid, fixed income, cash management funds and accounts, alternative investment products, and multiasset allocation strategies. Most of the investment funds offered are open-end mutual funds. Franklin Templeton offers taxable and tax free fixed income funds, hybrid funds, and growth-oriented equity funds. The wide range of SIP consists of products under hybrid, fixed income, cash management funds, and accounts. The investment management fees represent a major part of the revenues. The sales and distribution fees consisting of sales charges and distribution of SIP also constitute a large source of revenue.

The common stock of Franklin Resources is listed on the New York stock exchange (NYSE) and is included in the Standard & Poor's 500 Index. The company's stock began trading on the NYSE in 1986 under the ticker symbol "BEN," Franklin acquired LF Rothschild Fund Management Company in the year 1988. The Assets under Management (AUM) for Franklin increased from just over US$2 billion in year 1982 to over $40 billion in the year 1989. In 1992 through the acquisition of Templeton Investments, Franklin was able to expand its global footprint throughout Europe and Asia. Through this strategic acquisition of Templeton, the company was able to access strong portfolio of international equity funds. In 1996, Franklin Templeton bought Heine Securities Corporation which was the investment adviser to Mutual Series Fund, Inc. Franklin Templeton acquired Bissett in year 2000, Fiduciary Trust in 2001, and Darby in the year 2003. Franklin Templeton is the largest cross-border fund manager. A cross-border fund is one that sources less than 80% of its assets from investors in any single country. Franklin Templeton has over 650 professionals. The firm had $898 billion in AUM in the year 2013 which represented an increase of 6% over the amount of $845 billion in the year 2013. Franklin Templeton's AUM witnessed a compound annual growth rate of approximately 10% in the past decade. The operating revenue improved from $8.0 billion in year 2013 to 8.5 billion in year 2014. In 2014, the firm's AUM comprised of 59% equity and hybrid assets, 40% fixed income, and 1% cash management. The firm witnessed net outflows of $4.6 billion in 2014 compared to positive net inflows of $24 billion in year 2013. The company partners with nearly 250,000 financial professionals worldwide. In 2014 the Class A shares of Franklin Income fund were awarded five stars overall by Morning star. The hybrid strategies resulted in new net flows of $10 billion in the year 2014.

Franklin's SIPs are offered globally to retail, institutional, high net worth, and separate account clients, which include individual investors, qualified groups, trustees, tax-deferred (such as IRAs in the United States and retirement saving plans, or RSPs, in Canada) or money purchase plans, employee benefit and profit-sharing plans, trust companies, bank trust departments, and institutional investors. The firm's SIPs include portfolios managed for some of the world's largest corporations, endowments, charitable foundations, and pension funds, as well as wealthy individuals and other institutions.

20.1   Types of SIPs

The major SIPS of Franklin Resources are US Funds, Cross-border funds, Local/regional funds and other managed accounts, alternative investment products, and trusts. The US funds consisting of open-ended, close-ended funds and insurance products trust amounted to $491.4 billion of AUM as of September 30, 2014. The five largest US funds namely Franklin Income Fund, TIT—Templeton Global Bond Fund, FMSF—Franklin Mutual Global Discovery Fund, Templeton Growth Fund, Inc., and FMSF—Franklin Mutual Shares Fund amounted to 25% of the total AUM. The cross-border funds consisting of investment funds principally domiciled in Luxembourg and registered for sale to non-US investors in 39 countries, accounted for $167.7 billion of AUM as of September 30, 2014. The three largest cross-border funds—Templeton Global Bond Fund, FTIF—Templeton Global Total Return Fund, FTIF—Templeton Asian Growth Fund represented 10% of total AUM. The local/regional funds accounted for $47.5 billion of AUM as of September 2014. The managed accounts, alternative investment products, and trusts accounted for $191.4 billion of AUM as of September 2014 (Table 20.1).

20.2   Types of investment management and related services

1. Investment Management Services
    The company offers investment management services for SIP, sub-advised products, and managed accounts. The services include fundamental investment research and

Table 20.1 Acquisitions by Franklin

Year	Acquirer	Target
1992	Franklin	Templeton, Galbraith, and Hansberger
1996	Franklin Templeton	Mutual Series Fund, Inc., of Heine Securities Corporation
2000	Franklin Templeton	Ssangyong Templeton Investment Trust Management
2000	Franklin Templeton Investments	Bissett
2001	Franklin Templeton	Fiduciary Trust Company International
2002	Franklin Templeton Asset Management (India) Pvt Ltd	Pioneer ITI AMC
2003	Franklin Templeton	Darby Overseas Investments
2006	Franklin Templeton	Bradesco Templeton Asset Management, Brazil
2011	Franklin Templeton	Rensburg Fund Management Limited
2011	Franklin Templeton	Balanced Equity Management Pty. Limited

Source: Collated from Annual Report 2012.

valuation analyses, company research and analyses of suppliers, customers, and competitors. Most of the investment management agreements between subsidiaries and US funds are renewed every year after an initial 2-year term. Through this agreement, funds pay a monthly fee in arrears based on the fund's average daily net assets. The master/feeder fund of funds structure allows an investment advisor to manage a single portfolio of securities at the master fund level and have multiple feeder funds which invest into the master fund. Individual and institutional shareholders invest in the feeder funds which offer a variety of service and distribution options. In separately managed accounts, investors and their financial advisors choose an investment manager who creates a personalized portfolio to meet the investment requirements. The accounts are generally funded with securities in cash. The minimum for accounts are generally $100,000 or $250,000 depending on equity or fixed income investments.

2. Sales and Distribution

Sales and distribution services also generate a significant portion of the revenues for Franklin. Fund shares are basically sold through a large network of independent intermediaries which includes broker dealers, financial advisers, and third parties. Franklin/Templeton Distributors, Inc., acts as the principal underwriter and distributor of shares of majority of the open-end US funds. Majority of the retail funds are distributed with multiclass share structure. Class A shares are sold without a front-end sales charge to shareholders. Class B shares have no front-end sales charges, but instead have a declining schedule of sales charges if the investor redeems within a certain number of years with respect to original purchase date. Open US funds no longer issue Class B Shares. Class C shares though do not have front-end sales charge, have a back-end sales charge for redemptions within 12 months from the date of purchase. In the United States, Franklin Templeton offers Advisor class shares and Z shares in the Mutual series funds. These shares are offered to qualified financial intermediaries, institutions, and high net-worth clients. Money market funds are offered to investors without a sales charge. According to the company annual report 2012, around 1500 local, regional, and national banks, securities firms, and financial adviser firms offered Franklin Templeton open-end US Funds for sale. The open-end US Funds have adopted distribution plans under Rule 12b-1 under which the fund bears certain expenses related to the distribution of their shares such as expenses for marketing, advertising, printing, and sales promotion.

3. Shareholder and Transfer Agency Services

Franklin Templeton receives shareholder servicing fees for providing transfer agency services like providing customer statements, transaction processing, customer service, and tax reporting. The subsidiary Franklin Templeton Investor Services serves as shareholder servicing and dividend paying agent for the open-end funds.

4. High Net-Worth Investment Management Services

Franklin Templeton provides investment management and related services to high net-worth individuals and families, foundations, and institutional clients through the Fiduciary Trust. Fiduciary Trust Services include wealth management and estate and tax planning. The trust provides an integrated package of services known as Family Resource Management.

5. Institutional Investment Management

Franklin Templeton provides institutional investment management services to institutional clients with focus on endowment funds, government and corporate pension plans. The subsidiary Franklin Templeton Institutional offers a wide range of US and international equity, fixed income and alternative strategies through investment vehicles like separate accounts, open-end, closed-end and unregistered funds. Franklin Templeton markets and distributes SIP through subsidiaries like Franklin Templeton Financial Services Corp and Templeton/Franklin Investment.

6. Trust and Custody Services

The subsidiaries of Franklin Templeton offer trust, custody, and related services which include administration, performance measurement, estate planning, tax planning, and private banking. The company also provides planned giving administration and related custody services for nonprofit organizations like pooled income funds, charitable remainder trusts, charitable lead trusts, and gift annuities.

7. Management of Alternate Investment Products

This function is performed by the subsidiary Darby by sponsoring and managing funds that invest in private equity and mezzanine finance transactions in emerging markets in Asia, Latin America, and Central/Eastern Europe. These investment funds are offered by Darby to institutional and high net-worth individual investors through private placement. Franklin Templeton Institutional manages funds with exposure to global real estate opportunities. Franklin Adviser the investment adviser manages investment partnership which invests in derivatives products in global equity, government bond, and currency markets.

8. Private Banking

Fiduciary Trust provides private banking services to high net-worth clients who maintain trust, custody, and managed accounts. In 2012, Fiduciary Trust had assets worth $901.6 million and deposits of $611 million which were secured by Federal Deposit Insurance Corporation (FDIC). The products offered include loans secured by marketable securities, deposits accounts, and other banking services. The deposits include demand and savings deposits.

20.3   Investment products

Equity Investment products focus on growth, value, or both. Income portfolios consist of taxable and tax exempt money market instruments, tax exempt municipal bonds, global fixed income securities, fixed income debt securities of US government, and mortgage institutions like Governmental National Mortgage Association, Federal National Mortgage Association, and Federal Home Loan Mortgage Corporation.

The five largest US funds were Franklin Income Fund, Templeton Global Bond Fund, Mutual Global Discovery Fund, Templeton Growth Fund, and Franklin Tax Free Income Fund. In 2012, these five funds accounted for 24% of the total AUM. The cross-border products comprising a wide array of investment funds which are registered for sale to non-US investors in 39 countries represented 11% of total AUM in 2012 with a value of $143.6 billion. The three largest cross-border funds are Templeton Global Bond Fund, Templeton Global Total Return Fund, and Templeton Asian Growth Fund.

The equity funds are categorized on the basis of their investments in Asia Pacific, Canada, Europe, the Middle East and Africa, the United States, Emerging Market, and Global International. The hybrid funds invest primarily in the equities and fixed income securities of companies located in the above regions. The fixed income funds invest in debt securities offered by companies and government entities in different regions. Cash management funds invest primarily in money market instruments and short-term securities.

The close-end funds offered by Franklin Funds are Franklin Templeton Limited Duration Income Trust, Franklin Universal Trust, Templeton Dragon Fund, Templeton Emerging Market Fund, Templeton Emerging Markets Income Fund, Templeton Global Income Fund, Templeton Russia, and East European Fund, Inc.

Franklin Short Duration US Government Fund is an exchange traded fund which offers investors access to return and income from allocations involving a wide variety of US government securities. This ETF is designed with the flexibility to rotate allocations among multiple investment products which include Treasuries, Mortgage Backed Securities, Agency Adjustable Rate Mortgages, and Inflation Protected Securities (TIPs) in various market cycles.

The company has 250,000 advisor relationships worldwide.

Table 20.2 gives the number of different types of Franklin Templeton funds. Tables 20.5—20.9 gives the statistical highlights of the Assets Under Management (AUM).

Table 20.2   Franklin Templeton funds

Type	Number of funds
Franklin funds	94
Templeton funds	19
Mutual series	8

Table 20.3 **Number of investment professionals**

Year	Investment professionals
2000	243
2005	444
2010	534
2013	608
2014	648

Table 20.4 **Specialized investment teams**

Franklin equity group	Templeton emerging markets
Franklin Local Asset Management	Templeton Global Equity Group
Franklin Mutual Series	Templeton Strategic Emerging Markets
Franklin Real Asset Advisors	Darby Private Equity
Franklin Templeton Fixed Income Group	K2 Advisors
Franklin Templeton Solutions	Pelagos Capital Management

Table 20.5 **Assets under management (AUM) in billions of US dollars**

Year	AUM
2010	645
2011	660
2012	750
2013	845
2014	898

The 4-year average growth rate of AUM was approximately 9%. In the year 2011, the AUM increased by 2.3%. The growth rate of AUM was 13.6%, 12.6%, and 6.2% in the years 2012, 2013, and 2014, respectively.

Table 20.6 **Asset mix of AUM in percent**

Year	Equity	Fixed income	Hybrid	Cash
2010	43	39	17	1
2011	39	45	15	1
2012	39	45	15	1
2013	40	43	16	1
2014	41	40	18	1

The proportion of fixed income component was more in the AUM than the equity component during the period 2011–2013. By 2014, the equity proportion was higher by 1% compared to the fixed income component.

Table 20.7 **AUM by region in 2014**

Region	Share (%)
USA	66
EMEA	17
Asia Pacific	10
Canada	4
Latin America	3

Table 20.8 **AUM by client type in 2014**

Type	Share (%)
Retail	74
Institutional	24
High net worth	2

Table 20.9 **AUM by investment objective**

Investment objective	Value in billion dollars
Equity	371
Hybrid	159
Fixed income	361
Cash management	7
Total	898

Hybrid funds consist of asset allocation, balanced, flexible, alternative, and income-mixed funds. The fixed income funds consist of both long-term and short-term funds. Cash management consists of short-term liquid assets.

Table 20.10 **Operations summary in millions of dollars**

Year	2010	2011	2012	2013	2014
Operating revenues	5853	7140	7101	7985	8491.4
Operating income	1958.7	2659.8	2515.2	2921.3	3221.2
Net income	1445.7	1923.6	1931.4	2150.2	2384.3

The operating revenues improved from $5853 million in the year 2010 to $8491.4 million in the year 2014. The net income increased from $1445.7 million in the year 2010 to $ 2384.3 million in the year 2014.

Table 20.11 gives the growth rate in revenues and incomes on a year-on-year basis. The average growth rate for the 4-year period 2011−2014 was based on geometric mean.

Table 20.12 provides the financial highlights of Franklin during the period 2010−2014.

Table 20.11 Growth rate in operations highlights

Year	2011	2012	2013	2014
Operating revenues	0.22	−0.01	0.12	0.06
Operating income	0.36	−0.05	0.16	0.10
Net income	0.33	0.00	0.11	0.11

The highest growth rate on a year-on-year basis for revenues, operating income, and net income was in the year 2011. The operating income grew by 22% in the year 2011 while the net income grew by 33% in the year 2011. The average growth rate of operating revenues during the 4-year period 2011−2014 was 9.75%. The average growth rate of operating income and net income during the 4-year period 2011−2014 was approximately 13%.

Table 20.12 Financial data in millions of dollars

Year	2010	2011	2012	2013	2014
Total assets	10,708.1	13,775.8	14,751.5	15,390.3	16,357.1
Debt	979.9	998.2	1566.1	1197.7	1198.2
Franklin equity	7727	8524.7	9201.3	10,073.1	11,584.1
Operating cash flow	1651	1621.8	1066.2	2035.7	2138

The total assets grew from $10,708.1 million in year 2010 to $16,357.1 million in year 2014. The equity holding value improved from $7727 million in year 2010 to $11,584.1 million in year 2014. The total assets grew by 29% in the year 2011 compared to the previous year 2010. The average increase in total assets was 11% during the 4-year period 2011−2014. The average increase in debt was 57% in the year 2012. The maximum growth rate of equity of 15% was in the year 2014. The average growth rate of equity during the 4-year period of analysis was 11%. On average basis, the operating cash flow increased by 7% during the time period 2011−2014.

Table 20.13 Per share value

Year	2010	2011	2012	2013	2014
EPS	2.12	2.89	2.99	3.37	3.79
DPS	0.29	0.33	0.36	0.39	0.48
Book value	11.5	13.05	14.45	15.97	18.6

The EPS improved from $2.12 in year 2010 to $3.79 in year 2014. The DPS had been increasing over the period of analysis. The book value per share has been consistently increasing over the period of time. The average increase in EPS during the 5-year period was 15%. The average growth rate in the book value per share had been 12.7%. EPS denotes Earning Per Share and DPS denote Dividend Per Share.

Table 20.14 Profitability ratios

Year	2010	2011	2012	2013	2014
Net margin in %	29.87	30.62	28.48	28.28	29.27
Return on equity %	18.83	23.67	21.79	22.31	21.89
Return on invested capital %	17.82	20.15	17.29	17.89	18.42

The 5-year average net margin was 29%. The average return on equity and return on invested capital during the period was 21.6% and 18%, respectively.

20.4   Stock wealth creation

The stock price of Franklin Resources was analyzed over the 5-year period 2010–2014. The weekly returns for the stock were calculated for the above period based on data from Yahoo finance. The weekly returns for the market index S&P 500 index were also estimated for the above period. The yearly returns are estimated based on the weekly returns. Excess return was estimated as the difference between the stock returns and market index returns. The total cumulative excess returns for both the stock and index were also estimated. The cumulative abnormal return was also estimated for the above period (Tables 20.15 and 20.16). The detailed calculation are given in the worksheet stock return analysis of *Franklin Resources.xlsx*.

Table 20.15 **Yearly returns in percent**

Year	Franklin	S&P	Excess
2010	6.89	11.06	−4.17
2011	−8.67	2.29	−10.97
2012	33.69	15.86	17.83
2013	−37.9	22.68	−60.59
2014	−0.77	12.36	−13.13

The market index S&P 500 outperformed the stock of Franklin in all years of analysis except in the year 2012. Franklin stock had a yearly return of 33.69% while the market index returns for the period was 15.86%. The stock outperformed the market index by means of generating excess returns of approximately 18% in the year 2012. The cumulative total return for Franklin Resources during the period 2010–2014 was −6.26% while the S&P market index return was 64% during the above stated period. The total cumulative abnormal return *(CAR) during the above period was approximately −70% indicating that the stock has underperformed compared to the market index in most of the time period of analysis.

Table 20.16 **Excess value creation in millions of dollars**

Year	2010	2011	2012	2013	2014
Shares in million	682	666	643	634	625
Price per share	111.21	96.06	131.47	57.08	55.37
Market capitalization	75,845.22	63,975.96	84,535.21	36,188.72	34,606.25
Book value of equity	7727	8524.7	9201.3	10,073.1	11,584.1
Excess value created	68,118.22	55,451.26	75,333.91	26,115.62	23,022.15
BV as % of MV	10.18785	13.32485	10.88458	27.83492	33.47401

The market value of equity was much higher than the book value of equity during the entire period 2010–2014. The stock price used for estimating market capitalization was the closing price of the last day of trading in December of the year. Excess value created is estimated as the difference between the market value and book value of equity. The excess value created was $68,118.22 million in year 2010 which decreased to $23,022.15 million in the year 2014. In the year 2010, book value was only 10% of market value. In 2014, the book value as percent of market value increased to 33.47%. BV denotes book value of equity and MV denotes market value of equity.

20.5 Estimation of cost of equity

The beta is estimated by regressing the weekly returns of the Franklin stock on the returns of the market index S&P 500 during the 3-year period 2012−2014. The value of beta estimated is 1.71. The risk free rate is based on the monthly average yield of 10-year treasury bond rate during the period 2012−2014. The risk free rate is calculated as 2.18%.

Risk premium is assumed to be 5.5%.

Cost of equity = 2.18 + 1.71 ∗ 5.5 = 11.59%

The cost of equity is estimated as 11.59%.

20.6 Valuation

The valuation of Franklin Resources is estimated on the basis of dividend discount model.

20.6.1 Two stage DDM

The average growth rate of EPS during the 5-year period 2010−2014 was 24%. The average growth rate of DPS was 11% during the 5-year period. The average dividend payout (DPO) during the 5-year period was 12%. Table 20.17 gives the highlights of estimation of growth rates from fundamentals.

In the two stage growth model, the growth rate of earnings is assumed as 19%. The average DPO is assumed to be 12% based on historical estimation. The high growth period is assumed as 10 years.

EPS in year 2014 = $3.79
DPO = 12%.
Growth Rate = 19%

EPS in the first year of high growth period = 3.79 ∗ 1.19 = $4.51.

20.7 Stable phase inputs

The growth rate of earnings in the stable phase is assumed to be the growth rate of US economy. The average annual GDP growth rate of US economy during the past

Table 20.17 Estimation of growth rate from fundamentals

Year	2010	2011	2012	2013	2014
Retention ratio	0.86	0.89	0.88	0.88	0.87
ROE	0.19	0.24	0.22	0.22	0.22
Growth rate	0.16	0.21	0.19	0.20	0.19

The average growth rate of earnings estimated from fundamentals is 19%. ROE denotes return on equity.

4 years is taken as the growth rate of earnings in the stable phase period (Table 20.19).

The DPO in the stable growth period is estimated from fundamentals.

Growth rate = retention ratio * average return on equity of the industry sector.

Based on ICI fact book data, 2014, the average return on equity of the mutual fund industry is estimated as 16%.

Retention ratio = 2.15/16 = 0.13
DPO ratio = 1 − 0.13 = 0.87
EPS at the end of high growth period = $21.58
Growth rate in stable phase = 2.15%
EPS at the beginning of the stable period = 21.58 * 1.0215 = $22.05.

EPS at the beginning of the stable period	22.05
DPO	0.87
DPS at the beginning of stable period	19.18

Terminal value = DPS in stable period/(cost of equity − growth rate)
= 19.18/(0.1159 − 0.0215) = $203.18
Present value (PV) of the terminal value of dividends in stable phase = $67.86

The PV is obtained by discounting the terminal value for the 10-year period at the estimated discount rate of 11.59%.

Table 20.18 Present value (PV) of dividends in the high growth phase

Year	1	2	3	4	5	6	7	8	9	10
EPS	4.51	5.37	6.39	7.60	9.04	10.76	12.81	15.24	18.14	21.58
DPO	0.12	0.12	0.12	0.12	0.12	0.12	0.12	0.12	0.12	0.12
DPS	0.54	0.64	0.77	0.91	1.09	1.29	1.54	1.83	2.18	2.59
PV	0.49	0.52	0.55	0.59	0.63	0.67	0.71	0.76	0.81	0.87
Sum	6.59									

PV of dividends in the high growth period = $6.59.

Table 20.19 Annual GDP growth rate

Year	GDP growth rate
2010	2.5
2011	1.6
2012	2.3
2013	2.2
Average	2.15

The growth rate of earnings in stable period is assumed to be 2.15%.
Source: http://data.worldbank.org/indicator/NY.GDP.MKTP.KD.ZG

Table 20.20 Recent peer comparison

Company	Market cap	Net income	P/S	P/B	P/E	Div yield in %
Franklin Resources	31,892	2392	3.8	2.7	13.5	1
Black Rock	60,197	3294	5.6	2.2	18.9	2.2
Blackstone Group	47,462	1584	3.4	4.1	15.8	6.5
T. Rowe Price	21,154	1234	5.3	4.2	17.6	2.3

The market capitalization and net income of the firms are given in millions of US dollar. Black Rock had the highest market capitalization, price to sales ratio, and price to earnings ratio among the peer groups. The Blackstone Group had the highest dividend yield of 6.5% among the firms. Data were obtained from morningstar.com.

Table 20.21 Price multiple trends

Year	2010	2011	2012	2013	2014
P/E	15.8	11.1	13.6	16.3	14.8
P/B	3.1	2.5	3	3.5	3
P/S	4.1	3	3.7	4.5	4.1
P/cash flow	15.9	13.7	22.6	17.6	14.5

The above table gives the price multiple values of Franklin Resources during the period 2010–2014. The various ratios like price to earnings ratio, price to book ratio, price to sales ratio, and price to cash flow have been fluctuating over the 5-year period of analysis.

Value of Franklin Stock = PV of dividends during high growth period + PV of dividends in stable growth period
= 67.86 + 6.59 = $74.45

The value of Franklin stock as of the year 2014 is estimated as $74.45. On December 29, 2014, Franklin Resources was trading at $55.37 in the NYSE market.

20.8 Relative valuation

The relative value ratios of Franklin Resources are compared with peer groups like Black Rock, Blackstone, and T. Rowe Price (Tables 20.20). Table 20.21 compares the price multiple trends of Franklin Resources during the period 2010–2014.

References

For details of calculations of all analysis, see resources file *Franklin Resources.xlsx*.
Annual Reports of Franklin Resources.

Valuation of Pfizer

21

Pfizer was founded in 1894 by Charles Pfizer and Charles Erhart. By the 1950s, Pfizer was established in Belgium, Brazil, Canada, Cuba, Iran, Mexico, Panama, Puerto Rico, Turkey, and the United Kingdom. The company is headquartered in New York. The stock is listed in NYSE, LSE, Euronext, and Swiss exchanges.

During the 1980s and 1990s, Pfizer underwent a period of growth sustained by the discovery and marketing of Zoloft, Lipitor, Norvasc, Zithromax, Aricept, Diflucan, and Viagra. Pfizer has recently grown by mergers, including those with Warner−Lambert (2000), with Pharmacia (2003), and with Wyeth (2009).

Pfizer had the greatest number of blockbuster products in 2009 with 14, which includes 5 inherited through the acquisition of Wyeth. The majority of Pfizer revenues come from the manufacture and sale of biopharmaceutical products. In 2015, Pfizer entered into a definitive agreement to acquire Hospira Inc., the world's leading provider of injectable drugs and infusion technologies and a global leader in biosimilars, for $90 per share in cash, for a total enterprise value of approximately $17 billion.

Revenues in 2014 were $49.6 billion, which represented a decrease of 4% compared to 2013. The Research & Development (R&D) expenses went up by $1.7 billion. The income from continuing operations in 2014 was $9.1 billion, compared to $11.4 billion in 2013.

Pfizer has nine diverse healthcare businesses: primary care, specialty care, oncology, emerging markets, established products, consumer healthcare, nutrition, animal health, and capsugel. Pfizer has created two distinct research organizations. The Pharma Therapeutics R&D Group focuses on the discovery of small molecules and related modalities; the Bio Therapeutics R&D Group focuses on large-molecule research, including vaccines (Annual Reports of Pfizer).

In 2010, products like Lipitor, Enbrel, Lyrica, Prevnar/Prevenar 13, and Celebrex each delivered at least $2 billion in revenues. Products like Viagra Xalatan/Xalacom, Effexor, Norvasc, Prevnar/Prevenar (7-valent), Zyvox, Sutent, the Premarin family, Geodon/Zeldox, and Detrol/Detrol LA each surpassed $1 billion in revenues.

From 2014, Pfizer manages commercial operations through new global commercial structure consisting of two distinct businesses—an innovative products business and established products business.

In 2014, Pfizer entered into a collaborative agreement with OPKO to develop and commercialize OPKO's long-acting human growth hormone (hGH-CTP) for the treatment of growth hormone deficiency in adults and children. In the same year, Pfizer completed the acquisition of Baxter's portfolio of marketed vaccines for $635 million.

Again in year 2014, Pfizer completed the acquisition of InnoPharma, a privately held pharmaceutical development company, for an upfront cash payment of $225 million and contingent consideration of up to $135 million.

21.1   Growth perspective of Pfizer

Year	Milestones
1849–1899	1849 With $2500 borrowed from Charles Pfizer's father, cousins Charles Pfizer and Charles Erhart entrepreneurs from Germany, open Charles Pfizer & Company as a fine-chemicals business Their first product is a palatable form of santonin—an antiparasitic used to treat intestinal worms 1862 The first domestic production of tartaric acid and cream of tartar, products vital to the food and chemical industries, is launched by Pfizer 1868 The company now has a substantially increased product line and 150 new employees 1880 Pfizer soon becomes America's leading producer of citric acid 1899 A leader in the American chemical business, Pfizer marks its 50th anniversary
1900–1950	1906 Company sales exceed $3 million 1928 Alexander Fleming discovers the antibiotic properties of the penicillin mold, an event destined to make medical history and to change the course of Pfizer's future 1936 Pfizer becomes the world's leading producer of vitamin C 1939 Pfizer is widely recognized as a leader in fermentation technology 1940 By the late 1940s, Pfizer will become the established leader in the manufacture of vitamins 1944 Pfizer is successful in its efforts to mass-produce penicillin and becomes the world's largest producer of the "miracle drug" 1950 Terramycin (oxytetracycline), a broad-spectrum antibiotic that is the result of the Company's first discovery program, becomes the first pharmaceutical sold in the United States under the Pfizer label
1951–1999	1951 Expansion throughout the different parts of world 1952 Pfizer establishes an Agricultural Division dedicated to offering cutting-edge solutions to animal health problems 1953 After its acquisition, J.B. Roerig and Company, specialists in nutritional supplements, becomes a division of Pfizer

(Continued)

(Continued)

Year	Milestones
	1955
	Pfizer partners with Japan's Taito to manufacture and distribute antibiotics
	Pfizer acquires full ownership of Taito in 1983
	1961
	Pfizer begins a decade of substantial growth and establishes new World Headquarters in midtown Manhattan
	1967
	Vibramycin, the company's first once-a-day broad-spectrum antibiotic, is introduced and quickly becomes a top seller
	1971
	Pfizer acquires Mack Illertissen, a prosperous manufacturer of pharmaceutical, chemical, and consumer products oriented to the needs of the German marketplace
	1972
	Pfizer crosses the billion-dollar sales threshold
	Policy focus on R&D
	1976
	As America celebrates its 200th birthday, Pfizer celebrates over 125 years of explosive growth
	Pfizer introduces Minipress (prazosin HCI) in the United States for the control of high blood pressure
	1980
	Feldene piroxicam becomes one of the largest selling prescription anti-inflammatory medications in the world and, ultimately, Pfizer's first product to reach a total of a billion United States dollars in sales
	1984
	Glucotrol glipizide, for diabetes, is launched
	1988
	The agricultural division introduces several breakthrough products, including Dectomax (doramectin)
	1989
	Pfizer launches Procardia XL extended release tablets, an innovative once-a-day medication for angina and hypertension
	1990
	Diflucan fluconazole, a powerful antifungal, is launched in the United States and 15 additional countries
	1992
	Pfizer has a triple rollout of major new medicines: Zoloft (setraline hydrochloride) for treatment of depression, Norvasc (amlodipine besylate) for control of angina and hypertension, and Zithromax azithromycin) for respiratory and skin infections
	1995
	The Animal Health Division purchases SmithKline Beecham's animal health business, making Pfizer a world leader in the development and production of pharmaceuticals for livestock and companion animals

(*Continued*)

(Continued)

Year	Milestones
	1997
	Fortune® magazine names Pfizer the world's most admired pharmaceutical company. Pfizer continues its reign as most admired in 1998
	Discovered by Parke-Davis Research and introduced in 1997, Lipitor is the largest selling pharmaceutical of any kind worldwide
	1998
	Pfizer's roster of outstanding drugs grows with the launch of Viagra® (sildenafil citrate), a breakthrough treatment for erectile dysfunction
	Pfizer invests more than $3.3 billion in R&D
	1999
	Pfizer celebrates its 150th anniversary as one of the world's premier pharmaceutical companies
	Pfizer investment in research and development exceeds $4 billion for the first time
2000+	2000
	Pfizer and Warner–Lambert merge to form the new Pfizer, creating the world's fastest growing major pharmaceutical company
	2001
	Pfizer launches Geodon (ziprasidone), a new antipsychotic for the treatment of schizophrenia
	2002
	Pfizer invests an industry leading $5.1 billion in R&D and launches Vfend (voriconazole), an orally and intravenously administered antifungal indicated for treatment of serious fungal infections
	2003
	Pfizer invests more than $7.1 billion in R&D. On April 16, 2003, Pfizer Inc. and Pharmacia Corporation combine operations
	2004
	Pfizer Inc. is selected by Dow Jones and Co. to be included in the Dow Jones Industrial Average, which is the best-known stock market barometer in the world
	2007
	Pfizer launches Selzentry™ (maraviroc) tablets, the first in a new class of oral HIV medicines in more than 10 years
	2009
	On October 15, 2009, Pfizer acquires Wyeth, creating a company with a broad range of products and therapies
	2010
	Pfizer announces a diversified R&D platform named Pfizer Worldwide Research and Development, supporting excellence in small molecules, large molecules, and vaccine R&D

Source: http://www.pfizer.com/about/history/timeline

The present day Pfizer has resulted from the consolidation of the following major companies: Warner−Lambert; Pharmacia AB; Agouron, Monsanto (Searle); Esperion Therapeutics Inc., and Viruron Pharmaceuticals. In 2009, Pfizer acquired Wyeth. Table 21.1 provides the financial highlights of Pfizer during the period 2005−2014.

The average growth rate of revenues during the period 2006−2014 was −0.37%. The average net income growth rate was 1.36% during the 9-year period 2006−2014. The average growth rate of revenues during the period 2006−2009 was 3%, while the average growth rate of revenues during the period 2010−2014 was −0.16%. The average growth rate of operating income during the 4-year period was −2.29%, while the average growth rate of operating income during the 5-year period 2010−2014 was 2.48%. The average growth rate of net income was 1.66% during the period 2006−2009, while the net income registered an average growth rate of 1.13% during the period 2010−2014. The operating cash flow grew by 3% on an average basis during the period 2006−2009, while the average growth rate was only 0.35% during the period 2010−2014.

21.2 Performance analysis

The data for analysis were obtained from Morningstar.com and Annual Reports of Pfizer. Table 21.2 highlights the profitability ratios of Pfizer during the period 2005−2014.

21.3 Stock wealth creation

The stock returns are analyzed for the period of 5 years (2010−2014) based on weekly returns. The stock prices and DJIA index prices are obtained from yahoo finance. The excess returns are computed by estimating the difference between the

Table 21.1 Ten-year operating highlights in millions of US dollars

Year	2005	2006	2007	2008	2009	2010	2011	2012	2013	2014
Revenues	51,298	48,371	48,418	48,296	50,009	67,809	67,425	58,986	51,584	49,605
Operating income	11,881	12,124	7519	11,726	10,827	9422	15,241	13,221	16,727	12,240
Net income	8085	19,337	8144	8104	8635	8257	10,009	14,570	22,003	9135
Operating cash flow	14,733	17,594	13,353	18,238	16,587	11,454	20,240	17,054	17,765	16,883

The revenues improved from $51,298 million in the year 2005 to $49,605 million in the year 2014. The net income improved from $8085 million in the year 2005 to $9135 million in the year 2014. The revenues grew by 3.5% in the year 2009 compared to the year 2008 while the growth rate of revenues was approximately 36% in the year 2010. The year-on-year comparison reveals that the revenue growth rate had been negative during the period 2011−2014. The operating income grew by 56% in the year 2008 and 62% in 2011, respectively. The net income grew by 139% in the year 2006 and 51% in the year 2013. The operating cash flow grew by 77% in the year 2011.

stock and index returns. The cumulative excess returns are also estimated for the 5-year period based on weekly returns (Tables 21.5 and 21.6). The details of return calculation are given in the worksheet stock return analysis of *Pfizer.xlsx*.

21.4 Estimation of cost of equity and WACC

The cost of equity is estimated using the CAPM.

Cost of equity = Risk-free rate + Beta * Risk premium
Risk premium = Return on market index − Risk-free rate

Table 21.2 Profitability trends

Year	2005	2006	2007	2008	2009	2010	2011	2012	2013	2014
Net profit margin (%)	15.75	39.97	16.81	16.78	17.27	12.18	14.84	24.7	42.65	18.42
ROA (%)	6.7	16.64	7.08	7.16	5.33	4.05	5.23	7.8	12.3	5.35
ROE (%)	12.1	28.29	11.96	13.24	11.71	9.29	11.78	17.84	27.94	12.38
ROCE (%)	9.89	24.29	10.8	11.17	9.01	7.28	8.83	13.15	19.9	8.28

The net profit margin was highest in the year 2013. The profitability ratios of ROA, ROE, ROCE was highest in the year 2006. The average net profit margin was 21% during the period 2005−2009, while the average net profit margin was 22.6% during the period 2010−2014. The period 2005−2009 registered an average ROA of 8.58% in the year 2005−2009, while the average ROA fell to 6.95% during the period 2010−2014. The average ROE during the period 2005−2009 and 2010−2014 was approximately 15% and 16%, respectively. The average ROCE was 13% and 11.5% during the period 2005−2009 and 2010−2014, respectively.

Table 21.3 Liquidity ratios

Year	2005	2006	2007	2008	2009	2010	2011	2012	2013	2014
Current ratio	1.47	2.2	2.15	1.59	1.66	2.11	2.06	2.15	2.41	2.67
Quick ratio	1.14	1.76	1.65	1.24	1.12	1.51	1.78	1.9	1.79	2.07

The average current ratio during the period 2005−2009 was 1.81 which improved to 2.28 during the period 2010−2014.The average quick ratio was 1.38 during the period 2005−2009 which improved to 1.81 during the period 2010−2014.

Table 21.4 Efficiency ratios

Year	2005	2006	2007	2008	2009	2010	2011	2012	2013	2014
Payables period	104.8	101.4	69.6	90.4	125.6	94.1	95.1	130.4	142.7	127.1
Inventory turnover	1.34	1.26	1.97	1.68	1.06	1.56	1.87	1.53	1.45	1.62
Fixed assets turnover	2.89	2.87	2.99	3.33	2.77	3.24	3.74	3.76	3.84	4.11

The efficiency position for the firm has improved in the 5-year period 2010−2014 compared to the period 2005−2009. The payable period improved from 98 days during the period 2005−2009 to 118 days during the period 2010−2014 on an average basis. On a comparative basis, the average inventory ratio improved from 1.46 to 1.61. The average fixed assets turnover ratio during this period improved from 2.97 to 3.74.

Beta is estimated by regressing the weekly returns of Pfizer on market index DJIA returns during the 5-year period 2010−2014.

Beta = 0.45
Average return on market index based on 5-year period = 11.68%

Risk-free rate is based on the average monthly yield of 10-year treasury bond rate during the period 2012−2014.

Risk-free rate = 2.18%
Risk premium = 11.68 − 2.18 = 9.5%
Cost of equity = 2.18 + 0.45 * 9.5 = 6.46%

21.4.1   Cost of debt

The cost of debt is assumed as the yield to maturity on a long-term bond of Pfizer maturing in the year 2038. The yield to maturity is estimated as 5.19%.

Corporate tax rate = 35%
After-tax cost of debt = 5.19 * (1 − 0.35) = 3.37%

Table 21.5 Average yearly returns in percent

Year	Pfizer	DJIA	Excess returns
2010	−5.0	5.6	−10.57
2011	23.8	12.0	11.74
2012	18.8	5.7	13.11
2013	17.5	25.9	−8.46
2014	3.6	9.2	−5.58

The market index DJIA outperformed the stock in the years 2010, 2013, and 2014, respectively. The yearly average returns of Pfizer was higher in the years 2011 and 2012, respectively. Pfizer generated 11.7% and 13% higher returns than the market index during 2011 and 2012, respectively. The total cumulative weekly returns for Pfizer stock during the 5-year period 2010−2014 was 59%, while the total cumulative weekly returns for market index DJIA was 58% during the above period. The cumulative excess return during the period of analysis was 0.7%, suggesting that the stock outperformed the index by a slight margin.

Table 21.6 Excess value creation in millions of dollars

Year	2010	2011	2012	2013	2014
MV of equity	141,375.7	170,306.8	194,907.7	210,435.4	200,107.6
BV of equity	88,410.3	85,310.8	83,789.28	82,188.4	72,783.92
Excess value	52,965.44	84,996	111,118.4	128,247	127,323.7
BV as % of MV	62.54	50.09	42.99	39.06	36.37

The excess value created had been positive in all the years of analysis indicating that the market capitalization was greater than the book value of equity in every year. The book value as a percent of market value have decreased over the 5-year period. In 2010, the book value was 62.54% of the market value. By 2014, the book value as percent of market value dropped to 36%. The market capitalization each year was estimated based on the closing price of Pfizer stock on the last day of trading in the year. The year-on-year analysis reveals that market capitalization increased by approximately 20%, 14%, and 8% during 2011, 2012, and 2013, respectively. The market capitalization decreased by approximately 5% in the year 2014.

The weights used for estimation of cost of capital are the market value weights of equity and book value weight of debt.

Market value of equity in 2014 = 200,107.6 million
Book value of debt in 2014 = 36,682 million
Total value = 236,789.6 million

21.4.2 Market value weights

Weight of equity = 0.85
Weight of debt = 0.25
WACC = 0.85 * 6.46 + 0.15 * 3.37 = 5.98%

The weighted average cost of capital is 5.98%.

21.5 Valuation models

The detailed calculation for the valuation of Pfizer using different valuation models is given in the excel file Pfizer.xlsx.

21.5.1 Dividend discount model (Tables 21.7 and 21.8)

Table 21.7 **Dividend trends**

Year	2009	2010	2011	2012	2013	2014
EPS	1.23	1.02	1.27	1.94	3.19	1.42
DPS	0.8	0.72	0.8	0.88	0.96	1.04
DPO	0.65	0.71	0.63	0.45	0.30	0.73

The average growth rate of EPS during the 5-year period based on geometric mean was 2.9%. The average growth rate of DPS during the 5-year period based on geometric mean was 5.3%. The average DPO during the 6-year period was 58%.

Table 21.8 **Estimation of growth rate from fundamentals**

Year	2009	2010	2011	2012	2013	2014
Retention ratio	0.35	0.29	0.37	0.55	0.70	0.27
ROE	0.1171	0.093	0.1178	0.1784	0.2794	0.1238
Growth rate	0.04	0.03	0.04	0.10	0.20	0.03

Growth rate = Retention ratio * Return on equity
The average growth rate from fundamentals during the 6-year period 2009−2014 are calculated as 7%. The average DPO obtained from historical estimates during the 6-year period is 58%. This value is taken as the average DPO during the high growth period.

21.5.2 Two-stage DDM

High growth period = 10 years
Growth rate in earnings per share = 7%
DPO = 0.58
Cost of equity = 6.46%. Table 21.9 gives the present value calculation for dividends in the high growth phase.

5.2.1 Stable period inputs

The growth rate of US economy is assumed as the growth rate of earnings in the stable growth period.

Growth rate in stable growth period = 2.15%
Growth rate = Retention ratio * ROE of industry sector
ROE of pharma industry = 16.4%[1]
2.15% = Retention ratio * 16.4%
Retention ratio = 2.15/16.4 = 0.13
DPO in the stable period = 1 − 0.13 = 0.87
EPS at the end of high growth period = 2.79
EPS at beginning of stable period = 2.79 * 1.0215 = $5.62
DPO = 0.87
DPS in the stable period = 5.62 * 0.87 = $4.89
Terminal value of DPS = DPS/(Cost of equity − Growth rate)
4.89/(0.0646 − 0.215) = $113.45
Present value of the terminal value = $60.7
Value of Pfizer stock = PV of Pfizer in high growth phase + PV of Pfizer in stable growth phase = 60.7 + 8.47 = $69.1

Value of Pfizer stock using two-stage DDM = $69.1

21.5.3 One-stage DDM

DPS in the year 2014 = $1.04
Growth rate = 2.15%
Value = DPS (1 + Growth rate)/(Cost of equity − Growth rate) = 1.04 * 1.0215/(0.0646 − 0.0215) = $24.65

Table 21.9 **Present value of dividends in high growth phase**

Year	1	2	3	4	5	6	7	8	9	10
EPS	1.52	1.63	1.74	1.86	1.99	2.13	2.28	2.44	2.61	2.79
DPO	0.58	0.58	0.58	0.58	0.58	0.58	0.58	0.58	0.58	0.58
DPS	0.88	0.94	1.01	1.08	1.16	1.24	1.32	1.42	1.51	1.62
PV	0.83	0.83	0.84	0.84	0.84	0.85	0.85	0.86	0.86	0.87
Sum	8.47									

Present value of dividends in high growth period = $8.47.

---

[1] https://biz.yahoo.com/ic/510.html.

Value of Pfizer stock using one-stage DDM was $24.65.
Pfizer was trading at $31.15 in NYSE on December 29, 2014.

21.5.4   Estimation of value using FCFE model

The average growth rate of revenues of Pfizer during the period 2004–2014 was 0.9%. The average growth rate of net income during the time period 2004–2014 was 8.01%. These averages were based on geometric mean.

Pfizer have huge investments in R&D activities. Hence, it is essential to adjust R&D expenses as capital expenses instead of operating expenses.

Estimation of adjusted net capital expenditure = Net capital expenditure + R&D expenses in current period-amortization of research asset + Acquisition costs
Adjusted net income = Net income + Current year's R&D expense − Amortization of research asset in current year
Adjusted book value of equity = Book value of equity + Value of research asset

Research assets are amortized linearly over time. The life of research asset is assumed to be 5 years. The research assets are amortized 20% each year. The value of research asset and amortization expense calculation for the year 2014 is given in Table 21.10. For the rest of years calculation, see the work sheet FCFE of *Pfizer.xlsx*. The details of R&D variables estimation for different years is given in the Table 21.11.

21.5.5   Calculation of adjusted ROE

The adjusted net income and adjusted book value are estimated each year for the estimation of adjusted ROE. The net income is adjusted by adding R&D expenses and subtracting the amortized value of research asset from the net income. The value of research asset is added to the book value of equity to get adjusted book value of equity.

Table 21.10 Amortization and value of research estimation in the year 2014

Year	R&D expenses	Unamortized portion (%)	Million dollars	Amortization in 2014
Current (2014)	8393	100	8393	
−1	6678	80	5342.4	1335.6
−2	7870	60	4722	1574
−3	9112	40	3644.8	1822.4
−4	9413	20	1882.6	1882.6
−5	7913	0	0	1582.6
	Value of research asset		23,984.8	
	Amortization expense current year (2014)			8197.2

The values are given in millions of dollars.

Adjusted ROE = Adjusted net income in year t/Adjusted book value of equity in year t − 1.

Table 21.12 gives the calculation of adjusted ROE. Tables 21.13 and 21.14 shows the estimation of adjusted net capex and change in non cash working capital.

Table 21.11 R&D highlights in millions of dollars

Year	R&D expenses	Value of R&D asset	Amortization of R&D asset
2009	7913	24,991	8646.6
2010	9413	25,925.8	8478.2
2011	9112	26,495.8	8542
2012	7870	25,688.2	8677.6
2013	6678	23,789	8577.2
2014	8393	23,984.8	8197.2

Table 21.12 Calculation of adjusted ROE

Year	Adjusted net income	Adjusted book value of equity	Adjusted ROE
2009	7901.4	103,542.75	
2010	9191.8	114,336.1	0.088773
2011	10,579	111,806.6	0.092525
2012	13,762.4	109,477.48	0.123091
2013	20,103.8	105,977.4	0.183634
2014	9330.8	96,768.72	0.088045

Table 21.13 Estimation of adjusted net capital expenditure (in million dollars)

Year	2009	2010	2011	2012	2013	2014
Net capex	1205	1513	1660	1327	1465	1583
R&D expenses in current period	7913	9413	9112	7870	6678	8393
Amortization of research asset	8646.6	8478.2	8542	8677.6	8577.2	8197.2
Acquisitions expenses	4337	3214	2934	1880	1182	250
Adjusted net capex	4808.4	5661.8	5164	2399.4	747.8	2028.8
Adjusted net income	7901.4	9191.8	10579	13762.4	20,103.8	9330.8
Net capex/Adjusted net income	0.61	0.62	0.49	0.17	0.04	0.22

The net capex as a percent of adjusted net income improved from 61% in the year 2009 to 22% in the year 2014. The average net capex as a percent of adjusted net income was approximately 31% during the 5-year period 2010–2014. Adjusted net capital expenditure (Capex) = Net capital expenditures + R&D expenses in current period − Amortization of research asset + Acquisition expenses.

Tables 21.15 and 21.16 gives the estimation of reinvestment rate and growth rate from fundamentals.

21.5.6 Two-stage FCFE model

The growth rate estimated from both historical and fundamental is approximately 3%. Two-stage growth scenario is assumed in which the net income will grow by 3% in the first stage for 5 years and then by the growth rate of the economy in the stable stage period.

Table 21.14 Estimation of change in noncash working capital (in million dollars)

	2009	2010	2011	2012	2013	2014
Total current assets	61,670	60,468	57,728	61,415	56,244	57,702
Cash and cash equivalents	25,969	28,012	26,758	32,708	32,408	36,122
Noncash current assets	35,701	32,456	30,970	28,707	23,836	21,580
Total current liabilities	37,225	28,609	28,069	28,619	23,366	21,631
Interest-bearing short-term liabilities	5469	5623	4018	6424	6027	5141
Noninterest-bearing current liabilities	31,756	22,986	24,051	22,195	17,339	16,490
Noncash working capital	3945	9470	6919	6512	6497	5090
Change in noncash working capital		5525	−2551	−407	−15	−1407

Noncash current assets = Total current assets − cash and cash equivalents.
Noninterest-bearing current liabilities = Total current liabilities − interest-bearing current liabilities.
Noncash working capital = Noncash current assets − noninterest-bearing current liabilities.

Table 21.15 Estimation of reinvestment rate

Year	2010	2011	2012	2013	2014
Adjusted net Capex	5661.8	5164	2399.4	747.8	2028.8
Change in noncash working capital	5525	−2551	−407	−15	−1407
Total reinvestment	11,186.8	2613	1992.4	732.8	621.8
Adjusted net income	9191.8	10,579	13,762.4	20,103.8	9330.8
Reinvestment rate	1.22	0.25	0.14	0.036	0.067

Total reinvestment = Adjusted net capex + Change in noncash working capital.
Reinvestment rate = Total reinvestment/Adjusted net income.
The reinvestment rate was 25% in year 2011. By the year 2014, the reinvestment rate fell to 6.7%. The average reinvestment rate during the five year period 2010−2014 was 34%.
The growth rate of adjusted income was estimated for the 5-year period 2010−2014.The historical average growth rate (geometric mean) based on the above period was 3.4%. The growth rate estimated from fundamentals was 3%.

5.6.2 First-stage period inputs

Period of growth = 5 years
Reinvestment rate = 34%
Cost of equity = 6.46%
Adjusted net income in 2014 = 9330.8 million
Growth rate in net income = 3%

The present value calculation of FCFE in high growth period is given in Table 21.18.

Table 21.16 Estimation of growth rate from fundamentals

Year	2010	2011	2012	2013	2014
Adjusted ROE	0.09	0.09	0.12	0.18	0.09
Reinvestment rate	1.22	0.25	0.14	0.04	0.07
Growth rate	0.11	0.02	0.02	0.01	0.01

Growth rate = Adjusted ROE * Reinvestment rate
The average growth rate was estimated as 3% during the 5-year period.

Table 21.17 Estimation of FCFE in million dollars

Year	2010	2011	2012	2013	2014
Adjusted net income	9191.8	10,579	13,762.4	20,103.8	9330.8
Adjusted net capex	5661.8	5164	2399.4	747.8	2028.8
Change in noncash working capital	5525	−2551	−407	−15	−1407
Net debt issued	31,379	−5084	1489	−971	193
FCFE in millions of dollars	29,384	2882	13,259	18,400	8902

FCFE = Adjusted net income-adjusted net capex − Change in noncash working capital + Net debt issued.

Table 21.18 Present value of FCFE in first-stage period

Year	1	2	3	4	5
Net income	9610.7	9899.0	10,196.0	10,501.9	10,817.0
Reinvestment	3267.6	3365.7	3466.6	3570.6	3677.8
FCFE	6343.1	6533.4	6729.4	6931.3	7139.2
PV of FCFE	5958.18	5764.54	5577.19	5395.92	5220.55
Sum	27,916.38				

The present value of FCFE in the first stage is estimated as $27,916.38 million.

5.6.3 Stable period inputs

The growth rate in stable period after 5 years is assumed to be the average growth rate of US economy.

Growth rate in stable period = 2.15%
Growth rate = Reinvestment rate * ROE of pharma industry sector
ROE of pharma industry = 16.4%[1]
2.15 = Reinvestment rate * 16.4
Reinvestment rate = 2.15/16.4 = 13%

The reinvestment rate in the stable period is estimated as 13%.

Net income at the end of first stage of growth = 10,817 million
Net income in stable period = 10817 * (1.0215) = 11,049.52 million
Reinvestment = 11,049.52 * 0.13 = 1436.44 million
FCFE = 11,049.52 − 1436.44 = 9613.08 million
Terminal value = FCFE in stable period/(Cost of equity − Growth rate)
= 9613.08/(0.0646 − 0.0215) = 223,041.34 million
Present value of terminal value of FCFE = 163,099.66 million
Value of operating assets = PV of FCFE in first phase + PV of FCFE in stable period
= 27,916.38 + 163,099.66 = 191,016.04 million

Value of operating assets	$191,016.04
Cash and cash equivalents in 2014	36,122
Value of equity of Pfizer in million dollars	$227,138.04
Number of shares in million	6424
Value per share	35.36

The value of equity is estimated as $227.138 billion. The market capitalization of Pfizer as on May 5, 2015 was $209.26 billion. Value per share is estimated as $35.56.Pfizer was trading at $31.15 on December 29, 2014. The stock price of Pfizer as on May 5, 2015 was $34.32.

21.5.7 Constant growth FCFE model

In this model, we assume that there is only stage, i.e., stable growth period. The net income will grow at the US economic growth rate estimated as 2.15%.

Net income in 2014 = 9331 million
Reinvestment rate = 0.13
Reinvestment = 9331 * 0.13 = 1213.004 million
FCFE in the year 2014 = 9331 − 1213.004 = 8118 million
Value = FCFE in year 2014 * (1 + Growth rate)/(Cost of equity − Growth rate)
= 8118 * 1.0215/(0.0646 − 0.0215) = $192,397.42 million
Value per share = 192,397.42/6424 = $29.95
Value per share is estimated as $29.95.

21.5.8   FCFF valuation model

Adjusted operating earnings = Operating earnings + Current year's R&D expense −
Amortization of research asset
Adjusted book value of capital = Adjusted book value of equity + Debt
Adjusted book value of equity = Book value of equity + Research value of asset
(Tables 21.19−21.24).

Table 21.19 Adjusted book value of capital (million dollars)

Year	Adjusted BV of equity	Debt	Adjusted BV of capital
2009	103,542.75	48,662	152,204.75
2010	114,336.1	44,033	158,369.1
2011	111,806.6	38,949	150,755.6
2012	109,477.48	37,460	146,937.48
2013	105,977.4	36,489	142,466.4
2014	96,768.72	36,682	133,450.72

Table 21.20 Adjusted operating income and adjusted ROCE

Year	EBIT $(1-T)$	R&D expenses	Annual amortization	Adjusted EBIT $(1-T)$	Adjusted ROCE
2009	8120.25	7913	8646.6	7386.65	
2010	8298	9413	8478.2	9232.8	0.061
2011	11218	9112	8542	11,788	0.074
2012	10,659	7870	8677.6	9851.4	0.065
2013	12421	6678	8577.2	10,521.8	0.072
2014	9120	8393	8197.2	9315.8	0.065

The adjusted operating income (EBIT $(1-T)$ values are given in millions of dollars.
Adjusted EBIT $(1-T)$ = EBIT $(1-T)$ + Current year R&D Expenses − Annual amortization.
Adjusted ROCE = EBIT $(1-T)$ in year t/Adjusted book value of capital in year t − 1.

Table 21.21 Estimation of reinvestment rate from past data

Year	2010	2011	2012	2013	2014
Adjusted EBIT$(1-T)$	9232.8	11,788	9851.4	10,521.8	9315.8
Adjusted net capex	5661.8	5164	2399.4	747.8	2028.8
Change in noncash WC	5525	−2551	−407	−15	−1407
Reinvestment	11,186.8	2613	1992.4	732.8	621.8
Reinvestment/Adj EBIT $(1-T)$	1.21	0.22	0.20	0.07	0.07
Average	0.35				

The adjusted EBIT $(1-T)$ and reinvestment data values are in millions of dollars. The reinvestment rate is obtained
by dividing the sum of adjusted net capital expenditure and change in working capital by the adjusted operating
income (EBIT $(1-T)$. The average reinvestment rate during the period 2010−2014 was 35%. The geometric mean
based average value during the above period was 30%.

Table 21.22 Estimation of growth rate from historical

Year	2009	2010	2011	2012	2013	2014
Adjusted EBIT(1 − T)	7386.65	9232.8	11788	9851.4	10,521.8	9315.8
Growth rate		0.25	0.28	−0.16	0.07	−0.11

The values of adjusted EBIT (1 − T) are given in millions of dollars. The average growth rate for the five year period 2010−2014 based on geometric mean was approximately 5%.

Table 21.23 Estimation of growth rate from fundamentals

Year	2010	2011	2012	2013	2014
Adjusted ROCE	0.061	0.074	0.065	0.072	0.065
Reinvestment rate	1.21	0.22	0.20	0.07	0.07
Growth rate	0.073	0.016	0.013	0.005	0.004

The average growth rate based on geometric mean is estimated as 2.2%.

Table 21.24 Estimation of FCFF 2010−2014

Year	2010	2011	2012	2013	2014
Adjusted EBIT(1 − T)	9232.8	11,788	9851.4	10,521.8	9315.8
Adjusted net capex	5661.8	5164	2399.4	747.8	2028.8
Change in noncash WC	5525	−2551	−407	−15	−1407
FCFF	−1954	9175	7859	9789	8694

The FCFF improved from −1954 million in the year 2010 to 8694 million in the year 2014.

5.8.4   Two-stage FCFF model

High growth period = 5 years
Growth rate in EBIT (1 − T) = 5%
Reinvestment rate = 30%
WACC = 5.98%
Adjusted EBIT (1 − T) in 2014 = $9315.8 million
Adjusted EBIT (1 − T) in first year of high growth period = 9315.8 ∗ 1.05 = $9781.59 million.

Present value calculation of FCFF in high growth period is given in Table 21.25.

5.8.5   Stable period inputs

The growth rate of FCFF in the stable period is assumed to be the growth rate of the US economy, which is estimated as 2.15% as mentioned in Section 21.5.7.

Growth rate = Reinvestment rate ∗ Average return on invested capital of the industry sector

Table 21.25 Present value of FCFF in high growth period

Year	1	2	3	4	5
Adjusted EBIT (1 − T)	9781.59	10,270.67	10,784.20	11,323.41	11,889.58
Reinvestment	2934.48	3081.20	3235.26	3397.02	3566.88
FCFF	6847.11	7189.47	7548.94	7926.39	8322.71
PV	6460.76	6401.02	6341.83	6283.18	6225.08
Sum	31,711.87				

The present value of FCFF in the high growth period = $31,711.87 million.

The average return on capital employed is estimated as 11.33% based on the average ROCE of top 10 pharma companies in the year 2014.

Reinvestment rate = 18.9%
Adjusted EBIT (1 − T) at end of high growth period = $11,889.58 million
Adjusted EBIT (1 − T) in stable period = 11,889.58 ∗ 1.0215 = $12,145.21 million
Reinvestment rate = 0.189
Reinvestment = 12,145.21 ∗ 0.189 = $2295.44 million
FCFF in stable period = 12,145.21 − 2295.44 = $9849.77 million
Terminal value = FCFF in stable period/(WACC − growth rate) = 9849.77/ (0.0598 − 0.0215)
= $257,174.03 million
Present value of FCFF in stable period = $192,356.79 million.
Value of operating assets of Pfizer = PV of FCFF in high growth phase + PV of FCFF in stable growth phase
= 31,711.87 + 192,356.79 = $224,068.66 million

Value of operating assets	$224,068.66
Add cash and cash equivalents	36122
Value of Pfizer	$260,190.66
Subtract value of debt	36682
Value of equity	$223,508.66
Value of equity per share	34.79

Number of equity shares = 6424 million
Pfizer was trading at $34.12 in NYSE on May 6, 2015.
Value of equity per share based on FCFF was $34.79.

21.5.9 Constant growth FCFF model

EBIT (1 − T) in year 2014 = $9315.8 million
Reinvestment rate = 0.189
Reinvestment = $1760.69 million
FCFF in stable period = 9315.8 − 1760.69 = $7555.11 million
Value of operating assets = 7555.11/(0.0598 − 0.0215) = $201,502.58 million

Value of operating assets	201,502.58
Add cash and cash equivalents in 2014	36,122
Value of Pfizer	237,624.58
Subtract value of debt	36,682
Value of equity of Pfizer	200,942.58
Value of equity per share	31.28

Value of equity per share based on constant FCFF model is $31.28.

Summary of discounted cash flow valuation models

Two-stage DDM
  Value of Pfizer stock using two-stage DDM = $69.1
One-stage DDM
  Value of Pfizer stock using one-stage DDM was $24.65.
Two-stage FCFE model
  The value of equity is estimated as $227.138 billion. Value per share is estimated as $35.56.
Constant growth FCFE model
  Value per share is estimated as $29.95.
Two-stage FCFF model
  Value of equity per share based on FCFF was $34.79.
Constant growth FCFF model
  Value of equity per share based on constant FCFF model is $31.28.

Pfizer was trading at $31.15 in NYSE on December 29, 2014. The market capitalization of Pfizer as on May 5, 2015 was $209.26 billion. Pfizer was trading at $31.15 on December 29, 2014. The stock price of Pfizer as on May 5, 2015 was $34.32. Pfizer was trading at $34.12 in NYSE on May 6, 2015.

21.6 Relative valuation

The peer pharma companies chosen for comparison are Johnson & Johnson, Novartis, and Merck (Table 21.26−21.29).

The detailed step by step calculation involved in all valuation models is given in the resources file **Pfizer.xlsx**.

Table 21.26 Peer comparison highlights

Companies	Market cap	Net income	P/S	P/B	P/E	Div. yield (%)
Pfizer	209,116	9135	4.4	2.9	24.2	3.1
Johnson & Johnson	275,918	15,916	3.9	4.1	17.8	2.8
Novartis	248,341	10,210	4.7	3.5	24	2.6
Merck	171,682	11,920	4.2	3.5	14.9	2.9

The market capitalization and net income of these companies are given in millions of dollars. Johnson & Johnson has the highest market capitalization of $275.92 billion and net income of $15.916 billion among the peer companies. Johnson & Johnson have the highest P/B ratio among the four pharma majors. Novartis have the highest P/S ratio among the peer firms. Pfizer have the highest P/E ratio and dividend yield among the four companies.

Table 21.27 Pfizer price multiple trends

Year	2010	2011	2012	2013	2014
P/E	17.2	19.5	19.9	18.6	22.1
P/B	1.6	2	2.2	2.6	2.7
P/S	2.1	2.5	3.2	4.1	4
P/CF	12.3	8.4	11	11.9	11.8

The price-to-earnings (P/E) ratio have improved over the 5-year period. The P/E ratio has improved from 17.2 in 2010 to 22.1 in the year 2014.The price-to-book (P/B) ratio and price-to–sales (P/S) ratio has also improved over the 5-year period. The P/B ratio improved from 1.6 in 2010 to 2.7 in year 2014.The P/S ratio have improved from 2.1 in year 2010 to 4 in year 2014.The price-to-cash (P/C) flow ratio have been fluctuating over the 5-year period.

Table 21.28 Enterprise value and operating highlights

Firms	Pfizer	JNJ	Novartis	Merck
Market capitalization	200,107.6	299,488.48	224,793.16	166,281.1
Debt	36,682	18,760	20,411	21,403
Cash & cash equivalent	36,122	33,089	13,862	15,719
Enterprise value	200,667.6	285,159.5	231,342.2	171,965.1
Revenues	49,605	74,331	53,634	42,237
EBITDA	17,777	24,991	12,976	24,706
EBIT	12,240	20,959	11,089	5670

The values given are in millions of dollars. Enterprise value is obtained as sum of market capitalization plus debt minus cash and cash equivalents. Johnson & Johnson had the highest market capitalization among the peer companies.

Table **21.29** **Enterprise value multiples**

Multiples	Pfizer	JNJ	Novartis	Merck
EV/Revenues	4.0	3.8	4.31	4.07
EV/EBITDA	11.3	11.4	17.8	7.0
EV/EBIT	16.4	13.6	20.9	30.3

Lower the multiples, the more undervalued will be the stocks. Pfizer and JNJ have the lowest EV/Revenue multiples.

Reference

Annual Reports of Pfizer.

Part III

Case Studies on Mergers and Acquisition Valuation

Google's acquisition of Motorola—a valuation perspective* 22

I'm happy to announce the deal has closed. Motorola is a great American tech company, with a track record of over 80 years of innovation. It's a great time to be in the mobile business, and I'm confident that the team at Motorola will be creating the next generation of mobile devices that will improve lives for years to come.

Larry Page, CEO of Google.

22.1 Introduction

Google is a top web property in all major global market and has been the world's largest search engine. Google, the top online computer software and web search engine company, was founded by Larry Page and Sergey Brin in 1998. Starting from offering search in a single language, the company now offers dozens of products and services including various forms of advertising and web applications in scores of languages. Google also provides a variety of services for advertisers of all sizes.

Over the last decade, Google has emerged as the one of the biggest and most successful acquirer in the technology industry. Its core search advertising platform and biggest new businesses like Android, YouTube, and display advertising have all resulted from acquisitions.

Google has acquired over 150 companies, with its largest acquisition being the purchase of Motorola Mobility, a mobile device manufacturing subsidiary of Motorola. This acquisition was nearly four times larger than the previous largest purchase of online advertising company DoubleClick for $3.2 billion. It can be said that Google on an average had acquired more than one company per week since 2010.

Motorola Mobility Holdings Inc., the Mobile Devices division of Motorola is a communication corporation based in the United States. Its portfolio includes converged mobile devices, such as smartphones and tablets, wireless accessories, end-to-end video, and data delivery; management solutions including set-tops and data access devices. Motorola have a history of over eight decades in communications technology and products. Its major milestones include the introduction of the World's first portable cell phone and the StarTAC—the smallest and lightest phone.

* I acknowledge the contribution of former PG student of IMT Dubai, Mr M. N. Lokesh in preparing this chapter.

In the 1990s, Motorola had a leading position in the analog cell phone market, but was unable to capture the digital technology market making way for global rivals such as Nokia and Samsung. Motorola had shifted its operating system from their proprietary software to Google's Android operating system in 2009.

22.2 Merger highlights

In August 2011, Google Inc. and Motorola Mobility Holdings entered into a definitive agreement under which Google will acquire Motorola Mobility for $40.00 per share in cash, or a total of about $12.5 billion, which represented a premium of 63% to the closing price of Motorola Mobility shares on August 12, 2011.[1] The acquisition included a sizeable portfolio of patents owned by Motorola. The transaction was unanimously approved by the boards of directors of both companies. The deal information is given in Table 22.1.

22.3 Strategic reasons for the acquisition

The acquisition of Motorola Mobility by Google was eventful in the context that it was the first time an Internet company acquired an established hardware business. As of January 2011, Motorola Mobility held approximately 14,600 granted patents and 6700 pending applications worldwide. Google had 1000 odd patents at the time of acquisition. The acquisition of Motorola enabled Google to supercharge the Android ecosystem that would enhance competition in mobile computing.[2] Google expected to enhance its competitive advantage as Motorola Mobility had formidable strength in Android smartphones and devices along with market leadership position in the home devices and video solutions business. Google's strategy for the acquisition rationale was to build up the company's patent portfolio in order to protect Android from anticompetitive threats from Microsoft, Apple, and other companies.

Table 22.1 **Deal information**

Target	Motorola Mobility
Acquirer	Google Inc.
Acquisition date	22/05/2012
Acquirer fiscal year end prior to acquisition	31/12/2011
Stub year fraction	0.39
Offer price per share	$40.00
Target stock price	$24.45
Stock price as of (mm/dd/yyyy)	12/08/2011
Premium	63.0%
Acquirer stock price as on 12/08/2011	$563.77

[1] http://techcrunch.com/2011/08/15/breaking-google-buys-motorola-for-12-5-billion/.
[2] http://googleblog.blogspot.com/2011/08/supercharging-android-google-to-acquire.html.

Android, which is an open-source software, is vital to competition in the mobile device space. It has to be noted that Google had lost the bid for Nortel patents.

The transaction was subject to regulatory approvals from the United States, Europe, and other jurisdictions. The Motorola acquisition is considered as a means of protecting the viability of Android. Android system has been under the center of controversy involving patent infringement in which Android manufacturers HTC, Motorola, and Samsung were sued by Microsoft, Oracle, and Apple. Presently, more than 150 million Android devices have been activated worldwide through a network of about 39 manufacturers and 231 carriers in 123 countries.

Motorola had a successful stint as hardware integrator in the mobile industrial design world. The acquisition was aimed to create better user experience at reduced costs through hardware and software integration through innovation in mobile computing. The acquisition also fit into Google's strategy to enter home networking market via Motorola's connected home business.[3] The Android market is heavily fragmented and the developers face problems for designing applications. This acquisition was expected to provide Google a better Android system with lot of applications. This acquisition also provided the opportunity to Google to diversify into focused hardware products and mobile computing. Google could access all the product lines of MMI cell phones, set-top boxes, and tablets.

22.4   Financial breakdown of Motorola deal

Of the $12.4 billion total purchase price, $2.9 billion was cash acquired, $5.5 billion was attributed to patents and developed technology, $2.6 billion to goodwill, $730 million to customer relationships, and $670 million to other net assets acquired (Figure 22.1).

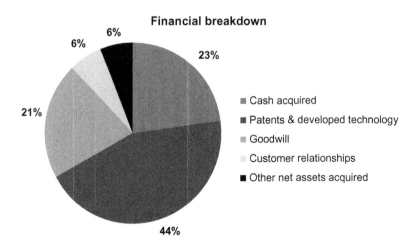

Figure 22.1 Details of financial transactions.

22.5   Valuation perspectives

22.5.1   Acquisition and stock wealth creation

The acquisition of Motorola by Google was announced on August 15, 2011. Google had paid $40 per share for Motorola. The share price of Motorola Mobile Holdings rose by approximately 58% within 1 week of announcement. On August 15, 2011, Motorola's share price was trading with a value of $24 approximately. By August 19, 2011, Motorola's share price rose to $37.88.

It is observed from Figure 22.2 that Motorola share price maintained a steady value during the postacquisition period of 9 months. The share price of target Motorola maintained a steady value during the period August 2011−May 2012. The stock price trend also indicates the concept of market efficiency, whereby the stock price of Motorola steadily increased on announcement of the acquisition and maintained the steady value (Figure 22.3).

In tune with the universal trend whereby acquirer company loses its share value on announcement of merger or acquisition, it is observed that Google lost approximately 10% of its share value in the week following the announcement. The downfall in the price is often attributed to the investors' skepticism about the success of the acquisition. On announcement day, Google was trading at $557.23. On 16th August, one day after announcement, the share price fell to $539. By 19th August, the share price fell to $490.92.

The week following the completion of the deal on May 23, 2012 also resulted in a decline in the share price for Google Inc. from $608 to $565 because of apprehensions in the market about the deal. The confusion was with respect to questions involving whether the deal was basically done by Google to acquire patents or to control the end-to-end experience of consumers and others expecting the margins to decline for the sake of future growth of Google.

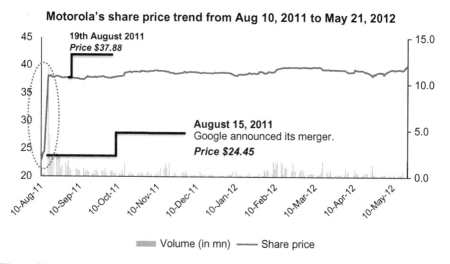

Figure 22.2 Postacquisition performance of Motorola's share price.

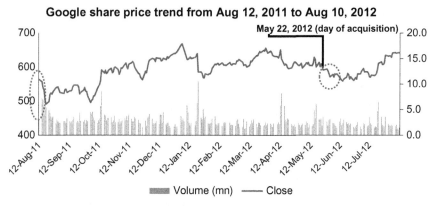

Figure 22.3 Google's share price trend analysis following acquisition announcement.

Table 22.2 Google and Motorola's share price daily returns and cumulative returns during announcement period

Day t	Google Inc.		Motorola Mobility	
	Returns (%)	Cumulative return (%)	Returns (%)	Cumulative return (%)
−5	−5.70	−5.70	−4.61	−4.61
−4	5.02	−0.68	7.34	2.73
−3	−4.26	−4.94	−0.35	2.38
−2	2.39	−2.55	4.69	7.07
−1	0.29	−2.26	1.37	8.44
0	−1.16	−3.42	55.91	64.35
1	−3.27	−6.69	−0.37	63.98
2	−1.09	−7.78	0.47	64.45
3	−5.30	−13.08	−0.81	63.64
4	−2.77	−15.85	0.01	63.65
5	1.48	−14.37	0.49	64.14

The cumulative return analysis shows that Google had a return of −15.91% during the time window of −15 to +15 days of announcement. At the same time, Motorola had a cumulative return of 55% during the time window of −15 to +15 days of acquisition announcement.

22.6 Returns analysis for different time windows of acquisition announcement

The returns analysis and cumulative return analysis during different time windows of acquisition announcement reveal huge gains for the target Motorola firm (Table 22.2).

On the announcement day, Google's share price return was −1.16%. Google's returns after +1 day of announcement was −3.27%. During the time window

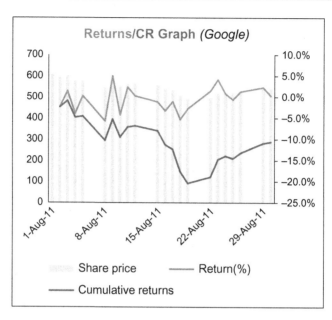

Figure 22.4 Google stock returns.

period of 3 days surrounding the announcement period (-1 to $+1$), the cumulative returns was -6.69% for Google shares. During the 11-day time window surrounding the announcement day (-5 to $+5$ days), the cumulative returns was -14.37%. On the announcement day, Motorola's share price return was approximately 56%. The cumulative return during the 2-day window period of -1 and the day of announcement was 64%. The cumulative return during the 11-day time window was approximately 64% (Figures 22.4 and 22.5).

22.7 Cumulative abnormal return analysis

The cumulative abnormal return (CAR) analysis is based on the excess returns the firms generate over and above the respective index during the time window of analysis. The cumulative abnormal returns for Google are based on the excess returns of Google shares over the market index of NASDAQ. The cumulative abnormal returns of Motorola are based on the excess returns of Motorola shares over the market index of NYSE.

Google had an excess return of -3.04% on the day of announcement and -2.3% on the day after announcement. Motorola had an excess return of 53.46% on the day of announcement and 0.81% on the day after announcement. The

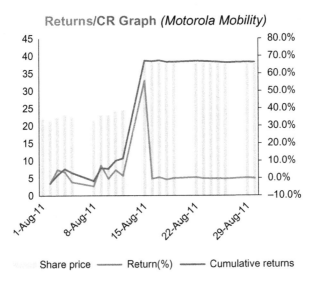

Figure 22.5 Motorola Mobility returns.

Table 22.3 Cumulative abnormal analysis for Google and Motorola

	Google Inc.	Motorola Mobility
Period	CAR (%)	CAR (%)
−30 to 30	14.07	78.45
−15 to 15	13.80	76.16
−5 to 5	14.51	79.75
−1 to 1	15.03	73.95

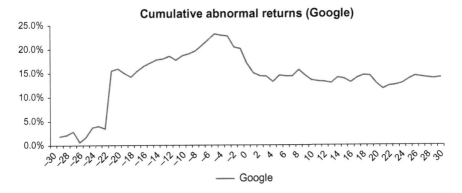

Figure 22.6 Google—CAR.

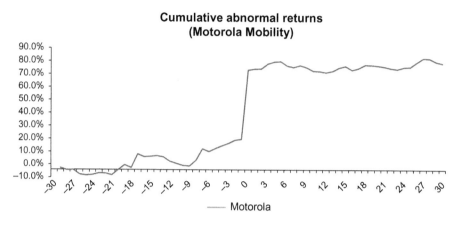

Figure 22.7 Motorola Mobility—CAR.

analysis reveals that during −30 to +30 days' time window, the cumulative abnormal return for Google was 14.07%, while for Motorola it was 78.45%. During the time window −1 to +1 period of announcement, the CAR for Google was 15.03% and for Motorola was 73.95% (Table 22.3, Figures 22.6 and 22.7).

22.8 Valuation—operating performance analysis

The operating performance analysis of Google and Motorola was based on discounted cash flow analysis and relative valuation. The fundamental discounted cash flow valuation model was based on two-stage growth model where cash flows were expected to have a high growth period followed by stable growth period. Another model for valuation used was the perpetuity growth model where it was assumed that the cash flows would be stable in perpetuity. The projections for the growth rate of revenues were based on management guidance reports, industry research, and analyst views on the performance of company's prospects. The percentage of revenue method was used to project the majority of the company's line items.

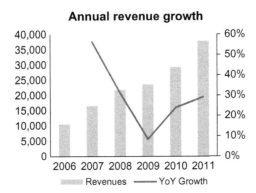

Figure 22.8 Annual growth rate.
Source: Annual reports.

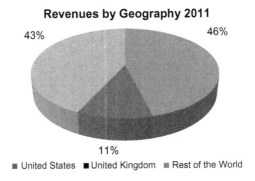

Figure 22.9 Revenue distribution by geographic regions.
Source: Annual reports.

22.8.1   Revenue highlights of Google Inc.

Google's advertisements are primarily aimed at users that access the internet via a traditional computer connection. Google dominates mobile search, with an over 99% market share, and the company continues to look for ways to monetize this. Google generated 96.4% of its total revenues through advertising in 2011. Google is also highly affected by foreign exchange rates. As we can see from the graph that around 54% of the company's revenue comes from outside the United States and hence change in foreign exchange rate can affect company's financial results (Figure 22.9, Table 22.4).

Table 22.4 Two-stage valuation model

Google Inc. ($ millions)	2011A	2012F	2013F	2014F	2015F	2016F
Net income[b]	10,237	11,104	14,043	16,589	19,256	21,954
Depreciation[c]	1396	2275	2715	3191	3670	4132
Amortization[c]	455	546	652	766	881	992
Stock-based compensation[c]	1974	2411	2810	3303	3798	4277
Interest*(1 − T)		56	54	53	42	40
Capital expenditure[d]	(3438)	(4550)	(5430)	(5744)	(6239)	(6611)
Investment in intangibles[e]	(1900)	(2048)	(2444)	(2872)	(3303)	(3719)
Changes in working capital[f]	595	373	(615)	(288)	(225)	(238)
Free cash flow to firm	9319	10,167	11,785	14,997	17,880	20,826

Valuation in million except per share	
Net present value (2012−2016)	56,546
Net terminal present value	87,277
Total enterprise value	1,43,823
Less: Debt	1217
Add: Cash and equivalents[g]	10,320
Add: Short-term investments[g]	28,798
Implied equity value	1,81,724
Number of shares outstanding	322.89
Share price (AED)	562.81

Google was trading for $563.77 as of August 12, 2011.

WACC for high growth assumptions		WACC for terminal value	
Market return[h]	13.31%	Market return	13.31%
Risk-free rate[i]	2.29%	Risk-free rate[i]	4.07%
Beta[j]	1.05	Beta[j]	1.13
Cost of equity	13.87%	Cost of equity	14.52%
Terminal growth rate[k]	2.00%	Terminal growth rate[k]	2.00%
After-tax cost of debt[l]	2.1%	After-tax cost of debt[l]	4.5%

Debt−equity structure		Debt−equity structure	
Total debt	1217	Total debt	3.362
Shareholders' equity	21,991	Shareholders' equity	1,57,696
Capitalization	53,208	Capitalization	1,61,058
Debt/Total capital	0.02	Debt/Total capital	0.02
Equity/Total capital	0.08	Equity/Total capital	0.08
WACC	13.60%	WACC	14.31%

(Continued)

Table 22.4 (Continued)

Notes:

b(In millions $)	Historical					Projected			
	2008A	2009A	2010A	2011A	2012E	2013E	2014E	2015E	2016E
Revenue built-up									
Google websites	14,414	15,723	19,444	26,145	31,635	37,963	44,606	51,297	57,709
YoY growth		9%	24%	34%	21%	20%	18%	15%	13%
Google Network websites	6715	7166	8792	10,386	12,152	14,278	16,848	19,375	21,797
YoY growth		7%	23%	18%	17%	18%	18%	15%	13%
Total advertising revenues	21,129	22,889	28,236	36,531	43,787	52,241	61,454	70,672	79,506
As % of revenue		96.8%	96.3%	96.4%	96.2%	96.2%	96.3%	96.3%	96.2%
Other revenues	667	762	1085	1374	1717.5	2061	2370	2726	3135
YoY growth		14%	42%	27%	25%	20%	15%	15%	15%
Total revenues	21,796	23,651	29,321	37,905	45,505	54,302	63,824	73,398	82,641
YoY growth		9%	24%	29%	20%	19%	18%	15%	13%

aTax rate: Google pays a tax rate significantly lower than usual federal rate of 35% because of overseas operations with lower taxes. The tax rate is projected to remain constant at 20% over the course of the DCF.
bRevenue was projected using a combination of Industry Analysis, Management Guidance from Annual Report, and the analysis of company's growth prospects. Total revenue is projected by breaking down the contribution by different operating segments and a growth rate was assigned for each segment each year.
cDepreciation, amortization and stock-based compensation is projected to remain constant as a percentage of revenues over the course of the discounted cash flows.
dCapital expenditures are projected to remain high and are calculated as a percentage of revenues. In 2011, the capital expenditures as percentage of revenues was 9.1% and is projected to reach up to 10% as per analysis of company's investments. The expenditures will be primary on the data center facilities. While this is trended down each year, the nominal value is still quite large and will depend on the company's growth.
eInvestment in intangibles are projected as a percentage of revenues and are expected increase in 2012 followed by a constant percentage increase every year. Intangible assets are patents and developed technology, Goodwill and trade names and other.
fNet working capital: Noncash current assets and liabilities such as Accounts Receivables, Inventories, and Accounts Payables were calculated based on the turnover days and projections were made based on historical data. Other noncash current assets and liabilities were projected as a % of revenues and cost of sales, respectively, and projected using historical data.
gCash and equivalents: As Google has a significant amount of cash and cash equivalents, these are very much valuable to shareholders. Cash and equivalents reported on the balance sheet were used and were added back to the firm value. The cash reported is very large, over $10 billion. Other investments were also added back to firm value that provides value to shareholders.
hExpected market return: 2-year NASDAQ return is calculated based on the mean and the standard deviation of the returns of the index (Exhibit 22.3).
iRisk-free rate: A 10-year treasury bond yield was used as the risk-free rate over the course of DCF. However, the terminal WACC was calculated using the 30-year treasury rate. Given the difference between the 10- and 30-year risk-free rates, the 30-year treasury rate better reflects the terminal value being discounted.
jBeta (Exhibit 22.2): One-year daily regression against NASDAQ composite is used to calculate the beta. While beta in equity research analysis report of S&P 500 was taken as 1.13, equal weighted average of both the values were taken which is coming to be around 1.04.
kTerminal growth rate: Terminal Growth rate is taken as 2% based on the Country's (US) GDP.
lCost of debt (Exhibit 21.1): Risk-free rate and default spread is taken into consideration while calculating the cost of debt. As debt is only roughly 2% of Google capital structure, this had very little effect on the valuation.
Source: http://www.treasury.gov/.

22.9 Two-stage valuation model for Motorola Mobility (Figure 22.10, Table 22.5)

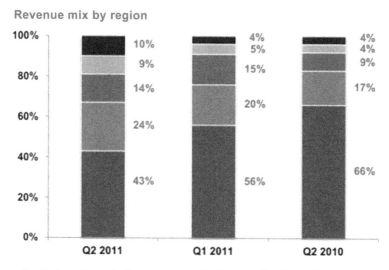

Figure 22.10 Mobile device.
Source: Company reports.

Table 22.5 **Motorola two-stage model**

Motorola Mobility Inc. ($ millions)	2011A	2012F	2013F	2014F	2015F	2016F
Net income[a]	*(249)*	*(212)*	*(29)*	*176*	*401*	*648*
Depreciation & amortization[b]	221	283	303	326	351	379
Stock-based compensation[b]	156	170	182	196	211	227
Interest*(1 − T)	(7)	0	0	0	0	0
Capital expenditure[c]	(200)	(141)	(152)	(163)	(176)	(189)
Investment in intangibles[c]	(210)	(227)	(245)	–	–	–
Changes in working capital[c]	275	135	51	67	73	79
Free cash flow to firm	*(14)*	*7*	*111*	*602*	*860*	*1143*

Valuation in mn except share price	As of August 2011					200
Net present value (2012–2016)	1255					
Net terminal present value	2845					
Total enterprise value	*4100*					

Table 22.5 (Continued)

Valuation in mn except share price	As of August 2011	200
Less: Debt	—	
Add: Cash and equivalents[d]	3026	
Add: Short-term investments[d]	119	
Implied equity value	*7,245*	
Number of shares outstanding	298.20	
Share price (AED)	*24.30*	

MM was trading at $24.55 as of August 12, 2011.

WACC assumptions		WACC for terminal value	
Market return[e]	13.31%	Market return[e]	13.31%
Risk-free rate[f]	2.24%	Risk-free rate[f]	4.07%
Beta[g]	1.5	Beta[g]	1.5
Cost of equity	*18.85%*	*Cost of equity*	*17.94%*
Terminal growth rate[h]	2.00%	Terminal growth rate[h]	2.00%
After-tax cost of debt[i]	*2.1%*	*After-tax cost of debt[i]*	*—*

Debt − equity structure		Debt − equity structure	
Total debt	—	Total debt	—
Shareholders' equity	5088	Shareholders' equity	5088
Capitalization	5088	Capitalization	5088
Debt/Total capital	—	Debt/Total capital	—
Equity/Total capital	1	Equity/Total capital	1
WACC	*18.85%*	*WACC*	*17.94%*

[a]*Revenue:* Projections were made based on the research of the company, management guidance and industry analysis. Revenue is projected to grow slowly this year and trend up till 2013. This is expected to decline slowly as the company will struggle to compete with some larger manufactures such as Apple, Samsung and HTC.
[b]*Depreciation, amortization and stock-based compensation is projected to remain constant as a percentage of revenues over the course of the discounted cash flows.*
[c]*Working capital and capital expenditure: Current Assets, Current Liabilities, Capital Expenditures, and Acquisitions are expected to remain a relatively constant portion of revenues.*
[d]*Cash and equivalents:* Cash and equivalents reported on the balance sheet were used and were added back to the firm value. Other investments were also added back to firm value that provides value to shareholders.
[e]*Expected market return:* Two-year NASDAQ return is calculated based on the mean and the standard deviation of the returns of the index (Exhibit 22.3).
[f]*Risk-free rate:* A 10-year treasury bond yield was used as the risk-free rate over the course of DCF. However, the terminal WACC was calculated using the 30-year treasury rate. Given the difference between the 10- and 30-year risk-free rates, the 30-year treasury rate better reflects the terminal value being discounted.
[g]*Beta:* Motorola Mobility was spun off in 2011; therefore, there is not enough historical data to calculate beta. Therefore, the beta of Nokia at 1.5 was used as Nokia had a similar line of business and was also losing market share rapidly to companies such as Apple and Samsung. To stay conservative, this higher beta was used.
[h]*Terminal growth rate:* Terminal growth rate is taken as 2% based on the Country's (US) GDP.
[i]*Cost of debt:* As there is no debt reported in the balance sheet; hence, there is no cost of debt is taken.
Source: http://www.treasury.gov/.

22.10   Zero growth or perpetuity model valuation for Motorola

Table 22.6 Zero growth valuation model -Motorola

($ millions)	Q2 2011
EBITDA	739.4
• Capital expenditure	96
• Change in working capital	(56)
Cost of equity	18.85%
Value of firm in perpetuity	3710.24
• Debt	0
Net value of firm in perpetuity	3710.24
/ No. of shares outstanding	298.20
Price per share	$12.44

22.11   Relative valuation for Google Inc.

Relative multiples (as of August 12, 2011) (Table 22.7)

Table 22.7 Comparison with Peer Group

Comparables (millions)	GOOG Google	AAPL Apple	MSFT Microsoft	Average	Median	Max	Min
Revenue	9026	28,571	17,367	18,321	17,367	28,571	9026
Operating income	2881	9379	6171	6143	6171	9379	2881
Net income	2505	7308	5874	5229	5874	7308	2505
Shareholder equity	51,991	69,348	87,083	69,474	69,348	87,083	51,991
No. of shares outstanding	323.9	927.1	8378.3	3209.7	927.1	8378.3	323.9
EPS	27.9	25.46	2.76	18.7	25.5	27.9	2.8
Operation income per share	33.2	32.93	3.24	23.1	32.9	33.2	3.2
Sales per share	103.2	108.2	8.4	73.3	103.2	108.2	8.4
Book value per share	161.0	74.8	6.81	80.9	74.8	161.0	6.8
P/E	20.2x	15.2x	10.0x	15.1x	15.2x	20.2x	10.0x
P/OP	17.0x	12.8x	8.6x	12.8x	12.8x	17.0x	8.6x
P/S	5.5x	3.6x	3.3x	4.1x	3.6x	5.5x	3.3x
P/BV	3.5x	5.2x	4.1x	4.2x	4.1x	5.2x	3.5x

At the time of acquisition, Google had higher relative multiple values except P/BV book ratio compared to its peers like Apple and Microsoft.

22.12 Cash flow to market value model

This model utilizes the ratio of cash flow to market capitalization. In this method, cash flow is measured as EBITDA is divided by the market capitalization. This valuation model is applied for Google Inc. and based on forecasted value; the ratio is expected to increase for Google for the period of analysis (Table 22.8).

Table 22.8 Cash flow to market value model

Google	2009A	2010A	2011A	2012F	2013F	2014F	2015F	2016F
EBITDA	9836	11,777	14,093	16,178	20,200	23,743	27,304	30,742
Market cap	1,97,010	1,90,840	2,09,200	2,33,420	3,74,420	3,74,420	3,74,420	3,74,420
EBITDA/ Market cap	0.050	0.062	0.067	0.069	0.054	0.063	0.073	0.082
Actual in 2012				0.067				

22.12.1 Google FCFF after acquiring Motorola (Table 22.9)

Table 22.9 FCFF Comparison

	2012 forecast without Motorola deal	2012 actual after acquiring Motorola
Net income	11,104	10,788
Depreciation	2275	1988
Amortization	546	974
Stock-based compensation	2411	2692
Interest*(1 − T)	56	56
Capex	(4550)	(3273)
Investment in intangibles	(2048)	(10,568)
Changes in working capital	373	127
Free cash flow to firm	*10,167*	*2784*

As we can observe from the above data that Google's Free cash flow to the firm dropped to $2784 million from a projection of $10,167 million because of acquiring Motorola Mobility, primarily because of the massive increase in Investment in intangibles.

22.12.2   MMI valuation at purchase price versus prior to deal (Table 22.10)

Table 22.10 Enterprise Value Multiple Comparison

In $ million	Purchase price	Prior to deal
Purchase price per share	40.00	24.47
MMI shares outstanding	298.2	298.2
Implied Equity Value	*11,928.00*	*7296.95*
Gross debt (2Q 11)	648	648
Cash (2Q 11)	3026	3026
Implied enterprise value	*9550.00*	*4918.95*
MMI EBITDA	739.4	739.4
EV/EBITDA	*12.9x*	*6.7x*

Google purchased MMI for $40 per share in cash, or a 63% premium to the stock's closing price. This implies a $12.5 billion purchase price for Motorola's equity, or about $9.55 billion in enterprise value, based on net cash of $2.4 billion at the end of 2Q 11. In turn, based on 2012 data and assuming no synergies, this implies a purchase multiple of 12.9x EV/EBITDA versus a 6.7x EV/EBITDA valuation of MMI prior to the announcement of the deal. Offering an EV/EBITDA multiple that is substantially higher than the average EV/EBITDA multiple for comparable transactions is usually an indication that the acquirer is overpaying for the target.

22.12.3   Accretion/dilution analysis (Table 22.11)

Table 22.11 Accretion/Dilution Analysis

	LTM			
	Acquirer	**Target**	**Adjustments**	*Pro forma*
Period ended	31/12/2011	31/12/2011		
Revenues	$37,905.0	$13,064.0		$50,969.0
EBITDA	*14,093.0*	*(142.0)*		*13,951.0*
Depreciation & amortization	1851.0	221.0		2072.0
EBIT	*12,242.0*	*(363.0)*		*11,879.0*
Interest expense, other nonoperating expense	(584.0)	10.0	(10.0)	0.0	(584.0)
Pretax income	*12,826.0*	*(148.0)*	*10.0*	*0.0*	*12,463.0*
Taxes	2589.0	101.0	2.0	0.0	2692.0
Net income	*10,237.0*	*(249.0)*	*8.0*	*0.0*	*9771.0*
Diluted shares outstanding (LTM weighted avg.)	328.5	297.1	(297.1)	0.0	328.5
EPS	*$31.16*	*$(0.84)*			*$29.74*

(*Continued*)

Table 22.11 (Continued)

	LTM
Acquirer diluted EPS	$31.16
Acquirer diluted shares outstanding	328.5
Acquirer net income	*10,237.0*
Target EPS	$(0.84)
Target diluted shares outstanding	297.1
Target net income	*(249.0)*
Combination adjustments	
Plus	
Combination pretax synergies	
Elimination of interest expense from refinanced debt	10.0
Less	
Interest expense on new acquisition debt	0.0
New interest expense on refinanced debt	0.0
Total pretax combination adjustments	10.0
Tax adjustments	(2.0)
Total combination adjustments	8.0
Pro forma net income	*9996.0*
New acquirer shares issued ('MM)	0.0
Pro forma diluted shares outstanding ('MM)	*328.5*
Pro forma diluted EPS	*$30.43*
Accretion/(Dilution)	*$(0.73)*
Accretion/(Dilution)	*(2.35%)*

22.12.4 Google sell off of Motorola to Lenovo

Google signed an agreement on January 29, 2014 to sell Motorola to Lenovo for $2.91 billion. A regulatory filing appeared to show that the Google bought a 5.94% stake in Lenovo for $750 million, according to Reuters. Google was said to have acquired 618.3 million shares of Lenovo at an average $1.213 per share on January 30, according to the report.

The investment was apparently part of the $2.91 billion deal to sell Motorola Mobility to Lenovo, which was announced a day earlier on January 29. In addition to $660 million in cash, Lenovo plans to pay $1.5 billion in the form of a 3-year promissory note.

Google will maintain ownership of the vast majority of the Motorola Mobility patent portfolio, including current patent applications and invention disclosures. As part of its ongoing relationship with Google, Lenovo will receive a license to this rich portfolio of patents and other intellectual property. Lenovo will also receive more than 2000 patent assets, as well as the Motorola Mobility brand and trademark portfolio.

On the intellectual property side, Motorola's patents have helped to create a level playing field, but the smartphone market is super competitive, and to thrive it helps to be all-in when it comes to making mobile devices. Motorola will be better served by Lenovo which has a rapidly growing smartphone business and is the largest (and fastest-growing) PC manufacturer in the world. This move will enable Google to devote the energy to driving innovation across the Android ecosystem, for the benefit of smartphone users everywhere. As a side note, this does not signal a larger shift for Google's other hardware efforts.

Google will retain the vast majority of Motorola's patents, which will continue to use to defend the entire Android ecosystem.

Google bought MMI in 2011 at $12.5 billion. It sold Motorola Home business to ARRIS in April 2013 at $2.5 billion. ARRIS paid Google approximately $2.2 billion in cash and issued Google 10.6 million shares of its common stock in connection with the transaction. On January 2014, Google announced that it will sell Motorola business to Lenovo in $2.91 billion but keeping the ownership of the Motorola's patent.

Empirically, Google bought MMI for $12.5 billion, in which the patents were bought at $5.5 billion which Google retained while selling the MMI to Lenovo at $2.9 billion. It already sold the Motorola Home Business at $2.5 billion.

In context of signaling theory, the acquisition of Motorola with cash gave a signal that the Google's management perceived that stock is undervalued. It is noteworthy to point out that Google stock price had doubled as acquisition signaling that market reacted in tune with the expectations.

Financial highlights Google Inc. ($ millions)

Variables	2008	2009	2010	2011
Revenues	21,796	23,651	29,321	37,905
Cash flow from operations	6632	8312	10,381	12,242
Net income	4227	6520	8505	10,237
EPS	13.31	20.41	26.31	29.76
Total assets	31,768	40,497	57,851	72,609

Source: Annual reports.

Financial highlights of Motorola Mobility in 2010

Revenue	11,460 million dollars
Net income	−79 million dollars
Total assets	6204 million dollars

Source: Annual reports.

22.12.5 Sensitivity analysis

GOOGLE (Target Share Price)

WACC	Terminal growth rates				
	1.0%	1.5%	2.0%	2.5%	3.0%
12.5%	544.42	555.69	567.91	581.21	595.74
13.0%	542.01	553.28	565.50	578.80	593.33
13.5%	539.65	550.92	563.14	576.44	590.97
14.0%	537.34	548.61	560.84	574.14	588.67
14.5%	535.09	546.36	558.58	571.88	586.41

Adjusted β	Terminal growth rates				
	1.0%	1.5%	2.0%	2.5%	3.0%
0.90	581.37	595.91	611.86	629.45	648.94
0.95	566.24	579.54	594.08	610.03	627.61
1.00	552.25	564.48	577.78	592.31	608.25
1.05	539.27	550.54	562.76	576.06	590.59
1.10	527.17	537.60	548.87	561.10	574.40

Motorola Mobility (Target Share Price)

WACC	Terminal growth rates				
	1.0%	1.5%	2.0%	2.5%	3.0%
16.00%	25.84	26.26	26.71	27.20	27.72
17.00%	25.01	25.38	25.77	26.20	26.65
18.85%	23.67	23.98	24.30	24.64	25.00
19.00%	23.58	23.87	24.19	24.52	24.88
20.00%	22.96	23.23	23.51	23.81	24.13

Adjusted β	Terminal growth rates				
	1.0%	1.5%	2.0%	2.5%	3.0%
1.00	28.67	29.28	29.95	30.68	31.48
1.05	28.00	28.57	29.18	29.84	30.57
1.20	26.27	26.72	27.20	27.72	28.27
1.35	24.86	25.22	25.61	26.02	26.47
1.50	23.67	23.98	24.30	24.64	25.00

Exhibit 22.1: Cost of debt

Interest coverage ratio	128.3	Net income/Interest
Default spread	0.40%	*Source*: pages.stern.nyu.edu
Risk-free rate	2.24%	US 10-year T-bond yield
Cost of debt	2.6%	Default spread + Risk-free rate
After-tax cost of debt	**2.11%**	Cost of debt*(1 − Tax rate)

Exhibit 22.2: Beta calculation

Beta is calculated by using the formula SLOPE (daily Stock price returns: daily index price returns). One-year price of Google and NASDAQ was taken, and the beta was calculated based on the above methodology.

Example

Date	Google	Returns	NASDAQ	Returns
12/08/2010	492.01		2190.27	
13/08/2010	486.35	− 0.0115	2173.48	− 0.00767
16/08/2010	485.59	− 0.00156	2181.87	0.00386
17/08/2010	490.52	0.010153	2209.44	0.012636
18/08/2010	482.15	− 0.01706	2215.7	0.002833
19/08/2010	467.97	− 0.02941	2178.95	− 0.01659
20/08/2010	462.02	− 0.01271	2179.76	0.000372

Slope of all the returns of Google daily stock price and NASDAQ daily index price will give us the beta, that is, how the company's stock is moving *vis-à-vis* the index on which it is listed.

Exhibit 22.3: Expected market return

Expected market return is calculated by taking the mean and standard deviation of the returns of NASDAQ index and then multiplying it by 252 (working days) to get the expected market return.

Example

Date	NASDAQ	Returns
12/08/2009	1998.72	
13/08/2009	2009.35	0.0053
14/08/2009	1985.52	−0.0119
17/08/2009	1930.84	−0.0279
18/08/2009	1955.92	0.01291
19/08/2009	1969.24	0.00679
20/08/2009	1989.22	0.01009

1. **Mean** = 0.0449% (average of returns).

2. **((STD DEV ^2)/2)** = 0.0079% (standard deviation).

3. **Total** = 0.0528% (1 + 2).

Expected return = 13.3137% *(Total*252)*.

Appendix 1: Cumulative returns for Google Inc.

Period	Returns (%)	Cumulative returns (%)	Period	Returns (%)	Cumulative returns (%)
− 15	0.12	0.12	1	− 3.27	− 13.09
− 14	0.57	0.69	2	− 1.09	− 14.18
− 13	− 2.46	− 1.77	3	− 5.30	− 19.48
− 12	0.61	− 1.16	4	− 2.77	− 22.25
− 11	− 1.19	− 2.35	5	1.48	− 20.77
− 10	0.51	− 1.84	6	4.15	− 16.62
− 9	− 2.37	− 4.21	7	0.86	− 15.76
− 8	1.48	− 2.73	8	− 0.62	− 16.38
− 7	− 3.93	− 6.66	9	1.31	− 15.07
− 6	0.26	− 6.40	10	2.32	− 12.75
− 5	− 5.70	− 12.10	11	0.30	− 12.45
− 4	5.02	− 7.08	12	0.05	− 12.40
− 3	− 4.26	− 11.34	13	− 1.56	− 13.96
− 2	2.39	− 8.95	14	− 1.44	− 15.40
− 1	0.29	− 8.66	15	− 0.51	− 15.91
0	− 1.16	− 9.82			

Appendix 2: Cumulative returns for Motorola Mobility Holdings

Period	Returns (%)	Cumulative returns (%)	Period	Returns (%)	Cumulative returns (%)
− 15	− 0.26	− 0.26	1	− 0.37	55.80
− 14	0.24	− 0.02	2	0.47	56.27
− 13	− 3.13	− 3.15	3	− 0.81	55.46
− 12	− 3.82	− 6.97	4	0.01	55.47
− 11	− 2.23	− 9.20	5	0.49	55.96
− 10	− 2.01	− 11.21	6	− 0.12	55.84
− 9	− 3.01	− 14.22	7	− 0.20	55.64
− 8	4.77	− 9.45	8	− 0.18	55.46
− 7	3.52	− 5.93	9	− 0.34	55.12
− 6	− 2.25	− 8.18	10	0.20	55.32
− 5	− 4.61	− 12.79	11	− 0.09	55.23
− 4	7.34	− 5.45	12	− 0.03	55.20
− 3	− 0.35	− 5.80	13	− 0.05	55.15
− 2	4.69	− 1.11	14	0.00	55.15
− 1	1.37	0.26	15	− 0.23	54.92
0	55.91	56.17			

Appendix 3: Cumulative abnormal returns (CAR) for Google Inc.

Period	Google returns (%)	NASDAQ returns (%)	Abnormal returns (%)	CAR (%)	Period	Google returns (%)	NASDAQ returns (%)	Abnormal returns (%)	CAR (%)
−30	2.89	1.53	1.36		1	−3.27	−1.24	−2.03	15.03
−29	2.19	0.35	1.84	1.84	2	−1.09	−0.47	−0.61	14.42
−28	0.55	0.29	0.26	2.10	3	−5.30	−5.22	−0.08	14.33
−27	2.10	1.36	0.74	2.83	4	−2.77	−1.62	−1.14	13.19
−26	−2.67	−0.45	−2.23	0.61	5	1.48	0.15	1.33	14.51
−25	−0.89	−2.00	1.11	1.72	6	4.15	4.29	−0.15	14.37
−24	1.28	−0.74	2.02	3.74	7	0.86	0.88	−0.02	14.34
−23	0.80	0.54	0.26	3.99	8	−0.62	−1.95	1.33	15.67
−22	−1.73	−1.22	−0.51	3.49	9	1.31	2.49	−1.18	14.49
−21	12.98	0.98	12.00	15.49	10	2.32	3.32	−1.00	13.50
−20	−0.45	−0.89	0.44	15.93	11	0.30	0.55	−0.25	13.25
−19	1.28	2.22	−0.94	14.98	12	0.05	0.13	−0.08	13.17
−18	−1.19	−0.43	−0.76	14.22	13	−1.56	−1.30	−0.27	12.90
−17	1.96	0.72	1.24	15.46	14	−1.44	−2.58	1.14	14.04
−16	1.85	0.86	0.99	16.45	15	−0.51	−0.26	−0.24	13.80
−15	0.12	−0.56	0.68	17.13	16	2.27	3.04	−0.77	13.03
−14	0.57	−0.10	0.67	17.81	17	0.17	−0.78	0.95	13.98
−13	−2.46	−2.65	0.19	17.99	18	−1.89	−2.42	0.53	14.51
−12	0.61	0.05	0.56	18.55	19	1.00	1.10	−0.09	14.41
−11	−1.19	−0.36	−0.83	17.72	20	−0.11	1.49	−1.60	12.82
−10	0.51	−0.43	0.94	18.66	21	0.48	1.60	−1.11	11.70
−9	−2.37	−2.75	0.38	19.04	22	1.97	1.34	0.63	12.33
−8	1.48	0.89	0.59	19.63	23	0.76	0.58	0.17	12.51
−7	−3.93	−5.08	1.14	20.77	24	0.00	−0.36	0.36	12.87
−6	0.26	−0.94	1.20	21.97	25	−0.01	−0.86	0.86	13.72
−5	−5.70	−6.90	1.20	23.17	26	−1.36	−2.01	0.65	14.37
−4	5.02	5.29	−0.28	22.89	27	−3.44	−3.25	−0.19	14.19
−3	−4.26	−4.09	−0.17	22.72	28	0.93	1.12	−0.19	14.00
−2	2.39	4.69	−2.30	20.42	29	1.21	1.35	−0.13	13.86
−1	0.29	0.61	−0.32	20.10	30	1.40	1.20	0.20	14.07
0	−1.16	1.88	−3.04	**17.06**					

Appendix 4: Cumulative abnormal returns (CAR) for Motorola Mobility Holdings

Period	MMI returns (%)	NYSE returns (%)	Abnormal returns (%)	CAR (%)	Period	MMI returns (%)	NYSE returns (%)	Abnormal returns (%)	CAR
− 30	6.51	1.28	5.23		1	− 0.37	− 1.18	0.81	73.95
− 29	− 2.96	− 0.25	− 2.71	− 2.71	2	0.47	0.33	0.14	74.09
− 28	− 1.65	− 0.10	− 1.55	− 4.26	3	− 0.81	− 4.58	3.76	77.86
− 27	1.07	0.95	0.12	− 4.14	4	0.01	− 1.54	1.56	79.41
− 26	− 4.28	− 0.78	− 3.51	− 7.65	5	0.49	0.15	0.34	79.75
− 25	− 2.91	− 2.16	− 0.75	− 8.40	6	− 0.12	3.28	− 3.40	76.35
− 24	0.00	− 0.44	0.44	− 7.96	7	− 0.20	0.88	− 1.08	75.27
− 23	1.97	0.66	1.31	− 6.65	8	− 0.18	− 1.70	1.51	76.79
− 22	− 0.86	− 0.68	− 0.19	− 6.83	9	− 0.34	1.34	− 1.69	75.10
− 21	− 0.89	0.44	− 1.33	− 8.17	10	0.20	2.82	− 2.62	72.47
− 20	2.94	− 1.11	4.05	− 4.11	11	− 0.09	0.18	− 0.28	72.20
− 19	5.25	1.46	3.79	− 0.32	12	− 0.03	0.86	− 0.89	71.31
− 18	− 1.86	0.33	− 2.19	− 2.51	13	− 0.05	− 1.13	1.08	72.38
− 17	12.16	1.57	10.59	8.08	14	0.00	− 2.59	2.59	74.97
− 16	− 2.13	− 0.04	− 2.09	5.99	15	− 0.23	− 1.42	1.19	76.16
− 15	− 0.26	− 0.60	0.34	6.33	16	− 0.04	2.90	− 2.94	73.23
− 14	0.24	− 0.31	0.55	6.88	17	− 0.05	− 1.33	1.28	74.50
− 13	− 3.13	− 2.14	− 0.99	5.89	18	− 0.24	− 2.93	2.69	77.19
− 12	− 3.82	− 0.36	− 3.46	2.43	19	− 0.19	0.03	− 0.22	76.97
− 11	− 2.23	− 0.55	− 1.68	0.76	20	0.40	0.89	− 0.49	76.48
− 10	− 2.01	− 0.48	− 1.53	− 0.77	21	0.53	1.25	− 0.72	75.76
− 9	− 3.01	− 2.60	− 0.41	− 1.18	22	0.61	1.81	− 1.20	74.56
− 8	4.77	0.27	4.49	3.31	23	− 0.42	0.26	− 0.68	73.88
− 7	3.52	− 5.41	8.93	12.24	24	− 0.11	− 1.55	1.44	75.32
− 6	− 2.25	− 0.13	− 2.13	10.11	25	0.05	− 0.24	0.30	75.62
− 5	− 4.61	− 7.05	2.44	12.56	26	0.26	− 3.27	3.53	79.15
− 4	7.34	5.25	2.08	14.64	27	− 0.42	− 3.65	3.23	82.38
− 3	− 0.35	− 2.16	1.81	16.46	28	0.37	0.66	− 0.29	82.09
− 2	4.69	2.20	2.49	18.94	29	0.04	2.51	− 2.47	79.62
− 1	1.37	0.64	0.73	19.67	30	0.30	1.47	− 1.17	78.45
0	55.91	2.45	53.46	**73.14**					

For details of calculation and analysis, see the resource files Valuation Analysis *-Google.xlsx* and Valuation Analysis *-Motorola Mobility.xlsx*.

References

<http://investor.google.com/releases/2011/0815.html>.
<http://techcrunch.com/2011/08/15/breaking-google-buys-motorola-for-12-5-billion/>.
<http://googleblog.blogspot.com/2011/08/supercharging-android-google-to-acquire.html>.

HP Compaq merger—valuation 23

23.1 Industry overview

In the late 1990s, the computer hardware industry was characterized by extreme competition between the top players, namely IBM, Dell, Compaq, and Hewlett-Packard (HP). It witnessed frequent product introductions and improvements in respect of product pricing and features arising due to changing customer requirements and transforming economics of the IT industry. Thus, in light of the radically changing industry, the participants had to equip quickly and profitably to the dynamics to sustain the market pressures. IBM and Dell performed well by following different strategies. Dell's ability to turnover inventory at a much faster rate dramatically changed the cost structure necessary to survive in the PC-making industry. While the former employed a full-service provider model, concentrating on its high growth, high margin businesses, and the later relied on a focus strategy principally aimed at the lower margin segments, namely personal computers and servers. On the contrary, Compaq, which was once the industry leader in PCs, faced challenges regaining its position in the industry. In such scenario, each of these participants was faced with a threat of dissolution or acquisition by a strong competitor. HP, one of the top in the industry, was evaluating its opportunities to expand into new and adjacent markets; it faced decline in sales growth. A change in the management was deemed as imperative by some critics, which was then followed by appointment of a new CEO, Carly Fiorina in July 1999. Fiorina was entrusted with the responsibility to a sustainable growth path for HP and take advantage of the Internet Age. Even after strengthening the cost structures and streamlining product lines, Fiorina did not achieve the desired objectives in terms of profitability. It was then in early 2001 that she explored the possibility of a business combination with Compaq and engaged investment banks to gain advice on the financial aspects of the same. The five main players in the enterprise hardware market were IBM, Sun, Dell, HP, and Compaq.

On September 3, 2001, the merger agreement was permitted by the boards of both the companies who then sought approval from their respective shareholders.

23.2 Company highlights

23.2.1 Acquirer company: HP

HP Company established in the year 1938 by two Stanford graduates—William Hewlett and David Packard—is a leading provider of computing and imaging solutions and services. It is focused on making technology. HP made total revenue from continuing operations of $48.8 billion in the fiscal year 2000. HP introduced its first PC in 1980 and its most successful product LaserJet in the year 1985. Table 23.1 provides the comparison of financial highlights of Dell , HP and Compaq in the period of merger.

Table 23.1 Financial highlights in period surrounding merger

Values ($ billion)	Dell	HP	Compaq
Sales (ttm)	31.2	44.2	33.6
EBITDA (ttm)	1.8	2.1	0.6
Net income (ttm)	1.3	0.7	-0.6
Operating margin	5.70%	2.90%	-2.30%
Profit margin	4.00%	1.60%	-1.70%
ROCE (ttm)	9.30%	2.20%	-2.40%
ROE (ttm)	24.40%	5.10%	-4.80%

Table 23.2 Worldwide high-end Unix servers in the year 2000

Firm	Factory revenues ($ million)	Market share (%)
Hewlett-Packard	512	11.4
Compaq	134	3.0

23.2.2 Target company: Compaq

Compaq Computer Corporation founded in 1983 is a leading global provider of enterprise technology and solutions. Compaq designs, develops, manufactures and markets hardware, software, solutions and services, including industry-leading enterprise storage and computing solutions, fault-tolerant business-critical solutions, communication products, and desktop and portable personal computers that are sold in more than 200 countries. Compaq's primary business divisions were Access, commercial and consumer PCs, Enterprise computing: servers and storage products and Global services. Compaq had successfully created a direct model in the PC Industry.

23.2.3 Performance statistics

Sun Microsystems with factory revenues of $2.1 billion had 47.1% market share in high-end Unix servers.

In the category of mid-range Unix servers, HP had revenues of $3.673 billion with market share of 30.3% in the year 2000. Compaq had revenues of $488 million with market share of 4%. Sun Microsystems with $2.8 billion in factory revenues had a market share of 23.5%. HP and Compaq's revenues and market share in the high end Unix servers segment is given in the Table 23.2.

23.3 Merger highlights

Hewlett-Packard and Compaq merged to create $87 billion global technology leader. The merger was aimed at creating world's number one position in servers, personal computers, hand held, imaging, and printing. The merger was aimed at creating leading positions in IT services, storage, and management software. The

Table 23.3 Projections for the combined firm in billions of dollars

Key facts (last four quarters)	HP	Compaq	*Pro forma* combined
Total revenues	47	40.4	87.4
Assets	32.4	23.9	56.3
Operating earnings	2.1	1.9	4

Source: http://www.hp.com/hpinfo/newsroom/press/2001/index.html, press release issued on September 3, 2001.

companies expected annual cost synergies of approximately $2.5 billion. Compaq shareholders received 0.6325 share of the new company for each share of Compaq. HP shareholders would own approximately 64% and Compaq shareholders 36% of the merged company. The premium paid to Compaq shareholders was approximately 18%. The deal financing involved issuance of 1.1 billion shares of HP common stock with a fair value of approximately $1.4 billion. The expected value of the deal can be assumed to be $24 billion based on the market price of $20.92, which was derived by averaging the closing price of three days surrounding the date of announcement. The announcement date was September 3, 2001. The merger agreement had a termination clause, which stated that HP or Compaq may terminate the agreement, and as a result, either HP or Compaq may be required to pay $675 million termination fee to other party in certain circumstances. The medium of exchange was stock. The ownership of Hewlett and Packard Families before merger was 18.6% and after merger the ownership dropped to 8.4%. The new merged HP was structured around four operating units—Imaging and Printing franchise, Access Device business, IT infrastructure business, and Service business. The new HP had operations in more than 160 countries and over 145,000 employees. The projections for the combined firm is given in Table 23.3.

23.4 Expected synergies

The merger was aimed to increase synergies for HP in desktop market and for Compaq in the servers market. The strategy was aimed to converge server families into IA64 [64-bit] Intel platform. The combination of the IT conglomerates was expected to provide the industry's most complete set of IT products and services for both businesses and consumers. As a result of the merger, the new HP was expected to be the primary global player in servers, imaging and printing and access devices (PCs and handhelds) as well as Top 3 player in IT services, storage, and management software. The merger facilitated the new entity to unify systems, architectures and promote aggressive direct and channel distribution models. The transaction was expected to be substantially accretive to HP's *pro forma* earnings per share in the first full year of combined operations based on achieving planned cost synergies. Cost synergies of approximately $2 billion were expected in fiscal 2003. The fully realized synergies were expected to be $2.5 billion by the mid-fiscal year 2004. The cost savings were expected from leveraging HP's new bulk to renegotiate

Table 23.4 **Breakdown of cost synergies**

Category	Anticipated cost savings ($ millions)
Administrative/IT costs	625
Cost of goods sold benefits	600
Sales management benefits	475
Research and development efficiencies	425
Indirect purchasing benefits	250
Marketing efficiencies	125
Total	2500

Source: HPQ S-4 Report filed January 14, 2002.

contracts for supplies such as memory chips and hard drives. The big chunk of savings amounting to $1.5 billion annually was expected from trimming the payroll. It was expected that by eliminating redundant administration functions, HP cost savings would reach $3 billion a year by 2004 (Table 23.4).

These anticipated synergies result from product rationalization; efficiencies in administration, procurement, manufacturing and marketing; and savings from improved direct distribution of PCs and servers. The merger was expected to significantly improve the profitability and operating margins in Enterprise Access and Services (Annual Reports of HP).

23.5 Impact of merger announcement on wealth creation

The merger was announced on September 4, 2001. The merger announcement led to an 18.1% fall in price of the HP shares from $23.21 as on August 31, 2001 to $19 as on September 4, 2001. The merger was approved with a margin majority on March 19, 2002 and the stock price closed at $18.80, which resulted in a fall of 2.34% from the previous day close. On announcement, the Compaq prices were down 34 cents closing at $12.35 (Figure 23.1).

The stock price returns of HP were analyzed for the time window of 41 days surrounding the merger announcement. HP had a cumulative return of −36% during the time window of −20 to +20 days surrounding the merger announcement. Table 23.5 gives the cumulative returns for HP in different time window periods surrounding the merger announcement. Table 23.6 gives the returns for HP during the merger time window period of −5 to +5 days.

The HP stock price fell by approximately 18% on the day of announcement. The stock price recovered and improved on the third day after announcement day. On the fifth day after announcement, the stock price fell by approximately 10%. The cumulative abnormal return (CAR) was also estimated based on the difference between stock returns and market index returns. The CAR for the period surrounding −40 to +40 days was approximately 30% (Figure 23.2).

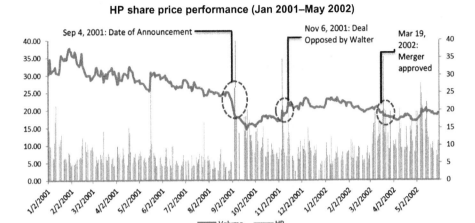

Figure 23.1 HP share price trend during merger event.

Table 23.5 **Cumulative returns of HP**

Period	Cumulative returns (%)
−20 to +20 days	−36
−10 to +10 days	−36.60
−5 to +5 days	−42
−1 to +1 days	−23

Zero is the announcement day.

Table 23.6 **Returns of HP**

Day	Returns (%)
−5	−0.44
−4	−1.64
−3	−2.68
−2	−2.30
−1	−0.81
0	−18.14
1	−4.16
2	−2.80
3	2.15
4	−1.05
5	−10.45

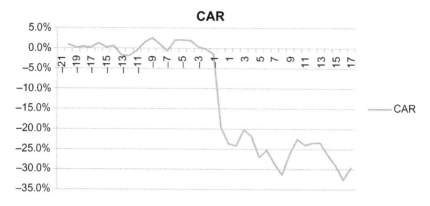

Figure 23.2 CAR of HP. CAR, cumulative abnormal return.

Table 23.7 **Operating performance**

Year	1998	1999	2000	2001	2002	2003	2004	2005
Sales	70,588	80,895	91,253	78,780	56,588	73,061	79,905	86,696
EBITDA	83,838	92,376	104,369	88,104	55,576	75,957	84,132	0
EBIT	13,250	11,481	13,116	9324	−1012	2896	4227	3473
Net Profit	202	4060	4266	−377	−903	2539	3497	2398

The values are given in millions of dollars. The average growth rate of these operating parameters in the premerger period (1998–2001) is compared the average growth rate of these variables in the postmerger period (2002–2005). The sales, EBITDA, EBIT, and net profit of HP and Compaq are combined in the premerger period 1998–2001. The merged firm data is used for postmerger comparison. The average growth rate of sales in the premerger period (1999–2001) was 3.7%. The average growth rate of sales in the postmerger period (2003–2005) was approximately 15%.

Table 23.8 **Profitability and liquidity position**

Year	1998	1999	2000	2001	2002	2003	2004	2005
ROA	0.09	0.10	0.11	0.01	−0.01	0.03	0.05	0.03
ROE	0.17	0.19	0.26	0.03	−0.02	0.07	0.09	0.06
Current ratio	1.56	1.51	1.53	1.53	1.54	1.61	1.50	1.38

The average return on asset of HP during the premerger period (1999–2001) was 7.8%. The average return on asset of HP during the postmerger period (2002–2005) was 2.45%. The average return on equity for HP during the premerger period and for postmerger period was 16.35% and 4.9%, respectively. The average current ratio in the premerger period declined from 1.53 to 1.51 in the postmerger period.

23.5.1 Operating performance analysis

The operating performance of HP is analyzed on the basis or premerger and postmerger period. Three years prior to merger is the premerger period and 3 years after merger is the postmerger period. The premerger data of both acquirer HP and target Compaq are added for the premerger years and compared with the postmerger data (Tables 23.7–23.10).

Table 23.9 Comparison of HP and Compaq in the year before merger completion

Firm	HP	Compaq
Total assets	32,584	23,689
Sales	45,226	33,554
EBITDA	2808	9262
EBIT	1439	7885
Net income	408	−785
ROA	10.87%	−3.31%
ROE	26.02%	−7.06%

The values of total assets, sales, and operating performance variables are in millions of dollars. The profitability position of HP was much better compared to Compaq in the year of merger announcement.

Table 23.10 Market capitalization in millions of dollars

Year	1998	1999	2000	2001	2002	2003	2004
Market capitalization	20,204.36	30,138.83	50,761.35	34,983.52	40,733.7	56,399.97	52,284.96

Table 23.11 Performance models

Year	1998	1999	2000	2001	2002	2003	2004
EBITDA/Mar Cap	0.24	0.17	0.10	0.08	0.03	0.10	0.13
EBITDA/Total assets	0.15	0.14	0.15	0.09	0.01	0.07	0.09
Sales/Mar Cap	1.95	1.41	0.96	1.29	1.39	1.30	1.53
Sales/Total assets	1.24	1.20	1.44	1.39	0.76	0.98	1.05

Table 23.11 highlights different ratios of performance measures in the pre- and postmerger years.

See the resource file HP Compaq .xlsx for details of analysis.

Reference

Annual Reports of HP.

Tata's acquisition of Corus—a valuation analysis

24

The steel industry witnessed a wave of consolidation of capacity since the year 2004. The prices of iron ore were rising, and on the other hand, requirement of steel from the emerging nations started to rise. To maintain market concentration, most players started indulging in price wars stressing the margins further. Consolidation for economies of scale became inevitable. The steel industry had long fragmented capacity. Consolidation would increase the pricing power with both suppliers and buyers. At the time of Tata Corus deal, the top 10 auto companies, which were the major buyers of steel controlled about 95% of the market (Aiyar, 2006). The top three ore companies control 75% of supply. Consolidation allows steel companies to adjust demand supply issues. Commodity cycles have eroded steel companies' profitability. Steel companies have responded to downturns with price cuts and in the process destroyed shareholder value. The top five steel companies control barely 20% of the business. The top 20 global steel companies account for 30% of the 1 billion capacity. In steel sector, the suppliers and buyers from steel makers are well consolidated. In iron ore supplies, the three major players—CVRD, Rio Tinto, and BHP Billiton—have three-fourth the market share and average margins of over 40%. Auto makers who buy finished steel are also well integrated with global six to seven major players. The steel industry grew by 6−7% annually during the period 1945−1975. This was due to the economic growth witnessed in the Europe and United States. During the period 1975−2000, the industry grew on an average by just 1%. In the 1990s, the growth was even lower at just 0.4%.

Tata Steel ranked 58 by production in 2005 bid for the UK-based Corus, which was four times its size, in the midst of fierce competition from resource-rich Brazilian company, Companhia Siderurgica Nacional (CSN), and finally bought it by offering 608 pence a share for acquiring the 1.01 billion outstanding shares in the year 2007. Thus, Tata outshined Brazilian rival CSN for the $12.1 billion to acquire Corus. The combined entity became the fifth largest producer in the world and second in Europe (Piya, 2007).

24.1 Highlights of Corus

In the year 1999, British Steel and the Dutch Koninklige Hoogovens merged to form Corus, the second largest steel maker in Europe. Corus is primarily engaged in the manufacture of semi-finished and finished carbon steel products. At the time of merger, Corus was the UK's largest steel company with a work force of 47,000 people spread across 40 countries (Annual Reports of Corus). Its production facilities are spread across various locations in the United Kingdom (14 million tons) and the Netherlands (6.8 million tons). It enjoys an exclusive presence in Western Europe and the United Kingdom, serving automobile, construction, engineering, and package sectors. Outside the United Kingdom and other regions of Europe, it has <20% market share. The main divisions consist of long product, strip product, distribution and building systems, and aluminum divisions. The long product division makes plates, sections, engineering billets, railway products, and custom-designed steel. Corus Group was renamed as Tata Steel Europe and had been a wholly owned subsidiary of Tata Steel since 2007.

Corus has plants in the United Kingdom, the Netherlands, Germany, France, Norway, and Belgium and is listed on the London, Amsterdam, and New York exchanges. Before the acquisition, Corus reached out to markets that Tata Steel did not have access to, including Europe, which accounted for 53% of Corus turnover.

24.2 Highlights of Tata Steel

Tata Steel belongs to the Tata Group founded by Jamsetji Tata in the year 1868. The Tata Group comprises over 100 operating companies in 7 business sectors. Established in 1907, Tata Steel is Asia's first and India's largest private sector steel company. Tata Steel founded India's first industrial city, now Jamshedpur, where it established India's first integrated steel plant in 1907. Tata Steel Group is among the top 10 global steel companies with an annual crude steel capacity of nearly 30 million tons per annum. It is now the world's second-most geographically diversified steel producer. The Group recorded a turnover of US$ 24.81 billion in the fiscal year 2014. Through the acquisition of Nat Steel Asia and Millennium Steel, Tata Steel created a manufacturing network in eight markets in South Asia and Pacific Rim countries. Tata Steel is a vertically integrated manufacturer. Tata Steel Group have operations in 26 countries and commercial presence in more than 50 countries. The company has approximately 80,000 employees across five continents. Tata Steel Group is among the top 10 global steel companies with an annual crude steel capacity of nearly 30 million tons per annum.

24.3 The bidding war

Tatas had great interest in Corus. Tatas initially started with 455 pence all cash bid per share on October 20, 2006. Thus, Corus was valued at £4.3 billion. CSN made its first bid on November 17, 2006, offering 475 pence per share. Tata upped the offer on 11th December, valuing the enterprise at £4.7 billion followed by the CSN offer of 515 pence and thereafter on 31st January. Tatas sealed the deal at 608 pence. The first counter bid by the CSN was the turning point in the whole episode in which a friendly negotiated deal turned into a fierce battle.

24.3.1 Timeline of the deal

Mid 2006	Tata Steel Chairman Ratan Tata made an offer of 455 pence per share to buy Corus
17/10/2006	Tata Steel makes a cash offer of GB 5.1billion pounds ($10 billion) bid for Corus worth 455 pence a share in cash
20/10/2006	Corus' Board of Directors recommend acceptance of Tata Steel's offer
17/11/2006	Companhia Siderurgica Nacional (CSN) of Brazil makes a bid of GBP 5.3 billion for Corus, worth 475 pence a share in cash
10/12/2006	Tata Steel raises its offer by 10% and makes an offer of GBP 5.5 billion including debt, worth 500 pence a share in cash
11/12/2006	CSN raises its formal offer for Corus from 500 pence to 515 pence a share in cash
21/1/2007	Corus accepts a 515 pence per share offer from CSN
27/1/2007	Tata Steel and CSN agreed to terms for an auction that will begin January 30 at 4:30 p.m. London time and end by 2:30 a.m. with an announcement of the winner by 3:00 a.m. There will be up to nine rounds of bidding
01/02/2007	Tata Steel wins a fiercely contested 8-h closed-door auction against Brazil's CSN for Corus. Tata Steel acquires 21.1% of the equity share capital for 608 pence per share ($11.7), besting the CSN bid of 603 pence

24.4 Market reaction during the acquisition process

Tata Steel had lost 1 billion dollars in market capitalization since it first announced its intention to buy Corus in October 2006. The BSE Sensex rose 18% during the same period. On the day the deal was stuck, opening lower at a gap of nearly 2% over its previous day's close of Rs. 519 on the BSE, the share was pounded to Rs. 461 within minutes of opening session. The 12% drop was among the steepest witnessed in the scrip since the takeover announcement was made. The deal had implied a high enterprise value/earnings before interest, taxes, depreciation and amortization (EV/EBITDA) multiple of 9 for Corus versus 4.6 for Tata Steel. Interestingly at the time of acquisition, CSN's market value has risen by about $1.6 billion as it lost the Corus bid. The share price of Corus in November 2005, when Tata Steel first placed a bid for acquisition was around 400 pence. However, Tata Steel eventually paid 608 pence, translating into an acquisition premium of 52%. Tata's price was neutral on the day when it announced its interest in buying Corus. As the deal became expensive, Tata's price took a negative turn. The stock went down significantly by 6.4% on December 11, 2006 when Tatas announced raising of bid to $9.2 billion. On January 31, 2007, the stock crashed by 10.5% when Tata Steel sealed the deal with the final bid of 608 pence per share, which valued Corus at above $12 billion.

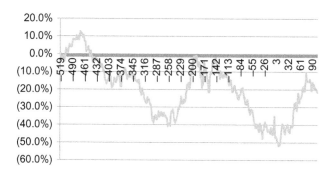

Figure 24.1 Cumulative abnormal returns of Tata Steel during the entire period of acquisition events.

Figure 24.1 highlights the CAR of Tata Steel stock during the acquisition period. The CAR analysis was done during the period January 2005–June 2007. The excess returns were found out by subtracting the daily returns of Tata Steel from the market index BSE SENSEX and then cumulating the returns for the above period.

24.5 Strategic reasons for the acquisition

The Corus acquisition facilitated Tata Steel to adopt the philosophy of deintegrated production. In this method, the focus would be to break up the supply chain and produce parts of it where it makes most economic sense. Low-cost, steel-producing countries like India, Brazil, Russia, and China are building enough of slab capacity on account of their proximity to iron ores. In order to market these slabs, expansion in a global level is very important. Corus' product portfolio would be a perfect fit for Tata Steel's deintegrated production strategy—make the raw or semi-finished steel in India and value add in Europe. In other words, Tata Steel's deintegrated strategy is two pronged: Steel making close to raw materials (iron ore, coal, gas) and production of finished steel in markets with a high rate of GDP growth where demand for finished steel from construction sector is high. Volumes in the steel business come from the construction and engineering sectors which are the core areas of Corus. Corus concentration on high end, value -added products could fit in well with Tata Steel's stated strategy which is to get "more from steel" via branding and value-added products. The acquisition was also expected to result in cost savings of $350 million per year. The deal was expected to increase Tata Steel's capacity exponentially and give it a wider customer and enhanced product portfolio. Significant cost savings were expected by exporting cheaper inputs (slabs) from India that would be processed in Corus' plants in the United Kingdom. The export of low-cost slabs from India would be the key to improve Corus' profitability. Tata Motors will have access to high value-added product mix and strong market positions in automotive, construction, and packaging. The combined entity would also emerge as the second largest tin plate maker in the world. The value creation in terms of synergies will result from sharing of manufacturing practices, shared services, and purchasing. Synergies will also result from sharing complementary strength. Corus have strong research and development (R&D) and product development capabilities for value-added products in the auto, construction, and packaging markets, which will complement what Tata Steel is doing in the fast growing Asian markets (Pallavi, 2007).

The powerful combination of low-cost stream production in India with the high-end downstream processing facilities of Corus improves the competitiveness of the European operations of Corus significantly. The combination also allows the cross-fertilization of R&D capabilities in the automotive, packaging and construction sectors, and transfer of technology, best practices and expertise. The steel makers in India enjoy a 20% cost advantage in slab making over its European peers. The ability to export surplus slabs, either from Tata Steel facilities or through acquisitions in low-cost regions, is one of the key drivers of the deal.

24.5.1   Funding highlights

Corus acquisition was routed through a special purpose vehicle (SPV) called Tata Steel, UK.

Total deal value = USD 12.1 billion

Warrants converted = 276 million. Converted preferential allocation of 2.85 crore warrants to ordinary shares at Rs. 484.2 a share

Rights issue = 732 million. Rights issue at 1:5 at Rs. 300 per share(a 40% discount to current price of Rs. 500 per share)

Preference issue : 870 million. Ratio—1:7 at 2% interest, convertible at a rate between Rs. 500 and Rs. 600 after 2 years

Foreign issue = 500 million

Quasi equity = 1250 million—By Tata Singapore

Internal accruals—600

Total equity = $4228 million

Debt

External commercial borrowing = 500 million

UK debt = 6140 million (By Tata Steel UK), (SPV created)

Tata Singapore = 1410 million

Total debt = $8050 million

24.6   Valuation perspective

24.6.1   Valuation of Corus

The statistics of IISI suggest that in the year 2005, the annual production of Corus was 18 million metric tons while that of Tata Steel was 5 million tons. In fiscal 2006, Corus turnover was $18 billion compared to Tata Steel's $4.64 billion. The enterprise value was estimated at $10 billion for Corus. Analysts often cite that Tata Steel had paid a price higher than what was paid for Arcelor. The EV/

Table 24.1 Financial highlights of Corus in millions of pounds

Year	2000	2001	2002	2003	2004	2005	2006
Turnover	11,698	7699	7188	7953	8373	9155	9733
Operating profit	−1156	−373	−425	−199	617	643	457
Net profit	−1042	−419	−458	−305	446	451	229
EPS in pence	−32.56	−13.04	−14.23	−9.25	46.4	48.14	21.01
Total assets	8398	7118	6431	6379	7269	7942	8080
Long-term debt	1766	1612	1428	1280	1407	1308	1236
Shareholders fund	3495	3061	2722	2796	3258	3378	3934

The total turnover in the year 2006 was 9.7 billion pounds. The total assets in the year 2006 amounted to 8.08 billion pounds. Corus was valued at $12 billion.
Source: Annual reports of Corus.

EBITDA for Corus was estimated at 7.6 times as against 5.4 times paid by Mittal Steel for Arcelor Steel. The price earnings ratio (the number of times the price is paid over the current year's earnings), at 14.8 times was also high. The acquisition price per ton in the case of Arcelor Mittal deal was $840 as against $750 paid by Tata Steel for the acquisition of Corus. The deal was valued at £5.2 billion with the rate of 608 pence per share. This estimated enterprise value was seven times Corus EBITDA for December 2005. The Mittal Steel Arcelor deal involved share swap along with cash. The Corus deal was all cash deal. Table 24.1 gives the financial highlights of Corus during the period 2000−2006.

24.6.2 Estimation of value of Corus using FCFF model

The 5-year average growth rate in sales was approximately 5%. The capital expenditure as a percent of sales was approximately 4%. The average noncash working capital as a percent of total turnover was approximately 15% during the period 2005−2006.

In the FCFF model, it is assumed that the growth rate of earning for Corus will be 5% for the next 10 years (2007−2016) and thereafter the growth rate assumed in stable growth period.

24.6.2.1 Cost of equity estimation

Risk-free rate = 4.50%. The risk-free rate is based on the average 10-year government bond yield during the period 2006.

Beta = 1.31
Risk premium = 5%
Cost of equity = 4.5 + 1.31 ∗ 5 = 11.05%
After-tax cost of debt = 3.85%
Weight of equity = 0.76
Weight of debt = 0.24

WACC = (11.05*0.76) + (3.85*0.24) = 9.18%
The weighted average cost of capital is 9.18%.
Sales in the year 2006 = 9733 million pounds
EBIT in the year 2006 = 457 million pounds

24.6.2.2 Input for first stage

It is assumed that the first stage comprises 10 years that is 2007−2016 and thereafter the stable period. Earnings grow at 5% for 10-year period and then at the growth rate of world economy assumed as 3%. Capex is assumed to be 4% of sales and depreciation to be 3% of sales. These values are on the basis of historical averages. Table 24.2 gives the present value calculation of FCFF of Corus in the high growth phase.

24.6.2.3 Stable phase inputs

The growth rate of world economy assumed to be 3% is taken as the growth rate of earnings in stable period.

EBIT (1 − T) in 2016 = 573.19 million pounds
EBIT (1 − T) in stable period = 590.38 million pounds
Growth rate = Reinvestment rate*Return on capital employed of the industry sector
3% = Reinvestment rate*6%
Reinvestment rate = 50%
EBIT (1 − T) in stable period = 573.19*1.03 = £590.39 million
Reinvestment = £295.19 million
FCFF in stable period = = £295.19 million
Terminal value = 295.19/(0.0918 − 0.03) = £4778.14 million
Present value of terminal price = £1879.43 million
Value of operating assets of Corus = = 1879.43 + 1447.5 = £3326.9 million
Add cash and cash equivalents in 2006 = £823 million
Total value of Corus = £4149.9 million
Value of Corus in dollars = $8299.5 million
The exchange rate was $1.95/£ on December 29, 2006.

24.6.3 Valuation summary

Book value of assets of Corus in 2006 was £8.08 billion, which amounted to $15.756 billion. The value of Corus was arrived at $8.3 billion approximately on the basis of FCFF-discounted cash flow valuation. The average value on the basis of book value of assets and FCFF comes to $12.03 billion. Tata Steel brought Corus at the price of $12 billion.

The detailed calculation for the FCFF model is given in the worksheet FCFF of *Corus.xlsx*.

Table 24.2 FCFF in first stage 2007–2016

Year	1	2	3	4	5	6	7	8	9	10
EBIT	479.9	503.8	529.0	555.5	583.3	612.4	643.0	675.2	709.0	744.4
EBIT(1 − T)	369.5	388.0	407.4	427.7	449.1	471.6	495.1	519.9	545.9	573.2
Net Capex	102.2	107.3	112.7	118.3	124.2	130.4	137.0	143.8	151.0	158.5
Change in working capital	132.9	76.6	80.5	84.5	88.7	93.2	97.8	102.7	107.9	113.2
FCFF	134.3	204.0	214.2	224.9	236.2	248.0	260.4	273.4	287.1	301.4
PV	123.0	171.1	164.6	158.3	152.2	146.4	140.8	135.4	130.2	125.3
Sum	1447.5									

The value of Corus in the first stage = £1.447 millions.

References

Aiyar, S., 2006. The art of the deal, cover story arcelor takeover. India Today. 36—42, July 10.

Annual Reports of Corus.

Pallavi, R., 2007. The man who bought corus...and the one who made it worth the buy. BusinessWorld. 36—37, 19th Feb.

Piya, S., 2007. Making corus work. Business World. 33, 19th Feb.

Glossary

Abandonment option The option to abandon a project is valuable in research and development as it provides the flexibility to abandon a project in the presence of negative results. An abandonment option can be applicable in the valuation of pharmaceutical firms on account of procedures used by pharmaceutical researchers and high costs involved in the development stages.

Accounting betas Accounting betas are estimated by regression of the company's return on assets against the average return on assets for large sample of firms as included in a market index.

Adjusted present value (APV) method APV method is used to value companies as well as projects. In the APV method, the value of the firm is obtained as its value as an all equity firm plus the discounted value of the interest tax shield from the debt funds.

Annual economic return Annual economic return (AER) is based on a firm's annual wealth creation performance. AER calculation is based on dividends and its timings and externally raised capital.

Average returns The average compound return earned per year over different years is called geometric average return. The return earned in an average year over different years is called arithmetic average return.

Beta It is the amount of systematic risk present in a particular risky asset in relation to that in an average risky asset. Portfolio beta can be calculated like portfolio expected return. Beta coefficient is the measure of sensitivity of a share price to movement in the market price.

Bond ratings Bond ratings are basically opinion about the credit quality of an issue like a bond or other debt obligation, which reflects the relative likelihood that it may default.

Bootstrapping The phenomena whereby shareholder value increases by the application of the bidder's higher bid to the target's earnings is known boot strapping. In other words, a high PE firm buys a low PE firm, resulting in a higher EPS for the merged firm.

Bottom-up approach for beta estimation Bottom-up approach method is used to calculate beta values for start-up firms and private companies that do not trade in the stock market.

CAMEL rating system CAMEL is an internal supervisory tool for evaluating the soundness of a financial institution. The CAMEL-based rating reviews different aspects of a bank with respect to a financial statement, funding sources, macroeconomic data, and cash flow.

Capital adequacy Maintaining an adequate level of capital is a critical element that is essential to maintaining balance along with a bank's risk exposure for the purpose of absorbing potential losses. The most widely used indicator of capital adequacy is the capital to risk weighted assets ratio known as CAR.

Capital asset pricing model (CAPM) CAPM considers risk in terms of a security's beta, which measures the systematic risk of a stock. CAPM expresses the expected return for an investment as the sum of the risk-free rate and expected risk premium.

Cash flow return on investment (CFROI) CFROI represents the sustainable cash flow a business generates as a percentage of the cash invested in the business. This measure can be interpreted as the internal rate of return (IRR) over the economic life of the assets.

Coefficient of variation (CV) Coefficient of variation is a measure of relative variability to indicate the risk per unit of return.

Conglomerate merger Conglomerate mergers occur when companies in different industry sectors merge. A pure conglomerate merger occurs when a firm in an industry with low demand growth relative to the economy acquires a firm operating in an industry with high expected demand growth.

Constant growth DDM (Gordon growth model) This model assumes that dividends for some firms grow at a steady rate. It can be assumed that dividends grow by a specific percentage each year.

Cost synergy Cost-based synergy aims for reducing incurred costs by combining similar assets in the merged businesses. Cost synergy can typically achieve economies of scale particularly for sales and marketing, administrative, operating, and/or research and development costs. Revenue-based synergy focuses on enhancing capabilities and revenues and combining complementary competencies.

Discounted cash flow valuation Valuation in which the value of any asset is the present value of expected future cash flows on that asset.

Diversification The process of spreading an investment across assets whereby the unsystematic or firm-specific risk is diversified is called diversification. A portfolio is a group of assets formed as a result of diversification.

Dividend discount model (DDM) Dividend discount model is the simplest and most direct version of the equity valuation model. This model of valuation assumes that the value of a firm's equity is the present value of the forecasted future dividends.

Dividend yield Dividend yield is an important measure of valuation. Dividend yield is equal to a company's annual dividend per share divided by its stock price per share.

Economic value (EV) EV is calculated as net operating income after taxes (NOPAT) minus the capital charge.

Efficient frontier Efficient frontier represents the set of portfolios which has the maximum return for any given level of risk or minimum risk for every level of return. The underlying principle behind the frontier set of risky portfolios is that in a universe of risky assets, investors can optimize their returns by combining risky assets that maximizes the expected return for any given level of risk.

Efficient market theory (EMT) EMT states that the price of an asset reflects all relevant information, which is available about the intrinsic value of the asset. A market in which prices always fully reflect available information is called "efficient."

Enterprise value-based multiples Enterprise value multiples are expressed as a ratio of capital investment to a financial metric, which is attributable to the providers of capital. Enterprise value (EV) equals market value of equity plus debt minus cash. Examples for enterprise value are EV/Sales, EV/EBITDA, and EV/EBIT.

Equity price-based multiples Equity value multiples are calculated using denominators relevant to equity holders. One of the most widely used multiple is the price earnings ratio commonly known as P/E or PER. Other price-based multiples are PEG, P/S, and P/B ratios.

Equity spread Equity spread is the difference between the ROE and the required return on equity (cost of equity).

Expected return Expected return is the return on a risky asset expected in the future. The expected return on an asset is equal to the sum of the possible returns multiplied by their probability.

FCFE FCFE is the residual cash flow available to shareholders. It is a measure of potential dividends that a firm can pay to its shareholders. It is the residual cash flow after taxes, interest expenses, and reinvestment needs.
FCFF = Net Income − Capital expenditure + Depreciation & amortization − Change in noncash working capital + New debt issued − Debt repayment.

FCFE valuation models Basically, there are two ways of estimating equity value through free cash flows. In the first method, the FCFF estimated is discounted by the weighted average cost of capital (WACC) to get the firm value. The value of the firm's debt is then subtracted to calculate the equity value. In the second method, the value of equity is obtained by discounting the FCFE cash flows by the required return on equity (cost of equity).

FCFF Free cash flow to firm (FCFF) is the sum of the cash flows to all the suppliers of capital to the firm, which includes stockholders, bondholders, and preference shareholders. The FCFF approach of valuation is more appropriate when the firm's FCFE is negative and when the capital structure is unstable.
FCFF = FCFE + Interest expense $(1 − T)$ + Principal repayments − New debt issues − Preferred dividends.

Financial synergy The resultant feature of corporate merger or acquisition on the cost of capital of the combined or acquiring firm is called financial synergy. It is the result of the lower cost of internal financing as compared to external financing.

Forward multiples Forward multiples are basically applied to a firm's next 12 months EBITDA or EBIT. This measure basically focuses on a firm's predicted earnings for the next year. Forward multiples are used to value high growth companies, which expect better future earnings in the future period.

Free cash flow Free cash flow is the after-tax cash flow available for all shareholders. Free cash flow is independent of financing and nonoperating items.

Fundamental beta Fundamental beta is basically used to calculate the beta of the unlisted firms. Fundamental is the product of a statistical model, which can be used to predict the fundamental risk of a security using market-related and financial data.

Holding period return The period for which the investment is made is called holding period and the return for the holding period is called the holding period return (HPR).

Horizontal merger Horizontal mergers take place when two merging companies produce similar products in the same industry. Horizontal mergers are meant to attain market power.

Implied value The implied value measure is based on forecasts of future by making *pro forma* income and balance sheet statements over a period of time.

Key performance indicators The metrics associated with value drivers are called key performance indicators (KPIs).

Managed earnings Corporate earnings are often manipulated by firms by practicing managed earnings by means of falsely inflating stock prices due to improperly reporting income, failure of capitalizing expenses, hiding losses in subsidiaries, or prematurely recognizing revenues.

Market value added (MVA) Market value added represents the wealth generated by a company for its shareholders. It equals the amount by which the market value of the company's stock exceeds the total capital invested in a company (including capital retained in the form of undistributed earnings).

Mean variance optimization Mean variance optimization is a quantitative tool for allocation of assets based on the tradeoff between risk and return.

Nonconstant growth DDM This model assumes abnormal growth rates over some finite length of time. This model allows for supernormal or abnormal growth rates over some period of time. The nonconstant growth model primarily consists of two-stage and three-stage growth model.

Operating synergy Facilitate firms to increase their operating income or growth or both. Operating synergy may result from economies of scale, which may arise from merger allowing the combined firm to become more cost efficient and profitable. The source of operating synergy may be attributed to greater pricing power, reduced competition, and higher market share, which may result in higher margins and operating income.

Operating working capital Operating working capital equals operating current assets minus current liabilities. The operating working capital is often referred to noncash operating working capital as excess cash and marketable securities are not included in working capital calculation.

Option to expand Firms can exercise options to expand for further investments or enter into a new market. Entering a large market or acquisition of a proprietary technology can be viewed as an option to expand. Options to expand are valued as call option.

Portfolio returns The expected return on a portfolio is calculated as the weighted average of the expected returns on the stocks which comprise the portfolio. The weights reflect the proportion of the portfolio invested in the stocks.

Portfolio risk Portfolio risk refers to the chances that an investment portfolio does not earn the expected or desired rate of return

Price earning growth (PEG) ratio PEG is calculated by dividing the P/E by the projected earnings growth rate of the firm.

Real options valuation It is a dynamic approach to valuation in terms of flexibility and growth opportunities. The real options approach is an extension of financial options theory. Options are contingent decisions that provide an opportunity to make decisions after uncertainty become relevant.

Relative valuation This multiple is an expression of market value of an asset relative to a key statistic that is assumed to relate to that value. The basic objective of relative valuation is to value assets based on how similar assets are currently priced in the market. In other words, relative valuation involves the use of similar comparable assets in valuing another asset.

Relative valuation Valuation that identifies whether a company is fairly valued relative to some benchmark group of companies in the same sector.

Revenue synergy Revenue-based synergy can be exploited if merging business develop new competencies, which allow them to command a price premium through higher innovation capabilities (product innovation, time to market, etc.) or boost sales volume through increased market coverage (geographic and product line extension).

Risk premium The excess return required from an investment in a risky asset over that required from a risk-free investment is called risk premium.

Risk The variability of returns is known as risk.

Semi strong form of efficient market In a semi-strong efficient market, stock prices reflect all publicly available information about economic fundamentals of the firm.

Shared values Shared values are policies and operating practices, which enhance the competitiveness of a company. In this concept, businesses have to focus on value with a societal perspective. Value is defined as benefits relative to costs. The approach to value creation has undergone transformational changes.

Sharpe ratio Sharpe ratio reflects the trade-off between the reward (the risk premium) and the risk (as measured by standard deviation or SD)

Single-stage FCFF model In this model, the value of the firm is equal to next period's FCFF discounted by the WACC minus the stable growth rate (g) in FCFF.

Strong form of efficient market In strong form, the highest level of market efficiency, prices reflect all public and private information.

Systematic risks Systematic risks have market wide effects and affect a large number of assets. Systematic risks are also known as market risks.

Terminal value Terminal value is the value of the firm's expected cash flow beyond the explicit forecast horizon. In practice, forecasts of dividends are made for a finite number of years and the truncation of the forecast horizon usually requires a terminal value or continuing value calculation at the horizon.

The option to delay The option to delay becomes valuable when an investment project which has a negative NPV presently will have a positive NPV in future as the riskiness of the project and cash flow may change due to new changes in the scenario.

Three-stage FCFE model This model can be applied to cover three stages of the growth life cycle of a company—an initial high phase of growth rate followed by slower growth period and finally the matured period. The model estimates the present value of expected free cash flow to equity over all the three stages of growth.

Three-stage FCFF model The three-stage model of FCFF is based on an initial high growth phase, a transition phase, and a stable phase period.

TOBIN Q ratio Tobin's q or the q ratio is the ratio of the market value of a company's assets (market value of outstanding stock plus debt) divided by the replacement cost of the company's assets or book value.

Total return The total return on any investment is the sum of the dividend and the capital gain. In percentage terms, the total return is equal to the dividend yield plus the capital gain yield.

Total shareholder return Stock price appreciation plus dividends.

Two-stage FCFE model This model assumes that the FCFE will have an initial high growth phase followed by stable growth phase. The model makes the assumption that there would be initially high growth earnings and large capital expenditures. The FCFE might be low or negative in the initial phase. In the stable phase on account of increased competition, earnings growth slows down and stabilizes.

Two-stage FCFF model This model is used when a firm's growth rate is expected to decelerate in the future and stabilize at a rate g. The two-stage model of FCFF is based on an initial high growth phase and a stable phase period.

Unsystematic risks These risks are those that affect a small number of assets. They are also known as unique or firm-specific risks.

Value capture model (VCM) VCM defines competition in an industry as a tension between the value generated from transactions that a firm undertakes with a given set of agents and the forgone value it could have generated from transactions with other agents.

Value driver A performance variable that impacts the results of a business such as production effectiveness or customer satisfaction. The three commonly cited financial drivers of value creation are sales, costs, and investments.

Value-based management VBM is an approach to management whereby the company's overall aspirations, analytical techniques, and management processes are aligned to help the company maximize its value by focusing management decision making on the key drivers of shareholder value.

Variance and standard deviation The two most commonly used measures of volatility are variance and its square root standard deviation. Variance is the average squared difference between the actual and average return.

Vertical merger Vertical mergers refer to a firm acquiring a supplier or distributor of one or more of its goods or services. Vertical mergers involve combinations of companies that have a buyer–seller relationship. Vertical mergers occur when two firms each working at different stages in the production of the same product combine.

Weak form of efficient market In weak form of efficiency, the future returns cannot be predicted from past returns or any other market-based indicator. In other words, past rates of return have no relation with future rates of returns.

Wealth creation It refers to changes in the wealth of shareholders on a periodic (annual) basis. In the case of stock exchange-listed firms, changes in shareholder wealth occur from changes in stock prices, dividends, equity issues during the period. Stock prices reflect the investors' expectation about future cash flows of the firm. Shareholder wealth is created when firms take investment decisions with positive NPV values.

Zero growth DDM model This model assumes that dividends have a zero growth rate. In other words, all dividends paid by a stock remain the same.

Index

Printed in the United States
By Bookmasters